Foundations of Modern Macroeconomics

Second Edition

Exercise and Solutions Manual

BEN J. HEIJDRA
LAURIE S. M. REIJNDERS
and
WARD E. ROMP

OXFORD

UNIVERSITY PRESS

OXFORD

UNIVERSITY PRESS

Great Clarendon Street, Oxford OX2 6DP

Oxford University Press is a department of the University of Oxford.
It furthers the University's objective of excellence in research, scholarship,
and education by publishing worldwide in

Oxford New York

Auckland Cape Town Dar es Salaam Hong Kong Karachi
Kuala Lumpur Madrid Melbourne Mexico City Nairobi
New Delhi Shanghai Taipei Toronto

With offices in

Argentina Austria Brazil Chile Czech Republic France Greece
Guatemala Hungary Italy Japan Poland Portugal Singapore
South Korea Switzerland Thailand Turkey Ukraine Vietnam

Oxford is a registered trade mark of Oxford University Press
in the UK and in certain other countries

Published in the United States
by Oxford University Press Inc., New York

British Library Cataloguing in Publication Data

Data available

Library of Congress Cataloging in Publication Data

Data available

Typeset by Ben J. Heijdra in LATEX,
Prelims typeset by SPI Publisher Services, Pondicherry, India
Printed in Great Britain
on acid-free paper by
CPI Antony Rowe, Chippenham, Wiltshire

ISBN 978-0-19-956440-8

1 3 5 7 9 10 8 6 4 2

Contents

viii

Preface

About the manual

The first edition of *Foundations of Modern Macroeconomics* did not include any end-of-chapter exercises, although I posted quite a few questions plus models answers on the website for the book. Over the years, many teachers using the book have approached me for such exercises. This *Exercise and Solutions Manual* is my response to their queries. In this manual you find a large number of exercises (plus extensive solutions) for each chapter. The aim of this manual is to allow the diligent student to further develop his or her skills in model-based macroeconomics. The manual includes three types of exercises:

- Short questions. These questions often ask the student to comment on statements regarding models discussed in the textbook. Typically, brief answers are sufficient for the student to demonstrate an understanding of the material under consideration. Sometimes, a short question asks the student to clarify a concept by explaining it verbally, or by giving examples.

- Relatively straightforward long questions. These questions are usually centered around a particular model. Students are asked to demonstrate an ability to derive conclusions regarding macroeconomic phenomena by solving the model. By learning to "play with" simple models, I expect that the student will be able to construct his or her own models after studying this manual.

- Relatively difficult long questions which are a bit more challenging. To warn the student, such questions are marked with a star ($\star$). Other than that, the objective behind these questions is the same as for the relatively easy ones. The student learns how to solve macroeconomic problems by using consistent and coherent macroeconomic models.

It must be stressed that the exercises and model solutions are *not* meant to emphasize a particular point of view about the field of macroeconomics or, for that matter, the macro-economy itself. They are simply a reflection of the type of models that have been used over the last four decades or so.

I have adopted the following notational system in this manual. The prefix Q is used to label information (equations, tables, figures) appearing in the questions themselves. So, for example, equation (Q1.2) refers to equation (2) in the question dealing with a topic from Chapter 1. In short, the syntax is Q$x.y$, where x is the chapter number and y is the object counter. The prefix A is used to label information appearing in the answers, with the similar syntax A$x.y$. Information from the main textbook features the syntax $x.y$.

About the authors

Although I use my role as the project's "Central Scrutinizer" to write this Preface, this edition of the manual carries two coauthors. The division of tasks was as follows. Over many years, I produced the vast majority of the exercises and model solutions that are found in this manual.

During the Spring and Summer of 2007, Ward E. Romp was employed as a part-time postdoctoral researcher at the University of Groningen where he had successfully defended his dissertation in February of that year. I was able to enlist Ward as a coauthor, and to get him to work on the manual on a part-time basis. Among other things, he had the rather thankless task of collecting exercises and model solutions from various locations on my hard disk drive and my equally chaotic paper filing system. He also contributed a number of exercises himself. These were typically based on the problem sets he produced whilst teaching part of the third year macro-economics course at the University of Groningen in 2005 and 2006. Ward also produced some rather ingenious LATEX 2_ε packages that are used to typeset this manual.

Laurie S.M. Reijnders is the coauthor who joined this project most recently. Laurie is a final-year bachelor student in both economics and econometrics, whose efforts on behalf of the main text have been documented in the Preface to that book. During the last half year or so, Laurie sacrificed one day each week to check the exercises and model answers for the first ten chapters of the book. Although these exercises had been proofed very thoroughly before, she was nevertheless able to substantially improve this part of the manual. The responsibility for the quality of the exercises and model answers for the later chapters must–alas–be shouldered to a large extent by myself.

Visible means of support

It somehow seems impossible to produce a book of this size without generating some typos and errors. Needless to say, all such errors and typos will be published as I become aware of them. I will make the errata documents available through my homepage:

http://www.heijdra.org

So please let me know about any typos and/or errors that you may spot. The contact address is:

info@heijdra.org

I will mention your name prominently on the website (as having contributed to the public good). Of course, your name will also feature in the Acknowledgements section in any future edition of this manual.

Eventually, the website will also include new exercises without model answers. These questions may be of use to teachers in need of suitable exam questions. I hereby solemnly declare that I will not release model solutions to these additional exercises to anybody!

Acknowledgements

Over the years I received useful comments on the problem sets on the website from many individuals. I thank these anonymous contributors for their efforts. The first edition of this manual has benefited from the detailed comments of Jochen O. Mierau (University of Groningen) and Jenny E. Ligthart (Tilburg University).

Ben J. Heijdra
University of Groningen, The Netherlands
April 2009

Chapter 1

Who is who in macroeconomics?

Question 1: Short questions

(a) Suppose that, in a closed economy, the central bank adjusts the money supply in such a manner that the interest rate, R, is constant. Derive the slope of the AD curve. Show what happens to the LM curve as a result of the central bank's policy.

(b) What do we mean with the notion that capital and labour are cooperative production factors? Can you give an example where this holds true?

(c) Assume that firm investment depends only weakly on the interest rate. Does that make the IS curve very steep or relatively flat? (In the usual diagram with the interest rate on the vertical axis and real output on the horizontal axis.)

(d) What are the two most important differences between the views of the classical and Keynesian economists?

(e) Consider the usual diagram with the real wage on the vertical axis and employment on the horizontal axis. Perfectly competitive firms use capital and labour to produce output. Why must *competitive* labour demand functions be downward sloping? Why must capital and labour be cooperative factors of production?

Question 2: The Cobb-Douglas production function

Consider the Cobb-Douglas production function:

$$Y = F(N, \bar{K}) = N^{\varepsilon} \bar{K}^{1-\varepsilon}, \quad 0 < \varepsilon < 1, \tag{Q1.1}$$

where Y is output, N is employment and $\bar{K}$ is the capital stock. The capital stock is fixed in the short run.

(a) Show that under perfect competition in the goods market the parameter ε corresponds to the national income share of wages.

(b) Derive the short-run labour demand and goods supply schedules, both in levels and in terms of relative changes.

(c) What are the real wage elasticities of labour demand and the supply of goods?

Question 3: The AS-AD model

Consider an economy with a representative profit maximizing producer with a Cobb-Douglas production function:

$$Y = N^\alpha \bar{K}^{1-\alpha}, \qquad 0 < \alpha < 1, \tag{Q1.2}$$

where Y is output, N labour, $\bar{K}$ the (fixed) capital stock, and α a share parameter. This producer maximizes short-run profits $\Pi = PY - WN$, with W denoting the nominal wage rate and P the price level.

(a) Derive the explicit expressions for the labour demand curve and the real wage elasticity of labour demand (ε_D). Does the partial derivative have the correct sign (i.e., does labour demand decrease if the real wage rate goes up)?

The same economy has a representative consumer who maximizes utility U that depends positively on consumption C and negatively on labour supply N.

$$U = C - \gamma \frac{N^{1+\sigma}}{1+\sigma}, \quad \gamma, \sigma > 0. \tag{Q1.3}$$

The consumer pays no taxes and cannot save or borrow, so she faces the expected budget constraint:

$$P^e C = WN. \tag{Q1.4}$$

(b) Derive the labour supply curve and the expected real wage elasticity of labour supply (ε_S). Which effect dominates, the income effect or the substitution effect?

(c) Derive the aggregate supply curve.

Suppose that the demand side of this economy is described (in the neighbourhood of the equilibrium) by the aggregate demand curve:

$$Y = \xi + \theta \frac{\bar{M}}{P} \tag{Q1.5}$$

where M/P is the real money supply.

(d) What is the interpretation and sign of θ? Explain.

(e) Derive graphically the short run effect (P^e given) and the long run effect of an unexpected monetary shock assuming that the adaptive expectations hypothesis holds:

$$P_{t+1}^e = P_t^e + \lambda \left[P_t - P_t^e \right]. \tag{Q1.6}$$

Is the model stable? What happens if consumers are blessed with perfect foresight?

Question 4: Consumption tax

A representative household has the following utility function:

$$U = \ln\left(C - \gamma\frac{N^{1+\sigma}}{1+\sigma}\right),\tag{Q1.7}$$

where U is utility, C is consumption, N is labour supply, and the parameters γ and σ are both positive. (The structure of the problem is such as to render the term in round brackets positive.) The household budget constraint is given by:

$$PC = WN + Z_0,\tag{Q1.8}$$

where Z_0 is exogenous non-labour income. The competitive labour demand is given by:

$$\ln N = \ln K_0 - \frac{1}{1-\alpha}\left[\ln(W/P) - \ln \alpha\right],\tag{Q1.9}$$

where K_0 is the exogenous capital stock and α is the efficiency parameter of labour in the production function ($0 < \alpha < 1$).

(a) Derive the labour supply function.

(b) Show what happens to optimal consumption and labour supply if non-labour income increases. Explain the intuition behind your results (preferably with the aid of a diagram).

(c) Introduce a consumption tax, t_C, and compute the effects it has on optimal consumption and labour supply.

(d) What kind of production function gives rise to a labour demand function as given in equation (Q1.9)?

(e) Assume labour market clearing. Compute the general equilibrium effect on employment and the real wage rate of the consumption tax introduced in part (c).

Question 5: Tax incidence

In the book we have developed a very simple model of the aggregate labour market. Suppose that we write this model as follows:

$$N^D = N^D(W/P, \bar{K}), \qquad N^D_{W/P} = \frac{1}{F_{NN}} < 0, \qquad N^D_{\bar{K}} = -\frac{F_N K}{F_{NN}} > 0,\tag{Q1.10}$$

$$W/P = g(N^S), \qquad g_N > 0,\tag{Q1.11}$$

$$[N \equiv] N^D = N^S,\tag{Q1.12}$$

where N^D is labour demand, W is the nominal wage, P is the price level, $\bar{K}$ is the capital stock, N^S is labour supply, and N is equilibrium employment. We assume that the expected price is equal to the actual price ($P^e = P$) and that the labour market is in equilibrium. Answer the following questions about this model. Use graphical means as much as possible.

(a) What do we assume implicitly in equation (Q1.11) about the income and sub-stitution effects in labour supply? Explain intuitively how these effects operate.

(b) Assume that the government introduces a so-called *payroll tax* (t_W), i.e. a tax levied on employers which is proportional to the firm's wage bill. The payroll tax is thus a tax on the use of labour by firms. This tax changes the definition of profit for the representative firm to: $\Pi \equiv PF(N, \bar{K}) - W(1 + t_W)N$. Explain the effect of the payroll tax on the demand for labour.

(c) Demonstrate the effects of an increase of the payroll tax on employment (N) and the gross real wage (W/P). Who ends up ultimately paying the payroll tax—the firms or the worker-households?

(d) Introduce a value-added (consumption) tax (t_C) in the simple labour market model. Explain what happens to employment (N) and the gross real wage (W/P). Who ultimately pays the tax?

(e) Use the insights from questions (b)–(d) to analyse the effects of a costly im-provement of labour conditions. Who pays the costs eventually and who be-nefits from the improvements?

Question 6: The Keynesian cross model

Consider a closed economy described by the following equations:

$$Y = C + I + G, \tag{Q1.13}$$
$$C = C_0 + c(Y - T), \qquad 0 < c < 1, \tag{Q1.14}$$

where Y, C, I, G, and T are, respectively, output, consumption, investment, govern-ment consumption, and taxes. C_0 represents the exogenous part of consumption and c is the marginal propensity to consume. Assume that prices are fixed and that I, G, and T are all exogenous.

(a) Recall that $Y = C + S + T$. Derive the *savings equation*, i.e. the expression relating S to aggregate income and the parameters of the model.

(b) Derive an expression for the equilibrium condition involving the savings equa-tion.

(c) Demonstrate the so-called *paradox of thrift* by computing the effects on out-put, saving, and consumption, of a decrease in C_0. Why do we call this phe-nomenon a paradox of thrift?

(d) Compute the output multiplier with respect to government consumption, dY/dG, under the assumption that the government finances its additional spend-ing by raising the tax (i.e. $dT = dG$). Explain the intuition behind thisso-called *Haavelmo* (balanced-budget) multiplier. Show the different rounds of the mul-tiplier process.

(e) Now assume that taxes depend positively on output, i.e. $T = tY$, where t is the marginal (and average) tax rate (it is assumed that $0 < t < 1$). Compute the output multiplier with respect to government consumption, dY/dG, under the assumption that the government finances its additional spending by selling bonds. Is the multiplier obtained here greater or smaller than the Haavelmo multiplier? Show what happens to consumption and the government deficit $(G - T)$. Explain your answers both formally and intuitively.

Question 7: The import leakage

We extend the model of question 6 by assuming that the economy is open to trade in goods and services. Assume that prices are fixed and that I, G, and T are all exogenous. The economy is described by the following equations:

$$Y = C + I + G + X \tag{Q1.15}$$
$$C = C_0 + c(Y - T), \qquad 0 < c < 1, \tag{Q1.16}$$
$$X = X_0 - mY, \qquad 0 < m < 1, \tag{Q1.17}$$

where X is net exports (exports minus imports), and m is the marginal propensity to import goods and services. The exogenous component of net exports is given by X_0.

(a) Solve the model by finding expressions for the endogenous variables (Y, C, and X) in terms of the exogenous variables (I, G, C_0, X_0, and T) and the parameters (c and m). These are the so-called *reduced-form* expressions for output, consumption, and net exports.

(b) Compute the output multiplier with respect to government consumption. Does the propensity to import increase or decrease this multiplier? Explain the intuition behind the import leakage.

(c) Compute the effect on output, consumption, and net exports of an increase in world trade (represented by an increase in X_0). Explain the intuition behind your results.

★ Question 8: The liquidity trap

A.C. Pigou was a colleague but not a big personal friend of Keynes. He refused to take the so-called *liquidity trap* seriously. He claimed (just like Blinder and Solow, to be studied in Chapter 2) that consumption also depends positively on real wealth (A, for "assets"), so that the economy can never find itself permanently in the "liquidity trap." Suppose that we write the consumption function as $C = C(Y - T, A)$ (with $0 < C_{Y-T} < 1$ and $C_A > 0$) and that wealth consists of real capital plus real money balances ($A = \bar{K} + M/P$). Explain that Pigou may well be right. Illustrate Pigou's argument graphically.

★ Question 9: The IS-LM-AS model with inflation

We can formulate the following classical macroeconomic model of a closed economy:

$$Y = C(Y - T) + I(R - \pi) + G, \quad 0 < C_{Y-T} < 1, \; I_{R-\pi} < 0, \quad \text{(Q1.18)}$$

$$M/P = l(Y, R), l_Y > 0, \qquad l_R < 0 \quad\quad\quad\quad\quad \text{(Q1.19)}$$

$$N^D = N^D(W/P, \bar{K}), \quad\quad\quad\quad\quad\quad\quad\quad \text{(Q1.20)}$$

$$W/P = g(N^S), \qquad g_N > 0, \quad\quad\quad\quad\quad\quad \text{(Q1.21)}$$

$$[N \equiv] \; N^D = N^S, \quad\quad\quad\quad\quad\quad\quad\quad\quad \text{(Q1.22)}$$

$$Y = F(N, \bar{K}), \quad\quad\quad\quad\quad\quad\quad\quad\quad\quad \text{(Q1.23)}$$

where Y is aggregate output, C is consumption, T is taxes, I is investment, R is the nominal interest rate, π is the anticipated inflation rate, G is government consumption, M is the money supply, P is the price level, N is labour, and W is the nominal wage. The endogenous variables are Y, P, N, R, and W. Exogenous are π, G, and $\bar{K}$. Technology features constant returns to scale.

(a) Interpret the equations.

(b) What are the effects of an adverse supply shock, proxied by a fall in the capital stock, on the price level, the real wage, employment and output?

(c) Why do fiscal and monetary policy not affect employment and output?

(d) What are the effects of a fiscal and a monetary expansion on the price level and the interest rate?

(e) Can you think of classical channels by which demand-side policies do affect employment and output?

Answers

Question 1: Short questions

(a) The effective LM curve is horizontal at the interest rate R_0. The AD curve is vertical, i.e. does not depend on the price level. See Figure A1.1.

(b) If capital and labour are cooperative production factors, then more capital increases the marginal productivity of labour and more labour increases the marginal productivity of capital. A simple example (see page 4 in the textbook): The use of robot mixers in the kitchen enhances the productivity of the cooks.

(c) The IS-curve describes equilibrium on the goods-market $Y = C(Y) + I(R) + G$. Total differentiation gives the slope of the IS-curve (with R the variable on the vertical axis and keeping G constant):

$$dY = C_Y dY + I_R dR \quad \Rightarrow \quad [1 - C_Y]dY = I_R dR \quad \Rightarrow \quad \frac{dR}{dY} = \frac{1 - C_Y}{I_R}$$

If investment depends only weakly on the interest rate, then I_R is very small, so dR/dY is large and the IS-curve is almost vertical (very steep).

(d) Their answers to two questions are different: (a) can the government affect the economy, and (b) should the government stabilize the economy. The classical economists say (a) maybe, and (b) no. The Keynesians say (a) yes, and (b) yes.

(e) Competitive labour demand functions take the form $W/P = F_N(N, K)$. They slope down in the $(W/P, N)$ space because there are diminishing returns to the labour input, $F_{NN}(N, K) < 0$.

With constant returns to scale and only two factors of production, it must be the case that $F_{NK} > 0$. This result is proved formally in Intermezzo 4.1.

Question 2: The Cobb-Douglas production function

(a) Under perfect competition the representative firm hires labour up to the point where the value of the marginal product of labour equals the nominal wage:

$$PF_N = W \tag{A1.1}$$

From the Cobb-Douglas equation (Q1.1) we get:

$$F_N = \varepsilon N^{\varepsilon-1} \bar{K}^{1-\varepsilon} = \varepsilon \frac{Y}{N}. \tag{A1.2}$$

By combing (A1.1) and (A1.2) we obtain:

$$[F_N =]\frac{W}{P} = \varepsilon \frac{Y}{N} \quad \Rightarrow \quad \varepsilon = \frac{WN}{PY}. \tag{A1.3}$$

Hence, ε represents the national income share of wages.

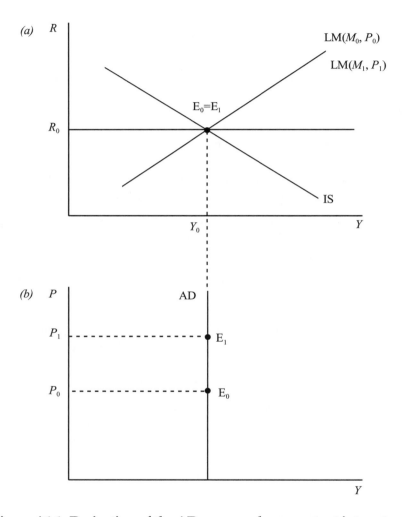

Figure A1.1: Derivation of the AD curve under a constant interest rate

(b) From equation (A1.1) and (A1.2) we get:

$$\varepsilon\left(\frac{N}{\bar{K}}\right)^{\varepsilon-1} = \frac{W}{P} \quad \Rightarrow \quad N = \bar{K}\left(\frac{W}{\varepsilon P}\right)^{\frac{1}{\varepsilon-1}}. \tag{A1.4}$$

By substituting (A1.4) into the Cobb-Douglas production function (Q1.1) we obtain the short-run supply of output:

$$Y = N^\varepsilon \bar{K}^{1-\varepsilon} = \left[\bar{K}\left(\frac{W}{\varepsilon P}\right)^{\frac{1}{\varepsilon-1}}\right]^\varepsilon \bar{K}^{1-\varepsilon} \quad \Rightarrow \quad Y = \bar{K}\left(\frac{W}{\varepsilon P}\right)^{\frac{\varepsilon}{\varepsilon-1}}. \tag{A1.5}$$

In terms of relative changes we derive in a straightforward fashion from (A1.4) and (A1.5):

$$\frac{dN}{N} = \frac{d\bar{K}}{\bar{K}} - \frac{1}{1-\varepsilon}\left[\frac{dW}{W} - \frac{dP}{P}\right],$$

$$\frac{dY}{Y} = \frac{d\bar{K}}{\bar{K}} - \frac{\varepsilon}{1-\varepsilon}\left[\frac{dW}{W} - \frac{dP}{P}\right].$$

(c) The wage elasticities of labour demand and output supply are, respectively, $1/(1-\varepsilon)$ and $\varepsilon/(1-\varepsilon)$ in absolute value.

Question 3: The AS-AD model

(a) The labour demand curve is obtained by setting marginal labour productivity equal to the real wage rate:

$$F_N(N, \bar{K}) = W/P \quad \Rightarrow \quad \alpha[\bar{K}/N]^{1-\alpha} = W/P \quad \Rightarrow$$

$$N = \bar{K}\left[\frac{W}{\alpha P}\right]^{\frac{1}{\alpha-1}} \tag{A1.6}$$

The real wage elasticity of labour demand is:

$$\varepsilon_D = -\frac{W/P}{N}\frac{\partial N}{\partial(W/P)}$$

Differentiate the labour demand equation (A1.6) with respect to W/P and we have:

$$\frac{\partial N}{\partial(W/P)} = -\frac{1}{1-\alpha}\frac{N}{W/P} \quad \Rightarrow \quad \varepsilon_D = \frac{1}{1-\alpha}.$$

Because $0 < \alpha < 1$, the real wage elasticity is always negative (real wages up, labour demand down, as expected).

(b) Substitute $C = WN/P^e$ into the utility function (Q1.3) and differentiate with respect to N, set the first order condition to 0 and we have the labour supply equation:

$$\frac{\partial U}{\partial N} = 0 : \gamma N^\sigma = W/P^e \quad \Rightarrow \quad W/P = \gamma\frac{P^e}{P}N^\sigma \tag{A1.7}$$

The real wage elasticity of labour supply is:

$$\varepsilon_S = \frac{W/P}{N} \frac{\partial N}{\partial (W/P)}$$

Differentiate the labour supply equation (A1.7) with respect to W/P and we have:

$$\frac{\partial N}{\partial (W/P)} = \frac{1}{\sigma} \frac{N}{W/P} \quad \Rightarrow \quad \varepsilon_S = \frac{1}{\sigma} > 0$$

The substitution effect dominates the income effect.

(c) Substitute W/P of the labour supply equation (A1.7) into the labour demand equation (A1.6):

$$N = \bar{K} \left[\frac{\gamma}{\alpha} \frac{P^e}{P} N^\sigma \right]^{\frac{1}{\alpha-1}} \quad \Rightarrow \quad N = \left[\frac{\alpha}{\gamma} \frac{P}{P^e} \bar{K}^{1-\alpha} \right]^{\frac{1}{1-\alpha+\sigma}}$$

This is the relation between N and P. As you can see, if P goes up, N goes up. Substitute the equilibrium level of labour into the production function, do all the math correctly and we have the aggregate supply curve:

$$Y = B \left(\frac{P}{P^e} \right)^\delta \tag{A1.8}$$

with:

$$\delta \equiv \frac{\alpha}{1-\alpha+\sigma}, \quad \beta \equiv \alpha \left[\frac{1-\alpha}{1-\alpha+\sigma} + \frac{1-\alpha}{\alpha} \right], \quad B \equiv \left[\frac{\alpha}{\gamma} \right]^\delta \bar{K}^\beta$$

(d) θ is the change in aggregate demand if *real* money balances increase 1 unit. From the IS-LM model we know that θ must be positive (LM curve shifts to the right).

(e) See Figure A1.2. The AD curve shifts to the right, households are surprised at impact and have not yet adjusted their expected price levels, the AS curve stays where it was. P and Y both increase from P_0 to P_1 resp. Y_0 to Y_1. In the following periods households adjust their expectations based on the previous forecasting error, and the AS-curve slowly shifts to the left until there is a new equilibrium at E_∞. The model is stable. If people are blessed with perfect foresight, they always supply the correct amount of labour, so the AS-curve is vertical and prices immediately jump to the new equilibrium E_∞.

Question 4: Consumption tax

(a) Here we can use the substitution method. (Do not use the Lagrangian, it makes the problem more difficult.) Substitute (Q1.8) into (Q1.7), transform the utility function ($\hat{U} = e^U$) and we have the simple utility function:

$$\hat{U} = (W/P)N + Z_0 - \gamma \frac{N^{1+\sigma}}{1+\sigma}$$

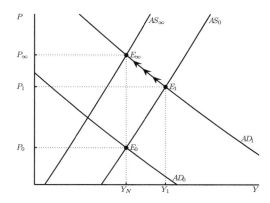

Figure A1.2: Effect of a monetary expansion under AEH

Differentiation with respect to N gives the labour supply equation:

$$\frac{\partial U}{\partial N} = 0 : N = \left[\frac{W/P}{\gamma}\right]^{\frac{1}{\sigma}}$$

(b) Consumption increases one-for-one but labour supply stays the same. There is no income effect in labour supply. Labour supply is given in the previous question, exogenous transfers do not enter the labour supply function, so apparently labour supply does not change. This means (through the budget equation) that all extra income is spent on consumption.

(c) The utility function (Q1.7) is unchanged, the new budget constraint is:

$$(1+t_C)PC = wN + Z_0 \quad \Rightarrow \quad C = \frac{(W/P)N + Z_0}{1 + t_C} \tag{A1.9}$$

Substitution of (A1.9) into the utility function (Q1.7) and transformation of that utility function gives:

$$\hat{U} = \frac{(W/P)N + Z_0}{1 + t_C} - \gamma \frac{N^{1+\sigma}}{1+\sigma}$$

Differentiation with respect to N gives the new labour supply equation:

$$\frac{\partial U}{\partial N} = 0 : N = \left[\frac{W/P}{(1+t_C)\gamma}\right]^{\frac{1}{\sigma}} \tag{A1.10}$$

Substitution of (A1.10) into the budget constraint (A1.9) gives optimal consumption:

$$C = \gamma \left[\frac{W/P}{(1+t_C)\gamma}\right]^{\frac{\sigma+1}{\sigma}} + \frac{Z_0}{1 + t_C} \tag{A1.11}$$

A higher consumption tax decreases both labour supply and consumption. Apparently the substitution effect dominates the income effect in the labour supply decision. To derive these effects formally, we differentiate the labour supply (A1.10) and optimal consumption function (A1.11) to obtain:

$$\frac{\partial N^S}{\partial t_C} = -\frac{\gamma}{\sigma(W/P)} \left[\frac{W/P}{(1+t_C)\gamma} \right]^{\frac{1+\sigma}{\sigma}} < 0$$

$$\frac{\partial C}{\partial t_C} = -\frac{\gamma^2(\sigma+1)}{\sigma(W/P)} \left[\frac{W/P}{(1+t_C)\gamma} \right]^{\frac{2\sigma+1}{\sigma}} - \frac{Z_0}{(1+t_C)^2} < 0$$

(d) A Cobb-Douglas production function. The firm's problem is:

$$\max_{\{N\}} \Pi = PY - WN \quad \text{subject to} \quad Y = N^\alpha K_0^{1-\alpha}$$

Substitution gives:

$$\max_{\{N\}} \Pi = PN^\alpha K_0^{1-\alpha} - WN$$

The first order constraint is the labour demand equation:

$$\alpha N^{\alpha-1} K^{1-\alpha} = \frac{W}{P}$$

Taking natural logarithms gives:

$$\ln \alpha - (1 - \alpha) [\ln N - \ln K_0] = \ln(W/P)$$

Rewriting gives the labour demand equation.

(e) Equating labour demand (Q1.9) and supply (A1.10) gives:

$$\left[\frac{w}{(1+t_C)\gamma} \right]^{1/\sigma} = K \left[\frac{\alpha}{w} \right]^{\frac{1}{1-\alpha}}$$

Rewriting yields:

$$w = (1+t_C)^{\frac{1-\alpha}{1-\alpha+\sigma}} B \quad \text{with} \quad B = \left[\gamma K^\sigma \alpha^{\frac{\sigma}{1-\alpha}} \right]^{\frac{1-\alpha}{1-\alpha+\sigma}}$$

Differentiation gives:

$$\frac{\partial w}{\partial t_C} = B \frac{1-\alpha}{1-\alpha+\sigma} (1+t_C)^{\frac{\sigma}{1-\alpha+\sigma}} > 0$$

By substituting the expression for w into the labour supply expression we find:

$$N = \left(\frac{B(1+t_C)^{\frac{1-\alpha}{1-\alpha+\sigma}}}{(1+t_C)\gamma} \right)^{1/\sigma} = \left(\frac{B}{\gamma} \right)^{1/\sigma} (1+t_C)^{\frac{-1}{1-\alpha+\sigma}},$$

from which we find immediately that:

$$\frac{\partial N}{\partial t_C} < 0$$

Question 5: Tax incidence

(a) We assume that the substitution effect (SE) dominates the income effect (IE). SE: if $W/P \uparrow$ then leisure is more expensive relative to consumption so the household consumes less leisure and thus supplies more labour. IE: if $W/P \uparrow$ the value of the time endowment increases and the household is richer. Because leisure (like goods consumption) is a normal good, one consumes more of it. Labour supply falls on that account.

(b) The firms sets its labour demand such that short-run profit is maximized. In formal terms we have:

$$\frac{d\Pi}{dN} = PF_N(N, \bar{K}) - W(1 + t_W) = 0 \quad \Rightarrow \quad F_N(N^D, \bar{K}) = (1 + t_W)(W/P)$$

where $w \equiv W/P$ is the *gross* real wage. This equation is the implicit demand for labour. By differentiating with respect to N^D and t_W (holding constant $\bar{K}$ and w) we find:

$$F_{NN}dN^D = (W/P)dt_W \quad \Rightarrow \quad \frac{dN^D}{dt_W} = \frac{(W/P)}{F_{NN}} < 0,$$

where the inequality follows from the fact that $F_{NN} < 0$. For a given real wage, an increase in t_W shifts the demand for labour curve to the left, see Figure A1.3.

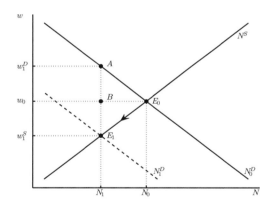

Figure A1.3: Effect of a payroll tax

(c) It follows directly from Figure A1.3 that equilibrium employment and the gross real wage both fall. The initial equilibrium is at point E_0 and the new equilibrium is at E_1. In E_0 we have $g(N_0) = (W/P)_0 = F_N(N_0, \bar{K})$ whilst in E_1 we have $g(N_1) = (W/P)_1^S$ and $F_N(N_1, \bar{K}) = (1 + t_W)(W/P)_1^S = (W/P)_1^D$. Both the firm and the household end up paying part of the tax. For the household the real wage used to be $(W/P)_0$ but it falls to $(W/P)_1^S$. The difference, $(W/P)_0 - (W/P)_1^S$ is the part of the tax implicitly paid by the household (see the segment E_1B in Figure A1.3). For the firm, the real wage used to be w_0 but inclusive of the tax it becomes $(W/P)_1^D = (1 + t_W)(W/P)_1^S$. The firm thus implicitly pays $(W/P)_1^D - (W/P)_0$ which is the segment AB in Figure A1.3.

(d) The value-added tax is a tax on the consumption of the worker (the supplier of labour). The household maximizes:

$$\max_{\{C,N^S\}} U \equiv U(C, 1 - N^S) \quad \text{subject to} \quad (1 + t_C)PC = N^S,$$

The first-order condition is:

$$\frac{U_{1-N}}{U_C} = \frac{(W/P)}{1 + t_C} \equiv w_C.$$

Ceteris paribus W/P, the real wage that concerns the household (the so-called *consumer wage*, w_C) falls if t_C is increased. If the substitution effect (SE) dominates the income effect (IE) then the increase in t_C leads to a reduction in labour supply. Equilibrium employment falls and the gross wage, W/P, rises. Part of the tax is paid by households (segment AB in Figure A1.4) and part is paid by the firms (segment BE_1).

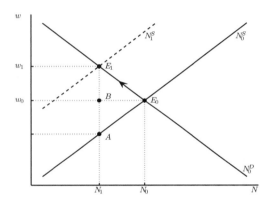

Figure A1.4: Effect of a value-added tax

(e) A mandatory improvement of labour conditions costs the company money. This can be seen as a payroll tax, it increases the costs per employee and the employee does not receive a higher wage. According to part (b) and (c), the labour demand curve shifts down and equilibrium employment and gross wage rate both go down. As with the tax, both the firm and the employee pay for part of the improvement. If the improved labour conditions lead to higher productivity, the labour demand curve will shift back somewhat, thus partially offsetting the initial shock.

Question 6: The Keynesian cross model

(a) From the information given in the question we derive:

$$\begin{aligned}
S &= Y - C - T \\
&= (Y - T) - C_0 - c(Y - T) \\
&= (1 - c)(Y - T) - C_0,
\end{aligned} \tag{A1.12}$$

where $1 - c$ thus represents the propensity to save out of disposable income. By adding T to both sides of equation (A1.12) we find the following expression:

$$S + T = (1 - c)(Y - T) - C_0 + T$$
$$= (1 - c)Y + cT - C_0. \tag{A1.13}$$

Equation (A1.13) is useful because it can be used in combination with the equilibrium condition derived in part (b).

(b) We know that $Y = C + I + G = C + S + T$. The second equality implies that the equilibrium condition can be written as:

$$I + G = S + T. \tag{A1.14}$$

The left-hand side is exogenous (in this model) and the right-hand side depends on Y according to equation (A1.13) above.

(c) The paradox of thrift in words: an exogenous increase in the thriftiness of the private sector ends up lowering income and leaving equilibrium saving unchanged. Presumably, increased thriftiness is good, but it ends up causing a bad effect on the economy. The increase in thriftiness is modelled by a decrease in C_0 (see equation (A1.12) above). Formally, we find by combining (A1.13)–(A1.14) that the equilibrium condition can be written as:

$$I + G = (1 - c)Y + cT - C_0. \tag{A1.15}$$

By differentiating both sides of (A1.15) with respect to C_0 (and noting that I, G, and T are exogenous) we obtain:

$$0 = (1 - c)\frac{dY}{dC_0} - \frac{dC_0}{dC_0} \quad \Rightarrow \quad \frac{dY}{dC_0} = \frac{1}{1 - c} > 1. \tag{A1.16}$$

From equation (A1.12) we get:

$$\frac{dS}{dC_0} = (1 - c)\frac{dY}{dC_0} - \frac{dC_0}{dC_0}$$
$$= (1 - c)\frac{1}{1 - c} - 1 = 0, \tag{A1.17}$$

where we have used (A1.16) in the final step. Hence, a decrease in C_0 leads to a decrease in Y but leaves S unchanged. The paradox of thrift has been illustrated in Figure A1.5.

(d) We compute the Haavelmo multiplier. By substituting equation (Q1.14) into (Q1.13) we obtain:

$$Y = C_0 + c(Y - T) + I + G \quad \Rightarrow$$
$$Y = \frac{C_0 - cT + I + G}{1 - c}. \tag{A1.18}$$

By differentiating equation (A1.18) we obtain:

$$dY = \frac{-cdT + dG}{1 - c} = \frac{-cdG + dG}{1 - c} = dG \quad \Rightarrow$$
$$\left(\frac{dY}{dG}\right)_{dG=dT} = 1, \tag{A1.19}$$

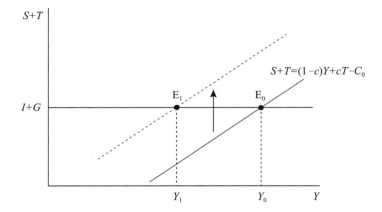

Figure A1.5: The paradox of thrift

Round	Effect on C	Effect on Y
1	$-cdG$	$(1-c)dG$
2	cdY_1	cdY_1
3	cdY_2	cdY_2
$\vdots$	$\vdots$	$\vdots$
n	cdY_{n-1}	cdY_{n-1}
sum	dC^n	dY^n

Table A1.1: The multiplier process

where we have imposed the balanced budget requirement, $dT = dG$, in going from the first to the second equality. To find out what happens to consumption we differentiate equation (Q1.14) with respect to G:

$$\left(\frac{dC}{dG}\right)_{dG=dT} = c\left[\left(\frac{dY}{dG}\right)_{dG=dT} - \frac{dT}{dG}\right]$$
$$= c[1-1] = 0, \tag{A1.20}$$

where we have used (A1.19) and $dT = dG$ in the final step.

The intuition behind the Haavelmo multiplier can be illustrated by explicitly tracing the multiplier process (as in done in the text) for the Kahn multiplier). In Table A1.1 we show the different "rounds" of the multiplier process.

In round 1 of the multiplier process consumption falls (due to the additional taxes) but income rises (because private consumption falls by cdG but public consumption rises by dG). In the second round the increase in output (and thus in household income) boosts consumption by cdY_1, where dY_1 is the income change in round 1. This in turn provides a boost to income in round 2. By gathering terms in the second column of Table A1.1 we get the cumulative change in consumption after n rounds of the multiplier process:

$$
\begin{aligned}
dC^n \equiv \sum_{i=1}^{n} dC_i &= -cdG + cdY_1 + c^2 dY_1 + c^3 dY_1 + \cdots + c^{n-1} dY_1 \\
&= -cdG + \left[c + c^2 + \cdots + c^{n-1} \right] (1-c) dG \\
&= -cdG - (1-c) dG + \left[1 + c + c^2 + \cdots + c^{n-1} \right] (1-c) dG \\
&= -dG + \left[1 + c + c^2 + \cdots + c^{n-1} \right] (1-c) dG. \qquad \text{(A1.21)}
\end{aligned}
$$

By letting $n \to \infty$ we find that the term in square brackets on the right-hand side of (A1.21) converges to $1/(1-c)$ so that:

$$
\lim_{n \to \infty} dC^n = -dG + \frac{1}{1-c} (1-c) dG = 0, \qquad \text{(A1.22)}
$$

which is—of course—the result we found analytically in equation (A1.20).

In a similar fashion we find for the output effect after n rounds:

$$
\begin{aligned}
dY^n \equiv \sum_{i=1}^{n} dY_i &= (1-c) dG + cdY_1 + c^2 dY_1 + c^3 dY_1 + \cdots + c^{n-1} dY_1 \\
&= (1-c) dG + \left[c + c^2 + \cdots + c^{n-1} \right] (1-c) dG \\
&= \left[1 + c + c^2 + \cdots + c^{n-1} \right] (1-c) dG. \qquad \text{(A1.23)}
\end{aligned}
$$

Letting $n \to \infty$ we find:

$$
\lim_{n \to \infty} dY^n = \frac{1}{1-c} (1-c) dG = 1, \qquad \text{(A1.24)}
$$

which again confirms the analytical result obtained in (A1.19) above. In Figure A1.6 we illustrate the Haavelmo multiplier graphically. The initial equilibrium is at E_0 and the final equilibrium is at E_1. The dashed line from E_0 to E_1 represents the rounds of the multiplier process.

(e) By using the new tax schedule, $T = tY$, in equation (Q1.14) and combining the resulting expression with (Q1.13) we obtain:

$$
Y = C_0 + c(Y - tY) + I + G \quad \Rightarrow \quad Y = \frac{C_0 + I + G}{1 - c(1-t)}. \qquad \text{(A1.25)}
$$

For consumption we find:

$$
\begin{aligned}
C &= C_0 + c(1-t)Y \\
&= C_0 + c(1-t) \frac{C_0 + I + G}{1 - c(1-t)} \\
&= \frac{C_0 + c(1-t)[I + G]}{1 - c(1-t)}, \qquad \text{(A1.26)}
\end{aligned}
$$

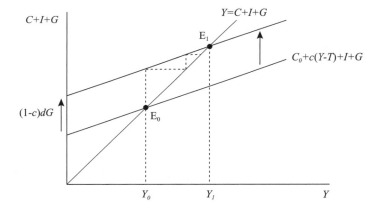

Figure A1.6: The Haavelmo multiplier

where we have used (A1.25) in going from the first to the second line. Similarly, we find for the deficit:

$$
\begin{aligned}
G - T &= G - tY \\
&= G - t \frac{C_0 + I + G}{1 - c(1 - t)} \\
&= \frac{-t[C_0 + I] + (1 - c)(1 - t)G}{1 - c(1 - t)},
\end{aligned}
\tag{A1.27}
$$

where we have used (A1.25) in going from the first to the second line.

By using (A1.25)–(A1.27) we immediately find the following multipliers:

$$
\frac{dY}{dG} = \frac{1}{1 - c(1 - t)} > 1,
\tag{A1.28}
$$

$$
\frac{dC}{dG} = \frac{c(1 - t)}{1 - c(1 - t)} > 0,
\tag{A1.29}
$$

$$
\frac{d(G - T)}{dG} = \frac{(1 - c)(1 - t)}{1 - c(1 - t)} > 0.
\tag{A1.30}
$$

The inequality in (A1.28) follows from the fact that $0 < c < 1$ and $0 < t < 1$ so that $0 < c(1 - t) < 1$ follows readily. The output multiplier is larger than the Haavelmo multiplier (given in (A1.19) above). In the text we explain the tax leakage in detail. By financing with bonds, which play no further role in the Keynesian Cross model, the dampening effect of taxation is reduced substantially. As equation (A1.29) shows, in this case consumption rises, whereas it stays the same in the Haavelmo case.

Question 7: The import leakage

(a) By substituting (Q1.16)–(Q1.17) into (Q1.15) we obtain:

$$\begin{aligned}
Y &= C_0 + c(Y - T) + I + G + X_0 - mY \\
&= C_0 - cT + I + G + X_0 + (c - m)Y \quad \Rightarrow \\
Y &= \frac{C_0 - cT + I + G + X_0}{1 - c + m}.
\end{aligned} \tag{A1.31}$$

By substituting (A1.31) into (Q1.16) we find the reduced form expression for consumption:

$$\begin{aligned}
C &= C_0 + c\left[\frac{C_0 - cT + I + G + X_0}{1 - c + m} - T\right] \\
&= \frac{(1 - c + m)(C_0 - cT) + c(C_0 - cT + I + G + X_0)}{1 - c + m} \\
&= \frac{(1 + m)(C_0 - cT) + c(I + G + X_0)}{1 - c + m}.
\end{aligned} \tag{A1.32}$$

Similarly, by substituting (A1.31) into (Q1.17) we find the reduced form expression for imports:

$$\begin{aligned}
X &= X_0 - m\,\frac{C_0 - cT + I + G + X_0}{1 - c + m} \\
&= \frac{(1 - c + m)X_0 - m(C_0 - cT + I + G + X_0)}{1 - c + m} \\
&= \frac{(1 - c)X_0 - m(C_0 - cT + I + G)}{1 - c + m}.
\end{aligned} \tag{A1.33}$$

(b) Since the reduced form expressions contain only exogenous variables we can obtain the multiplier directly from (A1.31). Indeed, by differentiating (A1.31) with respect to G we obtain:

$$\frac{dY}{dG} = \frac{1}{1 - c + m} > 0. \tag{A1.34}$$

Formally we find from (A1.34) that:

$$\frac{\partial\,(dY/dG)}{\partial m} = -\frac{1}{(1 - c + m)^2} < 0, \tag{A1.35}$$

from which we conclude that the multiplier falls as the import propensity gets larger. The import leakage implies that part of the additional income generated by the fiscal impulse leaks away in the form of imports from abroad. These imports are produced abroad and do not generate domestic income. Hence, they put a dampening effect on the multiplier.

(c) From the reduced form expressions for Y, C, and X (given in (A1.31)–(A1.33)

Round	Effect on C	Effect on X	Effect on Y
1	0	dX_0	dX_0
2	cdY_1	$-mdY_1$	$(c-m)dY_1$
3	cdY_2	$-mdY_2$	$(c-m)dY_2$
$\vdots$	$\vdots$	$\vdots$	$\vdots$
n	cdY_{n-1}	$-mdY_{n-1}$	$(c-m)dY_{n-1}$
sum	dC^n	dX^n	dY^n

Table A1.2: The multiplier process with an import leakage

above) we find the following effects:

$$\frac{dY}{dX_0} = \frac{1}{1-c+m} > 0, \tag{A1.36}$$

$$\frac{dC}{dX_0} = \frac{c}{1-c+m} > 0, \tag{A1.37}$$

$$\frac{dX}{dX_0} = \frac{1-c}{1-c+m} > 0. \tag{A1.38}$$

The increase in world trade leads to an increase in domestic demand because (net) exports increase. This creates additional income which leads to a boost in consumption and a slight fall in net exports (as imports increase). In Table A1.2 we trace the different rounds of the multiplier process.

By adding the entries on column 2 of Table A1.2 we obtain the cumulative effect on consumption after n rounds of the multiplier process:

$$dC^n = 0 + cdY_1 + c(c-m)dY_1 + c(c-m)^2dY_1 + \cdots + c(c-m)^{n-2}dY_1$$
$$= cdX_0 \left[1 + (c-m) + (c-m)^2 + \cdots + (c-m)^{n-2}\right]. \tag{A1.39}$$

Since $|c-m| < 1$ (see below) we find that the term in square brackets converges to $1/(1-(c-m))$ as $n \to \infty$. Hence, the effect on consumption ultimately converges to:

$$\lim_{n\to\infty} dC^n = cdX_0 \frac{1}{1-(c-m)} = \frac{c}{1-c+m}dX_0. \tag{A1.40}$$

This confirms the expression given in (A1.37) above. For exports we find:

$$dX^n = dX_0 - mdY_1 - m(c-m)dY_1 - m(c-m)^2dY_1 - \cdots$$
$$\qquad - m(c-m)^{n-2}dY_1$$
$$= dX_0 \left[1 - m(1 + (c-m) + (c-m)^2 + \cdots + (c-m)^{n-2})\right] \tag{A1.41}$$

$$\lim_{n\to\infty} dX^n = dX_0 \left[1 - \frac{m}{1-(c-m)}\right]$$
$$\qquad = \frac{1-c}{1-c+m}dX_0. \tag{A1.42}$$

Finally, for output we obtain:

$$dY^n = dX_0 + (c - m)dY_1 + (c - m)^2 dY_1 + \cdots + (c - m)^{n-1} dY_1$$

$$= dX_0 \left[1 + (c - m) + (c - m)^2 + \cdots + (c - m)^{n-1}\right] \quad \text{(A1.43)}$$

$$\lim_{n \to \infty} dY^n = dX_0 \left[\frac{1}{1 - (c - m)}\right]$$

$$= \frac{1}{1 - c + m} dX_0. \quad \text{(A1.44)}$$

It remains to show that $-1 < c - m < 1$. The first inequality implies $c > m - 1$ which holds because $c > 0$ and $m - 1 < 0$ (since $m < 1$). The second inequality implies $c < 1 + m$ which holds because $c < 1$ and $1 + m > 1$ (since $m > 0$).

Question 8: The liquidity trap

With the modification suggested by Pigou, the model for the closed economy finding itself in a "liquidity trap" is:

$$Y = C\left(Y - T(Y), \bar{K} + M/P\right) + I(R^{MIN}) + G,$$

$$M/P = l(R^{MIN}, Y).$$

A reduction in the price level leads to an increase in real money balances (M/P). Households feel wealthier and increase consumption accordingly. Aggregate demand for goods and services is boosted. As a result, the slope of the AD curve is negative even in the liquidity trap. The classical model is no longer inconsistent. In formal terms we have:

$$dY = C_{Y-T}(1 - T_Y)dY + \underbrace{\frac{l_R}{l_R}\left[d(M/P) - l_Y dY\right]}_{(\star)} + C_A d(M/P).$$

If $L_R \to -\infty$ then $R \to R^{MIN}$ and the term marked with $(\star)$ vanishes. The IS curve is price sensitive as is the AD curve:

$$\left(\frac{dY}{dP}\right)_{AD} = -\frac{C_A M/P^2}{1 - C_{Y-T}(1 - T_Y)} < 0.$$

Question 9: The IS-LM-AS model with inflation

(a) The only non-standard feature of the model is that investment now depends on the real interest rate, $R - \pi$. Accumulating physical capital is a real activity which thus involves the real rate of interest. In the standard IS-LM model prices are fixed so we need not distinguish real from nominal interest rates.

(b) The model features the classical dichotomy. Equations (Q1.20)–(Q1.23) constitute the aggregate supply side and determine unique values for the real wage, employment and output as a function of the exogenous capital stock (and parameters of technology and labour supply). With output determined by the supply side, equations (Q1.18)–(Q1.19) determine the interest rate and the price

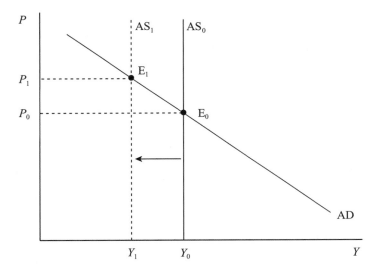

Figure A1.7: An adverse productivity shock in the classical model

level as a function of the exogenous parameters (G, M, T, and π). Prices are fully flexible.

The effect of a supply shock (proxied by a reduction in $\bar{K}$) can be studied with the aid of Figure A1.7. Equations (Q1.18)–(Q1.19) implicitly define the downward sloping AD curve:

$$Y = AD\left(\frac{M}{P}, G, T, \pi\right),\tag{A1.45}$$

with $AD_{M/P} > 0$, $AD_G > 0$, $AD_T < 0$, and $AD_\pi > 0$. The first three partial derivatives are standard but the fourth warrants some comment. In terms of an IS-LM diagram, an increase in π, leads *for a given nominal interest rate* to a decrease in the real interest rate, an increase in investment, and an outward shift in the IS curve. The new IS-LM equilibrium occurs at a higher nominal interest rate and a higher income level. In terms of the AD-AS diagram, the AD curve shifts out.

Equations (Q1.20)–(Q1.23) implicitly define the AS curve which is vertical in (P, Y) space and depends positively on the exogenous capital stock:

$$Y = AS(\bar{K}),\tag{A1.46}$$

with $AS_{\bar{K}} > 0$. An increase in $\bar{K}$ boosts labour demand (because the production factors are cooperative), and leads to an increase in equilibrium employment and a higher real wage. Output expands for two reasons: because of the direct effect of $\bar{K}$ itself and because of the induced employment effect.

In Figure A1.7, the decrease in $\bar{K}$ shifts the AS curve to the left. Output falls and the price level rises. The real wage falls because labour demand falls. The price increase lowers real money balances so that the LM curve shifts to the left. The interest rate increases and investment falls on that account. The decrease in output also causes a reduction in consumption.

(c) As is explained above, fiscal and monetary policy only affect the demand side of the model and thus only affect P and R. Prices and wages are fully flexible.

(d) *Fiscal policy*: An increase in G (or a decrease in T) shifts the IS and AD curves to the right. Since the AS curve is unaffected, the price level increases but output is unchanged. The increase in the price reduces real money balances and shifts LM to the left. On balance, output is unchanged and the interest rate is increased. Government consumption crowds out private investment one for one, i.e. $dI = -dG$.

Monetary policy: An increase in M shifts the LM and AD curves to the right. Since the AS curve is unaffected, the price level increases but output is unchanged. The increase in the price reduces real money balances and shifts LM back to its original position. On balance, output and the interest rate are unchanged but the price level is permanently higher. Real money balances are constant, however, so we have that $dP/P = dM/M$.

(e) One channel by which demand-side policies can affect the supply side runs via labour supply. Assume that labour supply contains a wealth effect, i.e. that equation (Q1.21) is replaced by:

$$N^S = N^S(W/P, A), \tag{A1.47}$$

where $A \equiv \bar{K} + M/P$ represents tangible assets. We expect that the wealth effect in labour supply is negative, i.e. $\partial N^S / \partial A < 0$. As households are wealthier they wish to consume more leisure and thus work less. The AS curve can be written as:

$$Y = AS(M/P, \bar{K}), \tag{A1.48}$$

with $AS_{M/P} < 0$. Both AD and AS are affected by fiscal and monetary policy. Because prices are flexible, monetary policy is still neutral. Fiscal policy shifts the AD curve to the right which leads to an increase in both equilibrium output and the price level. For a given money supply, real money balances fall which explains why output supply rises (households are less wealthy and supply more labour). In Chapter 15 we show that the new classical model of labour supply (based on intertemporal optimization) indeed gives rise to a broadly defined wealth effect in labour supply. It is shown there that human wealth (the present value of the after-tax time endowment) also affects labour supply. This implies that the present value of taxes also affects the supply side of the economy.

Another channel by which demand-side policies can affect the supply side runs via the capital accumulation identity, $\dot{K} = I(R - \pi) - \delta K$. If anything changes gross investment, then this will affect the capital stock (both during transition and in the steady state) which in turn will affect the supply side. More details are given in Chapter 14. Stock-flow interaction in IS-LM style models is studied in more detail in Chapter 2.

Chapter 2

Dynamics in aggregate demand and supply

Question 1: Short questions

(a) What is the so-called "correspondence principle" and why is it so useful in principle? Provide an example.

(b) What do we mean by "backward-looking stability "? And what is "forward-looking stability"? Provide and example of both concepts.

(c) Keynesians and monetarists engaged in a heated debate during the sixties and seventies of the previous century. Topic of the debate was the question of whether or not government consumption leads to crowding out of the capital stock. Explain why this debate could not be settled by simply appealing to the correspondence principle.

Question 2: The Keynesian cross model (continued)

Consider the following Keynesian cross model for the closed economy:

$$Y = C + I + G, \tag{Q2.1}$$
$$C = C_0 + c(Y - T), \qquad 0 < c < 1, \tag{Q2.2}$$
$$I = I_0 + \dot{Z}, \tag{Q2.3}$$
$$\dot{Y} = -\gamma \dot{Z}, \qquad \gamma > 0, \tag{Q2.4}$$

where Y is output, C is consumption, I is *actual* investment, G is government consumption, T is taxes, I_0 is *planned* investment, and Z is the stock of inventories. A variable with a dot denotes that variable's rate of change over time, i.e. $\dot{Z} \equiv dZ/dt$ and $\dot{Y} \equiv dY/dt$. C_0 and I_0 represent the exogenous parts of, respectively, consumption and investment, and c is the marginal propensity to consume. Assume that prices are fixed and that G and T are both exogenous.

(a) Interpret the equations of the model.

(b) Show that the model is stable. Illustrate your answer graphically by developing the phase diagram for the model.

(c) Show the effects over time on output, consumption, actual investment, and inventories, of a tax-financed increase in government consumption ($dT = dG$). Is the short-run output multiplier smaller or larger than the long-run output multiplier? Explain.

Question 3: The IS-LM model with capital accumulation

Consider the following simple model of the economy. Investment is endogenous and depends (among other things) on the level of the capital stock. The equations of the model are:

$$Y = C + I + G, \tag{Q2.5}$$
$$C = C_0 + cY, \tag{Q2.6}$$
$$\frac{M}{P} = \beta_0 Y + \beta_1 R, \tag{Q2.7}$$
$$\dot{K} = I - \delta K, \tag{Q2.8}$$
$$I = \alpha_0 R + \alpha_1 K + \alpha_2 Y. \tag{Q2.9}$$

Here c is the marginal propensity to consume ($0 < c < 1$), Y is aggregate output, C is consumption, M/P is the real money supply (exogenous), R is the interest rate, G is government consumption, I is gross investment, K is the capital stock, and $\dot{K} \equiv dK/dt$ is the time rate of change in K.

(a) Provide an economic interpretation for equations (Q2.5)-(Q2.9). What signs do you expect for α_0, α_1, α_2, β_0, en β_1?

(b) Derive the stability condition for this model. Illustrate your answer with a diagram.

(c) Derive the short-run and the long-run output multipliers with respect to an increase in government consumption.

Question 4: Stability of the IS-LM model

Consider the following short-run dynamics in the closed-economy IS-LM model. It is assumed that the price level is fixed and (for convenience) has been normalized to unity ($P = 1$):

$$\dot{R} = \phi_1 \left[I(Y, R) - M \right], \qquad\qquad \phi_1 > 0, \tag{Q2.10}$$
$$\dot{Y} = \phi_2 \left[C(Y - T) + I(R) + G - Y \right], \quad \phi_2 > 0, \tag{Q2.11}$$

where Y is output, R is the interest rate, M is the money stock, C is consumption, T is taxes, I is investment, and G is government consumption. As usual, a dot above a variables denotes that variable's time rate of change, i.e. $\dot{R} \equiv dR/dt$ and $\dot{Y} \equiv dY/dt$.

(a) Interpret these equations.

(b) Can you say something about the relative speeds of adjustment in the goods and financial markets?

(c) Use a two-dimensional phase diagram in order to derive the stability properties of this model and the qualitative nature of the transient adjustment paths for output and the interest rate associated with a fiscal expansion.

(d) ★ Derive the stability condition for this model mathematically.

Question 5: The Blinder-Solow model

Consider a closed economy with fixed prices ($P = P_0 = 1$ for convenience), a given stock of capital ($K = \bar{K}$) and wealth effects in the demand for money and the consumption function:

$$Y = C + I + G, \tag{Q2.12}$$
$$C = C(Y + B - T, A), \qquad 0 < C_{Y+B-T} < 1, \ C_A > 0, \tag{Q2.13}$$
$$I = I(R), \qquad I_R < 0, \tag{Q2.14}$$
$$T = T_0 + t(Y + B), \qquad 0 < t < 1, \tag{Q2.15}$$
$$M = l(Y, R, A), \qquad l_Y > 0, \ l_R < 0, \ 0 < l_A < 1, \tag{Q2.16}$$
$$A \equiv \bar{K} + M + B/R, \tag{Q2.17}$$
$$G + B = T + \dot{M} + (1/R)\dot{B}, \tag{Q2.18}$$

where Y is output, C is consumption, I is investment, G is government consumption, B is government debt, T is taxes, A is private wealth, R is the rate of interest, T_0 is the exogenous part of taxes, t is the marginal tax rate, $\bar{K}$ is the capital stock, and M is the money supply. As usual, a dot above a variables denotes that variable's time rate of change, i.e. $\dot{M} \equiv dM/dt$ and $\dot{B} \equiv dB/dt$.

(a) Interpret the equations of the model.

(b) In the book we derive reduced-form expressions for output and the nominal interest rate which we write here in short-hand notation as $Y = AD(G, B, M)$ and $R = H(G, B, M)$. Draw IS-LM style diagrams to motivate the signs of AD_G, AD_B, AD_M, H_G, H_B and H_M. Explain the intuition behind your results.

(c) Compute the "balanced-budget" output multiplier for the case in which the additional government consumption is financed by means of additional taxes. Assume that the government adjusts T_0 in order to ensure that $dG = dT$. Show that the required change in T_0 satisfies $0 < dT_0/dG < 1$. Explain your results graphically.

(d) Is the multiplier obtained in part c larger or smaller than the Haavelmo multiplier derived in Question 6(d) of Chapter 1? Explain any differences.

Question 6: Ricardian equivalence in the Blinder-Solow model

Some economists stress the importance of Ricardian equivalence, i.e. that bond finance or tax finance of a given stream of public spending is irrelevant for private consumption. The idea is that bond finance is perceived as postponed taxation, so that households save in order to provide for future taxation. A simple way to allow for this idea is to modify the Blinder-Solow model as follows:

$$C = C(Y^D, A), \qquad\qquad 0 < C_{YD} < 1, \, C_A > 0, \qquad\qquad (Q2.19)$$

$$Y^D \equiv Y + B - T - \dot{B}/R, \qquad\qquad\qquad\qquad (Q2.20)$$

$$M/P = l(Y, R, A), \qquad\qquad l_Y > 0, \, l_R < 0, \, 0 < l_A < 1, \qquad (Q2.21)$$

$$A \equiv \bar{K} + M/P, \qquad\qquad\qquad\qquad\qquad (Q2.22)$$

$$G + B = T + \dot{M} + (1/R)\dot{B}, \qquad\qquad\qquad\qquad (Q2.23)$$

$$T = T_0 + t(Y + B - \dot{B}/R), \quad 0 < t < 1, \qquad\qquad (Q2.24)$$

$$Y = C + I(R) + G, \qquad\qquad I_R < 0, \qquad\qquad\qquad (Q2.25)$$

where C is consumption, Y^D is disposable income, A is household wealth, Y is output, B is government debt, T is taxes, R is the interest rate, M is the money stock, P is the fixed price level, $\bar{K}$ is the capital stock, G is government consumption, T_0 is the lump-sum tax, t is the marginal tax, and I is investment. As usual, a dot above a variables denotes that variable's time rate of change, i.e. $\dot{M} \equiv dM/dt$ and $\dot{B} \equiv dB/dt$.

(a) Interpret the consumption function and the definition of private wealth, A. Why does this modification not alter the conclusions regarding money financing?

(b) Show that under bond financing disposable income is simply income minus government spending and thus demonstrate that private consumption rises only with income minus government spending.

(c) Show that a bond-financed and a tax-financed rise in public spending have identical effects on output, consumption and the interest rate and, furthermore, that the short-run and long-run effects coincide.

(d) Show that under bond financing the government debt explodes unless taxes rise strongly enough with government debt (or public spending is cut back severely enough as government debt explodes).

Question 7: The Blinder-Solow model with capital accumulation

Consider a Blinder-Solow model of a small open economy with an integrated capital market. Assume that the price level is fixed and has been normalized to unity ($P = 1$):

$$C = C(Y^D, A), \quad 0 < C_{YD} < 1, \, C_A > 0, \qquad\qquad (Q2.26)$$

$$Y^D \equiv Y + B + F - T, \qquad\qquad\qquad\qquad (Q2.27)$$

$$T = T_0 + t(Y + B + F), \quad 0 < t < 1, \qquad\qquad (Q2.28)$$

$$M = l(Y, R, A), \quad l_Y > 0, \, l_R < 0, \, 0 < l_A < 1, \qquad (Q2.29)$$

$$A \equiv \bar{K} + M + B/R + F/R^*, \qquad\qquad\qquad (Q2.30)$$

$$R = R^*, \qquad\qquad\qquad\qquad\qquad\qquad (Q2.31)$$

$$(1/R)\dot{B} = G + B - T - \dot{M}, \qquad\qquad\qquad\qquad (Q2.32)$$

$$(1/R)\dot{F} = F + [Y - C - I(R) - G], \quad I_R < 0, \qquad (Q2.33)$$

where C is consumption, Y^D is disposable income, A is wealth, Y is output, B is government bonds, F denotes net foreign asset holdings of the country, T is taxes, t is the marginal tax rate, M is the money supply, R is the domestic interest rate, $\bar{K}$ is the fixed capital stock, R^* is the world interest rate, G is government consumption, and I is investment.

(a) Interpret the equations of this model. Which are the endogenous variables? Which are the exogenous variables?

(b) Can you say something about the effectiveness of fiscal policy and stability under money finance? Show that $l_A > R^* l_Y$ is a *sufficient* stability condition.

(c) Can you say something about the effectiveness of fiscal policy and stability under bond finance?

Question 8: Adaptive expectations in a monetarist model

Consider the following monetarist model with adaptive expectations:

$$Mv = PY, \qquad\qquad v > 0, \tag{Q2.34}$$
$$\pi = \phi[y - y^*] + \pi^e, \qquad \phi > 0, \tag{Q2.35}$$
$$\dot{\pi}^e = \zeta[\pi - \pi^e], \qquad\qquad \zeta > 0, \tag{Q2.36}$$
$$\mu \equiv \dot{M}/M, \tag{Q2.37}$$

where M is the money supply, v is the velocity of circulation of the money supply (a constant), P is the price level, y is the logarithm of output ($y \equiv \ln Y$), π is the actual inflation rate ($\pi \equiv \dot{P}/P$), y^* is the logarithm of full employment output, π^e is expected inflation, and μ is the growth rate in the money supply.

(a) Interpret these equations. Which are the exogenous and which are the endogenous variables?

(b) Show that the reduced form of this model is given by:

$$\dot{y}/y = \mu - \pi^e - \phi[y - y^*], \tag{Q2.38}$$
$$\dot{\pi}^e = \zeta\phi[y - y^*]. \tag{Q2.39}$$

(c) Demonstrate mathematically the stability of this model (i.e. prove that the two eigenvalues have negative real parts).

(d) Use a phase diagram to derive the transient and steady-state effects on output and inflation of a monetary disinflation (a cut in the monetary growth rate μ).

Question 9: More on adaptive expectations

Consider the following log-linear macroeconomic model of a closed economy featuring adaptive expectations:

$$y = \theta(m - p) + \psi\pi^e + \zeta g, \quad \theta > 0,\ \psi > 0,\ \zeta > 0, \tag{Q2.40}$$
$$\pi = \phi[y - y^*] + \pi^e, \qquad\qquad \phi > 0, \tag{Q2.41}$$
$$\dot{\pi}^e = \lambda[\pi - \pi^e], \qquad\qquad \lambda > 0, \tag{Q2.42}$$

where y is output, m is the money supply, p is the price level, π^e is expected inflation, g is an index for fiscal policy, $\pi \equiv \dot{p}$ is actual inflation (recall that, if P stands for the price level, we have that $\pi \equiv \dot{P}/P = d \ln P/dt \equiv \dot{p}$), and y^* is full employment output. All variables are measured in logarithms and a dot above a variable denotes that variable's time rate of change. The endogenous variables are y, p, and π^e. The exogenous variables are g, m, and y^*. All parameters as well as y^* are assumed to be constant over time. The rate of nominal money growth is defined as $\mu \equiv \dot{m}$.

(a) Interpret the equations of the model.

(b) Show that in the short run (for a given expected inflation rate) the model has Keynesian features whilst it has classical features in the long run (with a variable expected inflation rate).

(c) Investigate the stability properties of the model by deriving a system of differential equations in π^e and y. Why is the model not automatically stable for all parameter values, as was the case for the monetarist model of question 8?

(d) Derive the impact, transitional, and long-run effects on output, the price *level*, actual inflation, and expected inflation, of an increase in the money growth rate. Assume that the parameters satisfy $\phi(\theta - \psi\lambda)^2 > 4\lambda\theta$.

(e) Derive the impact, transitional, and long-run effects on output, the price *level*, actual inflation, and expected inflation, of an increase in the index of fiscal policy. *Hint*: do not forget that the fiscal impulse causes a positive impact effect on output! Make the same assumption as in part (d).

Question 10: Optimization and computation

Suppose that we are considering a small open economy with a representative firm. This firm is a price taker in the markets for its inputs and its outputs. The interest rate and product prices are exogenously determined on world markets and for simplicity assumed (or expected) to be constant. Prices are normalized to $P = 1$. The capital stock depreciates at a constant rate $\delta > 0$, so the capital stock evolves according to

$$K_{t+1} = K_t + I_t - \delta K_t, \tag{Q2.43}$$

where I_t is investment in year t and K_t is the installed capital stock. Investment is costly, the representative firm has to pay adjustment costs to install extra capital. These adjustment costs are assumed to be quadratic in the level of investment. For the sake of simplicity assume that labour is completely irrelevant in the production process (the so-called AK-model). The representative firm chooses investment to maximize the present value of future and current profits. The firm's maximization problem is:

$$\max_{\{I_t\}} V = \sum_{t=0}^{\infty} \left(\frac{1}{1+R}\right)^t \Pi_t = \sum_{t=0}^{\infty} \left(\frac{1}{1+R}\right)^t \left(AK_t - I_t - bI_t^2\right), \tag{Q2.44}$$

where R is the interest rate, A is technology, and b is a strictly positive parameter.

(a) Solve the firm's optimization problem and find expressions for the steady-state levels of investment, capital and production.

Take as parameter values $A = 0.5$, $R = 0.03$, $\delta = 0.07$, and $b = 5$.

(b) What are the steady-state levels of production, capital, investment given these parameter values?

(c) Suppose that the economy is in the steady state. A large earthquake destroys 20% of the installed capital stock. What happens with capital, investment, and production over the next 10 years?

★ Question 11: The multiplier-accelerator model

[Based on Samuelson (1939)] Consider the Samuelson-Hansen discrete-time variant of the multiplier-accelerator model:

$$Y_t = C_t + I_t + G, \tag{Q2.45}$$
$$C_t = cY_{t-1}, \qquad 0 < c < 1, \tag{Q2.46}$$
$$I_t = v[C_t - C_{t-1}], \quad v > 0, \tag{Q2.47}$$

where Y_t is output, C_t is consumption, I_t is investment, G is (time-invariant) government consumption, c is the marginal propensity to consume, and v is the investment acceleration coefficient (vc is thus the desired capital-output ratio).

(a) Interpret the equations of the model.

(b) Define the marginal propensity to save as $s \equiv (1 - c)$. Show that the adjustment path in output after, say, a rise in public spending can be characterized by:

I $v \leq \frac{1-\sqrt{s}}{1+\sqrt{s}}$ stable monotonic adjustment

II $\frac{1-\sqrt{s}}{1+\sqrt{s}} < v < \frac{1}{1-s}$ stable cyclical adjustment

III $\frac{1}{1-s} < v < \frac{1+\sqrt{s}}{1-\sqrt{s}}$ explosive oscillations

IV $v \geq \frac{1+\sqrt{s}}{1-\sqrt{s}}$ steady, monotonic explosion

Illustrate your answers by constructing a diagram with v on the horizontal axis and c on the vertical axis displaying the various qualitative modes of dynamic adjustment.

Answers

Question 1: Short questions

(a) Correspondence principle: only use stable models. This gives information that is typically useful in comparative static exercises. Unstable models are useless because, following a shock, the system does not return to a meaningful equilibrium.

(b) Backward-looking stability: history determines where you are. No need to look at the future to know how the system evolves to the equilibrium. Forward-looking stability: both the past and the future determine the adjustment path. The forward-looking part typically deals with expectations.

(c) The correspondence principle is needed to ensure that the model is stable. But stable models can still lead to crowding out or to crowding in. It all depends on the slopes of IS and LM. See page 49 in the textbook.

Question 2: The Keynesian cross model (continued)

(a) Equation (Q2.1) is the national income identity. It holds trivially because I includes unintended inventory formation. Equation (Q2.2) is the standard Keynesian consumption function, featuring a marginal propensity to consume between 0 and 1. Equation (Q2.3) shows that actual investment equals planned investment (I_0, assumed to be exogenous) plus unintended inventory change ($\dot{Z}$). Equation (Q2.4) shows that firms are assumed to increase (decrease) production if inventories fall (rise). This equation introduces some rudimentary dynamics into the Keynesian Cross model.

(b) By substituting equations (Q2.2)–(Q2.3) into (Q2.1) we obtain:

$$Y = C_0 + c(Y - T) + I_0 + \dot{Z} + G \quad \Rightarrow$$
$$\dot{Z} = (1 - c)Y - [C_0 - cT + I_0 + G]. \tag{A2.1}$$

By substituting (Q2.4) into (A2.1) we obtain the differential equation for Y:

$$\dot{Y} = -\gamma(1 - c)Y + \gamma[C_0 - cT + I_0 + G]. \tag{A2.2}$$

Equation (A2.2) is a stable differential equation in Y because the coefficient for Y on the right-hand side is negative, i.e. $\partial\dot{Y}/\partial Y = -\gamma(1 - c) < 0$. Steady-state output is computed by setting $\dot{Y} = 0$ in (A2.2) and solving for Y:

$$Y^* = \frac{C_0 - cT + I_0 + G}{1 - c}. \tag{A2.3}$$

We draw the phase diagram for the model in Figure A2.1. The initial steady state is at point E_0 with output equal to Y_0^*. If actual output exceeds (falls short of) Y_0^* then $\dot{Y}$ is negative (positive). The adjustment process is stable.

(c) We derive from equation (A2.3) that the tax-financed increase in government consumption shifts the steady-state output level:

$$dY^* = \frac{-cdT + dG}{1 - c} = \frac{-cdG + dG}{1 - c} = dG \quad \Rightarrow \quad \frac{dY^*}{dG} = 1, \tag{A2.4}$$

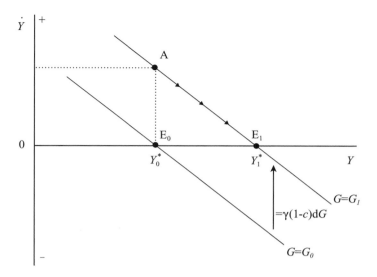

Figure A2.1: Stability of the Keynesian Cross model

where we have used the balanced-budget requirement, $dT = dG$, in going from the first to the second equality. Recall that (A2.4) is the famous Haavelmo multiplier. In graphical terms, the $\dot{Y}$ line is shifted vertically by $\gamma(1 - c)dG$ in Figure A2.1. At impact, actual output is unable to change instantaneously and is thus equal to Y_0^*. Demand is boosted, however, and unintended inventory reductions prompt a jump in $\dot{Y}$. The economy jumps from E_0 to A directly above it. Over time, the economy moves along the new $\dot{Y}$ line (labelled $G = G_1$) from A to E_1. The paths for the remaining variables are easily deduced. At impact, consumption falls (because the tax rises) and actual investment jumps down (because $\dot{Z} < 0$ at impact). Over time, the gradual increase in Y causes a gradual increase in consumption and the reduction in $\dot{Z}$ causes an increase in actual investment.

To find out what happens to steady-state consumption we use (Q2.2) and (A2.4):

$$\frac{dC^*}{dG} = c\left[\frac{dY^*}{dG} - \frac{dT}{dG}\right] = c(1 - 1) = 0. \tag{A2.5}$$

Because $\dot{Z} = 0$ in the steady state and I_0 is exogenous, there is no effect on investment:

$$\frac{dI^*}{dG} = 0. \tag{A2.6}$$

We plot the impulse-response diagram in Figure A2.2.

Obviously, the short-run output multiplier is zero because it takes time before output and production can be expanded. Running down inventories does not create additional household income because these goods were produced in the past. In the long run, however, output expands which does lead to additional household income. That is the reason why the long-run (steady-state) multiplier exceeds the short-run multiplier.

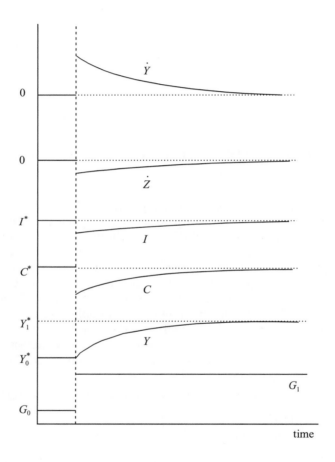

Figure A2.2: Impulse-response diagram Haavelmo multiplier

Question 3: The IS-LM model with capital accumulation

(a) Equation (Q2.5) is the national income identity. Equation (Q2.6) is the consumption function. Psychological law of Keynes: $0 < c < 1$. Equation (Q2.7) in the money market equilibrium condition. We expect $\beta_0 > 0$ (transactions motive) and $\beta_1 < 0$ (opportunity cost and speculative motive). Equation (Q2.8) is the capital accumulation identity, linking gross investment (I) with net investment ($\dot{K}$). Equation (Q2.9) is the optimal firm demand for investment. It can be motivated with a static version of Tobin's q theory. Investment depends on $I = F_K / (R + \delta)$. We expect $\alpha_0 < 0$ due to heavier discounting. Also, we expect $F_K \propto Y/K$, so that $\alpha_2 > 0$ and $\alpha_1 < 0$.

(b) Step 1: Solve (Q2.5)–(Q2.6) to get:

$$Y = \frac{C_0 + I + G}{1 - c}. \tag{A2.7}$$

Step 2: Solve equation (Q2.7) for R:

$$
\begin{aligned}
R &= \frac{1}{\beta_1} \left[\frac{M}{P} - \beta_0 Y \right] \\
&= \frac{1}{\beta_1} \left[\frac{M}{P} - \beta_0 \frac{C_0 + I + G}{1 - c} \right],
\end{aligned}
\tag{A2.8}
$$

Step 3: Use (A2.7) and (A2.8) in (Q2.9) to get quasi-reduced form expression for I:

$$
\begin{aligned}
I &= \alpha_0 R + \alpha_1 K + \alpha_2 Y \\
&= \frac{\alpha_0}{\beta_1} \left[\frac{M}{P} - \beta_0 \frac{C_0 + I + G}{1 - c} \right] + \alpha_1 K + \alpha_2 \frac{C_0 + I + G}{1 - c} \quad \Rightarrow \\
I &= \Omega \left[\frac{\alpha_0}{\beta_1} \frac{M}{P} + \alpha_1 K + \left(\alpha_2 - \frac{\alpha_0 \beta_0}{\beta_1} \right) \frac{C_0 + G}{1 - c} \right],
\end{aligned}
\tag{A2.9}
$$

where Ω is:

$$\Omega \equiv \frac{1 - c}{1 - c + \frac{\alpha_0 \beta_0}{\beta_1} - \alpha_2} \gtrless 0.$$

Step 4: Use (A2.9) in equation (Q2.8):

$$
\begin{aligned}
\dot{K} &= I - \delta K \\
&= \Omega \frac{\alpha_0}{\beta_1} \frac{M}{P} + \alpha_1 \Omega K + \left[\alpha_2 - \frac{\alpha_0 \beta_0}{\beta_1} \right] \Omega \frac{C_0 + G}{1 - c} - \delta K
\end{aligned}
\tag{A2.10}
$$

Step 5: The model is stable if and only if $\partial \dot{K} / \partial K < 0$:

$$\frac{\partial \dot{K}}{\partial K} = \alpha_1 \Omega - \delta < 0. \tag{A2.11}$$

Since $\alpha_1 < 0$ and $\delta > 0$ it follows that a sufficient condition for stability is $\Omega > 0$. This condition is not necessary: even if $\Omega < 0$ the condition may be satisfied. In the stable case, the phase diagram has a downward sloping $\dot{K}$ line.

(c) The short-run multiplier can be computed for a given $K = K_0$. We obtain:

$$(1 - c)Y = C_0 + \alpha_0 R + \alpha_1 K_0 + \alpha_2 Y + G,$$

$$R = \frac{1}{\beta_1} \left[\frac{M}{P} - \beta_0 Y \right],$$

so that:

$$(1 - c)Y = C_0 + \frac{\alpha_0}{\beta_1} \left[\frac{M}{P} - \beta_0 Y \right] + \alpha_1 K_0 + \alpha_2 Y + G$$

$$\left[1 - c + \frac{\alpha_0 \beta_0}{\beta_1} - \alpha_2 \right] Y = C_0 + \frac{\alpha_0}{\beta_1} \frac{M}{P} + \alpha_1 K_0 + G$$

$$\frac{1 - c}{\Omega} Y = C_0 + \frac{\alpha_0}{\beta_1} \frac{M}{P} + \alpha_1 K_0 + G$$

or:

$$\left(\frac{dY}{dG} \right)^{SR} = \frac{\Omega}{1 - c} \gtreqless 0.$$

In the "regular" case, $\Omega > 0$ and the multiplier is positive.

The long-run multiplier is computed by using (A2.10) and setting $\dot{K} = 0$ (stable case):

$$\delta dK = \alpha_1 \Omega dK + \left[\alpha_2 - \frac{\alpha_0 \beta_0}{\beta_1} \right] \Omega \frac{dG}{1 - c}$$

$$(\delta - \alpha_1 \Omega) dK = \left[\alpha_2 - \frac{\alpha_0 \beta_0}{\beta_1} \right] \Omega \frac{dG}{1 - c}$$

$$\left(\frac{dK}{dG} \right)^{LR} = \frac{1}{\delta - \alpha_1 \Omega} \left[\alpha_2 - \frac{\alpha_0 \beta_0}{\beta_1} \right] \frac{\Omega}{1 - c}$$

$$= \frac{1}{\delta - \alpha_1 \Omega} \left[\alpha_2 - \frac{\alpha_0 \beta_0}{\beta_1} \right] \left(\frac{dY}{dG} \right)^{SR} \gtreqless 0.$$

Question 4: Stability of the IS-LM model

(a) Equation (Q2.10) postulates that the interest rate rises if there is excess demand for money (EDM) and falls if there is excess supply of money (ESM). The intuition is as follows. If there is EDM there is automatically excess supply of bonds (ESB). Bond prices fall and the interest rate rises. Vice versa for ESM (and EDB). Equation (Q2.11) postulates that output rises if there is excess demand for goods (EDG) and falls if there is excess supply of goods (ESG). The intuition is, for example, provided by the adjustment of inventories studied in question 2 above.

(b) One would expect that the financial markets (for money and bonds) adjust much more quickly than the goods market. Hence, one would expect that ϕ_1 is much larger than ϕ_2. In the limiting case, financial adjustment is infinitely fast ($\phi_1 \to \infty$) and the economy is always on the LM curve.

(c) The phase diagram is drawn in Figure A2.3. The IS curve represents (R, Y) combinations for which output is constant over time:

$$\dot{Y} = 0 \quad \Leftrightarrow \quad Y = C(Y - T) + I(R) + G. \tag{A2.12}$$

By totally differentiating (Q2.11) with respect to Y, R, and G we get:

$$d\dot{Y} = \phi_2 \left[-(1 - C_{Y-T})dY + I_R dR + dG \right]. \tag{A2.13}$$

Equation (A2.13) contains all the information we need. First, by setting $dR = dG = 0$ we find that in points to the right (left) of the IS curve, output is falling (rising) over time:

$$\frac{\partial \dot{Y}}{\partial Y} = -\phi_2 (1 - C_{Y-T}) < 0, \tag{A2.14}$$

where the sign follows from the fact that $\phi_2 > 0$ and $0 < C_{Y-T} < 1$. This explains the horizontal arrows in Figure A2.3. Second, by setting $d\dot{Y} = dG = 0$ in (A2.13) we obtain the slope of the IS curve:

$$\left(\frac{\partial Y}{\partial R} \right)_{IS} = \frac{I_R}{1 - C_{Y-T}} < 0. \tag{A2.15}$$

Third, by setting $d\dot{Y} = dR = 0$ in (A2.13) we find that the IS curve shifts horizontally to the right if government consumption is increased:

$$\left(\frac{\partial Y}{\partial G} \right)_{d\dot{Y}=dR=0} = \frac{1}{1 - C_{Y-T}} > 1. \tag{A2.16}$$

The LM curve represents (R, Y) combinations for which the money market is in equilibrium:

$$\dot{R} = 0 \quad \Leftrightarrow \quad M = l(Y, R). \tag{A2.17}$$

By totally differentiating (Q2.10) with respect to Y and R we obtain $d\dot{R} = \phi_1 [l_Y dY + l_R dR]$, from which we derive:

$$\frac{\partial \dot{R}}{\partial R} = \phi_1 l_R < 0, \qquad \left(\frac{\partial Y}{\partial R} \right)_{LM} = -\frac{l_R}{l_Y} > 0. \tag{A2.18}$$

For points above (below) the LM curve, there is ESM and EDB (EDM and ESB) and the interest rate falls (rises). This explains the vertical arrows in Figure A2.3. The second result in (A2.18) shows that the LM curve slopes upwards.

The configuration of arrows in Figure A2.3 demonstrates that the equilibrium E_0 (where $\dot{R} = \dot{Y} = 0$) is stable. If the economy starts out in point A, then it may follow the stable trajectory through points B through E to eventually end up at E_0. In part (d) of this question we study the adjustment path more formally. (Make sure that you understand why the trajectory is vertical at points B and D and is horizontal at points C and E.)

In Figure A2.4 we show the effects of an increase in government consumption assuming that the economy starts out in the initial steady-state equilibrium E_0. The fiscal policy shifts the IS curve to the right (to IS_1). After this shock,

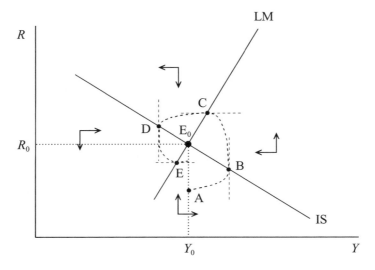

Figure A2.3: Stability of the IS-LM model

point E_0 is no longer the steady-state equilibrium: it is on the LM curve (so there is money market equilibrium) but it lies to the left of the new IS curve and thus features EDG. The arrows depict the dynamic forces associated with the new equilibrium E_1. Several types of adjustment paths towards the new equilibrium at E_1 are possible depending on the relative magnitudes of ϕ_1 and ϕ_2. If financial adjustment is very fast ($\phi_1 \to \infty$) then the economy moves along the LM curve from E_0 to E_1. If goods market adjustment is very fast ($\phi_2 \to \infty$) then the economy would move instantaneously from E_0 to A after which it would gradually move from A to E_1. In the intermediate case, with both ϕ_1 and ϕ_2 finite, but the former much larger than the latter, one would expect either monotonic adjustment (as with the dashed trajectory) or a case in which the trajectory approaches E_1 in a cyclical fashion (as drawn in Figure A2.3).

(d) (See Chiang (1984, pp. 638-645) for further details). Formally we can investigate local stability (near point E_1) by differentiating (Q2.10)–(Q2.11) with respect to R, Y, and G and writing the system in a single matrix equation:

$$\begin{bmatrix} d\dot{R} \\ d\dot{Y} \end{bmatrix} = \begin{bmatrix} \phi_1 l_R & \phi_1 l_Y \\ \phi_2 I_R & -\phi_2(1 - C_{Y-T}) \end{bmatrix} \begin{bmatrix} dR \\ dY \end{bmatrix} + \begin{bmatrix} 0 \\ \phi_2 dG \end{bmatrix}, \tag{A2.19}$$

where Δ is the Jacobian matrix on the right-hand side. It has the following determinant and trace:

$$|\Delta| \equiv \phi_1\phi_2[-l_R(1 - C_{Y-T}) - l_Y I_R] > 0, \tag{A2.20}$$

$$\operatorname{tr}\Delta \equiv \phi_1 l_R - \phi_2(1 - C_{Y-T}) < 0. \tag{A2.21}$$

The dynamic adjustment is regulated by the characteristic roots of the matrix Δ which we denote by λ_1 and λ_2. Recall that the determinant of Δ equals the product of its characteristic roots ($|\Delta| = \lambda_1\lambda_2$) whilst the trace of Δ equals the

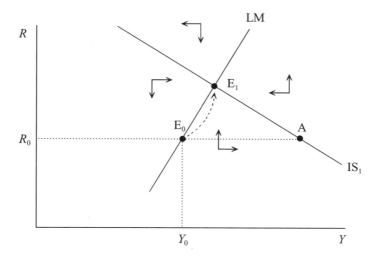

Figure A2.4: Adjustment after a fiscal impulse

sum of its roots ($\operatorname{tr}\Delta = \lambda_1 + \lambda_2$). Since $|\Delta| > 0$ and $\operatorname{tr}\Delta < 0$ it must be the case that both characteristic roots are negative (stable). The characteristic roots of Δ are the zeros of the characteristic equation of Δ, $A(\lambda) \equiv |\Delta - \lambda I| = 0$. After some manipulation we get:

$$
\begin{aligned}
A(\lambda) &= \begin{vmatrix} \phi_1 l_R - \lambda & \phi_1 l_Y \\ \phi_2 I_R & -\phi_2(1 - C_{Y-T}) - \lambda \end{vmatrix} \\
&= (\lambda - \phi_1 l_R)[\phi_2(1 - C_{Y-T}) + \lambda] - \phi_1 \phi_2 l_Y I_R \\
&= \lambda^2 - \operatorname{tr}\Delta\,\lambda + |\Delta| = 0.
\end{aligned}
\tag{A2.22}
$$

Equation (A2.22) is a quadratic equation in λ which has two roots:

$$
\lambda_1 = \frac{\operatorname{tr}\Delta + \sqrt{(\operatorname{tr}\Delta)^2 - 4|\Delta|}}{2},
\tag{A2.23}
$$

$$
\lambda_2 = \frac{\operatorname{tr}\Delta - \sqrt{(\operatorname{tr}\Delta)^2 - 4|\Delta|}}{2}.
\tag{A2.24}
$$

There are two cases that are possible, depending on the sign of $D \equiv (\operatorname{tr}\Delta)^2 - 4|\Delta|$.

- *Case 1:* If $D > 0$ then both roots are real and distinct. If $D = 0$ then the roots are the same. In both cases the equilibrium is a *stable node* (adjustment is monotonic as in the dashed trajectory in Figure A2.4).

- *Case 2:* If $D < 0$ then the roots are complex, i.e. $2\lambda_1 = \operatorname{tr}\Delta + i\sqrt{-D}$ and $2\lambda_2 = \operatorname{tr}\Delta - i\sqrt{-D}$ where i is the imaginary unit (which satisfies $i^2 = -1$). The equilibrium is in that case a *stable focus* (stable but cyclical adjustment towards E_1). The adjustment is stable because the characteristic roots have negative real parts (equalling $\operatorname{tr}\Delta/2$) but it is cyclical because these roots are complex.

Question 5: The Blinder-Solow model

(a) This model is explained in great detail in section 2.4 of the book. The only thing that has been changed here is the tax function. Instead of using the general functional form (2.61) we specify a particular (linear) tax schedule (Q2.15). This allows us to parameterize the lump-sum tax, T_0, and the marginal tax rate, t, that both play a role in the question.

(b) By using (Q2.12)–(Q2.15) and (Q2.17) we obtain the expression for the IS curve:

$$Y = C[(1 - t)(Y + B) - T_0, \bar{K} + M + B/R] + I(R) + G. \tag{A2.25}$$

By totally differentiating this expression with respect to Y, R, M, and B we obtain:

$$dY = C_{Y+B-T}(1 - t)(dY + dB) + C_A[dM + (1/R)dB - (B/R^2)dR]$$
$$+ I_R dR + dG \quad \Rightarrow$$

$$dY = \frac{[I_R - (B/R^2)C_A]dR + [C_{Y+B-T}(1 - t) + C_A/R]\,dB + C_A dM + dG}{1 - C_{Y+B-T}(1 - t)}. \tag{A2.26}$$

Equation (A2.26) can be used to characterize the IS curve. Setting $dB = dM = dG = 0$ we find the slope of the IS curve:

$$\left(\frac{dY}{dR}\right)_{IS} = \frac{I_R - (B/R^2)C_A}{1 - C_{Y+B-T}(1 - t)} < 0, \tag{A2.27}$$

where the sign follows from the fact that $I_R < 0, C_A > 0, 0 < C_{Y+B-T} < 1$, and $0 < t < 1$ (so that $0 < C_{Y+B-T}(1 - t) < 1$ and the denominator is positive). As in the standard IS-LM model without wealth effects the IS curve slopes down in the model with wealth effects. To find the horizontal directions in which B, M, and G shift the IS curve we hold the interest rate constant ($dR = 0$) and find from (A2.26):

$$\frac{\partial Y}{\partial M} = \frac{C_A}{1 - C_{Y+B-T}(1 - t)} > 0, \tag{A2.28}$$

$$\frac{\partial Y}{\partial B} = \frac{C_{Y+B-T}(1 - t) + C_A/R}{1 - C_{Y+B-T}(1 - t)} > 0, \tag{A2.29}$$

$$\frac{\partial Y}{\partial G} = \frac{1}{1 - C_{Y+B-T}(1 - t)} > 1. \tag{A2.30}$$

Increases in B or M shift the IS curve to the right because the additional wealth prompts households to expand consumption and boost aggregate demand. An increase in G shifts IS to the right because aggregate demand is stimulated by the additional government consumption. In all cases the denominator represent the multiplier effect. In Figure A2.5 we show the various effects on the IS curve. Although the magnitudes of the shift generally differ for the different variables (see (A2.28)–(A2.30)) we only show one rightward shift in Figure A2.5.

By using (Q2.16)–(Q2.17) we obtain the expression for the LM curve:

$$M = l[Y, R, \bar{K} + M + B/R]. \tag{A2.31}$$

By totally differentiating this expression with respect to Y, R, B, and M we obtain:

$$dM = l_Y dY + l_R dR + l_A[dM + (1/R)dB - (B/R^2)dR] \quad \Rightarrow$$

$$dY = \frac{(1-l_A)dM - (l_A/R)dB - [l_R - l_A B/R^2]dR}{l_Y}. \tag{A2.32}$$

Again we can find out all relevant information about the LM curve from (A2.32). The slope of the LM curve is obtained by setting $dM = dB = 0$:

$$\left(\frac{dY}{dR}\right)_{LM} = \frac{-l_R + l_A B/R^2}{l_Y} > 0, \tag{A2.33}$$

where the sign follows from the fact that $-l_R > 0$, $l_A > 0$, and $l_Y > 0$. As in the standard model, the LM curve slopes up. An increase in the interest rate now causes a wealth effect in money demand as it leads to a reduction in bond prices (see equation (2.59) in the text). To restore money market equilibrium, output has to rise by more than if there is no wealth term in money demand. Hence, as usually drawn (with R on the vertical and Y on the horizontal axis), the LM curve is flatter in the presence of wealth effects. The horizontal shifts in the LM curve are obtained by setting $dR = 0$ in (A2.32) and evaluating the various partial derivatives:

$$\frac{\partial Y}{\partial M} = \frac{1-l_A}{l_Y} > 0, \tag{A2.34}$$

$$\frac{\partial Y}{\partial B} = -\frac{l_A/R}{l_Y} < 0. \tag{A2.35}$$

An increase in the money supply shifts the LM curve to right. It increases both supply and (via the wealth effect) demand on the money market but the former effect dominates the latter effect (as l_A is less than unity). An increase in bonds increases the demand for money which shifts the LM curve to the left. All the effects have been illustrated in Figure A2.5.

Assume that the initial IS-LM equilibrium is at E_0 where output is Y_0 and the interest rate is R_0. An increase in B shifts the IS curve to the right and the LM curve to the left. The equilibrium shifts from E_0 to A, and the interest rate is unambiguously higher ($H_B > 0$) because both the consumption boost (the IS shift) and the increase in money demand (the LM shift) necessitate an interest rate increase. The effect on output is, however, ambiguous, as the consumption effect works in the opposite direction to the money demand effect. This explains why $AD_B \gtreqqless 0$. (We have drawn the case of $AD_B < 0$ in Figure A2.5.)

An increase in M shifts both the IS and LM curves to the right. The equilibrium shifts from E_0 to B, and output is unambiguously higher ($AD_M > 0$). The effect on the interest rate is ambiguous as the consumption effect (the IS shift) works in the opposite direction to the net money supply effect (the LM shift). This explains why $H_M \gtreqqless 0$. (We have drawn the case of $H_M > 0$ in Figure A2.5.)

Finally, if G increases the IS curve shifts to the right, the equilibrium shifts from E_0 to C, and both output and the interest rate increase ($AD_G > 0$ and $H_G > 0$).

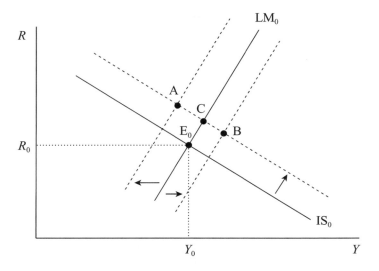

Figure A2.5: Effects of bonds, money, and government consumption

(c) The government uses T_0 to ensure that $dT = dG$. We can solve the problem in two steps. First we note that by using (Q2.12)–(Q2.14) and (Q2.17) the IS curve becomes:

$$Y = C[Y + B - T, \bar{K} + M + B/R] + I(R) + G, \tag{A2.36}$$

where it should be noted that we have *not* substituted (Q2.15) this time. Differentiating (A2.36) with respect to Y, T, R, and G (using $dT = dG$ and holding constant B, M, and $\bar{K}$) yields:

$$dY = dG + \frac{I_R - (B/R^2)C_A}{1 - C_{Y+B-T}} dR. \tag{A2.37}$$

From (A2.31) we obtain (again holding constant B, M, and $\bar{K}$):

$$dR = \frac{l_Y}{-l_R + l_A B/R^2} dY. \tag{A2.38}$$

Combining (A2.37)–(A2.38) yields the expression for the balanced-budget output multiplier:

$$dY = dG + \frac{I_R - C_A B/R^2}{1 - C_{Y+B-T}} \frac{l_Y}{-l_R + l_A B/R^2} dY \quad \Rightarrow$$

$$\left(\frac{dY}{dG}\right)_{dT=dG} = \frac{1 - C_{Y+B-T}}{1 - C_{Y+B-T} + \zeta l_Y}, \tag{A2.39}$$

where ζ is defined as:

$$\zeta \equiv \frac{C_A B/R^2 + |I_R|}{l_A B/R^2 + |l_R|} > 0. \tag{A2.40}$$

We can determine the required change in the lump-sum tax residually by using (Q2.15) in (Q2.18) and noting that $\dot{M} = \dot{B} = 0$ and $dM = dB = 0$:

$$dT = dG$$
$$dT_0 + tdY = dG \quad \Rightarrow$$
$$\frac{dT_0}{dG} = 1 - t\left(\frac{dY}{dG}\right)_{dT=dG}$$
$$= 1 - t\frac{1 - C_{Y+B-T}}{1 - C_{Y+B-T} + \zeta l_Y}. \tag{A2.41}$$

It follows from (A2.41) that $0 < dT_0/dG < 1$. Intuitively the lump-sum tax does not have to increase one-for-one with government consumption because the output expansion endogenously generates additional tax revenue provided the marginal tax rate is strictly positive (see the second term on the right-hand side of (A2.41)).

(d) Recall that the Haavelmo multiplier derived in question 6(d) of Chapter 1 is equal to unity. It is clear from (A2.39) that in the present setting the multiplier is positive but less than unity. The reason for the difference is that the interest rate changes as a result of the fiscal shock. This also happens in the standard IS-LM model without wealth effects but in the present model the interest rate operates via two channels. Even if both investment demand and money demand are interest insensitive (so that $I_R = l_R = 0$), the interest rate change still affects the multiplier because of the wealth effect caused by the revaluation of bonds (i.e. ζ is still positive if $I_R = l_R = 0$).

Question 6: Ricardian equivalence in the Blinder-Solow model

(a) Disposable income, Y^D, is now equal to:

$$Y^D \equiv Y + B - T - \frac{\dot{B}}{R}, \tag{A2.42}$$

whereas it is $Y^D \equiv Y + B - T$ in the standard Blinder-Solow model. In this view, the household understands that bond sales (with revenue $\dot{B}/R$) are really the same as delayed taxation. It therefore deducts them from income to compute disposable income. Equation (Q2.22) shows that the household does not view government bonds as net wealth–it is simply delayed taxation. (Ricardian equivalence is studied in more detail in Chapter 5.)

The conclusions regarding money financing are not affected by the change in the model because in that case $\dot{B} = 0$ (no additional bond emissions) and $dB = 0$ (constant stock of bonds). Hence, the treatment of government debt does not affect the conclusions.

(b) Under bond financing the money supply is constant ($\dot{M} = 0$ and $dM = 0$). Using (Q2.23) in (Q2.20) yields:

$$Y^D = Y + (B - T - \dot{B}/R)$$
$$= Y - G. \tag{A2.43}$$

By using (A2.43) and (Q2.22) in (Q2.19) the consumption function under bond financing is obtained:

$$C = C(Y - G, \bar{K} + M/P). \tag{A2.44}$$

Only the path of government consumption matters in the consumption function.

(c) Using (A2.44) and (Q2.25) we find that under bond financing the IS curve takes the following format:

$$Y = C(Y - G, \bar{K} + M/P) + I(R) + G. \tag{A2.45}$$

By differentiating the IS curve with respect to Y, R, and G we obtain:

$$dY = C_{YD}(dY - dG) + I_R dR + dG \quad \Rightarrow$$

$$dY = dG + \frac{I_R}{1 - C_{YD}} dR. \tag{A2.46}$$

From the LM curve (equations (Q2.21)–(Q2.22)) we obtain:

$$l_Y dY + l_R dR = 0 \quad \Rightarrow \quad dR = -\frac{l_Y}{l_R} dY. \tag{A2.47}$$

Combining (A2.46)–(A2.47) yields the multiplier:

$$dY = dG - \frac{I_R}{1 - C_{YD}} \frac{l_Y}{l_R} dY \quad \Rightarrow$$

$$\frac{dY}{dG} = \frac{1}{1 + \frac{I_R}{1-C_{YD}} \frac{l_Y}{l_R}} = \frac{1 - C_{YD}}{1 - C_{YD} + \frac{l_Y I_R}{l_R}}. \tag{A2.48}$$

Since $l_Y I_R / l_R$ is positive it follows that the multiplier lies between 0 and 1.

Under tax financing the government manipulates the lump-sum tax such that $dT = dG$. In this case, $\dot{B} = \dot{M} = 0$ and $dB = dM = 0$ so that differentiation of (Q2.19)–(Q2.20) also yields (A2.46). It follows that the multiplier under tax financing is also equal to the expression in (A2.48). Furthermore, there is no transitional dynamics in Y, C, I, and R in both cases. This explains why the short-run and long-run multipliers are identical. (Under bond financing there is dynamics in B but that has no effects on the IS-LM equilibrium because bonds are not part of household wealth.)

(d) Under bond financing we have $\dot{M} = 0$ so that the government budget identity (Q2.23) can be written as follows:

$$(1/R)\dot{B} = G + B - T_0 - t[AD(G, M/P) + B - \dot{B}/R], \tag{A2.49}$$

where $Y = AD(G, M/P)$ is the AD curve summarizing IS-LM equilibrium, and AD_G is the multiplier given in (A2.48) above. Equation (A2.49) can be rewritten as follows:

$$\dot{B} = RB + R \left[\frac{G - T_0 - tAD(G, M/P)}{1 - t} \right]. \tag{A2.50}$$

Equation (A2.50) is an unstable differential equation in B because the coefficient for B on the right-hand side is positive ($R > 0$). Unless the government increases T_0 (or decreases G), the government debt will explode according to (A2.50). (In section 13.4 of the text we study the debt stabilization rules suggested by Buiter.)

Question 7: The Blinder-Solow model with capital accumulation

(a) Equation (Q2.26) is the consumption function depending positively on disposable income (with a marginal propensity to consume between 0 and 1) and household wealth. Equation (Q2.27) provides the definition of disposable income. It includes interest income on both types of assets. Equation (Q2.28) is a linear tax function. Equation (Q2.29) is the money market equilibrium condition. Equation (Q2.30) is the definition of household wealth. It is the sum of physical capital, money, and the value of domestic and foreign bond holdings. Equation (Q2.31) is the interest parity condition, saying that identical assets (like domestic and foreign bonds in this model are) earn the same rate of return. The economy is operating under a system of fixed exchange rates so we do not have a term involving expected depreciation or appreciation of the exchange rate in (Q2.31). Equation (Q2.32) is the domestic government budget identity also found in the standard Blinder-Solow model. Finally, equation (Q2.33) is the expression for the current account, showing that the accumulation of foreign bonds equals interest earnings on foreign bonds (first term on the right-hand side) plus net exports (term in square brackets on the right-hand side). Net exports equals domestic production (Y) minus domestic absorption ($C + I + G$).

The endogenous variables in this model are: C, Y, Y^D, T, R, A, B, and F. The exogenous variables are: $\bar{K}$, M, T_0, t, R^*, and G. The money supply is not influenced by the accumulation of foreign bonds because these assets are held by the household and do not form part of the domestic money base.

(b) By substituting (Q2.30)–(Q2.31) into (Q2.29) we find that the money market equilibrium condition (i.e. the LM curve) reduces to:

$$M = l(Y, R^*, \bar{K} + M + (B + F)/R^*). \tag{A2.51}$$

By differentiating (A2.51) with respect to M, Y, B, and F, we find:

$$dM = l_Y dY + l_A \left[dM + (1/R^*)(dB + dF) \right] \quad \Leftrightarrow$$
$$dY = \frac{(1 - l_A)dM - (l_A/R^*)(dB + dF)}{l_Y}. \tag{A2.52}$$

A higher money supply raises short-run equilibrium output, whereas higher bond holdings (of either type) reduces it. By writing $Y = AD(M, B, F)$, we find the following partial derivatives from (A2.52): $AD_M = (1 - l_A)/l_Y > 0$ and $AD_B = AD_F = -(l_A/R^*)/l_Y < 0$. Note that we can now write:

$$dY = AD_M dM + AD_B dB + AD_f df. \tag{A2.53}$$

Under *money financing* we have $\dot{B} = dB = 0$ so that (Q2.32) can be rewritten, by using (Q2.28), as:

$$\dot{M} = G + B - T_0 - t(Y + B + F). \tag{A2.54}$$

By differentiating (A2.54) we obtain:

$$d\dot{M} = dG - t\left[dY + dF \right]$$
$$= dG - t[AD_M dM + (1 + AD_F)dF], \tag{A2.55}$$

where we have used (A2.52) and (A2.53) (and noted that $dB = 0$ in this scenario) in going from the first to the second line. For a given level of foreign bonds, the adjustment in the money stock is stable because the coefficient in front of dM on the right-hand side is negative (i.e. $\partial \dot{M}/\partial M = -tAD_M < 0$). But F will not remain constant, so the stability proof must take into account what happens to foreign bond holdings.

By substituting (Q2.26)–(Q2.28) and (Q2.30)–(Q2.31) into (Q2.33) we obtain the following expression for the current account:

$$
(1/R^*)\dot{F} = F + Y
$$
$$
- C\left((1-t)(Y+B+F) - T_0, \bar{K} + M + \frac{B+F}{R^*}\right) - I(R^*) - G. \quad \text{(A2.56)}
$$

By differentiating (A2.56) (again setting $dB = 0$) we obtain:

$$
\frac{1}{R^*}d\dot{F} = \alpha(dY + dF) - C_A dM - (C_A/R^*)dF - dG
$$
$$
= \alpha\left[AD_M dM + (1 + AD_F)dF\right] - C_A dM - \frac{C_A}{R^*}dF - dG, \quad \text{(A2.57)}
$$

where $\alpha \equiv 1 - C_{YD}(1 - t)$ and we have used (A2.53) in going from the first to the second line.

Equations (A2.55) and (A2.57) can be written in a single matrix equation as:

$$
\begin{bmatrix} d\dot{M} \\ d\dot{F} \end{bmatrix} = \Delta \begin{bmatrix} dM \\ dF \end{bmatrix} + \begin{bmatrix} 1 \\ -R^* \end{bmatrix} dG, \quad \text{(A2.58)}
$$

where the Jacobian matrix Δ is defined as:

$$
\Delta = \begin{bmatrix} -tAD_M & -t(1+AD_F) \\ R^*[\alpha AD_M - C_A] & \alpha R^*(1+AD_F) - C_A \end{bmatrix}. \quad \text{(A2.59)}
$$

In order to determine stability of the dynamical system (A2.58) we must compute the determinant and trace of Δ. The former is given by:

$$
|\Delta| \equiv -tR^* \begin{vmatrix} AD_M & 1 + AD_F \\ \alpha AD_M - C_A & \alpha(1+AD_F) - C_A/R^* \end{vmatrix}
$$
$$
= -tR^* C_A \left[-AD_M/R^* + 1 + AD_F\right]
$$
$$
= \frac{tC_A \left[1 - l_Y R^*\right]}{l_Y}, \quad \text{(A2.60)}
$$

where we have used the definitions of AD_M and AD_F (given below (A2.52)) in the final step. The *necessary condition* for the model to be stable is that both characteristic roots of Δ, denoted by λ_1 and λ_2, are negative, i.e. that $|\Delta| > 0$ (recall that $|\Delta| \equiv \lambda_1 \lambda_2$). Since t, C_A, l_Y, and R^* are all positive, the necessary condition for stability is thus:

$$
l_Y R^* < 1. \quad \text{(A2.61)}
$$

Note that the fulfilment of (A2.61) is not *sufficient* for stability since (A2.61) is also satisfied if both roots are positive (a situation of outright instability). All that (A2.61) ensures is that the (real parts of the) roots have the same sign. We must check the trace of Δ to find the necessary and sufficient condition for stability. We find from (A2.59):

$$\text{tr}\,\Delta = -tAD_M + \alpha R^*(1 + AD_F) - C_A. \tag{A2.62}$$

Since t, AD_M, and C_A are all positive, we know that the first and the third term on the right-hand side tend to make the trace negative. The second term on the right-hand side is, however, ambiguous as the sign of $1 + AD_F$ is ambiguous. Recall that the trace equals the sum of the characteristic roots ($\text{tr}\,\Delta \equiv \lambda_1 + \lambda_2$). Since the necessary stability condition ensures that the roots have the same sign, the sufficient condition is that the sum of these roots must be negative, i.e. $\text{tr}\,\Delta < 0$. To that effect we make the following assumption:

$$\text{tr}\,\Delta < 0 \quad \Leftrightarrow \quad C_A + tAD_M > \alpha R^*(1 + AD_F). \tag{A2.63}$$

Note that this trace condition is automatically satisfied if we make the assumption that $1 + AD_F < 0$ which is the case if $l_A > l_Y R^*$. A simple sufficient condition for overall stability of the model under money financing is thus:

$$l_Y R^* < l_A. \tag{A2.64}$$

Note that this condition automatically implies that (A2.61) holds because $l_A < 1$.

If both (A2.61) and (A2.63) are satisfied the model is stable and we can solve for the long-run effects of fiscal policy by setting $d\dot{M} = d\dot{F} = 0$ in (A2.58) and solving for the long-run multipliers:

$$\begin{bmatrix} \frac{dM}{dG} \\ \frac{dF}{dG} \end{bmatrix} = \Delta^{-1} \begin{bmatrix} -1 \\ R^* \end{bmatrix} = \frac{R^*}{|\Delta|} \begin{bmatrix} C_A/R^* + (t - \alpha)(1 + AD_F) \\ -[C_A + (t - \alpha)AD_M] \end{bmatrix}. \tag{A2.65}$$

Interestingly, we are unable to establish the signs of dM/dG and dF/dG even for the stable case. By substituting the definitions for α, AD_F, and AD_M into (A2.65) we obtain:

$$\frac{dM}{dG} = \frac{l_Y C_A - (l_Y R^* - l_A)(1 - t)(1 - C_{YD})}{l_Y |\Delta|} \gtreqless 0, \tag{A2.66}$$

$$\frac{dF}{dG} = \frac{-l_Y C_A + (1 - l_A)(1 - t)(1 - C_{YD})}{(1/R^*)l_Y |\Delta|} \lesseqgtr 0, \tag{A2.67}$$

If we assume that (A2.64) holds, then $dM/dG > 0$ but dF/dG is still ambiguous. The long-run output multiplier is obtained by using (A2.66)–(A2.67) in (A2.52) (and setting $dB = 0$):

$$\begin{aligned}
\frac{dY}{dG} &= \frac{1 - l_A}{l_Y} \frac{dM}{dG} - \frac{l_A}{l_Y R^*} \frac{dF}{dG} \\
&= \frac{(1 - l_A)\,[l_Y C_A - (l_Y R^* - l_A)(1 - t)(1 - C_{YD})]}{l_Y^2 |\Delta|} \\
&\quad - \frac{l_A[-l_Y C_A + (1 - l_A)(1 - t)(1 - C_{YD})]}{l_Y^2 |\Delta|} \\
&= \frac{l_Y C_A - (1 - l_A)(1 - t)(1 - C_{YD})l_Y R^*}{l_Y^2 |\Delta|} \gtreqless 0. \tag{A2.68}
\end{aligned}$$

It follows from (A2.68) that dY/dG is also ambiguous. This stands in stark contrast to the closed-economy case, for which the long-run multiplier must be positive (see equation (2.78) in the text). In this case, therefore, the Samuelsonian correspondence principle does not help in establishing the signs of the long-run effects on the money supply, the stock of foreign bonds, and output of a change in government consumption.

(c) Under *bond financing* we have $\dot{M} = dM = 0$ so that (Q2.32) can be rewritten, by using (Q2.28) and (Q2.31), as:

$$(1/R^*)\dot{B} = G + B - T_0 - t(Y + B + F). \tag{A2.69}$$

By differentiating (A2.69) we obtain:

$$\begin{aligned}
(1/R^*)d\dot{B} &= dG + dB - t(dY + dB + dF) \\
&= dG + dB - t\left[(1 + AD_B)\,dB + (1 + AD_F)\,dF\right] \\
&= dG + [1 - t\,(1 + AD_B)]\,dB - t\,(1 + AD_F)\,dF, \tag{A2.70}
\end{aligned}$$

where we have used (A2.52) (and noted that $dM = 0$ in this scenario) in going from the first to the second line. Note that for a given level of foreign bonds, the adjustment in the stock of domestic bonds may or may not be stable:

$$(1/R^*)\frac{\partial \dot{B}}{\partial B} = 1 - t\,(1 + AD_B). \tag{A2.71}$$

In the closed economy case, bond financing is stable if (and only if) the term on the right-hand side is negative (see equation (2.82) in the text). In the open economy case, we have to take into account the fact that the stock of foreign bonds is variable.

By differentiating (A2.56) (setting $dM = 0$) we obtain:

$$\begin{aligned}
(1/R^*)d\dot{F} &= \alpha(dY + dF) - (1 - \alpha)dB - (C_A/R^*)(dB + dF) - dG \\
&= \alpha\left[(1 + AD_F)\,dF + AD_B dB\right] - (1 - \alpha)dB \\
&\quad - (C_A/R^*)(dB + dF) - dG, \tag{A2.72}
\end{aligned}$$

where we have used (A2.52) in going from the first to the second line.

Equations (A2.70) and (A2.72) can be written in a single matrix equation as:

$$\begin{bmatrix} d\dot{B} \\ d\dot{F} \end{bmatrix} = \Delta \begin{bmatrix} dB \\ dF \end{bmatrix} + \begin{bmatrix} 1 \\ -R^* \end{bmatrix} dG, \tag{A2.73}$$

where the Jacobian matrix Δ is defined as:

$$\Delta = \begin{bmatrix} R^*[1 - t(1 + AD_B)] & -R^*t(1 + AD_F) \\ -R^*[1 - \alpha(1 + AD_B)] - C_A & \alpha R^*(1 + AD_F) - C_A \end{bmatrix}. \tag{A2.74}$$

The determinant of Δ is:

$$|\Delta| \equiv (R^*)^2\left[(\alpha - t)(1 + AD_B) - C_A/R^*\right], \tag{A2.75}$$

where we have used the fact that $AD_B = AD_F$ to simplify the expression. Since $\alpha - t = (1 - t)(1 - C_{YD}) > 0$ we find that a necessary condition for $|\Delta|$ to be positive is that $1 + AD_B$ is positive (just as in the closed-economy model–see equation (2.82) in the text). The trace of Δ is given by:

$$\operatorname{tr} \Delta = R^* \left[1 + (\alpha - t)(1 + AD_B) - C_A / R^* \right]. \tag{A2.76}$$

A necessary condition for stability is that the trace is negative. But that is only possible if $(\alpha - t)(1 + AD_B) - C_A / R^*$ is negative *and* less than -1. But then the determinant is negative also (see (A2.75)). Hence, the model is unstable as one root is negative and one is positive in that case. Since the model is unstable, there is no point in computing the multipliers. (Here we cannot make use of the saddle path property because both B and F are stocks, and stocks can't jump, no matter how hard they try.)

Question 8: Adaptive expectations in a monetarist model

(a) Equation (Q2.34) is Irving Fisher's *equation of exchange*. In itself it is a simple identity but by assuming that v is constant it becomes a behavioural equation relating the nominal money supply to nominal output. Equation (Q2.35) is an expectations-augmented Phillips curve in which *core* (expected) inflation drives up actual inflation even if output is at its full employment level. Equation (Q2.36) is the formulation of the adaptive expectations hypothesis (AEH) in continuous time. Finally, equation (Q2.37) is the definition of the growth rate in the nominal money supply. The endogenous variables are P, y, π, and π^e. The policy maker controls the money supply so M and μ are exogenous variables as is y^*.

(b) The reduce the dimensionality of the model somewhat we can take the time derivative of (Q2.34):

$$\frac{\dot{M}}{M} + \frac{\dot{v}}{v} = \frac{\dot{P}}{P} + \frac{\dot{y}}{y} \quad \Rightarrow$$
$$\mu = \pi + \frac{\dot{y}}{y}, \tag{A2.77}$$

where we have used (Q2.37), imposed the assumed constancy of v (so that $\dot{v}/v = 0$), and used the definition of π to get to the final expression. By using (A2.77) in (Q2.35) we find:

$$\pi = \phi[y - y^*] + \pi^e$$
$$\mu - \frac{\dot{y}}{y} = \phi[y - y^*] + \pi^e \quad \Rightarrow$$
$$\frac{\dot{y}}{y} = \mu - \pi^e - \phi[y - y^*], \tag{A2.78}$$

which is equation (Q2.38) in the question. By substituting (Q2.35) into (Q2.36) we obtain:

$$\dot{\pi}^e = \zeta\phi[y - y^*], \tag{A2.79}$$

which is equation (Q2.39) in the question.

(c) To prove (local) stability of the model we linearize it around the initial steady state. This steady state is such that output and expected inflation are both constant over time, i.e. $\dot{y}/y = \dot{\pi}^e = 0$ so that it follows from (A2.78)–(A2.79) that $y = y^*$ and $\pi^e = \mu$ (it thus also follows from (Q2.36) that actual inflation equals expected inflation, i.e. $\pi = \pi^e$ in the steady state). To linearise (A2.78) we first rewrite it as follows:

$$\dot{y} = [\mu - \pi^e - \phi[y - y^*]]\, y. \tag{A2.80}$$

Equation (A2.80) expresses $\dot{y}$ as a non-linear function of the endogenous variables (y and π^e) and the exogenous variables (μ and y^*). We denote this function by $\dot{y} = \Psi(y, \pi^e)$. By using a first-order Taylor approximation (see, e.g. (Chiang, 1984, pp. 256-258)) of this function around an initial steady state (where $y = y^*$ and $\pi^e = \mu_0$) we obtain:

$$\dot{y} \approx \Psi(y^*, \mu_0) + \frac{\partial \Psi}{\partial y}[y - y^*] + \frac{\partial \Psi}{\partial \pi^e}[\pi^e - \mu_0], \tag{A2.81}$$

where the partial derivatives $\partial \Psi/\partial y$ and $\partial \Psi/\partial \pi^e$ are all evaluated at the linearization point ($y = y^*$, $\pi^e = \mu_0$). We find that $\Psi(y^*, \mu_0) = 0$, $\partial \Psi/\partial y = -\phi y^*$ and $\partial \Psi/\partial \pi^e = -y^*$ so that (A2.81) reduces to:

$$\dot{y} = -\phi y^*[y - y^*] - y^*[\pi^e - \mu_0], \tag{A2.82}$$

where, from here one, we ignore the fact that (A2.82) is only an approximation to (A2.80). Since (A2.79) is already linear (in y) it does not need to be linearised. By combining (A2.82) and (A2.79) in a simple matrix equation we obtain:

$$\begin{bmatrix} \dot{y} \\ \dot{\pi}^e \end{bmatrix} = \begin{bmatrix} -\phi y^* & -y^* \\ \zeta \phi & 0 \end{bmatrix} \begin{bmatrix} y - y^* \\ \pi^e - \mu_0 \end{bmatrix}, \tag{A2.83}$$

where we denote the matrix on the right-hand side of (A2.83) by Δ. It has the following determinant and trace:

$$|\Delta| \equiv \lambda_1 \lambda_2 = \zeta \phi y^* > 0, \tag{A2.84}$$

$$\operatorname{tr}\Delta \equiv \lambda_1 + \lambda_2 = -\phi y^* < 0, \tag{A2.85}$$

where λ_1 and λ_2 are the characteristic roots of the matrix Δ. It follows from (A2.84)–(A2.85) that both roots are negative (if they are complex, they have negative real parts–see below). Hence, the model is stable.

The characteristic roots of Δ are the zeros of the characteristic equation of Δ, $A(\lambda) \equiv |\Delta - \lambda I| = 0$. After some manipulation we get:

$$A(\lambda) = \begin{vmatrix} -\phi y^* - \lambda & -y^* \\ \zeta \phi & -\lambda \end{vmatrix} = \lambda\,(\lambda + \phi y^*) + \zeta \phi y^*$$

$$= \lambda^2 - \operatorname{tr}\Delta\,\lambda + |\Delta| = 0. \tag{A2.86}$$

Equation (A2.86) is a quadratic equation in λ which has two roots:

$$\lambda_{1,2} = \frac{-\phi y^* \pm \sqrt{D}}{2}, \tag{A2.87}$$

where $D \equiv (\phi y^*)^2 - 4\zeta \phi y^*$. There are two possible cases that must be considered, depending on the sign of D.

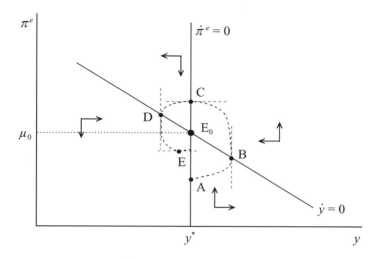

Figure A2.6: Stability in the monetarist model

(a) *Case 1*: If $D > 0$ then both roots are real and distinct. If $D = 0$ then the roots are the same. In both cases the equilibrium is a *stable node*.

(b) *Case 2*: If $D < 0$ then the roots are imaginary, i.e. $2\lambda_1 = -\phi y^* + i\sqrt{-D}$ and $2\lambda_2 = -\phi y^* - i\sqrt{-D}$ where $i = \sqrt{-1}$ is the imaginary unit. The equilibrium is in that case a *stable focus*.

(d) We present the phase diagram for the linearised model in Figure A2.6. The (linearised) expression for $\dot{y}$ is given in (A2.82) above. The $\dot{y} = 0$ line is given by:

$$\pi^e = \mu_0 - \phi[y - y^*]. \tag{A2.88}$$

This line is downward sloping in (π^e, y) space. For points above (below) the $\dot{y} = 0$ line, π^e is too high (too low) compared to μ_0, and output is falling (rising) over time, i.e. $\dot{y} < 0$ ($\dot{y} > 0$). The output dynamics is illustrated with horizontal arrows in Figure A2.6.

We derive from (A2.79) that the $\dot{\pi}^e = 0$ line is a vertical line for which $y = y^*$. For points to the right (left) of this line, output exceeds (falls short of) the full employment level so that expected inflation rises (falls) over time, i.e. $\dot{\pi}^e > 0$ ($\dot{\pi}^e < 0$). The dynamics of the expected inflation rate has been illustrated with vertical arrows in Figure A2.6.

The configuration of arrows in Figure A2.6 confirms that the model is stable. We sketch the adjustment path for the case where the equilibrium is a stable focus. The economy is initially in point A, where $\dot{\pi}^e = 0$ (because $y = y^*$) and $\dot{y} > 0$ (because $\pi^e < \mu_0$). The economy moves in north-easterly direction towards point B, where $\dot{y} = 0$ and $\dot{\pi}^e = 0$. Thereafter the economy moves from B to C to D to E, etcetera until it ultimately ends up in E_0.

In Figure A2.7 we show the dynamic effects of a monetary disinflation (a cut in the money growth rate from μ_0 to μ_1). It is clear from (A2.88) that this shock

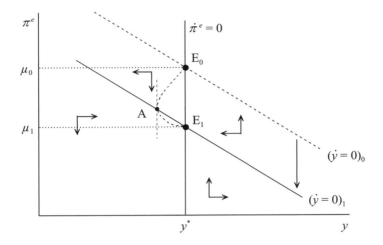

Figure A2.7: Disinflation in the monetarist model

shifts the $\dot{y} = 0$ line downwards, say from $(\dot{y} = 0)_0$ to $(\dot{y} = 0)_1$. The steady-state equilibrium shifts accordingly from E_0 to E_1 and ultimately the (expected and actual) inflation rate falls. In Figure A2.7 we sketch the adjustment trajectory, $E_0 A E_1$, under the assumption that the equilibrium is a stable node (the case of cyclical adjustment is easily visualized by looking at Figure A2.6). The disinflation policy brings down inflation in the long run at the expense of a short-run recession.

Question 9: More on adaptive expectations

(a) Equation (Q2.40) is the AD curve in logarithmic format. Real balances and fiscal policy both shift the AD curve to the right, so it is obvious that θ and ζ are both positive. The expected inflation term enters equation (Q2.41) because the IS curve depends (via investment demand) on the *real* interest rate, $R - \pi^e$, whereas the LM curve depends on the *nominal* interest rate, R. Ceteris paribus the nominal interest rate, an increase in expected inflation reduces the real interest rate, boosts investment, shifts the IS curve to the right, and stimulates output. Hence, according to this effect we have $\psi > 0$. Equation (Q2.41) is an expectations-augmented Phillips curve in which core (expected) inflation drives up actual inflation even if output is at its full employment level. Finally, equation (Q2.42) is the formulation of the adaptive expectations hypothesis (AEH) in continuous time.

(b) In the short run, the model is rather Keynesian because both p and π^e are predetermined. Essentially the model reacts like the standard IS-LM model in the short run. In the long run, p and π^e adjust such that $\pi = \pi^e = \mu$ and $y = y^*$. Since y^* is exogenous, demand management cannot affect it.

(c) To derive the system of differential equations we first substitute (Q2.41) into (Q2.42):

$$\dot{\pi}^e = \lambda \phi [y - y^*]. \tag{A2.89}$$

Next we differentiate (Q2.40) with respect to time (noting that θ, ψ, and ζ are all constant over time):

$$\dot{y} = \theta\,(\dot{m} - \dot{p}) + \psi\dot{\pi}^e + \zeta\dot{g}$$
$$= \theta(\mu - \pi) + \psi\dot{\pi}^e + \zeta\dot{g}, \tag{A2.90}$$

where we have used the definitions of inflation ($\pi \equiv \dot{p}$) and the money growth rate ($\mu \equiv \dot{m}$) in going from the first to the second line. By substituting (Q2.41) and (A2.89) into (A2.90) and simplifying we obtain:

$$\dot{y} = \theta[\mu - \phi[y - y^*] - \pi^e] + \psi\lambda\phi[y - y^*] + \zeta\dot{g}$$
$$= -\phi(\theta - \psi\lambda)[y - y^*] - \theta[\pi^e - \mu] + \zeta\dot{g}. \tag{A2.91}$$

By using (A2.89) and (A2.91) we can derive the following matrix expression:

$$\begin{bmatrix} \dot{y} \\ \dot{\pi}^e \end{bmatrix} = \begin{bmatrix} -\phi(\theta - \psi\lambda) & -\theta \\ \lambda\phi & 0 \end{bmatrix} \begin{bmatrix} y - y^* \\ \pi^e - \mu \end{bmatrix} + \begin{bmatrix} 0 \\ \zeta\dot{g} \end{bmatrix}, \tag{A2.92}$$

where we denote the matrix on the right-hand side as Δ. It has the following determinant and trace:

$$|\Delta| \equiv \lambda_1\lambda_2 = \lambda\phi\theta > 0, \tag{A2.93}$$

$$\text{tr}\,\Delta \equiv \lambda_1 + \lambda_2 = -\phi(\theta - \psi\lambda) \lesseqgtr 0, \tag{A2.94}$$

where λ_1 and λ_2 are the characteristic roots of the matrix Δ. It follows from (A2.93) that the two roots have the same sign. The model is only stable if these roots are negative, but that can only be the case if the trace of Δ is negative. Hence, the necessary and sufficient stability condition is that $\theta > \psi\lambda$ so that $\text{tr}\,\Delta < 0$.

Note that by setting $\theta = 1$ and $\psi = \zeta = 0$ the model collapses to the monetarist model of question 8. As we found in question 8, and as is confirmed by (A2.93)–(A2.94), the monetarist model is automatically stable. Stability is not guaranteed in the more general model of this question because the expected inflation term in the AD curve (Q2.40) represents a destabilizing influence. Recall that the position of the LM curve depends on real money balances (which are eroded by actual inflation) whereas the position of the IS curve depends on expected inflation which boosts output. So, if following a shock the expected inflation effect in IS (and thus AD) is strong (ψ is large) and if expectations are adjusted quickly (λ high) then the stabilizing effect of actual inflation (via the LM curve) may be dominated by the destabilizing effect of expected inflation (operating via the IS curve). See Scarth (1988, p. 60) for further insights on this issue.

(d) To study the effects of an increase in the money growth rate we first derive the effects on π^e and y in a phase diagram. By using the first row in (A2.92) (or, equivalently, equation (A2.89)) we find that the $\dot{\pi}^e = 0$ locus is given by:

$$\lambda\phi[y - y^*] = 0 \quad \Leftrightarrow \quad y = y^*. \tag{A2.95}$$

In Figure A2.8 the $\dot{\pi}^e = 0$ locus is vertical. For points to the right (left) of this curve, actual output exceeds (falls short of) its full employment level and

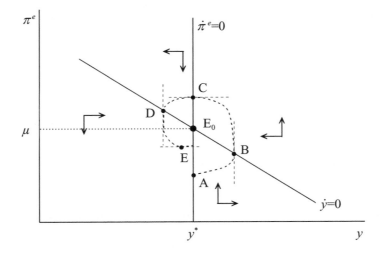

Figure A2.8: Stability in the AD-AS-AEH model

expected inflation rises (falls). This is indicated by the vertical arrows in Figure A2.8. The second row of (A2.92) (or, equivalently, equation (A2.91)) implies the following expression for the $\dot{y} = 0$ line:

$$\pi^e = \mu - \phi\frac{\theta - \psi\lambda}{\theta}[y - y^*], \qquad (A2.96)$$

where we have used the fact that the fiscal index is kept constant ($\dot{g} = 0$) in this experiment. In view of the stability condition, $\theta > \psi\lambda$, we find that the $\dot{y} = 0$ line slopes downwards and passes through the point $\pi^e = \mu$ for $y = y^*$. Note that (A2.91) implies $\partial\dot{y}/\partial y = -\phi(\theta - \psi\lambda) < 0$ (given the stability condition). Hence, for points to the right (left) of the $\dot{y} = 0$ line, output falls (increases) over time. This has been illustrated with horizontal arrows in Figure A2.8. Just as in the monetarist model of question 8, the steady-state equilibrium E_0 is either a *stable node* (if the characteristic roots of Δ are real) or a *stable focus* (if these roots are complex).

An increase in the money growth rate leaves the $\dot{\pi}^e = 0$ line unaffected but shifts the $\dot{y} = 0$ line up. The steady-state equilibrium shifts from E_0 to E_1 in Figure A2.9. At impact, nothing happens to π^e because that is a predetermined variable. Similarly, it follows from (Q2.40) that nothing happens to y either: p and π^e are predetermined as are the policy variables m and g. There is no jump in the level of m, but only its rate of change is increased. In Figure A2.9 we show the adjustment path under the assumption that the characteristic roots of Δ are real. This is justified because the assumption made in the question in fact ensures that the roots are real and distinct. Indeed, these characteristic roots are:

$$\zeta_{1,2} = \frac{-\phi(\theta - \psi\lambda) \pm \sqrt{D}}{2}, \quad D \equiv \phi[\phi(\psi\lambda - \theta)^2 - 4\lambda\theta] > 0, \qquad (A2.97)$$

where the sign of D is implied by the assumption made in the text.

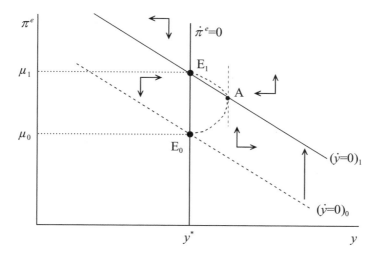

Figure A2.9: Money growth in the AD-AS-AEH model

In Figure A2.9, the transition path is given by the dashed line E_0AE_1. Expected inflation rises monotonically, but output rises during the early stages of transition and thereafter falls back towards its full employment level. In Figure A2.10 we show the time paths of the different variables. (These are so-called *impulse-response functions*.) At the bottom of the figure we show the impulse, consisting of an increase in the rate of money growth. This means that the time path for m (also drawn in Figure A2.10) is steeper after the shock. The path for output can be taken directly from the phase diagram in Figure A2.9. Points A in Figures A2.9 and A2.10 correspond. Since actual output is higher than full employment output during transition, it follows from (A2.89) (and from the phase diagram) that $\dot{\pi}^e$ is positive during transition. We can also derive from (A2.89) that $\ddot{\pi}^e = 0$ in point A (where $\dot{y} = 0$), i.e. the path for π^e attains an inflection point there. We conclude that the path for π^e takes the S-shaped form as drawn in Figure A2.10. It follows from (Q2.41) that the path for $\pi - \pi^e$ is proportional to the path for y, i.e. inflation in continually underestimated during transition (more on this in Chapter 3).

The path for the price level can best be described in relation to that of the money supply, i.e. Figure A2.10 reports the path for real money balances, $m - p$. At impact, both m and p are predetermined so nothing happens to $m - p$ either. In the long run, we find from (Q2.40) that:

$$y^* = \theta(m - p) + \psi\mu + \zeta g \quad \Rightarrow \quad \frac{d(m - p)}{d\mu} = -\frac{\psi}{\theta} < 0,$$

where we have used the fact that $y = y^*$, $\pi^e = \pi = \mu$ in the steady state and that g is constant by assumption. Real money balances fall in the long run. The higher inflation rate shifts out the IS curve and to restore output to its full employment level, the LM curve must shift to the left, i.e. real money balances must fall. During the early phase of transition, money growth outstrips actual inflation and real money balances increase over time. From (A2.90) we derive

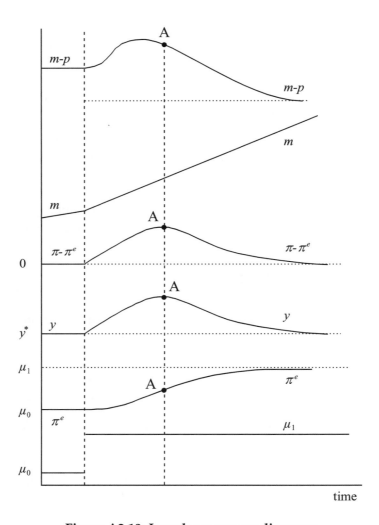

Figure A2.10: Impulse-response diagrams

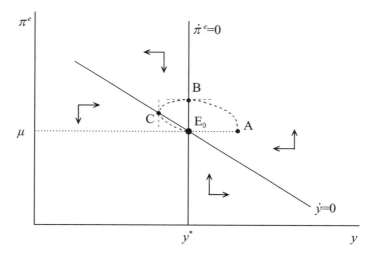

Figure A2.11: Fiscal policy in the AD-AS-AEH model

that in point A (where $\dot{y} = 0$), $\pi - \mu = (\psi/\theta)\dot{\pi}^e > 0$, i.e. real money balances have already started to decline over time in that point.

(e) We assume that the change in g is stepwise, i.e. $dg > 0$ but $\dot{g} = 0$ both before and after the shock. Looking at (A2.92) one would be tempted to conclude that nothing happens at all. But something does happen, namely an impact change in output. Indeed, we conclude from (Q2.40) that at impact (with m, p, and π^e all predetermined) the change in output is equal to $dy = \zeta dg$. In terms of Figure A2.11, nothing happens to the $\dot{\pi}^e = 0$ and $\dot{y} = 0$ lines, but the economy jumps from the initial steady state, E_0, to point A, directly to the right of E_0. The adjustment path is thereafter given by $ABCE_0$. (It is non-cyclical because of the assumption stated in part (d) of the question.) There is no long-run effect on output (as $y = y^*$ in the steady state) and no effect on actual and expected inflation (as $\pi^e = \pi = \mu$ in the steady state). The only thing that changes in the economy is the steady-state level of real money balances. Indeed, by using the steady-state version of (Q2.40) we find that:

$$y^* = \theta(m - p) + \psi\mu + \zeta g \quad \Rightarrow$$
$$\frac{d(m - p)}{dg} = -\frac{\zeta}{\theta} < 0. \tag{A2.98}$$

We draw the impulse-response functions for this fiscal policy shock in Figure A2.12. At the bottom of the diagram we show the shock, which is a stepwise increase in g. Expected inflation gradually rises at first, reaches a maximum at point B and thereafter gradually declines towards its initial level. Output increases at impact but declines thereafter. At point B it reaches its full employment level but it continues to decline because inflationary expectations are too high (relative to money growth). Eventually output reaches its lowest level at point C, after which it gradually rises towards y^* again. We conclude from equation (Q2.41) that $\pi - \pi^e$ is proportional to the path of output. The

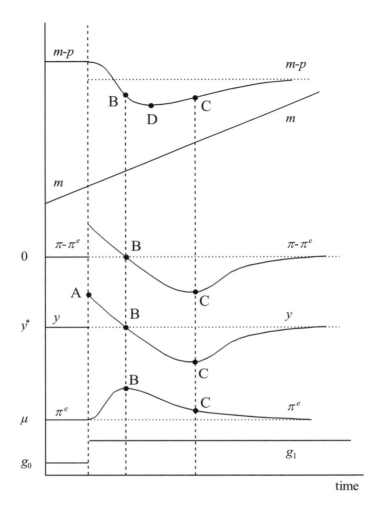

Figure A2.12: Impulse-response functions

nominal money growth rate is unaffected in this experiment so m continues to follow a linear trend line.

In order to determine the path of real balances, it is useful to derive the dynamical system characterizing the model directly in terms of (z, π^e) dynamics, where $z \equiv m - p$ is real money balances. We derive the dynamical equation for z as follows:

$$\dot{z} \equiv \dot{m} - \dot{p} = \mu - \pi$$
$$= \mu - \pi^e - \phi[\theta z + \psi \pi^e + \zeta g - y^*]$$
$$= -(1 + \phi \psi)\pi^e - \phi \theta z + \mu + \phi y^* - \phi \zeta g, \qquad (A2.99)$$

where we have used (Q2.40)–(Q2.41) to get from the first to the second line. By substituting (Q2.40)–(Q2.41) into (Q2.42) we obtain the dynamical equation for

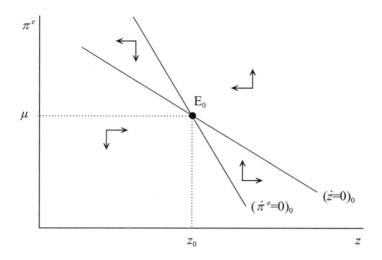

Figure A2.13: Real balances in the AD-AS-AEH model

π^e:

$$\dot{\pi}^e = \lambda\phi[\theta z + \psi\pi^e + \zeta g - y^*]. \tag{A2.100}$$

Equations (A2.99)–(A2.100) can be combined into one matrix equation as:

$$\begin{bmatrix} \dot{\pi}^e \\ \dot{z} \end{bmatrix} = \begin{bmatrix} \lambda\phi\psi & \lambda\phi\theta \\ -(1+\phi\psi) & -\phi\theta \end{bmatrix} \begin{bmatrix} \pi^e \\ z \end{bmatrix} + \begin{bmatrix} \lambda\phi(\zeta g - y^*) \\ \mu - \phi(\zeta g - y^*) \end{bmatrix}, \tag{A2.101}$$

where we denote the Jacobian matrix on the right-hand side by Δ^*. It is straightforward to derive that $|\Delta^*| = \lambda\phi\theta > 0$ and $\text{tr}\,\Delta^* = -\phi(\theta - \lambda\psi) < 0$ (by the stability condition). In Figure A2.13 we illustrate the phase diagram for the rewritten model.

We conclude from (A2.99):

$$\left(\frac{\partial \pi^e}{\partial z} \right)_{\dot{z}=0} = -\frac{\phi\theta}{1+\phi\psi} < 0, \tag{A2.102}$$

$$\left(\frac{\partial z}{\partial g} \right)_{\dot{z}=0} = -\frac{\zeta}{\theta} < 0, \tag{A2.103}$$

$$\frac{\partial \dot{z}}{\partial z} = -\phi\theta < 0. \tag{A2.104}$$

The $\dot{z} = 0$ line is downward sloping and shifts to the left if g is increased. For points to the right (left) of the $\dot{z} = 0$ line, money balances fall (rise), i.e. $\dot{z} < 0$ ($\dot{z} > 0$). This has been illustrated with horizontal arrows in Figure A2.13.

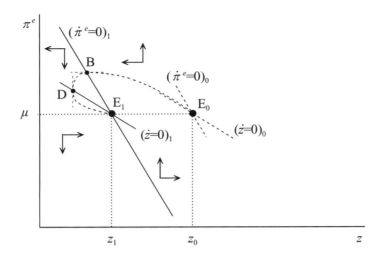

Figure A2.14: Fiscal policy and real money balances

We conclude from (A2.100):

$$\left(\frac{\partial \pi^e}{\partial z}\right)_{\dot{\pi}^e=0} = -\frac{\theta}{\psi} < 0, \tag{A2.105}$$

$$\left(\frac{\partial z}{\partial g}\right)_{\dot{\pi}^e=0} = -\frac{\zeta}{\theta} < 0, \tag{A2.106}$$

$$\frac{\partial \dot{\pi}^e}{\partial \pi^e} = \lambda \phi \psi > 0. \tag{A2.107}$$

The $\dot{\pi}^e = 0$ line is downward sloping (and steeper than the $\dot{z} = 0$ line) and shifts to the left (by the same amount as the $\dot{z} = 0$ line) if g is increased. For points above (below) the $\dot{\pi}^e = 0$ line, expected inflation rises (falls), i.e. $\dot{\pi}^e > 0$ ($\dot{\pi}^e < 0$). This has been illustrated with vertical arrows in Figure A2.13.

In Figure A2.14 we show the adjustment paths for π^e and z following the expansionary fiscal policy. Both the $\dot{z} = 0$ and $\dot{\pi}^e = 0$ lines shift to the left (by the same horizontal amount) and the steady-state equilibrium shifts from E_0 to E_1. The adjustment is non-cyclical and proceeds along E_0BDE_1. It is not difficult to show that point D must lie to the left of point C in Figure A2.12. Indeed, in point C we have $\dot{y} = 0$ and $\dot{\pi}^e < 0$ (and, of course, $\dot{g} = 0$) so that it follows from (A2.90) that $\theta(\pi - \mu) = \psi \dot{\pi}^e < 0$, i.e. $\mu > \pi$. Hence, in point C real money balances are rising. But this means that point C is to the right of point D in Figure A2.12.

Question 10: Optimization and computation

(a) Follow the steps in the book on pages 45–46 with $F_K = A$ and $P = P^I = 1$ and we obtain the first-order condition for investment:

$$I_{t+1} - \frac{1+R}{1-\delta}I_t + \frac{A - (R+\delta)}{2b(1-\delta)} = 0 \tag{A2.108}$$

Denote steady-state variables with a hat (e.g. $\hat{K}$). Setting $I_{t+1} = I_t$ in equation (A2.108) we get:

$$\hat{I} = \frac{1}{2b}\left[\frac{A}{R+\delta} - 1\right] \tag{A2.109}$$

Capital follows immediately from equation (Q2.43) with $K_{t+1} = K_t$, so $\hat{K} = \hat{I}/\delta$. Production follows from capital $\hat{Y} = A\hat{K}$.

(b) $\hat{I} = 0.4$, $\hat{K} = 5.714$, $Y = 2.857$.

(c) There is just one level of investment for which equation (A2.108) is stable. This implies that investment remains constant at $I_t = 0.4$. Capital was 5.714, but 20% is demolished in the earthquake, so $K_0 = (1 - 0.2) \times 5.714 = 4.571$. From this we can calculate the path of capital: $K_t = (1 - \delta)^t K_0 + \left[1 - (1 - \delta)^t\right] I/\delta$.

Question 11: The multiplier-accelerator model

(a) Equation (Q2.45) is the goods market clearing condition, (Q2.46) is the consumption function (c is the marginal propensity to consume), and (Q2.47) in an investment accelerator. By substituting (Q2.46) into (Q2.47) we get the form of this expression that is commonly reported in the literature:

$$I_t = vc[Y_{t-1} - Y_{t-2}]. \tag{A2.110}$$

(b) (See, e.g., Gandolfo (1971, pp. 55–56) for a more thorough treatment of this material.) By substituting (A2.110) and (Q2.46) into (Q2.45) we obtain a difference equation in output:

$$Y_t = cY_{t-1} + vc[Y_{t-1} - Y_{t-2}] + \bar{G} \quad \Leftrightarrow$$
$$Y_t - c(1+v)Y_{t-1} + vcY_{t-2} = \bar{G}. \tag{A2.111}$$

We first solve the homogeneous part of the equation:

$$Y_t - c(1+v)Y_{t-1} + vcY_{t-2} = 0. \tag{A2.112}$$

We try the solution $Y_t = A\lambda^t$ in (A2.112):

$$A\lambda^t - c(1+v)A\lambda^{t-1} + vcA\lambda^{t-2} = 0$$
$$A\lambda^{t-2}\left[\lambda^2 - c(1+v)\lambda + vc\right] = 0 \quad \Rightarrow \quad (\text{since } A\lambda^{t-2} \neq 0)$$
$$\lambda^2 - c(1+v)\lambda + vc = 0, \tag{A2.113}$$

where (A2.113) is the characteristic equation of the difference equation (A2.112). The roots of this quadratic equation are:

$$\lambda_{1,2} = \frac{c(1+v) \pm \sqrt{D}}{2}, \quad \text{with} \quad D \equiv c^2(1+v)^2 - 4vc. \tag{A2.114}$$

There are two things we need to know about these roots, namely (a) whether they are real or complex, and (b) whether they are smaller or greater than unity in absolute value. The first aspect regulates the type of adjustment (non-cyclical or cyclical) whereas the second aspect determines stability. We study a number of cases in turn.

Case 1: If $D > 0$ then both roots are real and distinct and both solutions solve (A2.112). The general solution to (A2.112) is thus:

$$Y_t = A_1\lambda_1^t + A_2\lambda_2^t, \tag{A2.115}$$

where A_1 and A_2 are arbitrary constants. The model is stable if both roots are less than unity in absolute value, i.e. if $|\lambda_1| < 1$ and $|\lambda_2| < 1$.

Case 2: If $D = 0$ the roots are real and equal to each other, i.e. $\lambda_1 = \lambda_2 = c(1+v)/2$. In that case, $A\lambda_1^t$ and $At\lambda_1^t$ are both solutions to (A2.112), so that the general solution to (A2.112) can be written as:

$$Y_t = A_1\lambda_1^t + A_2t\lambda_1^t, \tag{A2.116}$$

where A_1 and A_2 are again arbitrary constants. The model is stable if the root is less than unity in absolute value (i.e. $|\lambda_1| < 1$).

Case 3: If $D < 0$ then the roots are complex (conjugate) numbers of the form $\lambda_1 = \alpha + \beta i$ and $\lambda_2 = \alpha - \beta i$, where $i = \sqrt{-1}$, $\alpha \equiv c(1+v)/2$, and $\beta \equiv \sqrt{-D}/2$. The *modulus* (or *absolute value*) of λ_1 and λ_2 is defined as:

$$|\lambda_1| = |\lambda_2| = \sqrt{\alpha^2 + \beta^2}$$

$$= \sqrt{\frac{c^2(1+v)^2}{4} + \frac{(\sqrt{-D})^2}{4}}$$

$$= \sqrt{\frac{c^2(1+v)^2 + 4vc - c^2(1+v)^2}{4}} = \sqrt{vc}. \tag{A2.117}$$

Adjustment is stable (unstable) if and only if $|\lambda_1| = |\lambda_2| < 1$ ($|\lambda_1| = |\lambda_2| > 1$), i.e. if $vc < 1$ ($vc > 1$).

In Figure A2.15 we plot v on the horizontal and c on the vertical axis. Obviously we only need to consider values of c between 0 and 1. To determine for which (c, v) combinations the roots are real or complex we compute the $D = 0$ line. By using (A2.114) we obtain:

$$D = c(1+v)^2\left[c - \frac{4v}{(1+v)^2}\right]. \tag{A2.118}$$

Since both c and v are non-negative it follows from (A2.118) that the $D = 0$ line is described by:

$$c = \frac{4v}{(1+v)^2}. \tag{A2.119}$$

The properties of the $D = 0$ line are easily determined:

$$c(0) = 0, \qquad \frac{dc}{dv} = \frac{4(1-v)}{(1+v)^3}. \tag{A2.120}$$

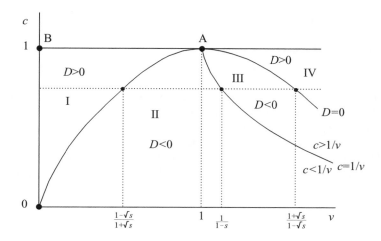

Figure A2.15: Regions of (in)stability

The $D = 0$ line goes through the origin, rises for $0 < v < 1$, attains a maximum at point A (where $v = c = 1$), and slopes downward for $v > 1$. It follows furthermore from (A2.118) that for points above (below) the $D = 0$ line, D is positive (negative). These sign configurations have been illustrated in Figure A2.15.

Below the $D = 0$ line (for which the roots are complex), we have stability if $vc < 1$ and instability if $vc > 1$ (see text below (A2.117)). In Figure A2.15, we draw the line $c = 1/v$ from point A. This line slopes downwards, and for points above (below) it, the adjustment is unstable (stable).

There are four distinct regions in Figure A2.15. To establish the boundaries of the different regions it is useful to describe the two branches of the $D = 0$ line as a function of $s \equiv 1 - c$. By using (A2.119) we find:

$$s \left[\equiv 1 - c \right] = \frac{(1+v)^2 - 4v}{(1+v)^2} = \frac{1 - 2v + v^2}{(1+v)^2}$$
$$= \left(\frac{1-v}{1+v} \right)^2.$$

Taking the square roots we find two solutions:

$$\frac{1-v}{1+v} = \sqrt{s} \quad \Leftrightarrow \quad v_1 = \frac{1 - \sqrt{s}}{1 + \sqrt{s}}, \tag{A2.121}$$

$$\frac{1-v}{1+v} = -\sqrt{s} \quad \Leftrightarrow \quad v_2 = \frac{1 + \sqrt{s}}{1 - \sqrt{s}}, \tag{A2.122}$$

from which it obvious that $v_1 < 1 < v_2$. The point for which $c = 1/v$ yields a third critical value for v, namely $v_3 = 1/(1-s)$. Since $1 - s = (1 - \sqrt{s})(1 + \sqrt{s})$ it follows that $1 < v_3 < v_2$.

In *region I*, v is relatively small, D is positive, and the roots are real and distinct. Since $v < 1$ it follows that $c(1 + v)/2 < c < 1$ and $cv < 1$. We know that

$\lambda_1\lambda_2 = vc$ and $\lambda_1 + \lambda_2 = c(1+v)$. Hence:

$$(1 - \lambda_1)(1 - \lambda_2) = 1 - (\lambda_1 + \lambda_2) + \lambda_1\lambda_2$$
$$= 1 - c(1+v) + vc = 1 - c > 0.$$

This establishes that both roots are between 0 and 1 so that adjustment in region I is stable and monotonic. In *region II*, stability is satisfied ($cv < 1$) but the roots are complex. The adjustment displays damped oscillation. In *region III*, stability is not satisfied (as $cv > 1$) and the roots are complex, so the adjustment displays explosive oscillations. Finally, in *region IV*, the stability is not satisfied (as $cv > 1$) but the roots are real, so the adjustment displays monotonic explosion.

Chapter 3

Rational expectations and economic policy

Question 1: Short questions

(a) Assume that you have a fair coin that you are going to toss 100 times. When *heads* come up you gain 1 euro and when *tails* come up you lose one euro. What is your rational expectation regarding your total gains after 100 rounds of tossing? How does your answer change if the probability of heads is 0.45? Explain.

(b) "The hypothesis of rational expectations assumes that everybody is a brilliant economist. Since brilliant economists are rather scarce, the assumption of rational expectations is absurd." Explain and evaluate this proposition.

(c) "If private agents form rational expectations, then monetary stabilization policy is both impossible and undesirable." Explain and evaluate this proposition.

(d) Consider the rational expectations model of Stanley Fischer. Explain intuitively why the so-called policy ineffectiveness proposition (PIP) still holds in this model provided wage contracts are set for only one period in advance.

Question 2: Stabilization of demand shocks

Assume that the logarithm of aggregate output in period t (y_t) can be written as:

$$y_t = -\delta[w_t - p_t], \qquad \delta > 0, \tag{Q3.1}$$

where w_t and p_t are, respectively, the logarithm of the nominal wage rate and the price level in period t. The logarithm of labour demand is:

$$n_t^D = -\alpha[w_t - p_t], \qquad \alpha > 0, \tag{Q3.2}$$

and the logarithm of labour supply is given by:

$$n_t^S = \beta[w_t - E_{t-1}p_t], \qquad \beta > 0, \tag{Q3.3}$$

where E_{t-1} is the conditional expectation based on information dated period $t-1$. Assume that the labour market is always in equilibrium.

(a) Derive the Lucas supply curve for this model.

(b) Assume that the aggregate demand curve for this economy can be written as $y_t = m_t - p_t + u_t$, where m_t is the nominal money supply and u_t is a normally distributed random shock term with mean zero and constant variance σ^2 (i.e. $u_t \sim N(0, \sigma^2)$). The money supply rule is given by $m_t = m_{t-1} + \mu$, where μ is a constant. Derive the rational expectations solutions for output and the price level. Show that the money supply does not affect real output.

(c) Compute the asymptotic variance of real output.

Question 3: Overlapping wage contracts and the REH

Consider an economy with two-period wage contracts. Labour demand depends on the actual price level, labour supply depends on the expected price level as usual. The labour market is described by the following labour demand and labour supply equation:

$$N_t^D = \Gamma_D \cdot \left[\frac{W_t}{P_t} \right]^{-\varepsilon_D} \qquad \text{and} \qquad N_t^S = \Gamma_S \cdot \left[\frac{W_t}{P_t^e} \right]^{\varepsilon_S}$$

With N^D and N^S the labour supply and labour demand (both in levels). Γ_D, Γ_S, ε_D and ε_S positive parameters. W_t is the nominal wage in period t, P_t is the actual price level, P_t^e is the expected price level to hold in period t at the time of the wage negotiations.

(a) Rewrite the labour demand and labour supply curves in logarithmic variables. What is the interpretation of ε_D and ε_S?

(b) Derive the logarithm of the nominal wage to hold in period t, agreed upon in, respectively, period $t-2$ and $t-1$ as a function of the expected price levels and the model parameters. Denote the log of the nominal wage rate in period t that results from the negotiations in period $t-2$ by $w_t(t-2)$ and in period $t-1$ by $w_t(t-1)$.

Suppose that the aggregate demand and aggregate supply equations are (in log levels):

$$y_t^D = m_t - p_t \qquad \text{and} \qquad y_t^S = \tfrac{1}{2}[\alpha + p_t - w_t(t-1) + u_t] + \tfrac{1}{2}[\alpha + p_t - w_t(t-2) + u_t]$$

with u_t an autocorrelated shock, $u_t = \rho u_{t-1} + \varepsilon_t$, $\varepsilon_t \sim N(0, \sigma^2)$ and $0 \le \rho < 1$.

(c) What is a typical example of a supply shock u_t? And what is an example of an *autocorrelated* shock?

(d) Derive the aggregate supply curve and the equilibrium price as a function of the expected price levels at the time of the wage negotiations.

(e) Derive $E_{t-2}p_t$, $E_{t-1}p_t$, p_t, and y_t as functions of the expected money supply and previous shocks.

Suppose that the monetary authorities set the money supply according to the following rule: $m_t = \mu_1 u_{t-1} + \mu_2 u_{t-2}$.

(f) What are the expectations in period $t - 1$ and $t - 2$ for the money supply in period t? What are the forecast errors?

(g) Derive aggregate production as a function of the exogenous shocks, using the results obtained under (f) and assuming that REH holds. What is the optimal money supply rule, provided that the authorities want to minimize fluctuations in the economy?

(h) What happens if there is no persistence in the shocks, i.e. $\rho = 0$? Does stabilization policy still work?

Question 4: A variation on the Muth model

Assume that the market for a particular commodity is described by the following model:

$$Q_t^D = a_0 - a_1 P_t + V_t, \qquad a_1 > 0, \tag{Q3.4}$$
$$Q_t^S = b_0 + b_1 P_t^e + U_t, \qquad b_1 > 0, \tag{Q3.5}$$
$$Q_t^D = Q_t^S \ [\equiv Q_t], \tag{Q3.6}$$

where Q_t^D is demand, P_t is the *actual* (market clearing) price, V_t is a stochastic shock term affecting demand, Q_t^S is supply, P_t^e is the *expected* price (i.e. the price that suppliers expect to hold in period t), U_t is a stochastic term affecting supply, and Q_t is the actual (market clearing) quantity traded in the market. It is assumed that the two stochastic shock terms, U_t and V_t, are independent and normally distributed white noise terms (there is no correlation between these terms and both terms display no autocorrelation): $U_t \sim N(0, \sigma_U^2)$ and $V_t \sim N(0, \sigma_V^2)$. Assume that expectations are formed according to the adaptive expectations hypothesis (AEH):

$$P_t^e = P_{t-1}^e + \lambda [P_{t-1} - P_{t-1}^e], \qquad \lambda > 0, \tag{Q3.7}$$

where λ regulates the speed at which expectations adjust.

(a) Interpret the equations of the model.

(b) Derive the stability condition for the model. Explain both formally and intuitively what you mean by stability in this model.

Next we replace the AEH assumption by the assumption of rational expectations (the REH). Instead of (Q3.7) we use:

$$P_t^e = E_{t-1} P_t, \tag{Q3.8}$$

where the expectations operator, E_{t-1}, denotes that agents form expectations using information dated period $t - 1$ and earlier. The information set of the agents thus includes P_{t-1}, P_{t-2}, etc., Q_{t-1}, Q_{t-2}, etc., as well as knowledge about the structure and parameters of the model.

(c) Derive expressions for equilibrium output and the price level for this case. Is the model stable? Explain.

Question 5: Expectational difference equations

Suppose that the stochastic process for Y_t is given by:

$$Y_t = \alpha_0 + \alpha_1 E_t Y_{t+1} + U_t, \qquad 0 < \alpha_1 < 1, \tag{Q3.9}$$

where α_0 and α_1 are constants, E_t is the conditional expectation (based on the period-t information set), and U_t is a stochastic shock term. We assume that this shock term features first-order autocorrelation:

$$U_t = \theta U_{t-1} + V_t, \qquad 0 < \theta < 1, \tag{Q3.10}$$

where θ is a constant and V_t is a white noise error term (with $E(V_t) = 0$ and $E(V_t^2) = \sigma^2$).

(a) Can you think of an economic example for which an expression like (Q3.9) arises naturally?

(b) Compute the rational expectations solution for Y_t. *Hint*: use the method of undetermined coefficients by trying a candidate solution of the form $Y_t = \pi_0 + \pi_1 U_t$ and computing those values for π_0 and π_1 for which the candidate solution is the correct solution.

(c) Compute the asymptotic variance of Y_t. Show that it depends positively on the autocorrelation parameter θ. Hint: first compute $Y_t - \theta Y_{t-1}$ and then write it as a difference equation.

Question 6: The Cagan model

[Based on (Cagan, 1956)] Phillip Cagan (one of Milton Friedman's friends) was very interested in the phenomenon of hyperinflation. He suggested that hyperinflation could be studied by looking at the demand for money equation. Assume that money demand, expressed in loglinear format, is given by:

$$m_t - p_t = \gamma - \alpha \left[r + E_t(p_{t+1} - p_t) \right] + u_t, \quad \alpha > 0, \tag{Q3.11}$$

where m_t is the money supply, p_t is the price level, u_t is a stochastic (white noise) error term, α and γ are constants, and r is the *real* interest rate (assumed to be constant). All variables are expressed in terms of logarithms. Assume that the money supply process is described by:

$$m_t = \mu_0 + \mu_1 m_{t-1} + e_t, \quad 0 < \mu_1 < 1, \tag{Q3.12}$$

where e_t is a (white noise) error term and μ_0 and μ_1 are parameters.

(a) Explain why we can interpret equation (Q3.11) as a money demand equation.

(b) Compute the rational expectations solution for the price level, p_t. Show that it can be written as a linear function of a constant, m_t and u_t.

Question 7: Fiscal policy under rational expectations

Consider the following loglinear model of a closed economy featuring rational expectations:

$$y_t = a_0 - a_1 \left[R_t - E_{t-1}(p_{t+1} - p_t) \right] + a_2 g_t + v_{1t}, \tag{Q3.13}$$

$$m_t - p_t = c_0 + c_1 y_t - c_2 R_t + v_{2t}, \tag{Q3.14}$$

$$y_t = \alpha_0 + \alpha_1 (p_t - E_{t-1} p_t) + \alpha_2 y_{t-1} + u_t, \tag{Q3.15}$$

$$g_t = \gamma_0 + \gamma_1 g_{t-1} + \gamma_2 y_{t-1} + e_t, \tag{Q3.16}$$

$$m_t = \mu_0 + m_{t-1}, \tag{Q3.17}$$

where y_t is output, R_t is the nominal interest rate, p_t is the price level, g_t is an index for fiscal policy, and m_t is the money supply. Furthermore, v_{1t}, v_{2t}, u_t, and e_t are stochastic (white noise) shock terms affecting the various equations of the model. These terms are independent from each other, feature no autocorrelation, and are normally distributed with mean zero and constant variance, i.e. $v_{1t} \sim N\left(0, \sigma_{v_1}^2\right)$, $v_{2t} \sim N\left(0, \sigma_{v_2}^2\right)$, $u_t \sim N\left(0, \sigma_u^2\right)$, and $e_t \sim N\left(0, \sigma_e^2\right)$. All variables, except the nominal interest rate R_t, are measured in logarithms. The parameters of the model satisfy: $a_1 > 0, a_2 > 0, c_1 > 0, c_2 > 0, \alpha_1 > 0, 0 < \alpha_2 < 1, 0 < \gamma_1 < 1$, and $\mu_0 > 0$.

(a) Interpret the equations of the model.

(b) Derive the expression for the AD curve for this model. Denote the coefficients for the AD curve by β_0, β_1, etcetera, and define the (composite) shock term entering this equation by v_t. State the stochastic properties of v_t.

(c) Find the rational expectations solution for output.

(d) Is fiscal policy ineffective in this model? What does your conclusion imply about the validity of the policy ineffectiveness proposition (PIP)?

(e) ★ Derive the rational expectations solution for the equilibrium price, p_t. Show that the price level moves one-for-one with the money stock.

Question 8: The labour market

Assume that the labour market is described by the following loglinear model:

$$n_t^D = \alpha_0 - \alpha_1 (w_t - p_t) + \alpha_2 n_{t-1} + u_{1t}, \qquad \alpha_1 > 0, \ 0 < \alpha_2 < 1, \tag{Q3.18}$$

$$n_t^S = \beta_0 + \beta_1 (w_t - E_{t-1} p_t) + u_{2t}, \qquad \beta_1 > 0, \tag{Q3.19}$$

$$n_t^D = n_t^S \ [\equiv n_t], \tag{Q3.20}$$

where n_t^D is the demand for labour, w_t is the nominal wage rate, p_t is the price level, n_t^S is the supply of labour, and n_t is equilibrium employment. The shock terms in labour demand and supply are independent from each other, feature no autocorrelation, and are normally distributed with mean zero and constant variance, i.e. $u_{1t} \sim N\left(0, \sigma_{u_1}^2\right)$ and $u_{2t} \sim N\left(0, \sigma_{u_2}^2\right)$. All variables are measured in logarithms. Expectations are formed according to the rational expectations hypothesis and E_{t-1} represents the objective expectation conditional upon the information set available in period $t - 1$.

(a) Interpret the equations of the model. Why does the lagged employment term (n_{t-1}) feature in the labour demand equation? What do we assume about the income and substitution effects in labour supply?

(b) Assume that the short-run production function can be written, in loglinear terms, as $y_t = \gamma_0 + \gamma_1 n_t$, where y_t is aggregate output and $0 < \gamma_1 < 1$. Show that the labour market model (Q3.18)–(Q3.20) in combination with the production function gives rise to the Lucas supply curve (LSC). State and explain any stability conditions that may be required.

(c) Derive the stochastic properties of the shock term of the LSC determined in part (c).

Question 9: Liquidity trap

[Based on McCallum (1983)] Consider the following loglinear model of a closed economy featuring rational expectations:

$$y_t - \bar{y} = \alpha_1 (p_t - E_{t-1} p_t) + \alpha_2 (y_{t-1} - \bar{y}) + u_t, \tag{Q3.21}$$

$$y_t = a_0 - a_1 \left[R_t - E_t (p_{t+1} - p_t) \right] + v_{1t}, \tag{Q3.22}$$

$$m_t - p_t = y_t - c_1 \left[R_t - R^{MIN} \right] + v_{2t}, \tag{Q3.23}$$

where y_t is actual output, $\bar{y}$ is full employment output (assumed to be constant), p_t is the price level, R_t is the nominal interest rate, m_t is the money supply, R^{MIN} is minimum interest rate (which is attained in the liquidity trap), and u_t, v_{1t}, and v_{2t} are stochastic (white noise) shock terms. These terms are independent from each other, feature no autocorrelation, and are normally distributed with mean zero and constant variance, i.e. $u_t \sim N\left(0, \sigma_u^2\right)$, $v_{1t} \sim N\left(0, \sigma_{v_1}^2\right)$, and $v_{2t} \sim N\left(0, \sigma_{v_2}^2\right)$. All variables except R and R^{MIN} are measured in logarithms. To keep the model as simple as possible we assume that the money supply is constant over time, i.e. $m_t = m$. The parameters of the model satisfy: $\alpha_1 > 0$, $0 < \alpha_2 < 1$, $a_1 > 0$, and $c_1 > 0$.

(a) Interpret the equations of the model.

(b) Derive the expression for the AD curve and denote its coefficients by β_0, β_1, and β_2 and its shock term by v_t. Explain what happens to the AD curve if the economy finds itself in a Keynesian liquidity trap.

(c) ★ Compute the rational expectations solution for output and the price level. Hint: use the method of undetermined coefficients and use trial solutions of the form $y_t = \pi_0 + \pi_1 y_{t-1} + \pi_2 u_t + \pi_3 v_t$ and $p_t = \omega_0 + \omega_1 y_{t-1} + \omega_2 u_t + \omega_3 v_t$.

(d) ★ Show that the model is internally inconsistent, and the price level is indeterminate, if the economy is in the liquidity trap. Demonstrate that Pigou's suggestion, that consumption depends on real money balances, leads to a consistent model again.

Question 10: PIP meets the Pigou effect

Consider the following loglinear model of a closed economy featuring rational expectations:

$$y_t = a_0 - a_1 r_t + a_2(m_t - p_t) + v_{1t}, \tag{Q3.24}$$
$$m_t - p_t = c_0 + c_1 y_t - c_2 R_t + v_{2t}, \tag{Q3.25}$$
$$y_t = \alpha_0 + \alpha_1(p_t - E_{t-1}p_t) + \alpha_2 y_{t-1} + \alpha_3 k_t + u_t, \tag{Q3.26}$$
$$k_{t+1} = \gamma_1 k_t + \gamma_2 r_t, \tag{Q3.27}$$
$$m_t = \mu_0 + \mu_1 m_{t-1} + \mu_2 y_{t-1} + e_t, \tag{Q3.28}$$
$$r_t \equiv R_t - E_{t-1}(p_{t+1} - p_t), \tag{Q3.29}$$

where y_t is output, r_t is the *real* interest rate, m_t is the money supply, p_t is the price level, R_t is the nominal interest rate, and k_t is the capital stock. Furthermore, v_{1t}, v_{2t}, u_t and e_t are stochastic (white noise) shock terms affecting the various equations of the model. These terms are independent from each other, feature no autocorrelation, and are normally distributed with mean zero and constant variance, i.e. $v_{1t} \sim N\left(0, \sigma_{v_1}^2\right)$, $v_{2t} \sim N\left(0, \sigma_{v_2}^2\right)$, $u_t \sim N\left(0, \sigma_u^2\right)$, and $e_t \sim N\left(0, \sigma_e^2\right)$. All variables, except the various interest rates (r_t and R_t) are measured in logarithms. The parameters of the model satisfy: $a_1 > 0$, $a_2 \geq 0$, $c_1 > 0$, $c_2 > 0$, $\alpha_1 > 0$, $0 < \alpha_2 < 1$, $\alpha_3 > 0$, $0 < \gamma_1 < 0$, $\gamma_2 < 0$, and $0 < \mu_1 \leq 1$.

(a) Interpret the equations of the model.

(b) Derive the expression for the AD curve and denote its coefficients by β_0, β_1, and β_2 and its shock term by v_t.

(c) Show that the expectational gap, $p_t - E_{t-1}p_t$, only depends on the shock terms of AD, AS, and the money supply rule (i.e. v_t, u_t, and e_t) but not on the parameters of the money supply rule (i.e. μ_0, μ_1, and μ_2).

(d) ★ Characterize the rational expectations solution for the model and show that the *policy ineffectiveness proposition* (PIP) does not hold, unless the real balance effect in the IS curve is absent.

McCallum (1980) argues that stabilization policy is not about stabilizing actual output (y_t) itself but rather about stabilizing the deviation of output relative to *capacity* output ($y_t - \bar{y}_t$). He suggests that in the context of the present model, capacity output should be measured as follows:

$$\bar{y}_t = \alpha_0 + \alpha_2 \bar{y}_{t-1} + \alpha_3 k_t + u_t. \tag{Q3.30}$$

(e) Can you give a rationale for the expression in (Q3.30)?

(f) Show that the reinterpreted PIP holds in the model because the path for $y_t - \bar{y}_t$ does not depend on the parameters of the money supply rule.

Question 11: PIP and the output gap

Consider the following loglinear model of a closed economy featuring rational expectations:

$$y_t = a_0 - a_1 r_t + a_2(m_t - p_t) + v_{1t}, \tag{Q3.31}$$

$$m_t - p_t = c_0 + c_1 y_t - c_2 R_t + v_{2t}, \tag{Q3.32}$$

$$y_t = \alpha_0 + \alpha_1(p_t - E_{t-1}p_t) + \alpha_2 y_{t-1} + \alpha_3 r_t + u_t, \tag{Q3.33}$$

$$m_t = \mu_0 + \mu_1 m_{t-1} + \mu_2 y_{t-1} + e_t, \tag{Q3.34}$$

$$r_t \equiv R_t - E_{t-1}(p_{t+1} - p_t), \tag{Q3.35}$$

where y_t is output, r_t is the *real* interest rate, m_t is the money supply, p_t is the price level, and R_t is the nominal interest rate. Furthermore, v_{1t}, v_{2t}, u_t and e_t are stochastic (white noise) shock terms affecting the various equations of the model. These terms are independent from each other, feature no autocorrelation, and are normally distributed with mean zero and constant variance, i.e. $v_{1t} \sim N\left(0, \sigma_{v_1}^2\right)$, $v_{2t} \sim N\left(0, \sigma_{v_2}^2\right)$, $u_t \sim N\left(0, \sigma_u^2\right)$, and $e_t \sim N\left(0, \sigma_e^2\right)$. All variables, except the various interest rates (r_t and R_t) are measured in logarithms. The parameters of the model satisfy: $a_1 > 0$, $a_2 \geq 0$, $c_1 > 0$, $c_2 > 0$, $\alpha_1 > 0$, $0 < \alpha_2 < 1$, and $\alpha_3 > 0$.

(a) Interpret the equations of the model.

(b) Show that the expectational gap, $p_t - E_{t-1}p_t$, only depends on the shock terms of IS, LM, AS, and the money supply rule (i.e. v_{1t}, v_{2t}, u_t, and e_t) but *not* on the parameters of the money supply rule (i.e. μ_0, μ_1, and μ_2).

(c) ★ Characterize the rational expectations solution for the model and show that the *policy ineffectiveness proposition* (PIP) does not hold, unless the real balance effect in the IS curve is absent.

(d) Define capacity output as $\bar{y}_t = \alpha_0 + \alpha_2 \bar{y}_{t-1} + \alpha_3 r_t + u_t$ and show that monetary policy cannot be used to stabilize the output gap, $y_t - \bar{y}_t$.

★ Question 12: Contemporaneous information

Consider the following model of a closed economy featuring rational expectations.

$$y_t = \alpha_0 + \alpha_1(p_t - E_{t-1}p_t) + u_t, \tag{Q3.36}$$

$$y_t = \beta_0 + \beta_1(m_t - p_t) + \beta_2 E_t(p_{t+1} - p_t) + v_t, \tag{Q3.37}$$

$$m_t = \mu_0 + \mu_1 m_{t-1} + \mu_2 y_{t-1} + e_t, \tag{Q3.38}$$

where y_t is output, p_t is the price level, m_t is the money supply, and u_t, v_t and e_t are stochastic (white noise) shock terms affecting the various equations of the model. These terms are independent from each other, feature no autocorrelation, and are normally distributed with mean zero and constant variance, i.e. $u_t \sim N\left(0, \sigma_u^2\right)$, $v_t \sim N\left(0, \sigma_v^2\right)$, and $e_t \sim N\left(0, \sigma_e^2\right)$. All variables are measured in logarithms. The parameters of the model satisfy: $\alpha_1 > 0$, $\beta_1 > 0$, $\beta_2 > 0$, and $0 < \mu_1 < 1$. The key thing to note is that agents are assumed to possess current aggregate information when estimating the future inflation rate, i.e. E_t (rather than E_{t-1}) features in equation (Q3.37).

(a) Interpret the equations of the model.

(b) Find the rational expectations solution for output and show that the *policy ineffectiveness proposition* (PIP) does not hold. Explain why this is the case.

(c) Compute the asymptotic variance of output. Should the government pursue a countercyclical monetary policy? Explain the intuition behind your results.

★ Question 13: Sticky prices

Consider the following model of a closed economy featuring rational expectations.

$$p_t = \tilde{p}_t - (1 - \theta)(\tilde{p}_t - E_{t-1}\tilde{p}_t), \tag{Q3.39}$$
$$y_t = \beta_0 + \beta_1(m_t - p_t) + \beta_2 E_{t-1}(p_{t+1} - p_t) + v_t, \tag{Q3.40}$$
$$m_t = \mu_0 + \mu_1 m_{t-1} + \mu_2 y_{t-1} + e_t, \tag{Q3.41}$$
$$\bar{y}_t = \zeta_0 + \bar{y}_{t-1} + u_t, \tag{Q3.42}$$

where p_t is the actual price level, $\tilde{p}_t$ is the *equilibrium* price level (see below), y_t is actual output, m_t is the money supply, and $\bar{y}_t$ is full employment output. In equation (Q3.39), $\tilde{p}_t$ is the price for which actual output, y_t, equals its exogenously given full employment level, $\bar{y}_t$. As usual, v_t, u_t and e_t are stochastic (white noise) shock terms affecting the various equations of the model. These terms are independent from each other, feature no autocorrelation, and are normally distributed with mean zero and constant variance, i.e. $v_t \sim N\left(0, \sigma_v^2\right)$, $e_t \sim N\left(0, \sigma_e^2\right)$, and $u_t \sim N\left(0, \sigma_u^2\right)$. All variables are measured in logarithms. The parameters of the model satisfy: $0 \le \theta \le 1$, $\beta_1 > 0$, $\beta_2 > 0$, and $0 < \mu_1 < 1$.

(a) Interpret the equations of the model.

(b) Consider the special case of the model for which $\theta = 1$. Compute the rational expectations solutions for output and the price level. Show that the *policy ineffectiveness proposition* (PIP) holds.

(c) Now use the general case of the model, with $0 < \theta < 1$, and solve for the rational expectations solution for output and the price level. Can the government pursue a countercyclical monetary policy? Explain the intuition behind your results.

(d) Compute the asymptotic variance of the output gap, $y_t - \bar{y}_t$. Does the degree of price stickiness, as parameterized by θ, increase or decrease output fluctuations in the economy? Explain.

★ Question 14: Automatic stabilizer

[Based on Scarth (1988, p. 190)] Consider the following Keynesian Cross model formulated in discrete time.

$$Y_t = C_t + I_t + \bar{G}, \tag{Q3.43}$$
$$C_t = c(1 - t)Y_t, \qquad 0 < c < 1, \; 0 < t < 1, \tag{Q3.44}$$
$$I_t = \bar{I} + vY_{t-1} + U_t, \qquad 0 < v < 1 - c(1 - t), \tag{Q3.45}$$

where Y_t is output, C_t is consumption, I_t is investment, $\bar{G}$ is exogenous government consumption, c is the marginal propensity to consume, t is the tax rate, $\bar{I}$ is the exogenous part of investment, and U_t is a stochastic term. It is assumed that U_t is distributed normally with mean zero and variance σ^2 (i.e. $U_t \sim N(0, \sigma^2)$ in the notation of Chapter 3) and that it features no autocorrelation.

(a) Interpret the equations of the model.

(b) Compute the asymptotic variances of output, consumption, and investment. (See Intermezzo 3.1 on the asymptotic variance in Chapter 3 if you are unfamiliar with the concept). Denote these asymptotic variances by, respectively, σ_Y^2, σ_C^2, and σ_I^2.

(c) Does the tax system act as an automatic stabilizer in this model? Explain both formally and intuitively.

Answers

Question 1: Short questions

(a) See any introduction to statistics. Each toss of the coin gives you an expected pay-off of $0.5 \times 1 - 0.5 \times 1 = 0$ euro. 100 tosses gives you an expected pay-off of $100 \times 0 = 0$ euro. If the probability of heads is 0.45, then the expected pay-off for one toss is $0.45 \times 1 - 0.55 \times 1 = -0.10$. If you toss 100 times, you expect a *negative* pay-off of $100 \times 0.10 = 10$ euro.

(b) False, all that the REH says is that the subjective expectation coincides with the objective expectation. Not everybody needs to be a brilliant economist. As long as there are no systematic mistakes, the REH is fine as an operating assumption.

(c) False, with multi-period nominal wage contracts, the policy maker has an informational advantage and thus can affect the economy. In this context it also should do so, because the asymptotic variance of output is reduced (stabilization).

(d) In this case the PIP still holds because the policy maker does not have an informational advantage over the public. It cannot react to stale information.

Question 2: Stabilization of demand shocks

(a) Labour market clearing implies $n_t^S = n_t^D$ or:

$$\beta[w_t - E_{t-1}p_t] = -\alpha[w_t - p_t] \quad \Leftrightarrow \quad w_t = \frac{\alpha p_t + \beta E_{t-1}p_t}{\alpha + \beta}. \tag{A3.1}$$

By using this expression for w_t in (Q3.1), we obtain:

$$\begin{aligned}
y_t &= -\delta[w_t - p_t] \\
&= -\delta\left[\frac{\alpha p_t + \beta E_{t-1}p_t}{\alpha + \beta} - p_t\right] \\
&= \gamma[p_t - E_{t-1}p_t], \quad \text{with} \quad \gamma \equiv \frac{\delta\beta}{\alpha + \beta} > 0.
\end{aligned} \tag{A3.2}$$

which is the Lucas supply curve.

(b) By using the aggregate demand curve and the Lucas supply curve we obtain:

$$\begin{aligned}
m_t - p_t + u_t &= \gamma[p_t - E_{t-1}p_t] \quad \Leftrightarrow \\
(1 + \gamma)p_t &= \gamma E_{t-1}p_t + m_t + u_t.
\end{aligned} \tag{A3.3}$$

Taking expectations we get:

$$\begin{aligned}
(1 + \gamma)E_{t-1}p_t &= \gamma E_{t-1}E_{t-1}p_t + E_{t-1}m_t + E_{t-1}u_t \\
&= \gamma E_{t-1}p_t + m_t,
\end{aligned} \tag{A3.4}$$

where we have used the fact that $E_{t-1}E_{t-1}p_t = E_{t-1}p_t$ (law of iterated expectations), $E_{t-1}m_t = m_t$ (no money supply surprises), and $E_{t-1}u_t = 0$ (best guess of future demand shock). Solving for $E_{t-1}p_t$ yields:

$$E_{t-1}p_t = m_t. \tag{A3.5}$$

Using (A3.5) in (A3.3) we get the rational expectations solution for p_t:

$$p_t = \frac{\gamma E_{t-1} p_t + m_t + u_t}{1 + \gamma} = \frac{\gamma m_t + m_t + u_t}{1 + \gamma} = m_t + \frac{u_t}{1 + \gamma}.$$

Finally, by using this in the aggregate demand curve we get:

$$y_t = m_t - p_t + u_t$$
$$= m_t - \left[m_t + \frac{u_t}{1 + \gamma} \right] + u_t$$
$$= \frac{\gamma}{1 + \gamma} u_t, \tag{A3.6}$$

which shows that money supply only affects price level but not real output.

(c) The asymptotic variance of output is obtained by using (A3.6):

$$\sigma_y^2 \equiv E_{t-\infty} \left[y_t - E_{t-\infty} y_t \right]^2$$
$$= E_{t-\infty} y_t^2$$
$$= \left(\frac{\gamma}{1 + \gamma} \right)^2 E_{t-\infty} u_t^2$$
$$= \left(\frac{\gamma}{1 + \gamma} \right)^2 \sigma^2. \tag{A3.7}$$

where we have used $E_{t-\infty} y_t = \frac{\gamma}{1 + \gamma} E_{t-\infty} u_t = 0$ in going from the first to the second line.

Question 3: Overlapping wage contracts and the REH

(a) $n_t^D = \gamma_D - \varepsilon_D [w_t - p_t]$ and $n_t^S = \gamma_S + \varepsilon_S [w_t - p_t^e]$, ε_D is the real wage elasticity of labour demand and ε_S is the expected real wage elasticity of labour supply.

(b) $w_t(t-1) = \gamma + E_{t-1} p_t$ and $w_t(t-2) = \gamma + E_{t-2} p_t$ with $\gamma \equiv \frac{\gamma_D - \gamma_S}{\varepsilon_D + \varepsilon_S}$.

(c) Oil price shocks, bad harvest, anything with a direct effect on supply.

(d) Equate aggregate demand and aggregate supply, follow the steps on page 77.

$$y_t^S = \beta + p_t - \tfrac{1}{2} [E_{t-2} p_t + E_{t-1} p_t] + u_t$$
$$p_t = \tfrac{1}{2} \left[m_t - \beta + \tfrac{1}{2} [E_{t-1} p_t + E_{t-2} p_t] - u_t \right]$$

with $\beta \equiv \alpha - \gamma$.

(e) Take expectations of the equilibrium price and solve for respectively E_{t-2} and

E_{t-1}.

$$E_{t-2}p_t = \tfrac{1}{2}E_{t-2}m_t - \tfrac{1}{2}\beta + \tfrac{1}{4}[E_{t-2}p_t + E_{t-2}p_t] - E_{t-2}u_t$$
$$= E_{t-2}m_t - \beta - \rho^2 u_{t-2}$$
$$E_{t-1}p_t = \tfrac{1}{2}E_{t-1}m_t - \tfrac{1}{2}\beta + \tfrac{1}{4}[E_{t-1}p_t + E_{t-2}p_t] - \tfrac{1}{2}E_{t-1}u_t$$
$$= \tfrac{2}{3}E_{t-1}m_t - \tfrac{2}{3}\beta + \tfrac{1}{3}E_{t-2}p_t - \tfrac{2}{3}\rho u_{t-1}$$
$$= \tfrac{2}{3}E_{t-1}m_t + \tfrac{1}{3}E_{t-2}m_t - \beta - \tfrac{2}{3}\rho u_{t-1} - \tfrac{1}{3}\rho^2 u_{t-2}$$
$$p_t = \tfrac{1}{2}m_t + \tfrac{1}{6}E_{t-1}m_t + \tfrac{1}{3}E_{t-2}m_t - \beta - \tfrac{1}{6}\rho u_{t-1} - \tfrac{1}{3}\rho^2 u_{t-2} - \tfrac{1}{2}u_t$$
$$y_t = \tfrac{1}{2}m_t - \tfrac{1}{6}E_{t-1}m_t - \tfrac{1}{3}E_{t-2}m_t + \beta + \tfrac{1}{6}\rho u_{t-1} + \tfrac{1}{3}\rho^2 u_{t-2} + \tfrac{1}{2}u_t$$

(f)
$$E_{t-2}m_t = [\mu_1\rho + \mu_2]u_{t-2} \qquad E_{t-1}m_t = m_t$$
$$m_t - E_{t-2}m_t = \mu_1\varepsilon_{t-1} \qquad m_t - E_{t-1}m_t = 0$$

(g)

$$y_t = \beta + \tfrac{1}{3}[m_t - E_{t-2}m_t] + \tfrac{1}{6}\rho u_{t-1} + \tfrac{1}{3}\rho^2 u_{t-2} + \tfrac{1}{2}u_t$$

Now use $m_t - E_{t-2}m_t = \mu_1\varepsilon_{t-1}$, $u_{t-1} = \rho u_{t-2} + \varepsilon_{t-1}$, and $u_t = \rho[\rho u_{t-2} + \varepsilon_{t-1}] + \varepsilon_t = \rho^2 u_{t-2} + \rho\varepsilon_{t-1} + \varepsilon_t$ and simple substitution gives the answer:

$$y_t = \beta + \tfrac{1}{2}\varepsilon_t + \tfrac{1}{3}[\mu_1 + 2\rho]\varepsilon_{t-1} + \rho^2 u_{t-2}$$

If $\mu_1 = -2\rho$, fluctuations are minimized.

(h) Previous supply shocks contain no information about future supply shocks. Stabilization still works, but it is optimal to do nothing, $\mu_1 = 0$!

Question 4: A variation on the Muth model

(a) Equation (Q3.4) is demand, (Q3.5) is supply, and (Q3.6) implicitly says that the current price, P_t, clears the market. We have generalized the model used in the text (given in (3.1)–(3.3)) by assuming that there are both demand and supply shocks. Demand shocks could be due to random changes in tastes, income, or prices of other commodities. Supply shocks are explained in the text. Equation (Q3.7) is the discrete-time expression for the adaptive expectations hypothesis (AEH).

(b) With stability we mean that the expectational errors go to zero eventually. Because there are random shocks in the model, the steady state will never actually be reached. But we can nevertheless study the stability issue by checking whether the deterministic part of the model is stable. The stochastic part is automatically stable because U_t and V_t are drawn from stationary probability distributions.

We solve the model in a number of steps. First we solve for the actual price, conditional on expectations and the stochastic error terms. We substitute equations (Q3.4)–(Q3.5) into (Q3.6):

$$b_0 + b_1 P_t^e + U_t = a_0 - a_1 P_t + V_t \quad \Leftrightarrow$$
$$a_1 P_t = (a_0 - b_0) - b_1 P_t^e + [V_t - U_t] \quad \Leftrightarrow$$
$$P_t = \frac{a_0 - b_0}{a_1} - \frac{b_1}{a_1}P_t^e + \frac{1}{a_1}[V_t - U_t]. \tag{A3.8}$$

It follows from (A3.8) that the lagged price is given by:

$$P_{t-1} = \frac{a_0 - b_0}{a_1} - \frac{b_1}{a_1}P_{t-1}^e + \frac{1}{a_1}\left[V_{t-1} - U_{t-1}\right].$$

(A3.9)

By substituting (A3.9) into (Q3.7) we obtain a difference equation for P_t^e:

$$P_t^e = (1-\lambda)P_{t-1}^e + \lambda\left[\frac{a_0 - b_0}{a_1} - \frac{b_1}{a_1}P_{t-1}^e + \frac{1}{a_1}[V_{t-1} - U_{t-1}]\right]$$

$$= \left[1 - \lambda\frac{a_1 + b_1}{a_1}\right]P_{t-1}^e + \lambda\frac{a_0 - b_0}{a_1} + \frac{\lambda}{a_1}[V_{t-1} - U_{t-1}].$$

(A3.10)

Stability requires the coefficient for P_{t-1}^e (the term in square brackets on the right-hand side) to be between 0 and 1 in absolute terms. It is clear that $\lambda > 0$ is a necessary (but not a sufficient) condition for stability. We look at the two cases in turn. The first stable case is the one associated with stable monotonic adjustment:

$$0 < 1 - \lambda\frac{a_1 + b_1}{a_1} < 1 \quad \Leftrightarrow$$

$$-1 < -\lambda\frac{a_1 + b_1}{a_1} < 0 \quad \Leftrightarrow$$

$$0 < \lambda\frac{a_1 + b_1}{a_1} < 1.$$

(A3.11)

The first inequality in (A3.11) holds automatically because λ, b_1, and a_1 are all assumed to be positive and the second inequality can be rewritten as:

$$0 < \lambda < \frac{a_1}{a_1 + b_1}, \qquad \text{(monotonic adjustment).}$$

(A3.12)

The second case is associated with stable cyclical adjustment:

$$-1 < 1 - \lambda\frac{a_1 + b_1}{a_1} < 0 \quad \Leftrightarrow$$

$$0 < 2 - \lambda\frac{a_1 + b_1}{a_1} < 1 \quad \Leftrightarrow$$

$$1 < \lambda\frac{a_1 + b_1}{a_1} < 2.$$

(A3.13)

The inequality in (A3.11) can be rewritten as:

$$\frac{a_1}{a_1 + b_1} < \lambda < \frac{2a_1}{a_1 + b_1}, \qquad \text{(cyclical adjustment).}$$

(A3.14)

Intuitively, the expectations adjustment parameter must work in the right direction (i.e. it must be positive) but it must not be so large that it grossly overcorrects expectational errors. In the monotonic case, the expectational gap is gradually closed and the expectational errors all have the same sign. In the cyclical case there is some over-correction but it is stable. The expectational errors alternate in sign.

(c) In order to compute the rational expectations solution of the model, we take the conditional expectation of (A3.8):

$$E_{t-1}P_t = E_{t-1}\left(\frac{a_0 - b_0}{a_1} - \frac{b_1}{a_1}P_t^e + \frac{1}{a_1}[V_t - U_t]\right)$$

$$= \frac{a_0 - b_0}{a_1} - \frac{b_1}{a_1}E_{t-1}P_t^e + \frac{1}{a_1}E_{t-1}(V_t - U_t)$$

$$= \frac{a_0 - b_0}{a_1} - \frac{b_1}{a_1}P_t^e. \qquad (A3.15)$$

We have used the fact that a_0, a_1, b_0, and b_1 are in the information set of the agent (they are known parameters) in going from the first to the second line. In going from the second to the third line we have incorporated the fact that the error terms both have an expected value of zero ($E_{t-1}U_t = 0$ and $E_{t-1}V_t = 0$), and that P_t^e is a non-stochastic constant (a subjective expectation held by suppliers in the market).

The rational expectations hypothesis (REH) says that the subjective expectation equals the objective expectation. By using (Q3.7) in (A3.15) we can solve for the expected price level:

$$P_t^e = \frac{a_0 - b_0}{a_1} - \frac{b_1}{a_1}P_t^e \quad \Leftrightarrow \quad P_t^e = \frac{a_0 - b_0}{a_1 + b_1}. \qquad (A3.16)$$

In this model, with error terms featuring an expected value of zero, the rationally expected price level is simply the equilibrium price implied by the deterministic part of the model.

To investigate stability of the model under the REH, we substitute (A3.16) into (A3.8) and solve for the actual equilibrium price level:

$$P_t = \frac{a_0 - b_0}{a_1} - \frac{b_1}{a_1}\frac{a_0 - b_0}{a_1 + b_1} + \frac{1}{a_1}[V_t - U_t] \quad \Leftrightarrow$$

$$P_t = \frac{a_0 - b_0}{a_1 + b_1} + \frac{1}{a_1}[V_t - U_t]. \qquad (A3.17)$$

It follows from (A3.17) that the model is automatically stable—no additional conditions need to be imposed on the parameters. The price (and thus equilibrium output) fluctuates because of random events affecting demand and/or supply but the expectation formation process does not itself introduce any potentially destabilizing effects into the market.

Question 5: Expectational difference equations

(a) Equation (Q3.9) is a so-called *expectational difference equation*. The actual realization of Y_t depends in part on the expectation regarding Y_{t+1}. Such equations are quite common in the economics literature. Blanchard and Fischer (1989, p. 215-217) give several examples. In one of these example, the arbitrage condition between a safe asset (say, a bank deposit which pays a constant interest rate, R) and shares (paying dividends, d_t) is written as:

$$R = \frac{d_t + E_t p_{t+1} - p_t}{p_t}, \qquad (A3.18)$$

where p_t is the price of the share at the beginning of period t. The left-hand side is the net yield on the bank deposit and the right-hand side is the yield on shares (i.e. the sum of dividend and the expected capital gain, expressed in terms of the market price of the share). By rewriting (A3.18) we find:

$$p_t = \frac{1}{1+R}\left[d_t + E_t p_{t+1}\right].$$
(A3.19)

If the process for d_t itself contains a stochastic term, equation (A3.19) has the same form as equation (Q3.9) in the question. Another example is the Cagan model, discussed in question 4.

(b) We can solve the expectational difference equations by repeated substitution (forward iteration) or by using the method of undetermined coefficients. We start with the latter method. The trial solution for Y_t is:

$$Y_t = \pi_0 + \pi_1 U_t,$$
(A3.20)

where π_0 and π_1 are the unknown coefficients that we wish to determine, i.e. we want to relate them to the parameters of the model (α_0, α_1, and θ). It follows from (A3.20) that Y_{t+1} can be written as:

$$Y_{t+1} = \pi_0 + \pi_1 U_{t+1}.$$
(A3.21)

By taking conditional expectations of (A3.21) and noting that (Q3.10) implies $U_{t+1} = \theta U_t + V_{t+1}$ we obtain:

$$
\begin{aligned}
2E_t Y_{t+1} &= \pi_0 + \pi_1 E_t U_{t+1} \\
&= \pi_0 + \pi_1 E_t \left(\theta U_t + V_{t+1}\right) \\
&= \pi_0 + \theta \pi_1 E_t U_t \quad \text{(because } E_t V_{t+1} = 0\text{)} \\
&= \pi_0 + \theta \pi_1 U_t \quad \text{(because } U_t \text{ is known in period } t\text{)}.
\end{aligned}
$$
(A3.22)

By substituting (A3.22) into (Q3.9) we obtain the following expression:

$$
\begin{aligned}
Y_t &= \alpha_0 + \alpha_1 \left[\pi_0 + \theta \pi_1 U_t\right] + U_t \\
&= \left(\alpha_0 + \alpha_1 \pi_0\right) + \left(1 + \alpha_1 \theta \pi_1\right) U_t.
\end{aligned}
$$
(A3.23)

The crucial thing to note is that (A3.23) has the same form as the trial solution (A3.20), i.e. it has a constant and a term involving U_t. However, these two solutions must not only have the same form but they must also be *identical*. The trial solution and the model solution implied by the trial solution must coincide. This requirement yields the following restrictions on the (previously undetermined) coefficients π_0 and π_1:

$$\pi_0 = \alpha_0 + \alpha_1 \pi_0 \Leftrightarrow \pi_0 = \frac{\alpha_0}{1-\alpha_1},$$
(A3.24)

$$\pi_1 = 1 + \alpha_1 \theta \pi_1 \Leftrightarrow \pi_1 = \frac{1}{1-\alpha_1 \theta}.$$
(A3.25)

By substituting (A3.24)-(A3.25) into (A3.20) we find the rational expectations solution for Y_t:

$$Y_t = \frac{\alpha_0}{1-\alpha_1} + \frac{1}{1-\alpha_1 \theta} U_t.$$
(A3.26)

The forward iteration method works as follows. We first write (Q3.9) for period $t + 1$.

$$Y_{t+1} = \alpha_0 + \alpha_1 E_{t+1} Y_{t+2} + U_{t+1}. \tag{A3.27}$$

Taking conditional expectations of (A3.27) yields:

$$\begin{aligned} E_t Y_{t+1} &= \alpha_0 + \alpha_1 E_t E_{t+1} Y_{t+2} + E_t U_{t+1} \\ &= \alpha_0 + \alpha_1 E_t Y_{t+2} + \theta U_t, \end{aligned} \tag{A3.28}$$

where we have used the *law of iterated expectations* ($E_t E_{t+1} Y_{t+2} = E_t Y_{t+2}$) and knowledge of the shock process ($E_t U_{t+1} = \theta U_t$) in going from the first to the second line. By using (A3.28) in (Q3.9) we find:

$$\begin{aligned} Y_t &= \alpha_0 + \alpha_1 [\alpha_0 + \alpha_1 E_t Y_{t+2} + \theta U_t] + U_t \\ &= \alpha_0(1 + \alpha_1) + \alpha_1^2 E_t Y_{t+2} + (1 + \alpha_1 \theta) U_t. \end{aligned} \tag{A3.29}$$

We have pushed the "problem" ahead of time since we now need to know $E_t Y_{t+2}$. Notice, however, that the influence of $E_t Y_{t+2}$ is dampened by the coefficient α_1^2 which is less than α_1 because $0 < \alpha_1 < 1$.

But we can continue this iteration process indefinitely. For period $t + 2$, for example, we find:

$$\begin{aligned} Y_{t+2} &= \alpha_0 + \alpha_1 E_{t+2} Y_{t+3} + U_{t+2} \quad \Rightarrow \\ E_t Y_{t+2} &= \alpha_0 + \alpha_1 E_t E_{t+2} Y_{t+3} + E_t U_{t+2} \\ &= \alpha_0 + \alpha_1 E_t Y_{t+3} + \theta^2 U_t, \end{aligned} \tag{A3.30}$$

where we have used $E_t E_{t+2} Y_{t+3} = E_t Y_{t+3}$ and $E_t U_{t+2} = \theta^2 U_t$ to get to (A3.30). Substitution of (A3.30) into (A3.29) yields:

$$\begin{aligned} Y_t &= \alpha_0(1 + \alpha_1) + \alpha_1^2 [\alpha_0 + \alpha_1 E_t Y_{t+3} + \theta^2 U_t] + (1 + \alpha_1 \theta) U_t \\ &= \alpha_0[1 + \alpha_1 + \alpha_1^2] + \alpha_1^3 E_t Y_{t+3} + [1 + \alpha_1 \theta + (\alpha_1 \theta)^2] U_t. \end{aligned} \tag{A3.31}$$

By now we recognize the emerging pattern and conclude that after N iterations we would get:

$$\begin{aligned} Y_t = \alpha_0 \left[1 + \alpha_1 + \alpha_1^2 + \cdots + \alpha_1^{N-1} \right] + \alpha_1^N E_t Y_{t+N} \\ + \left[1 + \alpha_1 \theta + (\alpha_1 \theta)^2 + \cdots + (\alpha_1 \theta)^{N-1} \right] U_t. \end{aligned} \tag{A3.32}$$

By letting $N \to \infty$ we terms in square brackets converge to, respectively, $1/(1 - \alpha_1)$ (as $0 < \alpha_1 < 1$) and $1/(1 - \alpha_1 \theta)$ (as $0 < \alpha_1 \theta < 1$) and $\alpha_1^N E_t Y_{t+N} \to 0$. As a result, equation (A3.32) converges to:

$$Y_t = \frac{\alpha_0}{1 - \alpha_1} + \frac{1}{1 - \alpha_1 \theta} U_t. \tag{A3.33}$$

Of course, since we are dealing with one and the same model, equation (A3.33) is identical to (A3.27) above.

(c) The asymptotic variance of Y_t is defined as follows (see Intermezzo 3.1 in Chapter 3):

$$\sigma_Y^2 \equiv E_{t-\infty}\left[Y_t - E_{t-\infty}Y_t\right]^2. \tag{A3.34}$$

Before computing σ_Y^2, we first derive a convenient expression for Y_t. By using (A3.27) or (A3.33) for periods t and $t-1$ we find:

$$Y_t - \theta Y_{t-1} = \frac{\alpha_0(1-\theta)}{1-\alpha_1} + \frac{1}{1-\alpha_1\theta}\left[U_t - \theta U_{t-1}\right] \quad\Rightarrow$$

$$Y_t = \frac{\alpha_0(1-\theta)}{1-\alpha_1} + \theta Y_{t-1} + \frac{1}{1-\alpha_1\theta}V_t, \tag{A3.35}$$

where we have used equation (Q3.10) to simplify the expression. The advantage of working with (A3.35) rather than (A3.27) is that the former is in the standard format dealt with in Intermezzo 3.1, whereas the latter is not. In particular, (A3.35) is a stable difference equation (because $0 < \theta < 1$) with a white noise shock term. Following the same steps as in Intermezzo 3.1 in Chapter 3 we find:

$$\sigma_Y^2 \equiv E_{t-\infty}\left[Y_t - E_{t-\infty}Y_t\right]^2$$
$$= E_{t-\infty}\left[\theta^2\left(Y_{t-1} - E_{t-\infty}Y_{t-1}\right)^2\right]$$
$$\quad + E_{t-\infty}\left[\left(\frac{1}{1-\alpha_1\theta}\right)^2 V_t^2 + \frac{2\theta(Y_{t-1} - E_{t-\infty}Y_{t-1})V_t}{1-\alpha_1\theta}\right]$$
$$= \theta^2\sigma_Y^2 + \left(\frac{1}{1-\alpha_1\theta}\right)^2\sigma_V^2, \tag{A3.36}$$

where we have used the fact that $E_{t-\infty}(Y_{t-1} - E_{t-\infty}Y_{t-1})V_t = 0$ to arrive at the final expression. By solving (A3.36) for σ_Y^2 we find:

$$\sigma_Y^2 = \frac{1}{1-\theta^2}\left(\frac{1}{1-\alpha_1\theta}\right)^2\sigma_V^2. \tag{A3.37}$$

It follows from (A3.37) that the closer θ gets to unity, the larger are the terms in round brackets on the right-hand side, and the larger is the asymptotic variance of Y_t.

Question 6: The Cagan model

(a) Since p_t is measured in logarithms we know that $p_{t+1} - p_t \equiv \ln(P_{t+1}/P_t)$, where P_t is the price expressed in level terms. But $P_{t+1} \equiv P_t + \Delta P_{t+1}$ so that $P_{t+1}/P_t = 1 + \pi_{t+1}$, where π_{t+1} represents the inflation rate between periods t and $t+1$. For small enough values of x we know that $\ln(1+x) \approx x$ so $\ln(P_{t+1}/P_t) \approx \pi_{t+1}$. But this means that the term in square brackets equals the nominal interest rate, i.e. $R_t = r + E_t\pi_{t+1}$. Equation (Q3.11) can thus be seen as a money demand equation which depends negatively on the nominal interest rate. Output does not feature in (Q3.11) because output effects are dwarfed by the inflation effect under hyperinflation.

(b) We can once again use the method of undetermined coefficients. Since we assume the availability of a period-t information set, we postulate the following trial solution:

$$p_t = \pi_0 + \pi_1 m_t + \pi_2 u_t, \tag{A3.38}$$

where π_0, π_1, and π_2 are the coefficients to be determined. It follows from (A3.38) that:

$$p_{t+1} = \pi_0 + \pi_1 m_{t+1} + \pi_2 u_{t+1}, \tag{A3.39}$$

so that $E_t p_{t+1}$ can be written as:

$$\begin{aligned}
E_t p_{t+1} &= \pi_0 + \pi_1 E_t m_{t+1} + \pi_2 E_t u_{t+1} \\
&= \pi_0 + \pi_1 \left[\mu_0 + \mu_1 m_t + E_t e_{t+1} \right] + \pi_2 E_t u_{t+1} \\
&= \pi_0 + \pi_1 \left[\mu_0 + \mu_1 m_t \right],
\end{aligned} \tag{A3.40}$$

where we have used (Q3.12) plus the fact that $E_t e_{t+1} = E_t u_{t+1} = 0$ to arrive at (A3.40). By substituting (A3.40) into (Q3.11) we find:

$$m_t - p_t = \gamma - \alpha \left[r + \pi_0 + \pi_1 \left[\mu_0 + \mu_1 m_t \right] - p_t \right] + u_t \quad \Rightarrow$$

$$p_t = \frac{-\gamma + \alpha \left[r + \pi_0 + \pi_1 \mu_0 \right]}{1 + \alpha} + \frac{1 + \alpha \pi_1 \mu_1}{1 + \alpha} m_t - \frac{1}{1 + \alpha} u_t. \tag{A3.41}$$

The trial solution (given in (A3.38)) and the model solution induced by the trial solution (given in (A3.41)) must be identical. We can find the π_i coefficients for which this is the case. By comparing (A3.38) and (A3.41) we find that the coefficients for u_t match if (and only if):

$$\pi_2 = -\frac{1}{1 + \alpha}. \tag{A3.42}$$

The coefficients for m_t coincide if (and only if):

$$\pi_1 = \frac{1 + \alpha \pi_1 \mu_1}{1 + \alpha} \quad \Leftrightarrow \quad \pi_1 = \frac{1}{1 + \alpha(1 - \mu_1)}. \tag{A3.43}$$

Finally, the constant terms are the same if (and only if):

$$\begin{aligned}
\pi_0 &= \frac{-\gamma + \alpha \left[r + \pi_0 + \pi_1 \mu_0 \right]}{1 + \alpha} \\
(1 + \alpha - \alpha) \pi_0 &= -\gamma + \alpha \left[r + \pi_1 \mu_0 \right] \\
\pi_0 &= -\gamma + \alpha r + \frac{\alpha \mu_0}{1 + \alpha(1 - \mu_1)},
\end{aligned} \tag{A3.44}$$

where we have used (A3.43) in the final step. By using (A3.42)–(A3.44) in (A3.38) we find the rational expectations solution for p_t in terms of parameters of the model.

$$p_t = -\gamma + \alpha r + \frac{\alpha \mu_0}{1 + \alpha(1 - \mu_1)} + \frac{1}{1 + \alpha(1 - \mu_1)} m_t - \frac{1}{1 + \alpha} u_t. \tag{A3.45}$$

Question 7: Fiscal policy under rational expectations

(a) Equation (Q3.13) is the IS curve. Investment depends negatively on the real interest rate (i.e. the nominal interest rate minus expected inflation) and positively on the index for fiscal policy. Equation (Q3.14) is the LM curve. The real supply of money (left-hand side) equals the real demand for money (right-hand side). Money demand is standard and depends negatively on the nominal interest rate and positively on output. Equation (Q3.15) is an expectations-augmented short-run aggregate supply curve featuring sluggish output adjustment. Finally, equation (Q3.16) is the fiscal policy rule followed by the government. Note that we now focus on fiscal, rather than monetary, policy. For simplicity, we assume in (Q3.17) that the money supply grows at an exogenously given rate μ_0. There is no shock term in (Q3.17) so the money supply can be forecasted perfectly by the economic agents.

(b) By solving the LM curve (given in (Q3.14)) for the nominal interest rate we find:

$$R_t = \frac{c_0 + c_1 y_t - m_t + p_t + v_{2t}}{c_2}. \tag{A3.46}$$

By substituting (A3.46) into the IS curve (given in (Q3.13)) and solving for output, we find the AD curve:

$$y_t = a_0 - a_1 \left[\frac{c_0 + c_1 y_t - m_t + p_t + v_{2t}}{c_2} - E_{t-1}(p_{t+1} - p_t) \right]$$
$$+ a_2 g_t + v_{1t}$$

$$y_t \left[1 + \frac{a_1 c_1}{c_2} \right] = \left[a_0 - \frac{a_1 c_0}{c_2} \right] + \frac{a_1}{c_2}(m_t - p_t) + a_1 E_{t-1}(p_{t+1} - p_t)$$
$$+ a_2 g_t + \left[v_{1t} - \frac{a_1}{c_2} v_{2t} \right]$$

$$y_t = \beta_0 + \beta_1(m_t - p_t) + \beta_2 E_{t-1}(p_{t+1} - p_t) + \beta_3 g_t + v_t, \tag{A3.47}$$

where $\beta_0, \beta_1, \beta_2, \beta_3$, and v_t are defined as:

$$\beta_0 \equiv \frac{a_0 c_2 - a_1 c_0}{c_2 + a_1 c_1} \lessgtr, \qquad \beta_1 \equiv \frac{a_1}{c_2 + a_1 c_1} > 0, \qquad \beta_2 \equiv \frac{a_1 c_2}{c_2 + a_1 c_1} > 0,$$

$$\beta_3 \equiv \frac{a_2 c_2}{c_2 + a_1 c_1} > 0, \qquad v_t \equiv \frac{c_2 v_{1t} - a_1 v_{2t}}{c_2 + a_1 c_1}.$$

The shock affecting the AD curve, v_t, is a composite expression featuring the shocks to IS and LM. The weights that these terms get in (A3.47) can be understood readily. A positive goods demand shock ($v_{1t} > 0$) shifts the IS curve to the right and expands output. A positive money demand shock ($v_{2t} > 0$), on the other hand, shifts LM to the left and reduces output.

Since $v_{1t} \sim N\left(0, \sigma_{v_1}^2\right)$ and $v_{2t} \sim N\left(0, \sigma_{v_2}^2\right)$ it follows from (A3.47) that $v_t \sim N\left(0, \sigma_v^2\right)$ (a linear combination of normally distributed variables is also normally distributed). Because v_{1t} and v_{2t} are assumed to be independent (so that

$E(v_{1t}v_{2t}) = 0$) the variance of v_t is given by the weighted sum of $\sigma_{v_1}^2$ and $\sigma_{v_2}^2$:

$$
\begin{aligned}
\sigma_v^2 &\equiv E(v_t - E(v_t))^2 \\
&= E(v_t^2) \quad \text{(as } E(v_t) = 0) \\
&= E\left(\left(\frac{c_2}{c_2 + a_1 c_1}\right)^2 v_{1t}^2 + \left(\frac{-a_1}{c_2 + a_1 c_1}\right)^2 v_{2t}^2\right) \quad \text{(as } E(v_{1t}v_{2t}) = 0) \\
&= \left(\frac{c_2}{c_2 + a_1 c_1}\right)^2 \sigma_{v_1}^2 + \left(\frac{a_1}{c_2 + a_1 c_1}\right)^2 \sigma_{v_2}^2.
\end{aligned}
$$

(A3.48)

The key thing to note is that the shocks to IS and LM do *not* offset each other in terms of the variance of the AD curve.

(c) The structure of the model is very similar to that of the basic Sargent-Wallace model used in section 3.2 of the text. We can therefore utilize a similar solution method. In the first step we use (Q3.15) and (A3.47) to solve for the equilibrium price level:

$$
p_t = \frac{\beta_0 - \alpha_0 + \alpha_1 E_{t-1} p_t + \beta_1 m_t + \beta_2 E_{t-1}(p_{t+1} - p_t) + \beta_3 g_t + v_t - u_t}{\alpha_1 + \beta_1}.
$$

(A3.49)

In the second step we take the conditional expectation of (A3.49):

$$
E_{t-1} p_t = \frac{\beta_0 - \alpha_0 + \alpha_1 E_{t-1} p_t + \beta_1 m_t + \beta_2 E_{t-1}(p_{t+1} - p_t) + \beta_3 E_{t-1} g_t}{\alpha_1 + \beta_1},
$$

(A3.50)

where we have used the law of iterated expectations (so that $E_{t-1} E_{t-1} p_t = E_{t-1} p_t$ and $E_{t-1} E_{t-1} p_{t+1} = E_{t-1} p_{t+1}$), recognized that the money supply is exogenous (so that $E_{t-1} m_t = m_t$), and incorporated the properties of the shock terms ($E_{t-1} v_t = E_{t-1} u_t = 0$). In the third step, we deduct (A3.50) from (A3.49) to get an expression for the expectational error:

$$
p_t - E_{t-1} p_t = \frac{\beta_3 \left[g_t - E_{t-1} g_t\right] + v_t - u_t}{\alpha_1 + \beta_1}.
$$

(A3.51)

According to (A3.51) only unexpected fiscal policy ($g_t - E_{t-1} g_t$) and the shock terms affecting AD and AS can give rise to an expectational error. By using equation (Q3.16) we find that:

$$
\begin{aligned}
g_t - E_{t-1} g_t &= \gamma_0 + \gamma_1 g_{t-1} + \gamma_2 y_{t-1} + e_t \\
&\quad - E_{t-1}\left[\gamma_0 + \gamma_1 g_{t-1} + \gamma_2 y_{t-1} + e_t\right] \\
&= e_t - E_{t-1} e_t = e_t,
\end{aligned}
$$

(A3.52)

where we have used the fact that g_{t-1} and y_{t-1} form part of the information set upon which E_{t-1} is based and that $E_{t-1} e_t = 0$. By using (A3.51)–(A3.52) in (Q3.15) we find the rational expectations solution for output:

$$
\begin{aligned}
y_t &= \alpha_0 + \alpha_1 \left[\frac{\beta_3 e_t + v_t - u_t}{\alpha_1 + \beta_1}\right] + \alpha_2 y_{t-1} + u_t \\
&= \alpha_0 + \alpha_2 y_{t-1} + \frac{\alpha_1 \beta_3 e_t + \alpha_1 v_t + \beta_1 u_t}{\alpha_1 + \beta_1}.
\end{aligned}
$$

(A3.53)

(d) Fiscal policy is ineffective in this model because it cannot affect output. According to (A3.53) only lagged output and the stochastic terms e_t, u_t, and v_t can affect output. The policy maker could follow a counter-cyclical policy rule (with $\gamma_2 < 0$) but this policy stance is well understood by the agents in the economy who do not let their real plans be affected by it. Intuitively, the PIP holds in this model because the model has strong classical features, such as perfectly flexible prices and clearing markets, and there is no informational asymmetry.

(e) To find the rational expectations solution for the equilibrium price, p_t, we could in principle use the method of forward iteration on (A3.49). To get some idea about what the solution will look like, we can first combine (A3.49) and (A3.50) to get an expectational difference equation for p_t which looks simple enough to solve. We can write (A3.49)–(A3.50) in a single matrix expression as:

$$
\begin{bmatrix} 1 & \frac{\beta_2 - \alpha_1}{\alpha_1 + \beta_1} \\ 0 & \frac{\beta_1 + \beta_2}{\alpha_1 + \beta_1} \end{bmatrix} \begin{bmatrix} p_t \\ E_{t-1} p_t \end{bmatrix} = \begin{bmatrix} \frac{\beta_0 - \alpha_0 + \beta_1 m_t + \beta_2 E_{t-1} p_{t+1} + \beta_3 g_t + w_t}{\alpha_1 + \beta_1} \\ \frac{\beta_0 - \alpha_0 + \beta_1 m_t + \beta_2 E_{t-1} p_{t+1} + \beta_3 E_{t-1} g_t}{\alpha_1 + \beta_1} \end{bmatrix} ,
\tag{A3.54}
$$

where $w_t \equiv v_t - u_t$ is a composite shock term. Denoting the matrix on the left-hand side of (A3.54) by Δ we find quite easily that:

$$
\Delta^{-1} = \begin{bmatrix} 1 & \frac{\alpha_1 - \beta_2}{\beta_1 + \beta_2} \\ 0 & \frac{\alpha_1 + \beta_1}{\beta_1 + \beta_2} \end{bmatrix} .
\tag{A3.55}
$$

By using (A3.55) in (A3.54) we find the following solution for p_t:

$$
\begin{aligned}
p_t &= \frac{\beta_0 - \alpha_0 + \beta_1 m_t + \beta_2 E_{t-1} p_{t+1} + \beta_3 g_t + w_t}{\alpha_1 + \beta_1} + \\
&\quad + \frac{\alpha_1 - \beta_2}{\beta_1 + \beta_2} \frac{\beta_0 - \alpha_0 + \beta_1 m_t + \beta_2 E_{t-1} p_{t+1} + \beta_3 E_{t-1} g_t}{\alpha_1 + \beta_1} \\
&= \frac{\beta_0 - \alpha_0 + \beta_1 m_t}{\beta_1 + \beta_2} + \frac{\beta_2}{\beta_1 + \beta_2} E_{t-1} p_{t+1} + \frac{\beta_3}{\alpha_1 + \beta_1} g_t \\
&\quad + \beta_3 \frac{\alpha_1 - \beta_2}{\beta_1 + \beta_2} E_{t-1} g_t + \frac{1}{\alpha_1 + \beta_1} w_t.
\end{aligned}
\tag{A3.56}
$$

The key thing to note is that (A3.56) is an expectational difference equation very much like the one studied in question 2 above. Since the parameter in front of $E_{t-1} p_{t+1}$ on the right-hand side of (A3.56) is between 0 and 1, we know that the forward iteration method will yield the rational expectations solution for p_t.

Furthermore, equation (A3.56) gives us a strong clue as to the form of the trial solution that would be useful if we want to use the method of undetermined coefficients. Indeed, we expect to find that the following trial solution will probably work:

$$
p_t = \pi_0 + \pi_1 m_t + \pi_2 g_t + \pi_3 g_{t-1} + \pi_4 y_{t-1} + \pi_5 w_t,
\tag{A3.57}
$$

where π_0, π_1, π_2, π_3, π_4 and π_5 are the coefficients to be determined. Note that, according to equation (Q3.16), $E_{t-1} g_t = \gamma_0 + \gamma_1 g_{t-1} + \gamma_2 y_{t-1}$ which is why (A3.57) contains g_{t-1} and y_{t-1}.

We now check whether (A3.57) has the correct form to solve (A3.56). By leading (A3.57) one period and taking conditional expectations we find:

$$
\begin{aligned}
E_{t-1}p_{t+1} &= E_{t-1}\left(\pi_0 + \pi_1 m_{t+1} + \pi_2 g_{t+1} + \pi_3 g_t + \pi_4 y_t + \pi_5 w_{t+1}\right) \\
&= \pi_0 + \pi_1(\mu_0 + m_t) + \pi_2 E_{t-1} g_{t+1} + \pi_3 E_{t-1} g_t + \pi_4 E_{t-1} y_t,
\end{aligned}
$$
(A3.58)

where we have used $E_{t-1}m_{t+1} = \mu_0 + E_{t-1}m_t = \mu_0 + m_t$ and $E_{t-1}w_{t+1} = 0$ in going from the first to the second line. By using equation (Q3.16) and taking conditional expectations we find that $E_{t-1}g_t$ can be written as:

$$
\begin{aligned}
E_{t-1}g_t &= E_{t-1}\left(\gamma_0 + \gamma_1 g_{t-1} + \gamma_2 y_{t-1} + e_t\right) \\
&= \gamma_0 + \gamma_1 g_{t-1} + \gamma_2 y_{t-1},
\end{aligned}
$$
(A3.59)

where we have used the fact that $E_{t-1}e_t = 0$ in going from the first to the second line. Similarly, by leading (Q3.16) one period and taking conditional expectations we find that $E_{t-1}g_{t+1}$ is:

$$
\begin{aligned}
E_{t-1}g_{t+1} &= E_{t-1}\left(\gamma_0 + \gamma_1 g_t + \gamma_2 y_t + e_{t+1}\right) \\
&= \gamma_0 + \gamma_1 E_{t-1} g_t + \gamma_2\left(\alpha_0 + \alpha_2 y_{t-1}\right),
\end{aligned}
$$
(A3.60)

where we have used the fact that $E_{t-1}e_{t+1} = 0$ and $E_{t-1}y_t = \alpha_0 + \alpha_2 y_{t-1}$ (by equation (A3.53)) in going from the first to the second line. By substituting (A3.59)–(A3.60) into (A3.58) we find the following expression for $E_{t-1}p_{t+1}$:

$$
\begin{aligned}
E_{t-1}p_{t+1} &= \pi_0 + \pi_1\mu_0 + \pi_2(\gamma_0 + \alpha_0\gamma_2) + \pi_4\alpha_0 + \pi_1 m_t \\
&\quad + (\pi_2\gamma_1 + \pi_3)E_{t-1}g_t + (\pi_2\gamma_2 + \pi_4)\alpha_2 y_{t-1} \\
&= \pi_0 + \pi_1\mu_0 + \pi_2(\gamma_0 + \alpha_0\gamma_2) + \pi_4\alpha_0 + \gamma_0(\pi_2\gamma_1 + \pi_3) \\
&\quad + \pi_1 m_t + \gamma_1(\pi_2\gamma_1 + \pi_3)g_{t-1} \\
&\quad + \left[\gamma_2(\pi_2\gamma_1 + \pi_3) + \alpha_2\left(\pi_2\gamma_2 + \pi_4\right)\right]y_{t-1}
\end{aligned}
$$
(A3.61)

By substituting (A3.59) and (A3.61) into (A3.56) we find the solution of the model that is implied by the trial solution (A3.57).

$$
\begin{aligned}
p_t =& \frac{\beta_0 - \alpha_0 + \beta_1 m_t + \beta_3 g_t}{\beta_1 + \beta_2} + +\beta_3\frac{\alpha_1 - \beta_2}{\beta_1 + \beta_2}\left[\gamma_0 + \gamma_1 g_{t-1} + \gamma_2 y_{t-1}\right] \\
&+ \frac{\beta_2}{\beta_1 + \beta_2}\left(\pi_0 + \pi_1\mu_0 + \pi_2(\gamma_0 + \alpha_0\gamma_2) + \pi_4\alpha_0 + \gamma_0(\pi_2\gamma_1 + \pi_3)\right. \\
&\quad + \pi_1 m_t + \gamma_1(\pi_2\gamma_1 + \pi_3)g_{t-1} \\
&\quad \left.+ \left[\gamma_2(\pi_2\gamma_1 + \pi_3 + \alpha_2\left(\pi_2\gamma_2 + \pi_4\right)\right]y_{t-1}\right) \\
&+ \frac{1}{\alpha_1 + \beta_1}w_t.
\end{aligned}
$$
(A3.62)

Equations (A3.62) and (A3.57) both express p_t in terms of a constant, m_t, g_t, g_{t-1}, y_{t-1}, and w_t. Furthermore, by choosing the appropriate π_i coefficients these two expressions can be made identical. We compute the π_i coefficients as follows. First, we note that w_t appears in only one place in (A3.62) so it follows readily from (A3.57) that:

$$\pi_5 = \frac{1}{\alpha_1 + \beta_1}. \tag{A3.63}$$

The terms for m_t in (A3.57) and (A3.62) coincide if:

$$\pi_1 = \frac{\beta_1}{\beta_1 + \beta_2} + \frac{\beta_2}{\beta_1 + \beta_2}\pi_1 \quad \Leftrightarrow \quad \pi_1 = 1. \tag{A3.64}$$

The price level moves one-for-one with the money stock, as was stated in the question. The terms for g_t coincide if:

$$\pi_2 = \frac{\beta_3}{\alpha_1 + \beta_1}. \tag{A3.65}$$

The terms for g_{t-1} coincide if:

$$\pi_3 = \beta_3\frac{\alpha_1 - \beta_2}{\beta_1 + \beta_2}\gamma_1 + \frac{\beta_2}{\beta_1 + \beta_2}\gamma_1(\pi_2\gamma_1 + \pi_3) \quad \Leftrightarrow$$

$$\left[1 - \frac{\beta_2\gamma_1}{\beta_1 + \beta_2}\right]\pi_3 = \frac{\gamma_1}{\beta_1 + \beta_2}\left[\beta_3(\alpha_1 - \beta_2) + \beta_2\gamma_1\frac{\beta_3}{\alpha_1 + \beta_1}\right] \quad \Leftrightarrow$$

$$\pi_3 = \frac{\gamma_1\beta_3}{\beta_1 + (1 - \gamma_1)\beta_2}\left[\alpha_1 + \beta_2\frac{\gamma_1 - \alpha_1 - \beta_1}{\alpha_1 + \beta_1}\right], \tag{A3.66}$$

where we have used (A3.65) to get from the first to the second line. The terms for y_{t-1} coincide if:

$$\pi_4 = \beta_3\frac{\alpha_1 - \beta_2}{\beta_1 + \beta_2}\gamma_2 + \frac{\beta_2}{\beta_1 + \beta_2}\left[\gamma_2(\pi_2\gamma_1 + \pi_3) + \alpha_2(\pi_2\gamma_2 + \pi_4)\right]$$

$$= \frac{\gamma_2}{\gamma_1}\pi_3 + \frac{\alpha_2\beta_2}{\beta_1 + \beta_2}(\pi_2\gamma_2 + \pi_4) \quad \Leftrightarrow$$

$$\left[1 - \frac{\alpha_2\beta_2}{\beta_1 + \beta_2}\right]\pi_4 = \frac{\gamma_2}{\gamma_1}\pi_3 + \frac{\alpha_2\beta_2\gamma_2}{\beta_1 + \beta_2}\frac{\beta_3}{\alpha_1 + \beta_1} \quad \Leftrightarrow$$

$$\pi_4 = \frac{\gamma_2\pi_3}{\gamma_1}\frac{\beta_1 + \beta_2}{\beta_1 + (1 - \alpha_2)\beta_2} + \frac{\alpha_2\beta_2\gamma_2}{\beta_1 + (1 - \alpha_2)\beta_2}\frac{\beta_3}{\alpha_1 + \beta_1}. \tag{A3.67}$$

Note that in going from the first to the second line we have exploited the fact that several terms for y_{t-1} are proportional to π_3 (which is given in (A3.66)). We have now expressed all the (interesting) π_i coefficients in terms of the structural parameters and we have thus found the rational expectations solution for the price level.

Question 8: The labour market

(a) Equation (Q3.18) is a *dynamic* labour demand function. The firm faces adjustment costs on labour (just like it does on capital investment in Chapter 2). A simple, though *ad hoc*, story could go as follows. Desired labour demand, $\bar{n}_t^D$, is a function of the real wage:

$$\bar{n}_t^D = \bar{\alpha}_0 - \bar{\alpha}_1\left[w_t - p_t\right], \tag{A3.68}$$

with $\bar{\alpha}_1 > 0$. Actual labour demand, n_t^D, is gradually changed according to a (stochastic) stock adjustment mechanism:

$$\Delta n_t^D = \lambda \left[\bar{n}_t^D - n_{t-1}^D \right] + u_{1t}, \quad 0 < \lambda < 1, \tag{A3.69}$$

where $\Delta n_t^D \equiv n_t^D - n_{t-1}^D$ and λ is the speed of adjustment in labour demand. By substituting (A3.68) into (A3.69) we obtain:

$$n_t^D = \lambda \left[\bar{\alpha}_0 - \bar{\alpha}_1 \left[w_t - p_t \right] - n_{t-1}^D \right] + n_{t-1}^D + u_{1t}$$

$$= \lambda \bar{\alpha}_0 - \lambda \bar{\alpha}_1 \left[w_t - p_t \right] + (1 - \lambda) n_{t-1}^D + u_{1t}. \tag{A3.70}$$

Equation (A3.70) is the same as (Q3.18) if we make the substitutions $\alpha_0 \equiv \lambda \bar{\alpha}_0$, $\alpha_1 \equiv \lambda \bar{\alpha}_1$, $\alpha_2 \equiv (1 - \lambda)$ and $n_{t-1}^D = n_{t-1}$ (market clearing also in the previous period).

Equation (Q3.19) is the logarithmic version of the expectations-augmented labour supply curve (see Chapter 1). Workers base their labour supply decision on the expected price level, $E_{t-1} p_t$. If the actual price level differs from the expected price level then the workers supply an "incorrect" amount of labour. By setting $\beta_1 > 0$ we are implicitly assuming that the substitution effect dominates the (absolute value of the) income effect in labour supply. This means that the labour supply function is upward sloping.

(b) By substituting (Q3.20) into (Q3.18)–(Q3.19) we obtain the following matrix expression:

$$\begin{bmatrix} 1 & \alpha_1 \\ 1 & -\beta_1 \end{bmatrix} \begin{bmatrix} n_t \\ w_t \end{bmatrix} = \begin{bmatrix} \alpha_0 + \alpha_1 p_t + \alpha_2 n_{t-1} + u_{1t} \\ \beta_0 - \beta_1 E_{t-1} p_t + u_{2t} \end{bmatrix}. \tag{A3.71}$$

The matrix on the left-hand side is denoted by Δ and has a determinant equal to $|\Delta| = -(\alpha_1 + \beta_1)$. The inverse of Δ is thus:

$$\Delta^{-1} \equiv \frac{1}{\alpha_1 + \beta_1} \begin{bmatrix} \beta_1 & \alpha_1 \\ 1 & -1 \end{bmatrix}. \tag{A3.72}$$

By using (A3.72) in (A3.71) we find the quasi-reduced form expressions for equilibrium employment and the nominal wage rate:

$$\begin{bmatrix} n_t \\ w_t \end{bmatrix} = \frac{1}{\alpha_1 + \beta_1} \begin{bmatrix} \beta_1 & \alpha_1 \\ 1 & -1 \end{bmatrix} \begin{bmatrix} \alpha_0 + \alpha_1 p_t + \alpha_2 n_{t-1} + u_{1t} \\ \beta_0 - \beta_1 E_{t-1} p_t + u_{2t} \end{bmatrix}$$

$$= \frac{1}{\alpha_1 + \beta_1} \begin{bmatrix} \beta_1 [\alpha_0 + \alpha_1 p_t + \alpha_2 n_{t-1} + u_{1t}] + \alpha_1 [\beta_0 - \beta_1 E_{t-1} p_t + u_{2t}] \\ [\alpha_0 + \alpha_1 p_t + \alpha_2 n_{t-1} + u_{1t}] - [\beta_0 - \beta_1 E_{t-1} p_t + u_{2t}] \end{bmatrix}. \tag{A3.73}$$

By gathering terms, the expression for equilibrium employment can be written more neatly as:

$$n_t = \frac{\alpha_0 \beta_1 + \alpha_1 \beta_0}{\alpha_1 + \beta_1} + \frac{\alpha_1 \beta_1}{\alpha_1 + \beta_1} \left[p_t - E_{t-1} p_t \right] + \frac{\alpha_2 \beta_1}{\alpha_1 + \beta_1} n_{t-1}$$

$$+ \frac{\beta_1}{\alpha_1 + \beta_1} u_{1t} + \frac{\alpha_1}{\alpha_1 + \beta_1} u_{2t}. \tag{A3.74}$$

Several features must be noted about this expression. First, the employment equation is stable if (and only if) the coefficient for n_{t-1} is less than unity in absolute value. Since $0 < \alpha_2 < 1$ and $0 < \beta_1/(\alpha_1+\beta_1) < 1$ this condition is automatically satisfied. The second key feature of (A3.74) is that the employment equation depends on the expectational error, $p_t - E_{t-1}p_t$, and not on p_t and $E_{t-1}p_t$ separately. This is the logic of the Lucas supply curve.

By substituting (A3.74) into the production function (and noting that $y_{t-1} = \gamma_0 + \gamma_1 n_{t-1}$) we obtain:

$$y_t = \gamma_0 + \gamma_1 \left[\frac{\alpha_0\beta_1 + \alpha_1\beta_0}{\alpha_1+\beta_1} + \frac{\alpha_1\beta_1}{\alpha_1+\beta_1}[p_t - E_{t-1}p_t] \right.$$
$$\left. + \frac{\alpha_2\beta_1}{\alpha_1+\beta_1}\frac{y_{t-1}-\gamma_0}{\gamma_1} + \frac{\beta_1 u_{1t}+\alpha_1 u_{2t}}{\alpha_1+\beta_1} \right]$$
$$\equiv \zeta_0 + \zeta_1[p_t - E_{t-1}p_t] + \zeta_2 y_{t-1} + u_t, \tag{A3.75}$$

where the ζ_i coefficients and the composite shock term are defined as follows:

$$\zeta_0 \equiv \gamma_0 + \gamma_1 \left[\frac{\alpha_0\beta_1+\alpha_1\beta_0}{\alpha_1+\beta_1} - \frac{\alpha_2\beta_1}{\alpha_1+\beta_1}\frac{\gamma_0}{\gamma_1} \right],$$
$$\zeta_1 \equiv \frac{\alpha_1\beta_1\gamma_1}{\alpha_1+\beta_1},$$
$$\zeta_2 \equiv \frac{\alpha_2\beta_1}{\alpha_1+\beta_1},$$
$$u_t \equiv \frac{\beta_1\gamma_1 u_{1t}+\alpha_1\gamma_1 u_{2t}}{\alpha_1+\beta_1}.$$

(c) In view of the properties of u_{1t} and u_{2t} it follows that the composite error term, u_t, is a normally distributed random variable with mean zero and a constant variance, i.e. $u_t \sim N(0,\sigma_u^2)$, where σ_u^2 is defined as:

$$\sigma_u^2 \equiv \left(\frac{\beta_1\gamma_1}{\alpha_1+\beta_1}\right)^2 \sigma_{u_1}^2 + \left(\frac{\alpha_1\gamma_1}{\alpha_1+\beta_1}\right)^2 \sigma_{u_2}^2, \tag{A3.76}$$

where we have also used the fact that u_{1t} and u_{2t} are independent ($E(u_{1t}u_{2t}) = 0$). Recall furthermore (from basic statistics) that a linear combination of normally distributed variables is itself a normally distributed variable.

Question 9: Liquidity trap

(a) Equation (Q3.21) is the Lucas supply curve. The lagged output term on the right-hand side can be justified by postulating adjustment costs in labour demand (see question 5 above). Equation (Q3.22) is the IS curve. There is a negative effect of the real interest rate via investment. Equation (Q3.23) is the LM curve. We have assumed that the income elasticity of money demand is equal to unity. In addition we allow for a liquidity trap (see Chapter 1) in that the nominal interest rate is assumed to have a lower bound, R^{MIN}. Formally the economy is in the liquidity trap if we let $c_1 \to \infty$ in (Q3.23).

(b) By rewriting (Q3.23) we obtain the following expression for the nominal interest rate:

$$R_t = R^{MIN} + \frac{y_t - (m_t - p_t) + v_{2t}}{c_1}.$$
(A3.77)

By substituting (A3.77) into (Q3.22) we obtain:

$$y_t = a_0 - a_1 R_t + a_1 E_t(p_{t+1} - p_t) + v_{1t}$$

$$= a_0 - a_1 \left[R^{MIN} + \frac{y_t - (m_t - p_t) + v_{2t}}{c_1} \right] + a_1 E_t(p_{t+1} - p_t) + v_{1t} \quad \Leftrightarrow$$

$$\left(1 + \frac{a_1}{c_1}\right) y_t = a_0 - a_1 R^{MIN} + \frac{a_1(m_t - p_t)}{c_1} + a_1 E_t(p_{t+1} - p_t) + v_{1t} - \frac{a_1 v_{2t}}{c_1}.$$
(A3.78)

By rearranging (A3.78) somewhat we obtain the following expression for the AD curve:

$$y_t = \beta_0 + \beta_1 E_t(p_{t+1} - p_t) + \beta_2(m_t - p_t) + v_t,$$
(A3.79)

where the β_i coefficients and the composite shock term u_t are defined as follows:

$$\beta_0 \equiv \frac{c_1}{a_1 + c_1} \left[a_0 - a_1 R^{MIN}\right], \qquad \beta_1 \equiv \frac{c_1 a_1}{a_1 + c_1},$$

$$\beta_2 \equiv \frac{a_1}{a_1 + c_1}, \qquad v_t \equiv \frac{c_1}{a_1 + c_1} v_{1t} - \frac{a_1}{a_1 + c_1} v_{2t}.$$

If the economy is in a liquidity trap, $c_1 \to \infty$, and (according to (A3.77)) $R_t \to R^{MIN}$. We find that $\beta_0 \to a_0 - a_1 R^{MIN}$, $\beta_1 \to a_1$, $\beta_2 \to 0$, and $v_t \to v_{1t}$. The real balance effect vanishes from the AD curve. Intuitively, this is because in the liquidity trap case, the AD curve coincides with the IS curve with $R_t = R^{MIN}$ imposed.

(c) We first solve the general case of the model and then investigate the implications of the liquidity trap. The model consists of the AS curve (given in equation (Q3.21)) and the AD curve (given in (A3.79) above). The trial solutions mentioned in the question are restated here for convenience:

$$y_t = \pi_0 + \pi_1 y_{t-1} + \pi_2 u_t + \pi_3 v_t,$$
(A3.80)

$$p_t = \omega_0 + \omega_1 y_{t-1} + \omega_2 u_t + \omega_3 v_t,$$
(A3.81)

where the π_i and ω_i coefficients must be determined. We derive the parameter restrictions in two steps.

Step 1. In the first step we use (A3.81) to derive:

$$E_t p_{t+1} = E_t \left(\omega_0 + \omega_1 y_t + \omega_2 u_{t+1} + \omega_3 v_{t+1}\right)$$

$$= \omega_0 + \omega_1 y_t,$$
(A3.82)

where we have used the fact that $E_t y_t = y_t$ and $E_t u_{t+1} = E_t v_{t+1} = 0$. By substituting (A3.81) and (A3.82) into the AD curve (A3.79) we find:

$$
\begin{aligned}
y_t &= \beta_0 + \beta_1 E_t(p_{t+1} - p_t) + \beta_2(m_t - p_t) + v_t \\
&= \beta_0 + \beta_1 \left[\omega_0 + \omega_1 y_t \right] - (\beta_1 + \beta_2) \left[\omega_0 + \omega_1 y_{t-1} + \omega_2 u_t + \omega_3 v_t \right] \\
&\quad + \beta_2 m + v_t \\
&= \frac{\beta_0 - \beta_2\omega_0 + \beta_2 m - (\beta_1 + \beta_2)\left[\omega_1 y_{t-1} + \omega_2 u_t\right] + \left[1 - (\beta_1 + \beta_2)\omega_3\right] v_t}{1 - \beta_1\omega_1},
\end{aligned}
$$

$$(A3.83)$$

where we have noted that the money supply is constant ($m_t = m$). Equation (A3.83) must be identical to the trial solution for output (given in (A3.80) above). This requirement yields four parameter restrictions:

$$\pi_0 = \frac{\beta_0 + \beta_2 m - \beta_2 \omega_0}{1 - \beta_1 \omega_1}, \tag{A3.84}$$

$$\pi_1 = -\frac{(\beta_1 + \beta_2)\omega_1}{1 - \beta_1 \omega_1}, \tag{A3.85}$$

$$\pi_3 = -\frac{(\beta_1 + \beta_2)\omega_2}{1 - \beta_1 \omega_1}, \tag{A3.86}$$

$$\pi_4 = \frac{1 - (\beta_1 + \beta_2)\omega_3}{1 - \beta_1 \omega_1}. \tag{A3.87}$$

So after completing the first step we have obtained four restrictions for eight parameters. To get the remaining four restrictions we must use the information contained in the AS curve (Q3.21).

Step 2. In the second step we derive from (A3.81) that:

$$
\begin{aligned}
p_t - E_{t-1}p_t &= \omega_0 + \omega_1 y_{t-1} + \omega_2 u_t + \omega_3 v_t \\
&\quad - E_{t-1}\left[\omega_0 + \omega_1 y_{t-1} + \omega_2 u_t + \omega_3 v_t \right] \\
&= \omega_2 u_t + \omega_3 v_t,
\end{aligned}
\tag{A3.88}
$$

where we have used the fact that $E_{t-1}y_{t-1} = y_{t-1}$ and $E_{t-1}u_t = E_{t-1}v_t = 0$. By substituting (A3.88) into the AS curve (Q3.21) we obtain:

$$
\begin{aligned}
y_t &= \bar{y} + \alpha_1(p_t - E_{t-1}p_t) + \alpha_2(y_{t-1} - \bar{y}) + u_t \\
&= \bar{y} + \alpha_1(\omega_2 u_t + \omega_3 v_t) + \alpha_2(y_{t-1} - \bar{y}) + u_t \\
&= (1 - \alpha_2)\bar{y} + \alpha_2 y_{t-1} + (1 + \alpha_1\omega_2)u_t + \alpha_1\omega_3 v_t.
\end{aligned}
\tag{A3.89}
$$

Equation (A3.89) must be identical to the trial solution for output (given in (A3.80) above). This yields the following parameter restrictions:

$$\pi_0 = (1 - \alpha_2)\bar{y}, \tag{A3.90}$$

$$\pi_1 = \alpha_2, \tag{A3.91}$$

$$\pi_2 = 1 + \alpha_1\omega_2, \tag{A3.92}$$

$$\pi_3 = \alpha_1\omega_3. \tag{A3.93}$$

So after completing both steps of the solution procedure, we possess eight restrictions (namely, (A3.84)–(A3.87) and (A3.90)–(A3.93)) involving eight unknown parameters (the π_i and ω_i parameters). Some subtle detective work will yield the solutions for these parameters in terms of the parameters of the model itself.

By using (A3.85) and (A3.91) we find:

$$\alpha_2 = -\frac{(\beta_1 + \beta_2)\omega_1}{1 - \beta_1\omega_1} \qquad \Leftrightarrow$$

$$(1 - \beta_1\omega_1)\alpha_2 = -(\beta_1 + \beta_2)\omega_1 \qquad \Leftrightarrow$$

$$\omega_1 = -\frac{\alpha_2}{(1 - \alpha_2)\beta_1 + \beta_2}. \qquad (A3.94)$$

We note the following auxiliary result from (A3.94) for future reference:

$$1 - \beta_1\omega_1 = \frac{\beta_1 + \beta_2}{(1 - \alpha_2)\beta_1 + \beta_2}. \qquad (A3.95)$$

By using (A3.90) and (A3.84) we obtain:

$$(1 - \alpha_2)\bar{y} = \frac{\beta_0 + \beta_2 m - \beta_2\omega_0}{1 - \beta_1\omega_1} \qquad \Leftrightarrow$$

$$\beta_2\omega_0 = -(1 - \alpha_2)\bar{y}\,(1 - \beta_1\omega_1) + \beta_0 + \beta_2 m \qquad \Leftrightarrow$$

$$\beta_2\omega_0 = \beta_0 + \beta_2 m - \frac{(1 - \alpha_2)(\beta_1 + \beta_2)\bar{y}}{(1 - \alpha_2)\beta_1 + \beta_2}, \qquad (A3.96)$$

where we have used (A3.95) in going from the second to the third line. (For future reference we note here that only $\beta_2\omega_0$ is determined.) By using (A3.86) and (A3.92) we find:

$$1 + \alpha_1\omega_2 = -\frac{(\beta_1 + \beta_2)\omega_2}{1 - \beta_1\omega_1} \qquad \Leftrightarrow$$

$$1 = -\left[\alpha_1 + (\beta_1 + \beta_2)\frac{(1 - \alpha_2)\beta_1 + \beta_2}{\beta_1 + \beta_2}\right]\omega_2 \qquad \Leftrightarrow$$

$$\omega_2 = -\frac{1}{\alpha_1 + (1 - \alpha_2)\beta_1 + \beta_2}, \qquad (A3.97)$$

where we have once again used (A3.95) in going from the first to the second line. Finally, by using (A3.87) and (A3.93) we obtain:

$$\alpha_1\omega_3 = \frac{1 - (\beta_1 + \beta_2)\omega_3}{1 - \beta_1\omega_1} \qquad \Leftrightarrow$$

$$\alpha_1\omega_3\,(1 - \beta_1\omega_1) = 1 - (\beta_1 + \beta_2)\omega_3 \qquad \Leftrightarrow$$

$$\omega_3 = \frac{(1 - \alpha_2)\beta_1 + \beta_2}{(\beta_1 + \beta_2)\,[\alpha_1 + (1 - \alpha_2)\beta_1 + \beta_2]}, \qquad (A3.98)$$

where we again used (A3.95) in going from the second to the third line. Since we have now expressed the π_i and ω_i coefficients in terms of the structural parameters we have fully determined the rational expectations solutions for output and the price level.

(d) If the economy is in a liquidity trap then $\beta_2 = 0$. It follows from (A3.96) that ω_0 is not determined in that case, i.e. the price level is *indeterminate*. Furthermore, both (A3.90) and the combination of (A3.84) and (A3.94) yield solutions for π_0 and there is guarantee that these solutions will be the same. Hence, the model is *inconsistent*.

If consumption depends on real money balances, as Pigou suggested, then the IS curve becomes:

$$y_t = a_0 - a_1 \left[R_t - E_t(p_{t+1} - p_t) \right] + a_2(m_t - p_t) + v_{1t}, \tag{A3.99}$$

where $a_2 > 0$. It follows that even if the economy is in the liquidity trap (so that $R_t = R^{MIN}$) the AD curve will contain a real balance effect and β_2 in (A3.79) will be positive. All parameters will be uniquely determined and the model will be consistent again.

Question 10: PIP meets the Pigou effect

(a) [This model is discussed in detail by McCallum (1980, pp. 726-727 and 741).] Equation (Q3.24) is the IS curve which depends negatively on the real interest rate (via investment) and positively on a real balance effect (via a wealth effect in consumption). Equation (Q3.25) is a standard LM curve. It depends positively on output (via the transactions motive) and negatively on the nominal interest rate (opportunity cost of holding money instead of bonds). Equation (Q3.26) is a Lucas supply function with an endogenous capacity effect included (the term involving the capital stock, k_t). The capital stock positively affects both labour demand (because capital and labour are cooperative production factors in a constant returns to scale production function) and output (directly via the production function). This explains why α_3 is positive. Equation (Q3.27) is the dynamic equation for the capital stock. Next period's capital stock, k_{t+1}, depends in part on the previous period's capital stock, k_t, and in part on current investment which depends negatively on the real interest rate. Finally, equation (Q3.28) is the money supply rule and (Q3.29) is the definition for the real interest rate.

(b) By substituting (Q3.25) and (Q3.29) into (Q3.24) we obtain the expression for the AD curve:

$$\begin{aligned} y_t &= a_0 - a_1 \left[R_t - E_{t-1}(p_{t+1} - p_t) \right] + a_2(m_t - p_t) + v_{1t} \\ &= a_0 - a_1 \frac{c_0 + c_1 y_t - (m_t - p_t) + v_{2t}}{c_2} + a_1 E_{t-1}(p_{t+1} - p_t) \\ &\quad + a_2(m_t - p_t) + v_{1t} \\ &= \beta_0 + \beta_1(m_t - p_t) + \beta_2 E_{t-1}(p_{t+1} - p_t) + v_t, \tag{A3.100} \end{aligned}$$

where the β_i coefficients and the composite shock term v_t are defined as:

$$\beta_0 \equiv \frac{a_0 c_2 - a_1 c_0}{a_1 c_1 + c_2}, \qquad \beta_1 \equiv \frac{a_1 + a_2 c_2}{a_1 c_1 + c_2}, \qquad \beta_2 \equiv \frac{a_1 c_2}{a_1 c_1 + c_2},$$

$$\beta_3 \equiv \frac{c_2}{a_1 c_1 + c_2}, \qquad \beta_4 \equiv \frac{a_1}{a_1 c_1 + c_2}, \qquad v_t \equiv \beta_3 v_{1t} - \beta_4 v_{2t}.$$

(c) By combining equations (Q3.26) and (A3.100) we obtain the following expression for p_t:

$$p_t = \frac{\beta_0 - \alpha_0 + \beta_1 m_t - \alpha_2 y_{t-1} - \alpha_3 k_t + v_t - u_t + \alpha_1 E_{t-1} p_t + \beta_2 E_{t-1}(p_{t+1} - p_t)}{\alpha_1 + \beta_1}.$$

$$(A3.101)$$

By taking the conditional expectation of (A3.101) we find:

$$E_{t-1}p_t = \frac{\beta_0 - \alpha_0 + \beta_1 E_{t-1}m_t - \alpha_2 y_{t-1} - \alpha_3 E_{t-1}k_t}{\alpha_1 + \beta_1}$$
$$+ \frac{\alpha_1 E_{t-1}p_t + \beta_2 E_{t-1}(p_{t+1} - p_t)}{\alpha_1 + \beta_1}, \qquad (A3.102)$$

where we have used the law of iterated expectations ($E_{t-1}E_{t-1}p_t = E_{t-1}p_t$ and $E_{t-1}E_{t-1}p_{t+1} = E_{t-1}p_{t+1}$), and noted that $E_{t-1}y_{t-1} = y_{t-1}$ and $E_{t-1}u_t = E_{t-1}v_t = 0$. By deducting (A3.102) from (A3.101) we find:

$$p_t - E_{t-1}p_t = \frac{\beta_1[m_t - E_{t-1}m_t] - \alpha_3[k_t - E_{t-1}k_t] + v_t - u_t}{\alpha_1 + \beta_1}. \qquad (A3.103)$$

From the money supply rule (Q3.28) we derive that $m_t - E_{t-1}m_t = e_t$ (because $E_{t-1}m_{t-1} = m_{t-1}$, $E_{t-1}y_{t-1} = y_{t-1}$, and $E_{t-1}e_t = 0$) and from the lagged version of equation (Q3.27) we obtain $k_t - E_{t-1}k_t = 0$ (because $E_{t-1}k_{t-1} = k_{t-1}$ and $E_{t-1}r_{t-1} = r_{t-1}$). By using these results in (A3.103) we obtain the desired expression for the expectational gap:

$$p_t - E_{t-1}p_t = \frac{\beta_1 e_t + v_t - u_t}{\alpha_1 + \beta_1}. \qquad (A3.104)$$

The key thing to note about (A3.103) is that it does not contain the parameters of the money supply rule. Indeed, equation (A3.104) is identical to equation (3.24) in the text.

(d) We cannot conclude from (A3.104) that the policy ineffectiveness proposition is valid in this model. This is because the Lucas supply curve (Q3.26) not only contains $p_t - E_{t-1}p_t$ but also the current capital stock, k_t. Only if k_t is also independent from the parameters of the money supply rule can we conclude that the PIP is valid. But k_t depends on the real interest rate, r_{t-1}, so we need to check whether this variable depends on the parameters of the money supply rule. In short, to investigate the validity of the PIP we must solve the model.

For convenience we restate the equations of the model here:

$$y_t = \alpha_0 + \alpha_1 \frac{\beta_1 e_t + \beta_3 v_{1t} - \beta_4 v_{2t} - u_t}{\alpha_1 + \beta_1} + \alpha_2 y_{t-1} + \alpha_3 k_t + u_t, \qquad (A3.105)$$

$$k_{t+1} = \gamma_1 k_t + \frac{\gamma_2}{a_1}[a_0 - y_t + v_{1t}]$$
$$+ \frac{a_2 \gamma_2}{a_1}\left[m_t - E_{t-1}p_t - \frac{\beta_1 e_t + \beta_3 v_{1t} - \beta_4 v_{2t} - u_t}{\alpha_1 + \beta_1}\right] \qquad (A3.106)$$

$$y_t = \beta_0 + \beta_1\left[m_t - E_{t-1}p_t - \frac{\beta_1 e_t + \beta_3 v_{1t} - \beta_4 v_{2t} - u_t}{\alpha_1 + \beta_1}\right]$$
$$+ \beta_2 E_{t-1}(p_{t+1} - p_t) + \beta_3 v_{1t} - \beta_4 v_{2t}, \qquad (A3.107)$$

$$m_t = \mu_0 + \mu_1 m_{t-1} + \mu_2 y_{t-1} + e_t. \qquad (A3.108)$$

Equation (A3.105) is the AS curve (Q3.26) with (A3.104) substituted and noting the expression for v_t (given in (A2b) above). Equation (A3.106) is obtained by using the capital accumulation equation (Q3.27) and substituting the solution for the real interest rate, r_t, which is implied by the IS curve. Equation (A3.107) is obtained by substituting (A3.104) and the expression for v_t (given in (A2b) above) into the AD curve (A3.100). Finally, equation (A3.108) is the money supply rule.

Without a real balance effect. It is easy to show that the PIP still holds if there is no real balance effect in the IS curve. In that case $a_2 = 0$ and it follows from (A3.105)–(A3.106) that the dynamic system for output and the capital stock does not depend on the parameters of the money supply rule:

$$\begin{bmatrix} 1 & 0 \\ \frac{\gamma_2}{a_1} & 1 \end{bmatrix} \begin{bmatrix} y_t \\ k_{t+1} \end{bmatrix} = \begin{bmatrix} \alpha_2 & \alpha_3 \\ 0 & \gamma_1 \end{bmatrix} \begin{bmatrix} y_{t-1} \\ k_t \end{bmatrix}$$
$$+ \begin{bmatrix} \alpha_0 + \alpha_1 \frac{\beta_1 e_t + \beta_3 v_{1t} - \beta_4 v_{2t}}{\alpha_1 + \beta_1} + \frac{\beta_1 u_t}{\alpha_1 + \beta_1} \\ \frac{\gamma_2}{a_1} [a_0 + v_{1t}] \end{bmatrix}. \quad \text{(A3.109)}$$

By inverting the matrix on the left-hand side, we can rewrite (A3.109) as follows:

$$\begin{bmatrix} y_t \\ k_{t+1} \end{bmatrix} = \Delta \begin{bmatrix} y_{t-1} \\ k_t \end{bmatrix} + \Gamma, \quad \text{(A3.110)}$$

where Δ and Γ are defined as:

$$\Delta \equiv \begin{bmatrix} \alpha_2 & \alpha_3 \\ -\frac{\gamma_2 \alpha_2}{a_1} & \gamma_1 - \frac{\alpha_3 \gamma_2}{a_1} \end{bmatrix}, \quad \text{(A3.111)}$$

$$\Gamma \equiv \begin{bmatrix} \alpha_0 + \alpha_1 \frac{\beta_1 e_t + \beta_3 v_{1t} - \beta_4 v_{2t}}{\alpha_1 + \beta_1} + \frac{\beta_1 u_t}{\alpha_1 + \beta_1} \\ \frac{\gamma_2}{a_1} [a_0 + v_{1t} - \alpha_0 - \alpha_1 \frac{\beta_1 e_t + \beta_3 v_{1t} - \beta_4 v_{2t}}{\alpha_1 + \beta_1} - \frac{\beta_1 u_t}{\alpha_1 + \beta_1}] \end{bmatrix}. \quad \text{(A3.112)}$$

We denote the characteristic roots of Δ by λ_1 and λ_2. Equation (A3.110) represents a stable system provided these characteristic roots are less than unity in absolute value (i.e. $|\lambda_1| < 1$ and $|\lambda_2| < 1$). (See Azariadis (1993, pp. 62-67) for further details on the stability issue.)

With a real balance effect. If there is a non-zero real balance effect in the IS curve ($a_2 \neq 0$), then (A3.105)–(A3.108) constitutes a simultaneous system in y_t, $E_{t-1} p_{t+1}$, m_t and k_{t+1} and the real and monetary subsystems do not separate. It is therefore to be expected that the PIP will not hold. To solve the model, it is most convenient to write it in the following format first.

$$\begin{bmatrix} y_t \\ k_{t+1} \\ E_{t-1} p_{t+1} \\ m_t \end{bmatrix} = \Delta \begin{bmatrix} y_{t-1} \\ k_t \\ E_{t-1} p_t \\ m_{t-1} \end{bmatrix} + \Gamma, \quad \text{(A3.113)}$$

where $\Delta \equiv \Delta_1^{-1}\Delta_2$ and $\Gamma \equiv \Delta_1^{-1}\Gamma_1$ and $\Delta_1, \Delta_2, \Gamma_1$ are defined as:

$$
\Delta_1 \equiv \begin{bmatrix} 1 & 0 & 0 & 0 \\ \frac{\gamma_2}{a_1} & 1 & 0 & -\frac{a_2\gamma_2}{a_1} \\ 1 & 0 & -\beta_2 & -\beta_1 \\ 0 & 0 & 0 & 1 \end{bmatrix},
$$

$$
\Delta_2 \equiv \begin{bmatrix} \alpha_2 & \alpha_3 & 0 & 0 \\ 0 & \gamma_1 & -\frac{a_2\gamma_2}{a_1} & 0 \\ 0 & 0 & -(\beta_1+\beta_2) & 0 \\ \mu_2 & 0 & 0 & \mu_1 \end{bmatrix},
$$

$$
\Gamma_1 \equiv \begin{bmatrix} \alpha_0 + \alpha_1 \frac{\beta_1 e_t + \beta_3 v_{1t} - \beta_4 v_{2t}}{\alpha_1 + \beta_1} + \frac{\beta_1 u_t}{\alpha_1 + \beta_1} \\ \frac{\gamma_2}{a_1}\left[a_0 + v_{1t} - a_2 \frac{\beta_1 e_t + \beta_3 v_{1t} - \beta_4 v_{2t} - u_t}{\alpha_1 + \beta_1}\right] \\ \beta_0 - \beta_1 \frac{\beta_1 e_t + \beta_3 v_{1t} - \beta_4 v_{2t} - u_t}{\alpha_1 + \beta_1} + \beta_3 v_{1t} - \beta_4 v_{2t} \\ \mu_0 + e_t \end{bmatrix}.
$$

In principle (A3.113) can be solved by using the methods of Blanchard and Kahn (1980). But it is clear that PIP will not hold, i.e. that output will generally be affected by monetary policy.

(e) McCallum (1980, p. 727) argues that capacity output in period t ($\bar{y}_t$) should be defined as that value of actual output that will materialize if there is (i) no expectational error in period t (so that $E_{t-1}p_t = p_t$) and (ii) output was equal to capacity output in the previous period also (so that $y_{t-1} = \bar{y}_{t-1}$). This is what the definition in equation (Q3.30) captures. It is obtained by substituting $E_{t-1}p_t = p_t$ and $y_{t-1} = \bar{y}_{t-1}$ in the AS curve (Q3.26).

(f) By using (Q3.26) and (Q3.30) we find the following expression for the output gap:

$$
y_t - \bar{y}_t = \alpha_1(p_t - E_{t-1}p_t) + \alpha_2\left[y_{t-1} - \bar{y}_{t-1}\right]. \tag{A3.114}
$$

Since we have already shown that $p_t - E_{t-1}p_t$ does not depend on the parameters of the money supply rule (see equation (A3.104) above) we conclude that the reinterpreted PIP holds in the model. Monetary policy cannot be used to stabilize the output gap.

Question 11: PIP and the output gap

(a) [This model is discussed in detail by McCallum (1980, p. 729).] Equation (Q3.31) is the IS curve which depends negatively on the real interest rate (via investment) and positively on a real balance effect (via a wealth effect in consumption). Equation (Q3.32) is a standard LM curve. It depends positively on output (via the transactions motive) and negatively on the nominal interest rate (opportunity cost of holding money instead of bonds). Equation (Q3.33) is a Lucas supply function with an endogenous capacity effect included (the term involving the real interest rate, r_t). The rationale behind this term is as follows. Labour supply depends positively on the real interest rate via the intertemporal substitution effect (see Chapter 15). If r_t is high (relative to the rate of time preference) then households postpone consumption of goods and leisure and thus increase labour supply. Finally, equation (Q3.34) is the money supply rule and (Q3.35) is the definition of the real interest rate.

(b) By substituting (Q3.35) into (Q3.32) and using (Q3.31) we can obtain the following matrix expression for output, y_t, and the real interest rate, r_t:

$$\begin{bmatrix} 1 & a_1 \\ c_1 & -c_2 \end{bmatrix} \begin{bmatrix} y_t \\ r_t \end{bmatrix} = \begin{bmatrix} a_0 + a_2(m_t - p_t) + v_{1t} \\ -c_0 + (m_t - p_t) + c_2 E_{t-1}(p_{t+1} - p_t) - v_{2t} \end{bmatrix}. \quad (A3.115)$$

By solving (A3.115) we obtain:

$$y_t = \beta_0 + \beta_1(m_t - p_t) + \beta_2 E_{t-1}(p_{t+1} - p_t) + \beta_3 v_{1t} - \beta_4 v_{2t}, \quad (A3.116)$$
$$r_t = \gamma_0 - \gamma_1(m_t - p_t) - \gamma_2 E_{t-1}(p_{t+1} - p_t) + \gamma_3 v_{1t} + \gamma_4 v_{2t}, \quad (A3.117)$$

where the β_i and γ_i coefficients are defined as:

$$\beta_0 \equiv \frac{a_0 c_2 - a_1 c_0}{a_1 c_1 + c_2}, \qquad \beta_1 \equiv \frac{a_1 + a_2 c_2}{a_1 c_1 + c_2}, \qquad \beta_2 \equiv \frac{a_1 c_2}{a_1 c_1 + c_2},$$

$$\beta_3 \equiv \frac{c_2}{a_1 c_1 + c_2}, \qquad \beta_4 \equiv \frac{a_1}{a_1 c_1 + c_2}, \qquad \gamma_0 \equiv \frac{a_0 c_1 + c_0}{a_1 c_1 + c_2},$$

$$\gamma_1 \equiv \frac{1 - a_2 c_1}{a_1 c_1 + c_2}, \qquad \gamma_2 \equiv \frac{c_2}{a_1 c_1 + c_2}, \qquad \gamma_3 \equiv \frac{c_1}{a_1 c_1 + c_2},$$

$$\gamma_4 \equiv \frac{1}{a_1 c_1 + c_2}.$$

Equation (A3.116) is the AD curve and equation (A3.117) is the quasi-reduced form expression for the real interest rate (similar to what we called the $H(\cdot)$ function in Chapter 2).

By substituting (A3.116)–(A3.117) into the AS curve (Q3.33) we find the following quasi-reduced form expression for p_t:

$$p_t = \frac{\beta_0 - \alpha_0 - \alpha_3 \gamma_0 + (\beta_1 + \alpha_3 \gamma_1) m_t - \alpha_2 y_{t-1}}{\alpha_1 + \beta_1 + \alpha_3 \gamma_1}$$

$$+ \frac{(\beta_2 + \alpha_3 \gamma_2) E_{t-1}(p_{t+1} - p_t)}{\alpha_1 + \beta_1 + \alpha_3 \gamma_1}$$

$$+ \frac{\alpha_1 E_{t-1} p_t + (\beta_3 - \alpha_3 \gamma_3) v_{1t} - (\beta_4 + \alpha_3 \gamma_4) v_{2t} - u_t}{\alpha_1 + \beta_1 + \alpha_3 \gamma_1}. \quad (A3.118)$$

By taking the conditional expectation of (A3.118) we find:

$$E_{t-1} p_t = \frac{\beta_0 - \alpha_0 - \alpha_3 \gamma_0 + (\beta_1 + \alpha_3 \gamma_1) E_{t-1} m_t - \alpha_2 y_{t-1}}{\alpha_1 + \beta_1 + \alpha_3 \gamma_1}$$

$$+ \frac{(\beta_2 + \alpha_3 \gamma_2) E_{t-1}(p_{t+1} - p_t) + \alpha_1 E_{t-1} p_t}{\alpha_1 + \beta_1 + \alpha_3 \gamma_1}, \quad (A3.119)$$

where we have used the law of iterated expectations ($E_{t-1} E_{t-1} p_t = E_{t-1} p_t$ and $E_{t-1} E_{t-1} p_{t+1} = E_{t-1} p_{t+1}$), and noted that $E_{t-1} y_{t-1} = y_{t-1}$ and $E_{t-1} u_t = E_{t-1} v_{1t} = E_{t-1} v_{2t} = 0$. By deducting (A3.119) from (A3.118) we find:

$$p_t - E_{t-1} p_t = \frac{(\beta_1 + \alpha_3 \gamma_1) e_t + (\beta_3 - \alpha_3 \gamma_3) v_{1t} - (\beta_4 + \alpha_3 \gamma_4) v_{2t} - u_t}{\alpha_1 + \beta_1 + \alpha_3 \gamma_1}, \quad (A3.120)$$

where we have used the money supply rule (Q3.34) by noting that $m_t - E_{t-1} m_t = e_t$. Just as in the model of question 10, the expectational gap does not contain the parameters of the money supply rule.

(c) *No real balance effect.* If there is no real balance effect in the IS curve (so that $a_2 = 0$) then equations (Q3.31) and (Q3.33) form a separate subsystem determining y_t and r_t independent from the monetary side of the model. Indeed, by solving (Q3.31) for the real interest rate, r_t, and substituting the result into (Q3.33) we obtain:

$$y_t = \frac{a_1}{a_1 + \alpha_3} \left[\alpha_0 + \alpha_1 \left[p_t - E_{t-1} p_t \right] + \alpha_2 y_{t-1} + \frac{\alpha_3}{a_1} \left(a_0 + v_{1t} \right) \right]. \quad \text{(A3.121)}$$

Since $\alpha_3 > 0$ it follows that $0 < a_1/(a_1 + \alpha_3) < 1$. Hence, equation (A3.121) is a stable (stochastic) difference equation in y_t. Since the expectational gap does not contain the parameters of the money supply rule (see (A3.120)), it follows that the PIP is valid in this case.

With a real balance effect. If there is a real balance effect in the IS curve (and $a_2 \neq 0$), then the system does not separate into a real and a monetary block. In principle the model can be solved by employing the methods of Blanchard and Kahn (1980).

(d) By using the proposed capacity measure in equation (Q3.33) we find the following expression for the output gap:

$$y_t - \bar{y}_t = \alpha_1 [p_t - E_{t-1} p_t] + \alpha_2 [y_{t-1} - \bar{y}_{t-1}]. \quad \text{(A3.122)}$$

Since we have already shown that $p_t - E_{t-1} p_t$ does not depend on the parameters of the money supply rule (see equation (A3.120) above) we conclude that the reinterpreted PIP holds in the model. Monetary policy cannot be used to stabilize the output gap.

Question 12: Contemporaneous information

(a) [A very similar model is discussed in detail by McCallum (1980, pp. 736-737 and 742-743).] Equation (Q3.36) is the expectations-augmented AS curve. Adjustment costs are abstracted from so there is no lagged output term in (Q3.36). Agents base their labour supply decisions on period-$t - 1$ dated information. Equation (Q3.37) is the AD curve which depends positively on real money balances and the expected future inflation rate. (Expected inflation enters the AD curve because the LM curve depends on the nominal rate of interest and the IS curve on the real interest rate, the difference between the two being the expected inflation rate.) It is implicitly assumed that agents possess period-t dated information when forming expectations about future inflation. Hence, the AD curve is based on contemporaneous information. Finally, equation (Q3.38) is the money supply rule.

(b) We solve the model by means of the method of undetermined coefficients. We postulate the following trial solutions for y_t and p_t:

$$y_t = \pi_0 + \pi_1 m_{t-1} + \pi_2 y_{t-1} + \pi_3 u_t + \pi_4 v_t + \pi_5 e_t, \quad \text{(A3.123)}$$
$$p_t = \omega_0 + \omega_1 m_{t-1} + \omega_2 y_{t-1} + \omega_3 u_t + \omega_4 v_t + \omega_5 e_t, \quad \text{(A3.124)}$$

where the π_i and ω_i parameters must be determined. It follows from (A3.124) that:

$$E_{t-1} p_t = \omega_0 + \omega_1 m_{t-1} + \omega_2 y_{t-1}, \quad \text{(A3.125)}$$

where we have used the fact that $E_{t-1}y_{t-1} = y_{t-1}$, $E_{t-1}m_{t-1} = m_{t-1}$, and $E_{t-1}u_t = E_{t-1}v_t = E_{t-1}e_t = 0$. By deducting (A3.125) from (A3.124) we obtain:

$$p_t - E_{t-1}p_t = \omega_3 u_t + \omega_4 v_t + \omega_5 e_t. \tag{A3.126}$$

By substituting (A3.126) into (Q3.36) and gathering terms we find:

$$y_t = \alpha_0 + (1 + \alpha_1 \omega_3)u_t + \alpha_1 \omega_4 v_t + \alpha_1 \omega_5 e_t. \tag{A3.127}$$

The requirement that (A3.123) and (A3.127) must be identical yields the following restrictions:

$$\pi_0 = \alpha_0, \tag{A3.128}$$
$$\pi_1 = 0, \tag{A3.129}$$
$$\pi_2 = 0, \tag{A3.130}$$
$$\pi_3 = 1 + \alpha_1 \omega_3, \tag{A3.131}$$
$$\pi_4 = \alpha_1 \omega_4, \tag{A3.132}$$
$$\pi_5 = \alpha_1 \omega_5. \tag{A3.133}$$

Next we use (A3.124) to compute $E_t p_{t+1}$:

$$
\begin{aligned}
E_t p_{t+1} &= E_t \left[\omega_0 + \omega_1 m_t + \omega_2 y_t + \omega_3 u_{t+1} + \omega_4 v_{t+1} + \omega_5 e_{t+1} \right] \\
&= \omega_0 + \omega_1 m_t + \omega_2 y_t, \tag{A3.134}
\end{aligned}
$$

where we have used the fact that $E_t y_t = y_t$, $E_t m_t = m_t$, and $E_t u_{t+1} = E_t v_{t+1} = E_t e_{t+1} = 0$. By substituting (A3.134) into the AD curve (Q3.37) we find:

$$
\begin{aligned}
y_t &= \beta_0 + \beta_1(m_t - p_t) + \beta_2 E_t(p_{t+1} - p_t) + v_t \\
&= \beta_0 + \beta_1 m_t - \beta_1 p_t + \beta_2(\omega_0 + \omega_1 m_t + \omega_2 y_t - p_t) + v_t \\
&= \beta_0 + \beta_2 \omega_0 + (\beta_1 + \beta_2 \omega_1)m_t - (\beta_1 + \beta_2)p_t + \beta_2 \omega_2 y_t + v_t \\
&= \frac{\beta_0 + \beta_2 \omega_0 + (\beta_1 + \beta_2 \omega_1)m_t - (\beta_1 + \beta_2)p_t + v_t}{1 - \beta_2 \omega_2}, \tag{A3.135}
\end{aligned}
$$

where we implicitly assume that $\beta_2 \omega_2 \neq 1$ (the validity of this assumption is verified below). By substituting (A3.124) and (Q3.38) into (A3.135) and collecting terms we arrive at the following expression:

$$
\begin{aligned}
y_t =& \frac{\beta_0 + (\beta_1 + \beta_2 \omega_1)\mu_0 - \beta_1 \omega_0}{1 - \beta_2 \omega_2} + \frac{(\beta_1 + \beta_2 \omega_1)\mu_1 - (\beta_1 + \beta_2)\omega_1}{1 - \beta_2 \omega_2} m_{t-1} \\
&+ \frac{(\beta_1 + \beta_2 \omega_1)\mu_2 - (\beta_1 + \beta_2)\omega_2}{1 - \beta_2 \omega_2} y_{t-1} - \frac{(\beta_1 + \beta_2)\omega_3}{1 - \beta_2 \omega_2} u_t \\
&+ \frac{1 - (\beta_1 + \beta_2)\omega_4}{1 - \beta_2 \omega_2} v_t + \frac{\beta_1 + \beta_2 \omega_1 - (\beta_1 + \beta_2)\omega_5}{1 - \beta_2 \omega_2} e_t. \tag{A3.136}
\end{aligned}
$$

Equation (A3.136) must be identical to (A3.123). This yields the remaining restrictions:

$$\pi_0 = \frac{\beta_0 + (\beta_1 + \beta_2\omega_1)\mu_0 - \beta_1\omega_0}{1 - \beta_2\omega_2}, \tag{A3.137}$$

$$\pi_1 = \frac{(\beta_1 + \beta_2\omega_1)\mu_1 - (\beta_1 + \beta_2)\omega_1}{1 - \beta_2\omega_2}, \tag{A3.138}$$

$$\pi_2 = \frac{(\beta_1 + \beta_2\omega_1)\mu_2 - (\beta_1 + \beta_2)\omega_2}{1 - \beta_2\omega_2}, \tag{A3.139}$$

$$\pi_3 = -\frac{(\beta_1 + \beta_2)\omega_3}{1 - \beta_2\omega_2}, \tag{A3.140}$$

$$\pi_4 = \frac{1 - (\beta_1 + \beta_2)\omega_4}{1 - \beta_2\omega_2}, \tag{A3.141}$$

$$\pi_5 = \frac{\beta_1 + \beta_2\omega_1 - (\beta_1 + \beta_2)\omega_5}{1 - \beta_2\omega_2}. \tag{A3.142}$$

By using (A3.128)–(A3.133) and (A3.137)–(A3.142) we can compute all the unknown coefficients. It follows from (A3.129) and (A3.138) that:

$$(\beta_1 + \beta_2)\omega_1 = (\beta_1 + \beta_2\omega_1)\mu_1 \quad \Leftrightarrow \quad \omega_1 = \frac{\beta_1\mu_1}{\beta_1 + \beta_2(1 - \mu_1)}. \tag{A3.143}$$

From (A3.130) and (A3.139) we get:

$$(\beta_1 + \beta_2)\omega_2 = (\beta_1 + \beta_2\omega_1)\mu_2 \quad \Leftrightarrow \quad \omega_2 = \frac{\beta_1\mu_2}{\beta_1 + \beta_2(1 - \mu_1)}, \tag{A3.144}$$

where we have substituted (A3.143) in going from the first to the second line. We compute from (A3.144) that:

$$1 - \beta_2\omega_2 = \frac{\beta_1 + \beta_2(1 - \mu_1 - \beta_1\mu_2)}{\beta_1 + \beta_2(1 - \mu_1)}, \tag{A3.145}$$

from which it follows that $\beta_2\omega_2 \neq 1$ provided the numerator of (A3.144) is non-zero. Since $0 < \mu_1 < 1$, the numerator of (A3.145) is certainly positive for counter-cyclical policy rules (for which $\mu_2 < 0$) or for a non-cyclical policy rule (for which $\mu_2 = 0$). All that the condition $\beta_2\omega_2 \neq 1$ rules out are highly procyclical policy rules. Since these do not make any sense anyway, we simply assume that $\mu_2 \leq 0$ from here on.

By using (A3.131) and (A3.140) we find:

$$1 + \alpha_1\omega_3 = -\frac{(\beta_1 + \beta_2)\omega_3}{1 - \beta_2\omega_2} \quad \Leftrightarrow \quad \omega_3 = -\frac{1 - \beta_2\omega_2}{\alpha_1(1 - \beta_2\omega_2) + \beta_1 + \beta_2}, \tag{A3.146}$$

where $1 - \beta_2\omega_2$ is given in (A3.145). By equating (A3.132) and (A3.141) we get:

$$\alpha_1\omega_4 = \frac{1 - (\beta_1 + \beta_2)\omega_4}{1 - \beta_2\omega_2} \quad \Leftrightarrow \quad \omega_4 = \frac{1}{\alpha_1(1 - \beta_2\omega_2) + \beta_1 + \beta_2}. \tag{A3.147}$$

By equating (A3.133) and (A3.142) we obtain:

$$\alpha_1\omega_5 = \frac{\beta_1 + \beta_2\omega_1 - (\beta_1 + \beta_2)\omega_5}{1 - \beta_2\omega_2} \Leftrightarrow \omega_5 = \frac{\beta_1 + \beta_2\omega_1}{\alpha_1(1 - \beta_2\omega_2) + \beta_1 + \beta_2}. \tag{A3.148}$$

Finally, we find the constant term by equating (A3.128) and (A3.137):

$$\alpha_0 = \frac{\beta_0 + (\beta_1 + \beta_2 \omega_1)\mu_0 - \beta_1 \omega_0}{1 - \beta_2 \omega_2} \quad \Leftrightarrow$$

$$\omega_0 = \frac{\beta_0 + (\beta_1 + \beta_2 \omega_1)\mu_0 - (1 - \beta_2 \omega_2)\alpha_0}{\beta_1}. \tag{A3.149}$$

Now that all the π_i and ω_i coefficients have been determined, we have completed the derivation of the rational expectations solution for output and the price level.

By substituting (A3.146)–(A3.148) into (A3.126) we find that the expectational gap can be written as:

$$p_t - E_{t-1}p_t = \omega_3 u_t + \omega_4 v_t + \omega_5 e_t$$

$$= \frac{-(1 - \beta_2 \omega_2)u_t + v_t + (\beta_1 + \beta_2 \omega_1)e_t}{\alpha_1(1 - \beta_2 \omega_2) + \beta_1 + \beta_2}. \tag{A3.150}$$

Since μ_1 and μ_2 appear in the definitions for ω_1 and ω_2 it is clear from (A3.150) that the policy ineffectiveness proposition is not valid in this model. By substituting (A3.150) into (Q3.36) and simplifying we obtain the rational expectations solution for output:

$$y_t = \alpha_0 + \frac{(\beta_1 + \beta_2)u_t + \alpha_1 v_t + \alpha_1(\beta_1 + \beta_2 \omega_1)e_t}{\alpha_1(1 - \beta_2 \omega_2) + \beta_1 + \beta_2}. \tag{A3.151}$$

The PIP does not hold in this model because there is an informational asymmetry between AS and AD. The former is based on period $t - 1$ dated information whereas the latter is based on period t dated information.

(c) The asymptotic variance of output is defined as:

$$\sigma_y^2 \equiv E_{t-\infty}\left[y_t - E_{t-\infty}y_t\right]^2. \tag{A3.152}$$

By using (A3.151) in (A3.152) we find after some straightforward computations:

$$\sigma_y^2 = \frac{(\beta_1 + \beta_2)^2 \sigma_u^2 + \alpha_1^2 \sigma_v^2 + \alpha_1^2(\beta_1 + \beta_2 \omega_1)^2 \sigma_e^2}{[\alpha_1(1 - \beta_2 \omega_2) + \beta_1 + \beta_2]^2}. \tag{A3.153}$$

Since the μ_2 parameter appears in the expression for ω_2 only (see (A3.144)) it follows from (A3.153) that countercyclical monetary policy can be used to reduce output fluctuations. Indeed, by using (A3.144) and (A3.153) we find:

$$\frac{\partial \sigma_y^2}{\partial \mu_2} = \frac{2\sigma_y^2}{\alpha_1(1 - \beta_2 \omega_2) + \beta_1 + \beta_2} \frac{\alpha_1 \beta_1 \beta_2}{\beta_1 + \beta_2(1 - \mu_1)} > 0. \tag{A3.154}$$

The lower is μ_2, the lower is the asymptotic variance of output.

Question 13: Sticky prices

(a) Equation (Q3.39) replaces the usual Lucas supply curve. It postulates that the *actual* price level, p_t, is a weighted average of the *equilibrium* price level, $\tilde{p}_t$, and the expectational error made (on the basis of period-$t - 1$ information) about this equilibrium price. The nice thing about (Q3.39) is that it nests various cases, depending on the magnitude of θ. If $\theta = 1$, prices are perfectly flexible, if $0 < \theta < 1$ the price is partially sticky (and dependent on "stale" information), and if $\theta = 0$ the price is completely predetermined. It thus incorporates both classical and Keynesian scenarios as special cases.

Equation (Q3.40) is the standard AD curve, which depends positively on real money balances and the expected future inflation rate. Equation (Q3.41) is the money supply rule, which incorporates counter-cyclical monetary policy if μ_2 is negative. Equation (Q3.42) is the expression for full employment output, which grows at rate ζ_0 and has a stochastic component u_t.

(b) In order to solve the general model (with $0 \leq \theta \leq 1$) we must first find the rational expectations solution for the equilibrium price level, $\tilde{p}_t$. If we set $\theta = 1$ it follows from equation (Q3.39) that $p_t = \tilde{p}_t$ and thus, by definition, that $y_t = \bar{y}_t$ for all time periods. So the rational expectations solution for output is simply the path for $\bar{y}_t$ (given in (Q3.42)):

$$y_t = \bar{y}_t \quad \Rightarrow \quad y_t = \zeta_0 + y_{t-1} + u_t. \tag{A3.155}$$

Hence it is obviously true that the policy ineffectiveness proposition is valid with perfectly flexible prices (equation (A3.155) does not contain the parameters of the money supply rule). By substituting $y_t = \bar{y}_t$ into (Q3.40) we find that the equilibrium price obeys the following expectational difference equation:

$$\bar{y}_t = \beta_0 + \beta_1(m_t - \tilde{p}_t) + \beta_2 E_{t-1}(\tilde{p}_{t+1} - \tilde{p}_t) + v_t. \tag{A3.156}$$

Since this expression contains expectations formed in period $t - 1$, we postulate the following trial solution:

$$\tilde{p}_t = \pi_0 + \pi_1 m_{t-1} + \pi_2 \bar{y}_{t-1} + \pi_3 v_t + \pi_4 e_t + \pi_5 u_t, \tag{A3.157}$$

where the π_i coefficients must be determined. It follows from (A3.157) that $E_{t-1}\tilde{p}_{t+1}$ is given by:

$$\begin{aligned} E_{t-1}\tilde{p}_{t+1} &= E_{t-1}(\pi_0 + \pi_1 m_t + \pi_2 \bar{y}_t + \pi_3 v_{t+1} + \pi_4 e_{t+1} + \pi_5 u_{t+1}) \\ &= \pi_0 + \pi_1 E_{t-1} m_t + \pi_2 E_{t-1}\bar{y}_t \\ &= \pi_0 + \pi_1 [\mu_0 + \mu_1 m_{t-1} + \mu_2 \bar{y}_{t-1}] + \pi_2 [\zeta_0 + \bar{y}_{t-1}], \end{aligned} \tag{A3.158}$$

where we have used the fact that $E_{t-1} v_{t+1} = E_{t-1} e_{t+1} = E_{t-1} u_{t+1} = 0$ in going from the first to the second line, and employed (Q3.41)–(Q3.42) as well as $E_{t-1} e_t = E_{t-1} u_t = 0$ in going from the second to the third line. It also follows from (A3.157) that $E_{t-1}\tilde{p}_t$ is equal to:

$$E_{t-1}\tilde{p}_t = \pi_0 + \pi_1 m_{t-1} + \pi_2 \bar{y}_{t-1}, \tag{A3.159}$$

where we have used the fact that $E_{t-1} v_t = E_{t-1} e_t = E_{t-1} u_t = 0$. By combining (A3.158) and (A3.159) we find the following expression for the expected future equilibrium inflation rate:

$$E_{t-1}(\tilde{p}_{t+1} - \tilde{p}_t) = \pi_1 \mu_0 + \pi_2 \zeta_0 - \pi_1(1 - \mu_1)m_{t-1} + \pi_1 \mu_2 \bar{y}_{t-1}. \tag{A3.160}$$

By substituting (A3.160) as well as (Q3.41)–(Q3.42) into (A3.156), and noting that $y_t = \bar{y}_t$, we can solve for $\tilde{p}_t$. After some manipulations we find:

$$\tilde{p}_t = \frac{\beta_0 + \beta_1 \mu_0 + \beta_2 \left[\pi_1 \mu_0 + \pi_2 \zeta_0\right] - \zeta_0}{\beta_1} + \frac{\beta_1 \mu_1 - \beta_2 \pi_1 (1 - \mu_1)}{\beta_1} m_{t-1}$$
$$+ \frac{\mu_2 (\beta_1 + \beta_2 \pi_1) - 1}{\beta_1} \bar{y}_{t-1} + \frac{1}{\beta_1} v_t + e_t - \frac{1}{\beta_1} u_t. \quad \text{(A3.161)}$$

Equations (A3.157) and (A3.161) must be identical. This requirement yields the following parameters restrictions:

$$\pi_0 \equiv \frac{\beta_0 + \beta_1 \mu_0 + \beta_2 \left(\pi_1 \mu_0 + \pi_2 \zeta_0\right) - \zeta_0}{\beta_1}, \quad \text{(A3.162)}$$

$$\pi_1 \equiv \frac{\beta_1 \mu_1 - \beta_2 \pi_1 (1 - \mu_1)}{\beta_1}, \quad \text{(A3.163)}$$

$$\pi_2 \equiv \frac{\mu_2 (\beta_1 + \beta_2 \pi_1) - 1}{\beta_1}, \quad \text{(A3.164)}$$

$$\pi_3 \equiv \frac{1}{\beta_1}, \quad \text{(A3.165)}$$

$$\pi_4 \equiv 1, \quad \text{(A3.166)}$$

$$\pi_5 \equiv -\frac{1}{\beta_1}. \quad \text{(A3.167)}$$

Equation (A3.163) can be solved for π_1:

$$\pi_1 = \frac{\beta_1 \mu_1}{\beta_1 + \beta_2 (1 - \mu_1)}. \quad \text{(A3.168)}$$

By using (A3.168) in (A3.164) we find the solution for π_2:

$$\pi_2 = -\frac{1}{\beta_1} \left[1 - \beta_1 \mu_2 \frac{\beta_1 + \beta_2}{\beta_1 + \beta_2 (1 - \mu_1)}\right]. \quad \text{(A3.169)}$$

Since π_1 and π_2 are both known, the constant term π_0 is also uniquely determined in (A3.162). After some manipulations we obtain:

$$\beta_1 \pi_0 \equiv \beta_0 + \mu_0 (\beta_1 + \beta_2 \pi_1) + \zeta_0 (\beta_2 \pi_2 - 1) \quad \Leftrightarrow$$
$$\pi_0 = \frac{\beta_0}{\beta_1} + \frac{\beta_1 + \beta_2}{\beta_1} \left[\frac{\beta_1 \mu_0 + \beta_2 \mu_2 \zeta_0}{\beta_1 + \beta_2 (1 - \mu_1)} - \frac{\zeta_0}{\beta_1}\right]. \quad \text{(A3.170)}$$

(c) To solve the general model, with $0 < \theta < 1$, we first use (A3.157) to compute:

$$\tilde{p}_t - E_{t-1} \tilde{p}_t = \pi_3 v_t + \pi_4 e_t + \pi_5 u_t$$
$$= \frac{v_t - u_t + \beta_1 e_t}{\beta_1}, \quad \text{(A3.171)}$$

where we have used (A3.165)–(A3.167) in the final step. By substituting (A3.171) into equation (Q3.39) we obtain the following expression for the actual price level:

$$p_t = \tilde{p}_t - (1 - \theta)(\tilde{p}_t - E_{t-1}\tilde{p}_t)$$

$$= \tilde{p}_t - (1 - \theta)\frac{v_t - u_t + \beta_1 e_t}{\beta_1} \tag{A3.172}$$

We derive from (A3.172) that expected actual future inflation equals expected equilibrium future inflation:

$$E_{t-1}(p_{t+1} - p_t) = E_{t-1}(\tilde{p}_{t+1} - \tilde{p}_t), \tag{A3.173}$$

where we have used the fact that $E_{t-1}v_{t+i} = E_{t-1}u_{t+i} = E_{t-1}e_{t+i} = 0$ for $i \geq 0$. By substituting (A3.172)–(A3.173) into equation (Q3.40) we obtain the following expression for actual output:

$$y_t = \beta_0 + \beta_1 \left[m_t - \tilde{p}_t + (1 - \theta)\frac{v_t - u_t + \beta_1 e_t}{\beta_1} \right] + \beta_2 E_{t-1}(\tilde{p}_{t+1} - \tilde{p}_t) + v_t \tag{A3.174}$$

By substituting (Q3.41), (A3.157), and (A3.160) into (A3.174), we obtain the following expression:

$$
\begin{aligned}
y_t =\ & [\beta_0 + \beta_1\mu_0 + \beta_2(\pi_1\mu_0 + \pi_2\zeta_0) - \beta_1\pi_0] \\
& + [\beta_1\mu_1 - \beta_2\pi_1(1 - \mu_1) - \beta_1\pi_1]\, m_{t-1} \\
& + [\mu_2(\beta_1 + \beta_2\pi_1) - \beta_1\pi_1]\, \bar{y}_{t-1} + [1 - \beta_1\pi_3 + 1 - \theta]\, v_t \\
& + \beta_1[1 - \pi_4 + 1 - \theta]\, e_t - \beta_1 \left[\pi_5 + \frac{1}{\beta_1} - \frac{\theta}{\beta_1} \right] u_t \\
=\ & \zeta_0 + \bar{y}_{t-1} + (1 - \theta)[v_t + \beta_1 e_t] + \theta u_t, \tag{A3.175}
\end{aligned}
$$

where we have used (A3.162)–(A3.167) in the final step. Since (A3.175) does not contain the parameters of the money supply rule, the policy ineffectiveness proposition holds despite the fact that prices are sticky. The reason for this is that the private agents and the policy maker possess the same information (unlike in the Fischer model). Any countercyclical policy will just affect the price level but not output. See also McCallum (1980, p. 731).

(d) By using (Q3.42) and (A3.175) we can derive the following expression for the output gap:

$$y_t - \bar{y}_t = (1 - \theta)[v_t - u_t + \beta_1 e_t]. \tag{A3.176}$$

The asymptotic variance of the output gap is given by:

$$
\begin{aligned}
\sigma_{y-\bar{y}}^2 &\equiv E_{t-\infty}\left[(y_t - \bar{y}_t) - E_{t-\infty}(y_t - \bar{y}_t)\right]^2 \\
&= (1 - \theta)^2 \left[\sigma_v^2 + \sigma_u^2 + \beta_1^2\sigma_v^2\right], \tag{A3.177}
\end{aligned}
$$

where we have incorporated the stochastic properties of the shock terms (mentioned in the question) in the final step. It is straightforward to derive that the asymptotic variance of the output gap increases as θ gets smaller, i.e. as the degree of price stickiness increases:

$$\frac{\partial \sigma_{y-\bar{y}}^2}{\partial \theta} = -2(1 - \theta) \left[\sigma_v^2 + \sigma_u^2 + \beta_1^2 \sigma_v^2 \right] < 0. \tag{A3.178}$$

Intuitively, increased price stickiness makes the slope of the AS curve flatter. This exacerbates the output effects of the shocks affecting the economy.

Question 14: Automatic stabilizer

(a) Equation (Q3.43) is the equilibrium condition in the goods market. Equation (Q3.44) shows that consumption is proportional to after-tax income, with the marginal propensity to consume between 0 and 1 (i.e. $0 < c(1 - t) < 1$). Equation (Q3.45) is a stochastic accelerator model of investment.

(b) To compute the asymptotic variances it is useful to first obtain the reduced form expression for output. By substituting (Q3.44)–(Q3.45) into (Q3.43) we obtain a difference equation in output:

$$Y_t = c(1 - t)Y_t + \bar{I} + vY_{t-1} + U_t + \bar{G} \quad \Rightarrow$$
$$Y_t = x + \lambda Y_{t-1} + \mu U_t, \tag{A3.179}$$

where x, λ, and μ are defined as follows:

$$x \equiv \frac{\bar{I} + \bar{G}}{1 - c(1 - t)}, \tag{A3.180}$$

$$\lambda \equiv \frac{v}{1 - c(1 - t)}, \tag{A3.181}$$

$$\mu \equiv \frac{1}{1 - c(1 - t)}. \tag{A3.182}$$

In equation (A3.180) the variable x summarizes the effects on output of the (constant) exogenous variables. By using the condition stated in the question ($0 < v < 1 - c(1 - t)$) we find from (A3.181) that the output persistence coefficient, λ, lies between 0 and 1. This means that the difference equation (A3.179) is stable. Furthermore, we observe from (A3.182) that the multiplier effect magnifies the effects of stochastic investment shocks (i.e. $\mu > 1$). Note finally, that it follows from (A3.181)–(A3.182) that λ and μ are related according to $\lambda = v\mu$. We use this result below to simplify the expressions.

The asymptotic variance of output is defined as follows:

$$\sigma_Y^2 \equiv E_{t-\infty} \left[Y_t - E_{t-\infty} Y_t \right]^2, \tag{A3.183}$$

where the expectations operator, $E_{t-\infty}$, indicates that we are computing the variance of the stochastic output process from the perspective of someone living at the beginning of time (no actual realizations of output and the error term are known; only the process (A3.179) is known). We know that:

$$E_{t-\infty} Y_t = E_{t-\infty} \left[x + \lambda Y_{t-1} + \mu U_t \right]$$
$$= x + \lambda E_{t-\infty} Y_{t-1} + \mu E_{t-\infty} U_t$$
$$= x + \lambda E_{t-\infty} Y_{t-1}, \tag{A3.184}$$

where we have used the fact that x is exogenous, λ is a known parameter, and the expected value of the error term is zero ($E_{t-\infty}U_t = 0$). It follows from (A3.179) and (A3.184) that:

$$Y_t - E_{t-\infty}Y_t = x + \lambda Y_{t-1} + \mu U_t - [x + \lambda E_{t-\infty}Y_{t-1}]$$
$$= \lambda [Y_{t-1} - E_{t-\infty}Y_{t-1}] + \mu U_t. \tag{A3.185}$$

By using (A3.185) in (A3.183) we obtain the following expression for σ_Y^2:

$$\sigma_Y^2 \equiv E_{t-\infty} [Y_t - E_{t-\infty}Y_t]^2$$
$$= E_{t-\infty} [\lambda [Y_{t-1} - E_{t-\infty}Y_{t-1}] + \mu U_t]^2$$
$$= E_{t-\infty} \left[\lambda^2 [Y_{t-1} - E_{t-\infty}Y_{t-1}]^2 + \mu^2 U_t^2 + 2\lambda\mu [Y_{t-1} - E_{t-\infty}Y_{t-1}] U_t \right]$$
$$= \lambda^2 E_{t-\infty} [Y_{t-1} - E_{t-\infty}Y_{t-1}]^2 + \mu^2 E_{t-\infty}U_t^2$$
$$+ 2\lambda\mu E_{t-\infty} [Y_{t-1} - E_{t-\infty}Y_{t-1}] U_t. \tag{A3.186}$$

We know that U_t is independent from lagged output ($E_{t-\infty}Y_{t-1}U_t = 0$) and that it has an expected value of zero ($E_{t-\infty}(E_{t-\infty}Y_{t-1})U_t = (E_{t-\infty}Y_{t-1})E_{t-\infty}U_t = 0$) so the third term on the right-hand side of (A3.186) drops out. Furthermore, we know that the output process (A3.179) is stationary (because $|\lambda| < 1$) so that the first term on the right-hand side is equal to σ_Y^2 also. Finally, we know that $E_{t-\infty}U_t^2 = \sigma^2$. By using all these results in (A3.186) we obtain the following expression:

$$\sigma_Y^2 = \lambda^2 \sigma_Y^2 + \mu^2 \sigma^2 \quad \Rightarrow \quad \sigma_Y^2 = \frac{\mu^2 \sigma^2}{1 - \lambda^2} = \frac{\lambda^2}{1 - \lambda^2} \frac{\sigma^2}{v^2}. \tag{A3.187}$$

The asymptotic variance of output is a multiple of the variance of the shock term in the investment equation. The shock multiplier, $\lambda^2/(1 - \lambda^2)$, is higher the more persistent is the output process, i.e. the closer is λ to unity in (A3.179).

To derive the asymptotic variance of C_t we could follow the same steps as for output but there is a quicker way which directly exploits equation (Q3.44). We derive:

$$\sigma_C^2 \equiv E_{t-\infty} [C_t - E_{t-\infty}C_t]^2$$
$$= E_{t-\infty} [c(1-t)Y_t - E_{t-\infty}c(1-t)Y_t]^2$$
$$= c^2(1-t)^2 E_{t-\infty} [Y_t - E_{t-\infty}Y_t]^2$$
$$= c^2(1-t)^2 \sigma_Y^2 = \frac{c^2(1-t)^2\lambda^2}{1-\lambda^2} \cdot \frac{\sigma^2}{v^2}, \tag{A3.188}$$

where we have used (A3.187) in the final step. Just like for output, the asymptotic variance of consumption is proportional to the variance of the shock term in the investment equation. This is, of course, not surprising because consumption is proportional to output.

Finally, to derive the asymptotic variance of investment we use equation (Q3.45):

$$\sigma_I^2 \equiv E_{t-\infty} [I_t - E_{t-\infty}I_t]^2$$
$$= E_{t-\infty} [\bar{I} + vY_{t-1} + U_t - \bar{I} - vE_{t-\infty}Y_{t-1}]^2$$
$$= v^2 E_{t-\infty} [Y_{t-1} - E_{t-\infty}Y_{t-1}]^2 + E_{t-\infty}U_t^2$$
$$= v^2 \sigma_Y^2 + \sigma^2. \tag{A3.189}$$

The asymptotic variance of investment has two sources, namely the variance induced by the variance in output (first term on the right-hand side) and the variance in the investment process itself (second term). By using (A3.187) in (A3.189) and simplifying we obtain:

$$\sigma_I^2 = v^2 \sigma_Y^2 + \sigma^2 = v^2 \frac{\lambda^2}{1 - \lambda^2} \frac{\sigma^2}{v^2} + \sigma^2 = \frac{1}{1 - \lambda^2} \sigma^2. \tag{A3.190}$$

(c) We use the asymptotic variances as measures for stabilization in the economy. We observe from (A3.181) that the tax rate affects the persistence parameter. By differentiating (A3.187) with respect to t we get:

$$
\begin{aligned}
\frac{\partial \sigma_Y^2}{\partial t} &= \frac{\sigma^2}{v^2} \frac{\partial \frac{1}{\lambda^{-2}-1}}{\partial t} = \frac{\sigma^2}{v^2} \frac{2\lambda^{-3}}{[\lambda^{-2} - 1]^2} \frac{\partial \lambda}{\partial t} \\
&= -\frac{\sigma^2}{v^2} \frac{2\lambda^{-3}}{[\lambda^{-2} - 1]^2} \frac{c}{1 - c(1 - t)} < 0.
\end{aligned}
\tag{A3.191}
$$

The tax acts as an automatic stabilizer. An increase in t reduces both output persistence (λ falls) and reduces the impact effect of shocks originating from the investment sector (μ falls). It is not difficult to derive from, respectively, (A3.188) and (A3.189), that the tax also reduces the asymptotic variances of consumption and investment.

Chapter 4

Anticipation effects and economic policy

Question 1: Short questions

(a) "A permanent (unanticipated) increase in the labour income tax causes an immediate boost in firm investment because employers want to replace workers by machines." Explain and evaluate this proposition.

(b) "A permanent investment subsidy stimulates long-run investment much more than a temporary subsidy does. The opposite holds in the impact period." Explain and evaluate this proposition.

(c) "An anticipated increase in the investment subsidy leads to an immediate reduction in firm investment." Explain and evaluate this proposition.

(d) Suppose you are a somewhat junior minister of Finance. To stimulate investment in green energy there is a subsidy on investment in capital that generates electricity in an environmental friendly way. However, due to its overwhelming success, this arrangement has become too expensive. There are simply too many small firms making use of this policy initiative. You reach the decision that you will have to abolish the subsidy. One of your advisers recommends to implement this change immediately to prevent a temporary rush. Another adviser disagrees, however, and tells you that it does not matter whether you announce it or not, since it will not have anticipation effects. How is it possible that these two persons reach different conclusions? With whom do you agree?

Question 2: The IS-LM model with sticky prices

Consider a closed economy with sticky prices and an efficient term structure of interest rates:

$$y = -\sigma R_L + g, \tag{Q4.1}$$

$$m - p = -\lambda R_S + \gamma y + \alpha, \tag{Q4.2}$$

$$\dot{p} = \phi(y - \bar{y}), \tag{Q4.3}$$

$$R_L - \frac{\dot{R}_L}{R_L} = R_S. \tag{Q4.4}$$

Here m is the logarithm of the money supply, g is the logarithm of (an indicator for) budgetary policy, p is the logarithm of the price level, y ($\bar{y}$) is the logarithm of the (natural) output level. R_L is the yield on long-term bonds ("perpetuities"), and R_S is the short-term interest rate.

(a) Provide a brief interpretation for these equations.

(b) Demonstrate the effect of an unanticipated and permanent increase in the natural output level ($\bar{y}$) on actual output, the long-term and short-term interest rates, the price level, and the real money supply. Show the effects in a diagram with time on the horizontal axis, and use t_A as the indicator for the time at which the shock in announced ("announcement time").

(c) Now redo part b for the case in which the shock is announced (i.e. becomes known to the public) *before* it actually takes place. The time at which the shock actually occurs (the "implementation time") is t_I, so we assume that $t_A < t_I$.

(d) Show that an unanticipated and permanent budgetary expansion (rise in g) leads to an immediate increase in the long-term interest rate. Show what happens (at impact, during transition, and in the long run) to output, the price level, and the short-term interest rate. Illustrate your answers in an impulse-response diagram.

(e) Show that an anticipated and permanent budgetary expansion (a future increase in g) will cause a recession at first and will only stimulate the economy further into the future. Show what happens (at impact, during transition, and in the long run) to output, the price level, and the short-term interest rate. Illustrate your answers in an impulse-response diagram.

(f) What happens to the long-term interest rate if the anticipated budgetary expansion (studied in the previous subquestion) does not take place? (At implementation time, t_I, the government announces that it will keep g unchanged). Illustrate your answers in an impulse-response diagram.

(g) ★ Assume that the *real* (rather than the nominal) long-term interest rate, $r_L \equiv R_L - \dot{p}$, features in equation (Q4.1). Assume furthermore that $0 < \sigma\phi < 1$. Study the (impact, transitional, and long-run) effects of an unanticipated and permanent technology shock (an increase in $\bar{y}$). Illustrate your answers in an impulse-response diagram.

★ Question 3: Leaning against the wind

[Based on Turnovsky (1979)] Consider the following model of a small open economy featuring perfect capital mobility and sluggish price adjustment:

$$y = -\eta R + \delta(e + p^* - p), \qquad\qquad \eta > 0, \quad 0 < \delta < 1, \qquad (Q4.5)$$
$$m - p = y - \lambda R, \qquad\qquad\qquad\qquad\qquad \lambda > 0, \qquad (Q4.6)$$
$$\dot{p} = \phi(y - \bar{y}), \qquad\qquad\qquad\qquad\qquad \phi > 0, \qquad (Q4.7)$$
$$R = R^* + \dot{e}, \qquad\qquad\qquad\qquad\qquad\qquad (Q4.8)$$

where y is actual output, R is the domestic interest rate, e is the nominal exchange rate, p^* is the exogenous foreign price level, p is the domestic price level, m is the nominal money supply, $\bar{y}$ is (exogenous) full employment output, and R^* is the exogenous world interest rate. All variables, except the two interest rates, are measured in logarithms. As usual, a dot above a variables denotes that variable's time rate of change, i.e. $\dot{p} \equiv dp/dt$ and $\dot{e} \equiv de/dt$. Assume that the policy maker adopts the following policy rule for the nominal money supply:

$$m - \bar{m} = -\mu(e - \bar{e}), \quad \mu \gtrless 0, \qquad\qquad\qquad (Q4.9)$$

where $\bar{m}$ is the exogenous component of money supply, $\bar{e}$ is the equilibrium exchange rate, and μ is a policy parameter.

(a) Interpret the equations of the model. Which are the endogenous and which are the exogenous variables? Explain why the policy rule embodies 'leaning against the wind' if $\mu > 0$. What do we mean by 'leaning with the wind'?

(b) Derive the steady-state values of p and e as a function of the exogenous variables (denote the steady-state level of p by $\bar{p}$).

(c) Show that the dynamic model can be written in the form: $\begin{bmatrix} \dot{p} \\ \dot{e} \end{bmatrix} = \Delta \begin{bmatrix} p - \bar{p} \\ e - \bar{e} \end{bmatrix}$ with Δ a 2×2 matrix. Hint: write the output gap and interest differential as $\begin{bmatrix} y - \bar{y} \\ R - R^* \end{bmatrix} = \Gamma \begin{bmatrix} p - \bar{p} \\ e - \bar{e} \end{bmatrix}$, and then use (Q4.5) and (Q4.7) to write $\begin{bmatrix} \dot{p} \\ \dot{e} \end{bmatrix} = \Xi \begin{bmatrix} y - \bar{y} \\ R - R^* \end{bmatrix}$.

(d) Under what condition(s) is the model saddle-point stable? Which is the jumping variable and which is the predetermined variable?

(e) Illustrate the phase diagram of the model for the case where the policy maker engages strongly in 'leaning against the wind' (so that $\eta\mu > \lambda\delta$).

(f) Assume that $\eta\mu = \lambda\delta$. Derive the (impact, transitional, and long-term) effects of an unanticipated and permanent increase in the foreign price level, p^*. Why is there no transitional dynamics in this case?

Question 4: The term structure of interest rates

Assume that there are two investment instruments: very *short-term bonds* and *perpetuities* (bonds with infinite term to maturity). The short-term bonds carry an interest rate of R_S whilst the perpetuities carry a coupon payment of unity and have an internal rate of return equal to R_L.

(a) Derive the condition for the efficient term structure of interest rates.

(b) Assume that the short-term interest rate is initially equal to R_S^0. Show the dynamic effects on the long-term interest rate, R_L, of an anticipated increase of the short-term interest rates in the future. As in the book, let t_A represent the time at which the news about the shock is received by the agents (the "announcement" time) and let t_I be the time at which the shock actually happens (the "implementation" time). The short-term interest rate is thus equal to R_S^0 for $t_A \leq t < t_I$ and equal to R_S^1 for $t > t_I$. Illustrate your answer with the aid of a phase diagram.

(c) Show what happens to the long-term interest rate when some time after t_A but before t_I, it becomes clear to the agents that the expected interest rate hike will not happen (and that the interest rate thus will remain equal to R_S^0 after t_I).

Question 5: Fiscal policy with fixed nominal wages and perfect foresight

[Based on Calvo (1980)] In this question we study an ad hoc dynamic IS-LM model of a closed economy. The nominal wage rate is assumed to be fixed, say at $\bar{W}$. Agents are blessed with perfect foresight. You are given the following information about the structure of the economy.

$$r + \delta = F_K(K, L), \qquad (Q4.10)$$

$$\frac{\bar{W}}{P} = F_L(K, L), \qquad (Q4.11)$$

$$Y = F(K, L), \qquad (Q4.12)$$

$$\frac{\bar{M}}{P} = L(Y, r + \pi^e, A), \qquad (Q4.13)$$

$$C = C(Y - T, r, A), \qquad (Q4.14)$$

$$A = K + \frac{\bar{M}}{P}, \qquad (Q4.15)$$

$$T = G, \qquad (Q4.16)$$

$$\dot{K} = Y - C - G - \delta K, \qquad (Q4.17)$$

$$\pi^e = \pi \left[\equiv \frac{\dot{P}}{P}\right], \qquad (Q4.18)$$

where r is the real interest rate, K is the capital stock, L is employment, P is the price level, Y is gross output, $\bar{M}$ is the money supply (fixed exogenously), π^e is the expected inflation rate, C is consumption, T is taxes, A is total wealth, G is useless government consumption, π is the actual inflation rate, and δ is the depreciation rate. The production function features constant returns to scale and has all the usual properties (see Intermezzo 4.3 in the book). The money demand function features the partial derivatives $L_Y > 0$, $L_R < 0$ (with $R \equiv r + \pi^e$), and $0 < L_A < 1$. The partial derivatives of the consumption function are given by $0 < C_{Y-T} < 1$, $C_r < 0$, and $C_A > 0$. As usual, a variable with a dot denotes that variable's time derivative, e.g. $\dot{K} \equiv dK/dt$.

(a) Provide a brief discussion of the economic rationale behind these equations.

(b) Prove that output can be written as $Y = \Phi(P) \cdot K$, with $\Phi'(P) > 0$. Also show that $r = \Psi(P) - \delta$ with $\Psi'(P) > 0$.

(c) Show that the core of this model can be written in terms of a fundamental system of differential equations in K and P.

(d) Prove that, evaluated at the steady state (in which $\dot{P} = \dot{K} = 0$), the economy has the following features:

$$\delta_{11} \equiv \frac{\partial \dot{K}}{\partial K} \gtrless 0, \qquad \delta_{12} \equiv \frac{\partial \dot{K}}{\partial P} > 0,$$

$$\delta_{21} \equiv \frac{\partial \dot{P}}{\partial K} > 0, \qquad \delta_{22} \equiv \frac{\partial \dot{P}}{\partial P} \gtrless 0.$$

(e) Show that there are four possible sign configurations for δ_{11} and δ_{22} for which the model is saddle-point stable. State the conditions that must hold and draw the phase diagrams for the four possible cases. Which variable is the jumping variable? And which one is the pre-determined (sticky variable)?

(f) Study the effects of an unanticipated and permanent increase in government consumption for the four cases. Derive the impact, transitional, and long-run effects on P and K and illustrate with phase diagrams.

Answers

Question 1: Short questions

(a) False, this is the reverse of Figure 4.9 in the book. As t_L rises, W goes up, less labour is demanded and (for a given K) F_K falls. This leads to a fall in investment, not an increase.

(b) True. A temporary investment subsidy has no permanent effects, a permanent investment subsidy has.

An investment subsidy decreases the costs of capital, so marginal productivity of capital must also decrease. Assuming decreasing, but positive marginal benefits, the total stock of capital must increase. This implies more investments to keep the total capital stock at its new, higher level. A temporary investment subsidy causes firms to bring their future investments forward to 'make hay while the sun shines'. This has a strong effect on current investment, no effect on long term investment.

(c) True, see Figure 4.6 in reverse. The anticipated increase prompt firms to decrease investment now (postpone) in order to get the higher subsidy later.

(d) The answer lies (as always) in the assumptions. Use the model of section 4.1.2. If the real wage is constant then we get the situation as described in Figure 4.2 of the book with a constant marginal product of capital. A lower investment subsidy shifts the $\dot{K} = 0$ line upward and to the left. The saddle path is horizontal and coincides with the $\dot{q} = 0$ line. It does not matter whether you announce your decision or not, investments only change at the time of the implementation, there are no announcement effects.

If labour is fixed instead of wages, then the marginal product of capital is no longer constant and we have the situation described in Figure 4.6 of the book. The $\dot{q} = 0$ line is now downward sloping. An anticipated abolition of the investment subsidy will result in a temporary rush of firms in order to get the subsidy while it exists (see the analysis in the book). If we surprise the investors and do not announce the abolition, then investment will go down immediately and we have (obviously) no anticipation effects.

Which assumption is more likely to hold? Given the fact that most investors that used this subsidy were small (single-person?) companies, it is unlikely that they will fire themselves. Any shock will have a direct impact on their wage, so the second scenario (fixed labour) is more likely.

Question 2: The IS-LM model with sticky prices

(a) Equation (Q4.1) is the IS curve. Investment is assumed to depend negatively on the long-term interest rate. Equation (Q4.2) is the LM curve. Money demand depends negatively on the short-term interest rate, and positively on output. Equation (Q4.3) is the Phillips curve, relating the price change to the output gap. Equation (Q4.4) is the expression for the efficient term structure of interest rates. The instantaneous yields on perpetuities and on short-run instruments are equalized. There are no unexploited arbitrage opportunities and perfect foresight is assumed.

(b) We must first derive the phase diagram of the model. By using (Q4.1)–(Q4.2) we can solve for R_S as a function of the exogenous variables (g, m, and $\bar{y}$) and the dynamic variables (p and R_L).

$$m - p = -\lambda R_S + \gamma[-\sigma R_L + g] + \alpha \quad \Rightarrow$$
$$R_S = \frac{-\gamma\sigma R_L + \gamma g + \alpha - (m - p)}{\lambda}. \tag{A4.1}$$

By using (Q4.1) in (Q4.3) and (A4.1) in (Q4.4) we find:

$$\dot{p} = \phi(-\sigma R_L + g - \bar{y}) \tag{A4.2}$$
$$\frac{\dot{R}_L}{R_L} = R_L - \left[\frac{-\gamma\sigma R_L + \gamma g + \alpha - m + p}{\lambda}\right] \tag{A4.3}$$
$$= \frac{(\lambda + \gamma\sigma)R_L - \gamma g + m - p - \alpha}{\lambda}. \tag{A4.4}$$

We have a dynamic system with one predetermined variable (the price, p) and one non-predetermined "jumping" variable (the long-term interest rate, R_L). We thus expect that the model exhibits the saddle path structure. We illustrate the phase diagram in Figure A4.1.

It follows from (A4.2) that the $\dot{p} = 0$ line is given by:

$$\dot{p} = 0 \quad \Leftrightarrow \quad R_L = \frac{g - \bar{y}}{\sigma}. \tag{A4.5}$$

Since both g and $\bar{y}$ are exogenous it follows that the $\dot{p} = 0$ line is horizontal. For points above (below) the line, the long-term interest rate is too high (low), investment is too low (high), output falls short of (exceeds) its full employment level, and the price falls (rises). These dynamic forces have been illustrated with horizontal arrows in Figure A4.1.

It follows from (A4.4) that the $\dot{R}_L = 0$ line can be written as:

$$\dot{R}_L = 0 \quad \Leftrightarrow \quad R_L = \frac{\gamma g + \alpha - (m - p)}{\lambda + \gamma\sigma}. \tag{A4.6}$$

For points above (below) this line, the long-term interest rate exceeds (falls short of) the short-term rate and the long-term rate rises (falls) over time. These dynamic forces have been illustrated with vertical arrows in the figure.

It follows from the configuration of arrows that the equilibrium at E_0 is saddle-point stable. The only convergent trajectory is given by SP, which is the saddle path associated with E_0. An unanticipated and permanent increase in $\bar{y}$ shifts the $\dot{p} = 0$ line down. See Figure A4.2. At impact the economy jumps to point A. In the long run, the equilibrium moves to E_1. Both p and $R_L = R_S$ go down. The effects on the other variables are easily deduced. See Figure A4.3.

(c) We use the intuitive solution principle to solve the dynamics of R_L and p:

- Jumps in R_L are allowed only at impact, i.e. for $t = t_A$.
- For $t_A \leq t < t_I$ the dynamic adjustment is determined by the old equilibrium.

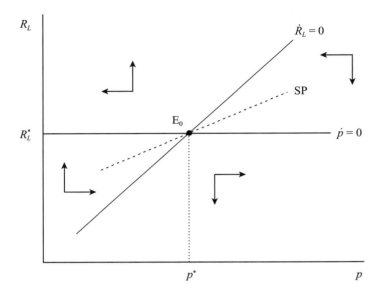

Figure A4.1: Phase diagram

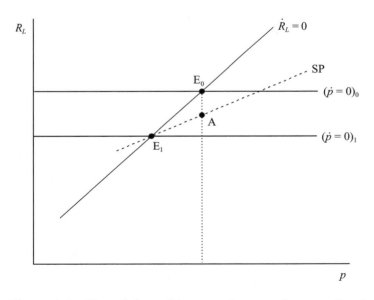

Figure A4.2: Unanticipated increase in natural output level

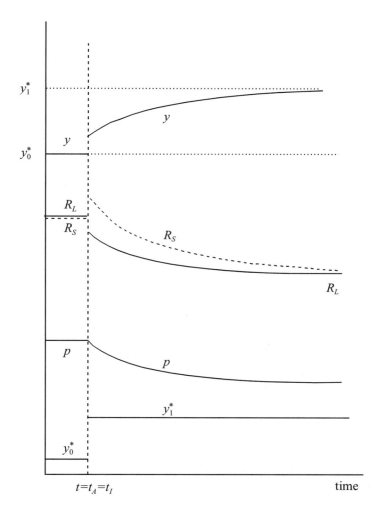

Figure A4.3: Impulse response diagrams

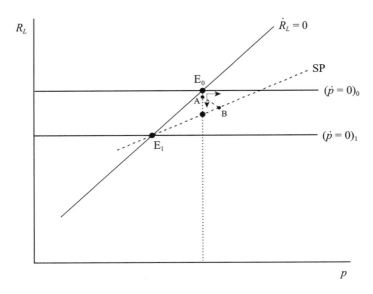

Figure A4.4: Anticipated increase in natural output level

- At $t = t_I$ the economy arrives smoothly (without jumps) at the saddle path associated with the new equilibrium.

The phase diagram is presented in Figure A4.4, where E_0 and E_1 are, respectively, the initial and new steady-state equilibria. The adjustment path is given by the jump from E_0 to A at impact ($t = t_A$), a gradual move from A to B (for $t_A < t < t_I$) and a gradual move from B to E_1 (for $t \geq t_I$). The intuitive principle shows why this is the case. At time $t = t_I$ the economy must be on the new saddle path SP. This furnishes point B. Between t_A and t_I the old dynamics (as shown by the arrows) are relevant, i.e. point B is approached from a north-westerly direction. This furnishes point A. There must be a downward jump in R_L at impact because otherwise the economy would never get to the new equilibrium without violation of the intuitive solution principle. It follows from Figure A4.4 that the adjustment in the long-term interest rate is monotonically decreasing, whereas the price level rises at first and only starts to fall after the shock has been implemented.

It is easy to show that the paths for y, R_S, and R_L are very similar to the ones shown above.

(d) An unanticipated and permanent budgetary expansion (a once-off rise in g) shifts both the $\dot{p} = 0$ and $\dot{R}_L = 0$ lines up in A4.1. To see which shift dominates, we first solve (A4.2)–(A4.4) for the steady-state price level, p^*.

$$\frac{g - \bar{y}}{\sigma} = \frac{\gamma g + \alpha + p^* - m}{\lambda + \gamma\sigma} \quad \Leftrightarrow \quad p^* = m - \alpha + \frac{\lambda g - (\lambda + \gamma\sigma)\bar{y}}{\sigma}. \quad \text{(A4.7)}$$

It follows from (A4.7) that $dp^*/dg = \lambda/\sigma > 0$, i.e. in Figure A4.5 the new equilibrium, E_1, lies north-east from the initial steady state, E_0. At impact, the price level is predetermined and the economy jumps from E_0 to A directly

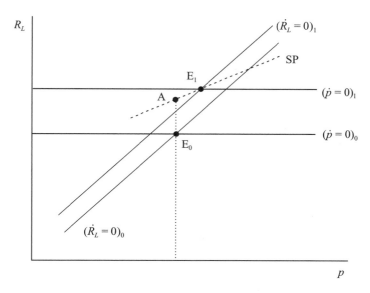

Figure A4.5: An unanticipated and permanent budgetary expansion

above it. During transition the economy moves along the new saddle path, SP, from A to E_1. In Figure A4.6 we show the impulse-response functions for the different variables. The shock hitting the system (the "impulse") is the step-wise change in g that occurs at time $t_A = t_I$, where t_A is the announcement date and t_I the implementation date. The paths for p and R_L can be inferred directly from Figure A4.5: p features no impact jump but rises gradually towards its new steady-state level; R_L jumps at impact and thereafter rises further towards its new steady-state level. Some smart detective work yields the remaining effects. First we note from Figures A4.5 and A4.6 that $\dot{p}$ is positive but declining throughout the transition phase. It follows from (Q4.3) that actual output jumps at impact and gradually returns to its full employment level during transition. In view of (Q4.1) it thus follows that at impact the boost in demand caused by the increase in g offsets the decline in investment caused by the increase in the long-term interest rate. Second, we note that $\dot{R}_L$ is positive but declining throughout transition. It follows from (Q4.4) that the short-run interest rate lies below the long-run interest rate throughout the transitional phase. Furthermore, it follows from (Q4.2) (plus the fact that m is exogenous and p is predetermined) that the impact jump in R_S is proportional to the impact jump in y.

In Figure A4.7 we show an "IS-LM" style diagram to illustrate the effect on output and the short-term interest rate. The (slightly unconventional) IS curve is given by (Q4.1) and is vertical as investment depends on the long-term interest rate (whereas the short-term interest rate is on the vertical axis of Figure A4.7). Since the initial equilibrium is such that $y = \bar{y}$, IS_0 represents the initial IS curve. The LM curve is given by (Q4.2) and is upward sloping as usual. The initial equilibrium is at E_0. The increase in g shifts the IS curve to the right (to IS_1). Nothing happens to the LM curve (because m is constant and p

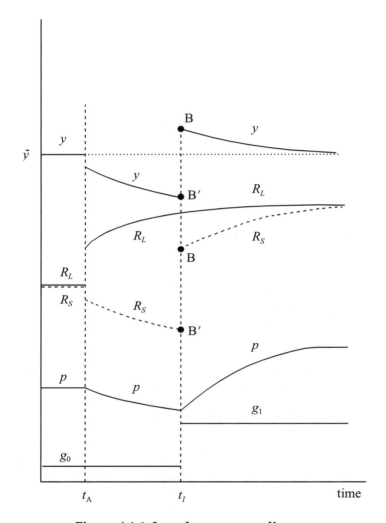

Figure A4.6: Impulse-response diagram

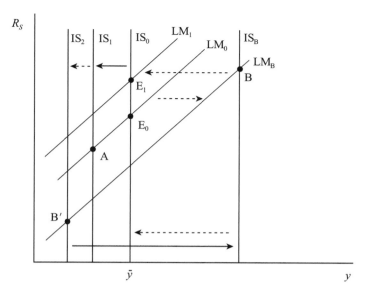

Figure A4.7: IS-LM effects

is predetermined) so at impact the equilibrium shifts from E_0 to A. The output increase causes an excess demand for money which is eliminated by the increase the short-term interest rate. During transition both IS and LM gradually shift to the left. The LM curve shifts because the price level rises and thus decreases the real money supply. IS shifts because the long-term interest rate increases which leads to a reduction in investment and output. Eventually, the new steady state at E_1 is attained.

(e) We use the intuitive solution principle to solve the dynamics of R_L and p:

- Jumps in R_L are allowed only at impact, i.e. for $t = t_A$.
- For $t_A \leq t < t_I$ the dynamic adjustment is determined by the old equilibrium.
- At $t = t_I$ the economy arrives smoothly (without jumps) at the saddle path associated with the new equilibrium.

The phase diagram is presented in Figure A4.8, where E_0 and E_1 are, respectively, the initial and new steady-state equilibria. The adjustment path is given by the jump from E_0 to A at impact ($t = t_A$), a gradual move from A to B (for $t_A < t < t_I$) and a gradual move from B to E_1 (for $t \geq t_I$). The intuitive principle shows why this is the case. At time $t = t_I$ the economy must be on the new saddle path SP. This furnishes point B. Between t_A and t_I the old dynamics (as shown by the arrows) are relevant, i.e. point B is approached from a southeasterly direction. This furnishes point A. There must be an upward jump in R_L at impact because otherwise the economy would never get to the new equilibrium without violation of the intuitive solution principle. It follows from Figure A4.8 that the adjustment in the long-term interest rate is monotonically

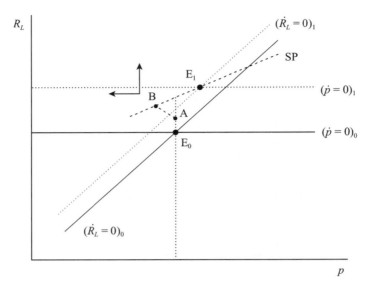

Figure A4.8: Anticipated and permanent fiscal policy

increasing, whereas the price level falls at first and only starts to rise after the shock has been implemented.

The impulse-response functions are presented in Figure A4.9. The paths for p and R_L (associated with the fiscal shock) can be taken directly from Figure A4.8. A little detective work furnishes the paths for the remaining variables. First we note from (Q4.1) that for $t_A \leq t < t_I$ the output effect is proportional to the effect on R_L (because g has not yet changed). Hence, output features a negative impact jump and declines thereafter because investment falls. At $t = t_I$, g rises and output jumps to a level higher than full employment output, $\bar{y}$. We observe that $\dot{p}$ is positive for $t \geq t_I$ so it follows from (Q4.3) that $y > \bar{y}$ during that time. Second, we note that $\dot{R}_L$ is positive throughout the adjustment. It thus follows from (Q4.4) that R_S lies below R_L throughout the adjustment period ($t \geq t_A$).

To determine the path for the short-term interest rate we use the IS-LM style diagram in Figure A4.10. The initial equilibrium is at E_0. At impact, the upward jump in R_L causes the IS curve to shift to the left (from IS_0 to IS_1) as investment is reduced. Since the LM curve is unaffected, the new equilibrium is at point A where both output and the short-term interest rate are lower than in the initial steady state. Hence, whereas the long-term interest rates increases at impact the short-term interest rate falls at impact.

Between t_A and t_I, R_L rises further (and IS gradually shifts further to the left from IS_1 to IS_2) and p falls (so that LM shifts to the right, from LM_0 to LM_B, because the real money supply increases). Both forces explain why the short-term interest falls further during that time. One "split second" before t_I the economy finds itself in point B′ in Figures A4.9 and A4.10. In t_I, however, g is increased, the IS curve shifts to the right (from IS_2 to IS_B), and the economy shifts instantaneously from point B′ to point B in Figure A4.10. The increased

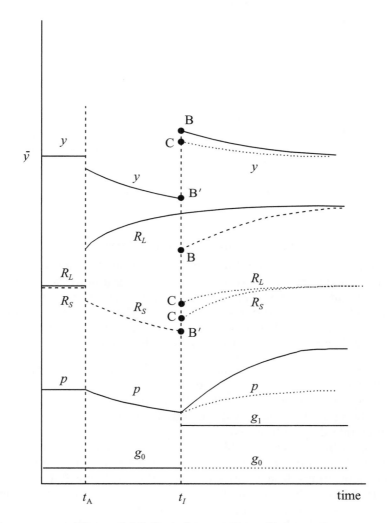

Figure A4.9: Impulse-response diagram

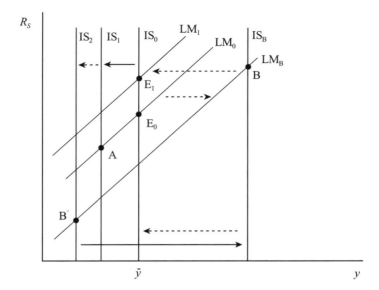

Figure A4.10: IS-LM effects

output leads to an increase in the short-term interest rate.

Transition after t_I is straightforward: output gradually returns to its full employment level and the short-term interest rate gradually catches up with the long-term rate. In terms of Figure A4.10, the IS curve gradually shifts from IS_B to IS_0 and the LM curve shifts from LM_B to LM_1. The ultimate equilibrium is at E_1. It features a higher short-term (and long-term) interest rate because the long-term increase in the price level has eroded the real money supply.

(f) Suppose that the economy has arrived at point B in Figure A4.8 (at time $t = t_I$) and that the policy maker at that time announces (unexpectedly) that g will not in fact be changed, i.e. that it will remain equal to g_0. This is a new shock facing the agents because they thought that g would change to g_1 at time $t = t_I$. We illustrate the resulting dynamics of p and R_L in Figure A4.11. Since g is unchanged the ultimate equilibrium is at E_0 and the dynamics of E_0 remain relevant. At the time that news about the new shock is received (i.e. at $t = t_I$), the economy jumps from point B to point C directly below it. Point C lies on the unique saddle path leading to the ultimate equilibrium E_0 and the price level is predetermined. After this impact shock, both the price level and the long-term interest rate gradually increase towards their respective long-term levels. Since nothing happens to g there are no long-term effects on any of the variables. The time paths for the different variables have been illustrated in Figure A4.12. In that figure the dotted lines are the paths associated with the new shock (the solid and dashed lines are the solutions found in part (c) above). The path of the long-term interest rate is deduced directly from Figure A4.11. Since R_L rises during transition ($\dot{R}_L > 0$) it follows from equation (Q4.4) that R_L exceeds R_S throughout the transition. Hence, the short-term interest rate *falls* at time t_I and rises thereafter. In terms of the IS-LM diagram in Figure A4.10, the reduction in R_L at time t_I shifts the IS curve to the right such that the new intersection with

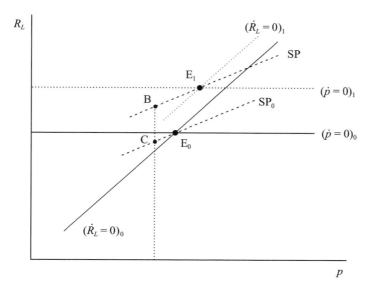

Figure A4.11: Announced policy not implemented

LM_B lies south-east from point E_0. This also explains why the output boost at t_I is smaller than if the fiscal increase had in fact occurred.

(g) The IS curve is now:

$$y = -\sigma [R_L - \dot{p}] + g. \tag{A4.8}$$

By substituting (A4.8) into (Q4.2) we can solve for the short-term interest rate:

$$R_S = \frac{-\gamma\sigma R_L + \gamma\sigma\dot{p} + \gamma g + \alpha - (m-p)}{\lambda}. \tag{A4.9}$$

By using (A4.9) in (Q4.4) we obtain:

$$\frac{\dot{R}_L}{R_L} = R_L - R_S$$
$$= \frac{(\lambda + \gamma\sigma)R_L - \gamma\sigma\dot{p} - \gamma g - \alpha + m - p}{\lambda}. \tag{A4.10}$$

By substituting (A4.8) into (Q4.3) we obtain:

$$\dot{p} = \phi\left[-\sigma R_L + \sigma\dot{p} + g - \bar{y}\right] \quad \Leftrightarrow$$
$$\dot{p} = \frac{\phi}{1 - \sigma\phi}\left[-\sigma R_L + g - \bar{y}\right], \tag{A4.11}$$

where the first term on the right-hand side is positive because $0 < \sigma\phi < 1$ and $\phi > 0$. By substituting (A4.11) into (A4.10) and simplifying we obtain:

$$\frac{\dot{R}_L}{R_L} = \frac{[\lambda(1 - \sigma\phi) + \gamma\sigma]R_L - \gamma g + (1 - \sigma\phi)(m - p - \alpha) + \gamma\sigma\phi\bar{y}}{\lambda(1 - \sigma\phi)}. \tag{A4.12}$$

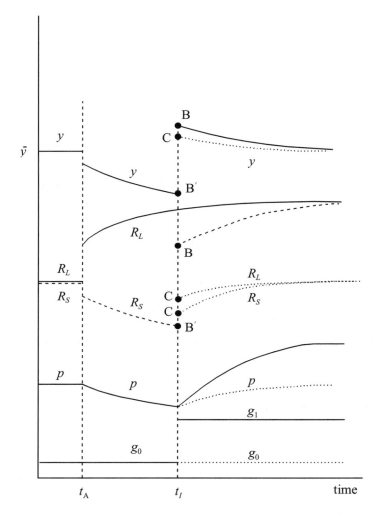

Figure A4.12: Impulse-response diagram

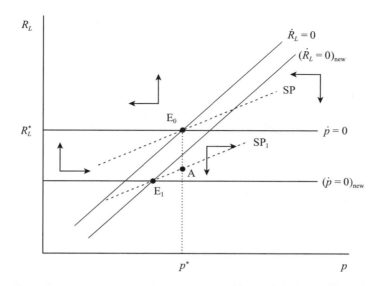

Figure A4.13: A permanent and unanticipated technology improvement

The dynamical system (A4.11)–(A4.12) is *qualitatively* very similar to the one studied in the previous parts. The phase diagram of the augmented model is presented in Figure A4.13. The $\dot{p} = 0$ line is still given by (A4.5). We derive from (A4.11) that:

$$\frac{\partial \dot{p}}{\partial R_L} = -\frac{\sigma \phi}{1 - \sigma \phi} < 0. \tag{A4.13}$$

Hence, points above (below) the $\dot{p} = 0$ line output falls short of (exceeds) its full employment level and prices fall (rise). See the horizontal arrows in Figure A4.13.

We derive the $\dot{R}_L = 0$ line from (A4.12). Its slope is given by:

$$\left(\frac{dR_L}{dp} \right)_{\dot{R}_L = 0} = \frac{1 - \sigma \phi}{\lambda(1 - \sigma \phi) + \gamma \sigma} > 0, \tag{A4.14}$$

where the sign follows readily from the assumption that $0 < \sigma \phi < 1$. We also derive from (A4.12) that:

$$\frac{\partial \left(\frac{\dot{R}_L}{R_L} \right)}{\partial R_L} = \frac{\lambda(1 - \sigma \phi) + \gamma \sigma}{\lambda(1 - \sigma \phi)} > 1. \tag{A4.15}$$

For points above (below) the $\dot{R}_L = 0$ line, the long-term interest rate rises (falls) over time. See the vertical arrows in Figure A4.13. Not surprisingly, the augmented model is saddle-point stable, and the initial equilibrium is at E_0.

Next we consider the effect of a permanent and unanticipated increase in $\bar{y}$. It follows from (A4.5) (or, equivalently, from (A4.11)) that the $\dot{p} = 0$ line shifts down. Similarly, it follows from (A4.12) that the $\dot{R}_L = 0$ line also shifts down. To figure out the long-run effects on R_L and p we set $\dot{R}_L = 0$ in (A4.12) and

$\dot{p} = 0$ in (A4.11) and differentiate the resulting expressions with respect to R_L, p, and $\bar{y}$. After some manipulations we find:

$$\begin{bmatrix} \lambda(1 - \sigma\phi) + \gamma\sigma & -(1 - \sigma\phi) \\ \sigma & 0 \end{bmatrix} \begin{bmatrix} dR_L(\infty) \\ dp(\infty) \end{bmatrix} = - \begin{bmatrix} \gamma\sigma\phi \\ 1 \end{bmatrix} d\bar{y}. \tag{A4.16}$$

The matrix on the left-hand side is denoted by Δ and has a determinant equal to $|\Delta| = \sigma(1 - \sigma\phi) > 0$. By Cramer's Rule (see Mathematical Appendix) we find:

$$\frac{dR_L(\infty)}{d\bar{y}} = \frac{\begin{vmatrix} -\gamma\sigma\phi & -(1 - \sigma\phi) \\ -1 & 0 \end{vmatrix}}{|\Delta|} = -\frac{1}{\sigma} < 0, \tag{A4.17}$$

$$\frac{dp(\infty)}{d\bar{y}} = \frac{\begin{vmatrix} \lambda(1 - \sigma\phi) + \gamma\sigma & -\gamma\sigma\phi \\ \sigma & -1 \end{vmatrix}}{|\Delta|} = -\frac{\lambda + \gamma\sigma}{\sigma} < 0. \tag{A4.18}$$

It follows from (A4.17)–(A4.18) that both R_L and p fall in the long run, i.e. in Figure A4.13 the vertical shift in the $\dot{p} = 0$ line dominates that in the $\dot{R}_L = 0$ line and E_1 lies south-west from E_0. At impact the price level is predetermined and the economy jumps from E_0 to point A directly below it. Thereafter, the economy moves gradually along the new saddle path, SP_1, from A to the new steady-state equilibrium at E_1. Both R_L and p move monotonically towards their new steady-state levels.

In Figure A4.14 we present the impulse-response diagram for the different variables. To deduce the path for the short-term interest rate we use IS-LM style diagram of Figure A4.15. The IS curve is obtained by substituting (A4.11) into (A4.8). After some manipulation we obtain:

$$y = -\sigma[R_L - \dot{p}] + g = -\sigma \left(\frac{R_L + \phi(\bar{y} - g)}{1 - \sigma\phi} \right) + g$$

$$= \frac{-\sigma(R_L + \phi\bar{y}) + g}{1 - \sigma\phi}. \tag{A4.19}$$

The increase in $\bar{y}$ leads to a fall in R_L so it is not a priori clear whether output will fall or rise at impact. The reasonable case appears to be that the real interest falls and output rises at impact. (It may be possible to prove this result by more formal means, i.e. by explicitly computing the impact jump.) In this case the IS curve shifts to the right in Figure A4.15, from IS_0 to IS_1. Since the position of the LM curve is given at impact, the economy moves from E_0 to A immediately, and both output and the short-term interest rate increase. Over time the IS curve continues to shift to the right and the LM shifts down. The long-run equilibrium is at E_1 where output is equal to its new full employment level and the nominal interest rate equals the new equilibrium long-term rate of interest.

Question 3: Leaning against the wind

(a) Equation (Q4.5) is the IS-curve for the open economy. Equation (Q4.6) is the LM-curve. Equation (Q4.7) is the price adjustment rule. Equation (Q4.8) is

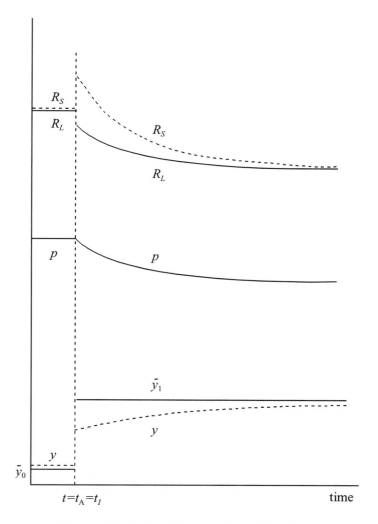

Figure A4.14: Impulse-response functions

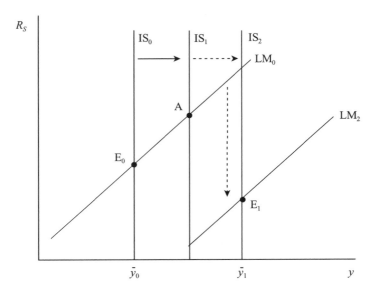

Figure A4.15: IS-LM effects following a technology improvement

the uncovered interest parity condition. The novel aspect of the model is in equation (Q4.9). There we postulate that the policy maker adjusts the money supply in the light of the exchange rate situation. Consider first the case of $\mu > 0$. If $e > \bar{e}$, then the domestic currency is undervalued relative to its equilibrium level (recall that the dimension of e is domestic currency per unit of foreign currency so a high value for e is a low value for the domestic currency). The policy maker cuts back the money supply (relative to its normal level, $\bar{m}$). With flexible exchange rates this means that the domestic currency appreciates somewhat, i.e. e becomes lower than it would have been without monetary adjustment (LM curve to the left, net capital inflows, excess demand for domestic currency, appreciation of the domestic currency, IS to the left). It is called 'leaning against the wind' because the monetary response moves the exchange rate in the direction of the equilibrium exchange rate.

In the opposite case, with $\mu < 0$, the policy maker engages in 'leaning with the wind.' In response to an undervalued currency ($e > \bar{e}$) the money supply is increased so that the currency moves further away from its equilibrium level (LM to the right, net capital outflows, excess supply of domestic currency, depreciation of the domestic currency, IS to the right).

In equation (Q4.9) it is assumed that $\bar{m}$ is an exogenously given component of money supply. Monetary policy in this model consists of a change in $\bar{m}$. The endogenous variables in the model are y, R, m, p, e, and $\bar{e}$. The exogenous variables are p^*, $\bar{y}$, R^*, and $\bar{m}$.

(b) In the steady state $\dot{p} = 0$ and $\dot{e} = 0$. This implies that output is at its natural (exogenous level) $y = \bar{y}$, the interest rate equals the world interest rate $R = R^*$ and the money supply is at the 'natural' level $m = \bar{m}$. Using this in the LM-equation (Q4.6) we find:

$$\bar{p} = \bar{m} - \bar{y} + \lambda R^* \tag{A4.20}$$

Substitution into the steady-state version of the IS-curve (Q4.5) gives for the equilibrium exchange rate:

$$
\begin{aligned}
\bar{y} &= -\eta R^* + \delta \left[\bar{e} + p^* - (\bar{m} - \bar{y} + \lambda R^*) \right] &\Leftrightarrow \\
\delta \bar{e} &= (1 - \delta)\bar{y} + (\eta + \lambda \delta) R^* + \delta(\bar{m} - p^*) &\Leftrightarrow \\
\bar{e} &= \bar{m} - p^* + \frac{1 - \delta}{\delta}\bar{y} + \frac{\eta + \lambda \delta}{\delta}R^*.
\end{aligned}
\tag{A4.21}
$$

In more convenient matrix notation we have:

$$
\begin{bmatrix} \bar{p} \\ \bar{e} \end{bmatrix} = \begin{bmatrix} 1 & \lambda & -1 & 0 \\ 1 & \frac{\eta + \lambda \delta}{\delta} & \frac{1-\delta}{\delta} & -1 \end{bmatrix} \begin{bmatrix} \bar{m} \\ R^* \\ \bar{y} \\ p^* \end{bmatrix}.
\tag{A4.22}
$$

Note that the steady-state levels $\bar{p}$ and $\bar{e}$ are fully determined by the exogenous variables and parameters of the model. Furthermore, foreign prices p^* have no direct influence on the domestic price level p, only on the steady-state exchange rate e (as would be expected).

(c) Equations (Q4.7) and (Q4.8) give (in matrix format):

$$
\begin{bmatrix} \dot{p} \\ \dot{e} \end{bmatrix} = \begin{bmatrix} \phi & 0 \\ 0 & 1 \end{bmatrix} \begin{bmatrix} y - \bar{y} \\ R - R^* \end{bmatrix}
\tag{A4.23}
$$

By subtracting the steady-state version of (Q4.5) from (Q4.5) we find: $y - \bar{y} = -\eta[R - R^*] + \delta[e - \bar{e}] - \delta[p - \bar{p}]$. Similarly, by subtracting the steady-state version of (Q4.6) from (Q4.6) and using (Q4.9) we find: $-\mu[e - \bar{e}] - [p - \bar{p}] = [y - \bar{y}] - \lambda[R - R^*]$. To simplify notation write these two equations in matrix format:

$$
\underbrace{\begin{bmatrix} 1 & \eta \\ 1 & -\lambda \end{bmatrix}}_{\equiv A} \begin{bmatrix} y - \bar{y} \\ R - R^* \end{bmatrix} = \underbrace{\begin{bmatrix} -\delta & \delta \\ -1 & -\mu \end{bmatrix}}_{\equiv B} \begin{bmatrix} p - \bar{p} \\ e - \bar{e} \end{bmatrix}
$$

Pre-multiply both sides by A^{-1} and we have:

$$
\begin{bmatrix} y - \bar{y} \\ R - R^* \end{bmatrix} = \frac{1}{\lambda + \eta} \begin{bmatrix} -[\eta + \delta \lambda] & \delta \lambda - \eta \mu \\ 1 - \delta & \delta + \mu \end{bmatrix} \begin{bmatrix} p - \bar{p} \\ e - \bar{e} \end{bmatrix}.
\tag{A4.24}
$$

Substitution of equation (A4.24) into (A4.23) gives the required result:

$$
\begin{aligned}
\begin{bmatrix} \dot{p} \\ \dot{e} \end{bmatrix} &= \frac{1}{\lambda + \eta} \begin{bmatrix} \phi & 0 \\ 0 & 1 \end{bmatrix} \begin{bmatrix} -[\eta + \delta \lambda] & \delta \lambda - \eta \mu \\ 1 - \delta & \delta + \mu \end{bmatrix} \begin{bmatrix} p - \bar{p} \\ e - \bar{e} \end{bmatrix} \\
&= \underbrace{\frac{1}{\lambda + \eta} \begin{bmatrix} -\phi[\eta + \delta \lambda] & \phi[\delta \lambda - \eta \mu] \\ 1 - \delta & \delta + \mu \end{bmatrix}}_{\equiv \Delta} \begin{bmatrix} p - \bar{p} \\ e - \bar{e} \end{bmatrix}.
\end{aligned}
\tag{A4.25}
$$

Denote the elements of Δ by δ_{ij}.

(d) The system (A4.25) is saddle-point stable if it has one negative (stable) eigenvalue and one positive (unstable) eigenvalue. The determinant of a matrix is the product of its eigenvalues, so the system is saddle-point stable if and only if its determinant is negative.

$$\det(\Delta) = -\frac{\phi}{(\eta + \lambda)^2} \left[(\eta + \delta\lambda)(\delta + \mu) + (1 - \delta)(\delta\lambda - \eta\mu) \right]$$
$$= -\frac{\delta(1 + \mu)\phi}{\eta + \lambda}$$

which is negative (given the restrictions on the parameters) if and only if $\mu + 1 > 0$.

(e) Setting $\dot{p} = 0$ and $\dot{e} = 0$ gives the two lines in (e, p)-space:

$$\dot{p} = 0: \quad [e - \bar{e}] = -\frac{\delta_{11}}{\delta_{12}}[p - \bar{p}] = -\frac{\eta + \delta\lambda}{\eta\mu - \delta\lambda}[p - \bar{p}]$$

$$\dot{e} = 0: \quad [e - \bar{e}] = -\frac{\delta_{21}}{\delta_{22}}[p - \bar{p}] = -\frac{1 - \delta}{\delta + \mu}[p - \bar{p}]$$

Both are downward sloping if $\eta\mu > \lambda\delta$. Differentiation of (A4.25) gives the stability characteristics:

$$\frac{\partial \dot{p}}{\partial p} = -\frac{\phi[\eta + \delta\lambda]}{\lambda + \eta} < 0, \qquad \frac{\partial \dot{e}}{\partial e} = \frac{\delta + \mu}{\lambda + \eta} > 0,$$

p is the stable (predetermined) variable, e is unstable (jumping) variable.

Finally we have to determine which line is steeper, the $\dot{p} = 0$ line or the $\dot{e} = 0$ line. Simple math gives:

$$\frac{\eta + \delta\lambda}{\eta\mu - \delta\lambda} - \frac{1 - \delta}{\delta + \mu} > 0 \quad \Leftrightarrow \quad \delta(\lambda + \eta)(1 + \mu) > 0$$

For $1 + \mu > 0$ the $\dot{p} = 0$ line is steeper. Finally we have all the information to draw the phase diagram and derive the saddle path. As can be seen from the arrows in Figure A4.16 there is one downward sloping saddle path.

(f) First we derive the phase diagram for this specific case under the old foreign price level. For $\eta\mu = \lambda\delta$ the dynamic system collapses to

$$\begin{bmatrix} \dot{p} \\ \dot{e} \end{bmatrix} = \frac{1}{\lambda + \eta} \begin{bmatrix} -\phi[\eta + \delta\lambda] & 0 \\ 1 - \delta & \delta + \mu \end{bmatrix} \begin{bmatrix} p - \bar{p} \\ e - \bar{e} \end{bmatrix}, \tag{A4.26}$$

that is, the deviation of the exchange rate from the steady state has no impact on the change of the price level. This is because the output gap $(y - \bar{y})$ has no impact on $\dot{p}$ as can be seen from equation (A4.24). As a result, the $\dot{p} = 0$ line is vertical.

Next, we have to analyse what happens to the positions of the $\dot{p} = 0$ and $\dot{e} = 0$ lines if the foreign price level increases. An exogenous shock has an impact on the steady-state values. The steady-state values are determined in equation (A4.22). As can be seen from this equation, an increase of the foreign price level

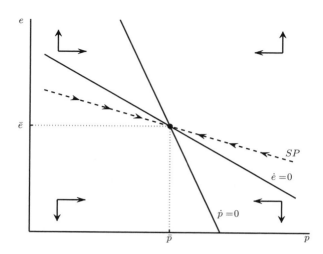

Figure A4.16: Saddle-point stability in the Turnovsky model

p^* has no impact on the steady-state value $\bar{p}$, but decreases $\bar{e}$. This means that the $\dot{p} = 0$ line stays where it is, but the $\dot{e} = 0$ line shifts downward and to the left. At the time of the shock, the exchange rate jumps to its new steady-state level $\bar{e}_1$ and the (sticky) prices stay at the original steady-state price level $\bar{p}$. See Figure A4.17 for a phase diagram.

Question 4: The term structure of interest rates

(a) The fundamental price of a perpetuity in the current period ($P_B(0)$) is equal to the present value of the coupon payments, using $R_L(0)$ for discounting:

$$P_B(0) \equiv \int_0^\infty 1 \cdot e^{-R_L(0)t} dt = -\frac{1}{R_L(0)} \left[e^{-R_L(0)t} \right]_0^\infty = \frac{1}{R_L(0)}. \qquad \text{(A4.27)}$$

Hence, the price of a perpetuity is the inverse of the yield on the perpetuity. The rate of return on investing in a perpetuity is equal to the coupon payment plus the capital gain, expressed in terms of the market value of the perpetuity:

$$\frac{1 + \dot{P}_B}{P_B} = \frac{1 - \frac{1}{R_L^2}\dot{R}_L}{\frac{1}{R_L}} = R_L - \frac{\dot{R}_L}{R_L}. \qquad \text{(A4.28)}$$

The rate of return on very short-term bonds (which do not carry a capital gain or loss) is equal to R_S. Since the two investment instruments are interchangeable as far as the investors are concerned, arbitrage will ensure that the rate of return on the two assets will be the same:

$$R_S = R_L - \frac{\dot{R}_L}{R_L}. \qquad \text{(A4.29)}$$

Equation (A4.29) represents the efficient term structure of interest rates. In general we can write the market price of perpetuities in period t as:

$$P_B(t) \equiv \frac{1}{R_L(t)} = \int_t^\infty \exp\left[-\int_t^\tau R_S(\mu)d\mu \right] d\tau. \qquad \text{(A4.30)}$$

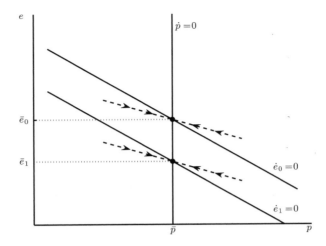

Figure A4.17: An increase of p^* with $\eta\mu = \lambda\delta$

Equation (A4.30) says that under an efficient term structure of interest rates, P_B consists of a stream of short-term interest rates.

If you really want to know, equation (A4.30) is derived as follows. First we note from (A4.28)–(A4.29) that P_B obeys the following linear differential equation.

$$\dot{P}_B = R_S P_B - 1. \tag{A4.31}$$

We define the following *integrating term*:

$$\Delta(t,\tau) \equiv \int_t^\tau R_S(\mu)d\mu. \tag{A4.32}$$

It follows from (A4.32) that $d\Delta(t,\tau)/d\tau = R_S(\tau)$. By multiplying both sides of (A4.31) by $e^{-\Delta(t,\tau)}$ we find:

$$e^{-\Delta(t,\tau)}\left[\dot{P}_B - R_S P_B\right] = -1 \times e^{-\Delta(t,\tau)} \quad \Leftrightarrow$$

$$\frac{d}{d\tau}\left[e^{-\Delta(t,\tau)}P_B\right] = -1 \times e^{-\Delta(t,\tau)} \quad \Leftrightarrow$$

$$d\left[e^{-\Delta(t,\tau)}P_B\right] = -1 \times e^{-\Delta(t,\tau)}d\tau. \tag{A4.33}$$

Integrating both sides of (A4.33) from t to ∞ we obtain:

$$\lim_{\tau \to \infty} e^{-\Delta(t,\tau)}P_B(\tau) - P_B(t) = -\int_t^\infty 1 \cdot e^{-\Delta(t,\tau)}d\tau. \tag{A4.34}$$

The first term on the left-hand side of (A4.34) equals zero by the NPG condition (see Intermezzo 2.2 on the cost of capital in Chapter 2). The remaining expression is identical to (A4.30).

(b) Formally, parts (b) and (c) of the question can be answered by using (A4.30). Fortunately, there is also a much easier graphical method by which these questions can be answered. By rewriting (A4.29) somewhat we obtain the following

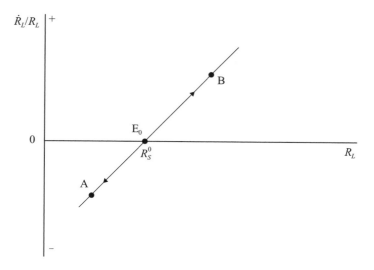

Figure A4.18: Efficient term structure of interest rates

(nonlinear) differential equation for R_L:

$$\frac{\dot{R}_L}{R_L} = R_L - R_S. \tag{A4.35}$$

In Figure A4.18 we characterize the dynamics of the long-term interest rate with the phase diagram. On the vertical axis we place $\dot{R}_L/R_L$ and on the horizontal axis we place R_L. Equation (A4.35) is a linear upward sloping schedule relating $\dot{R}_L/R_L$ to the difference between R_L and R_S. For points to the right (left) of this line, R_L exceeds (falls short of) R_S and $\dot{R}_L/R_L$ is positive (negative). We have indicated these dynamical forces with arrows in Figure A4.18. We reach the conclusion that the differential equation is *unstable*.

As is explained in the text, the instability of the differential equation is not a problem because R_L (or, alternatively, P_B) is an asset price which can jump at any instance of time. It is clear from Figure A4.18 that points like A and B are not equilibria. The only equilibrium point is point E_0, where the long-term interest rate equals the given short-term rate, i.e. $R_L = R_S^0$. Note that if the differential equation were stable, then all values for R_L would qualify as equilibrium points (because they would all eventually reach E_0) so the price of perpetuities would be indeterminate. Hence, the instability of (A4.35) is a desirable feature because it pins down a unique long-term interest rate and thus a unique market price of perpetuities.

In the question we postulate the following shock:

$$R_S = \begin{cases} R_S^0 & \text{for } t_A \leq t < t_I \\ R_S^1 & \text{for } t \geq t_I \end{cases}$$

where t_A is the announcement time and t_I the implementation time. We use the *intuitive solution principle* (mentioned in section 4.1.2.1 of the text).

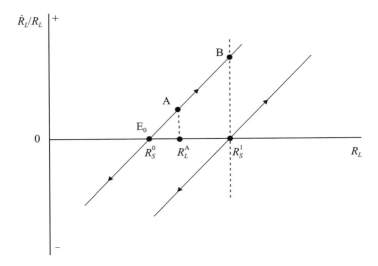

Figure A4.19: An anticipated increase in the short-term interest rate

- A jump in R_L (and thus in P_B) can only occur at the time the news about the shock reaches the agents, i.e. for $t = t_A$ (otherwise there would be anticipated infinitely large capital gains/losses, which cannot be a market equilibrium).

- Between announcement and implementation, $t_A \leq t < t_I$, the *old* equilibrium, E_0, determines the dynamic adjustment.

- At time $t = t_I$, the long-term interest rate (and thus the price of perpetuities) must reach its new equilibrium value in a continuous fashion, i.e. without having to jump discretely.

In Figure A4.19 we illustrate the adjustment path that is uniquely determined by the intuitive solution principle. Working backwards in time, we find that the economy must be in point B at time $t = t_I$. At that time the short term interest rate increases and $R_L = R_S^1$ is the new equilibrium long-term interest rate. For $t_A < t < t_I$ the economy must be on the trajectory associated with the old equilibrium. Finally, for $t = t_A$ the economy must jump to some point (say A) which is such that the path from A to B is covered in exactly the right amount of time.

We show the impulse-response diagram in Figure A4.20. Before the news about the shock was received, the short-term and long-term interest rates were the same and equal to R_S^0. At time t_A, the long-term rate jumps up (to point A) even though nothing has happened yet to the short-term rate. Between t_A and t_I, the long-term rate gradually rises until it reaches the new short-term rate R_S^1 exactly at time t_I (see point B). Thereafter, the short-term and long-term interest rates are the same again.

(c) Now assume that some time during transition it becomes clear that the interest rate will not in fact increase at time t_I at all but will stay constant. This is, in

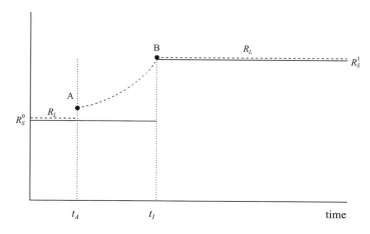

Figure A4.20: Impulse-response diagram

itself, *new information*. The only equilibrium that is possible is that the long-term interest rate will jump instantaneously to its old equilibrium value R_S^0. This jump does not violate the intuitive solution principle because the fact that the interest rate increase does not take place is an unanticipated shock itself.

Question 5: Fiscal policy with fixed nominal wages and perfect foresight

(a) Equations (Q4.10)-(Q4.11) are the marginal productivity conditions chosen by perfectly competitive firms not hindered by adjustment costs for investment. Equation (Q4.12) is the production function, and (Q4.13) is the money market equilibrium condition, equating the real supply of money (left-hand side) to the real demand for money (right-hand side). The money demand function has the usual features and includes a wealth effect (as in the Blinder-Solow model). Equation (Q4.14) is the consumption function. Apart from disposable income and wealth, consumption depends negatively on the real interest rate. Implicitly, saving is assumed to depend positively on the real interest rate. Equation (Q4.15) defines total financial wealth as the sum of real money balances and (claims on) the capital stock. Since there are no adjustment costs for investment, Tobin's q is equal to unity so that K also represents the value of the capital stock. Equation (Q4.16) is the government budget constraint. There are no bonds and the money supply is constant. Equation (Q4.17) shows that net capital accumulation equals the difference between net production, $Y - \delta K$, and total consumption by the private and public sectors, $C + G$. It is a closed economy, so there are no imports or exports. Last but not least, equation (Q4.18) shows that agents are blessed with perfect foresight, i.e. the expected inflation rate (left-hand side) is equal to the actual inflation rate (right-hand side).

(b) Since technology features constant returns to scale, the marginal products of labour and capital depend only on the capital intensity, $\kappa \equiv K/L$. (We also know that $F_{KL} > 0$ in the two-factor case.) From (Q4.11) we find that $\bar{W} =$

$PF_L(\kappa, 1)$. Totally differentiating this expression (and setting $d\bar{W} = 0$) we find that:

$$\frac{d\kappa}{dP} = -\frac{F_L(\kappa, 1)}{PF_{KL}(\kappa, 1)} < 0, \tag{A4.36}$$

i.e. and increase in P results in a decrease in the capital intensity of production. Write the implicit relationship as $\kappa = \phi(P)$.

But, using (Q4.11), output can be written as $Y = K \cdot F(1, 1/\kappa) = K \cdot F(1, 1/\phi(P))$. So we find that $\Phi(P) \equiv F(1, 1/\phi(P))$, with:

$$\Phi'(P) \equiv -F_L(1, 1/\phi(P)) \cdot \frac{\phi'(P)}{\phi(P)^2} > 0.$$

Finally, we can write (Q4.10) as $r + \delta = F_K(\kappa, 1) = F_K(\phi(\kappa), 1)$. Hence, $\Psi(P) \equiv F_K(\phi(\kappa), 1)$ with $\Psi'(P) = F_{KK}(\phi(\kappa), 1) \cdot \phi'(P) > 0$.

(c) By substituting (Q4.14)-(Q4.16) in (Q4.17) and noting $Y = \Phi(P)K$ and $r = \Psi(P) - \delta$ we find the differential equation for K:

$$\dot{K} = \Phi(P)K - C\left(\Phi(P)K - G, \Psi(P) - \delta, K + \frac{\bar{M}}{P}\right) - G - \delta K. \tag{A4.37}$$

Similarly, equation (Q4.13) can written as:

$$\frac{\bar{M}}{P} = L\left(\Phi(P)K, \Psi(P) - \delta + \pi^e, K + \frac{\bar{M}}{P}\right). \tag{A4.38}$$

But (A4.38) gives rise to an implicit function relating the expected inflation rate, π^e, to the endogenous variables, P and K, and the exogenous money supply, $\bar{M}$. We write this relationship as:

$$\pi^e = \Omega(P, K, \bar{M}), \tag{A4.39}$$

with partial derivatives:

$$\Omega_P \equiv -\frac{(1 - L_A)M/P^2 + L_Y K\Phi'(P) + L_R\Psi'(P)}{L_R} \lessgtr 0, \tag{A4.40}$$

$$\Omega_K \equiv -\frac{L_Y\Phi(P) + L_A}{L_R} > 0, \tag{A4.41}$$

$$\Omega_M \equiv \frac{1 - L_A}{P \cdot L_R} < 0. \tag{A4.42}$$

Using (A4.42) in (Q4.18) we obtain the fundamental differential equation for P:

$$\frac{\dot{P}}{P} = \Omega(P, K, \bar{M}). \tag{A4.43}$$

(d) Totally differentiating (A4.37) around the steady state we find $d\dot{K} = \delta_{11}dK + \delta_{12}dP$ with:

$$\delta_{11} \equiv [1 - C_{Y-T}] \cdot \Phi(P^*) - C_A - \delta \gtrless 0,$$

$$\delta_{12} \equiv [1 - C_{Y-T}] \cdot K^* \cdot \Phi'(P^*) - C_r \cdot \Psi'(P^*) + \frac{C_A\bar{M}}{(P^*)^2} > 0,$$

where P^* and K^* are the steady-state values for P and K respectively. The sign of δ_{11} is ambiguous because. An increase in K boosts saving, but it also increases consumption due to the wealth effect and necessitates higher replacement investment.

Totally differentiating (A4.43) around the steady state we find $d\dot{P} = P^* \cdot d\Omega = P^* \cdot [\Omega_K dK + \Omega_P dP]$. So we find immediately (from (A4.40)-(A4.41)) that $\delta_{21} \equiv P^* \Omega_K > 0$ and $\delta_{22} \equiv P^* \Omega_P \lessgtr 0$.

(e) Around the steady state, the system can be written as:

$$\begin{bmatrix} \dot{K} \\ \dot{P} \end{bmatrix} = \begin{bmatrix} \delta_{11} & \delta_{12} \\ \delta_{21} & \delta_{22} \end{bmatrix} \cdot \begin{bmatrix} K - K^* \\ P - P^* \end{bmatrix}.$$

It is saddle-point stable if the determinant of the matrix on the right hand side (which we denote by Δ) is negative so that there is one positive (unstable) root and one negative (stable) root. In all cases we must have:

$$|\Delta| \equiv \delta_{11}\delta_{22} - \delta_{12}\delta_{21} < 0. \tag{A4.44}$$

This leaves us with four cases.

- Case 1: $\delta_{11} < 0$ and $\delta_{22} < 0$.
- Case 2: $\delta_{11} > 0$ and $\delta_{22} < 0$.
- Case 3: $\delta_{11} < 0$ and $\delta_{22} > 0$.
- Case 4: $\delta_{11} > 0$ and $\delta_{22} > 0$.

To draw the phase diagrams we must define the isoclines. The $\dot{K} = 0$ line takes the form:

$$\left(\frac{dP}{dK} \right)_{\dot{K}=0} = -\frac{\delta_{11}}{\delta_{12}}, \tag{A4.45}$$

whilst the $\dot{P} = 0$ locus is given by:

$$\left(\frac{dP}{dK} \right)_{\dot{P}=0} = -\frac{\delta_{21}}{\delta_{22}}. \tag{A4.46}$$

For Case 1, both lines are upward sloping but the saddle-path condition (A4.44) implies that the $\dot{P} = 0$ line is steeper:

$$\left(\frac{dP}{dK} \right)_{\dot{P}=0} > \left(\frac{dP}{dK} \right)_{\dot{K}=0} \quad \Leftrightarrow$$

$$\frac{\delta_{21}}{-\delta_{22}} > \frac{-\delta_{11}}{\delta_{12}} \quad \Leftrightarrow$$

$$\delta_{12}\delta_{21} > -\delta_{11} \cdot -\delta_{22} \quad \Leftrightarrow$$

$$0 > |\Delta|.$$

The arrow configuration confirms saddle-path stability. See Figure A4.21.

The other cases are deduced in a similar way. See Figures A4.22 to A4.24.

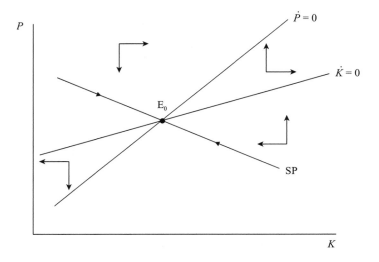

Figure A4.21: Case 1: Phase diagram

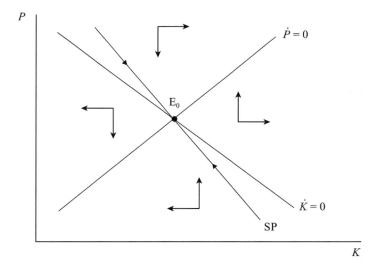

Figure A4.22: Case 2: Phase diagram

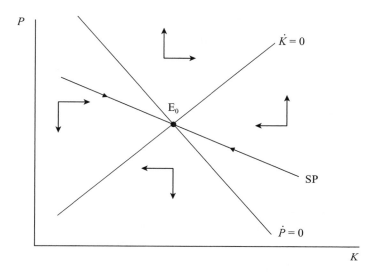

Figure A4.23: Case 3: Phase diagram

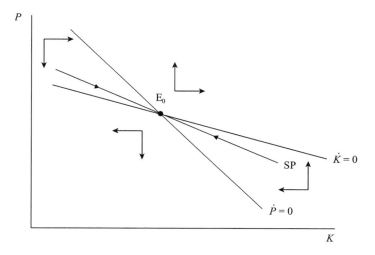

Figure A4.24: Case 4: Phase diagram

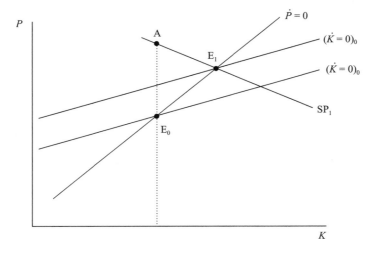

Figure A4.25: Case 1: Expansionary fiscal policy

(f) By using (A4.37) we can write $d\dot{K} = \delta_{11}dK + \delta_{12}dP - [1 - C_{Y-T}]\,dG$, so an increase in government consumption shifts up the $\dot{K} = 0$ line in all cases (because $\delta_{12} > 0$). We illustrate the transitional effects of an unanticipated and permanent increase in government consumption for Case 1 only. See Figure A4.25. At impact K is predetermined and P to the saddle path at point A. During transition, the economy moves along the saddle path from A to E_1. Fiscal policy increases the long-run price level and boosts the capital stock. The price overshoots its long-run level at impact.

The following effects are now easy to deduce:

- Also in Cases 2-4 the long-run price level increases.
- In the long-run the capital stock increases in Case 2, but decreases in Cases 3-4.
- There is price-level overshooting in Case 2, but not in Cases 3-4.

Chapter 5

The government budget deficit

Question 1: Short questions

(a) "Anticipated technological improvements will reduce the size of bequests that parents leave to their beloved offspring." True, false, or uncertain? Explain.

(b) "The Minister of Finance should not bother to engage in tax smoothing if the taxes are non-distortionary." True, false, or uncertain? Explain.

(c) "Most Europeans with a completed university education are in fact millionaires, even if they don't possess a lot of tangible assets." Defend this proposition by making use of the concept of total wealth.

(d) "A permanent reduction in government consumption must be accompanied by a reduction in the tax rates, both now and in the future." Explain and evaluate this proposition.

(e) "Ricardian equivalence does not hold if there exist distorting taxes, even if these taxes are held constant in the Ricardian experiment." Explain and evaluate this proposition.

(f) Why do people leave bequests in the overlapping-generation model? Under which two conditions would transfers flow from young to old agents? How would a pension system affect your answer?

Question 2: Tax smoothing

Use the theory of "tax smoothing" to answer the following questions.

(a) Explain what we mean by the golden rule of public finance. Explain the pros and cons of that rule.

(b) Explain how a temporary increase in government spending must be financed.

(c) Explain how a permanent increase in public spending should be financed.

(d) Use the model to demonstrate what happens to the time paths of taxes and public debt if the government consists of myopic ("short-sighted") politicians. (*Hint*: analyse the effects of a political rate of time preference, ρ_G, that is higher than the market rate of interest, r.

Question 3: The two-period model with tax smoothing

Use the two-period model of the representative household discussed extensively in the book:

$$V = U(C_1) + \frac{1}{1+\rho}U(C_2), \tag{Q5.1}$$

$$A_1 = (1 - t_1)Y_1 - C_1, \tag{Q5.2}$$

$$A_2 = (1 + r_1)A_1 + (1 - t_2)Y_2 - C_2, \tag{Q5.3}$$

where V is life-time utility, ρ is the rate of time preference, C_τ is consumption in period τ ($= 1, 2$) of the agent's life, Y_τ is the (exogenous) income in period τ, and A_τ is financial assets possessed by the household in period τ. Assume that the household borrows in the first period and pay back its debt in the second period. Assume furthermore that the periodic utility (or 'felicity') function, $U(\cdot)$, takes the following iso-elastic form:

$$U(C_\tau) \equiv \begin{cases} \frac{C_\tau^{1-1/\sigma}-1}{1-1/\sigma} & \text{for } \sigma > 0, \sigma \neq 1 \\ \ln(C_\tau) & \text{for } \sigma = 1 \end{cases} \tag{Q5.4}$$

(a) Interpret the model and derive the lifetime budget constraint. Explain what you assume about A_2.

Assume that the government only buys goods for its own consumption which it finances with the revenues from taxes or with debt. The government initially has no debt and exists, like everybody, just for two periods. The government can freely borrow or lend at the same interest rate as the households.

(b) Derive the budget identities for both periods and the intertemporal government budget constraint.

(c) Rewrite the household budget constraint using the government budget constraints and show that all tax parameters drop out of the household budget constraint.

(d) Derive the expressions for optimal consumption and savings plans (i.e. C_1, C_2, and $S_1 \equiv A_1$). Show that your expressions are the same as those in the book if and only if σ equals 1.

The government realizes that there are costs associated with tax collection. Suppose that the government minimizes the loss function L_G by setting t_1 and t_2.

$$L_G \equiv \tfrac{1}{2}t_1^2 Y_1 + \tfrac{1}{2}\frac{t_2^2 Y_2}{1+\rho_G} \tag{Q5.5}$$

(e) What is the optimal ratio of t_1 to t_2 if government expenditure is given?

(f) Use as parameter values $\sigma = 0.7$, $r_1 = 0.05$ ($= 5\%$ per period), $\rho = 0.08$, $\rho_G = 0.10$, $Y_1 = 15$, $Y_2 = 20$, $G_1 = G_2 = 4$. Solve the model for these parameter values. What is the household optimum if the government would have taxed income at 15% ($t_1 = 0.15$), or at $t_1 = 25\%$?

(g) What is the household optimum (C_1, C_2, and S_1) under the parameter values of the previous question if households cannot borrow, but are allowed to lend?

Question 4: Ricardian equivalence

Carefully explain why the Ricardian equivalence theorem is invalid if any of the following assumptions are made. (Be precise and concise and use figures if they facilitate your argument.)

(a) Labour supply is endogenous.

(b) Households have only limited access to capital markets.

(c) New generations of households are born.

(d) Households are risk averse, there is a tax on income, and future income is uncertain.

Question 5: Ricardian equivalence in the two-period model

Use the two-period model of the representative household discussed extensively in the book.

$$V = U(C_1) + \beta U(C_2), \tag{Q5.6}$$
$$A_1 = (1 + r_0)A_0 + (1 - t_1)Y_1 - C_1, \tag{Q5.7}$$
$$A_2 = (1 + r_1)A_1 + (1 - t_2)Y_2 - C_2, \tag{Q5.8}$$

where V is life-time utility, $\beta \equiv 1/(1+\rho)$ is the rate of felicity discounting due to time preference, C_τ is consumption in period τ ($= 1,2$) of the agent's life, Y_τ is the (exogenous) income in period τ, and A_τ is financial assets possessed by the household in period τ. Assume that the household saves in the first period of life in order to enjoy a pleasant retirement in the second period of life. Assume furthermore that the periodic utility (or "felicity") function, $U(\cdot)$, takes the following iso-elastic form:

$$U(C_\tau) \equiv \frac{C_\tau^{1-1/\sigma} - 1}{1 - 1/\sigma}, \qquad \sigma > 0, \sigma \neq 1. \tag{Q5.9}$$

(a) Interpret the model and derive the lifetime budget equation. Explain what you assume about A_2.

(b) Introduce the government and demonstrate Ricardian equivalence.

(c) Compute the expressions for optimal consumption and savings plans (i.e. C_1, C_2, and $S_1 \equiv A_1 - A_0$). Show that your expressions are the same as the ones in the book if and only if σ is equal to unity.

(d) Assume that there is a broad income tax (which also taxes interest income). Redo part (c). Show how consumption and saving depend on the income tax rate. Decompose the results for consumption in terms of the income effect, substitution effect, and the human wealth effect.

Answers

Question 1: Short questions

(a) True, parents leave bequest to their beloved offspring to increase their own utility (the children's utility enters the parents utility function). By leaving a bequest, the parents increase their children's utility and thus their own.

If technology improves in the future, the children's own income increases and hence their consumption. Due to decreasing marginal utility, the children value an extra unit of consumption less and the extra consumption that is made possible by the bequest has less value in utility terms. Parents will know this in advance (it is an anticipated technological improvement) and they will leave a smaller bequest to their children.

(b) False, even if taxes are non-distorting, there may be collection costs associated with tax collection, that is, a part of total production is used in the tax collection process and not available for consumption (or investment). In this setting, a policy maker will want to minimize total collection costs by smoothing taxes over time.

(c) True, their financial wealth may be low but their human wealth is typically rather high. Human wealth represents the market value of the time endowment. High skill translates into a high wage and thus high human wealth.

(d) In the positive theory of government spending and debt creation, this proposition is true. You minimize the distorting effect of taxation that way. In terms of Figure 5.5 in the textbook, the optimal point shifts from E_0^T to E_1^T and both t_1 and t_2 are cut.

(e) False, provided the distorting taxes are held constant, a Ricardian experiment which involves non-distorting taxes still leads to neutrality.

(f) People leave bequests to their offspring if they like them enough, and the offspring is not expected to be incredibly rich. There are two conditions under which transfers would flow from children to parents. First, if there is two-sided altruism in the model, i.e. if the children's utility function depends on the parents' welfare. Second, if it would be allowed by law for the parents to leave negative bequests (and the children could be somehow forced to accept this debt imposed on them by the parents). Certain pension systems induce flows of money to go from the young (workers) to the old (retirees). We study such pay-as-you-go schemes in Chapter 17.

Question 2: Tax smoothing

(a) The consolidated budget constraint of the government is given in equation (5.73) in the book:

$$[\Xi_1 \equiv] \ (1+r_0)B_0 + G_1^C + \frac{G_2^C}{1+r_1} + \frac{(r_1 - r_1^G)G_1^I}{1+r_1} = t_1 Y_1 + \frac{t_2 Y_2}{1+r_1}, \quad (A5.1)$$

where Ξ_1 is the present value of the net liabilities of the government. We immediately see the golden rule of public finance: to the extent that public investment projects earn a rate of return equal to the market rate of return (so that

$r_1^G = r_1$) they do not represent a net liability of the government. The government should borrow the funds to finance these investments. The advantage is that the government has no need to use distorting taxes in order to raise the revenues. The disadvantage are: (i) it is sensitive to political abuse (politicians will try to label government consumption items as if they are investment items); (ii) it is not easy to estimate the rate of return on public investment projects (politicians will have an incentive to overstate it). Private sector firms that continually invest in low-yielding projects will eventually go out of business. The government does not have that disciplining device.

(b) By a temporary increase in public consumption we mean the situation in which Ξ_1 is unchanged, i.e. G_1^C rises but G_2^C falls, such that the net liabilities of the government are unchanged. It is OK to leave the tax rates unchanged and to finance the temporary increase in government consumption with debt. This can be illustrated with the aid of Figure A5.1. For convenience, we assume that $r_1 = \rho_G$. In that figure the upward sloping line (labelled $t_1 = t_2$) is the tax smoothing line, whereas the solid downward sloping line is the consolidated budget constraint of the government (equation (A5.1)) rewritten in terms of output shares:

$$t_1 + \frac{1+\gamma}{1+r_1} t_2 = \xi_1, \tag{A5.2}$$

where $\xi_1 \equiv \Xi_1/Y_1$, $\gamma \equiv Y_2/Y_1 - 1$ is the growth rate in the economy, and ξ_1 is given by:

$$\xi_1 \equiv g_1^C + \frac{1+\gamma}{1+r_1} g_2^C + \frac{r_1 - r_1^G}{1+r_1} g_1^I + (1+r_0)b_0, \tag{A5.3}$$

where $g_t^C \equiv G_t^C/Y_t$, $g_1^I \equiv G_1^I/Y_1$, and $b_0 \equiv B_0/Y_1$. The deficit in period 1 can also be written in terms of output shares:

$$d_1 \equiv \frac{D_1}{Y_1} = rb_0 + g_1^C + g_1^I - t_1. \tag{A5.4}$$

The *spending point* is defined as the point where $d_1 = 0$, and is drawn as point E_0^S in Figure A5.1. The *optimal taxation point* is given by point E_0^T. A temporary increase in government consumption implies that the spending point moves *along the initial budget line* from E_0^S to E_1^S. The optimal taxation point is unaffected. Since the tax rates are not changed but spending in the first period is increased, it follow from (A5.4) that the deficit in period 1 is increased $(dd_1/dg_1^C = 1)$.

(c) A permanent increase in government spending implies that ξ_1 itself increases. In terms of Figure A5.1, the budget line shifts out. Assuming that the spending increase takes place in the second period, the spending point moves from E_0^S to E_2^S. The optimal tax point shifts from E_0^T to E_1^T so both tax rates are increased immediately (in anticipation of the higher spending in the second period).

(d) The Euler equation for the government's optimal tax plan is given by equation (5.79) in the book:

$$\frac{t_1}{t_2} = \frac{1+r_1}{1+\rho_G}. \tag{A5.5}$$

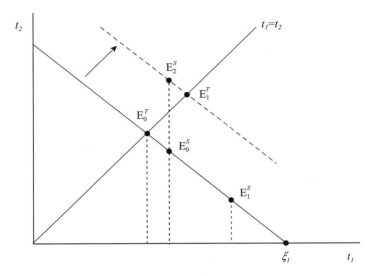

Figure A5.1: Temporary and permanent spending shocks

It follows that a short-sighted government has the tendency to postpone taxation, i.e. to set t_1 much lower than t_2. To figure out what happens to public debt we note that the deficit in period 1 is given by (A5.4) above. Since the policy maker chooses a low tax rate in the first period it runs a large deficit in that period. As a result the debt in the second period is large. Recall that $D_1 + D_2 + B_0 = 0$. By rewriting this expression in terms of income shares we get:

$$\frac{D_1}{Y_1} + \frac{D_2}{Y_2}\frac{Y_2}{Y_1} + \frac{B_0}{Y_1} = 0 \quad \Leftrightarrow \quad d_1 + (1+\gamma)d_2 + b_0 = 0 \quad \Leftrightarrow$$

$$-d_2 = \frac{d_1 + b_0}{1+\gamma}. \tag{A5.6}$$

The surplus in the second period must be large due to the myopic nature of the policy maker.

Question 3: The two-period model with tax smoothing

(a) According to (Q5.1), lifetime utility (V) is the sum of utility in the current period and weighted utility in the second period. The household discounts future utility because it exhibits time preference. Equations (Q5.2) and (Q5.3) are budget *identities*, i.e. they hold by definition. We obtain the lifetime budget *constraint* by setting $A_2 = 0$. It makes no sense for the household to die with positive assets (i.e. $A_2 \leq 0$) and capital markets will not allow the household to die indebted (i.e. $A_2 \geq 0$). Combing the two inequalities yields $A_2 = 0$ as the solvency condition. By substituting (Q5.2) into (Q5.3) and setting $A_2 = 0$ we find the household budget constraint:

$$C_1 + \frac{C_2}{1+r_1} = (1-t_1)Y_1 + \frac{(1-t_2)Y_2}{1+r_1}. \tag{A5.7}$$

(b) Government expenditures consist of government consumption G and interest payments on debt. Initially the government has no debt ($B_0 = 0$), so the government has no interest expenditures in the first period. The government has to pay all its debt before the world ends, that is, $B_2 = 0$. This gives the following two expressions:

$$D_1 \equiv G_1 - t_1 Y_1 = B_1 \tag{A5.8}$$
$$D_2 \equiv r B_1 + G_2 - t_2 Y_2 = B_2 - B_1 = -B_1. \tag{A5.9}$$

Solving the second budget identity for B_1 and substitution into the first identity gives:

$$B_1 = G_1 - t_1 Y_1 = \frac{t_2 Y_2 - G_2}{1 + r_1} \quad \Rightarrow \quad G_1 + \frac{G_2}{1 + r_1} = t_1 Y_1 + \frac{t_2 Y_2}{1 + r_1} \tag{A5.10}$$

This intertemporal budget constraint simply states that the present value of all the government's expenditures must be equal to the present value of its tax revenues.

(c) Rewrite equation (A5.7):

$$C_1 + \frac{C_2}{1 + r_1} = +Y_1 + \frac{Y_2}{1 + r} - \left(t_1 Y_1 + \frac{t_2 Y_2}{1 + r} \right)$$

and recognise that the term within brackets is exactly equal to the governments tax revenues. Now use the GBC to get

$$C_1 + \frac{C_2}{1 + r_1} = Y_1 + \frac{Y_2}{1 + r_1} - \left(G_1 + \frac{G_2}{1 + r_1} \right) \quad \Leftrightarrow \tag{A5.11}$$
$$C_1 + \frac{C_2}{1 + r_1} = Y_1 - G_1 + \frac{Y_2 - G_2}{1 + r_1} \equiv \Omega. \tag{A5.12}$$

This last equation is the household budget constraint, taking into account that the government must eventually pay all its debt. There are no tax parameters equation (A5.12), this means that the tax parameters do not enter the household optimization problem.

(d) Households maximize V by setting C_1 and C_2. The corresponding Lagrangian is

$$\mathcal{L} = U(C_1) + \frac{U(C_2)}{1 + \rho} + \lambda \left[\Omega - C_1 - \frac{C_2}{1 + r_1} \right]$$

The first order conditions are

$$\frac{\partial \mathcal{L}}{\partial C_1} = 0 : U'(C_1) = \lambda \tag{A5.13}$$
$$\frac{\partial \mathcal{L}}{\partial C_2} = 0 : \frac{U'(C_2)}{1 + \rho} = \frac{\lambda}{1 + r_1} \tag{A5.14}$$

Combining (A5.13) and (A5.14) yields the Euler equation:

$$\frac{U'(C_1)}{U'(C_2)} = \frac{1 + r_1}{1 + \rho}. \tag{A5.15}$$

Government variables		Household variables	
t_1	0.223	$(1-t_1)Y_1$	11.649
t_2	0.234	$(1-t_2)Y_2$	15.319
$t_1 Y_1$	3.351	C_1	13.568
$t_1 Y_1$	4.681	C_2	13.303
D_1	0.649	S_1	-1.920
D_2	-0.649	S_2	1.920
B_1	0.649	A_1	-1.920
B_2	0.000	A_2	0.000

Table A5.1: Solution to the 2-period representative household model

Differentiating the instantaneous utility function (Q5.4) gives $U'(C) = C^{-1/\sigma}$. Using this in the Euler equation gives:

$$\frac{C_2}{C_1} = \left[\frac{1+r_1}{1+\rho}\right]^{\sigma}. \tag{A5.16}$$

which is only equal to equation (5.15) in the textbook if $\sigma = 1$.

We now know the relation between C_1 and C_2. Substitute the Euler equation into the HBC (A5.12) and find:

$$C_2\left[\frac{1+\rho}{1+r_1}\right]^{\sigma} + \frac{C_2}{1+r_1} = \Omega \quad \Rightarrow \quad C_2 = \left(\left[\frac{1+\rho}{1+r_1}\right]^{\sigma} + \frac{1}{1+r_1}\right)^{-1}\Omega \tag{A5.17}$$

$$C_1 + \frac{[1+r_1]^{\sigma-1}}{[1+\rho]^{\sigma}}C_1 = \Omega \quad \Rightarrow \quad C_1 = \left(1 + \frac{[1+r_1]^{\sigma-1}}{[1+\rho]^{\sigma}}\right)^{-1}\Omega \tag{A5.18}$$

(e) This is exactly the problem on page 140 in the textbook! Note that the growth of the economy (γ in the textbook) cancels in the government optimum so we end up with expression (5.79) in the textbook:

$$t_2 = \frac{1+\rho_G}{1+r_1}t_1 \tag{A5.19}$$

(f) Derive the growth rates of taxes using equation (A5.19), present value of after tax income Ω (equation (A5.12)), consumption in periods 1 and 2 (equations (A5.18) and (A5.17)) and taxes in both periods (using equation (A5.10) and (A5.19)). With these variables known, it is easy to derive all other relevant variables like the government deficit in both periods, savings etc... In a program like MS-Excel this is quite easy to implement (see Table A5.1) (There is one problem: savings equilibrium. As you can see from the figures in the table, national savings are not 0. We can solve this by postulating an open economy framework. The interest rate is fixed and the rest of the world fills the savings gap.)

For households it does not matter how taxes evolve, in this basic setup, Ricardian equivalence holds.

(g) As can be seen from Table A5.1 households would like to borrow in the first period. If this is not possible, they will choose the best possible option, that is, they will consume all of their after tax income in the first period $C_1 = (1 - t_1)Y_1$. Savings are zero and second period consumption is equal to second period after tax income $C_2 = (1 - t_2)Y_2$. In Figure A5.2 households would like to consume point E_1, but are restricted to their original after-tax income endowment point E_0.

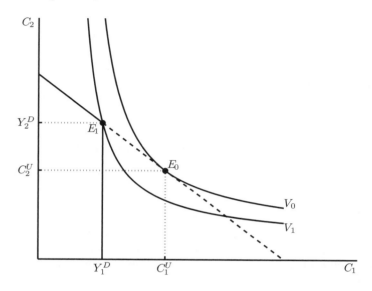

Figure A5.2: Borrowing constraints for households

Question 4: Ricardian equivalence

(a) If labour supply is endogenous then the tax rates will themselves introduce distortions. Whereas income is exogenously given in the standard case discussed in the text, with endogenous labour supply Y_1 and Y_2 will depend on the tax rates in the two periods. The Ricardian experiment (a cut in t_1 and an increase in t_2) will then affect the present value of income of the households. As a result, Ricardian equivalence will not generally hold any more. See section 5.1.2 in the book.

(b) When households have only limited access to the capital markets Ricardian equivalence will not generally hold any more. In section 5.1.3 in the text we show that a household which faces binding borrowing constraints will be unable to attain its optimal consumption point. Instead, it will choose a second-best optimal consumption plan that is restricted by income in the two periods. A tax cut in the current period moves the income-endowment point in the direction of the optimal consumption point and makes the household better off. Consumption in the two periods is affected and Ricardian equivalence does not hold.

(c) When new generations are born which are not altruistically linked with existing generations, then the future tax load will be carried by more shoulders. As a result, a tax cut now will make current generations better off and will prompt them to consume more. Ricardian equivalence will not hold. If, on the other hand, the new generations are altruistically linked with the present generations then Ricardian equivalence will hold again. The reason is that positive bequests will ensure that present and future generations are connected to each other.

(d) When households are risk averse and future income is stochastic, then they will engage in so-called *precautionary savings*. A tax cut now, matched by a tax increase later, will ensure that precautionary savings fall. The reason is that the future tax increase reduces the variance of future after-tax income. A temporary tax cut thus boosts consumption, which is inconsistent with Ricardian equivalence.

Question 5: Ricardian equivalence in the two-period model

(a) According to (Q5.6), lifetime utility (V) is the sum of felicity in the current period and weighted felicity in the second period. The household discounts future felicity because it exhibits time preference. Equations (Q5.7) and (Q5.8) are budget *identities*, i.e. they hold by definition. We obtain the lifetime budget *constraint* by setting $A_2 = 0$. It makes no sense for the household to die with positive assets (i.e. $A_2 \leq 0$) and capital markets will not allow the household to die indebted (i.e. $A_2 \geq 0$). Combing the two inequalities yields $A_2 = 0$ as the solvency condition. By substituting (Q5.7) into (Q5.8) and setting $A_2 = 0$ we find the household budget constraint:

$$C_1 + \frac{C_2}{1+r_1} = (1+r_0)A_0 + (1-t_1)Y_1 + \frac{(1-t_2)Y_2}{1+r_1} \equiv \Omega. \qquad \text{(A5.20)}$$

(b) The government budget identities are:

$$rB_0 + G_1 - t_1Y_1 = B_1 - B_0, \qquad \text{(A5.21)}$$
$$rB_1 + G_2 - t_2Y_2 = B_2 - B_1 = -B_1, \qquad \text{(A5.22)}$$

where B_τ is government debt in period τ $(= 1, 2)$. The solvency condition for the government is $B_2 = 0$. By combining (A5.21) and (A5.22) and setting $B_2 = 0$ we find the budget constraint of the government:

$$(1+r_0)B_0 + G_1 + \frac{G_2}{1+r_1} = t_1Y_1 + \frac{t_2Y_2}{1+r_1}. \qquad \text{(A5.23)}$$

Since government bonds are the only financial asset in this economy, $A_\tau = B_\tau$. By using this in (A5.20) and (A5.23) we find:

$$(1+r_0)A_0 = C_1 + \frac{C_2}{1+r_1} - \left[(1-t_1)Y_1 + \frac{(1-t_2)Y_2}{1+r_1}\right]$$
$$= t_1Y_1 + \frac{t_2Y_2}{1+r_1} - \left[G_1 + \frac{G_2}{1+r_1}\right], \qquad \text{(A5.24)}$$

or:

$$C_1 + \frac{C_2}{1+r} = Y_1 - G_1 + \frac{Y_2 - G_2}{1+r}. \tag{A5.25}$$

The tax parameters drop out of the rewritten household budget constraint. The path of taxes does not matter for the real equilibrium in the economy.

(c) The Lagrangian associated with the optimization problem is:

$$\mathcal{L} \equiv \frac{C_1^{1-1/\sigma} - 1}{1 - 1/\sigma} + \frac{1}{1+\rho} \frac{C_2^{1-1/\sigma} - 1}{1 - 1/\sigma} + \lambda \left[\Omega - C_1 - \frac{C_2}{1+r} \right]. \tag{A5.26}$$

The first-order conditions are the budget constraint (A5.20) and:

$$\frac{\partial \mathcal{L}}{\partial C_1} = C_1^{-1/\sigma} - \lambda = 0, \tag{A5.27}$$

$$\frac{\partial \mathcal{L}}{\partial C_2} = \beta C_2^{-1/\sigma} - \frac{\lambda}{1+r_1} = 0. \tag{A5.28}$$

By combining (A5.27)-(A5.28), the so-called consumption Euler equation is obtained:

$$\lambda = C_1^{-1/\sigma} = \beta(1+r_1)C_2^{-1/\sigma} \quad \Rightarrow \quad \left(\frac{C_2}{C_1} \right)^{1/\sigma} = \beta(1+r_1) \quad \Rightarrow$$

$$\frac{C_2}{C_1} = [\beta(1+r_1)]^{\sigma}. \tag{A5.29}$$

Note that (A5.29) is the same as equation (5.15) in the book if $\sigma = 1$ (recall that $\beta \equiv 1/(1+\rho)$).

Next we find the levels of C_1 and C_2 by combining (A5.29) and the budget constraint (A5.20). We obtain:

$$C_1 + \frac{[\beta(1+r_1)]^{\sigma} C_1}{1+r_1} = \Omega$$

$$C_1 \left[1 + \beta^{\sigma}(1+r_1)^{\sigma-1} \right] = \Omega$$

$$C_1 = \frac{\Omega}{1 + \beta^{\sigma}(1+r_1)^{\sigma-1}}. \tag{A5.30}$$

It follows from (A5.30) and (A5.29) that C_2 is:

$$C_2 = [\beta(1+r_1)]^{\sigma} C_1 = \frac{[\beta(1+r_1)]^{\sigma} \Omega}{1 + \beta^{\sigma}(1+r_1)^{\sigma-1}}. \tag{A5.31}$$

If $\sigma = 1$, then (A5.30) and (A5.31) coincide with the expressions found in equation (5.16) in the book.

Finally, by noting that $S_1 \equiv A_1 - A_0$ we find:

$$S_1 = A_1 - A_0 = r_0 A_0 + (1 - t_1)Y_1 - C_1$$

$$= r_0 A_0 + (1 - t_1)Y_1 - \frac{\Omega}{1 + \beta^{\sigma}(1+r_1)^{\sigma-1}}$$

$$= r_0 A_0 + \frac{\beta^{\sigma}(1+r_1)^{\sigma-1} \cdot (1 - t_1)Y_1 - \left[(1+r_0) A_0 + (1 - t_2)\frac{Y_2}{1+r_1} \right]}{1 + \beta^{\sigma}(1+r_1)^{\sigma-1}},$$

$$\tag{A5.32}$$

where we have used the definition of Ω in the final step.

(d) If interest income is taxed, then the household budget constraint becomes:

$$C_1 + \frac{C_2}{1+r^*} = [1 + r(1-t_1)] A_0 + (1-t_1)Y_1 + \frac{(1-t_2)Y_2}{1+r^*} \equiv \Omega^*, \quad \text{(A5.33)}$$

where $r^* \equiv r_1(1-t_2)$. Retracing the steps performed in part (c) we find:

$$C_1 = \frac{\Omega^*}{1 + \beta^\sigma (1+r^*)^{\sigma-1}}, \quad \text{(A5.34)}$$

$$C_2 = \frac{[\beta(1+r^*)]^\sigma \, \Omega^*}{1 + \beta^\sigma (1+r^*)^{\sigma-1}}. \quad \text{(A5.35)}$$

The effects of taxes in the two periods are as follows. The effect of t_1 operates only via household wealth and leaves the intertemporal trade-off between C_1 and C_2 unchanged:

$$\frac{\partial \Omega^*}{\partial t_1} = -(r_0 A_0 + Y_1) < 0. \quad \text{(A5.36)}$$

In terms of Figure A5.3, the lifetime budget constraint shifts inward in a parallel fashion. If the initial equilibrium is at E_0 (where lifetime utility is V_0), after the tax increase the new equilibrium will be at E_1 (where lifetime utility is lower). The straight line from the origin, labelled EE, is the Euler equation:

$$\frac{C_2}{C_1} = \beta^\sigma [1 + r_1(1-t_2)]^\sigma. \quad \text{(A5.37)}$$

Since t_1 does not affect the intertemporal trade-off between C_1 and C_2, E_0 and E_1 lie on the same EE line. The move from E_0 to E_1 only causes an income effect (IE).

An increase in the tax rate in the second period has more complicated effects. First, it follows from the definition of r^* that the after-tax interest rate falls:

$$\frac{\partial r^*}{\partial t_2} = -r_1 < 0. \quad \text{(A5.38)}$$

Second, it follows from the definition of Ω^* in (A5.33) that wealth falls:

$$\frac{\partial \Omega^*}{\partial t_2} = Y_2 \frac{-(1+r^*) + r_1(1-t_2)}{(1+r^*)^2} = -\frac{Y_2}{(1+r^*)^2} < 0. \quad \text{(A5.39)}$$

In terms of Figure A5.4, the equilibrium shifts from E_0 to E_1. We can decompose the total effect into the income effect (IE), the substitution effect (SE), and the human wealth effect (HWE). The decrease in the after-tax interest rate, given by (A5.38), is represented by the counter-clockwise rotation of the budget line from its initial position to the dashed line aa. The decrease in wealth, as given in (A5.39), is represented by the parallel shift of the aa line to the bb line. In order to discover the pure substitution effect we draw the auxiliary line cc, which is parallel to both aa and bb, in order to find the tangency point E' along the old indifference curve, V_0.

The total effect can now be decomposed as follows:

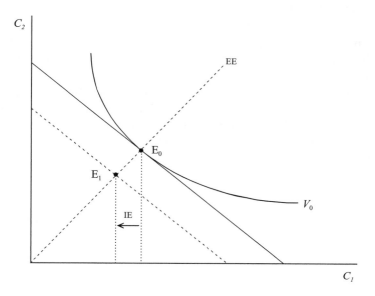

Figure A5.3: Increase in current tax rate

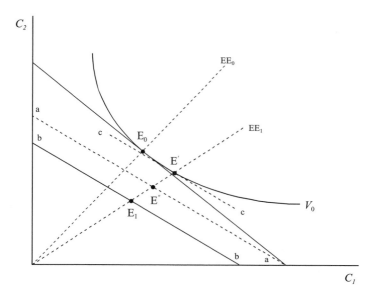

Figure A5.4: Increase in future tax rate

- The substitution effect (SE) is represented by the move from E_0 to E'. The decrease in the after-tax interest rate causes an increase in consumption in the first period and a decrease in future consumption.

- The income effect (IE) is represented by the move from E' to E''. Since the household is poorer as a result of the tax increase, less of both goods is consumed.

- The human wealth effect (HWE) is represented by the move from E'' to E_1. Though future income is discounted less heavily (because r^* falls) the reduction in after-tax future income dominates this discounting effect (see (A5.39)). Because the household is poorer, consumption of both goods is decreased.

Chapter 6

A closer look at the labour market

Question 1: Short questions

(a) Explain in general terms how the theory of efficiency wages can explain relatively high youth unemployment.

(b) "An increase in the minimum wage leads to an increase in the unemployment rate experienced by unskilled workers and an increase in the real wage received by skilled workers." Explain and evaluate this proposition.

Question 2: Two-sector model with a skill-biased productivity shock

Consider the two-sector labour market model discussed in section 6.2.1 in the text. Assume, however, that the production function facing the representative firm is given by:

$$Y = G\left(N_U, Z_S N_S, \bar{K}\right) \equiv F\left(N_U, Z_S N_S\right), \qquad (Q6.1)$$

where $G\left(\cdot\right)$ features constant returns to scale in the three production factors (skilled and unskilled labour and capital), and $F\left(\cdot\right)$ features diminishing returns to scale because $\bar{K}$ is held fixed in the short run. We assume that $F_{SU} < 0$. The term Z_S is an exogenous productivity term, representing the labour efficiency of skilled workers. The rest of the model is unchanged. Supplies of the two labour types is exogenous:

$$N_S^S = \bar{N}_S, \qquad N_U^S = \bar{N}_U. \qquad (Q6.2)$$

(a) Derive expressions for the competitive demands for the two types of labour.

(b) Explain how an exogenous increase in Z_S affects the labour market if there is no minimum wage and wages are perfectly flexible. Explain your answer in a two-panel diagram such as Figure 6.3 in the text.

(c) Redo part (b) for the case in which the minimum wage, $\bar{w}$, is initially binding in the market for unskilled labour only. Explain your answer in a two-panel diagram such as Figure 6.3 in the text.

Question 3: Progressive taxation

In Chapter 1 we took an informal look at the way in which the representative household chooses its optimal supply of labour. In this question we look more precisely at this matter. In particular, we focus on the interaction between a progressive tax system and the labour supply decision. The representative household has a utility function which depends on consumption, C, and leisure, $1 - N$, according to:

$$U = U(C, 1 - N), \tag{Q6.3}$$

where the time endowment is unity and where N is labour supply. We assume that the utility function is homothetic. The budget restriction is as usual:

$$C = WN - T, \tag{Q6.4}$$

where T is the amount of tax paid by the household, and we set the price equal to $P = 1$. Tax payments are assumed to depend on wage income according to:

$$T = t_M WN - \theta, \quad \theta > 0, \quad 0 < t_M < 1. \tag{Q6.5}$$

According to (Q6.5), the household receives θ from the government (regardless of whether it works or not) but must pay taxes over its wage income equal to $t_M WN$.

(a) Compute the average tax rate, $t_A \equiv T/(WN)$, and the marginal tax rate, $dT/d(WN)$. Show that the tax system is indeed a progressive one.

(b) Show that at the optimal point, the marginal rate of substitution between leisure and consumption can be written as follows:

$$\frac{U_{1-N}}{U_C} = W(1 - t_M). \tag{Q6.6}$$

Explain intuitively why the *marginal* (rather than the *average*) tax rate features in this expression.

The substitution elasticity between consumption and leisure is formally defined as follows:

$$\sigma_{CM} = \frac{\%\text{ge change in } \Delta C/(1-N)}{\%\text{ge change in } U_{1-N}/U_C} \equiv \frac{d \ln(C/(1-N))}{d \ln(U_{1-N}/U_C)} > 0. \tag{Q6.7}$$

This coefficient measures the degree of substitutability between consumption and leisure in the utility function. If σ_{CM} is very high then substitution is quite easy, whereas substitution is difficult if σ_{CM} is low.

(c) Draw the indifference curves for the following three cases: $\sigma_{CM} = 0$, $\sigma_{CM} = 1$, and $\sigma_{CM} \to \infty$.

(d) Show that the two first-order conditions for utility maximization can be loglinearized as follows:

$$\tilde{C} + \left[\frac{N}{1-N}\right] \tilde{N} = \sigma_{CM}[\tilde{W} - \tilde{t}_M],$$

$$\tilde{C} = \tilde{W} - \tilde{t}_A + \tilde{N},$$

where $\tilde{C} \equiv dC/C$, $\tilde{N} \equiv dN/N$, $\tilde{W} \equiv dW/W$, $\tilde{t}_M \equiv dt_M/[1 - t_M]$, and $\tilde{t}_A \equiv dt_A/[1 - t_A]$. Derive the loglinearized expressions for labour supply and consumption.

(e) Show (for the two cases $\sigma_{CM} = 0$ and $\sigma_{CM} = 1$) what happens to consumption and labour supply if the tax system is made more progressive. Assume that the average tax rate (evaluated at the initial optimum) remains unchanged. Explain your answers with the aid of diagrams.

Question 4: Indivisible labour

Assume that jobs come in a fixed number of hours per day. In this setting, a household either has no work at all ($N = 0$) or works an exogenously determined number of hours per day ($N = \bar{N} < 1$). If the household does not work, it receives an unemployment benefit equal to B. Unemployment benefits are not taxed. The budget restriction of an unemployed household is then:

$$PC = B, \tag{Q6.8}$$

where P is the price level and C is consumption. An employed household has the usual budget restriction:

$$PC = W\bar{N}(1 - t), \tag{Q6.9}$$

where t is the (constant) tax rate and W is the nominal wage. Assume that the unemployment benefit is proportional to the *after-tax* income of the employed households.

$$B = \gamma W\bar{N}(1 - t), \tag{Q6.10}$$

where γ is the so-called *replacement rate* ($0 < \gamma < 1$). The utility function of household i is given by:

$$U^i(C, 1 - N) \equiv C^\alpha (1 - N)^{\beta_i}, \tag{Q6.11}$$

where $\alpha > 0$ and $\beta_i \geq 0$.

(a) Derive the labour supply decision for household i. Show that it depends on the magnitude of β_i. (*Hint*: do not differentiate anything.)

(b) Assume that the population size is Z and that the β_i's are distributed uniformly over the interval $[0, \bar{\beta}]$. Show that the replacement rate exerts a negative influence on aggregate labour supply in this economy.

(c) Assume now that the unemployment benefit is proportional to *gross* wage income, i.e. $B = \gamma W\bar{N}$. Assume furthermore that $\gamma < 1 - t$. Redo part (a) and derive the effect on aggregate labour supply of a higher tax rate.

Question 5: Efficiency wages

(a) Provide three reasons why it may be advantageous for a firm to pay its workers a wage in excess of the market clearing wage.

(b) Explain why unemployment is a "necessary evil" for firms to get a well - disciplined labour force in the Shapiro and Stiglitz (1984) model. Is unemployment voluntary or involuntary in this model?

Answers

Question 1: Short questions

(a) The basic underlying hypothesis of efficiency wages is that the net productivity of workers depends positively on the wage rate they receive. More specifically, the effort of a company's employees depends positively on the gap between the wage rate workers receive and the expected wage rate outside the firm. A profit maximizing firm will pay its workers a mark-up over the outside option and this mark-up will increase if the productivity-enhancing effect is stronger.

However, the higher the wage rate is that the firm pays to its workers, the less workers it will hire and unemployment will be higher.

The young's effort is very sensitive to difference in the wage they receive and the expected wage they get outside their current job, which would imply that the markup for the young is high, but also that unemployment among the young will be higher.

(b) True, provided the minimum wage is binding for the unskilled only. See Figure 6.3 in the book. If $\bar{w}$ increases, $w_U = \bar{w}$ increases. Demand for skilled workers increases as does w_S. This boosts the demand for unskilled workers a little.

Question 2: Two-sector model with a skill-biased productivity shock

(a) The representative firm maximizes profit by choosing the optimal production level:

$$\max_{\{N_U, N_S\}} \Pi \equiv PF(N_U, Z_S N_S) - W_U N_U - W_S N_S. \tag{A6.1}$$

This gives us the usual marginal productivity conditions:

$$F_U(N_U, Z_S N_S) = w_U, \tag{A6.2}$$

$$F_S(N_U, Z_S N_S) = \frac{w_S}{Z_S} \equiv \tilde{w}_S, \tag{A6.3}$$

where $w_S \equiv W_S/P$, $w_U \equiv W_U/P$ (note that $F_S(N_U, Z_S N_S) \equiv \partial F / \partial (Z_S N_S)$ is the marginal product of efficiency units of skilled labour). In (A6.3), $\tilde{w}_S$ is the real wage for efficiency units of labour. Total differentiation of the two equations gives:

$$\begin{bmatrix} dN_S \\ dN_U \end{bmatrix} = \frac{1}{\Delta} \cdot \begin{bmatrix} F_{UU} & -F_{SU} \\ -F_{SU}Z_S & F_{SS}Z_S \end{bmatrix} \begin{bmatrix} d\tilde{w}_S - F_{SS}N_S dZ_S \\ dw_U - F_{SU}N_S dZ_S \end{bmatrix}, \tag{A6.4}$$

where $\Delta \equiv \Delta \equiv Z_S \cdot [F_{SS}F_{UU} - F_{SU}^2] > 0$ is a positive constant.

From (A6.4) we can derive:

$$\frac{\partial N_S^D}{\partial \tilde{w}_S} = \frac{F_{UU}}{\Delta} < 0, \qquad \frac{\partial N_U^D}{\partial w_U} = \frac{F_{SS}}{\Delta} < 0, \tag{A6.5}$$

$$\frac{\partial N_S^D}{\partial w_U} = -\frac{F_{SU}}{\Delta} > 0, \qquad \frac{\partial N_U^D}{\partial \tilde{w}_S} = -\frac{F_{SU}Z_S}{\Delta} > 0. \tag{A6.6}$$

These effects are the same as in the text–see equations (6.12) and (6.13). Demand curves slope down and an increase in the price of one factor leads to an increase in the demand for the other factor.

(b) The effect of an increase in Z_S can also be obtained from (A6.4):

$$\frac{\partial N_S^D}{\partial Z_S} = -\frac{[F_{SS}F_{UU} - F_{SU}^2] N_S}{\Delta} = -\frac{N_S}{Z_S} < 0, \tag{A6.7}$$

$$\frac{\partial N_U^D}{\partial Z_S} = \frac{[F_{SU}F_{SS} - F_{SU}F_{SS}] N_S}{\Delta} = 0. \tag{A6.8}$$

Holding constant real wages, $\tilde{w}_S$ and w_U, the technology shock reduces the demand for skilled labour and leaves the demand for unskilled labour unaffected.

We can obtain the general equilibrium effects by recognizing that under flexible wages, $dN_S = dN_U = 0$ (demands equal fixed supplies). Using this in (A6.4) we find:

$$d\tilde{w}_S = F_{SS}N_S dZ_S < 0, \qquad dw_U = F_{SU}N_S dZ_S < 0.$$

In terms of Figure A6.1, an increase in Z_S shifts the equilibrium from E_0 to E_1.

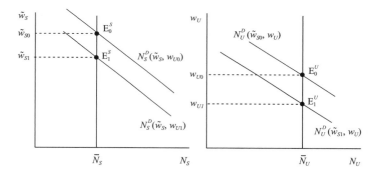

Figure A6.1: A skill-biased shock and wages

(c) Now unemployment of unskilled workers will exist, both before and after the shock. See Figure A6.2. In the left-hand panel the productivity shock shifts labour demand from $N_S^D(\tilde{w}_S, \tilde{w})_0$ to $N_S^D(\tilde{w}_S, \tilde{w})_1$ and the skilled rental rate falls, from $\tilde{w}_{S0}$ to $\tilde{w}_{S1}$. In the right-hand panel, labour demand shifts because of the reduction in the skilled rental rate, from $N_U^D(\tilde{w}_{S0}, w_U)$ to $N_U^D(\tilde{w}_{S1}, w_U)$. Unemployment gets worse because the minimum wage becomes a more binding constraint than before the shock.

Question 3: Progressive taxation

(a) The average tax rate, t_A, is defined as:

$$t_A \equiv \frac{T}{WN} = \frac{t_M WN - \theta}{WN} = t_M - \frac{\theta}{WN}. \tag{A6.9}$$

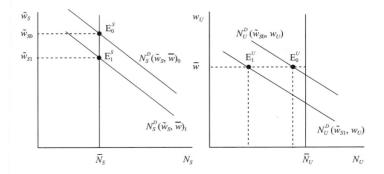

Figure A6.2: A skill-biased shock and unemployment

The tax system is progressive if the average tax rate increases with the tax base (labour income in this case). By differentiating (A6.9) with respect to WN we obtain:

$$\frac{dt_A}{d(WN)} = \frac{\theta}{(WN)^2} > 0, \tag{A6.10}$$

where the sign follows from the fact that we assume $\theta > 0$. Hence, the tax system is progressive.

The marginal tax rate, t_M, is defined as:

$$t_M = \frac{dT(WN)}{WN} > 0. \tag{A6.11}$$

By assumption the marginal tax is constant (i.e. does not depend on income). The tax curve has been illustrated in Figure A6.3. The marginal tax rate is constant (equal to the slope of the tax curve) but the average tax rate increases with WN. In points A and B, t_M is the same but t_A is higher in the latter point ($t_A^B > t_A^A$).

(b) The household chooses consumption, C, and labour supply, $1 - N$, in order to maximize the utility function (Q6.3) subject to the budget constraint (Q6.4). The Lagrangian expression is:

$$\mathcal{L} \equiv U(C, 1 - N) + \lambda[WN - T(WN) - C], \tag{A6.12}$$

The first-order necessary conditions are the constraint and:

$$\frac{\partial \mathcal{L}}{\partial C} = 0: \quad U_C = \lambda, \tag{A6.13}$$

$$\frac{\partial \mathcal{L}}{\partial N} = 0: \quad U_{1-N} = \lambda W(1 - t_M). \tag{A6.14}$$

Substitution of (A6.13) into (A6.14) gives the required expression for the marginal rate of substitution between leisure and consumption:

$$\lambda = U_C = \frac{U_{1-N}}{W(1 - t_M)} \quad \Rightarrow \quad \frac{U_{1-N}}{U_C} = W(1 - t_M). \tag{Q6.6}$$

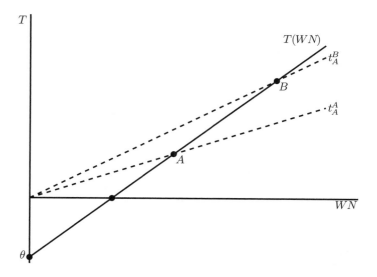

Figure A6.3: A progressive tax schedule

Hence, the *marginal* tax rate features in the first-order condition for labour supply. Intuitively, this is because the household is making a marginal decision concerning consumption and labour supply. It will take into account that the average tax rates increases as more labour is supplied.

(c) The three cases correspond to, respectively, no substitution at all (Leontief, $\sigma_{CM} = 0$), relatively easy substitution (Cobb-Douglas, $\sigma_{CM} = 1$), and perfect substitution (Linear, $\sigma_{CM} \to \infty$). In Figures A6.4–A6.6, the three cases have been illustrated.

Consider first Figure A6.4, $\sigma_{CM} = 0$. Along a given indifference curve, we obtain by differentiation:

$$dU = U_C dC + U_{1-N} d(1 - N) = 0 \quad \Rightarrow \quad \frac{dC}{d(1 - N)} = -\frac{U_{1-N}}{U_C}. \quad (A6.15)$$

For points on the indifference curve U_0 that lie above point A, we have $U_C = 0$ (additional consumption gives no extra utility), i.e. $dC/d(1 - N) = -\infty$ there. For points on the indifference curve U_0 that lie to the right of point A we have $U_{1-N} = 0$ (additional leisure gives no extra utility), i.e. $dC/d(1 - N) = 0$ there. The household will always choose to be in the kink. This means that, no matter what happens to the marginal rate of substitution between leisure and consumption, the ratio between C and $1 - N$ is constant. This means that the numerator of (Q6.7) (and thus σ_{CM} itself) is always zero.

Next, we consider Figure A6.5, which assumes that the utility function is Cobb-Douglas:

$$U = C^\alpha [1 - N]^{1-\alpha}, \quad (A6.16)$$

with $0 < \alpha < 1$. The marginal rate of substitution between leisure and con-

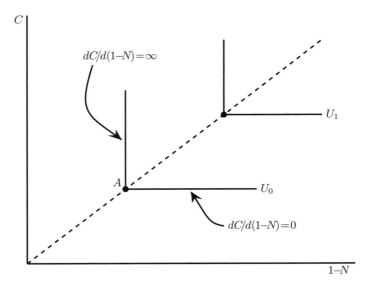

Figure A6.4: Leontief utility function

sumption for the Cobb-Douglas utility function is:

$$\frac{U_{1-N}}{U_C} = \frac{(1-\alpha)C^\alpha[1-N]^{-\alpha}}{\alpha C^{\alpha-1}[1-N]^{1-\alpha}} = \frac{1-\alpha}{\alpha}\frac{C}{1-N}. \tag{A6.17}$$

By taking logarithms and totally differentiating we get:

$$d\ln\left(\frac{U_{1-N}}{U_C}\right) = d\ln\left(\frac{C}{1-N}\right). \tag{A6.18}$$

By using this in the definition of σ_{CM} (in equation (Q6.7)) we find that $\sigma_{CM} = 1$ for the Cobb-Douglas utility function.

Finally, we consider Figure A6.6, which assumes that the utility function is linear:

$$U = \beta_0 + \beta_1 C + \beta_2[1-N], \tag{A6.19}$$

where β_1 and β_2 are positive constants. For this utility function, U_C, U_{1-N}, and thus the marginal rate of substitution between leisure and consumption are all constant, i.e. $U_{1-N}/U_C = \beta_2/\beta_1$. It follows that $d\ln(U_{1-N}/U_C) = 0$ regardless of $C/(1-N)$. Using this result in the definition of σ_{CM} (in equation (Q6.7)) shows that $\sigma_{CM} \to \infty$ for the linear utility function.

(d) The two relevant first order conditions are the equation for the marginal rate of substitution (Q6.6) and the (slightly rewritten) budget constraint (Q6.4):

$$\frac{U_{1-N}}{U_C} = W(1-t_M) \tag{Q6.6}$$

$$C = (1-t_A)WN \tag{Q6.4}$$

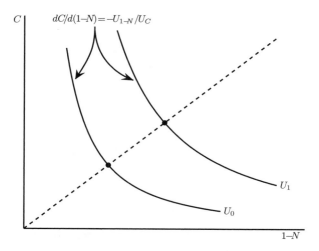

Figure A6.5: Cobb-Douglas utility function

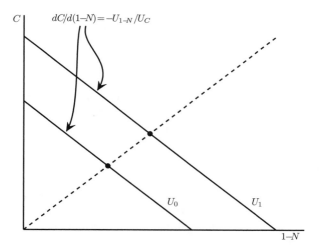

Figure A6.6: Linear utility function

with our knowledge of loglinearization we can skip all tedious steps and we can immediately write:

$$\frac{1}{\sigma_{CM}}\left[\tilde{C}+\frac{N}{1-N}\tilde{N}\right]=\tilde{W}-\tilde{t}_M \quad \Rightarrow \quad \tilde{C}+\frac{N}{1-N}\tilde{N}=\sigma_{CM}[\tilde{W}-\tilde{t}_M]$$

$$\tilde{C}=-\tilde{t}_A+\tilde{W}+\tilde{N}$$

or in matrix notation:

$$\begin{bmatrix} 1 & \frac{N}{1-N} \\ 1 & -1 \end{bmatrix}\begin{bmatrix} \tilde{C} \\ \tilde{N} \end{bmatrix}=\begin{bmatrix} \sigma_{CM} & -\sigma_{CM} & 0 \\ 1 & 0 & -1 \end{bmatrix}\begin{bmatrix} \tilde{W} \\ \tilde{t}_M \\ \tilde{t}_A \end{bmatrix} \tag{A6.20}$$

The first matrix is always non-singular (determinant is $-1/(1-N)$) and can be inverted as:

$$\begin{bmatrix} 1 & \frac{N}{1-N} \\ 1 & -1 \end{bmatrix}^{-1}=\begin{bmatrix} 1-N & N \\ 1-N & -[1-N] \end{bmatrix}$$

Pre-multiplying equation (A6.20) with this inverse matrix gives the required result (in matrix notation):

$$\begin{bmatrix} \tilde{C} \\ \tilde{N} \end{bmatrix}=\begin{bmatrix} \sigma[1-N]+N & -\sigma[1-N] & -N \\ [\sigma-1][1-N] & -\sigma[1-N] & 1-N \end{bmatrix}\begin{bmatrix} \tilde{W} \\ \tilde{t}_M \\ \tilde{t}_A \end{bmatrix} \tag{A6.21}$$

(e) In the book we define the index of progressivity of the tax system as (see equation (6.51)):

$$s \equiv \frac{1-t_M}{1-t_A}. \tag{A6.22}$$

A decrease in s represents a move towards a more progressive tax system. By log-linearization of equation (A6.22) we find:

$$\tilde{s}=\tilde{t}_A-\tilde{t}_M, \tag{A6.23}$$

where $\tilde{s} \equiv ds/s$. In the question we keep the average tax rate constant ($\tilde{t}_A=0$) and increase the progressivity of the tax system by raising the marginal tax rate ($\tilde{s}=-\tilde{t}_M < 0$). It follows from (A6.21) that consumption and labour supply react according to:

$$\tilde{C}=\tilde{N}=-\sigma_{CM}[1-N]\tilde{t}_M, \tag{A6.24}$$

where we have used the fact that the wage is unchanged (i.e. $\tilde{W}=0$ and we are only looking at the labour supply response for a given gross wage rate). We can conclude that labour supply falls unambiguously unless $\sigma_{CM}=0$ in which case it stays the same.

Consider Figure A6.7, which is based on the assumption that $\sigma_{CM}=0$ (no substitution). Since utility depends on (consumption and) leisure, it is helpful to rewrite the budget restriction in terms of leisure also. After some manipulations we find that (Q6.4) can be written as:

$$C=\theta+(1-t_M)\cdot W-W(1-t_M)\cdot[1-N]. \tag{A6.25}$$

Even if the household does not work at all ($N = 0$) it can still consume the lump-sum hand out from the government ($C = \theta$ in that case). The budget restriction is drawn in Figure A6.7 as the straight line BC. The household is initially at point E_0. If the marginal tax rate is increased, the budget constraint rotates in a counter-clockwise fashion and becomes the dashed line BD. In the absence of any counter-measures, the household would choose point A on the new budget line. In this experiment however, we must ensure that the average tax rate (evaluated at the initial optimum E_0) is not changed. We denote the initial average tax rate by $\bar{t}_A$. Since, by definition, the household budget constraint can also be written as $C = W(1 - t_A)N$, it follows that the new choice point must lie along the following line:

$$C = W(1 - \bar{t}_A) - W(1 - \bar{t}_A)[1 - N]. \tag{A6.26}$$

This line is drawn in Figure A6.7 as the straight line EF. Since $t_M > t_A$ for a progressive tax system, it is straightforward to show that EF is steeper than BC ($t_M > t_A$). Because both W and $\bar{t}_A$ are held constant, the position of the 'alternative' budget line is not affected by the change in the marginal tax rate.

It is now clear where the new choice point must lie as it must satisfy the following criteria:

- It must lie on the line EF (so that the average tax is constant).
- It must be on the dashed line from the origin (because households want to consume goods and leisure in that proportion).
- There must be a tangency with a line parallel to BD.

It follows from these requirements that the choice point must be E_0. In order to keep the average tax rate constant, the policy maker must increase θ so that the budget line BD shifts in a parallel fashion such that it passes through point E_0. The household continues to choose E_0 and neither consumption nor labour supply are changed.

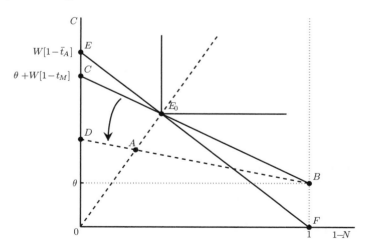

Figure A6.7: Increasing tax progressivity ($\sigma_{CM} = 0$)

Next we consider the Cobb-Douglas case ($\sigma_{CM} = 1$) in Figure A6.8. Equations (A6.25) and (A6.26) are drawn as, respectively, BC and FE. The initial equilibrium point is at E_0 (indifference curves are not drawn to avoid cluttering the diagram). The increase in the marginal tax rate rotates the budget line BC to the dashed line BD. In the absence of changes to θ, the household would choose point A. It follows from (Q6.6) that the household wants to choose a lower $C/(1 - N)$ ratio, i.e. the expansion path rotates clockwise from 0G to 0H. Point A, however, does not satisfy the requirement that the average tax must remain constant as it does not lie on the line EF. To satisfy that requirement the government must increase θ such that the budget line shifts in a parallel fashion to intersect 0H and EF in point E_1. Because the utility function is homothetic, there is a tangency between the new budget line and an indifference curve at point E_1.

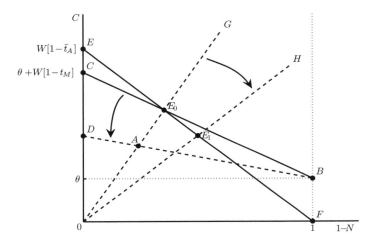

Figure A6.8: Increasing tax progressivity ($\sigma_{CM} = 1$)

Question 4: Indivisible labour

(a) Household i maximizes utility, $U^i = C^\alpha (1 - N)^{\beta_i}$, subject to the budget constraint:

$$PC = \begin{cases} B & \text{if } N = 0 \\ W\bar{N}(1 - t) & \text{if } N = \bar{N} \end{cases} \qquad (A6.27)$$

There are only two options for the household to check. It will choose $N = 0$ if this yields higher utility than $N = \bar{N}$ and vice versa. By substituting $N = 0$ and $N = \bar{N}$ into the utility function (Q6.11) we obtain:

$$U^i = \begin{cases} U^i_{N=0} \equiv \left(\frac{B}{P}\right)^\alpha & \text{if } N = 0 \\ U^i_{N=\bar{N}} \equiv \left(\frac{W\bar{N}(1-t)}{P}\right)^\alpha (1 - \bar{N})^{\beta_i} & \text{if } N = \bar{N} \end{cases} \qquad (A6.28)$$

But, according to equation (Q6.10), we have $B = \gamma W\bar{N}(1 - t)$ so the first expression in (A6.28) can be rewritten as:

$$U^i_{N=0} = \left(\frac{B}{P}\right)^\alpha = \left(\frac{\gamma W\bar{N}(1 - t)}{P}\right)^\alpha. \tag{A6.29}$$

By using (A6.29) and the second expression in (A6.28) we obtain:

$$\frac{U^i_{N=\bar{N}}}{U^i_{N=0}} = \frac{\left(\frac{W\bar{N}(1-t)}{P}\right)^\alpha (1 - \bar{N})^{\beta_i}}{\left(\frac{\gamma W\bar{N}(1-t)}{P}\right)^\alpha} = \gamma^{-\alpha}(1 - \bar{N})^{\beta_i}. \tag{A6.30}$$

It follows that the household makes the following labour supply choice:

$$N^S_i = \begin{cases} 0 & \text{if } \gamma^{-\alpha}(1 - \bar{N})^{\beta_i} < 1 \\ \bar{N} & \text{if } \gamma^{-\alpha}(1 - \bar{N})^{\beta_i} > 1 \end{cases} \tag{A6.31}$$

The *marginal household* is indifferent between working and not working, i.e. it has a $\beta_i = \beta_M$ such that $\gamma^{-\alpha}(1 - \bar{N})^{\beta_M} = 1$. By taking logarithms on both sides of this expression we can solve for β_M:

$$-\alpha \ln \gamma + \beta_M \ln(1 - \bar{N}) = 0 \quad \Leftrightarrow \quad \beta_M = \frac{\alpha \ln \gamma}{\ln(1 - \bar{N})} > 0, \tag{A6.32}$$

where the sign follows from the fact that $0 < \gamma < 1$ and $0 < \bar{N} < 1$ (so that $\ln \gamma < 0$ and $\ln(1 - \bar{N}) < 0$). Households whose β_i exceeds β_M prefer not to work (they like leisure "too much") whereas households with a β_i smaller than β_M choose to work. (Someone with $\beta_i = 0$ is the proverbial *workaholic*.)

(b) The β_i coefficients are distributed uniformly over the interval $[0, \bar{\beta}]$. The frequency distribution of β_i's in the population is drawn in Figure A6.9. All households with a $\beta_i \leq \beta_M$ are workers whereas all households with a $\beta_i > \beta_M$ are "loungers". Since the population size is Z, there are thus $(\bar{\beta} - \beta_M)Z/\bar{\beta}$ loungers and $\beta_M Z/\bar{\beta}$ workers (who each work $\bar{N}$ hours). Aggregate labour supply is thus:

$$N^S = \frac{\beta_M Z \bar{N}}{\bar{\beta}}. \tag{A6.33}$$

The macroeconomic labour supply curve is drawn in Figure A6.10. Note that this aggregate labour supply curve is vertical because β_M does not depend on the wage rate (due to the fact that unemployment benefits are linked to the wage rate).

If γ is increased, then it follows from (A6.32)–(A6.33) that:

$$\frac{\partial \beta_M}{\partial \gamma} = \frac{\alpha}{\gamma \ln(1 - \bar{N})} < 0, \qquad \frac{\partial N^S}{\partial \gamma} = \frac{Z\bar{N}}{\bar{\beta}} \frac{\partial \beta_M}{\partial \gamma} < 0, \tag{A6.34}$$

where the signs follow from the fact that $\ln(1 - \bar{N}) < 0$. The reduction in β_M causes the aggregate labour supply curve to shift to the left, as is indicated in Figure A6.10.

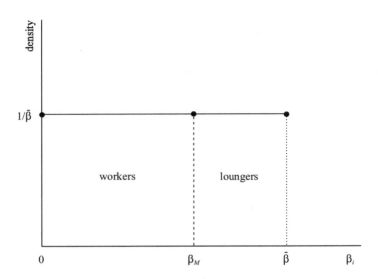

Figure A6.9: Distribution of β_i coefficients in the population

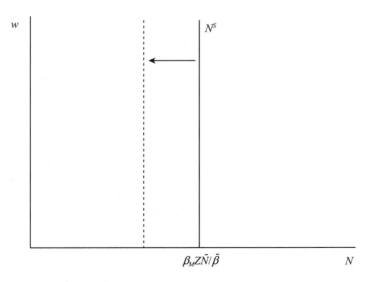

Figure A6.10: Aggregate labour supply with indivisible labour

(c) Now we assume that the unemployment benefits are linked to the gross wage, i.e. $B = \gamma W \bar{N}$. By substituting this into the first expression in (A6.28) we obtain:

$$U^i_{N=0} = \left(\frac{B}{P}\right)^\alpha = \left(\frac{\gamma W \bar{N}}{P}\right)^\alpha = \left(\frac{\gamma}{1-t}\right)^\alpha \left(\frac{W\bar{N}(1-t)}{P}\right)^\alpha. \qquad \text{(A6.35)}$$

By using (A6.35) and the second expression in (A6.28) we find:

$$\frac{U^i_{N=\bar{N}}}{U^i_{N=0}} = \frac{\left(\frac{W\bar{N}(1-t)}{P}\right)^\alpha (1-\bar{N})^{\beta_i}}{\left(\frac{\gamma}{1-t}\right)^\alpha \left(\frac{W\bar{N}(1-t)}{P}\right)^\alpha} = \left(\frac{1-t}{\gamma}\right)^\alpha (1-\bar{N})^{\beta_i}. \qquad \text{(A6.36)}$$

The marginal household now has a $\beta_i = \beta_M$ equal to:

$$\alpha\left[\ln(1-t) - \ln\gamma\right] + \beta_M \ln(1-\bar{N}) = 0 \qquad \Leftrightarrow$$
$$\beta_M = \frac{\alpha\left[\ln\gamma - \ln(1-t)\right]}{\ln(1-\bar{N})} > 0, \qquad \text{(A6.37)}$$

where the sign follows from the fact that $\ln(1-\bar{N}) < 0$ and the assumption that $\gamma < 1 - t$.

An increase in the tax rate, leads to an increase in $\gamma/(1-t)$ and thus to an increase in the *effective* replacement rate. This implies that β_M falls so that aggregate labour supply falls.

Question 5: Efficiency wages

(a) The three magic words are recruit, retain, and motivate.

- *Recruit* Make sure that the best workers choose to join your firm (rather than your competitor's firm).

- *Retain* Make sure that your employees do not quit to go to another firm.

- *Motivate* Make sure that your employees provide sufficient effort on the job.

(b) In the Shapiro-Stiglitz model, unemployment acts as a worker discipline device. If they are caught shirking (not expending sufficient effort) then the firm can fire the worker. If there were no unemployment, then there would be no way to punish the worker because he/she would immediately find the same kind of job. In the internal solution of the Shapiro-Stiglitz model, there is non-zero unemployment and the threat of unemployment provides the firm with an effective instrument to limit shirking.

Chapter 7

Trade unions and the labour market

Question 1: Short questions

(a) Why does a monopoly union not choose to set wages such that all its members are employed?

(b) "Breaking the power of trade unions is good for the investment climate in this country." Explain and evaluate this proposition.

(c) Explain why the iso-profit function must be horizontal at the point where it intersects the demand for labour.

Question 2: Small talk...

On your day off you take a ride in Vienna's *Riesenrad* and overhear a shabbily dressed, quite conservative, economist making a number of rather strong claims. Since you are an economist yourself, you feel obliged to comment on the statements. Here are the claims:

(a) "In order to attain full employment of labour it is absolutely essential that union power is broken down as much as possible."

(b) "Highly centralized unions or perfect competition on the labour market are both good for the employment level in an economy. Medium-sized unions, on the other hand, are very bad for employment."

(c) "Higher unemployment benefits lead to higher wage claims and thus to higher unemployment. The degree of corporatism influences this relationship."

Question 3: The Blanchard-Summers model

Use the Blanchard-Summers model (see textbook, section 7.3) on fiscal increasing returns.

$$Y = F(L, \bar{K}), \tag{Q7.1}$$
$$w = F_L(L, \bar{K}), \tag{Q7.2}$$
$$tY = G + \beta w(1 - t)[N - L]. \tag{Q7.3}$$

(a) Provide a brief interpretation of the equations.

(b) Assume that the after-tax real wage is constant. This may be, for example, because of union influence. Show that the model admits two equilibria, namely a 'good' and a 'bad' equilibrium.

(c) In order to judge the stability properties of the model we postulate that the tax rate moves gradually over time to re-establish government budget balance. Equation (Q7.3) is replaced by:

$$\dot{t} = \gamma[G + \beta w(1 - t)[N - L] - tY]. \tag{Q7.4}$$

Show that the model is unstable around the bad equilibrium but stable around the good equilibrium. What do you conclude from this result?

Question 4: Variable unemployment benefits

Assume that the unemployment benefits are linked to the net market wage rate. Use a simple union model to discuss the effects of the following:

(a) Higher unemployment benefits.

(b) More intense competition on the goods market (due to, for example, increased European integration).

(c) A more progressive tax system.

(d) A higher employers tax on labour (t_E).

(e) A higher average tax rate on workers (t_A).

Question 5: The two-sector labour market model

Consider the two-sector model of the labour market. In the first sector (the primary sector) unions are prevalent, whilst in the second sector (the secondary sector) the labour market is characterized by perfect competition.

(a) Show that there will be unemployment if the unemployment benefits are "too high." Explain the mechanism.

(b) Show what happens if "union bashing" leads to the elimination of trade unions in the primary sector.

(c) Show the effects of a wage subsidy on labour in the secondary sector.

Answers

Question 1: Short questions

(a) A trade union does not only care about the number of employed. Rather, it cares about the 'average utility level of its members'. Decreasing its wage claims might increase the number of employed and thus the number of members that receive a wage instead of the low unemployment benefit, but it decreases the wage received by the workers. A monopoly labour union sets the wage rate that maximizes the 'average utility level of its members' subject to the labour demand equation (that is, companies choose the number of employed given the wage rate set by the union). Even if it is possible to set a wage that brings full employment (if the unemployment benefit is not too high), then the labour union would not set this wage rate because the second effect above would dominate the first. Like a monopolist in the goods market, the union restricts output (i.e. employment) and thus drives up wages and union utility.

(b) Depends, it is true for the right-to-manage and monopoly union models. With less powerful unions one gets closer to the competitive outcome. It is not true for the efficient bargaining case.

(c) Profit is defined as:

$$\pi(w, L) \equiv F(L, \bar{K}) - wL,$$

so that the iso-profit line has the slope:

$$\left(\frac{dw}{dL}\right)_{d\pi=0} = -\frac{\pi_L}{\pi_w}.$$

But $\pi_w = -L$ is always negative, so the slope of the iso-profit line is determined by the sign of $\pi_L = F_L(L, \bar{K}) - w$. Obviously, $\pi_L = 0$ for $w = F_L(L, \bar{K})$ which is the labour demand curve.

Question 2: Small talk...

(a) The validity of this statement depends on the type of union model one uses. In the monopoly union model and in the right-to-manage model the statement is correct. In the first model breaking union power would presumably rob it of its monopoly power (e.g. by allowing other unions to enter or by forbidding unions altogether). In the extreme case, the wage would be driven to its reservation level (B) and employment would be expanded from L^M to L^C in Figure 7.3.

In the right-to-manage model, breaking union power could be interpreted as a decrease in λ, the relative bargaining power of the union in the generalized Nash bargaining model. This would move the solution in the direction of the competitive solution (point C in Figure 7.4) and expand employment.

In the efficient bargaining model, however, the statement is incorrect. In that model, breaking union power can be interpreted as a decrease in the share of output that goes to the workers ("wage moderation"), i.e. a reduction in k in equation (7.22). In terms of Figure 7.5, this shifts the equity locus to the left and reduces both the wage and employment. Jobs are turned into profits (rewards to capital owners).

(b) This statement touches on the idea of corporatism, discussed in section 7.2 of the book. With weak (small) trade unions or with a competitive labour market, there is little unemployment and low wages (see Figure 7.7 in the book). A large (centralized) trade union also chooses a high employment-low gross wages solution because it tends to 'internalize' the government budget constraint. It knows that high wage claims cause unemployment, high outlays on unemployment benefits, and thus high labour income taxes and low after-tax wages for the workers.

In the intermediate case, with medium sized unions, the economy is in the worst of both worlds. The unions are large enough to cause damage (demand high wages and cause unemployment) but they are too small to take the government budget constraint into account.

(c) This statement is true for all trade union models considered. With a high degree of corporatism, the large unions will lower their markup to avoid causing too much unemployment and excessively high labour income taxes.

Question 3: The Blanchard-Summers model

(a) Equation (Q7.1) is a constant returns to scale production function, (Q7.2) is the labour demand function, (Q7.3) is the government budget constraint. It is a short term model, i.e. capital is exogenous and constant. The tax rate is t, so total tax revenues are tY. The government pays an unemployment benefit to the unemployed, which is linked to the after tax wage rate ($w_N \equiv w(1-t)$). The unemployment benefit equals the replacement ratio β times the after tax wage rate. This means that total unemployment benefits are $\beta w(1-t)[N-L]$. The tax rate is endogenous and ensures that the government budget constraint holds.

The model contains four endogenous variables, Y, L, w, and t. To solve this model we need one extra restriction.

(b) We follow the steps in the book. First derive the relationship between the after tax wage rate and employment (equation (7.27) in the book):

$$w_N \equiv w(1-t) = F_L(L, \bar{K}) \cdot \left[\frac{F(L, \bar{K}) - G - \beta w(1-t)[N-L]}{F(L, \bar{K})} \right] \quad \text{(A7.1)}$$

In Intermezzo 7.1 the first derivative of w_N with respect to L is derived:

$$\frac{dw_N}{dL} = \frac{(1-t)w_N}{(1-\omega_G)L} \cdot \left[-\frac{1-\omega_L}{\sigma} + \left(\beta + \frac{t}{1-t} \right) \omega_L \right] \quad \text{(A7.2)}$$

with $\omega_G \equiv G/Y$ the share of government consumption in total production, σ the elasticity of substitution, and $\omega_L \equiv wL/Y$ the share of labour income in output.

The sign of dw_N/dL is determined by the term within square brackets. For a high enough σ or β, this term is positive for high values of t and negative for small values of t. If we use the government budget constraint (Q7.3) we see that t is high for low employment levels and low for high employment levels (the unemployment benefit must be financed with tax revenues). This means that (A7.1) is humped shaped.

The relation between w_N and L is drawn in Figure A7.1. For a given after tax wage rate $\bar{w}_N$ there might be two levels of employment, one low (bad) equilibrium L^B and one high (good) equilibrium L^G.

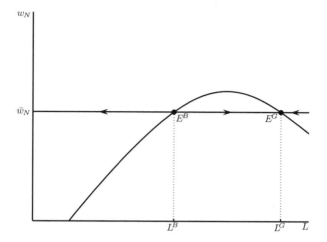

Figure A7.1: Fiscal increasing returns

(c) This equation states that taxes increase ($\dot{t} > 0$) if the government has a deficit, taxes decrease ($\dot{t} < 0$) if the government has a surplus.

In Intermezzo 7.1 it is shown how to derive the linearized version of (Q7.4).

$$\frac{d\dot{t}}{dt} = \frac{\gamma\sigma Y}{1-\omega_L}\left[-\frac{1-\omega_L}{\sigma} + \left(\beta + \frac{t}{1-t}\right)\omega_L\right] \tag{A7.3}$$

The sign of this derivative is determined by the term within square brackets, but this is exactly equal to the term that determines the sign in equation (A7.2)! This means that $d\dot{t}/dt > 0$ (an unstable situation) if $dw/dL > 0$ and $d\dot{t}/dt < 0$ (a stable situation) if $dw/dL < 0$. So the equilibrium E^B in Figure A7.1 is unstable and E^G is stable.

Question 4: Variable unemployment benefits

We are free to choose the simplest union model around. This is, of course, the monopoly union model with logarithmic member preferences and a constant elasticity of labour demand. In part (b) of the question we must say something about the market in which the firm sells its product. To do so we must expand the model somewhat. In part (d) we must introduce the employers' tax on labour into the model.

(a) According to equation (7.9) in the book, the monopoly union sets the wage according to:

$$\frac{u(w) - u(B)}{wu_w} = \frac{1}{\varepsilon_D}. \tag{A7.4}$$

Assuming that $u(\cdot)$ is logarithmic, we obtain:

$$w = e^{1/\varepsilon_D}B. \tag{A7.5}$$

If ε_D is constant, it follows directly from (A7.5) that an increase in B leads to an increase in the wage. Since labour demand slopes downwards, employment drops off and unemployment increases.

(b) To study the effect of the firm's market power in the goods market we must move beyond the perfectly competitive model of the firm used in Chapter 7 (because there the firm has *zero* market power). Assume that the typical firm j has (a little bit of) market power and faces a downward sloping (inverse) demand curve for its product:

$$P_j = P(Y_j), \tag{A7.6}$$

with $P'(\cdot) < 0$. The firm's short-run profit, Π_j, is defined by:

$$\Pi_j \equiv P_j F(L_j, \bar{K}) - W L_j, \tag{A7.7}$$

where $F(\cdot)$ is a constant returns to scale production function, L_j is labour input, and W is the nominal wage. The firm's output is given by $Y_j = F(L_j, \bar{K})$. The firm chooses its price, P_j, and its demand for labour, L_j, such that (A7.7) is maximized, taking into account that lower output produces a higher product price according to (A7.6). By inserting $P_j = P(F(L_j, \bar{K}))$ into (A7.7) we obtain profits in terms of L_j only:

$$\Pi_j \equiv P(F(L_j, \bar{K})) F(L_j, \bar{K}) - W L_j. \tag{A7.8}$$

Maximizing (A7.8) with respect to L_j yields the following first-order condition:

$$\frac{d\Pi_j}{dL_j} = P(\cdot) F_L + F(\cdot) P'(\cdot) F_L - W = 0, \tag{A7.9}$$

where $F_L \equiv \partial F / \partial L_j$ is the marginal product of labour. By rearranging (A7.9) somewhat, we obtain:

$$F_L \left[P(\cdot) + F(\cdot) P'(\cdot) \right] = W \quad \Leftrightarrow$$
$$F_L P(\cdot) \left[1 + Y_j \frac{P'(\cdot)}{P(\cdot)} \right] = W \quad \Leftrightarrow$$
$$F_L P_j \left[1 - \frac{1}{\eta_D} \right] = W \quad \Leftrightarrow$$
$$F_L = \frac{\eta_D}{\eta_D - 1} \frac{W}{P_j}, \tag{A7.10}$$

where $\eta_D \equiv -P(\cdot) / (Y_j P'(\cdot)) > 0$ is the absolute value of the price elasticity of firm j's demand curve.

According to (A7.10), a firm with some market power equates the marginal product of labour (left-hand side) to a gross markup (the first term on the right-hand side) *times* the real wage rate. This markup, $\eta_D / (\eta_D - 1)$ exceeds unity (because $\eta_D > 1$) and is decreasing in the demand elasticity, η_D. (In the perfectly competitive case, $\eta_D \to \infty$ and the markup is unity.) Hence, the higher is η_D, the more competitive is the goods market, the lower in the markup, and the higher is the demand for labour at a given real wage rate. We conclude that the demand for labour depends negatively on the markup and thus positively on the demand elasticity, η_D.

$$L^D = L^D(\underset{-}{w}, \underset{+}{\eta_D}, \underset{+}{\bar{K}}) \tag{A7.11}$$

If we look at the markup expression for the trade union (equation (A7.5) above) we see that it is not the *level* of labour demand that matters but rather the *elasticity* of the labour demand curve. If this elasticity is constant (as we assume) then nothing happens to the real wage if competitiveness is increased. In terms of Figure A7.2, labour demand shifts to the right and the union's optimal point shifts from M_0 to M_1. Employment increases from L_0^M to L_1^M and unemployment decreases.

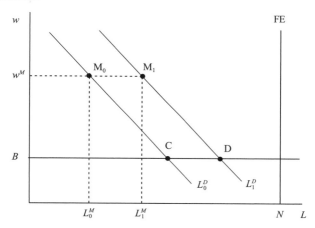

Figure A7.2: Increased goods market competition and the monopoly union

(c) This issue is explained in detail in section 7.5.1 of the book. A fall in the degree of progressivity (a rise in s in equation (7.42)) increases both the wage rate and unemployment.

(d) Assume that the representative firm is perfectly competitive. Short-run profit is defined as:

$$\Pi = PF(L, \bar{K}) - W(1 + t_E)L, \tag{A7.12}$$

where t_E is the payroll tax. Short-run profit maximization yields the marginal productivity condition for labour:

$$F_L(L, \bar{K}) = (1 + t_E)\left(\frac{W}{P}\right). \tag{A7.13}$$

An increase in t_E shifts labour demand to the left. With a constant elasticity of labour demand, the union does not change the real wage, so employment falls and unemployment increases.

(e) This issue is explained in detail in section 7.5.1 of the book. An increase in the average tax, t_A, increases both the wage and unemployment–see equation (7.42).

Question 5: The two-sector labour market model

(a) See section 7.1.4 in the book.

(b) Consider Figure 7.6 in the book. If the unions are banished from the primary sector, there will be entry of secondary sector workers into the primary sector until wages are equalized in the two sectors. The economy will go to point C, and (for the case drawn in the figure) unemployment will disappear. This is because w^C is strictly above the unemployment benefit, B.

(c) We again refer to Figure 7.6 in the book. A wage subsidy in the secondary sector will stimulate labour demand in that sector, i.e. $L_2^D(w_2)$ will shift to the left. Unemployment in the secondary sector will decrease as a result.

Chapter 8

Search in the labour market

Question 1: Short questions

(a) "An increase in the employers tax on labour ("payroll tax") will lead to an increase in unemployment, a lower real wage, and a longer unemployment duration." Explain and evaluate this proposition.

(b) Explain why the value of a vacancy is zero in the standard labour market search model. Explain also that it can never be negative, even if there are restrictions on the numbers of vacancies that can be posted.

(c) What do we mean by a Beveridge curve? What could make the Beveridge curve shift?

(d) Explain how modern search theory uses the so-called *matching function*. How can we use this function to compute the probability that a job seeker finds a job? And, vice versa, how can we find the probability that an employer with a vacancy finds a worker? Provide examples with the aid of a Cobb-Douglas matching function.

Question 2: Search unemployment

Consider the following search-theoretic model of the labour market:

$$F_K(K, Z_0) = r + \delta, \tag{Q8.1}$$

$$\frac{\gamma_0}{q(\theta)} = \frac{F_L\left(K(r+\delta), Z_0\right) - w}{r + s}, \tag{Q8.2}$$

$$w = (1 - \beta)z + \beta\left[F_L\left(K(r+\delta), Z_0\right) + \theta\gamma_0\right], \tag{Q8.3}$$

$$U = \frac{s}{s + \theta q(\theta)}, \tag{Q8.4}$$

where U is the unemployment rate, s is the (exogenous) job destruction rate, $\theta \equiv V/U$ is the labour market pressure index, V is the vacancy rate, K is the capital stock, w is the real wage, z is the (exogenous) income of job seekers, r is the (exogenous) real interest rate, γ_0 is the employer's (flow) search cost, and β is the relative bargaining power of the worker. The underlying production function is written in general terms as $F(K, Z_0 L)$ where Z_0 is an exogenous index of (what economists call) *labour-augmenting technological change* and L is employment. The technology features constant returns to scale and you are reminded of the fact that the model applies to single job firms (i.e. $L = 1$).

(a) Give a brief interpretation of these equations.

(b) Assume that the policy maker decides to provide a subsidy to the employers for the search costs they have to incur. Show what happens to unemployment, vacancies, and the real wage rate as a result of this policy measure.

(c) Assume that there is a once-off *increase* in the efficiency parameter Z_0 (techno-logical progress). Show what happens to the marginal products of capital and labour (F_K and F_L) as a result of the shock.

(d) Show what happens to unemployment, vacancies, and the real wage rate as a result of the change in technology mentioned in part (c). Illustrate your answer with a two-panel diagram as used in the book.

(e) Show what happens to unemployment, vacancies, and the real wage rate if the interest rate rises. Illustrate with the aid of a diagram and explain the economic intuition.

(f) Assume that the policy maker decides to provide a subsidy to the employers for the search costs they have to incur. As a result of this policy measure, γ_0 is reduced. Show what happens to unemployment, vacancies, and the real wage rate as a result of this policy measure.

Question 3: A CES matching function

Assume that the matching function is given by:

$$XN = \left[(1 - \alpha) (Z_U UN)^{(\sigma-1)/\sigma} + \alpha (Z_V VN)^{(\sigma-1)/\sigma} \right]^{\sigma/(\sigma-1)}, \qquad 0 < \alpha < 1, \quad \text{(Q8.5)}$$

where XN is the total number of matches (X is the matching *rate*), UN is the number of unemployed job seekers (U is the unemployment *rate*), and VN is the number of vacancies (V is the vacancy *rate*). Z_U and Z_V are exogenous shift factors. The labour market tightness variable is denoted by $\theta \equiv V/U$.

(a) Show that the matching function is linear homogeneous (i.e., it features con-stant returns to scale). Explain which economic phenomena can be captured by the shift factors, Z_U and Z_V.

(b) Explain why this matching function only makes economic sense if $0 < \sigma \leq 1$.

(c) Compute the implied functions $q(\theta, Z_U, Z_V)$, $f(\theta, Z_U, Z_V)$, and $\eta(\theta, Z_U, Z_V)$. Verify that $f(\theta, Z_U, Z_V) = \theta \cdot q(\theta, Z_U, Z_V)$. Show how these functions depend on θ and on the shift factors, Z_U and Z_V.

(d) Consider the market equilibrium model given in equations (8.25)-(8.28) in the book. Show what happens to the wage rate, labour market tightness, and the equilibrium unemployment rate, if unemployed workers search more actively.

(e) Redo part (d), but assume that firms with a vacancy become a little more adept at locating willing unemployed workers.

Question 4: Downward real wage rigidity

Consider the basic labour market search model with a payroll tax as presented in section 8.2.1 in the book. The key equations of this model are restated here:

$$\frac{\bar{F}_L - w \cdot (1 + t_E)}{r + s} = \frac{\gamma_0}{q(\theta)},$$ (Q8.6)

$$w = (1 - \beta)z + \beta \cdot \frac{\bar{F}_L + \theta\gamma_0}{1 + t_E},$$ (Q8.7)

$$U = \frac{s}{s + \theta q(\theta)},$$ (Q8.8)

where $\bar{F}_L$ is the (fixed) marginal product of labour ($\bar{F}_L \equiv F_L(K(r + \delta), 1)$, where $K(r + \delta)$ is the optimal capital stock per active firm), t_E is the payroll tax, and $f(\theta) = \theta q(\theta)$.

(a) Compute the comparative static effects on w, θ, U, and V of an increase in the payroll tax.

(b) Denote the initial equilibrium real (consumer) wage rate by w_0. Assume that this real wage rate is inflexible in a downward direction. Following an exogenous shock, workers are willing to negotiate with firms about wage increases but are not willing to accept any wage decrease. Characterize such an equilibrium, using a two-panel figure like Figure 8.1 in the book.

(c) Show that, in the scenario sketched in part (b), the economy reacts differently to an increase and a decrease in the payroll tax. Explain the economic intuition behind your results.

★ Question 5: Dynamics of unemployment and vacancies

[Based on Pissarides (2000)] In this question we study the dynamic adjustment pattern of unemployment and vacancies outside the steady state. We ignore capital altogether and assume that labour is the only factor of production, attracting a constant marginal product, $\bar{F}_L$. You are given the information that outside the steady state, the key arbitrage equations are given by:

$$rJ_V = -\gamma_0 + q(\theta)[J_O - J_V] + \dot{J}_V,$$ (Q8.9)
$$rJ_O = \bar{F}_L - w - sJ_O + \dot{J}_O,$$ (Q8.10)
$$rY_U = z + \theta q(\theta)[Y_E - Y_U] + \dot{Y}_U,$$ (Q8.11)
$$rY_E = w - s[Y_E - Y_U] + \dot{Y}_E,$$ (Q8.12)

where the notation is explained in the book and where $\dot{x} \equiv dx/dt$ is the time derivative of x. The wage equation is given by:

$$w = (1 - \beta)z + \beta[\bar{F}_L + \theta\gamma_0],$$ (Q8.13)

whilst the unemployment rate changes over time according to:

$$\dot{U} = s \cdot (1 - U) - \theta q(\theta) \cdot U.$$ (Q8.14)

There is free entry/exit of firms with a vacancy. The matching function is Cobb-Douglas, i.e. $X = U^\eta V^{1-\eta}$, with $0 < \eta < 1$.

(a) Explain the economic intuition behind the dynamic terms appearing in (Q8.9)-(Q8.12) and (Q8.14).

(b) Prove that there is a unique perfect foresight solution for wages, vacancies, and labour market tightness, satisfying $\dot{w} = \dot{J}_O = \dot{\theta} = 0$.

(c) Derive the system of differential equations for U and θ and prove that this system is saddle-point stable. Illustrate your answer with the help of a graph, featuring U on the horizontal axis and θ on the vertical axis.

(d) Suppose that the unemployment rate is higher than its steady-state value. Show how vacancies and the unemployment rate converge over time. Employ the usual diagram, featuring U on the horizontal axis and V on the vertical axis.

(e) Compute the effects of an increase in z, both at impact, over time, and in the long run. Illustrate your answers with diagrams of the type employed in earlier parts of this question.

Answers

Question 1: Short questions

(a) True, a higher t_E shifts the ZP curve down as the value of an occupied job is reduced. The increase in the tax also puts downward pressure on wages as the firm shift part of the burden to employees. As a result, both w and θ fall. Unemployment rises and vacancies fall. Since $\theta \equiv V/U$ falls it is harder to locate a job and unemployment duration increases. See Figure 8.3 in the textbook.

(b) We typically assume that $J_V = 0$ in the matching model. This is because it is assumed that there is free entry or exit of firms with a vacancy. Exit or entry ensures that there are no excess (i.e. positive) profits to be had. If there is a restriction on the number of vacancies, we must distinguish two cases. If the restriction is binding (too low from the market's perspective), it will ensure that $J_V > 0$, i.e. it is valuable to possess a license to search for a worker in that case. If the restriction is non-binding (again from the market's perspective), then the licenses are not scarce, i.e. they are worthless ($J_V = 0$). Nobody can be forced to open a vacancy if this would result in a loss.

(c) The *Beveridge curve* is the combination of vacancies (V) and unemployment (U) for which the flow from employment to unemployment exactly matches the reverse flow from unemployment to employment. Put differently, it plots *equilibrium* (steady-state) unemployment as a function of the number of vacancies. In the matching model the Beveridge curve is given by:

$$U = \frac{s}{s + f(\theta)},$$

where U is the unemployment rate, s is the (exogenous) job destruction rate, f is the job finding rate of the workers, and $\theta \equiv V/U$ is the labour market tightness variable. We typically draw the Beveridge curve in (V, U) space–see for example panel (b) of Figures 8.1–8.5. The Beveridge curve is downward sloping: for a given unemployment rate, a reduction in V leads to a fall in the instantaneous probability of finding a job (i.e. f falls). For points below the Beveridge curve the unemployment rate is thus less than the rate required for flow equilibrium in the labour market ($U < s/(s + f)$). To restore flow equilibrium (and return to the Beveridge curve) the unemployment rate must increase.

The Beveridge curve is shifted if job destruction changes or if (ceteris paribus θ) the job finding rate changes. The latter could take place if the matching process becomes more productive, e.g. because of better information transmission in the labour market (see below).

(d) The matching function describes the relation between the number of unemployed, the number of vacancies and the number of successful matches on the labour market in a period (in a discrete time model) or at any moment in time (in a continuous time model). In modern search theory it is assumed that it takes time until a company with a vacancy and an unemployed looking for a job find each other. The number of matches increases as the number of unemployed and/or the number of vacancies increase.

If we assume that the matching function is of the Cobb-Douglas type, then we may write the number of matches XN (where X is the matching rate and N the exogenously given labour force) as

$$XN = (UN)^a (VN)^{1-\alpha} \tag{A8.1}$$

The probability that an employer with a vacancy finds an unemployed (q) equals the number of matches divided by the number of vacancies.

$$q \equiv \frac{XN}{VN} = \frac{(UN)^\alpha (VN)^{1-\alpha}}{VN} = \left(\frac{U}{V}\right)^\alpha = \theta^{-\alpha}$$

The probability that an unemployed finds a job (f) equals the number of matches divided by the number of unemployed.

$$f \equiv \frac{XN}{UN} = \frac{(UN)^a (VN)^{1-\alpha}}{UN} = \left(\frac{U}{V}\right)^{\alpha-1} = \theta^{1-\alpha}$$

Question 2: Search unemployment

(a) Equation (Q8.1) is the marginal productivity condition for capital, determining the optimal capital stock (and thus the optimal size of production) of each firm with a filled job. Equation (Q8.2) is a zero profit condition implied by the free entry/exit of firms. Equation (Q8.3) is the wage setting rule that follows from the generalised Nash bargaining between a firm with a vacancy and a potential employee. Equation (Q8.4) is the Beveridge curve that determines the equilibrium unemployment rate.

(b) The firm's search costs γ_0 decreases, the zero profit function in Figure 8.1 (in the textbook) shifts up because to keep zero-profit with decreasing search costs, wage costs must go up (given θ). The wage setting rule shifts down because expected foregone search costs are going down as a result of the subsidy. The effect on θ is clear, it will increase. Hence, equilibrium unemployment will decrease and the number of vacancies will increase. The effect on the wage rate is not unambiguous a priori. With mathematical methods we can derive the ultimate effect on w.

By differentiating (Q8.2)–(Q8.3) we get:

$$\frac{\gamma_0}{q(\theta)}\left[\frac{d\gamma_0}{\gamma_0} - \frac{dq(\theta)}{q(\theta)}\right] = -\frac{dw}{r+s}$$

$$dw = \beta\gamma_0\theta\left[\frac{d\gamma_0}{\gamma_0} + \frac{d\theta}{\theta}\right]$$

But $dq(\theta)/q(\theta) = -\eta(\theta)d\theta/\theta$ (with $0 < \eta(\theta) < 1$) and $(r+s)\gamma_0/q(\theta) = F_L - w$ so the system can be written as:

$$\begin{bmatrix} \eta(w - F_L) & -1 \\ -\beta\gamma_0\theta & 1 \end{bmatrix} \begin{bmatrix} \tilde{\theta} \\ dw \end{bmatrix} = \begin{bmatrix} F_L - w \\ \beta\gamma_0\theta \end{bmatrix} \tilde{\gamma}_0.$$

The determinant of the matrix on the left-hand side is $|\Delta| = -[\eta(F_L - w) + \beta\gamma_0\theta] < 0$. Using Cramer's Rule we get for θ:

$$\frac{\gamma_0}{\theta}\frac{\partial\theta}{\partial\gamma_0} = \frac{1}{|\Delta|}\begin{vmatrix} F_L - w & -1 \\ \beta\gamma_0\theta & 1 \end{vmatrix} = \frac{\beta\gamma_0\theta + (F_L - w)}{|\Delta|} < 0.$$

For the wage rate we obtain:

$$\gamma_0 \frac{\partial w}{\partial \gamma_0} = \frac{1}{|\Delta|} \begin{vmatrix} \eta(w - F_L) & F_L - w \\ -\beta\gamma_0\theta & \beta\gamma_0\theta \end{vmatrix} = \frac{\beta\gamma_0\theta(F_L - w)[1 - \eta]}{|\Delta|} < 0.$$

Conclusion: since γ_0 goes down, both w and θ increase as a result of the subsidy.

(c) Technology features constant returns to scale. Hence F_K and $F_N \equiv \frac{\partial F}{\partial (Z_0 L)}$ depend only on K/Z_0 (since $L = 1$). Thus, for a given interest rate, F_K stays the same. $F_L = Z_0 F_N$ (where $N \equiv Z_0 L$). But F_N is constant so that F_L increases. Readers of Chapter 13 will find this result easy to understand: in the question we assume that there is (once-off) labour-augmenting technological progress.

(d) From the previous question we know that F_L increases. This shifts both the zero profit curve and the wage setting curve up. The zero profit curve shifts up because the benefits of filling a vacancy go up, the wage setting curve goes up because the workers demand a piece of the cake. Differentiating (Q8.2)–(Q8.3) we get:

$$-\frac{(r + s)\gamma_0}{q(\theta)} \frac{dq(\theta)}{q(\theta)} = dF_L - dw$$

$$dw = \beta \left[dF_L + \gamma_0\theta \frac{d\theta}{\theta} \right]$$

But $dq(\theta)/q(\theta) = -\eta(\theta)d\theta/\theta$ (with $0 < \eta(\theta) < 1$) and $(r + s)\gamma_0/q(\theta) = F_L - w$ so the system can be written as:

$$\begin{bmatrix} \eta(w - F_L) & -1 \\ -\beta\gamma_0\theta & 1 \end{bmatrix} \begin{bmatrix} \tilde{\theta} \\ dw \end{bmatrix} = \begin{bmatrix} -1 \\ \beta \end{bmatrix} dF_L.$$

The determinant of the matrix on the left-hand side is $|\Delta| = -[\eta(F_L - w) + \beta\gamma_0\theta] < 0$. Using Cramer's Rule we get for θ:

$$\frac{1}{\theta} \frac{\partial\theta}{\partial F_L} = \frac{1}{|\Delta|} \begin{vmatrix} -1 & -1 \\ \beta & 1 \end{vmatrix} = \frac{\beta - 1}{|\Delta|} > 0.$$

For the wage rate we obtain:

$$\frac{\partial w}{\partial F_L} = \frac{1}{|\Delta|} \begin{vmatrix} \eta(w - F_L) & -1 \\ -\beta\gamma_0\theta & \beta \end{vmatrix} = \frac{-\beta[\gamma_0\theta + \eta(F_L - w)]}{|\Delta|} > 0.$$

Conclusion: the wage goes up (workers benefit), unemployment goes down, and vacancies go up.

(e) If the interest rate rises then several things happen. First, it follows from equation (Q8.1) that firms scale down production, i.e. they reduce the stock of capital per worker. The reduction in K leads to a reduction in the marginal product of labour (appearing in (Q8.2) and (Q8.3)) because the two production factors are cooperative. Second, it follows from equation (Q8.2) that the value of occupied job becomes smaller because $F_L - w$ is discounted more heavily. In terms of Figure A8.1, the ZP condition (defined by (Q8.2)) shifts down as does the

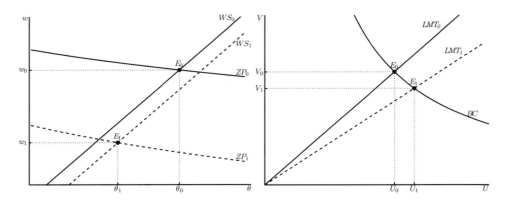

Figure A8.1: The effects of a higher interest rate

WS curve (defined by (Q8.3)). The wage rate unambiguously declines but the effect on labour market tightness appears to be ambiguous from the diagram. It can be shown mathematically, however, that θ falls as a result of the increase in r. We follow the same approach as in Appendix A of Chapter 8. First we loglinearize equations (Q8.2)-(Q8.3), holding constant z, δ, and β. (We allow γ_0 to vary because we need this later in this question). We loglinearize (Q8.2) and totally differentiate (Q8.3).

$$\tilde{\gamma} + \eta\tilde{\theta} = \frac{dF_L - dw}{F_L - w} - \frac{r}{r+s}\tilde{r}, \tag{A8.2}$$

where we used the definition of η in equation (8.4) in the text. For sake of simplicity (later on) we do not loglinearize F_L and w. Differentiation of equation (Q8.3) yields:

$$dw = \beta dF_L + \beta\theta\gamma_0\tilde{\gamma}_0 + \beta\gamma_0\theta\tilde{\theta}. \tag{A8.3}$$

Equations (A8.2)–(A8.3) can be used to solve for $\tilde{\theta}$ and dw in terms of $\tilde{r}$, dF_L, and $\tilde{\gamma}_0$:

$$\begin{bmatrix} \eta(F_L - w) & 1 \\ -\beta\gamma_0\theta & 1 \end{bmatrix} \begin{bmatrix} \tilde{\theta} \\ dw \end{bmatrix} = \begin{bmatrix} dF_L - (F_L - w)[\tilde{\gamma}_0 + (\frac{r}{r+s})\tilde{r}] \\ \beta\gamma_0\theta\tilde{\gamma}_0 + \beta dF_L \end{bmatrix} \tag{A8.4}$$

The matrix on the left-hand side has a positive determinant ($\Delta \equiv \eta(F_L - w) + \beta\gamma_0\theta > 0$), so it possesses a unique inverse:

$$\begin{bmatrix} -\eta(F_L - w) & -1 \\ -\beta\gamma_0\theta & 1 \end{bmatrix}^{-1} = \frac{1}{\Delta}\begin{bmatrix} 1 & -1 \\ \beta\gamma_0\theta & \eta(F_L - w) \end{bmatrix} \tag{A8.5}$$

Using (A8.5) in (A8.4) yields:

$$\begin{bmatrix} \tilde{\theta} \\ dw \end{bmatrix} = \frac{1}{\Delta}\begin{bmatrix} 1 & -1 \\ \beta\gamma_0\theta & \eta(F_L - w) \end{bmatrix}\begin{bmatrix} dF_L - (F_L - w)[\tilde{\gamma}_0 + \frac{r}{r+s}\tilde{r}] \\ \beta\gamma_0\theta\tilde{\gamma}_0 + \beta dF_L \end{bmatrix} \tag{A8.6}$$

$$= \frac{1}{\Delta}\begin{bmatrix} -\frac{r(F_L-w)}{r+s} & 1-\beta & -[F_L - w + \beta\gamma_0\theta] \\ -\frac{\beta\gamma_0\theta r(F_L-w)}{r+s} & \beta[\eta(F_L - w) + \gamma_0\theta] & -(1-\eta)\beta\gamma_0\theta(F_L - w) \end{bmatrix}\begin{bmatrix} \tilde{r} \\ dF_L \\ \tilde{\gamma}_0 \end{bmatrix}$$

By setting $\tilde{\gamma}_0 = 0$ we obtain the result for $\tilde{\theta}$ from the first line of (A6):

$$\tilde{\theta} = -\frac{F_L - w}{\Delta}\frac{r}{r+s}\tilde{r} + \frac{1-\beta}{\Delta}dF_L < 0. \tag{A8.7}$$

As a result of the increase in the interest rate, the labour market tightness variable falls for two reasons. First, the firm's surplus per occupied job is discounted more heavily, thus reducing the value of occupied jobs and decreasing the supply of vacancies. This *rent discounting effect* is represented by the first term on the right-hand side of (A8.7). Second, the interest rate increase prompts the firm to scale down by hiring less capital. This leads to a reduction in the marginal product of capital. This *labour productivity effect* is represented by the second term on the right-hand side of (A8.7).

In terms of Figure A8.1, panel (a), the equilibrium shifts from E_0 to E_1, and both w and θ fall. In panel (b) the labour market tightness line rotates in a clockwise fashion, from LMT_0 to LMT_1, unemployment increases and vacancies fall.

(f) A reduction in the firms' search costs affects both the zero profit condition (Q8.2) and the wage setting equation (Q8.3). In terms of Figure A8.2, the ZP curve shifts up if γ_0 falls. Intuitively, for a given value of θ, expected vacancy costs $\gamma_0/q(\theta)$ fall, so to restore zero-profit equilibrium the discounted value of rents earned on labour $((F_L - w)/(r+s))$ must fall also, i.e. the wage must rise. The WS curve shifts down. Intuitively, in the Nash bargaining outcome,

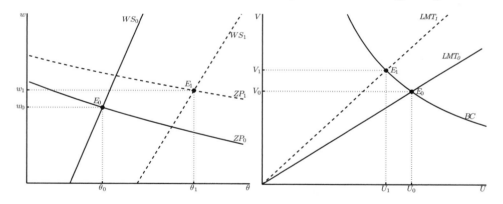

Figure A8.2: The effects of a reduction in the firm search costs

the workers capture a part of the foregone search costs ($\theta\gamma_0$) in the form of higher wages–see equation (8.24) in the book. If these costs decline the wage falls also.

By setting $\tilde{r} = dF_L = 0$ in (A8.6) we obtain:

$$\begin{bmatrix} \tilde{\theta} \\ dw \end{bmatrix} = -\frac{1}{\Delta}\begin{bmatrix} F_L - w + \beta\gamma_0\theta \\ (1-\eta)\beta\gamma_0\theta[F_L - w] \end{bmatrix}\tilde{\gamma}_0 \tag{A8.8}$$

We observe from (A8.8) that a decrease in γ_0 leads to an increase in both θ and w (remember $\Delta > 0$). Hence, in terms of Figure A8.2, panel (a), the equilibrium shifts from E_0 to E_1. In panel (b), the labour market tightness condition rotates counterclockwise from LMT_0 to LMT_1. Unemployment falls and vacancies increase.

Question 3: A CES matching function

(a) We must prove that multiplication of UN and VN by $\lambda > 0$ gives a matching total of λXN. To get more compact expressions, we define $\rho \equiv (\sigma - 1)/\sigma$. We write (Q8.5) as $XN = G(UN, VN)$ and find:

$$
\begin{aligned}
G(\lambda UN, \lambda VN) &= \left[(1 - \alpha)(Z_U \lambda UN)^\rho + \alpha (Z_V \lambda VN)^\rho \right]^{1/\rho} \\
&= \left[\lambda^\rho \cdot \left[(1 - \alpha)(Z_U \lambda UN)^\rho + \alpha (Z_V VN)^\rho \right] \right]^{1/\rho} \\
&= \lambda \cdot G(UN, VN).
\end{aligned}
$$

The shift factor Z_U captures how actively the job seekers are searching for a job. Similarly, the shift factor Z_V measures how keenly firms with a vacancy are seeking potential workers.

(b) If σ is greater than unity ($\rho > 0$), then (Q8.5) implies that there can be matches between job seekers and vacancies even if one of the parties is absent from the market, i.e. $G(0, VN)$ and $G(UN, 0)$ are both positive and well defined–the inputs UN and VN are non-essential in that case. This does not make any economic sense. Note that the Cobb-Douglas specification is allowed because both inputs are essential.

(c) We know from the definition in (8.2) that:

$$
\begin{aligned}
q &\equiv \frac{G(UN, VN)}{VN} = \left[(1 - \alpha)\left(Z_U \frac{UN}{VN} \right)^\rho + \alpha \left(Z_V \frac{VN}{VN} \right)^\rho \right]^{1/\rho} \\
&= \left[(1 - \alpha)\left(\frac{Z_U}{\theta} \right)^\rho + \alpha Z_V^\rho \right]^{1/\rho} \\
&\equiv q(\theta, Z_U, Z_V). \qquad\qquad\qquad\qquad\qquad\qquad\qquad\text{(A8.9)}
\end{aligned}
$$

Similarly, using the definition for f in (8.5) we obtain:

$$
\begin{aligned}
f &\equiv \frac{G(UN, VN)}{UN} = \left[(1 - \alpha)\left(Z_U \frac{UN}{UN} \right)^\rho + \alpha \left(Z_V \frac{VN}{UN} \right)^\rho \right]^{1/\rho} \\
&= \left[(1 - \alpha) Z_U^\rho + \alpha (Z_V \cdot \theta)^\rho \right]^{1\sigma/(\sigma-1)} \\
&\equiv f(\theta, Z_U, Z_V). \qquad\qquad\qquad\qquad\qquad\qquad\qquad\text{(A8.10)}
\end{aligned}
$$

To verify that $f(\theta, Z_U, Z_V) = \theta \cdot q(\theta, Z_U, Z_V)$ we multiply (A8.9) by θ:

$$
\begin{aligned}
\theta \cdot q(\theta, Z_U, Z_V) &= \theta \cdot \left[(1 - \alpha)\left(\frac{Z_U}{\theta} \right)^\rho + \alpha Z_V^\rho \right]^{1/\rho} \\
&= \left[\theta^\rho \cdot \left((1 - \alpha)\left(\frac{Z_U}{\theta} \right)^\rho + \alpha Z_V^\rho \right) \right]^{1/\rho} \\
&= \left[(1 - \alpha) Z_U^\rho + \alpha (Z_V \cdot \theta)^\rho \right]^{1/\rho} \\
&\equiv f(\theta, Z_U, Z_V). \qquad\qquad\qquad\qquad\qquad\qquad\qquad\text{(A8.11)}
\end{aligned}
$$

Using (A8.9) we can find the partial derivatives of the $q\left(\theta, Z_U, Z_V\right)$ function:

$$
\begin{aligned}
\frac{\partial q\left(\theta, Z_U, Z_V\right)}{\partial \theta} &= \frac{\sigma}{\sigma-1} \cdot\left[(1-\alpha)\left(\frac{Z_U}{\theta}\right)^{(\sigma-1)/\sigma}+\alpha Z_V^{(\sigma-1)/\sigma}\right]^{\sigma/(\sigma-1)-1} \\
&\quad \times \frac{\sigma-1}{\sigma}(1-\alpha)\left(\frac{Z_U}{\theta}\right)^{(\sigma-1)/\sigma-1} \cdot-\frac{Z_U}{\theta^2} \\
&= \left[(1-\alpha)\left(\frac{Z_U}{\theta}\right)^{(\sigma-1)/\sigma}+\alpha Z_V^{(\sigma-1)/\sigma}\right]^{1/(\sigma-1)} \\
&\quad \times(1-\alpha)\left(\frac{Z_U}{\theta}\right)^{-1/\sigma} \cdot-\frac{Z_U}{\theta^2} \\
&= \left[q^{(\sigma-1)/\sigma}\right]^{1/(\sigma-1)}(1-\alpha)\left(\frac{Z_U}{\theta}\right)^{-1/\sigma} \cdot-\frac{Z_U}{\theta^2} \\
&= -(1-\alpha)\frac{Z_U}{\theta^2}\left(\frac{\theta q}{Z_U}\right)^{1/\sigma}<0, \tag{A8.12}
\end{aligned}
$$

$$
\begin{aligned}
\frac{\partial q\left(\theta, Z_U, Z_V\right)}{\partial Z_U} &= \left[(1-\alpha)\left(\frac{Z_U}{\theta}\right)^{(\sigma-1)/\sigma}+\alpha Z_V^{(\sigma-1)/\sigma}\right]^{1/(\sigma-1)} \\
&\quad \times(1-\alpha)\left(\frac{Z_U}{\theta}\right)^{-1/\sigma} \cdot \frac{1}{\theta} \\
&= (1-\alpha)\frac{1}{\theta^2}\left(\frac{\theta q}{Z_U}\right)^{1/\sigma}>0, \tag{A8.13}
\end{aligned}
$$

$$
\begin{aligned}
\frac{\partial q\left(\theta, Z_U, Z_V\right)}{\partial Z_V} &= \left[(1-\alpha)\left(\frac{Z_U}{\theta}\right)^{(\sigma-1)/\sigma}+\alpha Z_V^{(\sigma-1)/\sigma}\right]^{1/(\sigma-1)} \alpha Z_V^{-1/\sigma} \\
&= \alpha\left(\frac{q}{Z_V}\right)^{1/\sigma}>0. \tag{A8.14}
\end{aligned}
$$

To obtain $\eta\left(\theta, Z_U, Z_V\right)$ we note from (8.4) in the book that:

$$
\begin{aligned}
\eta\left(\theta, Z_U, Z_V\right) &\equiv -\frac{\theta}{q} \cdot \frac{\partial q\left(\theta, Z_U, Z_V\right)}{\partial \theta} \\
&= \frac{\theta}{q} \cdot(1-\alpha)\frac{Z_U}{\theta^2}\left(\frac{\theta q}{Z_U}\right)^{1/\sigma} \\
&= (1-\alpha)\frac{Z_U}{q\theta}\left(\frac{\theta q}{Z_U}\right)^{1/\sigma} \\
&= (1-\alpha)\cdot\left(\frac{f}{Z_U}\right)^{(1-\sigma)/\sigma}>0. \tag{A8.15}
\end{aligned}
$$

From (A8.10) we can derive:

$$
1=(1-\alpha)\left(\frac{f}{Z_U}\right)^{(1-\sigma)/\sigma}+\alpha\left(\frac{q}{Z_V}\right)^{(1-\sigma)/\sigma}, \tag{A8.16}
$$

so it is clear that $\eta\left(\theta, Z_U, Z_V\right)$ is positive but less than unity.

The partial derivatives for $f\left(\theta, Z_U, Z_V\right)$ are very easy to get:

$$
\begin{aligned}
\frac{\partial f\left(\theta, Z_U, Z_V\right)}{\partial \theta} &= q\left(\theta, Z_U, Z_V\right) + \theta \cdot \frac{\partial q\left(\theta, Z_U, Z_V\right)}{\partial \theta} \\
&= q \cdot \left[1 + \frac{\theta}{q} \cdot \frac{\partial q\left(\theta, Z_U, Z_V\right)}{\partial \theta}\right] \\
&= q \cdot \left[1 - \eta\left(\theta, Z_U, Z_V\right)\right] > 0, \quad\quad\quad (A8.17)
\end{aligned}
$$

$$
\frac{\partial f\left(\theta, Z_U, Z_V\right)}{\partial Z_U} = \theta \cdot \frac{\partial q\left(\theta, Z_U, Z_V\right)}{\partial Z_U} = \frac{1-\alpha}{\theta}\left(\frac{\theta q}{Z_U}\right)^{1/\sigma} > 0, \quad (A8.18)
$$

$$
\frac{\partial f\left(\theta, Z_U, Z_V\right)}{\partial Z_V} = \theta \cdot \frac{\partial q\left(\theta, Z_U, Z_V\right)}{\partial Z_V} = \alpha\theta\left(\frac{q}{Z_V}\right)^{1/\sigma} > 0. \quad (A8.19)
$$

(d) The model is given by:

$$
\frac{\bar{F}_L - w}{r+s} = \frac{\gamma_0}{q(\theta, Z_U, Z_V)}, \quad\quad\quad (A8.20)
$$

$$
w = (1-\beta)z + \beta\left[\bar{F}_L + \theta\gamma_0\right], \quad\quad\quad (A8.21)
$$

$$
U = \frac{s}{s + f(\theta, Z_U, Z_V)}, \quad\quad\quad (A8.22)
$$

where $\bar{F}_L$ is the (fixed) marginal product of labour. Figure A8.3 shows what happens to the equilibrium if Z_U increases. Nothing happens to the wage setting curve (A8.21), but the zero-profit condition (A8.20) shifts up. Holding constant θ, and increase in Z_U increases q and decreases γ_0/q. This means that the left-hand side of (A8.20) decreases as well, i.e. w rises. In the right-hand panel, the LMT curve rotates counter-clockwise, say from LMT_0 to LMT_1.

The Beveridge curve shifts inward (toward the origin), say from BC_0 to BC_1. This effect can be ascertained by noting that $[s + f(\theta, Z_U, Z_V)] \cdot U = s$ so that:

$$
\left[s + f - \theta\frac{\partial f}{\partial \theta}\right] \cdot dU = -\frac{\partial f}{\partial \theta} \cdot dV - U\frac{\partial f}{\partial Z_U}dZ_U, \quad\quad\quad (A8.23)
$$

where the term in square brackets on the left-hand side is positive (because $f - \theta\frac{\partial f}{\partial \theta} = f\left[1 - \frac{\theta}{f}\frac{\partial f}{\partial \theta}\right] = f\eta > 0$).

(e) The effects of an increase in Z_V are exactly the same qualitatively as those of an increase in Z_U.

Question 4: Downward real wage rigidity

(a) The effect on w and θ can be gleaned from the sub-system (Q8.6)-(Q8.7). Totally differentiating these expressions, holding constant $r, s, \gamma_0, \beta, \bar{F}_L$, and z we find:

$$
(1 + t_E)\, dw + w\, dt_E = \frac{\gamma_0(r+s)}{\theta q(\theta)} \cdot \frac{\theta q'(\theta)}{q(\theta)}\, d\theta, \quad\quad\quad (A8.24)
$$

$$
(1 + t_E)\, dw + w\, dt_E = (1-\beta)z\, dt_E + \beta\gamma_0 d\theta. \quad\quad\quad (A8.25)
$$

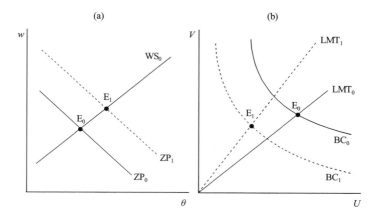

Figure A8.3: More efficient job seekers or vacancy fillers

By noting that $\eta(\theta) \equiv -\theta q'(\theta)/q(\theta)$ we can write (A8.24)-(A8.25) in matrix notation:

$$\begin{bmatrix} 1+t_E & \eta(\theta)\frac{\gamma_0(r+s)}{\theta q(\theta)} \\ -(1+t_E) & \beta\gamma_0 \end{bmatrix} \cdot \begin{bmatrix} dw \\ d\theta \end{bmatrix} = \begin{bmatrix} -w \\ w-(1-\beta)z \end{bmatrix} \cdot dt_E.$$

The determinant of the matrix, Δ, on the left-hand side is positive:

$$|\Delta| = (1+t_E) \cdot \left[\beta\gamma_0 + \eta(\theta)\frac{\gamma_0(r+s)}{\theta q(\theta)}\right] > 0.$$

The comparative static results are thus:

$$\begin{bmatrix} dw/dt_E \\ d\theta/dt_E \end{bmatrix} = \frac{1}{|\Delta|} \cdot \begin{bmatrix} \beta\gamma_0 & -\eta(\theta)\frac{\gamma_0(r+s)}{\theta q(\theta)} \\ 1+t_E & 1+t_E \end{bmatrix} \cdot \begin{bmatrix} -w \\ w-(1-\beta)z \end{bmatrix}$$

$$= \frac{1}{|\Delta|} \cdot \begin{bmatrix} -\beta\gamma_0 w - \eta(\theta)\frac{\gamma_0(r+s)}{\theta q(\theta)}[w-(1-\beta)z] \\ -(1-\beta)(1+t_E)z \end{bmatrix}. \tag{A8.26}$$

Since $w > (1-\beta)z$ it follows readily that $dw/dt_E < 0$ and $d\theta/dt_E < 0$. It follows readily that $dV/dt_E < 0$ and $dU/dt_E > 0$. This case has been illustrated in the book–see Figure 8.3.

(b) See Figure A8.4. Nothing happens to the zero-profit condition. The effective wage setting curve is given by the horizontal segment passing through E_2 and E_0 to the left of θ_0, and the upward sloping segment of the WS_0 curve to the right of θ_0.

(c) We know from part (a) that a decrease in t_E reseults in an increase in θ and w. So for this case, downward wage rigidity is not a problem.

An increase in the payroll tax, however, results in a decrease in both θ and w (if wages are flexible). This is illustrated in Figure A8.4 by the shift from point E_0 to E_1. With downward wage rigidity, however, the wage will be maintained

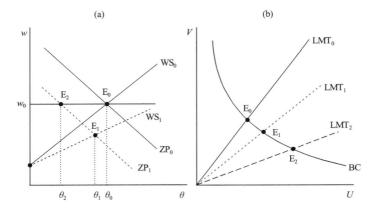

Figure A8.4: The payroll tax under downward real wage rigidity

at $w = w_0$. The constrained equilibrium is at point E_2. Firms cut back on vacancies because the tax-inclusive wage rate has increased. With downward real wage rigidity, the effects on V and U are amplified compared to the case of flexible real wages. Under downward real wage rigidity, quantity movements take the place of price (i.e., real wage) movements.

Question 5: Dynamics of unemployment and vacancies

(a) In (Q8.9)-(Q8.12), the dynamic terms represent a second type of capital gain (if positive) or loss (if negative) that may be obtained outside the steady state. This capital gains does not arise from changing status (say from vacancy to filled job or unemployed to employed), but because the value of the asset itself may change over time. Since agents are forward looking, they take these perfectly anticipated capital gains and losses into account in valuing the asset under consideration.

In equation (Q8.14), the dynamics in the unemployment rate is just the difference between the instantaneous flow into unemployment due to job destruction (first term on the right-hand side) and the instantaneous flow out of unemployment due to successful matching.

(b) There is instantaneous free entry/exit of firms with a vacancy, so $J_V = \dot{J}_V = 0$ at all times. By using this result in (Q8.9)-(Q8.10) we obtain:

$$J_O = \frac{\gamma_0}{q(\theta)}, \tag{A8.27}$$

$$\dot{J}_O = (r+s) J_O + w - \bar{F}_L. \tag{A8.28}$$

The wage rate only depends on the endogenous variable, θ. Similarly, (A8.27) shows that J_O only depends on θ so that we can use (A8.28) to derive a differential equation for labour market tightness. By differentiating (A8.27) with respect to time we find:

$$\dot{J}_O = -J_O \cdot \frac{\dot{q}(\theta)}{q(\theta)}. \tag{A8.29}$$

Substituting (A8.27), (A8.29), and (Q8.13) into (A8.28) and rearranging we find:

$$
\begin{aligned}
-J_O \cdot \frac{\dot{q}(\theta)}{q(\theta)} &= (r+s) J_O + (1-\beta)z + \beta \left[\bar{F}_L + \theta \gamma_0 \right] - \bar{F}_L \\
-\frac{\dot{q}(\theta)}{q(\theta)} &= (r+s) + \frac{(1-\beta)(z-\bar{F}_L) + \beta \theta \gamma_0}{J_O} \\
&= (r+s) + \left[(1-\beta)(z-\bar{F}_L) + \beta \theta \gamma_0 \right] \cdot \frac{q(\theta)}{\gamma_0}.
\end{aligned}
$$
(A8.30)

The matching function implies that:

$$
q(\theta) = \theta^{-\eta},
$$
(A8.31)

so that:

$$
-\frac{\dot{q}(\theta)}{q(\theta)} = \eta \cdot \frac{\dot{\theta}}{\theta}.
$$
(A8.32)

Using these results in (A8.30) we find the differential equation for labour market tightness:

$$
\begin{aligned}
\eta \cdot \frac{\dot{\theta}}{\theta} &= (r+s) + \left[(1-\beta)(z-\bar{F}_L) + \beta \theta \gamma_0 \right] \cdot \frac{\theta^{-\eta}}{\gamma_0} \quad \Leftrightarrow \\
\eta \cdot \dot{\theta} &= (r+s)\theta + \left[(1-\beta)(z-\bar{F}_L) + \beta \theta \gamma_0 \right] \cdot \frac{\theta^{1-\eta}}{\gamma_0}.
\end{aligned}
$$
(A8.33)

Since the term in square brackets on the right-hand side is positive and $0 < \eta < 1$, equation (A8.33) represents an unstable differential equation in θ. The only economically sensible solution for this differential equation is the steady-state solution, i.e. $\dot{\theta} = 0$ at all times. Following a *time-invariant* shock to one of the exogenous variables appearing in (A8.33), θ immediately jumps to its new steady-state value, θ^*. Since J_V and w only depend on θ, they also have this property.

(c) Since $\theta q(\theta) = \theta^{1-\eta}$, equation (Q8.14) can be written as:

$$
\dot{U} = s \cdot (1-U) - \theta^{1-\eta} \cdot U,
$$
(A8.34)

i.e. $\dot{U}$ depends negatively on both U and θ. We recall from (A8.33) that $\dot{\theta}$ only depends on θ. Qualitatively, the dynamic system can thus be written as:

$$
\begin{bmatrix} \dot{U} \\ \dot{\theta} \end{bmatrix} = \begin{bmatrix} \delta_{11} & \delta_{12} \\ 0 & \delta_{22} \end{bmatrix} \cdot \begin{bmatrix} \dot{U} \\ \dot{\theta} \end{bmatrix},
$$
(A8.35)

with $\delta_{11} < 0$, $\delta_{12} < 0$, and $\delta_{22} > 0$. Since the determinant of the Jacobian matrix is equal to $\delta_{11}\delta_{22}$ and is negative, we must have characteristic roots of opposite sign. The (U, θ)-dynamics is saddle-point stable, with U representing the predetermined (sticky) variable and θ constituting the jumping variable.

In Figure A8.5 the iso-clines and dynamic forces are illustrated. Not surprisingly, in view of the results found in part (b), the $\dot{\theta} = 0$ line coincides with the saddle path for this system. The unique equilibrium is at point E_0. Steady-state unemployment is U^* and the steady-state labour market tightness variable equals θ^*.

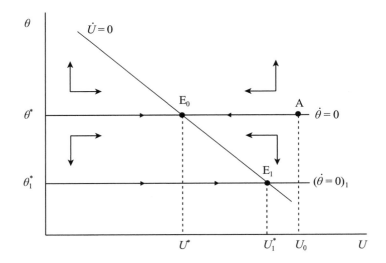

Figure A8.5: Phase diagram for unemployment and labour market tightness

(d) In Figure A8.6 the economy is initially located at point A, where $U_0 > U^*$ and $V_0 > V^*$. Since $\theta = \theta^*$, the economy gradually moves along the LMT curve (repesenting $\dot{\theta} = 0$ in the (V, U) diagram) toward the steady-state equilibrium, E_0.

(e) It is shown in the book (in Figure 8.1) that an increase in z leads to an increase in w and a decrease in θ. Since there is no transitional dynamics in these variables, the steady-state values for w and θ jump at impact. The decrease in θ^* is represented in Figure A8.5 by an downward shift in the saddle path. The dynamics of U and of U and V are illustrated in, respectively, Figures A8.5 and A8.6.

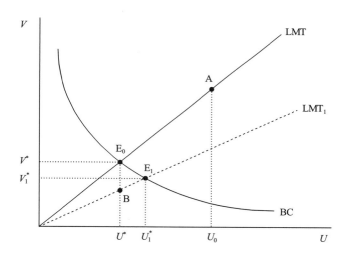

Figure A8.6: Vacancy-unemployment dynamics around the Beveridge curve

Chapter 9

Macroeconomic policy, credibility, and politics

Question 1: Short questions

(a) Explain why central bankers are often recruited from the more conservative ranks of society. Explain the link with Ulysses strategy concerning the Sirens.

(b) "The central bank should not focus on inflation, but should do what is best for the economy: stimulate production!" Explain and evaluate this proposition.

(c) "An ambitious government that wants to stimulate production is excellent for the economy." Explain and evaluate this proposition.

★ Question 2: Capital taxation and income inequality

Consider a two period model. People differ only with respect to their initial capital endowment K_1^i. The distribution of the initial capital endowment is skewed towards the right, as is shown in Figure Q9.1. This implies that the average capital endowment is larger than the median capital endowment, $\bar{K}_1 > K_1^M$.

The lifetime utility function of individual i is given by:

$$U^i = \ln C_1^i + \frac{C_2^i}{1+\rho}, \tag{Q9.1}$$

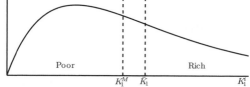

Figure Q9.1: The frequency distribution of initial capital endowment

with C_t^i consumption of individual i in period t and ρ the rate of time preference. Capital is the only production factor in this economy, marginal capital productivity is denoted by b. This implies that each individual's income before taxes and transfers in period t is given by:

$$Y_t^i = bK_t^i, \qquad t = 1, 2. \tag{Q9.2}$$

At the beginning of period 2 everyone receives a lump-sum transfer Z. This transfer Z is financed by a capital income tax t_K on income in period 2. The corresponding government budget constraint is:

$$Z = t_K b \bar{K}_2 \tag{Q9.3}$$

People vote by simple majority on the size of the capital income tax at the beginning of period 1. The government budget constraint determines the lump-sum transfer.

(a) Show that the intertemporal budget constraint of individual i can be written as:

$$C_2^i = Z + [1 + b(1 - t_K)][(1 + b)K_1^i - C_1^i] \tag{Q9.4}$$

(b) Derive optimal consumption C_1^i and C_2^i given the initial capital endowment K_1^i, the lump-sum transfer Z and the capital income tax t_K.

(c) Show that the (transformed) indirect utility function of individual i can be written as:

$$V^i = -\ln(1 + b(1 - t_K)) - \frac{t_K b}{1 + b(1 - t_K)} + \frac{t_K b(1 + b)}{1 + \rho}[\bar{K}_1 - K_1^i] \tag{Q9.5}$$

(d) Use the median voter theorem to derive the capital income tax t_K as an (implicit) function of the median capital endowment K_1^M.

(e) Show that the capital income tax increases if the initial capital endowment is more skewed towards the right (i.e. there are more very wealthy people, $\bar{K}_1 - K_1^M$ increases).

(f) Suppose that the people vote again on the lump-sum transfer and the capital income tax at the beginning of period 2. Are the at the beginning of period 1 announced capital income tax and lump-sum transfer time-consistent? What are the consequences for savings and consumption if the rational expectations hypothesis holds?

Question 3: Choice of policy instrument

[Based on Poole (1970)] In this question we study the classic paper by Poole (1970). This paper shows how optimal economic policy was typically determined in the literature predating the rational expectations revolution of the early 1970s. Assume that the closed economy is described by the simple (log-linear) IS-LM model:

$$y_t = \alpha_0 - \alpha_1 R_t + u_t, \qquad \alpha_1 > 0, \tag{Q9.6}$$
$$m_t - p_t = \beta_0 + \beta_1 y_t - \beta_2 R_t + v_t, \qquad \beta_1 > 0, \beta_2 > 0, \tag{Q9.7}$$

where y_t is output, R_t is the nominal interest rate, u_t is a stochastic shock term affecting the IS curve, m_t is the nominal money supply, p_t is the price level, and v_t is a stochastic term affecting the LM curve. It is assumed that the two stochastic shock terms, u_t and v_t, are independent and normally distributed white noise terms (there is no correlation between these terms and both terms display no autocorrelation): $u_t \sim N(0, \sigma_u^2)$ and $v_t \sim N(0, \sigma_v^2)$. All variables except the interest rate are measured in logarithms. Assume furthermore that the price level is fixed and can be normalized to unity (so that $p_t \equiv \ln P_t = 0$ in (Q9.7)).

The policy maker is concerned about stabilizing the economy and wishes to use monetary policy in order to minimize the following loss function:

$$\Omega \equiv E\left(y_t - y^*\right)^2, \tag{Q9.8}$$

where Ω is a measure of social loss (the volatility of output around its target level) and y^* is the (fixed) target level of output, e.g. full employment output. The policy maker can choose one of two instruments of monetary policy. It can control the money supply and let the interest rate settle at its equilibrium level determined in the economy. Alternatively, it can peg the interest rate and let the money supply settle at the equilibrium level determined in the market.

(a) Interpret the equations of the model.

(b) Show that in the *deterministic case*, with both u_t and v_t identically equal to zero in all periods, the two instruments of monetary policy are completely equivalent, i.e. it does not matter which one is used.

(c) Now assume that the IS curve is subject to stochastic shocks but the LM curve is deterministic (i.e. $u_t \sim N(0, \sigma_u^2)$ and $v_t \equiv 0$ for all periods). Show that the rational policy maker will choose the money supply instrument. Illustrate your answer both formally and with the aid of a diagram.

(d) Now assume that the LM curve is subject to stochastic shocks but the IS curve is deterministic (i.e. $u_t \equiv 0$ for all periods and $v_t \sim N(0, \sigma_v^2)$). Show that the rational policy maker will now choose the interest rate instrument. Illustrate your answer both formally and with the aid of a diagram.

(e) Use the general stochastic model, with both u_t and v_t non-zero, and derive the value of the loss function (Q9.8) under the two monetary instruments. Show that the money supply instrument is preferred to the interest rate instrument if the following condition holds:

$$\frac{\alpha_1^2 \sigma_v^2 + \beta_2^2 \sigma_u^2}{(\alpha_1 \beta_1 + \beta_2)^2} < \sigma_u^2.$$

Explain your result intuitively.

Question 4: Rules versus discretion

The supply of goods is determined by:

$$y = \bar{y} + \alpha\left[\pi - \pi^e\right] + \varepsilon, \tag{Q9.9}$$

where y is output, $\bar{y}$ is full employment output, π is inflation, π^e is expected inflation, and ε is a stochastic disturbance term with zero mean ($E(\varepsilon) = 0$) and constant
variance ($E(\varepsilon^2) = \sigma^2$). The preferences of citizen i are represented by:

$$\Omega_i = \frac{1}{2}[y - y^*]^2 + \frac{\beta_i}{2}\pi^2, \qquad\qquad\qquad\qquad (Q9.10)$$

where y^* is the optimal output level (from the perspective of all citizens). Each citizen tries to attain a minimum level of Ω_i, so equation (Q9.10) can be interpreted
as a "regret function" stating the welfare costs associated with being away from the
optimum ($y = y^*, \pi = 0$).

(a) Interpret these two equations.

(b) "Just like Ulysses, the President of the ECB should tie himself to the mast of
a zero-inflation rule." Discuss this proposition in the light of the literature on
"rules versus discretion." Assume in this part of the question that the preferences of the population are homogeneous (so that $\beta_i = \beta$). Explain the importance of the quantity $\bar{y} - y^*$ to your conclusion.

(c) Now assume that the population features heterogeneous preferences. Assume
furthermore that there is asymmetric information. In particular, when the
wages are set, the realization of the supply shock, ε, is unknown. The central
banker, on the other hand, is assumed to know this realization when he/she
sets monetary policy and determines the inflation rate. Explain why a majority
decision will lead to the appointment of a central banker who is more "right-
wing" than the population itself.

Question 5: Political business cycles

[Based on Nordhaus (1975)] In this question we study the political business cycle under the assumption that private agents feature adaptive expectations about inflation.
The macroeconomic environment is summarized by the following two equations:

$$\pi(t) = \Phi(U(t)) + \alpha \cdot \pi^e(t), \qquad 0 < \alpha \leq 1, \qquad (Q9.11)$$
$$\dot{\pi}^e(t) = \beta \cdot [\pi(t) - \pi^e(t)], \qquad \beta > 0, \qquad\qquad (Q9.12)$$

where $\pi(t)$ is the actual inflation rate at time t, $\pi^e(t)$ is the expected inflation rate at
that time, $U(t)$ is the unemployment rate. It is assumed that $\Phi'(\cdot) < 0$. The voting
public dislikes both inflation and unemployment, and the aggregate voting function
at time t is given by:

$$v(t) \equiv V(U(t), \pi(t)), \qquad\qquad\qquad\qquad (Q9.13)$$

with $V_U \equiv \partial V/\partial U < 0$, and $V_\pi \equiv \partial V/\partial \pi < 0$. Intuitively, $v(t)$ represents the
performance score that the incumbent party receives from the public at time t. At
time $t = 0$, the incumbent has just won the election. There are elections every T
period, i.e. the next election will be held at time $t = T$. The incumbent party's
objective function at time $t = 0$ is given by:

$$\Omega \equiv \int_0^T V(U(t), \pi(t)) \cdot e^{\rho t}dt, \qquad \rho > 0, \qquad (Q9.14)$$

The higher is $\Omega(0)$, the higher will be the appreciation of the public for this administration's economic policies. The parameter ρ measures the rate of decay of the public's memory. If ρ is large, the public hardly recalls the early performance of the policy maker by the time the election occurs. Vice versa, if ρ is small the public has a long memory. The policy maker maximizes Ω by $\pi(t)$ and $U(t)$ optimally, taking into account the constraints imposed by (Q9.11)-(Q9.12). At time $t = 0$, the expected inflation rate equals $\pi^e(0) = \pi_0^e$.

(a) Briefly explain the economic intuition behind equations (Q9.11)-(Q9.12).

(b) Formulate the incumbent party's optimization problem as an optimal control problem. Explain which are the control and state variables. Derive the first-order conditions.

(c) Solve the incumbent party's optimization problem. Assume that $V(U(t), \pi(t)) = -U(t)^2 - \eta\pi(t)$ and $\Phi(U(t)) = \gamma_0 - \gamma_1 U(t)$, with $\eta > 0$, $\gamma_0 > 0$, and $\gamma_1 > 0$. Prove that the policy maker chooses a declining path for unemployment over the term of its administration. Assume that $\rho \neq (1-\alpha)\beta$. (Just in case you forgot, you are reminded of the fact that $e^{ax} > 1 - a$ for $x > 0$ regardless of the sign of a.)

(d) ★ Derive the fundamental differential equation for $\pi^e(t)$, and prove that it is stable. Compute the expected inflation rate at time T, and write it as $\pi^e(T)$. State the condition that must hold in order for $\pi^e(T)$ to be equal to π_0^e.

Answers

Question 1: Short questions

(a) This is a commitment device to ensure that inflation remains relatively low. By choosing somebody who is more inflation averse that himself, the median voter commits to a better outcome (which he cannot produce himself). Ulysses also used a commitment device by tying himself to the mast.

(b) In terms of the model used throughout the chapter, a central bank that stimulates production instead of targeting on inflation has a low β. From equations (9.10) and (9.11) we know that a low β leads to high inflation, but the expected (and average) production is still equal to the natural level of production. A central bank that focuses on production only leads to higher inflation in the long run.

(c) The answer to this question depends on how the government wants to stimulate production. If the government has a long term focus, the only way to stimulate aggregate production is either to increase productivity or by stimulating investment, thereby increasing the capital stock. To analyse these policies, we would need a dynamic growth model which is one of the topics of Chapter 13.

If the government has a short term focus, then it can stimulate production either by fiscal or monetary policy. The effectiveness of both policies crucially depends on the exchange rate system and capital mobility (see Table 10.1 in the textbook).

Moreover, from Chapter 9 we know that an over-ambitious government (target production is much higher than natural production) might lead to higher inflation because the optimal enforceable rule inflation (equation (9.35)) increases as $y^* - \bar{y}$ increases. This is because the optimal enforceable region decreases.

Question 2: Capital taxation and income inequality

(a) A household's budget restrictions in periods 1 and 2 are:

$$C_1^i + [K_2^i - K_1^i] = Y_1^i \quad \Rightarrow \quad C_1^i + [K_2^i - K_1^i] = bK_1^i \tag{A9.1}$$
$$C_2^i = Z + K_2^i + (1 - t_K)bK_2^i \quad \Rightarrow \quad C_2^i = Z + [1 + b(1 - t_K)]K_2^i \tag{A9.2}$$

Equation (A9.1) is obvious, the only income is capital income which an individual can save and add to the initial capital endowment or consume. Note that nobody pays taxes or receives transfers in the first period. In the second period each individual receives Z in lump-sum transfers, but has to pay taxes over his/her capital income. Finally, since the world ends at the end of period two, there is no reason to have any capital left, so each individual can consume its entire accumulated capital stock.

Combining equations (A9.1) and (A9.2) yields the required expression.

(b) Each individual maximizes his/her utility (Q9.1) subject to the intertemporal budget constraint (Q9.4). The corresponding Lagrangian is:

$$\mathcal{L}^i = \ln C_1^i + \frac{C_2^i}{1 + \rho} + \lambda \left[Z + [1 + b(1 - t_K)][(1 + b)K_1^i - C_1^i] - C_2^i \right] \tag{A9.3}$$

The first order conditions:

$$\frac{\partial \mathcal{L}}{\partial C_1^i} = 0 : \quad \frac{1}{C_1^i} = \lambda [1 + b(1 - t_K)]$$

$$\frac{\partial \mathcal{L}}{\partial C_2^i} = 0 : \quad \frac{1}{1 + \rho} = \lambda$$

These first order conditions together with the intertemporal budget constraint (Q9.4) give:

$$C_1^i = \frac{1 + \rho}{1 + b(1 - t_K)} \tag{A9.4}$$

$$C_2^i = Z + [1 + b(1 - t_K)](1 + b)K_1^i - (1 + \rho) \tag{A9.5}$$

Later on we will need an expression for K_2^i. Use (A9.1) and (A9.4) to get:

$$K_2^i = (1 + b)K_1^i - C_1 = (1 + b)K_1^i - \frac{1 + \rho}{1 + b(1 - t_K)} \tag{A9.6}$$

(c) Substitute equations (A9.4) and (A9.5) into the utility function (Q9.1). The result is the indirect utility function (utility as a function of income, transfer and tax rate):

$$\hat{V}^i = \ln \left(\frac{1 + \rho}{1 + b(1 - t_K)} \right) + \frac{Z + [1 + b(1 - t_K)](1 + b)K_1^i - (1 + \rho)}{1 + \rho}$$

$$= \ln(1 + \rho) - \ln(1 + b(1 - t_K)) + \frac{Z + [1 + b(1 - t_K)](1 + b)K_1^i}{1 + \rho} - 1 \tag{A9.7}$$

Dropping the terms with only exogenous variables and parameters (note: t_K and Z are *not* exogenous) gives:

$$\hat{V}^i = -\ln(1 + b(1 - t_K)) + \frac{Z - t_K b(1 + b)K_1^i}{1 + \rho}$$

Use the government budget constraint (Q9.3) to substitute Z out of this equation:

$$\hat{V}^i = -\ln(1 + b(1 - t_K)) + \frac{t_K b \bar{K}_2 - t_K b(1 + b)K_1^i}{1 + \rho} \tag{A9.8}$$

From (A9.6) we can derive an expression for $\bar{K}_2$:

$$\bar{K}_2 = (1 + b)\bar{K}_1 - \frac{1 + \rho}{1 + b(1 - t_K)} \tag{A9.9}$$

and substitution into (A9.8) gives:

$$\hat{V}^i = -\ln(1 + b(1 - t_K)) - \frac{t_K b}{1 + b(1 - t_K)} + \frac{t_K b(1 + b)\bar{K}_1 - t_K b(1 + b)K_1^i}{1 + \rho}$$

Collect terms and we have the required result.

(d) The median voter theorem states that the median voter determines the result of the election, in this case the capital income tax. This median voter will choose t_K such that his/her utility is maximized, given his/her initial capital endowment K_1^M. Maximization of (Q9.5) with $K_1^i = K_1^M$ gives the first order condition:

$$\frac{\partial V^M}{\partial t_K} = \frac{b}{1 + b(1 - t_K)} - \frac{b[1 + b(1 - t_K)] + b^2 t_K}{[1 + b(1 - t_K)]^2} + \frac{b(1 + b)}{1 + \rho}[\bar{K}_1 - K_1^M]$$

$$= \frac{b}{1 + b(1 - t_K)} - \frac{b(1 + b)}{[1 + b(1 - t_K)]^2} + \frac{b(1 + b)}{1 + \rho}[\bar{K}_1 - K_1^M]$$

$$= \frac{-b^2 t_K}{[1 + b(1 - t_K)]^2} + \frac{b(1 + b)}{1 + \rho}[\bar{K}_1 - K_1^M] = 0$$

Rewriting gives:

$$\frac{b t_K}{[1 + b(1 - t_K)]^2} = \frac{1 + b}{1 + \rho}[\bar{K}_1 - K_1^M] \qquad \text{(A9.10)}$$

(e) Equation (A9.10) implicitly defines t_K as a function of $\bar{K}_1 - K_1^M$. Total differentiation gives:

$$\frac{b[1 + b(1 - t_K)]^2 + 2b^2 t_K[1 + b(1 - t_K)]}{[1 + b(1 - t_K)]^4} dt_K = \frac{1 + b}{1 + \rho}d(\bar{K}_1 - K_1^M) \quad \Rightarrow$$

$$\frac{b + b^2 - b^2 t_K + 2b^2 t_K}{[1 + b(1 - t_K)]^3} dt_K = \frac{1 + b}{1 + \rho}d(\bar{K}_1 - K_1^M) \quad \Rightarrow$$

$$\frac{b[1 + b(1 + t_K)]}{[1 + b(1 - t_K)]^3} dt_K = \frac{1 + b}{1 + \rho}d(\bar{K}_1 - K_1^M) \quad \Rightarrow$$

$$\frac{dt_K}{d(\bar{K}_1 - K_1^M)} = \frac{1 + b}{1 + \rho} \cdot \frac{[1 + b(1 - t_K)]^3}{b[1 + b(1 + t_K)]} > 0$$

From this it is obvious that if $\bar{K}_1 - K_1^M$ increases, t_K increases.

The economic intuition is that there are gains to be made from the viewpoint of the median voter to tax the wealthy and divide the revenues equally over the entire population. Although the median voter will have to pay some capital income tax, the benefits are larger (because of the skewed initial distribution). The median voter will not fully tax capital income since this will take away the incentive to save and thereby reduces the tax base.

Note that if the median voter's initial capital endowment is exactly equal to the mean, he/she will opt for no capital tax at all, he/she is *not* indifferent!

(f) At the beginning of the second period, the existing capital stocks K_2^i are given. The median voter realises this and maximizes his/her utility given only the second period's budget restriction (A9.2). The optimization problem for the median voter is now:

$$\max U^M = C_2^M \quad \text{s.t.} \quad C_2^M = Z + [1 + b(1 - t_K)]K_2^M \qquad \text{(A9.11)}$$

which results in the obvious indirect utility function:

$$\hat{V}^M = Z + [1 + b(1 - t_K)]K_2^M \qquad \text{(A9.12)}$$

Combine this with the government budget constraint (Q9.3), drop all the exogenous terms and we have:

$$V^M = t_K b [\bar{K}_2 - K_2^M] \tag{A9.13}$$

It is easily seen from (A9.13) that for $\bar{K}_2 > K_2^M$ the median voter will pick the maximum capital income tax, that is, $t_K = 1$. The earlier announced tax rate is time-inconsistent.

People will realise this according to the rational expectations hypothesis and will not believe the earlier announced capital income tax. Everybody will maximize his/her utility given that $t_K = 1$. Setting $t_K = 1$ in equation (A9.4) gives $C_1 = 1 + \rho$ which clearly shows that people save less.

Question 3: Choice of policy instrument

(a) Equation (Q9.6) is the IS curve. Demand for goods is affected negatively by the interest rate (through investment) and there are stochastic demand shocks, represented by u_t. Equation (Q9.7) is the LM curve. The demand for real money balances (in logarithms) depends positively on output (transactions demand) and negatively on the nominal interest rate (opportunity cost of holding money). We abstract from (expected) inflation, so the nominal interest rate features in the IS curve.

Equation (Q9.8) is the *objective function* of the policy maker. The policy maker wishes to steer actual output, y_t, as closely as possible to some exogenously given *target* output level, y^*. Both positive and negative deviations of actual from target output are not appreciated by the policy maker. The policy maker must either use the interest rate or the money supply as its *instrument*.

(b) In the deterministic case, both stochastic shocks are identically equal to zero ($u_t = v_t = 0$ for all t). It is easy to show that in that case both instruments serve equally well to stabilize output. In fact, they are completely identical. The equivalence result is shown in Figure A9.1. Assume that the economy is initially in point E_0 where output falls short of its target level ($y_t < y^*$).

Under the *interest rate instrument* the policy maker sets $R = R^*$, where R^* is the interest rate for which the IS curve gives an output level equal to y^*–see point A in Figure A9.1. The LM curve is not very informative under the interest rate instrument because the money supply is endogenous, i.e. if the policy maker sets $R = R^*$ then the money supply will adjust such that IS_0 and the dashed LM curve, LM_1, intersect at point A. R^* can be computed by substituting $y = y^*$ (and $u_t = 0$) into the IS curve and solving for R^*:

$$y^* = \alpha_0 - \alpha_1 R^* \quad \Leftrightarrow \quad R^* = \frac{\alpha_0 - y^*}{\alpha_1}. \tag{A9.14}$$

The money supply that will result is computed by substituting $y_t = y^*$ and $R_t = R^*$ (and, of course, $p_t = 0$ and $v_t = 0$) in the LM curve (Q9.7). We obtain:

$$\begin{aligned} m_t &= \beta_0 + \beta_1 [\alpha_0 - \alpha_1 R^*] - \beta_2 R^* \\ &= \beta_0 + \alpha_0 \beta_1 - (\alpha_1 \beta_1 + \beta_2) R^*. \end{aligned} \tag{A9.15}$$

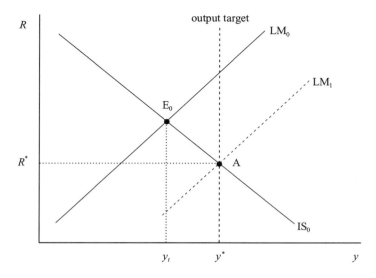

Figure A9.1: Money supply and interest rate instruments

Under the *money supply instrument*, the policy maker sets the money supply, m^*, such that the IS-LM equilibrium occurs at an output level of y^*. This is obviously also at point A. The endogenous variables under this policy instrument are output and the interest rate. The correct money supply is thus:

$$m^* = \beta_0 + \alpha_0\beta_1 - (\alpha_1\beta_1 + \beta_2)R^* \tag{A9.16}$$

$$= \beta_0 + \alpha_0\beta_1 - (\alpha_1\beta_1 + \beta_2)\frac{\alpha_0 - y^*}{\alpha_1}. \tag{A9.17}$$

The two instruments are equivalent and both hit the output target exactly, i.e. $y_t = y^*$ for all t and $\Omega = 0$. The instrument equivalency result breaks down in a stochastic setting, as parts (c)–(e) of this question illustrate.

(c) If only the IS curve is subject to stochastic shocks, then the money supply and interest rate instruments are no longer equivalent. Under the interest rate instrument, the policy maker will set R^* such that the IS curve is *expected* to yield an output level of y^*, i.e. R^* will be set according to the value given in (A9.14). The actual output level is, of course, stochastic, because demand for goods is subject to stochastic shocks that the policy maker (and the public) cannot forecast. Hence, actual output is obtained by substituting R^* (from (A9.14)) into equation (Q9.6):

$$y_t = \alpha_0 - \alpha_1 R^* + u_t$$

$$= \alpha_0 - \alpha_1 \frac{\alpha_0 - y^*}{\alpha_1} + u_t$$

$$= y^* + u_t. \tag{A9.18}$$

Given the interest rate instrument, actual output fluctuates randomly around its target level y^*. The asymptotic variance of output will thus be:

$$\sigma_y^2\Big|_{R=R^*} = \sigma_u^2. \tag{A9.19}$$

Under the money supply instrument, the policy maker sets the money supply such that the expected IS-LM intersection occurs at an output level equal to y^*, i.e. it sets $m = m^*$, where m^* is given in (A9.16) or (A9.17). Since the IS curve shifts stochastically, the actual IS-LM intersection will be somewhere along the given LM curve based on $m = m^*$. To find actual output level, we first solve equations (Q9.6)–(Q9.7) for output:

$$y_t = \alpha_0 - \frac{\alpha_1}{\beta_2}[\beta_0 + \beta_1 y_t + v_t - m_t + p_t] + u_t \quad \Rightarrow$$

$$y_t = \frac{\alpha_0 \beta_2 - \alpha_1 \beta_0 + \alpha_1 m^* + \beta_2 u_t}{\beta_2 + \alpha_1 \beta_1}, \tag{A9.20}$$

where we have substituted $p_t = v_t = 0$ and $m_t = m^*$ for all t in going from the first to the second line. By substituting the expression for m^* (given in (A9.17)) into (A9.20), we obtain an even simpler expression:

$$y_t = y^* + \frac{\beta_2}{\beta_2 + \alpha_1 \beta_1} u_t. \tag{A9.21}$$

Actual output fluctuates randomly around its target level, just like for the interest rate instrument. The crucial difference between the two instruments is, however, that the effect of the IS shocks is dampened somewhat under the money supply instrument–the coefficient in front of u_t in (A9.21) is between 0 and 1. The asymptotic variance of output is:

$$\left. \sigma_y^2 \right|_{m=m^*} = \left(\frac{\beta_2}{\beta_2 + \alpha_1 \beta_1} \right)^2 \sigma_u^2. \tag{A9.22}$$

Since the term in round brackets is between 0 and 1, it follows that:

$$\left. \sigma_y^2 \right|_{m=m^*} < \left. \sigma_y^2 \right|_{R=R^*}. \tag{A9.23}$$

Hence a rational policy maker (one who wants to reduce output fluctuations) chooses the money supply instrument if the LM curve does not fluctuate.

In terms of Figure A9.2, this result can be explained as follows. Let IS_0 be the expected position of the IS curve, i.e. equation (Q9.6) for $E(u_t) = 0$, and let IS_1 and IS_2 be the IS curves for a given positive and negative IS shock respectively. The deterministic equilibrium is at point E_0, where $y = y^*$ and $R = R^*$. Under the interest rate instrument, the policy maker maintains $R = R^*$ so that the economy fluctuates between points A and B and output fluctuates between y_t^A and y_t^B. Under the money supply instrument, the money supply is set such that IS_0 and LM_0 intersect at point E_0. As a result, the economy fluctuates between points C and D, and output fluctuates between y_t^C and y_t^D. Output fluctuations are smaller under the money supply rule because interest rate movements act as automatic stabilizers. With a positive IS shock, the interest rate rises under the money supply rule so that investment and thus output demand is dampened somewhat.

(d) If only the LM curve is subject to stochastic shocks, then the instruments are also not equivalent. Now the IS curve is not subject to fluctuations but the LM curve fluctuates randomly. In terms of Figure A9.3, the IS curve is given by IS_0

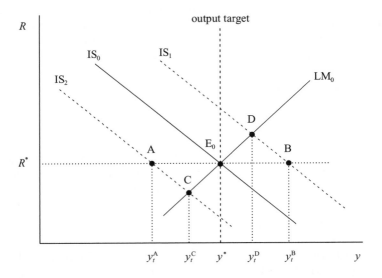

Figure A9.2: Instruments and output fluctuations (deterministic LM curve)

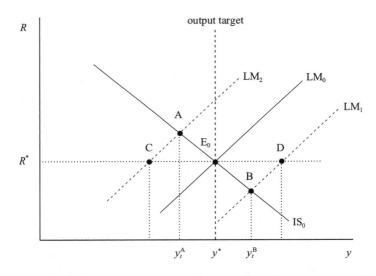

Figure A9.3: Instruments and output fluctuations (deterministic IS curve)

and the expected position of the LM curve is LM_0. LM_1 and LM_2 are associated with, respectively, a positive and a negative money demand shock.

Under the interest rate instrument, the policy maker maintains $R = R^*$ and lets the money supply be determined endogenously. As a result, the economy stays in point E_0. (The economy does not go to points C and D because in these points the money supply is not in equilibrium.) Output is given by (A9.21) but, since $u_t = 0$ here, it does not fluctuate at all. There is perfect stabilization in this case and the asymptotic variance of output is zero.

Under the money supply rule, the economy fluctuates between points A and B and output fluctuates between y_t^A and y_t^B. To compute actual output under the money supply instrument, we solve equations (Q9.6)–(Q9.7) for output:

$$y_t = \alpha_0 - \frac{\alpha_1}{\beta_2}[\beta_0 + \beta_1 y_t + v_t - m_t + p_t] + u_t \Rightarrow$$

$$y_t = \frac{\alpha_0 \beta_2 - \alpha_1 \beta_0 + \alpha_1 m^* - \alpha_1 v_t}{\beta_2 + \alpha_1 \beta_1}, \tag{A9.24}$$

where we have set $p_t = u_t = 0$ and $m_t = m^*$ for all t in going from the first to the second line. By substituting (A9.17) into (A9.24) we obtain an even simpler expression for output:

$$y_t = y^* - \frac{\alpha_1}{\beta_2 + \alpha_1 \beta_1} v_t. \tag{A9.25}$$

The asymptotic variance of output under the money supply instrument is thus:

$$\sigma_y^2 \Big|_{m=m^*} = \left(\frac{\alpha_1}{\beta_2 + \alpha_1 \beta_1} \right)^2 \sigma_v^2. \tag{A9.26}$$

Since output can be perfectly stabilized under the interest rate instrument, the rational policy maker prefers this instrument over the money supply instrument.

(e) To solve the general instrument choice problem, we first solve (Q9.6)–(Q9.7) for output. After some manipulation we obtain for the interest rate instrument:

$$y_t = y^* + u_t, \tag{A9.27}$$

and for the money supply instrument:

$$y_t = y^* + \frac{\beta_2 u_t - \alpha_1 v_t}{\beta_2 + \alpha_1 \beta_1}. \tag{A9.28}$$

The asymptotic variance of output under the interest rate instrument is obtained from (A9.27):

$$\sigma_y^2 \Big|_{R=R^*} = \sigma_u^2. \tag{A9.29}$$

The asymptotic variance under the money supply rule is obtained from (A9.28):

$$\sigma_y^2 \Big|_{m=m^*} = \frac{\beta_2^2 \sigma_u^2 + \alpha_1^2 \sigma_v^2}{(\beta_2 + \alpha_1 \beta_1)^2}, \tag{A9.30}$$

where we have used the fact that u_t and v_t are independent random variables (so that $E(u_t v_t) = 0$).

It is easy to rewrite the quadratic loss function, given in equation (Q9.8), in terms of the asymptotic variance of output:

$$\Omega \equiv E\left(y_t - y^*\right)^2 = E\left(y_t - E(y_t)\right)^2 \equiv \sigma_y^2, \qquad (A9.31)$$

where we have used the fact that $E(y_t) = y^*$ under both instruments (see equations (A9.27) and (A9.28)). Hence, the rational policy maker chooses that policy instrument for which σ_y^2 is lowest. By comparing (A9.29) and (A9.30), we find that the money supply instrument is the preferred instrument if (and only if):

$$\frac{\beta_2^2 \sigma_u^2 + \alpha_1^2 \sigma_v^2}{(\beta_2 + \alpha_1 \beta_1)^2} < \sigma_u^2 \quad \Leftrightarrow \quad \frac{\sigma_u^2}{\sigma_v^2} > \frac{\alpha_1}{\beta_1\left(2\beta_2 + \alpha_1\beta_1\right)}. \qquad (A9.32)$$

According to (A9.32), the money supply instrument is optimal if the variance of the IS shocks is large relative to that of the LM shocks. The intuition behind this result is provided by the answer to part (c). Interest rate fluctuations dampen the output fluctuations in that case.

Question 4: Rules versus discretion

(a) Equation (Q9.9) is the Lucas supply curve. Equation (Q9.10) is the objective function of individual i in the population.

(b) If we assume that all citizens have the same coefficient of relative inflation aversion, it does not matter who is the central banker. We can thus use the model that is discussed in detail in section 9.1.2 of the book. If (before the ECB era) the Dutch central banker can somehow commit to follow the behaviour of some (more inflation-averse) central banker (say, the German one), then he/she can effectively mitigate the effects of dynamic inconsistency somewhat. Even if the other central banker follows discretionary policy, the resulting inflation rate will be lower than the inflation rate the domestic central banker would choose. As a result, welfare would be higher. As is clear from equation (9.41), delegation to somebody else only occurs if $\bar{y} \neq y^*$.

(c) This question is studied in detail in section 9.2 of the book. By choosing a person more conservative than him-/herself, the median voter commits to a lower discretionary inflation rate. Like in part (b) of this question, this leads to an increase in social welfare because the adverse effects of dynamic inconsistency are mitigated somewhat.

Question 5: Political business cycles

(a) Equation (Q9.11) is an expectations–augmented Phillips curve. In the short run there is a trade-off between inflation and unemployment. This is represented by the $\Phi\left(\cdot\right)$ function. Inflation, however, also depends on expected inflation, $\pi^e\left(t\right)$. This is a shift-variable in the Phillips curve. Equation (Q9.12) shows that the expected inflation rate is adjusted adaptively, i.e. the model incorporates the AEH (studied in detail in Chapter 1 of the book).

(b) The incumbent party maximizes Ω subject to (Q9.11)-(Q9.12). The initial condition is $\pi^e(0) = \pi_0^e$ and $\pi(T)$ can be freely chosen. The Hamiltonian for this problem is:

$$\mathcal{H} \equiv V(U(t), \pi(t)) \cdot e^{\rho t}dt + \lambda(t) \cdot [\beta \cdot [\pi(t) - \pi^e(t)]]$$
$$+ \mu(t) \cdot [\pi(t) - \Phi(U(t)) - \alpha \cdot \pi^e(t)],$$

where $U(t)$ and $\pi(t)$ are the control variables, $\pi^e(t)$ is the state variable, $\lambda(t)$ is the co-state variable, and $\mu(t)$ is the Lagrange multiplier associated with the constraint (Q9.11).

The first-order conditions are, respectively,

$$\frac{\partial \mathcal{H}}{\partial U(t)} = V_U(U(t), \pi(t)) e^{\rho t} - \mu(t) \Phi'(U(t)) = 0, \tag{A9.33}$$

$$\frac{\partial \mathcal{H}}{\partial \pi(t)} = V_\pi(U(t), \pi(t)) e^{\rho t} + \beta \lambda(t) + \mu(t) = 0, \tag{A9.34}$$

for the control variables, and:

$$\dot{\lambda}(t) = -\frac{\partial \mathcal{H}}{\partial \pi^e(t)} = \beta \lambda(t) + \alpha \mu(t), \tag{A9.35}$$

for the state variable. Of course, $\partial \mathcal{H}/\partial \lambda(t) = \dot{\pi}^e(t)$ just gives us back the state equation (Q9.12), whilst $\partial \mathcal{H}/\partial \mu(t) = 0$ slings back (Q9.11) at us. Given that $\pi^e(T)$ is free, we must also have that:

$$\lambda(T) = 0. \tag{A9.36}$$

(c) Using these specific functional forms, we can write the first-order conditions (A9.33)-(A9.35) as:

$$U(t) = \frac{\gamma_1}{2} \mu(t) e^{-\rho t}, \tag{A9.37}$$

$$\beta \lambda(t) + \mu(t) = \eta e^{\rho t}. \tag{A9.38}$$

By substituting (A9.37) into (A9.38) we find:

$$U(t) = \frac{\gamma_1}{2} \cdot [\eta - \beta \lambda(t) e^{-\rho t}]. \tag{A9.39}$$

Once we know the path of $\lambda(t)$, the path of $U(t)$ follows readily from (A9.39). By using (A9.38) in (A9.35) we obtain the differential equation for $\lambda(t)$:

$$\dot{\lambda}(t) = (1 - \alpha)\beta \lambda(t) + \alpha \eta e^{\rho t}. \tag{A9.40}$$

Since $0 < \alpha \leq 1$ and $\beta > 0$, this is an unstable differential equation which we solve forward in time, taking into account the terminal condition (A9.36). Here are the juiciest steps in the derivation:

$$\dot{\lambda}(t) - (1 - \alpha)\beta \lambda(t) = \alpha \eta e^{\rho t}$$

$$\frac{d}{dt}\left[\lambda(t) e^{-(1-\alpha)\beta t}\right] = \alpha \eta e^{\rho t} e^{-(1-\alpha)\beta t}$$

$$d\left[\lambda(t) e^{-(1-\alpha)\beta t}\right] = \alpha \eta e^{\rho t} e^{-(1-\alpha)\beta t} dt.$$

Integrating both sides from s to T ($0 \leq s \leq T$) we thus find:

$$
\int_s^T d\left[\lambda\left(t\right)e^{-(1-\alpha)\beta t}\right] = \alpha\eta \int_s^T e^{\rho t}e^{-(1-\alpha)\beta t}dt
$$

$$
\lambda\left(T\right)e^{-(1-\alpha)\beta T} - \lambda\left(s\right)e^{-(1-\alpha)\beta s} = \frac{\alpha\eta}{\rho-(1-\alpha)\beta}
$$
$$
\cdot\left[e^{[\rho-(1-\alpha)\beta]T} - e^{[\rho-(1-\alpha)\beta]s}\right].
$$

Finally, setting $\lambda\left(T\right) = 0$ and re-arranging we obtain:

$$
-\lambda\left(s\right)\cdot e^{-\rho s} = \frac{\alpha\eta}{\rho-(1-\alpha)\beta}\cdot\left[e^{[\rho-(1-\alpha)\beta](T-s)} - 1\right]. \tag{A9.41}
$$

By setting $s = t$ and substituting (A9.41) into (A9.39) we find the path for unemployment:

$$
U\left(t\right) = \frac{\eta\gamma_1}{2}\cdot\left[1+\alpha\beta\cdot\frac{e^{[\rho-(1-\alpha)\beta](T-t)}-1}{\rho-(1-\alpha)\beta}\right], \qquad \text{(for } 0 \leq t \leq T\text{). (A9.42)}
$$

We observe from (A9.42) that:

$$
\frac{dU\left(t\right)}{dt} = -\frac{\alpha\beta\eta\gamma_1}{2}e^{[\rho-(1-\alpha)\beta](T-t)} < 0.
$$

The policy maker starts with a high unemployment rate, and lets it fall over time. At the end of its term in office, unemployment equals:

$$
U\left(T\right) = U_T^* \equiv \frac{\eta\gamma_1}{2}. \tag{A9.43}
$$

(d) The economic system is given by:

$$
\pi\left(t\right) = \gamma_0 - \gamma_1 U\left(t\right) + \alpha\pi^e\left(t\right), \tag{A9.44}
$$
$$
\dot{\pi}^e\left(t\right) = \beta\left[\pi\left(t\right) - \pi^e\left(t\right)\right], \tag{A9.45}
$$
$$
U\left(t\right) = U_T^*\cdot\left[1+\alpha\beta\cdot\frac{e^{\rho^*(T-t)}-1}{\rho^*}\right], \tag{A9.46}
$$

where $\rho^* \equiv \rho - (1-\alpha)\beta$. Substituting (A9.44) and (A9.46) into (A9.45) we find the fundamental differential equation for $\pi^e\left(t\right)$ for $0 \leq t \leq T$:

$$
\dot{\pi}^e\left(t\right) = \beta\left[\gamma_0 - \gamma_1 U_T^*\cdot\left[1+\alpha\beta\cdot\frac{e^{\rho^*(T-t)}-1}{\rho^*}\right] - (1-\alpha)\pi^e\left(t\right)\right]
$$
$$
= -\beta\left(1-\alpha\right)\pi^e\left(t\right) + \beta\left[\gamma_0 - \gamma_1 U_T^*\cdot\left[1+\alpha\beta\cdot\frac{e^{\rho^*(T-t)}-1}{\rho^*}\right]\right]. \tag{A9.47}
$$

Since the coefficient in front of $\pi^e\left(t\right)$ on the right-hand side is negative, we surmise that the differential equation is stable. But there is a time-varying shock term on the right-hand side also, so we must dig a little deeper.

To compute $\pi^e(T)$ we must solve this differential equation (backwards in time) subject to the initial condition, $\pi^e(0) = \pi_0^e$. We show some steps. First we define the forcing term, $G(T-t)$:

$$
\begin{aligned}
G(T-t) &= \gamma_0 - \gamma_1 U_T^* \cdot \left[1 + \alpha\beta \cdot \frac{e^{\rho^*(T-t)} - 1}{\rho^*}\right] \\
&\equiv \zeta_0 - \zeta_1 \cdot e^{\rho^*(T-t)},
\end{aligned}
\tag{A9.48}
$$

with:

$$
\zeta_0 \equiv \gamma_0 - \gamma_1 U_T^* \cdot \left[1 - \frac{\alpha\beta}{\rho^*}\right], \qquad \zeta_1 \equiv \frac{\gamma_1 U_T^* \alpha\beta}{\rho^*}.
$$

Next, we write the fundamental differential equation as:

$$
\dot{\pi}^e(t) + \beta(1-\alpha)\pi^e(t) = \beta G(T-t).
$$

This implies that:

$$
\begin{aligned}
\frac{d}{dt}\left[\pi^e(t)e^{(1-\alpha)\beta t}\right] &= \beta G(T-t)e^{(1-\alpha)\beta t} &&\Rightarrow \\
\int_0^s d\left[\pi^e(t)e^{(1-\alpha)\beta t}\right] &= \beta \int_0^s G(T-t)e^{(1-\alpha)\beta t}dt &&\Leftrightarrow \\
\pi^e(s)e^{(1-\alpha)\beta s} - \pi^e(0) &= \beta \int_0^s G(T-t)e^{(1-\alpha)\beta t}dt &&\Leftrightarrow
\end{aligned}
$$

$$
\pi^e(s) = \pi_0^e e^{-(1-\alpha)\beta s} + \beta \int_0^s G(T-t)e^{(1-\alpha)\beta(t-s)}dt.
\tag{A9.49}
$$

The final expression shows that $\pi^e(s)$ is a weighted average of the initial condition and the time-varying shock. For $\pi^e(T)$ we find:

$$
\pi^e(T) = \pi_0^e e^{-(1-\alpha)\beta T} + \beta \int_0^T G(T-t)e^{(1-\alpha)\beta(t-T)}dt.
$$

By setting $\pi^e(T) = \pi_0^e$ we find the condition that is asked for in the question:

$$
\pi_0^e = \beta \cdot \frac{\int_0^T G(T-t)e^{(1-\alpha)\beta(t-T)}dt}{1 - e^{-(1-\alpha)\beta T}}.
\tag{A9.50}
$$

If (A9.50) is satisfied, then the economy passes through the same (π_0^e, U_T^*) point in all election years. It displays a stable saw-tooth pattern in unemployment and inflation over time–see Figure 8 in Nordhaus (1975, p. 185).

Chapter 10

The open economy

Question 1: Short questions

(a) "A necessary condition for exchange rate overshooting to occur in Dornbusch-style models (featuring perfect capital mobility and flexible exchange rates) is that prices are sufficiently flexible." True, false, or uncertain? Explain.

(b) If financial capital is completely immobile internationally and the economy operates under a system of fixed exchange rates, then a bond financed increase in government consumption will lead to an increase in the interest rate and crowding out of investment. True or false? Explain.

(c) "In a two-country setting, uncoordinated fiscal policy always leads to excessive spending by governments of the individual countries." True, false, or uncertain? Explain.

Question 2: The Mundell-Fleming model

Consider an open economy IS-LM model with perfect capital mobility (also known as the Mundell-Fleming model). Assume that we extend the IS-LM model by introducing international trade. Assume furthermore that the price level is fixed (say $P = P_0$) and that domestic and foreign bonds are perfect substitutes. The extended model is given by:

$$Y = C + I + G + X \tag{Q10.1}$$
$$C = C(Y - T) \quad 0 < C_{Y-T} < 1 \tag{Q10.2}$$
$$I = I(r), \quad I_r < 0 \tag{Q10.3}$$
$$T = T(Y), \quad 0 < T_Y < 1 \tag{Q10.4}$$
$$M/P = k(Y) + l(r) \tag{Q10.5}$$
$$X \equiv EX(E) - IM(E, Y)E, \quad EX_E > 0,\ IM_E < 0,\ IM_Y > 0 \tag{Q10.6}$$
$$r = r^* + \dot{E}/E \tag{Q10.7}$$

where Y, C, I, G, T, and r are, respectively, output, consumption, investment, government consumption, taxes, and the interest rate. Furthermore, r^* is the foreign interest rate, EX is exports, IM is imports, E is the exchange rate (euros per unit of foreign currency), and X is net exports. Use this model to answer the following questions. Assume that the expectations regarding the exchange rate are perfectly inelastic (so that there is no speculation on the market for foreign exchange and the $\dot{E}/E$ term can be put equal to zero).

(a) Interpret the equations.

(b) Explain the so-called *Marshall-Lerner condition*.

(c) Why is there less scope for Keynesian countercyclical policy in an open economy with flexible exchange rate? How effective is monetary policy in such a situation?

(d) Can the government of a less-than-fully employed economy stimulate employment without putting pressure on the interest rate (and the foreign exchange rate)? Show how the government can engineer an appreciation of the currency without harming employment. Distinguish the two cases of fixed and flexible exchange rates.

(e) Explain why a small open economy with fixed exchange rates is extremely sensitive to shocks in world trade. Is it possible to use monetary or fiscal policy to counter the effects of world trade shocks?

Question 3: The Dornbusch model

Consider the following model of a small open economy featuring perfect capital mobility and sluggish price adjustment.

$$y = -\eta r + g + \delta[p^* + e - p], \qquad \eta > 0, \quad 0 < \delta < 1, \qquad \text{(Q10.8)}$$
$$m - p = y - \lambda r, \qquad \lambda > 0, \qquad \text{(Q10.9)}$$
$$\dot{p} = \phi[y - \bar{y}], \qquad \phi > 0, \qquad \text{(Q10.10)}$$
$$r = r^* + \dot{e}, \qquad \text{(Q10.11)}$$

where y is actual output, r is the domestic interest rate, g is an index for fiscal policy, e is the nominal exchange rate, p^* is the exogenous foreign price level, p is the domestic price level, m is the nominal money supply, $\bar{y}$ is full employment output, and r^* is the exogenous world interest rate. All variables, except the two interest rates, are measured in logarithms. As usual, a dot above a variables denotes that variable's time rate of change, i.e. $\dot{p} \equiv dp/dt$ and $\dot{e} \equiv de/dt$.

(a) Interpret the equations of the model.

(b) Suppose that the economy operates under a system of *fixed exchange rates* ($e = \bar{e}$). What are the endogenous variables? What is the coefficient of monetary accommodation (i.e. $\partial m/\partial p$) in this model? Derive the (impact, transitional, and long-term) effects of an expansionary fiscal policy (an increase in g).

(c) Now assume that the economy operates under a system of *flexible exchange rates*. Derive the model's phase diagram for the nominal exchange rate, e, and the domestic price level, p.

(d) Derive the (impact, transitional, and long-term) effects of an unanticipated and permanent expansionary fiscal policy.

(e) Show that under flexible exchange rates an unanticipated and permanent increase in the money supply leads to overshooting of the exchange rate in the short-term.

(f) Derive the (impact, transitional, and long-term) effects of an anticipated and permanent increase in the money supply.

(g) Show how your answer to parts (e) and (f) change if domestic prices are perfectly flexible, i.e. if $\phi \to \infty$ in equation (Q10.10).

Question 4: The Buiter-Miller model

[Based on Buiter and Miller (1982)] Consider the following model of a small open economy featuring perfect capital mobility and sluggish price adjustment.

$$y = -\eta\,[r - \dot{p}_C] + \delta[p^* + e - p], \qquad \eta > 0, \quad 0 < \delta, \gamma < 1, \qquad \text{(Q10.12)}$$
$$m - p_C = y - \lambda r, \qquad \lambda > 0, \qquad\qquad\qquad \text{(Q10.13)}$$
$$p_C \equiv \alpha p + (1 - \alpha)[p^* + e], \qquad 0 < \alpha < 1, \qquad\qquad \text{(Q10.14)}$$
$$\dot{p} = \phi(y - \bar{y}), \qquad \phi > 0, \qquad\qquad\qquad \text{(Q10.15)}$$
$$r = r^* + \dot{e}, \qquad\qquad\qquad\qquad \text{(Q10.16)}$$

where y is actual output, r is the domestic interest rate, p_C is the price index for goods used in the domestic economy, e is the nominal exchange rate, p^* is the exogenous (and constant) foreign price level, p is the price of domestically produced goods, $\bar{y}$ is full employment output, m is the (constant) nominal money supply, and r^* is the exogenous world interest rate. All variables, except the two interest rates, are measured in logarithms. As usual, a dot above a variables denotes that variable's time rate of change, i.e. $\dot{p} \equiv dp/dt$ and $\dot{e} \equiv de/dt$. We define the auxiliary variables $l \equiv m - p$ (measure of "liquidity") and $c \equiv p^* + e - p$ (index for "competitiveness").

(a) Interpret the equations of the model. Which are the endogenous and which are the exogenous variables?

(b) Derive the dynamical system for this model in terms of l and c. Show that the model is saddle-point stable provided $\lambda + \alpha\eta(1 - \lambda\phi) > 0$. Which is the predetermined variable? Which is the jumping variable?

(c) Construct the phase diagram for the model. (Many saddle-point stable slope configurations are possible. Assume that the $\dot{c} = 0$ line is upward sloping and $\dot{l} = 0$ line is downward sloping. State the corresponding parameter assumptions.)

(d) Derive the (impact, transitional, and long-term) effects on c and l of an unanticipated and permanent increase in the money supply. Does overshooting of the exchange rate occur in this model?

Question 5: Dynamics of foreign reserves

Consider the following model of a small open economy with fixed prices ($P = P_0 = 1$ for convenience) operating under a regime of fixed exchange rates.

$$Y = C(Y) + I(r) + G + X(Y, E), \tag{Q10.17}$$
$$D + F = l(Y, r), \tag{Q10.18}$$
$$\dot{F} = X(Y, E) + KI(r - r^*), \tag{Q10.19}$$

where Y is output, C is consumption, I is investment, r is the domestic interest rate, G is government consumption, X is net exports, E is the nominal exchange rate (domestic currency per unit of foreign currency), D is domestic credit (government bonds in the hands of the central bank), F is the stock of foreign exchange reserves (measured in units of the domestic currency), and KI is net capital inflows. As usual, a dot above a variable denotes that variable's time derivative, i.e. $\dot{F} \equiv dF/dt$. We make the usual assumptions regarding the partial derivatives of the various functions: $0 < C_Y < 1$, $X_Y < 0$, $I_r < 0$, $X_E > 0$, $l_Y > 0$, $l_r < 0$, and $KI_r > 0$.

(a) Interpret the equations of the model. What do we assume about the Marshall-Lerner condition? Which are the endogenous variables? Which are the exogenous variables?

(b) Derive the fundamental differential equation for the stock of foreign exchange reserves and show that the model is stable. Show that the speed of adjustment increases as the degree of capital mobility increases and illustrate your argument with the aid of a diagram.

(c) Derive the so-called BP curve, representing (r, Y) combinations for which the balance of payments is in equilibrium ($\dot{F} = 0$). Assume that the BP curve is flatter than the LM curve (when drawn in the usual diagram with r on the vertical axis and Y on the horizontal axis). Show that this is the case if the following condition holds: $X_Y l_r < l_Y KI_r$. Give an economic interpretation for this condition.

(d) Derive the impact, transitional, and long-run effects on the endogenous variables of an increase in government consumption. Assume that the condition mentioned in part (c) holds. Illustrate your answer with graphs and explain the economic intuition.

(e) Derive the impact, transitional, and long-run effects on the endogenous variables of monetary policy. Illustrate your answers with a graph and explain the intuition.

★ Question 6: Price flexibility in the Mundell-Fleming model

[Based on Mark (2001)] Consider the following Mundell-Fleming type model of a small open economy:

$$m_t - p_t = y_t - \alpha r_t, \quad \alpha > 0, \tag{Q10.20}$$

$$y_t = -\beta \left[r_t - (E_t p_{t+1} - p_t) \right] + \gamma [p^* + e_t - p_t] + d_t, \quad \beta > 0, \ \gamma > 0, \tag{Q10.21}$$

$$r_t = r^* + E_t e_{t+1} - e_t, \tag{Q10.22}$$

$$p_t = \tilde{p}_t - (1 - \theta)[\tilde{p}_t - E_{t-1}\tilde{p}_t], \quad 0 \le \theta \le 1, \tag{Q10.23}$$

$$m_t = m_{t-1} + v_t, \tag{Q10.24}$$

$$y_t = \bar{y}_{t-1} + z_t, \tag{Q10.25}$$

$$d_t = d_{t-1} + u_t, \tag{Q10.26}$$

where m_t is the nominal money supply, p_t is the actual domestic price level, y_t is output, r_t is the domestic (nominal) interest rate, e_t is the nominal exchange rate, p^* is the world price level (we normalize $p^* = 0$), r^* is the world (nominal) interest rate, and $\tilde{p}_t$ is the *equilibrium* domestic price level, and $\bar{y}_t$ is the full employment level of output. In equation (Q10.23), $\tilde{p}_t$ is the price for which actual output, y_t, equals its exogenously given full employment level, $\bar{y}_t$. All variables except r_t and r^* are in logarithms. E_t and E_{t-1} denote conditional expectations based on, respectively, period-t and period-$t - 1$ information. It is assumed that agents hold rational expectations. The shock terms, u_t and v_t, are independent from each other and are both normally distributed with mean zero and constant variance, i.e. $u_t \sim N\left(0, \sigma_u^2\right)$ and $v_t \sim N\left(0, \sigma_v^2\right)$. They also features no serial correlation.

(a) Provide a brief interpretation of these equations.

(b) Consider the special case of the model for which $\theta = 1$. Define the *real* exchange rate as $q_t \equiv p^* + e_t - p_t$. Solve for the rational expectations solutions for the real exchange rate, the domestic price, and the nominal exchange rate. Denote these solutions by, respectively, $\tilde{q}_t$, $\tilde{p}_t$, and $\tilde{e}_t$.

(c) Show that the money supply does not affect the equilibrium real exchange rate, $\tilde{q}_t$. Explain intuitively why this is the case.

(d) Now use the general case of the model, with $0 < \theta < 1$, and solve for the rational expectations solution for the real exchange rate, the domestic price, the nominal exchange rate, and output.

(e) Does the classical dichotomy still hold for the sticky-price model solved in part (d)? Can you find evidence for the overshooting property? Explain.

Answers

Question 1: Short questions

(a) False, a necessary condition for overshooting is that prices are sticky, i.e. $\phi \ll \infty$. If $\phi \to \infty$, then prices are perfectly flexible, $y = \bar{y}$ at all times, and over-shooting cannot occur (see section 10.3.1.1).

(b) True, see Figure 10.2 in the book. The IS curve shifts out and output increases. Imports increase and the current account is in deficit. The money supply declines as foreign reserves are lost in the maintenance of the exchange rate. The LM curve shifts up and the interest rate increases. In the long run no effect on output and lower investment.

(c) This is uncertain as it depends on further details of the two-country environment. The issue of policy coordination is studied in section 10.2.4 of the book. If there exists nominal wage rigidity in both regions, then individual regions spend too little in the uncoordinated regime. This is because individual fiscal policy is a locomotive policy, and regions ignore the spill-over effects in the uncoordinated scenario. The opposite holds if both countries experience real wage rigidity. There uncoordinated spending is too high.

Question 2: The Mundell-Fleming model

(a) Equation (Q10.1) is the national income identity; (Q10.2) is the consumption function: consumption depends on disposable income and the MPC is between 0 and 1; (Q10.3) is the investment function: investment depends negatively on the rate of interest as this represents the "cost of funds" if a firm wants to invest; (Q10.4) is the tax function: T_Y is the marginal tax rate which is between 0 and 1; (Q10.5) is the demand for real money balances: it depends positively on output via the transactions motive and negatively on the interest rate (cash management and the speculative demand for money); (Q10.6) is the equation for net exports (equalling exports, EX, minus imports expressed in terms of the domestic good, $E \cdot IM$): import quantities depend on the price of domestic goods relative to the price of foreign goods; (Q10.7) is the interest parity condition according to which financial investments should have the same rate of return domestically and abroad. The correction term, $\dot{E}/E$, is needed to express the rate of return in the same currency.

(b) The Marshall-Lerner condition answers the question about what happens to net exports if the exchange rate of a country changes. The exchange rate, E, is defined as domestic currency per unit of foreign currency (e.g. euros per US dollar for an European). Hence, a *devaluation* (under fixed exchange rates) or *depreciation* (under flexible exchange rates) amounts to an *increase* in E. We want to know the sign of $\partial X/\partial E$. We partially differentiate equation (Q10.6) with respect to E:

$$\frac{\partial X}{\partial E} = \frac{\partial EX}{\partial E} - IM\frac{\partial E}{\partial E} - E\frac{\partial IM}{\partial E}$$

$$= EX_E - IM\left(1 + \frac{E \cdot IM_E}{IM}\right)$$

$$= \frac{Y}{E}\left[\frac{EX}{Y}\frac{E \cdot EX_E}{EX} - \frac{E \cdot IM}{Y}\left(1 + \frac{E \cdot IM_E}{IM}\right)\right]$$

$$= \frac{Y}{E}\left[\omega_X\varepsilon_X - \omega_M(1 - \varepsilon_M)\right], \tag{A10.1}$$

where the shares (ω_X and ω_M) and the elasticities (ε_X and ε_M) are defined as:

$$\omega_X \equiv \frac{EX}{Y} \qquad \varepsilon_X \equiv \frac{E \cdot EX_E}{EX} > 0 \tag{A10.2}$$

$$\omega_M \equiv \frac{E \cdot IM}{Y} \qquad \varepsilon_M \equiv -\frac{E \cdot IM_E}{IM} > 0 \tag{A10.3}$$

Hence, $\partial X/\partial E > 0$ if (and only if) the term in square brackets on the right-hand side of (A10.1) is positive, i.e. if:

$$\omega_X\varepsilon_X - \omega_M(1 - \varepsilon_M) > 0. \tag{A10.4}$$

For the special case in which *net* exports are initially zero (so that $EX = E \cdot IM$ and thus $\omega_X = \omega_M$) we obtain an expression for the Marshall-Lerner condition that is often reported in textbooks:

$$\varepsilon_X + \varepsilon_M - 1 > 0. \tag{A10.5}$$

The sum of the export and import elasticities must exceed unity for the Marshall-Lerner condition to hold.

(c) Under flexible exchange rates and with perfect capital mobility:

- There is equilibrium on the balance of payments (which is the sum of the trade account and the capital account).

- The monetary authority does not intervene on the market for foreign exchange (the FOREX market) as it lets the currency fluctuate freely. As a result, the stock of foreign assets of the central bank stays constant. This means that the domestic money supply is constant also.

- The domestic interest rate is equal to the (exogenous) foreign interest rate, i.e. $r = r^*$.

We can write the resulting model as follows:

$$Y = C(Y - T(Y)) + I(r^*) + G + X(Y, E), \quad \text{(IS curve)}, \tag{A10.6}$$

$$M/P_0 = k(Y) + l(r^*), \quad \text{(LM curve)}. \tag{A10.7}$$

In mathematical terms, the IS equation contains two endogenous variables (Y and E) whilst the LM equation only contains Y. It follows that the model is

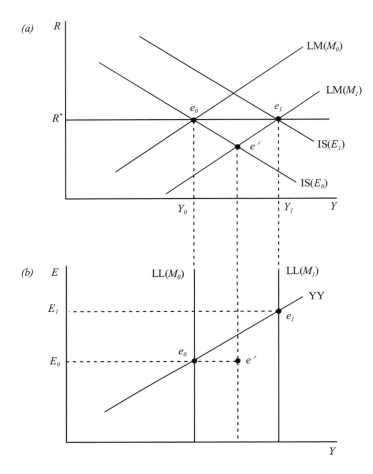

Figure A10.1: Monetary policy with flexible exchange rates

recursive and can be solved in a very simple fashion. From the LM equation (A10.7) we find that monetary policy affects output:

$$\frac{1}{P_0}dM = k_Y dY \quad \Rightarrow \quad \frac{dY}{dM} = \frac{1}{k_Y P_0} > 0, \tag{A10.8}$$

while fiscal policy does not ($dY/dG = 0$). An increase in G thus only affects the exchange rate. Indeed, from the IS equation (A10.6) we obtain:

$$dG + X_E dE = 0 \quad \Rightarrow \quad \frac{dE}{dG} = -\frac{1}{X_E} < 0. \tag{A10.9}$$

(provided the Marshall-Lerner condition is satisfied). An increase in government consumption thus leads to an appreciation of the domestic currency. Fiscal and monetary policy can also be illustrated graphically. See Figures A10.1 and A10.2.

(d) *Flexible exchange rates:* $M \uparrow$ so LM shifts to the right $\Rightarrow$ domestic interest rate lower than world interest rate $\Rightarrow$ net outflow of financial capital $\Rightarrow$ depreci-

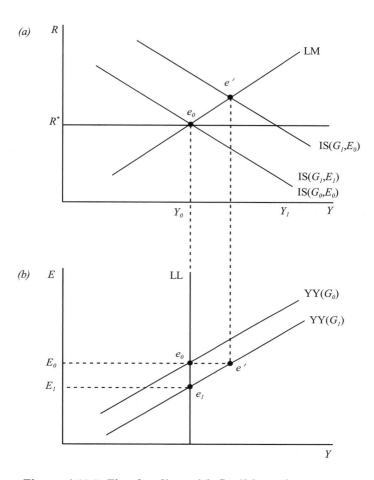

Figure A10.2: Fiscal policy with flexible exchange rates

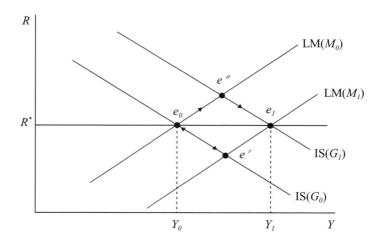

Figure A10.3: Fiscal and monetary policy with fixed exchange rates

ation of the exchange rate $\Rightarrow EX \uparrow$ and $IM \downarrow \Rightarrow$ (if the ML condition holds) $X \uparrow$ $\Rightarrow$ IS to the right. Output and employment are both higher but the exchange rate has depreciated. [See Figure A10.1].

Fixed exchange rates: $G \uparrow \Rightarrow$ IS shifts to the right $\Rightarrow$ domestic interest rate higher than world interest rate $\Rightarrow$ net inflow of financial capital $\Rightarrow$ increase in the domestic money supply $\Rightarrow$ LM to the right. Output and employment both higher as is the money supply. [See Figure A10.3]

(e) Assume that there is a negative export shock: ceteris paribus output and the exchange rate, $X \downarrow \Rightarrow$ IS to the left $\Rightarrow$ domestic interest rate lower than the world interest rate $\Rightarrow$ net outflow of financial capital $\Rightarrow$ reduction in the money supply $\Rightarrow$ LM *also* to the left. Output and employment are very sensitive because the shock is magnified by the monetary contraction. Monetary policy is not useful. Fiscal policy is (see part (d) above).

Question 3: The Dornbusch model

(a) Equation (Q10.8) is the IS curve for a small open economy. The real exchange rate, $p^* + e - p$, positively affects net exports, i.e. it is implicitly assumed that the Marshall-Lerner condition is satisfied. Equation (Q10.9) is the LM curve. The demand for real money balances features a unitary income elasticity. Equation (Q10.10) is the Phillips curve. The domestic price level rises (falls) if actual output exceeds (falls short of) full employment output. Finally, equation (Q10.11) is the uncovered interest parity condition. Under perfect capital mobility the yields on domestic and foreign financial assets are equalized. The yield on domestic assets is r whereas the yield on foreign assets, expressed in terms of the domestic currency, is $r^* + \dot{e}$. The dimension of e is domestic currency per unit of foreign currency (e.g. euros per US dollar). Hence, an increase in e represents a depreciation (or devaluation) of the domestic currency. Similarly, a rise in the real exchange rate, $p^* + e - p$, is called a real depreciation.

(b) Under fixed exchange rates, e is kept equal to some constant level $\bar{e}$ by the policy maker. The policy maker thus intervenes in the foreign exchange market such that this target exchange rate is maintained. If the fixed exchange rate is credible to the agents then they expect neither a devaluation nor a revaluation of the currency, i.e. $\dot{e} = 0$. This means that the domestic interest rate equals the foreign interest rate at all times, i.e. $r = r^*$. The endogenous variables in the model are thus y, p, and m. By engaging in foreign exchange transactions the monetary base is affected, which in turn implies that the money supply is endogenous (see Chapter 11).

By substituting (Q10.8) into (Q10.11) and setting $e = \bar{e}$ and $r = r^*$ we obtain the following differential equation for p:

$$\dot{p} = \phi[-\eta r^* + g + \delta[p^* + \bar{e} - p] - \bar{y}]. \tag{A10.10}$$

It follows from (A10.10) that the price adjustment mechanism is stable, i.e. $\partial \dot{p}/\partial p = -\phi\delta < 0$. By substituting (Q10.8) into (Q10.9) and setting $e = \bar{e}$ and $r = r^*$ we obtain the following equation for m:

$$m - p = -\eta r^* + g + \delta[p^* + \bar{e} - p] - \lambda r^* \quad \Leftrightarrow$$
$$m = (1 - \delta)p - (\eta + \lambda)r^* + g + \delta[p^* + \bar{e}]. \tag{A10.11}$$

Since the path for p is stable, it follows from (A10.11) that the path for the money supply is also stable. The coefficient for monetary accommodation is equal to $1 - \delta$. We study the effects of an expansionary fiscal policy with the aid of Figure A10.4. In the top panel we plot the IS curve, with $r = r^*$ and $e = \bar{e}$ substituted in. It is downward sloping in (y, p) space because a higher domestic price level worsens the real exchange rate. The $\dot{p} = 0$ line is obtained from (Q10.10). If y exceeds (falls short of) $\bar{y}$, then $\dot{p} > 0$ ($\dot{p} < 0$). Stable adjustment proceeds along the relevant IS curve. In the bottom panel of Figure A10.4 we plot the induced money supply, as given by (A10.11). Suppose that the economy is initially at point E_0 and assume that g is increased. As a result of this policy shock, IS shifts up (from IS_0 to IS_1) and the LM curve shifts up (from LM_0 to LM_1). Since the domestic price level is predetermined, the economy jumps from E_0 to point A directly above it in both panels. Both output and the money supply increase at impact:

$$\frac{dy(0)}{dg} = \frac{dm(0)}{dg} = 1, \tag{A10.12}$$

where the notation $dx(0)/dg$ represents the impact effect on variable x (the impact period is normalized to equal 0).

At point A, output is larger than its full employment level so that the domestic price rises gradually over time ($\dot{p} > 0$). In the top panel the economy moves gradually from point A to the ultimate equilibrium at E_1. In the bottom panel the economy moves along LM_1 from A to E_1. There is no long-run effect on output (as $y = \bar{y}$ in the steady state) but the domestic money supply and price level both increase:

$$\frac{dm(\infty)}{dg} = \frac{dp(\infty)}{dg} = \frac{1}{\delta}, \tag{A10.13}$$

where the notation $dx(\infty)/dg$ represents the long-run effect on variable x. To restore output to its full employment level, the real exchange rate must appreciate (i.e. domestic goods must become more expensive to foreigners). Since both $\bar{e}$ and p^* are fixed by assumption, the domestic price increase causes this real appreciation.

(c) Under flexible exchange rates the domestic interest rate is no longer equal to the foreign interest rate during the transitional phase. Since the exchange rate is flexible the policy maker does not intervene in the foreign exchange market and the money supply is constant (a policy variable). The phase diagram for e and p can be derived as follows. First we use (Q10.8)–(Q10.9) to obtain quasi-reduced-form expressions for output and the domestic interest rate.

$$y = -\eta \frac{y - m + p}{\lambda} + g + \delta[p^* + e - p) \quad \Leftrightarrow$$

$$y\left[1 + \frac{\eta}{\lambda}\right] = \frac{\eta}{\lambda}[m - p] + g + \delta[p^* + e - p] \quad \Leftrightarrow$$

$$y = \frac{\eta[m - p] + \lambda g + \lambda\delta[p^* + e - p]}{\lambda + \eta}. \tag{A10.14}$$

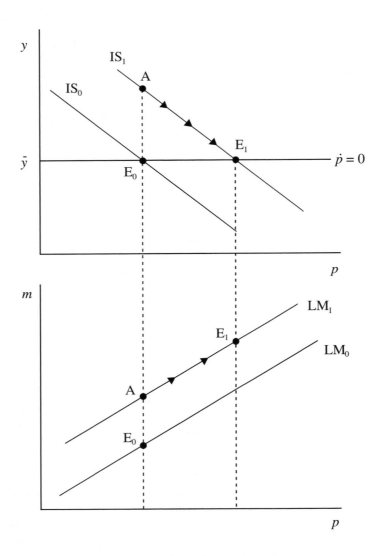

Figure A10.4: Fiscal policy under fixed exchange rates

By substituting (A10.14) into (Q10.9) we find the expression for the domestic interest rate:

$$\lambda r = y - [m - p]$$
$$= \frac{\eta[m-p] + \lambda g + \lambda\delta[p^* + e - p]}{\lambda + \eta} - [m - p] \quad \Leftrightarrow$$
$$r = \frac{-[m-p] + g + \delta[p^* + e - p]}{\lambda + \eta}. \tag{A10.15}$$

By substituting (A10.14) into (Q10.10) (and gathering terms) we obtain the expression for domestic inflation, $\dot{p}$:

$$\dot{p} = \phi \left[\frac{-(\eta + \lambda\delta)p + \lambda\delta e + \eta m + \lambda g + \lambda\delta p^*}{\lambda + \eta} - \bar{y} \right]. \tag{A10.16}$$

Similarly, by substituting (A10.15) into (Q10.11) (and gathering terms) we obtain the expressions for nominal exchange rate depreciation:

$$\dot{e} = \frac{(1 - \delta)p + \delta e - m + g + \delta p^*}{\lambda + \eta} - r^*. \tag{A10.17}$$

Equations (A10.16)–(A10.17) together constitute the dynamical system for p and e. This system can be characterized with the aid of a phase diagram as in Figure A10.5. We derive the following results from equation (A10.16):

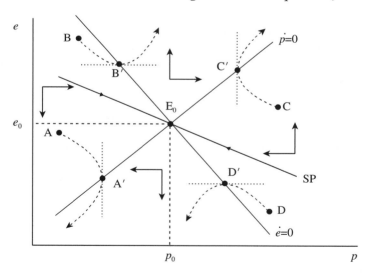

Figure A10.5: Phase diagram for the Dornbusch model

$$\left(\frac{de}{dp} \right)_{\dot{p}=0} = \frac{\eta + \lambda\delta}{\lambda\delta} > 1, \tag{A10.18}$$

$$\frac{\partial \dot{p}}{\partial e} = \frac{\phi\lambda\delta}{\lambda + \eta} > 0. \tag{A10.19}$$

Equation (A10.18) shows that $\dot{p} = 0$ line is upward sloping in (e, p) space, whereas (A10.19) says that domestic inflation is positive (negative) for points above (below) the $\dot{p} = 0$ line. (Intuitively, a nominal depreciation stimulates domestic output which boosts inflation, and vice versa.) The dynamic forces acting on the domestic price level have been illustrated with horizontal arrows in Figure A10.5.

We derive the following results from equation (A10.17):

$$\left(\frac{de}{dp}\right)_{\dot{e}=0} = -\frac{1-\delta}{\delta} < 0, \tag{A10.20}$$

$$\frac{\partial \dot{e}}{\partial e} = \frac{\delta}{\lambda + \eta} > 0. \tag{A10.21}$$

According to (A10.20), the $\dot{e} = 0$ line is downward sloping in (e, p) space. Equation (A10.21) says that points above (below) the $\dot{e} = 0$ line are such that the domestic interest rate exceeds (falls short of) the foreign interest rate so that $\dot{e} > 0$ ($\dot{e} < 0$). The dynamic forces acting on the nominal exchange rate have been illustrated with vertical arrows in Figure A10.5.

The configuration of arrows in Figure A10.5 suggests that only one of all possible trajectories converges to the steady-state equilibrium, E_0. Four unstable trajectories have been drawn starting from points A through D. The stable trajectory is the saddle path, SP. The model is saddle-point stable with the domestic price level acting as the *predetermined* ('non-jumping') variable and the nominal exchange rate acting as the *non-predetermined* ('jumping') variable.

(d) We can now study the effects of an unanticipated and permanent increase in g. We first compute the long-run effects on e and p. By setting $\dot{p} = 0$ in (A10.16) and $\dot{e} = 0$ in (A10.17) we obtain the following matrix expression for the steady-state p and e:

$$\begin{bmatrix} -(\eta + \lambda\delta) & \lambda\delta \\ 1 - \delta & \delta \end{bmatrix} \begin{bmatrix} p(\infty) \\ e(\infty) \end{bmatrix} = \begin{bmatrix} -\eta m - \lambda g - \lambda\delta p^* + (\lambda + \eta)\bar{y} \\ m - g - \delta p^* + (\lambda + \eta)r^* \end{bmatrix}. \tag{A10.22}$$

The matrix on the left-hand side is denoted by Δ. We find that $|\Delta| = -\delta(\lambda + \eta)$ and:

$$\Delta^{-1} = \frac{1}{\delta(\lambda + \eta)} \begin{bmatrix} -\delta & \lambda\delta \\ 1 - \delta & \eta + \lambda\delta \end{bmatrix}. \tag{A10.23}$$

Combining with (A10.22) yields the reduced-form expressions:

$$\begin{bmatrix} p(\infty) \\ e(\infty) \end{bmatrix} = \frac{1}{\delta(\lambda + \eta)} \begin{bmatrix} -\delta & \lambda\delta \\ 1 - \delta & \eta + \lambda\delta \end{bmatrix} \begin{bmatrix} -\eta m - \lambda g - \lambda\delta p^* + (\lambda + \eta)\bar{y} \\ m - g - \delta p^* + (\lambda + \eta)r^* \end{bmatrix}$$

$$= \begin{bmatrix} m - \bar{y} + \lambda r^* \\ m - p^* - \frac{1}{\delta}g + \frac{1-\delta}{\delta}\bar{y} + \frac{\eta+\lambda\delta}{\delta}r^* \end{bmatrix}. \tag{A10.24}$$

By differentiating (A10.22) with respect to g (holding constant m, p^*, $\bar{y}$, and r^*) we find the long-run results on the domestic price level and the nominal exchange rate:

$$\frac{dp(\infty)}{dg} = 0, \qquad \frac{de(\infty)}{dg} = -\frac{1}{\delta} < 0. \tag{A10.25}$$

There is no long-run effect on the price level but the exchange rate appreciates as a result of the fiscal shock. In terms of Figure A10.6, the fiscal shock shifts both the $\dot{p} = 0$ and $\dot{e} = 0$ lines down (by the same vertical amount), and the steady-state equilibrium shifts from E_0 to E_1. There is no transitional dynamics because the price level is unaffected by the policy shock. Output and the domestic interest rate are thus also unaffected by the fiscal policy.

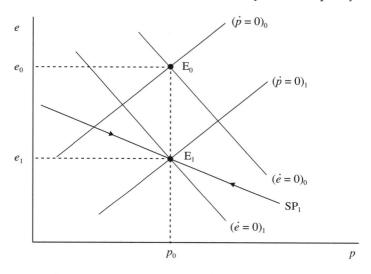

Figure A10.6: Unanticipated and permanent fiscal policy

(e) To study the effects of an increase in the money supply we first compute the steady-state results by differentiating (A10.24) with respect to m (holding constant g, p^*, $\bar{y}$, and r^*):

$$\frac{dp(\infty)}{dm} = \frac{de(\infty)}{dm} = 1. \tag{A10.26}$$

Both the domestic price level and the nominal exchange rate rise by the same amount in the long run. There is thus no long-run effect on the *real* exchange rate. In the top panel of Figure A10.7, the $\dot{p} = 0$ line shifts to the right (from $(\dot{p} = 0)_0$ to $(\dot{p} = 0)_1$) whilst the $\dot{e} = 0$ line shifts up (from $(\dot{e} = 0)_0$ to $(\dot{e} = 0)_1$). The results in (A10.26) imply that the steady-state equilibria E_0 and E_1 lie on a straight line with a 45 degree slope (see the dashed line in the top panel). The transitional dynamics is as follows. At impact the domestic price level is predetermined and the economy jumps from E_0 to point A directly above it. The nominal exchange rate depreciates from e_0 to e'. In point A, output exceeds its full employment level because the real exchange rate has depreciated and net exports have risen. Over time the domestic price level increases and the economy moves gradually along the saddle path from A to E_1. There is *overshooting* of the exchange rate in that the impact depreciation is larger than the long-run depreciation. Because $\dot{e}$ is negative during transition, it follows from equation (Q10.11) that the domestic interest rate falls short of the foreign interest rate during that time.

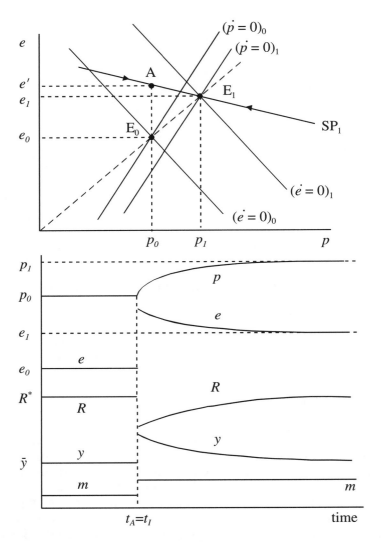

Figure A10.7: Unanticipated and permanent increase in the money supply

(f) We use the intuitive solution principle to study the effects of an anticipated and permanent increase in the money supply. According to this principle:

- Jumps in e are allowed only at impact, i.e. for $t = t_A$.
- For $t_A \leq t < t_I$ the dynamic adjustment is determined by the old equilibrium.
- At $t = t_I$ the economy arrives smoothly (without jumps) at the saddle path associated with the new equilibrium.

The phase diagram is presented in Figure A10.8, where E_0 and E_1 are, respectively, the initial and new steady-state. Obviously the long-run effects of the shock are the same as in part (e). The transition path is, however, quite different from that studied in part (e). Using the intuitive solution principle we find that the stable trajectory arrives at point B (on the then relevant saddle path SP_1) at time $t = t_I$. The old dynamics for $t_A \leq t < t_I$ implies that point B is approached from a south-westerly direction. At impact the price level is predetermined, so the economy jumps from E_0 to A. We thus conclude from the upper panel of Figure A10.8 that the price level adjusts monotonically towards its new (higher level) whilst the adjustment in the nominal exchange rate is non-monotonic. For $t_A \leq t < t_I$ the exchange rate depreciates whereas for $t \geq t_I$ it appreciates. Hence, there is still overshooting of the exchange rate. The path for the domestic interest rate follows readily from equation (Q10.11) and the information regarding $\dot{e}$: $r > r^*$ (for $t_A \leq t < t_I$) and $r < r^*$ (for $t \geq t_I$). It jumps down at time t_I because at that time the money supply is increased (see equation (A10.15)). The time profile of the interest rate is obtained by differentiating (A10.15) with respect to time:

$$\dot{r} = \frac{(1-\delta)\dot{p} + \delta\dot{e}}{\lambda + \eta}, \tag{A10.27}$$

where we have used the fact that $\dot{m} = \dot{g} = \dot{p}^* = 0$. For $t_A \leq t < t_I$ we have $\dot{p} > 0$ and $\dot{e} > 0$ so the domestic interest rate rises during that time. In contrast, for $t \geq t_I$ we have $\dot{p} > 0$ and $\dot{e} < 0$ so the net effect on $\dot{r}$ is not a priori clear. Since r eventually has to equal r^*, we simply assume that $\dot{r}$ is positive after t_I. (This result may be provable with more formal means beyond the scope of this chapter.) The time profile for output is obtained by differentiating (A10.14) with respect to time:

$$\dot{y} = \frac{-(\eta + \lambda\delta)\dot{p} + \lambda\delta\dot{e}}{\lambda + \eta}, \tag{A10.28}$$

where we have again used the fact that $\dot{m} = \dot{g} = \dot{p}^* = 0$. For $t_A \leq t < t_I$ we have $\dot{p} > 0$ and $\dot{e} > 0$ so the effect on output is ambiguous during that time. (We assume in Figure A10.8 that output falls. Again, this may be provable by more formal means beyond the scope of this chapter.) For $t \geq t_I$ we have $\dot{p} > 0$ and $\dot{e} < 0$ so that output falls during that time.

(g) If the domestic price is perfectly flexible (and $\phi \to \infty$) it follows from (Q10.10) that output is always equal to its full employment level ($y = \bar{y}$). We can thus solve (Q10.8)-(Q10.9) for the domestic interest rate and price level as a function

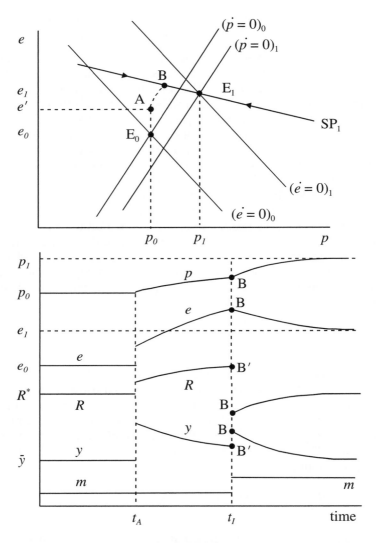

Figure A10.8: Anticipated and permanent increase in the money supply

of the nominal exchange rate and the remaining exogenous variables ($\bar{y}$, g, m, and p^*).

$$\begin{bmatrix} \eta & \delta \\ \lambda & -1 \end{bmatrix} \begin{bmatrix} r \\ p \end{bmatrix} = \begin{bmatrix} g + \delta[p^* + e] - \bar{y} \\ \bar{y} - m \end{bmatrix}. \tag{A10.29}$$

The matrix on the left-hand side is denoted by Δ. We find that $|\Delta| = -(\eta + \lambda\delta)$ and:

$$\Delta^{-1} = \frac{1}{\eta + \lambda\delta} \begin{bmatrix} 1 & \delta \\ \lambda & -\eta \end{bmatrix}. \tag{A10.30}$$

Combining these two equations yields the reduced-form expressions:

$$\begin{bmatrix} r \\ p \end{bmatrix} = \frac{1}{\eta + \lambda\delta} \begin{bmatrix} 1 & \delta \\ \lambda & -\eta \end{bmatrix} \begin{bmatrix} g + \delta[p^* + e] - \bar{y} \\ \bar{y} - m \end{bmatrix}$$

$$= \frac{1}{\eta + \lambda\delta} \begin{bmatrix} -(1 - \delta)\bar{y} - \delta m + g + \delta[p^* + e] \\ -(\lambda + \eta)\bar{y} + \eta m + \lambda g + \lambda\delta[p^* + e] \end{bmatrix}. \tag{A10.31}$$

By using the reduced-form expression for r in (Q10.11) we obtain:

$$\dot{e} = r - r^*$$

$$= \frac{-(\lambda + \eta)\bar{y} + \eta m + \lambda g + \lambda\delta[p^* + e]}{\eta + \lambda\delta} - r^*. \tag{A10.32}$$

This is an unstable differential equation in the nominal exchange rate. The only economically sensible solution for the exchange rate is such that convergence to the steady state is ensured. We study the effects of monetary policy in Figure

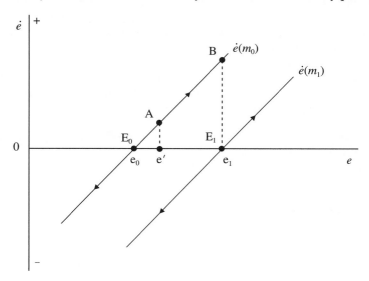

Figure A10.9: Exchange rate dynamics with perfectly flexible prices

A10.9, which has $\dot{e}$ on the vertical axis and e on the horizontal axis. The initial steady state is at E_0. An permanent increase in the money supply shifts the $\dot{e}$

line to the right, from $\dot{e}(m_0)$ to $\dot{e}(m_1)$. If the shock is *unanticipated* then the only stable solution is that the economy jumps at impact ($t = t_A = t_I$) from E_0 to E_1. Any other change in the exchange rate would never get the economy to the new steady-state equilibrium. The key thing to note is that there is no longer exchange rate overshooting.

If the policy shock is anticipated, then the intuitive solution principle suggests that the economy will arrive at point B for $t = t_I$. For $t_A \leq t < t_I$, the old dynamics (given by the $\dot{e}(m_0)$ line) determine the adjustment of the exchange rate. At time $t = t_A$, the exchange rate jumps such that the path from A to B is covered precisely during the transitional phase. Again we reach the conclusion that there is no overshooting of the exchange rate. In Chapter 11 we show that price stickiness is a necessary (but not a sufficient) condition for the overshooting result to hold (see section 10.3.1).

Question 4: The Buiter-Miller model

(a) Equation (Q10.12) is the IS curve for the open economy. The demand for output depends negatively on the (appropriately defined) real interest rate, $r - \dot{p}_C$, where p_C is the price index for goods used for consumption and investment in the domestic economy. Output demand depends positively on the real exchange rate, $p^* + e - p$, and we thus assume implicitly that the Marshall-Lerner condition is valid. Equation (Q10.13) is the LM curve, featuring a unit-elastic demand for real money balances. Again the price index p_C is used to deflate the nominal money supply. Equation (Q10.14) is the definition of the price index. It is a weighted average of the price of domestically produced goods (p) and the domestic currency price of foreign goods ($p^* + e$). In section 10.1.4.1 we show in detail how the Armington trick can be used to rationalize such a price index. Intuitively, we assume that the *composite* good used domestically is a Cobb-Douglas combination of domestically produced and foreign-produced goods, with weights α and $1 - \alpha$, respectively. Equation (Q10.15) is the price adjustment rule stating that the domestic price level rises (falls) if actual output exceeds (falls short of) full employment output. Finally, equation (Q10.16) is the uncovered interest parity condition. The endogenous variables are y, r, p_C, e, and p. The exogenous variables are p^*, m, $\bar{y}$, and r^*.

(b) By differentiating (Q10.14) with respect to time (and noting that α and $\dot{p}^*$ are constant over time) we find:

$$\dot{p}_C \equiv \alpha \dot{p} + (1 - \alpha)\dot{e}. \tag{A10.33}$$

By substituting (A10.33) into (Q10.12) we obtain:

$$y = -\eta [r - \alpha \dot{p} - (1 - \alpha)\dot{e}] + \delta[p^* + e - p]. \tag{A10.34}$$

Similarly, by substituting (Q10.14) into (Q10.13) we find:

$$m - \alpha p - (1 - \alpha)[p^* + e] = y - \lambda r. \tag{A10.35}$$

Next we rewrite the system in terms of $l \equiv m - p$ and $c \equiv p^* + e - p$. Equation

(A10.34) can be rewritten as:

$$
\begin{aligned}
y &= -\eta r + \alpha \eta \dot{p} + (1 - \alpha)\eta \dot{e} + \delta[p^* + e - p] \\
&= -\eta r + (1 - \alpha)\eta(\dot{e} - \dot{p}) + [(1 - \alpha)\eta + \alpha\eta]\,\dot{p} + \delta[p^* + e - p] \\
&= -\eta r + (1 - \alpha)\eta \dot{c} - \eta l + \delta c + \eta \dot{m},
\end{aligned} \tag{A10.36}
$$

where we have used the fact that $l \equiv \dot{m} - \dot{p}$ and $\dot{c} \equiv \dot{e} - \dot{p}$ (since $\dot{p}^* = 0$ by assumption). Equation (A10.35) can similarly be rewritten in terms of l and c:

$$
\begin{aligned}
y - \lambda r &= m - \alpha p - (1 - \alpha)[p^* + e] \\
&= m - p - (1 - \alpha)[p^* + e - p] \\
&= l - (1 - \alpha)c.
\end{aligned} \tag{A10.37}
$$

We can rewrite the price adjustment equation (Q10.15) as follows:

$$
-\dot{p} = \phi(\bar{y} - y) \quad \Leftrightarrow \quad \dot{m} - \dot{p} = \phi(\bar{y} - y) + \dot{m} \quad \Leftrightarrow
$$
$$
l = -\phi y + \phi \bar{y} + \dot{m}. \tag{A10.38}
$$

Finally, by using (Q10.15) and (Q10.16), we obtain the following expression:

$$
\begin{aligned}
\dot{e} - \dot{p} &= r - r^* - \phi(y - \bar{y}) \\
\dot{c} &= r - \phi y - r^* + \phi \bar{y}.
\end{aligned} \tag{A10.39}
$$

We can now solve (A10.37) and (A10.39) for y and r, conditional upon $\dot{c}, l, c, r^*$, and $\bar{y}$. In matrix notation we get:

$$
\begin{aligned}
\begin{bmatrix} y \\ r \end{bmatrix} &= \begin{bmatrix} 1 & -\lambda \\ -\phi & 1 \end{bmatrix}^{-1} \begin{bmatrix} l - (1-\alpha)c \\ \dot{c} + r^* - \phi \bar{y} \end{bmatrix} \\
&= \frac{1}{1 - \lambda\phi} \begin{bmatrix} 1 & \lambda \\ \phi & 1 \end{bmatrix} \begin{bmatrix} l - (1-\alpha)c \\ \dot{c} + r^* - \phi \bar{y} \end{bmatrix} \\
&= \frac{1}{1 - \lambda\phi} \begin{bmatrix} l - (1-\alpha)c + \lambda\left[\dot{c} + r^* - \phi \bar{y}\right] \\ \phi\left[l - (1-\alpha)c\right] + \dot{c} + r^* - \phi \bar{y} \end{bmatrix}.
\end{aligned} \tag{A10.40}
$$

By substituting the solutions for y and r (given in (A10.40)) into (A10.36) we find:

$$
[\lambda + \lambda\eta - (1-\alpha)\eta(1 - \lambda\phi)]\,\dot{c} + \eta(1 - \lambda\phi)l = [\delta(1 - \lambda\phi) + (1-\alpha)(1 + \eta\phi)]\,c
$$
$$
- (1 + \eta\phi)l + \eta(1 - \lambda\phi)\dot{m} - (\lambda + \eta)(r^* - \phi \bar{y}). \tag{A10.41}
$$

Similarly, by substituting the solution for y into (A10.38) we obtain after some manipulations:

$$
\lambda\phi\dot{c} + (1 - \lambda\phi)l = (1 - \alpha)\phi c - \phi l + (1 - \lambda\phi)\dot{m} - \lambda\phi r^* + \phi \bar{y}. \tag{A10.42}
$$

Equations (A10.41)–(A10.42) can be written in a single matrix equations as:

$$
\Delta_1 \begin{bmatrix} \dot{c} \\ l \end{bmatrix} = \Delta_2 \begin{bmatrix} c \\ l \end{bmatrix} + \Gamma_1 \begin{bmatrix} \dot{m} \\ r^* \\ \phi \bar{y} \end{bmatrix}, \tag{A10.43}
$$

where the matrices Δ_1, Δ_2, and Γ_1 are defined as follows:

$$\Delta_1 \equiv \begin{bmatrix} \lambda + \eta - (1 - \alpha)\eta(1 - \lambda\phi) & \eta(1 - \lambda\phi) \\ \lambda\phi & 1 - \lambda\phi \end{bmatrix}, \tag{A10.44}$$

$$\Delta_2 \equiv \begin{bmatrix} \delta(1 - \lambda\phi) + (1 - \alpha)(1 + \eta\phi) & -(1 + \eta\phi) \\ (1 - \alpha)\phi & -\phi \end{bmatrix}, \tag{A10.45}$$

$$\Gamma_1 \equiv \begin{bmatrix} \eta(1 - \lambda\phi) & -(\lambda + \eta) & \lambda + \eta \\ 1 - \lambda\phi & -\lambda\phi & 1 \end{bmatrix}. \tag{A10.46}$$

The determinant of Δ_1 is given by:

$$|\Delta_1| = (1 - \lambda\phi)\left[\lambda + \alpha\eta(1 - \lambda\phi)\right]. \tag{A10.47}$$

Provided $|\Delta_1| \neq 0$, Δ_1^{-1} exists and is equal to:

$$\Delta_1^{-1} \equiv \frac{1}{(1 - \lambda\phi)\left[\lambda + \alpha\eta(1 - \lambda\phi)\right]} \begin{bmatrix} 1 - \lambda\phi & -\eta(1 - \lambda\phi) \\ -\lambda\phi & \lambda + \eta - (1 - \alpha)\eta(1 - \lambda\phi) \end{bmatrix}. \tag{A10.48}$$

By using (A10.48) in (A10.43) we find that the dynamical system can be written in the standard format as:

$$\begin{bmatrix} \dot{c} \\ \dot{l} \end{bmatrix} = \Delta \begin{bmatrix} c \\ l \end{bmatrix} + \Gamma \begin{bmatrix} \dot{m} \\ r^* \\ \phi\bar{y} \end{bmatrix}, \tag{A10.49}$$

where Δ and Γ are given by:

$$\Delta \equiv \Delta_1^{-1}\Delta_2 = \begin{bmatrix} \frac{1 - \alpha + \delta(1 - \lambda\phi)}{\lambda + \alpha\eta(1 - \lambda\phi)} & -\frac{1}{\lambda + \alpha\eta(1 - \lambda\phi)} \\ \frac{\phi[-\lambda\delta + (1 - \alpha)\alpha\eta]}{\lambda + \alpha\eta(1 - \lambda\phi)} & -\frac{\alpha\eta\phi}{\lambda + \alpha\eta(1 - \lambda\phi)} \end{bmatrix}, \tag{A10.50}$$

$$\Gamma \equiv \Delta_1^{-1}\Gamma_1 = \begin{bmatrix} 0 & -\frac{\lambda + \eta(1 - \lambda\phi)}{\lambda + \alpha\eta(1 - \lambda\phi)} & \frac{\lambda}{\lambda + \alpha\eta(1 - \lambda\phi)} \\ 1 & \frac{(1 - \alpha)\eta\lambda\phi}{\lambda + \alpha\eta(1 - \lambda\phi)} & \frac{\lambda + \alpha\eta}{\lambda + \alpha\eta(1 - \lambda\phi)} \end{bmatrix}. \tag{A10.51}$$

The determinant of Δ is equal to:

$$\begin{aligned} |\Delta| &= \frac{\phi}{[\lambda + \alpha\eta(1 - \lambda\phi)]^2} \begin{vmatrix} 1 - \alpha + \delta(1 - \lambda\phi) & -1 \\ -\lambda\delta + (1 - \alpha)\alpha\eta & -\alpha\eta \end{vmatrix} \\ &= -\frac{\delta\phi}{\lambda + \alpha\eta(1 - \lambda\phi)}. \end{aligned} \tag{A10.52}$$

Saddle-point stability requires that $|\Delta|$ is negative. Since δ and ϕ are both positive, the necessary and sufficient stability condition is thus that the denominator of (A10.52) is positive, i.e. $\lambda + \alpha\eta(1 - \lambda\phi) > 0$. This is the condition stated in the question.

Under saddle-point stability, the competitiveness index is the jumping variable (as the nominal exchange rate can jump if news becomes available) and the liquidity index is the pre-determined variable. It can only jump when the money supply jumps (p itself is pre-determined and cannot jump at all but m is a policy variable which can jump discretely).

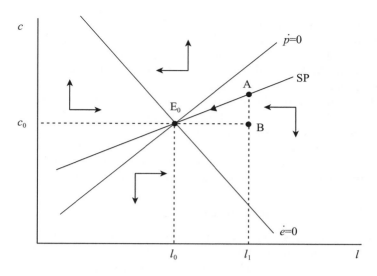

Figure A10.10: Monetary policy and overshooting

(c) Next we construct the phase diagram presented in Figure A10.10. The $\dot{c} = 0$ line is obtained from the first line of (A10.49):

$$[1 - \alpha + \delta(1 - \lambda\phi)]\,c - l = [\lambda + \eta(1 - \lambda\phi)]\,r^* - \lambda\phi\bar{y}. \qquad (A10.53)$$

The slope of the $\dot{c} = 0$ line is ambiguous as the sign of $1 - \lambda\phi$ is ambiguous. In Figure A10.10 we assume that $1 - \lambda\phi > 0$ so that the term in square brackets on the left-hand side of (A10.53) is positive and the $\dot{c} = 0$ line is upward sloping. For points above (below) the $\dot{c} = 0$ line, the competitiveness index rises (falls) over time:

$$\frac{\partial \dot{c}}{\partial c} = \frac{1 - \alpha + \delta(1 - \lambda\phi)}{\lambda + \alpha\eta(1 - \lambda\phi)} > 0. \qquad (A10.54)$$

The $\dot{l} = 0$ line is obtained from the second line of (A10.49):

$$[-\lambda\delta + (1 - \alpha)\alpha\eta]\,c - \alpha\eta l = -(1 - \alpha)\eta\lambda r^* - (\lambda + \alpha\eta)\bar{y}. \qquad (A10.55)$$

The slope of the $\dot{l} = 0$ line is also ambiguous because the sign of the term in square brackets on the left-hand side of (A10.55) is not unambiguous. In Figure A10.10 we assume that this term is negative so that the $\dot{l} = 0$ line slopes downward. For points to the right (left) of the $\dot{l} = 0$ line, the liquidity index falls:

$$\frac{\partial \dot{l}}{\partial l} = -\frac{\alpha\eta\phi}{\lambda + \alpha\eta(1 - \lambda\phi)} < 0. \qquad (A10.56)$$

The arrow configuration in Figure A10.10 confirms that the model is saddle-path stable.

(d) We study a step-wise increase in the money supply for which announcement and implementation dates coincide. Hence, $\dot{m} = 0$ both before and after the shock, so it would appear (from (A10.49)–(A10.51)) that nothing affects the dynamical system for c and l. This is not correct, however, because the impact jump in m causes an equal-sized impact jump in l (as p is predetermined). In terms of Figure A10.10, the liquidity index jumps at impact from l_0 to l_1. If the competitiveness index were to remain unchanged (and the economy would stay in point B) then the steady-state equilibrium E_0 would not be reached. The only stable trajectory reaching E_0 is the saddle path SP. Hence, at impact the economy jumps from E_0 to point A on this saddle path. Since the saddle path is upward sloping, overshooting still occurs in this model. There is no long-run effect of the money supply increase on c but there is a positive effect on competitiveness both on impact and during transition (a real depreciation).

Question 5: Dynamics of foreign reserves

(a) Equation (Q10.17) is the goods market equilibrium condition for a small open economy (the IS curve). Equation (Q10.18) is the money market equilibrium condition (LM curve). The left-hand side of (Q10.18) is the monetary base. We abstract from a private (fractional reserve) banking system so that the monetary base equals the money supply. Equation (Q10.19) is the balance of payments: the sum of net exports plus net capital inflows equals the change in foreign exchange holdings by the central bank. We assume that a devaluation of the currency (a rise in E) raises net exports, i.e. the Marshall-Lerner condition is assumed to hold. The endogenous variables are output, the domestic interest rate, and the stock of foreign exchange reserves (Y, r, and F). Exogenous are G, D, r^*, and E.

(b) Equations (Q10.17)–(Q10.18) summarize the IS-LM equilibrium and yield equilibrium values for Y and r conditional upon the stock of foreign exchange reserves (F) and the exogenous variables (G, D, r^*, and E). As in Chapter 2 in the text, we write these implicit relations as follows:

$$Y = AD(F, D, G, E), \qquad \text{(A10.57)}$$
$$r = H(F, D, G, E). \qquad \text{(A10.58)}$$

In order to examine the stability issue, we need expressions for the partial derivatives of AD and H with respect to F (which we denote by, respectively, AD_F and H_F). To examine the policy shocks in parts (c) and (d) of the question we need to know AD_G, H_G, AD_D and H_D. Intuitively, the signs of these expressions are easily obtained. An increase in F or D shifts the LM curve to the right which leads to an increase in output and a fall in the domestic interest rate, i.e. $AD_F = AD_D > 0$ and $H_F = H_D < 0$. An increase in G or E shifts the IS curve to the right which leads to an increase in both output and the domestic interest rate, i.e. $AD_G > 0$, $H_G > 0$, $AD_E > 0$ and $H_E > 0$.

Formally, we obtain the partial derivatives by totally differentiating (Q10.17)–(Q10.18) with respect to all the variables. After some manipulation we obtain the following matrix expression:

$$\begin{bmatrix} 1 - C_Y - X_Y & -I_r \\ l_Y & l_r \end{bmatrix} \begin{bmatrix} dY \\ dr \end{bmatrix} = \begin{bmatrix} dG + X_E dE \\ dF + dD \end{bmatrix}, \qquad \text{(A10.59)}$$

where we denote the two-by-two matrix on the left-hand side by Δ. The determinant of this matrix is:

$$|\Delta| \equiv l_r(1 - C_Y - X_Y) + I_r l_Y < 0, \tag{A10.60}$$

where the sign follows from the fact that $l_r < 0$, $I_r < 0$, $l_Y > 0$, $1 - C_Y > 0$, and $-X_Y > 0$. The inverse of Δ is:

$$\Delta^{-1} = \frac{1}{|\Delta|} \begin{bmatrix} l_r & I_r \\ -l_Y & 1 - C_Y - X_Y \end{bmatrix}. \tag{A10.61}$$

Using (A10.61) and (A10.59) we obtain:

$$\begin{bmatrix} dY \\ dr \end{bmatrix} = \frac{1}{|\Delta|} \begin{bmatrix} l_r(dG + X_E dE) + I_r(dF + dD) \\ -l_Y(dG + X_E dE) + (1 - C_Y - X_Y)(dF + dD) \end{bmatrix}. \tag{A10.62}$$

By allowing only one differential on the right-hand side of (A10.62) to be non-zero we obtain the partial derivatives we are after. For example, by setting $dG = dE = dD = 0$ and $dF \neq 0$ we find:

$$[AD_F \equiv] \frac{\partial Y}{\partial F} = \frac{I_r}{l_r(1 - C_Y - X_Y) + I_r l_Y} > 0, \tag{A10.63}$$

$$[H_F \equiv] \frac{\partial r}{\partial F} = \frac{1 - C_Y - X_Y}{l_r(1 - C_Y - X_Y) + I_r l_Y} < 0. \tag{A10.64}$$

To investigate the stability of the model we differentiate (Q10.19) with respect to F taking into account the induced effect on output and the interest rate:

$$\frac{\partial \dot{F}}{\partial F} = X_Y AD_F + KI_r H_F < 0, \tag{A10.65}$$

where the sign follows readily because $X_Y < 0$, $AD_F > 0$ (see (A10.63)), $KI_r > 0$, and $H_F < 0$ (see (A10.64)). It follows from (A10.65) that the model is stable. Furthermore, the larger is the degree of capital mobility, the larger is KI_r, and the faster is the rate at which the stock of foreign exchange reserves adjusts toward its steady-state level. In the special case of perfect capital mobility ($KI_r \to \infty$) adjustment is instantaneous. Paths with finite and infinite adjustment speeds have been illustrated in Figure A10.11. Under perfect capital mobility ($KI_r \to \infty$) adjustment is instantaneous, say from E_0 to E_1. In contrast, under imperfect capital mobility ($KI_r \ll \infty$) adjustment is only gradual as represented by the dashed path originating from point E_0.

(c) The BP curve represents (r, Y) combinations for which the balance of payments is in equilibrium ($\dot{F} = 0$). By setting $\dot{F} = 0$ in (Q10.19) and differentiating with respect to r and Y (holding constant E and r^*) we find $X_Y dY + KI_r dr = 0$ or:

$$\left(\frac{dr}{dY}\right)_{BP} = -\frac{X_Y}{KI_r} > 0. \tag{A10.66}$$

The slope of the LM curve is obtained by differentiating (Q10.18) with respect to r and Y (holding constant D and F):

$$\left(\frac{dr}{dY}\right)_{LM} = -\frac{l_Y}{l_r} > 0. \tag{A10.67}$$

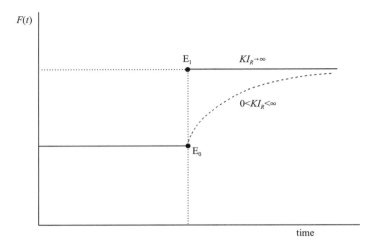

Figure A10.11: Adjustment speed and capital mobility

By comparing the two slopes in (A10.66) and (A10.67) we find that the BP curve is flatter if:

$$\left(\frac{dr}{dY}\right)_{LM} > \left(\frac{dr}{dY}\right)_{BP} \quad \Leftrightarrow \quad -\frac{l_Y}{l_r} > -\frac{X_Y}{KI_r} \quad \Leftrightarrow \quad X_Y l_r - l_Y KI_r < 0, \quad \text{(A10.68)}$$

where the final expression is the condition stated in the question. Note that the condition is trivially met under perfect capital mobility because $KI_r \to \infty$ in that case. The economic interpretation of (A10.68) is that capital must be sufficiently mobile. If (A10.68) holds, then the *impact* effect of an increase in G is to shift the balance of payments into a surplus. Despite the fact that imports increase (and net exports fall), the domestic interest rate rises by enough to attract additional net capital inflows which dominate the reduction in net exports. (Technically this result is stated in (A10.71) below.)

(d) We derive from (Q10.19) and (A10.62) that:

$$d\dot{F} = -\gamma_F dF + \gamma_G dG, \quad \text{(A10.69)}$$

where γ_F and γ_G are defined as follows:

$$\gamma_F \equiv -(X_Y AD_F + KI_r H_F) > 0, \quad \text{(A10.70)}$$

$$\gamma_G \equiv X_Y AD_G + KI_R H_G = \frac{X_Y l_R - l_Y KI_R}{l_R(1 - C_Y - X_Y) + I_R l_Y} > 0, \quad \text{(A10.71)}$$

where the sign of γ_G in (A10.71) follows from the condition (A10.68). The adjustment in the stock of foreign exchange reserves is shown in Figure A10.12. Fiscal policy causes a balance of payments surplus and the economy jumps from E_0 to A directly above it. Over time, reserves gradually increase as the economy moves from A to E_1.

To figure out what happens to the remaining variables we draw the IS-LM-BP diagram in Figure A10.13. The IS curve shifts to the right from $IS(G_0)$ to

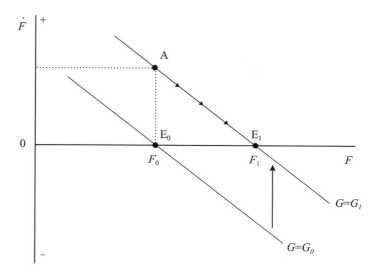

Figure A10.12: Adjustment in the stock of foreign exchange reserves

$IS(G_1)$. At impact F (and the money supply) is predetermined so the LM curve stays put. Equilibrium shifts from E_0 to A, and both output and the interest rate rise. In point A there is a balance of payments surplus ($\dot{F} > 0$ there) so that the stock of foreign exchange reserves (and thus the money supply) starts to rise. Over time the LM curve shifts from $LM(F_0)$ to $LM(F_1)$. The economy moves gradually from A to E_1. The domestic interest rate overshoots during transition but the adjustment in output is monotonic. The impulse-response diagrams are presented in Figure A10.14.

(e) Monetary policy consists of a so-called *open market operation*, i.e. the purchase of bonds by the central bank on the open market ($dD > 0$). This raises the monetary base and thus increases the money supply. By differentiating (Q10.19) with respect to F and D, taking into account the induced effects on Y and r, we obtain:

$$d\dot{F} = -\gamma_F dF - \gamma_D dD, \tag{A10.72}$$

where γ_F is defined in (A10.70) and γ_D is:

$$\gamma_D \equiv -(X_Y AD_D + KI_r H_D) > 0. \tag{A10.73}$$

Inspection of (A10.62) reveals, of course, that $AD_D = AD_F$ and $H_D = H_F$ so that $\gamma_D = \gamma_F$ and (A10.72) can be written more compactly as:

$$d\dot{F} = -\gamma_F(dF + dD). \tag{A10.74}$$

As we saw above, the model is stable (because $-\gamma_F < 0$). In the steady state, expansionary monetary policy leads to a loss of foreign exchange reserves (i.e. $dF/dD = -1$ in the long run). In Figures A10.15–A10.17 we present, respectively, the phase diagram, the IS-LM-BP diagram, and the impulse response functions.

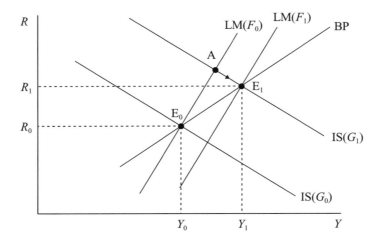

Figure A10.13: IS-LM-BP equilibrium

Question 6: Price flexibility in the Mundell-Fleming model

(a) Mark (2001) presents a slightly more general version of this model. We follow
his solution method closely.] Equation (Q10.20) is the demand for real money
balances, featuring a unit output elasticity and a negative semi-elasticity for
the nominal interest rate. Equation (Q10.21) is the IS curve for the small open
economy. Output demand depends negatively on the expected real interest
rate (first term on the right-hand side) and positively on the real exchange rate
(second term). The real exchange rate measures the relative price of foreign
goods so the effect on domestic output demand is positive (implicitly it is thus
assumed that the Marshall-Lerner condition is satisfied). The IS curve is also
affected by a random demand shock term, d_t. Equation (Q10.22) is the uncovered interest parity expression, stating that yields on domestic and foreign
assets are the same (when measured in the same currency). Equation (Q10.23)
is a sticky-price adjustment rule. The variable $\tilde{p}_t$ represents the (hypothetical)
price for which y_t equals $\bar{y}_t$. In equation (Q10.23) $E_{t-1}\tilde{p}_t$ is the predetermined
part of the price level, i.e. it is based on period-$t-1$ information. The pricing
equation allows for three interesting cases, depending on the magnitude of θ.

   (a) *Perfect price flexibility.* If $\theta = 1$ then (Q10.23) reduces to $p_t = \tilde{p}_t$, i.e. the
   actual price equals the equilibrium price.

   (b) *Complete price stickiness.* If $\theta = 0$ then (Q10.23) reduces to $p_t = E_{t-1}\tilde{p}_t$, i.e.
   the actual price is set on the basis of information available in the previous
   period and is completely pre-determined in the current period.

   (c) *Intermediate price flexibility.* If $0 < \theta < 1$ then the current price is imper-
   fectly flexible.

Equation (Q10.24) is the money supply rule, stating that the policy maker aims
for constant money supply but that there are stochastic shocks in the money
supply process. Equation (Q10.25) is the exogenous stochastic path for $\bar{y}_t$,
where z_t is the stochastic supply term. Finally, equation (Q10.26) shows the

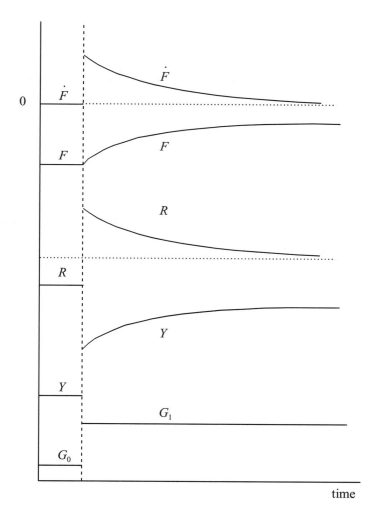

Figure A10.14: Fiscal policy in the IS-LM-BP model

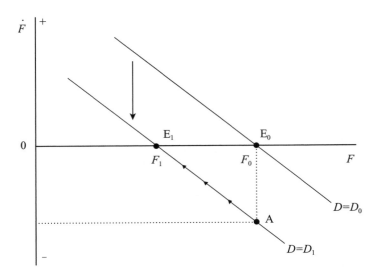

Figure A10.15: Adjustment in the stock of foreign exchange reserves

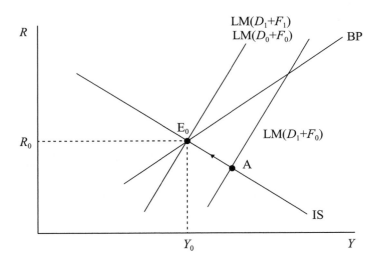

Figure A10.16: IS-LM-BP equilibrium

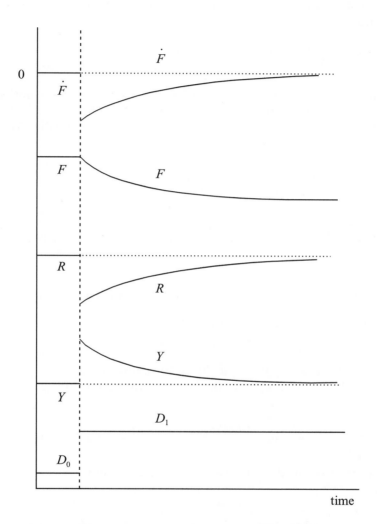

Figure A10.17: Monetary policy in the IS-LM-BP model

stochastic process for the demand shock, d_t, where u_t is the stochastic demand term.

(b) We use tildes above variables to denote realizations under pure price flexibility. If $\theta = 1$ it follows from (Q10.23) that $p_t = \tilde{p}_t$ and thus that $\tilde{y}_t = \bar{y}_t$. The domestic price is perfectly flexible and output is equal to its full employment level at all times. By substituting (Q10.22) into (Q10.21) and noting that $\tilde{y}_t = \bar{y}_t$ we find:

$$
\begin{aligned}
\bar{y}_t &= -\beta \left[r^* + E_t(\tilde{e}_{t+1} - \tilde{p}_{t+1}) - (\tilde{e}_t - \tilde{p}_t) \right] + \gamma(\tilde{e}_t - \tilde{p}_t) + d_t \\
&= -\beta r^* - \beta E_t \tilde{q}_{t+1} + (\beta + \gamma)\tilde{q}_t + d_t,
\end{aligned} \tag{A10.75}
$$

where we have used the definition of the real exchange rate (mentioned in the question) in going from the first to the second line ($q_t \equiv e_t - p_t$). By rewriting (A10.75) we find the expectational difference equation for the real exchange rate under pure price flexibility:

$$
\tilde{q}_t = \frac{\beta r^* + \bar{y}_t - d_t}{\beta + \gamma} + \frac{\beta}{\beta + \gamma} E_t \tilde{q}_{t+1}. \tag{A10.76}
$$

Since the coefficient in front of $E_t q_{t+1}$ is between 0 and 1, the expectational difference equation is stable and forward iteration will yield a solution. The form of (A10.76) suggests that the following trial solution will be appropriate:

$$
q_t = \pi_{q0} + \pi_{q1} \left[\bar{y}_t - d_t \right]. \tag{A10.77}
$$

Equation (A10.77) implies that $E_t q_{t+1}$ can be written as:

$$
\begin{aligned}
E_t q_{t+1} &= E_t \left[\pi_{q0} + \pi_{q1} \left(\bar{y}_{t+1} - d_{t+1} \right) \right] \\
&= \pi_{q0} + \pi_{q1}(\bar{y}_t - d_t),
\end{aligned} \tag{A10.78}
$$

where we have used (Q10.25)-(Q10.26), by noting that $E_t \bar{y}_{t+1} = \bar{y}_t$, and $E_t d_{t+1} = d_t$ (since $E_t z_{t+1} = E_t u_{t+1} = 0$). By substituting (A10.78) and (A10.77) into (A10.76) we find:

$$
\pi_{q0} + \pi_{q1} \left[\bar{y}_t - d_t \right] = \frac{\beta r^* + \bar{y}_t - d_t}{\beta + \gamma} + \frac{\beta}{\beta + \gamma} \left[\pi_{q0} + \pi_{q1}(\bar{y}_t - d_t) \right].
$$

This expression must hold for all $(\bar{y}_t - d_t)$, so we find:

$$
\left[1 - \frac{\beta}{\beta + \gamma} \right] \pi_{q0} = \frac{\beta r^*}{\beta + \gamma} \quad \Rightarrow \quad \pi_{q0} = \frac{\beta r^*}{\gamma},
$$

$$
\left[1 - \frac{\beta}{\beta + \gamma} \right] \pi_{q1} = \frac{1}{\beta + \gamma} \quad \Rightarrow \quad \pi_{q1} = \frac{1}{\gamma},
$$

so that the REH solution for $\tilde{q}_t$ is:

$$
\tilde{q}_t = \frac{\beta r^* + \bar{y}_t - d_t}{\gamma}. \tag{A10.79}
$$

According to (A10.79) the equilibrium flex-price real exchange rate depends positively on the foreign interest rate and output supply and negatively on the domestic demand shock. Monetary shocks play no role. For future use we note that (A10.79) implies:

$$E_t \tilde{q}_{t+1} = E_t \left[\frac{\beta r^* + \bar{y}_{t+1} - d_{t+1}}{\gamma} \right] = \frac{\beta r^* + \bar{y}_t - d_t}{\gamma} = \tilde{q}_t \qquad (A10.80)$$

To solve for the equilibrium price, $\tilde{p}_t$, we combine (Q10.20) and (Q10.22) and note that $\tilde{y}_t = \bar{y}_t$:

$$m_t - \tilde{p}_t = \bar{y}_t - \alpha \left[r^* + E_t \tilde{e}_{t+1} - \tilde{e}_t \right] \quad \Rightarrow$$

$$(1 + \alpha)\tilde{p}_t = m_t - \bar{y}_t + \alpha \left[r^* + E_t (\tilde{e}_{t+1} - \tilde{p}_{t+1}) - (\tilde{e}_t - \tilde{p}_t) \right] + \alpha E_t \tilde{p}_{t+1} \quad \Rightarrow$$

$$\tilde{p}_t = \frac{\alpha r^* + m_t - \bar{y}_t}{1 + \alpha} + \frac{\alpha}{1 + \alpha} \left[E_t \tilde{q}_{t+1} - \tilde{q}_t \right] + \frac{\alpha}{1 + \alpha} E_t \tilde{p}_{t+1}$$

$$= \frac{\alpha r^* + m_t - \bar{y}_t}{1 + \alpha} + \frac{\alpha}{1 + \alpha} E_t \tilde{p}_{t+1}, \qquad (A10.81)$$

where we have used (A10.80) in the final step. This expectational difference equation is stable because the coefficient in front of $E_t \tilde{p}_{t+1}$ is between 0 and 1. We can again use the method of undetermined coefficients to solve (A10.81). The trial solution $\tilde{p}_t = \pi_{p0} + \pi_{p1} [m_t - \bar{y}_t]$ is fine, and–upon substitution in (A10.81)–yields the following REH solution for $\tilde{p}_t$:

$$\tilde{p}_t = \alpha r^* + m_t - \bar{y}_t. \qquad (A10.82)$$

A nominal shock (change in m_t) raises the domestic price level, as is to be expected. An increase in domestic supply depresses the domestic price level.

Now that we have the rational expectations solution for both the real exchange rate (A10.79) and the domestic price level (A10.82), we can easily deduce the implied solution for the nominal exchange rate (under perfect price flexibility):

$$\tilde{e}_t = \tilde{q}_t + \tilde{p}_t = m_t + \frac{(\alpha\gamma + \beta) r^* + (1 - \gamma)\bar{y}_t - d_t}{\gamma}. \qquad (A10.83)$$

An increase in m_t increases e_t one-for-one; this is a nominal depreciation. The effect of output supply on the nominal exchange rate depends on the sign of $1 - \gamma$.

(c) As is clear from (A10.79), the money supply does not affect the equilibrium *real* exchange rate. With perfect price flexibility, the model is quite classical and thus features the classical dichotomy according to which nominal variables do not affect real variables. It follows from, respectively, (A10.82) and (A10.83) that the equilibrium domestic price and the *nominal* exchange rate are affected one-for-one by the money supply.

(d) In summary, the flex-price system is fully characterized by:

$$\tilde{q}_t = \frac{\beta r^* + \bar{y}_t - d_t}{\gamma},$$

$$\tilde{p}_t = \alpha r^* + m_t - \bar{y}_t,$$

$$m_t = m_{t-1} + v_t,$$

$$\bar{y}_t = \bar{y}_{t-1} + z_t,$$

$$d_t = d_{t-1} + u_t,$$

$$\tilde{y}_t = \bar{y}_t.$$

To solve the general (sticky-price) version of the model, with $0 < \theta < 1$, we must take equation (Q10.23) into account. First we note from (A10.82) that $\tilde{p}_t - E_{t-1}\tilde{p}_t$ can be written as:

$$\tilde{p}_t - E_{t-1}\tilde{p}_t = (m_t - E_{t-1}m_t) - (\bar{y}_t - E_{t-1}\bar{y}_t) = v_t - z_t. \tag{A10.84}$$

According to (A10.84), agents can misestimate the equilibrium price either because there is a monetary surprise (v_t) or because there is a shock to the IS curve (z_t).

By using (A10.84) in (Q10.23) we find:

$$p_t = \tilde{p}_t - (1 - \theta)(v_t - z_t). \tag{A10.85}$$

For future use we note some useful results:

$$E_t p_{t+1} = E_t \tilde{p}_{t+1} = \tilde{p}_t, \tag{A10.86}$$
$$E_t p_{t+1} - p_t = (1 - \theta)(v_t - z_t), \tag{A10.87}$$
$$p_t = \alpha r^* + m_t - \bar{y}_t - (1 - \theta)(v_t - z_t). \tag{A10.88}$$

The first task at hand is to derive the expectational difference equation for q_t. Here are the steps. First, we substitute (Q10.21) into (Q10.20) to get:

$$m_t - p_t = -(\alpha + \beta) r_t + \beta [E_t p_{t+1} - p_t] + \gamma (e_t - p_t) + d_t. \tag{A10.89}$$

Next we substitute (Q10.22) into (A10.89) and note that $q_t \equiv e_t - p_t$ to get:

$$m_t - p_t = d_t - (\alpha + \beta) r^* - (\alpha + \beta)[E_t q_{t+1} - q_t] - \alpha [E_t p_{t+1} - p_t] + \gamma q_t. \tag{A10.90}$$

By substituting (A10.88) and (A10.87) into (A10.90) and collecting terms we find the expectational difference equation for the real exchange rate under stick prices:

$$q_t = \frac{\beta r^* + \bar{y}_t - d_t + (1 + \alpha)(1 - \theta)[v_t - z_t]}{\alpha + \beta + \gamma} + \frac{\alpha + \beta}{\alpha + \beta + \gamma} E_t q_{t+1}. \tag{A10.91}$$

Since the coefficient in front of $E_t q_{t+1}$ on the right-hand side is between 0 and 1, the expectational difference equation is stable and can be solved by forward iteration. Since it is so much fun, we use the method of undetermined coefficients again. The trial solution $q_t = \pi_0 + \pi_1 [\bar{y}_t - d_t] + \pi_2 [v_t - z_t]$ turns out to be just fine. Upon substitution in (A10.90) it yields the REH solution for the real exchange rate:

$$q_t = \frac{\beta r^* + \bar{y}_t - d_t}{\gamma} + \frac{(1 - \theta)(1 + \alpha)[v_t - z_t]}{\alpha + \beta + \gamma}. \tag{A10.92}$$

Since $e_t = q_t + p_t$, we can use (A10.88) and (A10.92) find the REH solution for the nominal exchange rate under sticky prices:

$$e_t = m_t + \frac{(\alpha\gamma + \beta) r^* + (1 - \gamma) \bar{y}_t - d_t}{\gamma} + \frac{1 - \beta - \gamma}{\alpha + \beta + \gamma}(1 - \theta)(v_t - z_t). \tag{A10.93}$$

(e) By using (A10.79) in (A10.92) we find that the real exchange rate under sticky prices can be written as:

$$q_t = \tilde{q}_t + (1 - \theta) \frac{1 + \alpha}{\alpha + \beta + \gamma} (v_t - z_t). \tag{A10.94}$$

Under sticky prices, the nominal shock (the v_t term) affects the real exchange rate. The classical dichotomy does not hold in the short run.

By using (A10.83) in (A10.93) we find that the real exchange rate under sticky prices can be written as:

$$e_t = \tilde{e}_t + (1 - \theta) \frac{1 - \beta - \gamma}{\alpha + \beta + \gamma} (v_t - z_t). \tag{A10.95}$$

Provided $\beta + \gamma < 1$, the nominal shock causes the nominal exchange rate to rise above its flex-price value. This is a form of the overshooting property of the Dornbusch model.

Chapter 11

Money

Question 1: Short questions

(a) According to Milton Friedman the optimal rate of inflation is zero. True, false, or uncertain? Explain.

(b) Explain the constrained optimization problem (the choices of $\bar{Z}$ and σ_Z) leading to the first-order condition (11.69) in the book. Derive equation (11.82) in the book.

(c) What is Friedman's "full liquidity result". Explain intuitively what it means. State the main reasons why this result may not be valid.

(d) What are the three major roles played by money? Explain which of these roles is the most distinguishing feature of money. Give examples.

(e) Consider the Bewley model discussed in section 11.3 of the book. Assume that the utility function is logarithmic, i.e. $U(C_t) = \ln C_t$. Show what happens to optimal consumption in the two periods and money holdings if the inflation rate, π_1, is increased. Illustrate your result, using a diagram like Figure 11.2 in the text. Assume that the income endowment point is to the right of the optimal consumption point (both before and after the shock).

Question 2: Optimal money growth

The representative agent is infinitely lived and has the following lifetime utility function:

$$V = \sum_{t=1}^{\infty} \left(\frac{1}{1+\rho} \right)^{t-1} U(C_t, 1 - L_t, m_t), \tag{Q11.1}$$

where the felicity function, $U(\cdot)$, has the usual properties: (i) there is positive but diminishing marginal felicity for both consumption and leisure, (ii) there exists a satiation level for real money balances, $\bar{m}$, and (iii) marginal felicity of real money is diminishing. We abstract from physical capital, and assume that the representative household can shift resources through time by means of government bonds and/or money. The periodic budget constraint in period t ($= 1, 2, \ldots.$) is given in nominal terms by:

$$(1 + R_{t-1})B_{t-1} + W_t(1 - \tau_t)L_t + M_{t-1} + P_t T_t = P_t C_t + M_t + B_t, \qquad \text{(Q11.2)}$$

where B_{t-1} is the stock of government bonds held at the end of period $t-1$, R_{t-1} is the nominal interest on government bonds paid at the end of period $t-1$, M_t is the stock of money balances at the beginning of period t, W_t is the nominal wage rate, τ_t is the proportional tax on labour income, and $P_t T_t$ is transfers received from the government.

The firm sector is very simple. There is no capital in the economy and goods are produced with labour only. The production function is given by $Y_t = L_t$ and the perfectly competitive representative firm maximizes profits, $\Pi_t \equiv P_t Y_t - W_t L_t$, given this linear technology.

The government budget identity is given in nominal terms by:

$$R_{t-1}B_{t-1} + P_t G_t + P_t T_t = \tau_t W_t L_t + (M_t - M_{t-1}) + (B_t - B_{t-1}), \qquad \text{(Q11.3)}$$

where G_t is the consumption of goods by the government. The sum of spending on interest payments on outstanding debt plus government consumption and transfers to households (left-hand side) must be equal to the sum of the labour income tax revenue, newly issued money balances, and newly issued government debt (right-hand side).

(a) Rewrite the periodic budget constraints for the household and the government in real terms. Use the definitions $m_t \equiv M_t/P_t$, $b_t \equiv B_t/P_t$, $w_t \equiv W_t/P_t$, $\pi_t \equiv P_{t+1}/P_t - 1$, and $r_t \equiv P_t(1 + R_t)/P_{t+1} - 1$.

(b) Prove that firm behaviour ensures that $w_t = 1$ and $\Pi_t = 0$. Prove that $Y_t = C_t + G_t = w_t L_t$.

Define the following discounting factor:

$$q_t^0 \equiv \begin{cases} 1 & \text{for } t = 1 \\ \prod_{i=1}^{t-1} \frac{1}{1+r_i} & \text{for } t = 2, 3, \ldots \end{cases} \qquad \text{(Q11.4)}$$

and assume that the following transversality conditions are satisfied:

$$\lim_{k \to \infty} q_{k+1}^0 b_{k+1} = 0, \qquad \lim_{k \to \infty} \frac{q_{k+1}^0 m_{k+1}}{1 + R_{t+k}} = 0. \qquad \text{(Q11.5)}$$

(c) ★ Prove that the household lifetime budget constraint can be written as:

$$a_0 = \sum_{t=1}^{\infty} q_t^0 \cdot \left[C_t + \frac{R_t}{1 + R_t} \cdot m_t - w_t(1 - \tau_t)L_t - T_t \right], \qquad \text{(Q11.6)}$$

where $a_0 \equiv (1 + r_0)b_0 + m_0/(1 + \pi_0)$. Provide an intuitive interpretation for (Q11.6).

(d) Set up the Lagrangian expression for the household's optimization problem, using λ as the Lagrange multiplier. Derive and interpret the first-order necessary conditions characterizing the household's optimal plans regarding consumption, labour supply, and money holdings.

(e) ★ Substitute the first-order conditions (derived in the previous subquestion) into the household lifetime budget constraint (Q11.6). Show that the adjusted lifetime budget constraint can be written as:

$$a_0 U_C(x_1) = \sum_{t=1}^{\infty} \left(\frac{1}{1+\rho}\right)^{t-1} [U_C(x_t)[C_t - T_t] + U_m(x_t)m_t - U_{1-L}(x_t)L_t],$$

(Q11.7)

where $U_C(x_t) \equiv \frac{\partial U(x_t)}{\partial C_t}$, $U_{1-L}(x_t) \equiv \frac{\partial U(x_t)}{\partial [1-L_t]}$, $U_m(x_t) \equiv \frac{\partial U(x_t)}{\partial m_t}$, and $x_t \equiv (C_t, 1-L_t, m_t)$.

(f) ★ Derive the optimal money growth rate under the assumption that the policy maker can freely adjust the level of transfers T_t in each period. Show that it is optimal for the policy maker to satiate the representative household with money balances. Prove that it is optimal to set $\tau_t = R_t = 0$, $\pi_t = \mu_t = -\rho/(1+\rho)$.

(g) ★ Next, derive the optimal money growth rate under the assumption that the policy maker does not have access to lump-sum transfers T_t in any period. Show that the Friedman rule no longer applies in this case.

Question 3: Monetary superneutrality

[Based on Marini and Ploeg (1988)] In this question we study monetary superneutrality in an overlapping generations model of the Blanchard-Yaari type. The theoretical details of this model are discussed in Chapter 16. Here we simply study its monetary properties. At time t, the lifetime utility function of a household of vintage $v \leq t$ is given by:

$$E\Lambda(v,t) \equiv \int_t^{\infty} \ln U(v,\tau) e^{(\rho+\beta)(t-\tau)} d\tau,$$

(Q11.8)

where $U(\cdot)$ is a CES sub-felicity function:

$$U(v,\tau) \equiv \left[\varepsilon C(v,\tau)^{(\sigma-1)/\sigma} + (1-\varepsilon)M(v,\tau)^{(\sigma-1)/\sigma}\right]^{\sigma/(\sigma-1)}, \quad 0 < \varepsilon < 1, \sigma > 0,$$

(Q11.9)

where $C(v,\tau)$ and $M(v,\tau)$ denote, respectively, consumption and *real* money balances of the household at time τ. The household's budget identity is:

$$\dot{A}(v,\tau) = [r(\tau)+\beta] A(v,\tau) + W(\tau) - T(\tau) - C(v,\tau) - [r(\tau)+\pi(\tau)] M(v,\tau),$$

(Q11.10)

where $\pi(\tau)$ is the inflation rate. The monetary authority sets a constant rate of growth, θ, of the *nominal* money supply so that the real money supply changes according to:

$$\dot{M}(\tau) = [\theta - \pi(\tau)] M(\tau).$$

(Q11.11)

The production side of the model is very simple. For simplicity we assume that the production function is Cobb-Douglas, i.e. $Y(t) = K(t)^\alpha L(t)^{1-\alpha}$. Labour supply is exogenous so $L(t) = 1$. We consider a closed economy, so the goods market clearing condition is given by $Y(t) = C(t) + I(t) + G(t)$.

(a) Interpret equations (Q11.10) and (Q11.11) of the model. Make sure you explain why the inflation rate appears in these equations.

(b) Use the method of two-stage budgeting to solve the optimization problem for individual households.

(c) Derive the aggregate consumption rule, the aggregate consumption Euler equation, and the differential equations for aggregate human and financial wealth for the model.

(d) State the government budget identity and the solvency condition for the government.

(e) Show that the model features *superneutrality* of money if and only if the birth/death rate is zero and the sub-felicity function is Cobb-Douglas ($\sigma = 1$). Show that, for the case with $\beta = 0$ and $\sigma = 1$, an unanticipated and permanent increase in the money growth rate leads to a discrete jump in the price level at impact but causes no further transitional dynamics. Show the phase diagram for real money balances and the impulse response functions for inflation, the price level, and the nominal money supply.

(f) Assume that $\beta > 0$, $\sigma = 1$, $B(\tau) = 0$ (for all τ), and that the government balances its budget by means of lump-sum taxes. Show that an increase in the money growth rate leads to a steady state increase in consumption and the capital stock but causes an ambiguous effect on real money balances. Explain the intuition behind your results.

(g) Make the same assumption as in part (f) and derive the long-run effects on capital, consumption, and real money balances of a tax-financed increase in government consumption. Explain the intuition behind your results.

★ Question 4: Cash-in-advance constraint in continuous time

[Based on Kam (2004)] In this question we consider the cash-in-advance model in continuous time. Less than fully confident readers may want to attempt this question after studying the Ramsey model of Chapter 13. The infinitely-lived representative household has a lifetime utility function of the form:

$$V \equiv \int_0^\infty U\left(C\left(t\right)\right) e^{-\rho t} dt, \tag{Q11.12}$$

where $C(t)$ is consumption at time t, ρ is the rate of time preference ($\rho > 0$), and $U(\cdot)$ is the felicity function featuring $U'(\cdot) > 0$ and $U''(\cdot) < 0$. The household budget identity is given by:

$$\dot{A}(t) = F\left(K\left(t\right)\right) + T\left(t\right) - C\left(t\right) - \pi\left(t\right) m\left(t\right), \tag{Q11.13}$$

where $F(\cdot)$ is the production function (featuring $F'(\cdot) > 0$ and $F''(\cdot) < 0$), $A(t)$ is the stock of assets, $T(t)$ is transfers received from the government, $\pi(t)$ is the inflation rate ($\pi(t) > 0$), and $m(t)$ is the real stock of money balances. As usual, we have that $\dot{A}(t) \equiv dA(t)/dt$. Total wealth consists of real money balances plus the capital stock, i.e. $A(t) \equiv K(t) + m(t)$. Finally, the cash-in-advance (CIA) constraint is given by:

$$m(t) \geq C(t). \tag{Q11.14}$$

The household is blessed with perfect foresight and takes the path of government transfers as given.

(a) Briefly comment on the household budget identity (Q11.13) and the CIA constraint (Q11.14).

(b) Explain why the CIA constraint will hold with equality. Show that (Q11.13) can be rewritten as follows:

$$\dot{A}(t) = F(A(t) - C(t)) + T(t) - [1 + \pi(t)]C(t). \tag{Q11.15}$$

(c) Solve the household's optimization problem by means of optimal control methods.

(d) Use stars to designate steady-state variables. Let μ stand for the policy determined growth rate in the nominal money supply. Prove that $\pi^* = \mu$, $T^* = \pi^* m^*$, and $dK^*/d\mu = dC^*/d\mu = 0$.

★ Question 5: Cash-in-advance with labour supply

[Based on Mansoorian and Mohsin (2004)] In this question we use the cash-in-advance (CIA) constraint and endogenize the labour supply decision. Less than fully confident readers may want to attempt this question after studying the Ramsey model of Chapter 13. The infinitely-lived representative household has a lifetime utility function of the form:

$$\Lambda \equiv \int_0^\infty U(C(t), 1 - L(t)) e^{-\rho t} dt, \tag{Q11.16}$$

where $C(t)$ is consumption at time t, $L(t)$ is labour supply ($1 - L(t)$ is leisure), ρ is the rate of time preference ($\rho > 0$), and $U(\cdot)$ is the felicity function. It has the usual features:

$$U_C \equiv \frac{\partial U}{\partial C} > 0, \quad U_{1-L} \equiv \frac{\partial U}{\partial (1 - L)} > 0,$$

$$U_{CC} \equiv \frac{\partial^2 U}{\partial C^2} < 0, \quad U_{1-L, 1-L} \equiv \frac{\partial^2 U}{\partial (1 - L)^2} < 0,$$

$$U_{CC} U_{1-L, 1-L} - (U_{C, 1-L})^2 > 0,$$

where $U_{C, 1-L} \equiv \frac{\partial^2 U}{\partial C \partial (1 - L)}$. The household budget identity is given by:

$$\dot{A}(t) = r(t)A(t) + w(t)L(t) + T(t) - C(t) - [r(t) + \pi(t)]m(t), \tag{Q11.17}$$

where $A(t)$ is the stock of tangible assets, $r(t)$ is the real interest rate, $w(t)$ is the real wage rate, $T(t)$ is transfers received from the government, $\pi(t)$ is the inflation rate ($\pi(t) > 0$), and $m(t)$ is the real stock of money balances. Obviously, $r(t) + \pi(t)$ is the nominal interest rate. As usual, we have that $\dot{A}(t) \equiv dA(t)/dt$. Total wealth consists of real money balances plus the value of the capital stock:

$$A(t) \equiv V(t) + m(t). \tag{Q11.18}$$

The cash-in-advance (CIA) constraint is given by:

$$m(t) \geq C(t). \tag{Q11.19}$$

The household is blessed with perfect foresight and takes the path of government transfers as given.

The perfectly competitive firm maximizes the value of the firm,

$$V(0) \equiv \int_0^\infty [F(K(t), L(t)) - w(t)L(t) - I(t)] e^{-R(t)} dt, \tag{Q11.20}$$

where $R(t) \equiv \int_0^t r(s)\,ds$ is the cumulative interest factor, and $I(t)$ is gross investment, and $F(\cdot)$ features constant returns to scale. The firm faces the capital accumulation identity, $\dot{K}(t) = I(t) - \delta K(t)$, and takes as given the initial capital stock, $K(0)$. The choice variables are $I(t)$ and $L(t)$ (and thus $K(t)$).

(a) Solve the household's optimization problem by means of optimal control methods.

(b) Solve the firm's optimization problem by means of optimal control methods. Prove that $V(0) = K(0)$ in the optimum.

(c) Use stars to designate steady-state variables. Let μ stand for the policy determined growth rate in the nominal money supply. Compute $dK^*/d\mu$, $dL^*/d\mu$, $dC^*/d\mu$, and $d\lambda^*/d\mu$. Show that only the sign of $d\lambda^*/d\mu$ depends on the sign of $U_{C,1-L}$.

(d) Illustrate the effects on C^* and $1 - L^*$ of an increase in μ in a diagram. Assume that $U(C, 1-L)$ is homothetic.

Answers

Question 1: Short questions

(a) False. The opportunity costs of holding money (the nominal interest rate) should be equal to zero.

(b) The objective function (11.65) can be written as:

$$E(U(\check{Z})) = U(\bar{Z}) - \eta\sigma_Z^2. \tag{A11.1}$$

The expression for $\bar{Z}$ (given in (11.67) can be rewritten in terms of σ_Z:

$$
\begin{aligned}
\bar{Z} &= S \cdot \left[(1 + r^M)\omega + (1 + \bar{r})(1 - \omega) \right] \\
&= S \cdot \left[1 + r^M + (1 - \omega)\left(\bar{r} - r^M\right) \right] \\
&= S \cdot \left[1 + r^M + \frac{\sigma_Z}{S\sigma_R}\left(\bar{r} - r^M\right) \right] \\
&= \left(1 + r^M\right)S + \frac{\sigma_Z}{\sigma_R}\left(\bar{r} - r^M\right),
\end{aligned}
\tag{A11.2}
$$

where we have used $\sigma_Z^2 \equiv S^2(1 - \omega)^2\sigma_R^2$ to eliminate $1 - \omega$. The exogenous parameters are r^M, $\bar{r}$, σ_R, and S. The investor chooses $\bar{Z}$ and σ_Z in order to maximize (A11.1) subject to (A11.2). The Lagrangian is:

$$\mathcal{L} \equiv U(\bar{Z}) - \eta\sigma_Z^2 + \lambda \cdot \left[\left(1 + r^M\right)S + \frac{\sigma_Z}{\sigma_R}\left(\bar{r} - r^M\right) - \bar{Z} \right],$$

from which we obtain the first-order conditions:

$$
\begin{aligned}
\frac{\partial\mathcal{L}}{\partial\bar{Z}} &= U'(\bar{Z}) - \lambda = 0, \\
\frac{\partial\mathcal{L}}{\partial\sigma_Z} &= -2\eta\sigma_Z - \lambda\frac{\bar{r} - r^M}{\sigma_R} = 0.
\end{aligned}
$$

Combining we thus get:

$$
\begin{aligned}
\frac{1}{\lambda} &= \frac{1}{U'(\bar{Z})} = \frac{1}{2\eta\sigma_Z}\frac{\bar{r} - r^M}{\sigma_R} \\
\frac{2\eta\sigma_Z}{U'(\bar{Z})} &= \frac{\bar{r} - r^M}{\sigma_R},
\end{aligned}
$$

which is (11.69) in the text.

To derive equation (11.82) it is more convenient to work with equation (11.73) in the book which directly addresses the optimal choice of ω. Equation (11.76) writes the first-order condition for ω^* as:

$$
\begin{aligned}
\Phi\left(\omega^*, \sigma_R^2\right) &\equiv -U'\left(S\left[(1 + r^M)\omega^* + (1 + \bar{r})(1 - \omega^*)\right]\right)S\left(\bar{r} - r^M\right) \\
&\quad + 2\eta S^2(1 - \omega^*)\sigma_R^2 = 0.
\end{aligned}
\tag{A11.3}
$$

To get the uncompensated effect of a change in σ_R we use:

$$\frac{\partial \Phi\left(\omega^*, \sigma_R^2\right)}{\partial \omega^*} d\omega^* + \frac{\partial \Phi\left(\omega^*, \sigma_R^2\right)}{\partial \sigma_R} d\sigma_R = 0,$$

or:

$$\frac{d\omega^*}{d\sigma_R} = -\frac{\frac{\partial \Phi\left(\omega^*, \sigma_R^2\right)}{\partial \sigma_R}}{\frac{\partial \Phi\left(\omega^*, \sigma_R^2\right)}{\partial \omega^*}}.$$

We find from (A11.3) that:

$$\frac{\partial \Phi\left(\omega^*, \sigma_R^2\right)}{\partial \omega^*} = U''(\bar{Z})S^2\left(\bar{r} - r^M\right)^2 - 2\eta S^2 \sigma_R^2$$

$$= -2\eta S^2\left[\left(\bar{r} - r^M\right)^2 + \sigma_R^2\right],$$

$$\frac{\partial \Phi\left(\omega^*, \sigma_R^2\right)}{\partial \sigma_R} = 4\eta S^2(1 - \omega^*)\sigma_R.$$

It follows that:

$$\left(\frac{d\omega^*}{d\sigma_R}\right)_{UC} = \frac{2(1 - \omega^*)\sigma_R}{\left(\bar{r} - r^M\right)^2 + \sigma_R^2} > 0. \tag{A11.4}$$

(In the text we use partial derivative notation for comparative static effects.)

As is explained in footnote 16 on page 342 of the text, the effect on ω^* of a (hypothetical) lump-sum change in $\bar{Z}$ is given by:

$$\frac{\partial \omega^*}{\partial \bar{Z}} = -\frac{\partial \Phi/\partial \bar{Z}}{\partial \Phi/\partial \omega^*} = \frac{\bar{r} - r^M}{S\left[\left(\bar{r} - r^M\right)^2 + \sigma_R^2\right]} \tag{A11.5}$$

Using (A11.4) and (A11.5) we can verify (11.82) in the text.

(c) The full liquidity result states that the money supply should be expanded to the point where the marginal benefit of money is (close to) zero and agents are flooded with liquidity (money balances). Money is cheap to produce and people should not economize on something that is not scarce. The nominal interest rate must be set to zero since it represents the opportunity cost of holding money. Main reasons why it may not be valid: (i) there may be distorting taxes, (ii) preferences may be non-separable, (iii) optimal taxation argument for inflation taxation. See sections 11.4.3.2 and 11.4.3.3 in the text.

(d) Main functions: (i) medium of exchange, (ii) medium of account, and (iii) store of value. See section 11.1. The first one is the most fundamental feature of money.

(e) The relevant first-order condition is given by equation (11.33):

$$\frac{U'(C_2)}{U'(C_1)} = (1 + \rho)(1 + \pi_1),$$

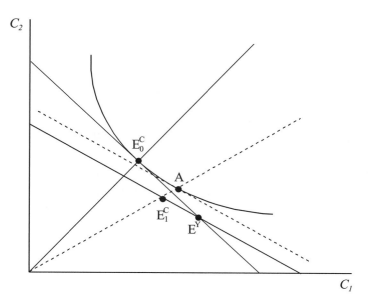

Figure A11.1: Inflation increase in the Bewley model

or:

$$\frac{C_2}{C_1} = \frac{1}{(1+\rho)(1+\pi_1)}.$$

This is a ray from the origin in Figure A11.1. An increase in π_1 flattens this line. Since $m_1 > 0$ (before and after the shock) we can consolidate the lifetime budget constraint:

$$C_1 + (1+\pi_1)\,C_2 = Y_1 + \frac{m_0}{1+\pi_0} + (1+\pi_1)\,Y_2.$$

An increase in π_1 rotates the budget constraint around the income endowment point in a counter-clockwise fashion. The new equilibrium is at E_1^C, C_2 falls, C_1 rises, and m_1 falls. There is less need for money as a store of value because the consumption point moves closer to the income endowment point. The shock produces income and substitution effects. The SE is the move from E_0^C to A and the IE is the move from A to E_1^C.

Question 2: Optimal money growth

(a) From (Q11.2) we find by dividing by P_t:

$$(1+R_{t-1})\frac{B_{t-1}}{P_{t-1}}\frac{P_{t-1}}{P_t} + \frac{W_t}{P_t}(1-\tau_t)L_t + \frac{M_{t-1}}{P_{t-1}}\frac{P_{t-1}}{P_t} + T_t = C_t + \frac{M_t}{P_t} + \frac{B_t}{P_t}$$

$$(1+R_{t-1})\frac{P_{t-1}}{P_t}b_{t-1} + w_t(1-\tau_t)L_t + m_{t-1}\frac{P_{t-1}}{P_t} + T_t = C_t + m_t + b_t$$

$$(1+r_{t-1})b_{t-1} + w_t(1-\tau_t)L_t + \frac{m_{t-1}}{1+\pi_{t-1}} + T_t = \cdots. \quad (A11.6)$$

From (Q11.3) we find in a similar fashion that:

$$(1 + r_{t-1})b_{t-1} + G_t + T_t = \tau_t w_t L_t + m_t - \frac{m_{t-1}}{1 + \pi_{t-1}} + b_t. \tag{A11.7}$$

(b) The first-order condition for profit maximization is $d\Pi_t / dL_t = P_t - W_t = 0$ or $w_t = 1$. By combining (A11.6) and (A11.7) we find that $w_t L_t = C_t + G_t$. But $w_t = 1$ and $L_t = Y_t$ so we find that $Y_t = C_t + G_t$. Provided the household and government budget identities are satisfied, so is the economy-wide resource constraint.

(c) The household's budget identity (A11.6) is a difference equation in bond holdings, b_t, which can be solved forward in time by repeated substitutions. After some tedious but straightforward manipulations we find the following general expression:

$$
\begin{aligned}
a_0 &= \sum_{t=1}^{1+k} q_t^0 \cdot \left[C_t + \frac{R_t}{1 + R_t} m_t - w_t (1 - \tau_t) L_t - T_t \right] \\
&\quad + q_{k+1}^0 b_{k+1} + q_{k+1}^0 \cdot \frac{m_{k+1}}{1 + R_{k+1}}.
\end{aligned}
\tag{A11.8}
$$

By letting $k \to \infty$, and noting (Q11.5) we find that (A11.8) simplifies to (Q11.6).

(d) The household chooses sequences for its consumption, labour supply, and real money balances (i.e. $\{C_t\}_{t=1}^\infty$, $\{L_t\}_{t=1}^\infty$, and $\{m_t\}_{t=1}^\infty$) in order to maximize lifetime utility (Q11.1) subject to the lifetime budget constraint (Q11.6). The Lagrangian expression associated with this optimization programme is:

$$
\begin{aligned}
\mathcal{L} &\equiv \sum_{t=1}^\infty \left(\frac{1}{1+\rho} \right)^{t-1} U(C_t, 1 - L_t, m_t) \\
&\quad + \lambda \cdot \left[a_0 - \sum_{t=1}^\infty q_t^0 \left[C_t + \frac{R_t}{1 + R_t} m_t - w_t (1 - \tau_t) L_t - T_t \right] \right],
\end{aligned}
$$

where λ is the Lagrangian multiplier. The first-order conditions for an interior optimum are the constraint (Q11.6) and:

$$\frac{\partial \mathcal{L}}{\partial C_t} = 0: \quad \left(\frac{1}{1+\rho} \right)^{t-1} U_C(x_t) = \lambda q_t^0, \tag{A11.9}$$

$$\frac{\partial \mathcal{L}}{\partial L_t} = 0: \quad \left(\frac{1}{1+\rho} \right)^{t-1} U_{1-L}(x_t) = \lambda q_t^0 w_t (1 - \tau_t), \tag{A11.10}$$

$$\frac{\partial \mathcal{L}}{\partial m_t} = 0: \quad \left(\frac{1}{1+\rho} \right)^{t-1} U_m(x_t) = \lambda q_t^0 \cdot \frac{R_t}{1 + R_t}. \tag{A11.11}$$

By eliminating the Lagrange multiplier from these expressions we obtain the usual conditions equating marginal rates of substitution to relative prices:

$$\frac{U_{1-L}(x_t)}{U_C(x_t)} = w_t (1 - \tau_t), \tag{A11.12}$$

$$\frac{U_m(x_t)}{U_C(x_t)} = \frac{R_t}{1 + R_t}, \tag{A11.13}$$

where $U_C(x_t) \equiv \frac{\partial U(x_t)}{\partial C_t}$, $U_{1-L}(x_t) \equiv \frac{\partial U(x_t)}{\partial [1-L_t]}$, $U_m(x_t) \equiv \frac{\partial U(x_t)}{\partial m_t}$, and $x_t \equiv (C_t, 1 - L_t, m_t)$. In each period, the marginal rate of substitution between leisure and consumption should be equated to the after-tax wage rate, whilst the marginal rate of substitution between real money balances and consumption should be equated to the opportunity cost of holding real money balances.

(e) The adjusted budget constraint is obtained by substituting the household's first-order conditions (A11.9)-(A11.11) into the regular, unadjusted, household budget constraint (Q11.6). After some manipulation we obtain the following expression:

$$
\begin{aligned}
a_0 &= \sum_{t=1}^{\infty} q_t^0 \left[C_t - T_t \right] + \sum_{t=1}^{\infty} q_t^0 \frac{R_t}{1 + R_t} m_t - \sum_{t=1}^{\infty} q_t^0 W_t (1 - \tau_t) L_t \\
&= \frac{1}{\lambda} \sum_{t=1}^{\infty} \left(\frac{1}{1 + \rho} \right)^{t-1} \left[U_C(x_t) \left[C_t - T_t \right] \right. \\
&\quad \left. + U_m(x_t) m_t - U_{1-L}(x_t) L_t \right].
\end{aligned}
\tag{A11.14}
$$

By applying (A11.9) for $t = 1$ and noting that $q_1^0 = 1$ we derive that λ equals the marginal utility of consumption in the first period, i.e. $\lambda = U_C(x_1)$. By substituting this result in (A11.14) we obtain (Q11.7). The advantage of working with (Q11.7) instead of with (Q11.6) is that the former expression no longer contains the distorting tax instruments of the government (namely τ_t and μ_t). This facilitates the characterization of the optimal taxation problem because the social planning problem can be conducted directly in quantities (rather than in terms of tax rates).

(f) The social planner chooses sequences for consumption, employment, and real money balances (i.e. $\{C_t\}_{t=1}^{\infty}$, $\{L_t\}_{t=1}^{\infty}$, and $\{m_t\}_{t=1}^{\infty}$) in order to maximize lifetime utility of the representative household (Q11.1) subject to the adjusted household budget constraint (Q11.7) and the economy-wide resource constraint $L_t = C_t + G_t$. We assume that the sequence of government consumption, $\{G_t\}_{t=1}^{\infty}$, is exogenously given. The Lagrangian associated with this optimization programme is:

$$
\begin{aligned}
\mathcal{L}_G &\equiv \sum_{t=1}^{\infty} \left(\frac{1}{1 + \rho} \right)^{t-1} \left[U(C_t, 1 - L_t, m_t) + \lambda_t^G \left[L_t - C_t - G_t \right] \right. \\
&\quad \left. + \theta^G \left(U_C(x_t) \left[C_t - T_t \right] + U_m(x_t) m_t - U_{1-L}(x_t) L_t \right) \right] \\
&\quad - \theta^G a_0 U_C(x_1),
\end{aligned}
\tag{A11.15}
$$

where θ^G is the Lagrange multiplier for the adjusted household budget constraint and $\{\lambda_t^G\}_{t=1}^{\infty}$ is the sequence of Lagrange multipliers for the resource constraint.

Assume that the policy maker can freely adjust the level of transfers (or taxes, if negative), T_t, in each period. The first-order conditions for the sequence of transfers, $\{T_t\}_{t=1}^{\infty}$, take the following form:

$$
\frac{\partial \mathcal{L}_G}{\partial T_t} = -\theta^G \left(\frac{1}{1 + \rho} \right)^{t-1} U_C(x_t) = 0.
\tag{A11.16}
$$

But, since the discounting factor on the right-hand side of (A11.16) is strictly positive, and we have ruled out satiation of consumption ($U_C(x_t) > 0$), it follows from (A11.16) that $\theta^G = 0$. Intuitively, the availability of the lump-sum instruments means that the adjusted household budget constraint does not represent a constraint on the social optimization programme. The remaining first-order conditions of the social plan are obtained by setting $\partial \mathcal{L}_G / \partial C_t = \partial \mathcal{L}_G / \partial L_t = \partial \mathcal{L}_G / \partial m_t = 0$ (for $t = 1, 2, ...$) and noting that $\theta^G = 0$. After some straightforward manipulation we find:

$$\frac{U_{1-L}(x_t)}{U_C(x_t)} = 1, \tag{A11.17}$$

$$U_m(x_t) = 0. \tag{A11.18}$$

Equation (A11.17) shows that the marginal rate of substitution between leisure and consumption should be equated to the marginal rate of transformation between labour and goods (which is unity since the production function is linear). Equation (A11.18) is the Friedman rule requiring the policy maker to satiate the representative household with money balances. Equations (A11.17)-(A11.18) characterize the socially optimal allocation in terms of quantities. In the final step we must find out what tax instruments the planner can use to ensure that these conditions hold in the decentralized economy. By comparing (A11.17)-(A11.18) to the first-order conditions for the household, given in (A11.12)-(A11.13), we find that they coincide if there is no tax on labour income and the nominal interest rate is zero, i.e. $\tau_t = R_t = 0$. With a constant level of government consumption ($G_t = G$ for all t) the optimal allocation is constant, i.e. $C_t = C$, $L_t = L$, $b_t = b$, $m_t = m$, $W_t = W$, and $T_t = T$ for all t. The real interest rate is equal to the rate of pure time preference, $r_t = \rho$, and, since the nominal rate is zero, it follows that the rate of inflation is constant and equal to $\pi_t = -\rho/(1+\rho)$. Since m is constant, the rate of money growth equals the rate of inflation, i.e. $\mu_t = -\rho/(1+\rho)$.

(g) Assume now that lump-sum taxes/transfers are not available, i.e. $T_t = 0$ for all t. In the absence of such an instrument the policy maker is forced to raise the required revenue, needed to finance the government's consumption path, in a distortionary fashion, i.e. by means of a tax on labour income and/or by means of money growth (the inflation tax). In the remainder of this subsection we briefly sketch the complications which arise in this setting. As before, the social planner chooses sequences $\{C_t\}_{t=1}^{\infty}$, $\{L_t\}_{t=1}^{\infty}$, and $\{m_t\}_{t=1}^{\infty}$) which maximize (Q11.1) subject to (Q11.7) and the resource constraint $L_t = C_t + G_t$. We now assume, however, that $T_t = 0$ for all t.

The first-order condition for an interior solution for real money balances is given by $\partial \mathcal{L}_G / \partial m_t = 0$ for all t. By using (A11.15) we derive the following conditions for, respectively, m_1 and m_t ($t = 2, 3, ...$):

$$0 = U_m(x_1) + \theta^G [U_m(x_1) + m_1 U_{mm}(x_1)] + \theta^G (1 + r_0) U_{Cm}(x_1), \tag{A11.19}$$

$$0 = U_m(x_t) + \theta^G [U_m(x_t) + m_t U_{mm}(x_t)], \tag{A11.20}$$

where the term involving $U_{Cm}(x_1)$ appearing in (A11.19) is due to the fact that the marginal utility of consumption in the first period in general depends on real money balances. In contrast to the lump-sum case, the Lagrange multiplier θ^G is now strictly positive. Intuitively, θ^G measures the utility cost of raising government revenue through distortionary taxes (Ljungqvist and Sargent (2000, p. 323)). An immediate consequence which follows from the first-order conditions (A11.19)-(A11.20) is that the full liquidity rule is no longer optimal even if the felicity function is separable in consumption and real money balances (so that $U_{Cm}(x_t) = 0$). Indeed, in the separable case (A11.19) and (A11.20) coincide and can be simplified to:

$$U_m(x_t) = -m_t U_{mm}(x_t) \frac{\theta^G}{1 + \theta^G} > 0. \tag{A11.21}$$

The optimal level of real money balances falls short of its satiation level and the Friedman result no longer obtains in this setting.

Question 3: Monetary superneutrality

(a) Denoting nominal variables by the superscript N we find that the budget identity of the household is:

$$\dot{B}^N(v,\tau) + \dot{M}^N(v,\tau) + \dot{V}^N(v,\tau) = \left[R^N(\tau) + \beta \right] \left[B^N(v,\tau) + V^N(v,\tau) \right]$$
$$+ \beta M^N(v,\tau) + W^N(\tau) - T^N(\tau) - P(\tau)C(v,\tau), \quad \text{(A11.22)}$$

where B^N is nominal bond holdings, M^N is the nominal money holdings, V^N is the nominal value of shares, R^N is the nominal interest rate, W^N is the nominal wage, T^N is nominal lump-sum taxes, and P is the price of the homogeneous good. Equation (A11.22) incorporates two notions. First, it is based on the Keynesian assumption that claims on physical capital and government bonds are perfect substitutes ensuring equalization of their *ex ante* rate of return. Second, though money holdings do not attract an interest rate they do attract a payment from the life-insurance company: upon death, all assets including money holdings revert to the insurance company.

By dividing (A11.22) by P we find:

$$\frac{\dot{B}^N(v,\tau)}{P(\tau)} + \frac{\dot{M}^N(v,\tau)}{P(\tau)} + \frac{\dot{V}^N(v,\tau)}{P(\tau)} = \left[R^N(\tau) + \beta \right] [B(v,\tau) + V(v,\tau)]$$
$$+ \beta M(v,\tau) + W(\tau) - T(\tau) - C(v,\tau), \quad \text{(A11.23)}$$

where $B \equiv B^N/P$, $V \equiv V^N/P$, $M \equiv M^N/P$, $W \equiv W^N/P$, and $T \equiv T^N/P$. By definition we have that $\dot{X}^N/P = \dot{X} + \pi X$, where $\pi \equiv \dot{P}/P$ (for $X \in \{B, V, M\}$). Since there are no adjustment costs on investment, Tobin's q is unity and $V(v,\tau) = K(v,\tau)$. Using these results in (A11.23) we find:

$$\dot{B}(v,\tau) + \dot{M}(v,\tau) + \dot{K}(v,\tau) = \left[R^N(\tau) - \pi(\tau) + \beta \right] [B(v,\tau) + V(v,\tau)]$$
$$+ [\beta - \pi(\tau)] M(v,\tau) + W(\tau) - T(\tau) - C(v,\tau)$$
$$= [r(\tau) + \beta] [B(v,\tau) + M(v,\tau) + K(v,\tau)]$$
$$- R^N(\tau)M(v,\tau) + W(\tau) - T(\tau) - C(v,\tau), \quad \text{(A11.24)}$$

where we have used the definition $r(\tau) \equiv R^N(\tau) - \pi(\tau)$. By noting that $A \equiv B + M + K$ we find that (A11.24) coincides with equation (Q11.10) in the question. The inflation rate appears in equation (Q11.10) because the nominal interest rate, $r + \pi$, represents the opportunity cost of holding money.

Equation (Q11.11) is derived as follows. The monetary authority adopts the following growth rule for the nominal money supply:

$$\dot{M}^N(\tau) = \theta(\tau) M^N(\tau). \tag{A11.25}$$

By noting that $\dot{M}^N/P = \dot{M} + \pi M$ we can rewrite (A11.25) as follows:

$$\frac{\dot{M}^N(\tau)}{P(\tau)} = \theta(\tau) \frac{M^N(\tau)}{P(\tau)} \quad \Leftrightarrow$$

$$\dot{M}(\tau) + \pi(\tau) M(\tau) = \theta(\tau) M(\tau) \quad \Leftrightarrow$$

$$\dot{M}(\tau) = [\theta(\tau) - \pi(\tau)] M(\tau). \tag{A11.26}$$

Equation (A11.26) is identical to equation (Q11.11) in the question for a constant rate of money growth. If the inflation rate is higher (lower) than the nominal money growth rate, then the real money supply falls (increases) over time. The inflation rate appears in equation (Q11.11) because the money growth rule applies to the nominal money supply but we are interested in the growth rate of the real money supply.

(b) *Stage 1.* We define full consumption as the sum of spending on consumption and real money balances:

$$X(v, \tau) \equiv C(v, \tau) + [r(\tau) + \pi(\tau)] M(v, \tau). \tag{A11.27}$$

We postulate that:

$$P_U(\tau) U(v, \tau) = X(v, \tau). \tag{A11.28}$$

By using (A11.27) in (Q11.10) and (A11.28) in (Q11.8) we find that the Hamiltonian for the dynamic optimization problem is:

$$\mathcal{H} \equiv \ln\left(\frac{X(v, \tau)}{P_U(\tau)}\right) + \mu(\tau)\left[(r(\tau) + \beta) A(v, \tau) + W(\tau) - T(\tau) - X(v, \tau)\right], \tag{A11.29}$$

where $X(v, \tau)$ is the control variable, $A(v, \tau)$ is the state variable, and $\mu(\tau)$ is the co-state variable. The first-order conditions are $\partial H/\partial X(v, \tau) = 0$ and $-\partial H/\partial A(v, \tau) = \dot{\mu}(\tau) - [r(\tau) + \beta]\mu(\tau)$ or:

$$\frac{1}{X(v, \tau)} = \mu(\tau), \tag{A11.30}$$

$$\frac{\dot{\mu}(\tau)}{\mu(\tau)} = \rho - r(\tau). \tag{A11.31}$$

By combining (A11.30)–(A11.31) we find the Euler equation for *full* consumption:

$$\frac{\dot{X}(v, \tau)}{X(v, \tau)} = r(\tau) - \rho. \tag{A11.32}$$

The household budget constraint is derived by integrating equation (Q11.10) (with (A11.27) inserted) forward in time and imposing the NPG condition $\lim_{\tau \to \infty} A(v, \tau) e^{-R^A(t, \tau)} = 0$:

$$A(v, t) + H(t) = \int_t^\infty X(v, \tau) e^{-R^A(t, \tau)} d\tau, \tag{A11.33}$$

where human wealth is:

$$H(t) \equiv \int_t^\infty [W(\tau) - T(\tau)] e^{-R^A(t, \tau)} d\tau. \tag{A11.34}$$

From the Euler equation (A11.32) we derive:

$$X(v, \tau) = X(v, t) e^{R^A(t, \tau) - (\rho + \beta)(\tau - t)},$$

so that (A11.33) can be rewritten as:

$$X(v, t) = (\rho + \beta) [A(v, t) + H(t)]. \tag{A11.35}$$

Full consumption in the planning period is proportional to total wealth in that period.

Stage 2. Next we determine $C(v, \tau)$ and $M(v, \tau)$ such that $U(v, \tau)$ is maximized subject to the restriction (A11.27), taking $X(v, \tau)$ as given. The Lagrangian is:

$$\mathcal{L} \equiv \left[\varepsilon C(v, \tau)^{(\sigma-1)/\sigma} + (1 - \varepsilon) M(v, \tau)^{(\sigma-1)/\sigma} \right]^{\sigma/(\sigma-1)}$$
$$+ \lambda(\tau) [X(v, \tau) - C(v, \tau) - [r(\tau) + \pi(\tau)] M(v, \tau)]. \tag{A11.36}$$

The first-order conditions are the constraint and $\partial \mathcal{L} / \partial C(v, \tau) = \partial \mathcal{L} / \partial M(v, \tau) = 0$. We find:

$$[\cdot]^{1/(\sigma-1)} \varepsilon C(v, \tau)^{-1/\sigma} = \lambda(\tau), \tag{A11.37}$$

$$[\cdot]^{1/(\sigma-1)} (1 - \varepsilon) M(v, \tau)^{-1/\sigma} = \lambda(\tau) [r(\tau) + \pi(\tau)], \tag{A11.38}$$

or, after eliminating $\lambda(\tau)$:

$$\frac{(1 - \varepsilon) M(v, \tau)^{-1/\sigma}}{\varepsilon C(v, \tau)^{-1/\sigma}} = [r(\tau) + \pi(\tau)]. \tag{A11.39}$$

According to (A11.39), the marginal rate of substitution between money balances and consumption should be equated to the nominal interest rate. By using (A11.39) in the constraint (A11.27), we find after some manipulations:

$$C(v, \tau) = \omega(r(\tau) + \pi(\tau)) X(v, \tau), \tag{A11.40}$$

$$[r(\tau) + \pi(\tau)] M(v, \tau) = [1 - \omega(r(\tau) + \pi(\tau))] X(v, \tau), \tag{A11.41}$$

where $\omega(\cdot)$ is the share of goods consumption in full consumption. It is defined as follows:

$$\omega(\cdot) \equiv \frac{\varepsilon^\sigma}{\varepsilon^\sigma + (1 - \varepsilon)^\sigma [r(\tau) + \pi(\tau)]^{1-\sigma}}. \tag{A11.42}$$

For future reference we note that (i) $\omega(\cdot) = \varepsilon$ for the Cobb-Douglas case ($\sigma = 1$), and (ii) $\omega(\cdot)$ has the following elasticity:

$$\eta_\omega \equiv \frac{[r(\tau) + \pi(\tau)]\, \omega'(\cdot)}{\omega(\cdot)} \equiv (\sigma - 1)\,[1 - \omega(\cdot)]. \tag{A11.43}$$

Using (A11.41) and noting (A11.43) we find that the interest elasticity of money demand is negative (and equal to $\eta_\omega - \sigma = -[1 + (\sigma - 1)\omega(\cdot)]$).

(c) Aggregation of (Q11.10), (A11.35), and (A11.40)–(A11.41) is straightforward and results (for period t) in:

$$\dot{A}(t) = r(t)A(t) + W(t) - T(t) - X(t), \tag{A11.44}$$

$$X(t) = (\rho + \beta)\,[A(t) + H(t)], \tag{A11.45}$$

$$C(t) = \omega(r(t) + \pi(t))X(t), \tag{A11.46}$$

$$[r(t) + \pi(t)]\,M(t) = [1 - \omega(r(t) + \pi(t))]\,X(t). \tag{A11.47}$$

The Euler equation for full consumption is derived in the following manner:

$$\dot{X}(t) = \beta X(t,t) - \beta X(t) + \beta \int_{-\infty}^{t} \dot{X}(v,t)e^{\beta(v-t)}dv$$

$$= \beta(\rho + \beta)H(t) - \beta(\rho + \beta)\,[A(t) + H(t)] + [r(t) - \rho]\,X(t) \quad \Rightarrow$$

$$\frac{\dot{X}(t)}{X(t)} = [r(t) - \rho] - \beta(\rho + \beta)\frac{A(t)}{C(t)}, \tag{A11.48}$$

where we have used (A11.32) in going from the first to the second line. Finally, the differential equation for (individual and aggregate) human wealth is obtained by differentiating (A11.34) with respect to time:

$$\dot{H}(t) = [r(t) + \beta]\,H(t) - [W(\tau) - T(t)]. \tag{A11.49}$$

(d) We derive the government budget identity as follows. In nominal terms we have:

$$\dot{M}^N + \dot{B}^N + T^N = R^N B^N + PG, \tag{A11.50}$$

$$\dot{M}^N = \theta M^N. \tag{A11.51}$$

By substituting (A11.51) into (A11.50) and dividing by P we find:

$$\theta \frac{M^N}{P} + \frac{\dot{B}^N}{P} + \frac{T^N}{P} = R^N \frac{B^N}{P} + G \quad \Leftrightarrow \quad \dot{B} + \theta M + T = rB + G, \tag{A11.52}$$

where $r \equiv R^N - \pi$, $\pi \equiv \dot{P}/P$, and we have (again) used $\dot{B}^N/P = \dot{B} + \pi B$. According to (A11.52), outlays of the government, consisting of interest payments plus government consumption, is covered by new bond issues, seigniorage, and lump-sum taxes.

By integrating equation (A11.52) forward in time and imposing the appropriate NPG condition, $\lim_{\tau \to \infty} B(\tau)e^{-R(t,\tau)} = 0$, we find the government budget restriction:

$$B(t) = \int_{t}^{\infty} [\theta(\tau)M(\tau) + T(\tau) - G(\tau)]\, e^{-R(t,\tau)}d\tau. \tag{A11.53}$$

Outstanding debt must be covered (in present value terms) by future primary surpluses.

(e) The marginal productivity conditions for the competitive representative firm are, for the Cobb-Douglas technology, given by:

$$r(t) + \delta = \alpha K(t)^{\alpha-1}, \qquad W(t) = (1-\alpha)K^{\alpha}. \tag{A11.54}$$

The system of differential equations characterizing the economy is:

$$\dot{K}(t) = K(t)^{\alpha} - \omega\left(r(t) + \pi(t)\right)X(t) - G(t) - \delta K(t), \tag{A11.55}$$

$$\frac{\dot{X}(t)}{X(t)} = r(t) - \rho - \beta(\rho+\beta)\frac{B(t) + K(t) + M(t)}{X(t)}, \tag{A11.56}$$

$$\dot{M}(t) = [r(t) + \theta(t)]M(t) - [1 - \omega(r(t) + \pi(t))]X(t), \tag{A11.57}$$

$$\dot{B}(t) = r(t)B(t) + G(t) - \theta(\tau)M(\tau) - T(\tau), \tag{A11.58}$$

where $r(t)$ depends on $K(t)$ (see (A11.54)) and $B(t)$ must satisfy the restriction (A11.53). Equation (A11.56) is obtained from (Q11.11) by noting that $\theta - \pi = (r+\theta) - (r+\pi)$ and by using (A11.47).

By superneutrality of money we mean that the money growth rate does not affect the real economy, either during transition or in the long run. It is straightforward to show that superneutrality holds provided the birth/death rate is zero ($\beta = 0$) *and* sub-felicity is weakly separable in consumption and money balances ($\sigma = 1$). If both requirements are met, then the dynamical system dichotomizes into real and monetary subsystems. Indeed, if $\beta = 0$ the generational turnover term disappears from (A11.56) and if $\sigma = 1$ goods consumption does not depend on the nominal interest rate ($\omega(\cdot) = \varepsilon$ in (A11.55)) and the real subsystem simplifies to:

$$\dot{K}(t) = K(t)^{\alpha} - \varepsilon X(t) - G(t) - \delta K(t), \tag{A11.59}$$

$$\frac{\dot{X}(t)}{X(t)} = \alpha K(t)^{\alpha-1} - (\rho+\delta) \tag{A11.60}$$

The money growth rate does not appear anywhere in (A11.59)–(A11.60) so $K(t)$, $X(t)$, $r(t)$, and $C(t)$ are unaffected by it.

The monetary part of the model simplifies to:

$$\dot{M}(t) = [r(t) + \theta(t)]M(t) - (1-\varepsilon)X(t), \tag{A11.61}$$

where $r(t)$ and $X(t)$ are determined in the real subsystem (A11.59)–(A11.60). Equation (A11.61) is an unstable differential equation in real money balances (as the nominal interest rate is positive) so $M(t)$ must be a jumping variable to ensure economically sensible conclusions. The mechanism ensuring jumps in real money balances is, of course, the adjustment in the price level. The nominal money supply is predetermined (in the assumed absence of open market operations) so an increase in P leads to a discrete jump in M.

To study the dynamic effects of an unanticipated and permanent increase in the money growth rate, we assume for simplicity that the economy is initially in the steady state, i.e. $r(t) = \rho$ and $X(t) = X$ (a constant) in (A11.61). In Figure A11.2, we present the phase diagram for real money balances. The initial steady-state equilibrium is at E_0 where $\pi_0 = \theta_0$. An increase in the money growth rate rotates the $\dot{M}(t)$ line counter-clockwise (around point A on the

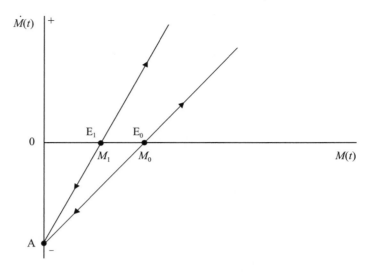

Figure A11.2: Monetary superneutrality

vertical axis) and shifts the steady-state equilibrium to E_1. Since the shock is permanent and unanticipated, the economy jumps at impact from E_0 to E_1 and real money balances fall from M_0 to M_1. Households economize on real money balances because the additional money growth causes additional inflation which drives up the nominal interest rate.

In Figure A11.3 we show the impulse-response functions. Since real money balances feature no further transitional dynamics following the impact jump, the inflation rate remains equal to the money growth rate. At impact the (logarithm of the) price level jumps after which it follows a steeper path over time. The nominal money supply does not feature a jump but starts to grow at a higher rate after the shock.

(f) The economy can in this case be characterized by the following differential equations:

$$\dot{K}(t) = K(t)^\alpha - C(t) - G(t) - \delta K(t), \tag{A11.62}$$

$$\frac{\dot{C}(t)}{C(t)} = r(t) - \rho - \beta\varepsilon(\rho + \beta)\frac{K(t) + M(t)}{C(t)}, \tag{A11.63}$$

$$\dot{M}(t) = [r(t) + \theta(t)]\,M(t) - \frac{1-\varepsilon}{\varepsilon}C(t), \tag{A11.64}$$

where we have used the fact that $C(t) = \varepsilon X(t)$ in various places. Of the state variables, two are non-predetermined 'jumping' variables (X and M) whilst the third is predetermined (K). To study its stability properties, we first linearize the model around the initial steady state (for which $\dot{K} = \dot{C} = \dot{M} = 0$).

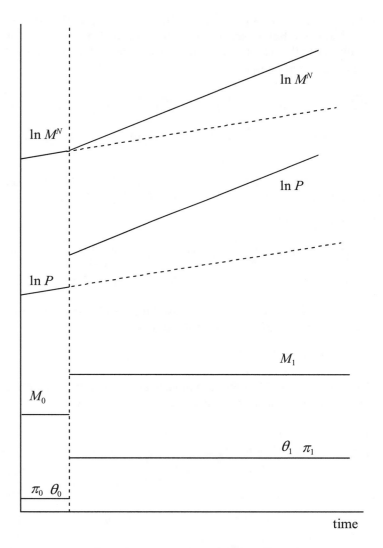

Figure A11.3: Impulse-response functions

Linearizing (A11.62) yields:

$$\frac{d\dot{K}(t)}{K} = \alpha K^{\alpha-1}\frac{dK(t)}{K} - \frac{C}{K}\frac{dC(t)}{C} - \frac{dG(t)}{K} - \delta\frac{dK(t)}{K} \quad \Leftrightarrow$$

$$\dot{\tilde{K}}(t) = r\tilde{K}(t) - \omega_C\tilde{C}(t) - \tilde{G}(t), \tag{A11.65}$$

where $\dot{\tilde{K}}(t) \equiv dK(t)/K$, $\tilde{K}(t) \equiv dK(t)/K$, $\tilde{C}(t) \equiv dC(t)/C$, $\tilde{G}(t) \equiv dG(t)/K$, $\omega_C \equiv C/K$ and we have used the fact that in the steady state $r + \delta = \alpha K^{\alpha-1}$. Note finally that all variables without a time index refer to values.

Linearizing (A11.63) yields:

$$\frac{d\dot{C}(t)}{C} = (r - \rho)\frac{dC(t)}{C} + dr(t) - \frac{\beta\varepsilon(\rho+\beta)}{C}[dK(t) + dM(t)] \quad \Leftrightarrow$$

$$\dot{\tilde{C}}(t) = (r - \rho)\tilde{C}(t) + dr(t) - (r - \rho)[\omega_K\tilde{K}(t) + (1 - \omega_K)\tilde{M}(t)], \tag{A11.66}$$

where $\dot{\tilde{C}}(t) \equiv d\dot{C}(t)/C$, $\tilde{M}(t) \equiv dM(t)/M$, $\omega_K \equiv K/(K + M)$, and we have used the fact that $\beta\varepsilon(\rho + \beta)/C = (r - \rho)/(K + M)$ in the steady state.

Linearizing (A11.64) yields:

$$\frac{d\dot{M}(t)}{M} = (r + \theta)\frac{dM(t)}{M} + dr(t) + d\theta(t) - \frac{(1 - \varepsilon)C}{\varepsilon M}\frac{dC(t)}{C} \quad \Leftrightarrow$$

$$\dot{\tilde{M}}(t) = (r + \theta)\tilde{M}(t) + dr(t) + d\theta(t) - (r + \theta)\tilde{C}(t), \tag{A11.67}$$

where $\dot{\tilde{M}}(t) \equiv d\dot{M}(t)/M$ and we have used the steady state version of (A11.64). Finally, by using (A11.54) we can write $dr(t)$ as:

$$dr(t) = -(1 - \alpha)(r + \delta)\tilde{K}(t). \tag{A11.68}$$

By collecting (A11.65)–(A11.68), the linearized system of differential equations can now be written in a single matrix equation as follows:

$$\begin{bmatrix} \dot{\tilde{K}}(t) \\ \dot{\tilde{C}}(t) \\ \dot{\tilde{M}}(t) \end{bmatrix} = \Delta \begin{bmatrix} \tilde{K}(t) \\ \tilde{C}(t) \\ \tilde{M}(t) \end{bmatrix} - \Gamma, \tag{A11.69}$$

where Δ and Γ are defined as:

$$\Delta \equiv \begin{bmatrix} r & -\omega_C & 0 \\ -[(r - \rho)\omega_K + (1 - \alpha)(r + \delta)] & r - \rho & -(r - \rho)(1 - \omega_K) \\ -(1 - \alpha)(r + \delta) & -(r + \theta) & r + \theta \end{bmatrix}, \tag{A11.70}$$

$$\Gamma \equiv \begin{bmatrix} \tilde{G}(t) \\ 0 \\ -d\theta(t) \end{bmatrix}. \tag{A11.71}$$

Saddle-point stability holds if (and only if) Δ possesses one stable and two unstable characteristic roots. We denote these roots by $-\lambda_1 < 0$, $\lambda_2 > 0$, and $\lambda_3 > 0$ and recall that $|\Delta| = -\lambda_1\lambda_2\lambda_3$ so that saddle-path stability requires

$|\Delta| < 0$. Since $\text{tr}\Delta = \lambda_2 + \lambda_3 - \lambda_1 = 3r + \theta - \rho > 0$ (since $r > \rho$ and $r + \theta > 0$) we find that there is at least one positive root. It is rather tedious to check under which conditions $|\Delta| < 0$ holds so, for the purpose of this question, we simply assume saddle-point stability.

We are now in the position to compute the long-run effects of an increase in the rate of money growth. By setting $\dot{K}(t) = \dot{C}(t) = \dot{M}(t) = 0$ in (A11.69) and using Cramer's Rule we find the long-run effect on the capital stock:

$$\frac{\tilde{K}(\infty)}{d\theta} = \frac{1}{|\Delta|} \begin{vmatrix} 0 & -\omega_C & 0 \\ 0 & r - \rho & -(r-\rho)(1-\omega_K) \\ -1 & -(r+\theta) & r+\theta \end{vmatrix}$$

$$= \frac{(r-\rho)\,\omega_C(1-\omega_K)}{-|\Delta|} > 0, \tag{A11.72}$$

where the sign follows from the fact that $r > \rho$ and $-|\Delta| > 0$. Similarly, the long-run effect on consumption is:

$$\frac{\tilde{C}(\infty)}{d\theta} = \frac{1}{|\Delta|} \begin{vmatrix} r & 0 & 0 \\ -[(r-\rho)\,\omega_K + (1-\alpha)(r+\delta)] & 0 & -(r-\rho)(1-\omega_K) \\ -(1-\alpha)(r+\delta) & -1 & r+\theta \end{vmatrix}$$

$$= \frac{(r-\rho)\,r(1-\omega_K)}{-|\Delta|} > 0, \tag{A11.73}$$

whilst the long-run effect on real money balances is:

$$\frac{\tilde{M}(\infty)}{d\theta} = \frac{1}{|\Delta|} \begin{vmatrix} r & -\omega_C & 0 \\ -[(r-\rho)\,\omega_K + (1-\alpha)(r+\delta)] & r-\rho & 0 \\ -(1-\alpha)(r+\delta) & -(r+\theta) & -1 \end{vmatrix}$$

$$= \frac{r(r-\rho) - \omega_C\,[(r-\rho)\,\omega_K + (1-\alpha)(r+\delta)]}{-|\Delta|} \lessgtr 0. \tag{A11.74}$$

As Marini and van der Ploeg (1988, p. 778) point out, the effect on the capital stock resembles the conventional Mundell-Tobin effect. The increase in the money growth rate increases long-run inflation one-for-one but leads to a fall in the real interest rate. In the representative-agent model this latter effect is impossible because the rate of time preference pins down the long-run real interest rate in that model (as $\beta = 0$ and $r = \rho$). The effect on money balances is ambiguous in the OLG model because there are two effects operating in opposite directions. On the one hand, the nominal interest rate rises, which prompts a decrease in the demand for real money balances. On the other hand, consumption rises, which causes an increase in the demand for real money balances. In the representative-agent model only the first effect survives and money demand falls in the long run.

(g) In the present scenario the government budget constraint (A11.58) simplifies to $T(t) = G(t) - \theta M(t)$ which can be ignored since $T(t)$ does not appear anywhere in (A11.62)–(A11.64). Under the assumption of saddle-point stability ($|\Delta| < 0$) the long-run effects of an increase in G can be computed by using (A11.69)–(A11.71) (and setting $d\theta(t) = 0$). The long-run effect on the capital stock is:

$$\frac{\tilde{K}(\infty)}{\tilde{G}} = \frac{1}{|\Delta|} \begin{vmatrix} 1 & -\omega_C & 0 \\ 0 & r - \rho & -(r-\rho)(1-\omega_K) \\ 0 & -(r+\theta) & r+\theta \end{vmatrix}$$

$$= \frac{(r-\rho)\,\omega_K\,(r+\theta)}{|\Delta|} < 0. \qquad (A11.75)$$

Similarly, the long-run effect on consumption is:

$$\frac{\tilde{C}(\infty)}{\tilde{G}} = \frac{1}{|\Delta|} \begin{vmatrix} r & 1 & 0 \\ -[(r-\rho)\,\omega_K + (1-\alpha)(r+\delta)] & 0 & -(r-\rho)(1-\omega_K) \\ -(1-\alpha)(r+\delta) & 0 & r+\theta \end{vmatrix} < 0. \qquad (A11.76)$$

whilst the long-run effect on real money balances is:

$$\frac{\tilde{M}(\infty)}{\tilde{G}} = \frac{1}{|\Delta|} \begin{vmatrix} r & -\omega_C & 1 \\ -[(r-\rho)\,\omega_K + (1-\alpha)(r+\delta)] & r-\rho & 0 \\ -(1-\alpha)(r+\delta) & -(r+\theta) & 0 \end{vmatrix} < 0. \quad (A11.77)$$

Question 4: Cash-in-advance constraint in continuous time

(a) The household budget constraint has some interesting features:

- We model a household producer supplying a unit of labour ($L = 1$) and accumulating capital. The production function could be written as $F(K,1)$ and implicit input payments exhaust output, $F(K,1) = wL + (r+\delta)K$.
- The inflation tax is given by $\pi(t)\,m(t)$.
- The difference between total income, $F(K(t)) + T(t)$, and total spending, $C(t) + \pi(t)\,m(t)$, is saved.

The CIA constraint has the following features:

- $M(t) \geq P(t)\,C(t)$, where $M(t)$ is the nominal money supply and $P(t)$ is the price level. Money buys goods. In real terms we thus get $m(t) \equiv M(t)/P(t) \geq C(t)$.
- Sometimes the CIA constraint is written to include the real transfers, i.e. $m(t) + T(t) \geq C(t)$.
- We implicitly assume that no cash is needed for capital accumulation purposes.

(b) There is no direct utility from holding money ($m(t)$ is not in the felicity function). These balances are costly to hold since $\pi(t) > 0$. As a result, the household holds as little money as possible, i.e. $m(t) = C(t)$. Substituting this result into (Q11.13) and noting that $K(t) = A(t) - m(t) = A(t) - C(t)$ we find (Q11.15).

(c) The current-value Hamiltonian is:

$$\mathcal{H}_C \equiv U(C(t)) + \lambda(t) \cdot [F(A(t) - C(t)) + T(t) - [1 + \pi(t)]\,C(t)],$$

and the first-order conditions are:

$$\frac{\partial \mathcal{H}_C}{\partial C(t)} = U'(C(t)) - \lambda(t) \cdot \left[F'(A(t) - C(t)) + 1 + \pi(t) \right] = 0,$$

$$\dot{\lambda}(t) = \rho \lambda(t) - \frac{\partial \mathcal{H}_C}{\partial A(t)} = \left[\rho - F'(A(t) - C(t)) \right] \lambda(t),$$

$$\lim_{t \to \infty} \lambda(t) A(t) e^{-\rho t} = 0.$$

In summary, noting that $K(t) = A(t) - C(t)$ we can write the first two conditions as:

$$U'(C(t)) = \lambda(t) \cdot \left[F'(K(t)) + 1 + \pi(t) \right],$$

$$\frac{\dot{\lambda}(t)}{\lambda(t)} = \rho - F'(K(t)).$$

(d) The growth rate of the nominal money supply is defined as:

$$\mu \equiv \frac{\dot{M}(t)}{M(t)},$$

where μ is a policy variables and $\dot{M}(t) \equiv dM(t)/dt$. It follows that $\dot{M}(t)/P(t) = \mu m(t)$. But we also know that:

$$\dot{m}(t) = \frac{\dot{M}(t)}{P(t)} - \frac{M(t)}{P(t)^2} \cdot \dot{P}(t)$$

$$= \frac{\dot{M}(t)}{P(t)} - m(t) \pi(t),$$

where $\pi(t) \equiv \dot{P}(t)/P(t)$. Using these results we find that real money balances change over time according to:

$$\dot{m}(t) = \left[\mu - \pi(t) \right] \cdot m(t).$$

In the steady state we have that $\dot{m}(t) = 0$ so that $\pi^* = \mu$.

Newly created money is transferred to the household, i.e. $\dot{M}(t) = P(t) T(t)$. It follows that:

$$T(t) \equiv \frac{\dot{M}(t)}{P(t)} = \dot{m}(t) + m(t) \pi(t).$$

In the steady state $\dot{m}(t) = 0$ so that $T^* = \pi^* m^* = \pi^* C^*$.

The steady-state system (satisfying $\dot{C}(t) = \dot{m}(t) = \dot{A}(t) = \dot{\lambda}(t) = 0$) is given by:

$$U'(C^*) = \lambda^* \cdot \left[F'(K(t)) + 1 + \mu \right],$$

$$\rho = F'(K^*),$$

$$0 = F(K^*) + \mu C^* - \left[1 + \mu \right] C^* \qquad \Leftrightarrow$$

$$C^* = F(K^*).$$

It follows immediately that K^* and C^* only depend on ρ. Hence $dK^*/d\mu = dC^*/d\mu = 0$. The only variable that is affected by μ is the co-state variable, i.e. $d\lambda^*/d\mu < 0$

Question 5: Cash-in-advance with labour supply

(a) The current-value Hamiltonian is:

$$\mathcal{H}_C^H \equiv U\left(C\left(t\right),1-L\left(t\right)\right)$$
$$+ \lambda\left(t\right) \cdot \left[r\left(t\right)A\left(t\right)+w\left(t\right)L\left(t\right)+T\left(t\right)-C\left(t\right)-\left[r\left(t\right)+\pi\left(t\right)\right]m\left(t\right)\right],$$

where we have used the fact that $m\left(t\right) = C\left(t\right)$. The first-order conditions are:

$$\frac{\partial \mathcal{H}_C^H}{\partial C\left(t\right)} = U_C\left(\cdot\right) - \lambda\left(t\right) \cdot \left[1 + r\left(t\right) + \pi\left(t\right)\right] = 0,$$

$$\frac{\partial \mathcal{H}_C^H}{\partial L\left(t\right)} = -U_{1-L}\left(\cdot\right) + \lambda\left(t\right) \cdot w\left(t\right) = 0,$$

$$\dot{\lambda}\left(t\right) = \rho\lambda\left(t\right) - \frac{\partial \mathcal{H}_C^H}{\partial A\left(t\right)} = \left[\rho - r\left(t\right)\right]\lambda\left(t\right),$$

$$\lim_{t\to\infty} \lambda\left(t\right)A\left(t\right)e^{-\rho t} = 0.$$

(b) The current-value Hamiltonian is:

$$\mathcal{H}_C^F \equiv F\left(K\left(t\right),L\left(t\right)\right) - w\left(t\right)L\left(t\right) - I\left(t\right) + \zeta\left(t\right) \cdot \left[I\left(t\right) - \delta K\left(t\right)\right].$$

The first-order conditions are:

$$\frac{\partial \mathcal{H}_C^F}{\partial L\left(t\right)} = F_L\left(\cdot\right) - \zeta\left(t\right) \cdot w\left(t\right) = 0,$$

$$\frac{\partial \mathcal{H}_C^F}{\partial I\left(t\right)} = -1 + \zeta\left(t\right) = 0,$$

$$\dot{\zeta}\left(t\right) = r\left(t\right)\zeta\left(t\right) - \frac{\partial \mathcal{H}_C^F}{\partial K\left(t\right)} = \left[r\left(t\right)+\delta\right]\zeta\left(t\right) - F_K\left(\cdot\right),$$

$$\lim_{t\to\infty} \zeta\left(t\right)K\left(t\right)e^{-R(t)} = 0.$$

The proof of $V\left(0\right) = K\left(0\right)$ is standard and can be found in section 13.5.2 in the book.

(c) In the steady state we have $\dot{C}\left(t\right) = \dot{m}\left(t\right) = \dot{K}\left(t\right) = \dot{\lambda}\left(t\right) = 0$ and $\pi^* = \mu$ so that the system simplifies to:

$$U_C\left(C^*,1-L^*\right) = \lambda^* \cdot \left[1 + r^* + \mu\right],$$
$$U_{1-L}\left(C^*,1-L^*\right) = \lambda^* \cdot w^*,$$
$$r^* = F_K\left(K^*,L^*\right) - \delta = \rho,$$
$$w^* = F_L\left(K^*,L^*\right),$$
$$F\left(K^*,L^*\right) = C^* + \delta K^*.$$

Since technology features constant returns, we can write $r^* = F_K\left(\kappa^*,1\right) - \delta = \rho$, $w^* = F_L\left(\kappa^*,1\right)$, and $F\left(K^*,L^*\right) = L^* \cdot F\left(\kappa^*,1\right)$, where $\kappa^* \equiv K^*/L^*$ is the capital intensity. It follows that κ^*, r^* and w^* are fixed (independent of μ) and the core system is:

$$
\begin{aligned}
U_C\left(C^*, 1 - L^*\right) &= \lambda^* \cdot [1 + \rho + \mu], \\
U_{1-L}\left(C^*, 1 - L^*\right) &= \lambda^* \cdot w^*, \\
L^* \cdot [F\left(\kappa^*, 1\right) - \delta \kappa^*] &= C^*.
\end{aligned}
$$

This system determines C^*, L^*, and λ^* as a function of μ. Total differentiation yields:

$$
\Delta \cdot \begin{bmatrix} dC^* \\ dL^* \\ d\lambda^* \end{bmatrix} = \begin{bmatrix} \lambda^* \\ 0 \\ 0 \end{bmatrix} \cdot d\mu
$$

where Δ is given by:

$$
\Delta \equiv \begin{bmatrix} U_{CC} & -U_{C,1-L} & -(1 + \rho + \mu) \\ -U_{C,1-L} & U_{1-L,1-L} & w^* \\ -1 & C^*/L^* & 0 \end{bmatrix}.
$$

The determinant of Δ is:

$$
\begin{aligned}
|\Delta| &= w^* U_{C,1-L} - (1 + \rho + \mu) U_{1-L,1-L} - \frac{C^*}{L^*} [w^* U_{CC} - (1 + \rho + \mu) U_{C,1-L}] \\
&= \frac{1}{\lambda^*} \left[-\left(U_C U_{1-L,1-L} + \frac{C^*}{L^*} U_{1-L} U_{CC} \right) + U_{C,1-L} \cdot \left(U_{1-L} + \frac{C^*}{L^*} U_C \right) \right].
\end{aligned}
$$

Clearly, for $U_{C,1-L} \geq 0$ it follows readily that $|\Delta| > 0$. We assume that $|\Delta| > 0$ from here on.

By Cramer's Rule we find:

$$
\frac{dC^*}{d\mu} = \frac{1}{|\Delta|} \cdot \begin{vmatrix} \lambda^* & -U_{C,1-L} & -(1 + \rho + \mu) \\ 0 & U_{1-L,1-L} & w^* \\ 0 & C^*/L^* & 0 \end{vmatrix} = -\frac{1}{|\Delta|} \frac{\lambda^* w^* C^*}{L^*} < 0,
$$

$$
\frac{dL^*}{d\mu} = \frac{1}{\kappa^*} \frac{dK^*}{d\mu} = \frac{1}{|\Delta|} \cdot \begin{vmatrix} U_{CC} & \lambda^* & -(1 + \rho + \mu) \\ -U_{C,1-L} & 0 & w^* \\ -1 & 0 & 0 \end{vmatrix} = -\frac{\lambda^* w^*}{|\Delta|} < 0,
$$

$$
\frac{d\lambda^*}{d\mu} = \frac{1}{|\Delta|} \cdot \begin{vmatrix} U_{CC} & -U_{C,1-L} & \lambda^* \\ -U_{C,1-L} & U_{1-L,1-L} & 0 \\ -1 & C^*/L^* & 0 \end{vmatrix} = -\frac{1}{|\Delta|} \cdot \lambda^* \left[\frac{U_{C,1-L} C^*}{L^*} - U_{1-L,1-L} \right] \gtrless 0.
$$

So only in the last expression does the cross term, $U_{C,1-L}$, show up.

(d) Optimal consumption is such that:

$$
\frac{U_{1-L}\left(C^*, 1 - L^*\right)}{U_C\left(C^*, 1 - L^*\right)} = \frac{w^*}{1 + \rho + \mu}.
$$

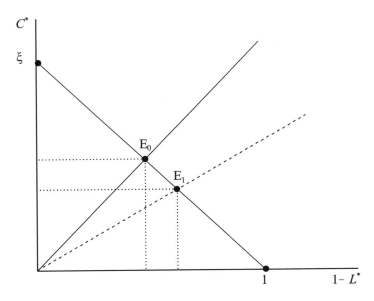

Figure A11.4: The effect of nominal money growth on consumption and labour supply

For a homothetic felicity function this represents a ray from the origin–see Figure A11.4. We also know that:

$$C^* = \xi - \xi \cdot [1 - L^*],$$

where $\xi \equiv F(\kappa^*, 1) - \delta \kappa^* > 0$ is a constant. This is a downward sloping line in the figure. The initial equilibrium is at point E_0. An increase in μ rotates the line from the origin in a clockwise fashion. The new equilibrium is at point E_1: C^* falls and $1 - L^*$ increases, i.e. L^* falls also. Since κ^* is constant, K^* also decreases. Inflation hurts capital accumulation.

Chapter 12

New Keynesian economics

Question 1: Short questions

(a) In this chapter we use models of monopolistic competition. In what sense do such model incorporate elements of *monopoly*? And where does the *competition* come in?

(b) Why is the multiplier derived in section 12.1 only "Keynesian" and not Keynesian?

(c) Explain why we must assume the existence of positive fixed cost of production in the monopolistic competition model with free entry or exit of firms.

Question 2: Cost function for a Dixit-Stiglitz technology

The technology of the final goods sector is given by:

$$Y \equiv N^{\eta} \cdot \left[\frac{1}{N} \cdot \sum_{i=1}^{N} X_i^{1/\mu} \right]^{\mu}, \qquad \mu > 1, \ 1 \leq \eta \leq 2, \tag{Q12.1}$$

where Y is output, X_i is the amount of input i used in production, and N is the number of input varieties. The price of input i is denoted by P_i so that total cost is equal to:

$$TC_Y \equiv \sum_{i=1}^{N} P_i X_i. \tag{Q12.2}$$

The firm is a cost minimizer.

(a) Prove that the production function (Q12.1) features constant returns to scale.

(b) Prove that the production function features returns to specialization, provided $\eta > 1$.

(c) Derive the cost function and the derived input demand functions. Prove that the cost function is homogeneous of degree one in prices.

(d) Verify Shephard's Lemma, i.e. the result that the partial derivative of the cost function with respect to P_i yields an expression for the derived demand for factor i.

Question 3: The multiplier when taxes are distortionary

Consider the static model of monopolistic competition presented in section 12.1.1 in the book. Assume that the tax function is given by:

$$T = T_0 + \tau_L \cdot WL, \qquad 0 < \tau_L < 1, \tag{Q12.3}$$

where T_0 is a constant and τ_L is the marginal tax rate. The rest of the model is unchanged. Assume that the economy is initially in a zero-profit equilibrium and that T_0 is positive.

(a) Derive expressions for the representative household's optimal choices of composite consumption, C, consumption of variety j, C_j, and labour supply, L. Use the method of two-stage budgeting.

(b) Explain how C, C_j, and L are affected by (i) the lump-sum part of the tax schedule, and (ii) the marginal tax rate.

(c) Compute the short-run spending multipliers under the assumption that the government adjusts T_0 to balance the budget. Explain the intuition.

(d) Redo part (c) but now assume that the government adjusts τ_L to balance the budget. Assume that the economy is on the upward sloping part of the Laffer curve. Explain the intuition.

(e) Assume that an anti-government party wins the elections and achieves control over macroeconomic policy. Assume that the new government cuts the number of civil servants and uses the cost savings to reduce the marginal tax rate on labour. Show what happens to the economy in the short run.

★ Question 4: Consumers in the New Keynesian model

[Loosely based on Yun (1996)] In this question we study household behaviour in the New Keynesian model. The infinitely-lived representative household features the following lifetime utility function:

$$\Lambda_t \equiv \sum_{\tau=t}^{\infty} \left(\frac{1}{1+\rho} \right)^{\tau-t} \cdot U\left(C_\tau, L_\tau, m_\tau\right), \tag{Q12.4}$$

where C_τ is composite consumption, L_τ is labour hours, m_τ is real money balances, and ρ is the pure rate of time preference. To keep matters simple, the felicity function is additively separable:

$$U\left(C_\tau, L_\tau, m_\tau\right) \equiv \frac{C_\tau^{1-1/\sigma} - 1}{1-1/\sigma} - \gamma_L \frac{L_\tau^{1+\theta}}{1+\theta} + \gamma_M \frac{m_\tau^{1-1/\eta} - 1}{1-1/\eta}, \tag{Q12.5}$$

where σ, γ_L, θ, γ_M, and η are positive parameters. The household exhibits preference for diversity and composite consumption is given by:

$$C_\tau \equiv \left[\sum_{j=1}^{N} C_{j,\tau}^{1/\mu} \right]^{\mu}, \qquad \mu > 1, \tag{Q12.6}$$

where N is the (fixed) number of existing varieties, $C_{j,\tau}$ is a consumption good of variety j at time τ, μ is a parameter ($\mu > 1$). The price of variety j at time τ is denoted by $P_{j,\tau}$.

The household periodic budget identity is given by:

$$W_\tau L_\tau + (1 + R_{\tau-1}) B_{\tau-1} + M_{\tau-1} + P_\tau T_\tau = P_\tau C_\tau + M_\tau + B_\tau, \qquad (Q12.7)$$

where W_τ is the nominal wage rate, $B_{\tau-1}$ is the stock of single-period bonds at the end of period $\tau - 1$, $R_{\tau-1}$ is the nominal interest rate received on such bonds, $M_{\tau-1}$ is cash balances at the end of period $\tau - 1$ (and thus at the beginning of period τ), and $P_\tau T_\tau$ is nominal transfers. Real money balances are defined as $m_\tau \equiv M_\tau / P_\tau$.

(a) Prove that (Q12.6) indeed implies a preference for diversity on the part of the household.

(b) For a given level of C_τ, the household chooses the consumption good varieties, $C_{j,\tau}$, such that total spending, $\sum_{j=1}^{N} P_{j,\tau} C_{j,\tau}$, is minimized. Derive expressions for the true price index, P_τ, and the conditional demand for variety j. Show that $\sum_{j=1}^{N} P_{j,\tau} C_{j,\tau} = P_\tau C_\tau$.

(c) Solve the household's optimization problem using the Lagrangian method.

(d) Loglinearize the key household decision rules around a steady-state path featuring a constant inflation rate π^*. Along this path, all real variables are constant.

★ Question 5: Producers in the New Keynesian model

[Based on Yun (1996) and Hornstein and Wolman (2007)] In this question we study producer behaviour in the New Keynesian model. This question continues question 4 and employs the notation introduced there. There are N small firms, where N is a large constant. Each firm j produces a unique variety of the consumption good, denoted at time τ by $C_{j,\tau}$. We abstract from capital and the production function facing firm j is given by:

$$C_{j,\tau} = A_\tau \cdot L_{j,\tau}, \qquad (Q12.8)$$

where A_τ is an index of general technology (common to all firms), and $L_{j,\tau}$ is the labour input by the firm at time τ. Labour is perfectly mobile across firms so that in period τ each firm is confronted with the same nominal wage rate, W_τ. The demand curve facing firm j when it charges price $P_{j,\tau}$ is given by:

$$\frac{C_{j,\tau}}{C_\tau} = \left(\frac{P_\tau}{P_{j,\tau}} \right)^\varepsilon, \qquad (Q12.9)$$

where $\varepsilon \equiv \mu / (\mu - 1) > 1$ is the price elasticity of demand (in absolute terms), C_τ is aggregate consumption, and P_τ is the aggregate price index. Both C_τ and P_τ are treated parametrically by individual firms. Nominal profit in period τ is defined as:

$$\Pi_{j,\tau} \equiv P_{j,\tau} C_{j,\tau} - W_\tau L_{j,\tau} = \left(P_{j,\tau} - \frac{W_\tau}{A_\tau} \right) \cdot C_{j,\tau}, \qquad (Q12.10)$$

where we have used (Q12.8) in the final step.

We adopt the Calvo (1983) price setting friction. Each period of time "nature" draws a signal to the firm which may be a "green light" or a "red light" with probabilities η and $1 - \eta$, respectively. These probabilities are the same for all firms in the economy. A firm which has just received a green light can change its price optimally in that period but must maintain that price (corrected for the core inflation rate, π^*) until the next green light is received. The objective function for a firm that has received a green light at the start of period t is given by:

$$
\Omega_t^G \equiv \left[\left(Q_{t,t} - \frac{W_t}{A_t} \right) \cdot \left(\frac{P_t}{Q_{t,t}} \right)^\varepsilon \cdot C_t \right]
$$

$$
+ \frac{1 - \eta}{1 + R_{t+1}} \cdot \left[\left((1 + \pi^*) Q_{t,t} - \frac{W_{t+1}}{A_{t+1}} \right) \cdot \left(\frac{P_{t+1}}{(1 + \pi^*) Q_{t,t}} \right)^\varepsilon \cdot C_{t+1} \right]
$$

$$
+ \frac{(1 - \eta)^2}{(1 + R_{t+1})(1 + R_{\tau+2})} \cdot \left[\left((1 + \pi^*)^2 Q_{t,t} - \frac{W_{t+2}}{A_{t+2}} \right) \right.
$$

$$
\left. \times \left(\frac{P_{t+2}}{(1 + \pi^*)^2 Q_{t,t}} \right)^\varepsilon \cdot C_{t+2} \right] + \cdots , \tag{Q12.11}
$$

where $Q_{t,t}$ is the price set by the firm at time t, and in general:

$$
Q_{t,t+k} \equiv (1 + \pi^*)^k \cdot Q_{t,t}, \qquad (\text{for } k = 1, 2, \cdots), \tag{Q12.12}
$$

where the first subscript denotes the time the price decision is made (period t), and the second subscript designates the time for which the price is relevant (period $t + k$). Until the next green light, the firm maintains the inflation corrected price.

(a) Explain intuitively why (Q12.11) is the correct objective function for the firm facing a price setting decision in period t.

(b) Derive the optimal price set at time t, $Q_{t,t}$.

(c) Derive an expression for the aggregate price index, P_t. Show that it can be written in terms of $Q_{t,t}$ and P_{t-1}.

(d) Write the relative price of a re-optimizing firm at time t as $q_{t,t} \equiv Q_{t,t}/P_t$. Prove that $q_{t,t}$ can be written as:

$$
1 = \left[\eta q_{t,t}^{1/(1-\mu)} + (1 - \eta) \left(\frac{1 + \pi^*}{1 + \pi_t} \right)^{1/(1-\mu)} \right]^{1-\mu}, \tag{Q12.13}
$$

$$
q_{t,t} = \mu \cdot \frac{\Phi_{N,t}}{\Phi_{D,t}}, \tag{Q12.14}
$$

$$
\Phi_{N,t} = mc_t \cdot C_t + \frac{(1 - \eta)(1 + \pi^*)}{1 + R_{t+1}} \left(\frac{1 + \pi_{t+1}}{1 + \pi^*} \right)^{1+\varepsilon} \cdot \Phi_{N,t+1}, \tag{Q12.15}
$$

$$
\Phi_{D,t} = C_t + \frac{(1 - \eta)(1 + \pi^*)}{1 + R_{t+1}} \left(\frac{1 + \pi_{t+1}}{1 + \pi^*} \right)^\varepsilon \cdot \Phi_{D,t+1}, \tag{Q12.16}
$$

where $mc_t \equiv W_t/(A_t P_t)$ is real marginal cost, and $1 + \pi_t \equiv P_t/P_{t-1}$ is the inflation rate.

Question 6: Monetary policy in the New Keynesian model

[Based on Clarida, Galí, and Getler (1999)] Consider the following basic New Keynesian model of a closed economy.

$$x_t = -\phi \cdot [R_t - E_t(\pi_{t+1})] + E_t(x_{t+1}) + d_t, \qquad \phi > 0, \qquad \text{(Q12.17)}$$
$$\pi_t = \lambda x_t + \beta E_t(\pi_{t+1}) + s_t, \qquad \lambda > 0, \beta > 0, \qquad \text{(Q12.18)}$$
$$d_t = \rho_D d_{t-1} + \varepsilon_t, \qquad 0 \le \rho_D \le 1, \qquad \text{(Q12.19)}$$
$$s_t = \rho_S s_{t-1} + \eta_t, \qquad 0 \le \rho_S \le 1, \qquad \text{(Q12.20)}$$

where $x_t \equiv y_t - z_t$ is the output gap (the difference between actual stochastic output, y_t, and the natural output level, z_t), R_t is the nominal interest rate, $\pi_t \equiv P_t/P_{t-1} - 1$ is the inflation rate (P_t being the price level), d_t is a stochastic demand shock, and s_t is a stochastic supply shock. Except for R_t and π_t, all variables are measured in logarithms. The innovation terms, ε_t and η_t, are independent and identically distributed random variables with mean zero ($E_t(\varepsilon_t) = E_t(\eta_t) = 0$) and constant variances ($E_t(\varepsilon_t^2) = \sigma_\varepsilon^2$ and $E_t(\eta_t^2) = \sigma_\eta^2$). Equation (Q12.17) is a New Keynesian "IS curve" relating the current output gap negatively to the real interest rate, and positively to the expected future output gap and the demand shock. Equation (Q12.18) is a New Keynesian "Phillips curve" relating the inflation rate to the output gap, expected future inflation, and the supply shock. The nominal interest rate is assumed to be the instrument of monetary policy. The private sector is blessed with rational expectations.

The central bank has the following objective function which it wants to minimize:

$$\Omega_t \equiv \frac{1}{2} E_t \left[\sum_{i=0}^{\infty} \beta^i \cdot \left[\alpha x_{t+i}^2 + \pi_{t+i}^2 \right] \right], \qquad \text{(Q12.21)}$$

where $\alpha > 0$ is the relative weight placed on output gap fluctuations.

(a) Show that in this model the current output gap depends not only on the current real interest rate and demand shock, but also on the expected value of future real interest rates and demand shocks.

(b) Show how the New Keynesian Phillips curve differs from the standard expectation augmented Phillips curve. Show that in the New Keynesian Phillips curve there is no lagged dependence in inflation.

(c) ★ Under *discretionary* monetary policy the central bank chooses in period t the value of R_{t+i} (and thus x_{t+i} and π_{t+i}) such that Ω_t is minimized subject to (Q12.17)-(Q12.18). The central bank takes as given the inflation expectations of the private sector. It re-optimizes in each period. Solve the optimization problem and find the optimal discretionary solutions for π_t, R_t, and x_t.

(d) ★ Assume that the policy maker *commits* him/herself to follow a simple policy rule of the following form:

$$x_t^c = -\omega \cdot s_t, \qquad \omega > 0, \qquad \text{(Q12.22)}$$

where x_t^c is the value of the output gap that is attained under this policy rule, and ω is the parameter of the policy rule. The central bank understands that its rule influences private sector inflationary expectations, and takes this dependence into account. Find the optimal value of ω.

(e) Prove that the optimal rule-based inflation is lower than under discretion, and that welfare is higher under the rule than under discretion.

Answers

Question 1: Short questions

(a) On monopoly: in these models, each (small) producer faces a downward slop-ing demand curve and thus has a tiny bit of marker power which can be ex-ploited. Exploitation is limited because there are close substitutes available. But the price will be set above marginal cost, just like a true monopolist will do.

On competition: in these models there are many small producers who com-pete with each other, taking each others prices parametrically. So there is no strategic interaction between producers in that sense. Each producer is a small agent in the overall market. (In contrast, in an oligopoly setting individual firms very much condition their behaviour on the behaviour of their few com-petitors.)

(b) It is "Keynesian" because it has some features reminiscent of Keynesian eco-nomics. For example, the output multiplier is larger under monopolistic com-petition than under perfect competetition–see equation (12.20). This is because the additional profit income boosts consumption somewhat. Also, there is an intimate link between the size of the multiplier and the welfare effect of public spending under monopolistic competition (and absent under perfect competition)–see equation (12.40).

It has un-Keynesian features as well. For example, private consumption falls as a result of an increase in public consumption–see equation (12.21). The main effect operates via the labour supply channel, a new classical mechanism. In Keynesian theory, public consumption helps boost aggregate demand when it is too low. The usual assumption in Keynesian economics is that of price and/or wage stickiness. The New Keynesian model uses monopolistic price setting in addition to the Calvo trick of infrequent price setting moments.

(c) The fixed costs are given by F in (12.10) and incurred if a firm is active, i.e. pro-duces a positive amount of output. In the presence of fixed costs, the firm faces increasing returns to scale at firm level because average cost falls as output ex-pands. Each firm sets its price as a markup on its marginal cost, thus covering its fixed cost. With free entry or exit of firms, a zero-profit equilibrium is at-tained. The scale of each active firm is equal to $\bar{Y} = F/[(\mu - 1)k]$. Hence, if F were zero, the equilibrium size of individual firms would be indeterminate.

Question 2: Cost function for a Dixit-Stiglitz technology

(a) Let us write the production function in general terms as:

$$Y = F(N; X_1, X_2, \cdots, X_N). \tag{A12.1}$$

Suppose we hold N constant but multiply every input by a positive scalar, λ. We get from (Q12.1):

$$
\begin{aligned}
F\left(N; \lambda X_1, \lambda X_2, \cdots, \lambda X_N\right) &= N^\eta \cdot \left[\frac{1}{N} \cdot \sum_{i=1}^{N} (\lambda X_i)^{1/\mu}\right]^\mu \\
&= N^\eta \cdot \left[\lambda^{1/\mu} \frac{1}{N} \cdot \sum_{i=1}^{N} X_i^{1/\mu}\right]^\mu \\
&= \lambda N^\eta \cdot \left[\frac{1}{N} \cdot \sum_{i=1}^{N} (\lambda X_i)^{1/\mu}\right]^\mu \\
&= \lambda F\left(N; X_1, X_2, \cdots, X_N\right).
\end{aligned} \tag{A12.2}
$$

Hence, output is also multiplied by λ, so (Q12.1) features constant returns to the inputs, X_i.

(b) "Returns to specialization" is the production counterpart to what we call "preference for diversity" in the utility function. Following the treatment of the latter in section 12.1 we define average returns to specialization as:

$$
ARTS \equiv \frac{F\left(N; \frac{X}{N}, \frac{X}{N}, \cdots, \frac{X}{N}\right)}{F\left(1; X, 0, \cdots, 0\right)}. \tag{A12.3}
$$

The numerator represents output that is produced if N varieties are employed and each variety is set equal to $X_i = X/N$. We find:

$$
\begin{aligned}
F\left(N; \frac{X}{N}, \frac{X}{N}, \cdots, \frac{X}{N}\right) &= N^\eta \cdot \left[\frac{1}{N} \cdot \sum_{i=1}^{N} \left(\frac{X}{N}\right)^{1/\mu}\right]^\mu \\
&= N^\eta \cdot \left[\frac{1}{N} \cdot \left(\frac{X}{N}\right)^{1/\mu} \sum_{i=1}^{N} 1\right]^\mu \\
&= X N^\eta \cdot \left[\frac{1}{N} \cdot \left(\frac{1}{N}\right)^{1/\mu} \cdot N\right]^\mu \\
&= X N^{\eta-1}.
\end{aligned} \tag{A12.4}
$$

The denominator represents output that is produced if only one variety is employed ($N = 1$), say $X_1 = X$ and $X_2 = X_3 = \cdots X_N = 0$ (it does not matter which particular input we use because the model is symmetric). Now we find:

$$
F\left(1; X, 0, \cdots, 0\right) = 1^\eta \cdot \left[\frac{1}{1} \cdot X^{1/\mu}\right]^\mu = X. \tag{A12.5}
$$

By using (A12.4) and (A12.5) in (A12.3) we find:

$$
ARTS \equiv N^{\eta-1} \equiv \phi(N).
$$

The elasticity of this function with respect to N is the marginal returns to specialization:

$$
MRTS \equiv \frac{N\phi'(N)}{\phi(N)} = \eta - 1.
$$

(c) The cost function minimizes total cost (by choice of inputs) of producing a given level of output (taking as given input prices, P_i). Note that (Q12.1) can be rewritten as:

$$Y^* = \left[\sum_{i=1}^{N} X_i^{1/\mu} \right]^{\mu}, \tag{A12.6}$$

$Y^* \equiv Y N^{\mu - \eta}$ is transformed output. We derive the minimum cost of producing Y^*. The Lagrangian for this problem is:

$$\mathcal{L} \equiv \sum_{i=1}^{N} P_i X_i + \lambda \cdot \left[Y^* - \left[\sum_{i=1}^{N} X_i^{1/\mu} \right]^{\mu} \right],$$

where λ is the Lagrange multiplier. The first-order conditions are:

$$P_i = \lambda \mu \cdot \left[\sum_{i=1}^{N} X_i^{1/\mu} \right]^{\mu - 1} \cdot \frac{1}{\mu} X_i^{(1-\mu)/\mu}, \qquad \text{(for all } i\text{)}.$$

Compare two varieties, i and j and we obtain:

$$\frac{P_i}{P_j} = \left(\frac{X_i}{X_j} \right)^{(1-\mu)/\mu}, \tag{A12.7}$$

or:

$$X_i^{1/\mu} = X_j^{1/\mu} P_j^{1/(\mu - 1)} P_i^{1/(1-\mu)}.$$

Summing over all $i = 1, \cdots, N$ we thus get:

$$\sum_{i=1}^{N} X_i^{1/\mu} = X_j^{1/\mu} P_j^{1/(\mu - 1)} \cdot \sum_{i=1}^{N} P_i^{1/(1-\mu)}.$$

Raising both sides to the power μ we get:

$$Y^* = \left[\sum_{i=1}^{N} X_i^{1/\mu} \right]^{\mu} = X_j P_j^{\mu/(\mu - 1)} \cdot \left[\sum_{i=1}^{N} P_i^{1/(1-\mu)} \right]^{\mu}, \tag{A12.8}$$

where we have used (A12.6). By rewriting somewhat we find that spending on input j equals:

$$P_j X_j = \frac{Y^*}{\left[\sum_{i=1}^{N} P_i^{1/(1-\mu)} \right]^{\mu}} \cdot P_j^{1/(1-\mu)}. \tag{A12.9}$$

This expression is the derived demand for input j.

Total cost equals the sum of spending on all inputs, i.e. summing over $j =$

$1, \cdots, N$ we find from (A12.9):

$$
\begin{aligned}
TC_Y &\equiv \sum_{j=1}^{N} P_j X_j = \sum_{j=1}^{N} \frac{Y^*}{\left[\sum_{i=1}^{N} P_i^{1/(1-\mu)}\right]^{\mu}} \cdot P_j^{1/(1-\mu)} \\
&= \frac{Y^*}{\left[\sum_{i=1}^{N} P_i^{1/(1-\mu)}\right]^{\mu}} \cdot \left[\sum_{j=1}^{N} P_j^{1/(1-\mu)}\right] \\
&= Y^* \cdot \left[\sum_{i=1}^{N} P_i^{1/(1-\mu)}\right]^{1-\mu}.
\end{aligned}
$$

Noting the definition of Y^* we can thus find the final expression in terms of output itself (rather than transformed output):

$$
TC_Y \equiv N^{\mu-\eta} Y \cdot \left[\sum_{i=1}^{N} P_i^{1/(1-\mu)}\right]^{1-\mu}. \tag{A12.10}
$$

(d) By partially differentiating (A12.10) with respect to some j we find:

$$
\begin{aligned}
\frac{\partial TC_Y}{\partial P_j} &= N^{\mu-\eta} Y \cdot (1-\mu) \left[\sum_{i=1}^{N} P_i^{1/(1-\mu)}\right]^{-\mu} \frac{1}{1-\mu} P_j^{1/(1-\mu)-1} \\
&= N^{\mu-\eta} Y \cdot \left[\sum_{i=1}^{N} P_i^{1/(1-\mu)}\right]^{-\mu} P_j^{\mu/(1-\mu)}. \tag{A12.11}
\end{aligned}
$$

But this is just the derived demand for X_j given above (in equation (A12.9)). Hence, for any input j we have that:

$$
X_j = \frac{\partial TC_Y}{\partial P_j}. \tag{A12.12}
$$

This is Shephard's Lemma (or the derivative property of the cost function).

Question 3: The multiplier when taxes are distortionary

(a) The representative household maximizes utility,

$$
U \equiv C^{\alpha} (1-L)^{1-\alpha}, \quad 0 < \alpha < 1, \tag{A12.13}
$$

subject to the budget constraint:

$$
\sum_{j=1}^{N} P_j C_j = (1-\tau_L) WL + \Pi - T_0, \tag{A12.14}
$$

where C is defined as in the book:

$$
C \equiv N^{\eta} \left[N^{-1} \sum_{j=1}^{N} C_j^{(\theta-1)/\theta}\right]^{\theta/(\theta-1)}, \quad \theta > 1, \ \eta \geq 1. \tag{A12.15}
$$

The method of two-stage budgeting is explained in detail in Intermezzo 12.1. The top level problem asserts that $P \cdot C = \sum_{j=1}^{N} P_j C_j$ and writes the budget constraint (A12.14) as $PC = (1 - \tau_L) WL + \Pi - T_0$. The top-level choice is about C and L. The Lagrangian is:

$$\mathcal{L} \equiv C^\alpha (1 - L)^{1-\alpha} + \lambda \cdot [(1 - \tau_L) WL + \Pi - T_0 - PC],$$

and the first-order conditions are:

$$\frac{\partial \mathcal{L}}{\partial C} = \alpha C^{\alpha-1}(1 - L)^{1-\alpha} - \lambda P = 0,$$
$$\frac{\partial \mathcal{L}}{\partial L} = -(1 - \alpha) C^\alpha (1 - L)^{-\alpha} + \lambda (1 - \tau_L) W = 0.$$

Eliminating λ we thus get:

$$\frac{\lambda (1 - \tau_L) W}{\lambda P} = \frac{(1 - \alpha) C^\alpha (1 - L)^{-\alpha}}{\alpha C^{\alpha-1}(1 - L)^{1-\alpha}} \quad \Leftrightarrow$$
$$\frac{(1 - \tau_L) W}{P} = \frac{1 - \alpha}{\alpha} \cdot \frac{C}{1 - L}. \tag{A12.16}$$

For a given real wage rate, W/P, and increase in τ_L decreases the ratio $C/(1 - L)$. By using (A12.16) in the slightly rewritten budget constraint we find:

$$PC + W(1 - \tau_L)(1 - L) = (1 - \tau_L) W + \Pi - T_0$$
$$PC + \frac{1 - \alpha}{\alpha} \cdot PC = \cdots$$
$$PC = \alpha \cdot [(1 - \tau_L) W + \Pi - T_0] \tag{A12.17}$$

Using (A12.17) in (A12.16) we find:

$$(1 - \tau_L) W(1 - L) = \frac{1 - \alpha}{\alpha} \cdot PC$$
$$= (1 - \alpha) \cdot [(1 - \tau_L) W + \Pi - T_0]. \tag{A12.18}$$

The indirect utility function is:

$$V = \frac{I_F}{P_V},$$

with:

$$I_F \equiv (1 - \tau_L) W + \Pi - T_0,$$
$$P_V \equiv \left(\frac{P}{\alpha}\right)^\alpha \left(\frac{(1 - \tau_L) W}{1 - \alpha}\right)^{1-\alpha}.$$

The bottom-level problem is solved exactly as in Intermezzo 12.1. We thus find that:

$$P \equiv N^{-\eta} \left[N^{-\theta} \sum_{j=1}^{N} P_j^{1-\theta}\right]^{1/(1-\theta)}, \tag{A12.19}$$
$$\frac{C_j}{C} = N^{-(\theta+\eta)+\eta\theta} \left(\frac{P_j}{P}\right)^{-\theta}, \quad j = 1, \ldots, N. \tag{A12.20}$$

(b) From (A12.17) we find the required partial equilibrium results:

$$\frac{\partial C}{\partial T_0} = -\frac{\alpha}{P} < 0, \qquad \frac{\partial C}{\partial \tau_L} = -\frac{\alpha W}{P} < 0.$$

Both lead to a reduction in consumption. (The effects on C_j follow trivially from (A12.20).) From (A12.18) we find the results for labour supply:

$$
\begin{aligned}
-\frac{\partial L}{\partial T_0} &= (1-\alpha) \cdot \frac{\partial}{\partial T_0} \left[\frac{(1-\tau_L)\,W + \Pi - T_0}{(1-\tau_L)\,W} \right] = -\frac{1-\alpha}{(1-\tau_L)\,W} < 0, \\
-\frac{\partial L}{\partial \tau_L} &= (1-\alpha) \cdot \frac{\partial}{\partial \tau_L} \left[\frac{(1-\tau_L)\,W + \Pi - T_0}{(1-\tau_L)\,W} \right] \\
&= (1-\alpha) \cdot \frac{\partial}{\partial \tau_L} \left[1 + \frac{\Pi - T_0}{(1-\tau_L)\,W} \right] \\
&= (1-\alpha) \frac{[\Pi - T_0] \cdot W}{[(1-\tau_L)\,W]^2}.
\end{aligned}
$$

It follows that $\partial L / \partial T_0 > 0$, i.e. the income effect increases labour supply. Also, the sign of $\partial L / \partial \tau_L$ is determined by the sign of $-[\Pi - T_0]$. Since $\Pi = 0$ initially and $T_0 > 0$, $\Pi - T_0 < 0$ then $\partial L / \partial \tau_L < 0$, i.e. the substitution effect dominates the income effect in labour supply.

(c) The full model is given by:

$$
\begin{aligned}
Y &= C + G, & \text{(A12.21)} \\
PC &= \alpha I_F, & \text{(A12.22)} \\
I_F &\equiv (1-\tau_L)\,W + \Pi - T_0, & \text{(A12.23)} \\
\Pi &= \frac{1}{\theta} PY - WNF, & \text{(A12.24)} \\
\tau_L WL + T_0 &= PG + WL_G, & \text{(A12.25)} \\
P &= N^{1-\eta} \mu W k, & \text{(A12.26)} \\
(1-\tau_L)\,W(1-L) &= (1-\alpha)\,I_F. & \text{(A12.27)}
\end{aligned}
$$

Compared to the model in Table 12.1 in the book, only (A12.23) and (A12.25) are affected.

To derive the short-run results, we note that $N = N_0$ (fixed) so that $w \equiv W/P = N_0^{\eta-1} / (\mu k) = w_0$ (fixed). The core expressions are:

$$
\begin{aligned}
Y &= \alpha\,(1-\tau_L)\,w_0 + \alpha \frac{\Pi - T_0}{P} + G, \\
\frac{\Pi}{P} &= \frac{1}{\theta} Y - w_0 N_0 F, \\
\tau_L w_0 L &= G + w_0 L_G - \frac{T_0}{P}, \\
L &= \alpha - \frac{1-\alpha}{(1-\tau_L)\,w_0} \frac{\Pi - T_0}{P}. & \text{(A12.28)}
\end{aligned}
$$

The endogenous variables are Y, Π/P, L, and one of T_0/P and τ_L.

For the lump-sum tax case we find:

$$dY = \frac{\alpha}{\theta}dY - \alpha d\frac{T_0}{P} + dG,$$

$$\tau_L w_0 dL = dG - d\frac{T_0}{P},$$

$$(1-\tau_L)\,w_0 dL = -(1-\alpha)\left[\frac{1}{\theta}dY - d\frac{T_0}{P}\right].$$

In matrix format:

$$\begin{bmatrix} 1-\alpha/\theta & 0 & \alpha \\ 0 & \tau_L w_0 & 1 \\ -(1-\alpha)/\theta & -(1-\tau_L)\,w_0 & 1-\alpha \end{bmatrix} \cdot \begin{bmatrix} dY \\ dL \\ d(T_0/P) \end{bmatrix} = \begin{bmatrix} 1 \\ 1 \\ 0 \end{bmatrix} \cdot dG.$$

The determinant of the matrix on the left-hand side is:

$$|\Delta| = \tau_L\,(1-\alpha)\,w_0 + (1-\tau_L)\,w_0\left[1-\frac{\alpha}{\theta}\right] > 0.$$

Using Cramer's Rule we find the comparative static results:

$$\frac{dY}{dG} = \frac{1}{|\Delta|} \cdot \begin{vmatrix} 1 & 0 & \alpha \\ 1 & \tau_L w_0 & 1 \\ 0 & -(1-\tau_L)\,w_0 & 1-\alpha \end{vmatrix} = \frac{(1-\alpha)\,w_0}{|\Delta|} > 0,$$

$$\frac{dL}{dG} = \frac{1}{|\Delta|} \cdot \begin{vmatrix} 1-\alpha/\theta & 1 & \alpha \\ 0 & 1 & 1 \\ -(1-\alpha)/\theta & 0 & 1-\alpha \end{vmatrix} = \frac{(1-\alpha)\,(1-1/\theta)}{|\Delta|} > 0,$$

$$\frac{d(T_0/P)}{dG} = \frac{1}{|\Delta|} \cdot \begin{vmatrix} 1-\alpha/\theta & 0 & 1 \\ 0 & \tau_L w_0 & 1 \\ -(1-\alpha)/\theta & -(1-\tau_L)\,w_0 & 0 \end{vmatrix}$$

$$= \frac{\tau_L\frac{1-\alpha}{\theta}w_0 + (1-\tau_L)\,w_0\left[1-\frac{\alpha}{\theta}\right]}{|\Delta|} > 0.$$

If τ_L is strictly positive, we find that $\frac{d(T_0/P)}{dG} < 1$ because the employment expansion generates additional tax revenue (and thus reduces the needed increase in T_0/P). The intuition behind these results is simple. The tax increase induces an income effect which prompts the household to increase labour supply (and thus production).

(d) When the government keeps T_0/P constant and instead changes τ_L to balance the budget we find:

$$dY = -\alpha w_0 d\tau_L + \frac{\alpha}{\theta}dY + dG,$$

$$\tau_L w_0 dL + w_0 L d\tau_L = dG,$$

$$-(1-\tau_L)\,w_0 dL - w_0(1-L)d\tau_L = (1-\alpha)\left[\frac{1}{\theta}dY - w_0 d\tau_L\right].$$

In matrix format we obtain:

$$
\begin{bmatrix}
1 - \alpha/\theta & 0 & \alpha w_0 \\
0 & \tau_L w_0 & w_0 L \\
-(1-\alpha)/\theta & -(1-\tau_L) w_0 & (L-\alpha) w_0
\end{bmatrix}
\cdot
\begin{bmatrix}
dY \\
dL \\
d\tau_L
\end{bmatrix}
=
\begin{bmatrix}
1 \\
1 \\
0
\end{bmatrix}
\cdot dG.
$$

The determinant of the matrix on the left-hand side is:

$$
|\Delta^*| = \frac{w_0^2}{\theta} \cdot [(\theta - \alpha)(L - \alpha \tau_L) + \alpha(1-\alpha)\tau_L] > 0.
$$

(We know that $|\Delta^*| > 0$ because the economy is on the upward sloping part of the Laffer curve, i.e. the tax rate must increase if government consumption goes up. See equation (A12.29) below.) The output multiplier is thus:

$$
\frac{dY}{dG} = \frac{1}{|\Delta^*|} \cdot
\begin{vmatrix}
1 & 0 & \alpha w_0 \\
1 & \tau_L w_0 & w_0 L \\
0 & -(1-\tau_L) w_0 & (L-\alpha) w_0
\end{vmatrix}
= \frac{(L-\alpha) w_0^2}{|\Delta^*|} > 0,
$$

where we assume that $T_0 > \Pi = 0$ so that $L > \alpha$ (see (A12.28) above)). For employment and the tax rate we find:

$$
\frac{dL}{dG} = \frac{1}{|\Delta^*|} \cdot
\begin{vmatrix}
1-\alpha/\theta & 1 & \alpha w_0 \\
0 & 1 & w_0 L \\
-(1-\alpha)/\theta & 0 & (L-\alpha) w_0
\end{vmatrix}
= \frac{(L-\alpha)(1-1/\theta) w_0}{|\Delta^*|} > 0,
$$

$$
\frac{d\tau_L}{dG} = \frac{1}{|\Delta^*|} \cdot
\begin{vmatrix}
1-\alpha/\theta & 0 & 1 \\
0 & \tau_L w_0 & 1 \\
-(1-\alpha)/\theta & -(1-\tau_L) w_0 & 0
\end{vmatrix}
$$

$$
= \frac{\tau_L(1-\alpha) w_0 + (1-\tau_L) w_0 (\theta - \alpha)}{\theta \cdot |\Delta^*|} > 0. \tag{A12.29}
$$

Because there is negative non-labour income ($\Pi - T_0 < 0$), the income effect dominates the substitution effect in labour supply. The tax increase increases labour supply and thus output.

(e) For this scenario we find:

$$
dY = -\alpha w_0 d\tau_L + \frac{\alpha}{\theta} dY,
$$

$$
\tau_L w_0 dL + w_0 L d\tau_L = w_0 dL_G,
$$

$$
-(1-\tau_L) w_0 dL - w_0(1-L) d\tau_L = (1-\alpha)\left[\frac{1}{\theta} dY - w_0 d\tau_L\right].
$$

In matrix format:

$$
\begin{bmatrix}
1-\alpha/\theta & 0 & \alpha w_0 \\
0 & \tau_L w_0 & w_0 L \\
-(1-\alpha)/\theta & -(1-\tau_L) w_0 & (L-\alpha) w_0
\end{bmatrix}
\cdot
\begin{bmatrix}
dY \\
dL \\
d\tau_L
\end{bmatrix}
=
\begin{bmatrix}
0 \\
1 \\
0
\end{bmatrix}
\cdot w_0 dL_G.
$$

The comparative static effects are thus:

$$
\frac{dY}{dL_G} = \frac{1}{|\Delta^*|} \cdot
\begin{vmatrix}
0 & 0 & \alpha w_0 \\
1 & \tau_L w_0 & w_0 L \\
0 & -(1-\tau_L) w_0 & (L-\alpha) w_0
\end{vmatrix}
= -\frac{\alpha(1-\tau_L) w_0^2}{|\Delta^*|} < 0,
$$

$$\frac{dL}{dL_G} = \frac{1}{|\Delta^*|} \cdot \begin{vmatrix} 1 - \alpha/\theta & 0 & \alpha w_0 \\ 0 & 1 & w_0 L \\ -(1-\alpha)/\theta & 0 & (L-\alpha)w_0 \end{vmatrix} = \frac{[(\theta-\alpha)L - \alpha(\theta-1)]w_0}{\theta \cdot |\Delta^*|} < 0,$$

$$\frac{d\tau_L}{dL_G} = \frac{1}{|\Delta^*|} \cdot \begin{vmatrix} 1 - \alpha/\theta & 0 & 0 \\ 0 & \tau_L w_0 & 1 \\ -(1-\alpha)/\theta & -(1-\tau_L)w_0 & 0 \end{vmatrix} = \frac{[1-\alpha/\theta](1-\tau_L)w_0}{|\Delta^*|} > 0.$$

By firing "useless" civil servants, the tax rate falls, and output and private employment increase.

Question 4: Consumers in the New Keynesian model

(a) Note that (Q12.6) can be written as:

$$C_\tau \equiv N^\eta \cdot \left[N^{-1} \sum_{j=1}^{N} C_{j,\tau}^{1/\mu} \right]^\mu, \tag{A12.30}$$

with $\eta = \mu$. In the text it is shown that $\eta > 1$ implies a preference for diversity.

(b) The derivations are structurally the same as for part (c) of question 2 above. The Lagrangian is:

$$\mathcal{L} \equiv \sum_{j=1}^{N} P_{j,\tau} X_{j,\tau} + \lambda \cdot \left[C_\tau - \left[\sum_{j=1}^{N} C_{j,\tau}^{1/\mu} \right]^\mu \right],$$

and the first-order conditions are:

$$\frac{P_{i,\tau}}{P_{j,\tau}} = \left(\frac{C_{i,\tau}}{C_{j\tau}} \right)^{(1-\mu)/\mu}.$$

It follows that total spending is:

$$\sum_{j=1}^{N} P_{j,\tau} C_{j,\tau} = C_\tau \cdot \left[\sum_{j=1}^{N} P_{j,\tau}^{1/(1-\mu)} \right]^{1-\mu} \equiv P_\tau C_\tau, \tag{A12.31}$$

where P_τ is the true price index:

$$P_\tau \equiv \left[\sum_{j=1}^{N} P_{j,\tau}^{1/(1-\mu)} \right]^{1-\mu}. \tag{A12.32}$$

The conditional demand curve is:

$$\frac{C_{j,\tau}}{C_\tau} = \left(\frac{P_\tau}{P_{j,\tau}} \right)^\varepsilon, \tag{A12.33}$$

where $\varepsilon \equiv \mu/(\mu-1) > 1$ is the price elasticity of demand (in absolute terms).

(c) The household chooses sequences for C_τ, L_τ, B_τ, and M_τ in order to maximize lifetime utility subject to the budget identity (and a solvency condition). The Lagrangian expression is:

$$\mathcal{L}_t \equiv \sum_{\tau=t}^{\infty} \left(\frac{1}{1+\rho}\right)^{\tau-t} \cdot \left[\frac{C_\tau^{1-1/\sigma}-1}{1-1/\sigma} - \gamma_L \frac{L_\tau^{1+\theta}}{1+\theta} + \gamma_M \frac{(M_\tau/P_\tau)^{1-1/\eta}-1}{1-1/\eta} \right.$$

$$\left. - \lambda_\tau \cdot \left[B_\tau + M_\tau + P_\tau C_\tau - W_\tau L_\tau - (1+R_{\tau-1})B_{\tau-1} - M_{\tau-1} - P_\tau T_\tau \right] \right],$$

where λ_τ is the Lagrange multiplier for the constraint in period τ. The first-order conditions for this problem (for $\tau = t, t+1, t+2, ...$) are:

$$\frac{\partial \mathcal{L}_t}{\partial C_\tau} = \left(\frac{1}{1+\rho}\right)^{\tau-t} \left[C_\tau^{-1/\sigma} - \lambda_\tau P_\tau \right] = 0,$$

$$\frac{\partial \mathcal{L}_t}{\partial L_\tau} = \left(\frac{1}{1+\rho}\right)^{\tau-t} \left[-\gamma_L L_\tau^\theta + \lambda_\tau W_\tau \right] = 0,$$

$$\frac{\partial \mathcal{L}_t}{\partial M_\tau} = \left(\frac{1}{1+\rho}\right)^{\tau-t} \left[-\lambda_\tau + \frac{\gamma_M}{P_\tau} \cdot \left(\frac{M_\tau}{P_\tau}\right)^{-1/\eta} + \frac{\lambda_{\tau+1}}{1+\rho} \right] = 0,$$

$$\frac{\partial \mathcal{L}_t}{\partial B_\tau} = \left(\frac{1}{1+\rho}\right)^{\tau-t} \left[-\lambda_\tau + (1+R_\tau)\frac{\lambda_{\tau+1}}{1+\rho} \right] = 0.$$

For the planning period ($\tau = t$) these first-order conditions can be written in a more compact format as:

$$C_t^{-1/\sigma} = \lambda_t P_t, \tag{A12.34}$$

$$\gamma_L L_t^\theta = \lambda_t W_t, \tag{A12.35}$$

$$\lambda_t = \frac{\gamma_M}{P_t} \cdot \left(\frac{M_t}{P_t}\right)^{-1/\eta} + \frac{\lambda_{\tau+1}}{1+\rho}, \tag{A12.36}$$

$$\lambda_t = (1+R_t)\frac{\lambda_{t+1}}{1+\rho}. \tag{A12.37}$$

By combining (A12.34) and (A12.35) we find:

$$\gamma_L L_t^\theta C_t^{1/\sigma} = \frac{W_t}{P_t}, \tag{A12.38}$$

i.e. the marginal rate of substitution between labour and consumption is equated to the real wage rate. By using (A12.36)-(A12.37) we find:

$$[\lambda_t =] \quad \frac{\gamma_M}{P_t} \cdot \left(\frac{M_t}{P_t}\right)^{-1/\eta} + \frac{\lambda_{t+1}}{1+\rho} = (1+R_t)\frac{\lambda_{t+1}}{1+\rho} \quad \Leftrightarrow$$

$$\gamma_M \cdot \left(\frac{M_t}{P_t}\right)^{-1/\eta} = \frac{R_t}{1+R_t}\lambda_t P_t \quad \Leftrightarrow$$

$$\gamma_M \cdot \left(\frac{M_t}{P_t}\right)^{-1/\eta} = \frac{R_t}{1+R_t}C_t^{-1/\sigma}, \tag{A12.39}$$

where we have used (A12.37) in going from the first to the second line, and
(A12.34) in going from the second to the third line. Equation (A12.39) says
that the marginal rate of substitution between real money balances and consumption is equated to the nominal interest rate factor, $R_t / (1 + R_t)$ (see also
Chapter 11).

Finally, by using (A12.34) and (A12.37) we find:

$$
\frac{1}{P_t} C_t^{-1/\sigma} = \frac{1 + R_t}{1 + \rho} \frac{1}{P_{t+1}} C_{t+1}^{-1/\sigma} \quad \Leftrightarrow
$$
$$
\left(\frac{C_{t+1}}{C_t} \right)^{1/\sigma} = \frac{1 + r_t}{1 + \rho}, \tag{A12.40}
$$

where we have used the definition of the real interest rate:

$$
1 + r_t \equiv \frac{P_t (1 + R_t)}{P_{t+1}} = \frac{1 + R_t}{1 + \pi_{t+1}}, \tag{A12.41}
$$

where $\pi_{t+1} \equiv (P_{t+1} - P_t) / P_t$ is the (expected) inflation rate. The key expressions characterizing the household's decisions are (A12.38)-(A12.40).

(d) Taking logarithms, equation (A12.34) can be written as:

$$
\ln \gamma_L + \theta \ln L_t + \frac{1}{\sigma} \ln C_t = \ln W_t - \ln P_t. \tag{A12.42}
$$

Along the steady-state path (denoted by stars), we thus obtain:

$$
\ln \gamma_L + \theta \ln L^* + \frac{1}{\sigma} \ln C^* = \ln W_t^* - \ln P_t^*. \tag{A12.43}
$$

Deducting (A12.43) from (A12.44) we obtain:

$$
\theta \tilde{L}_t + \frac{1}{\sigma} \tilde{C}_t = \tilde{W}_t - \tilde{P}_t,
$$

where $\tilde{L}_t \equiv \ln (L_t/L^*)$, $\tilde{C}_t \equiv \ln (C_t/C^*)$, $\tilde{W}_t \equiv \ln (W_t/W_t^*)$, and $\tilde{P}_t \equiv \ln (P_t/P_t^*)$.
Similarly, from (A12.39) we find:

$$
\ln \gamma_M - \frac{1}{\eta} [\ln M_t - \ln P_t] + \frac{1}{\sigma} \ln C_t = \ln \left(\frac{R_t}{1 + R_t} \right),
$$
$$
\ln \gamma_M - \frac{1}{\eta} [\ln M_t^* - \ln P_t^*] + \frac{1}{\sigma} \ln C^* = \ln \left(\frac{R^*}{1 + R^*} \right),
$$

where $R^* = r^* + \pi^* = \rho + \pi^*$ is the steady-state nominal interest rate. Around
$R_t = R^*$, we can use the approximation:

$$
\ln \left(\frac{R_t}{1 + R_t} \right) \approx \ln \left(\frac{R^*}{1 + R^*} \right) + \frac{1 + R^*}{R^*} \frac{(1 + R^*) \cdot 1 - R^* \cdot 1}{(1 + R^*)^2} \cdot [R_t - R^*]
$$
$$
= \ln \left(\frac{R^*}{1 + R^*} \right) + \frac{1}{R^*} \cdot \left[\frac{R_t - R^*}{R^*} \right].
$$

We thus find:

$$-\frac{1}{\eta} \left[\tilde{M}_t - \tilde{P}_t \right] + \frac{1}{\sigma} \tilde{C}_t = \frac{1}{R^*} \cdot \left[\frac{R_t - R^*}{R^*} \right], \tag{A12.44}$$

where $\tilde{M}_t \equiv \ln \left(M_t / M_t^* \right)$.

From (A12.40) we find:

$$\begin{aligned}
\ln C_{t+1} - \ln C_t &= \sigma \cdot \left[\ln \left(1 + r_t \right) - \ln \left(1 + \rho \right) \right], \\
\ln C^* - \ln C^* &= \sigma \cdot \left[\ln \left(1 + \rho \right) - \ln \left(1 + \rho \right) \right],
\end{aligned}$$

so that:

$$\tilde{C}_{t+1} - \tilde{C}_t = \sigma \cdot \ln \left(\frac{1 + r_t}{1 + \rho} \right) \approx \sigma \cdot \frac{r_t - \rho}{1 + \rho},$$

where we have used the following approximation (for $r_t \approx r^* = \rho$):

$$\ln \left(\frac{1 + r_t}{1 + \rho} \right) \approx \ln \left(\frac{1 + \rho}{1 + \rho} \right) + \frac{1 + \rho}{1 + \rho} \frac{1}{1 + \rho} \cdot \left[r_t - \rho \right] = \frac{r_t - \rho}{1 + \rho}.$$

Finally, the relationship (A12.41) can be used to deduce:

$$\begin{aligned}
1 + R_t &= 1 + r_t + \pi_{t+1} + r_t \pi_{t+1}, \\
1 + R^* &= 1 + \rho + \pi^* + \rho \pi^*,
\end{aligned}$$

so that:

$$R_t - R^* \approx \left(r_t - \rho \right) + \left(\pi_{t+1} - \pi^* \right),$$

where we ignore the cross term, $r_t \pi_{t+1} - \rho \pi^*$.

Summarizing, the household's (approximated) decision rules are given by:

$$\begin{aligned}
\theta \tilde{L}_t + \frac{1}{\sigma} \tilde{C}_t &= \tilde{W}_t - \tilde{P}_t \\
-\frac{1}{\eta} \left[\tilde{M}_t - \tilde{P}_t \right] + \frac{1}{\sigma} \tilde{C}_t &= \frac{1}{R^*} \cdot \left[\frac{R_t - R^*}{R^*} \right], \\
\tilde{C}_{t+1} - \tilde{C}_t &= \sigma \cdot \frac{r_t - \rho}{1 + \rho}, \\
R_t - R^* &= \left(r_t - \rho \right) + \left(\pi_{t+1} - \pi^* \right).
\end{aligned}$$

Question 5: Producers in the New Keynesian model

(a) A lot of the intuition is explained in section 12.3.3 in the book, though in terms of a cost minimization problem (rather than a profit maximization problem). Key features of (Q12.11) are:

- The firm chooses $Q_{t,t}$ at time t and re-optimizes with probability η in period $t + 1$. If the firm gets a green light in period $t + 1$, it re-optimizes. It formulates Ω_{t+1}^G and chooses $Q_{t+1,t+1}$. This choice does not affect the choice of $Q_{t,t}$ in period t.

- There is a probability $1 - \eta$ that there is a red light in period $t + 1$. In that case the firm sets $Q_{t,t+1} = (1 + \pi^*) Q_{t,t}$ (the inflation correction) but faces marginal cost W_{t+1}/A_{t+1} and the aggregate price index P_{t+1}.

- The probability that there are two red lights in a row (periods $t + 1$ and $t + 2$) is $(1 - \eta)^2$. In that case, the price is $Q_{t,t+2} = (1 + \pi^*)^2 Q_{t,t}$, and the firm faces marginal cost W_{t+2}/A_{t+2} and the aggregate price index P_{t+2}.

- Because time is involved and profits are in nominal terms, the firm discounts future profits at the nominal interest rate.

(b) The optimal $Q_{t,t}$ is set such that Ω_t^G is maximized. Differentiating Ω_t^G with respect to $Q_{t,t}$ (holding constant the aggregate variables, $P_{t+\tau}$, $C_{t+\tau}$, $A_{t+\tau}$, $W_{t+\tau}$, and $R_{t+\tau}$) we find:

$$
\begin{aligned}
\frac{d\Omega_t^G}{dQ_{t,t}} &= \left[1 - \varepsilon \cdot \frac{Q_{t,t} - MC_t}{Q_{t,t}}\right] \cdot \left(\frac{P_t}{Q_{t,t}}\right)^\varepsilon \cdot C_t \\
&+ \frac{(1 - \eta)(1 + \pi^*)}{1 + R_{t+1}} \cdot \left[1 - \varepsilon \cdot \frac{(1 + \pi^*) Q_{t,t} - MC_{t+1}}{(1 + \pi^*) Q_{t,t}}\right] \\
&\times \left(\frac{P_{t+1}}{(1 + \pi^*) Q_{t,t}}\right)^\varepsilon \cdot C_{t+1} \\
&+ \frac{(1 - \eta)^2 (1 + \pi^*)^2}{(1 + R_{t+1})(1 + R_{t+2})} \cdot \left[1 - \varepsilon \cdot \frac{(1 + \pi^*)^2 Q_{t,t} - MC_{t+2}}{(1 + \pi^*)^2 Q_{t,t}}\right] \\
&\times \left(\frac{P_{t+2}}{(1 + \pi^*)^2 Q_{t,t}}\right)^\varepsilon \cdot C_{t+2} + \cdots,
\end{aligned}
$$

where $MC_{t+\tau} \equiv W_{t+\tau}/A_{t+\tau}$ stands for marginal cost at time $t + \tau$. Several simplifications can be made. First, the terms in square brackets can be written as:

$$
\begin{aligned}
\left[1 - \varepsilon \cdot \frac{Q_{t,t} - MC_t}{Q_{t,t}}\right] &= 1 - \varepsilon + \varepsilon \frac{MC_t}{Q_{t,t}} \\
&= \frac{1 - \varepsilon}{Q_{t,t}} \cdot [Q_{t,t} - \mu \cdot MC_t],
\end{aligned}
$$

where $\mu \equiv \varepsilon/(\varepsilon - 1)$ is the markup. Similarly, for later periods we find:

$$
\begin{aligned}
\left[1 - \varepsilon \cdot \frac{(1 + \pi^*)^k Q_{t,t} - MC_{t+k}}{(1 + \pi^*)^k Q_{t,t}}\right] &= 1 - \varepsilon + \varepsilon \frac{MC_{t+k}}{(1 + \pi^*)^k Q_{t,t}} \\
&= \frac{1 - \varepsilon}{Q_{t,t}} \cdot \left[Q_{t,t} - \mu \cdot \frac{MC_{t+k}}{(1 + \pi^*)^k}\right].
\end{aligned}
$$

Gathering results, we find the first-order condition:

$$
\begin{aligned}
\frac{Q_{t,t}^{1+\varepsilon}}{1-\varepsilon} \cdot \frac{d\Omega_t^G}{dQ_{t,t}} &= [Q_{t,t} - \mu \cdot MC_t] \cdot P_t^\varepsilon \cdot C_t \\
&+ \frac{(1-\eta)(1+\pi^*)}{1+R_{t+1}} \cdot \left[Q_{t,t} - \mu \cdot \frac{MC_{t+1}}{1+\pi^*} \right] \cdot \left(\frac{P_{t+1}}{1+\pi^*} \right)^\varepsilon \cdot C_{t+1} \\
&+ \frac{(1-\eta)^2 (1+\pi^*)^2}{(1+R_{t+1})(1+R_{t+2})} \cdot \left[Q_{t,t} - \mu \cdot \frac{MC_{t+2}}{(1+\pi^*)^2} \right] \cdot \left(\frac{P_{t+2}}{(1+\pi^*)^2} \right)^\varepsilon \cdot C_{t+2} \\
&+ \cdots = 0,
\end{aligned}
$$

Solving for $Q_{t,t}$ we find:

$$
\Xi_D \cdot Q_{t,t} = \mu \cdot \Xi_N,
$$

where Ξ_D and Ξ_N are defined as:

$$
\Xi_D \equiv P_t^\varepsilon C_t + \frac{(1-\eta)(1+\pi^*)^{1-\varepsilon}}{1+R_{t+1}} P_{t+1}^\varepsilon C_{t+1} + \frac{(1-\eta)^2 (1+\pi^*)^{2(1-\varepsilon)}}{(1+R_{t+1})(1+R_{t+2})} P_{t+2}^\varepsilon C_{t+2} + \cdots,
$$

and:

$$
\begin{aligned}
\Xi_N \equiv\ & MC_t P_t^\varepsilon C_t + \frac{(1-\eta)(1+\pi^*)^{-\varepsilon}}{1+R_{t+1}} MC_{t+1} P_{t+1}^\varepsilon C_{t+1} \\
& + \frac{(1-\eta)^2 (1+\pi^*)^{-2\varepsilon}}{(1+R_{t+1})(1+R_{t+2})} MC_{t+2} P_{t+2}^\varepsilon C_{t+2} + \cdots.
\end{aligned}
$$

In compact notation we can write:

$$
Q_{t,t} = \mu \cdot \frac{\sum_{k=0}^{\infty} (1-\eta)^k (1+\pi^*)^{-\varepsilon k} D_{t,t+k} MC_{t+k} P_{t+k}^\varepsilon C_{t+k}}{\sum_{k=0}^{\infty} (1-\eta)^k (1+\pi^*)^{(1-\varepsilon)k} D_{t,t+k} P_{t+k}^\varepsilon C_{t+k}}, \qquad \text{(A12.45)}
$$

where $D_{t,t+k}$ is a discounting factor, such that $D_{t,t} = 1$ and:

$$
D_{t,k} \equiv \frac{1}{1+R_{t+1}} \cdot \frac{1}{1+R_{t+2}} \cdots \frac{1}{1+R_{t+k}}, \qquad \text{(for } k = 1,2,\cdots). \quad \text{(A12.46)}
$$

(c) As is explained in the text, $\eta(1-\eta)^s$ is the fraction of firms which last changed their prices in period $t-s$. The aggregate price index in period t is given by:

$$
\begin{aligned}
P_t^{1/(1-\mu)} &\equiv \sum_{j=1}^{N} P_{j,t}^{1/(1-\mu)} \\
&= \eta Q_{t,t}^{1/(1-\mu)} + \eta (1-\eta) Q_{t-1,t}^{1/(1-\mu)} + \eta (1-\eta)^2 Q_{t-2,t}^{1/(1-\mu)} + \cdots \\
&= \eta Q_{t,t}^{1/(1-\mu)} + \eta (1-\eta) \left[(1+\pi^*) Q_{t-t,t-1} \right]^{1/(1-\mu)} \\
&\quad + \eta (1-\eta)^2 \left[(1+\pi^*)^2 Q_{t-2,t-2} \right]^{1/(1-\mu)} + \cdots. \quad \text{(A12.47)}
\end{aligned}
$$

The aggregate price index one period before is given by:

$$
\begin{aligned}
P_{t-1}^{1/(1-\mu)} &\equiv \sum_{j=1}^{N} P_{j,t-1}^{1/(1-\mu)} \\
&= \eta Q_{t-1,t-1}^{1/(1-\mu)} + \eta\,(1-\eta)\,Q_{t-2,t-1}^{1/(1-\mu)} + \eta\,(1-\eta)^2\,Q_{t-3,t-1}^{1/(1-\mu)} + \cdots \\
&= \frac{(1+\pi^*)^{-1/(1-\mu)}}{1-\eta} \cdot \Big[\eta\,(1-\eta)\,[(1+\pi^*)\,Q_{t-1,t-1}]^{1/(1-\mu)} \\
&\quad + \eta\,(1-\eta)^2\,\big[(1+\pi^*)^2\,Q_{t-2,t-2}\big]^{1/(1-\mu)} \\
&\quad + \eta\,(1-\eta)^3\,\big[(1+\pi^*)^3\,Q_{t-3,t-3}\big]^{1/(1-\mu)} + \cdots \Big] \\
&= \frac{(1+\pi^*)^{-1/(1-\mu)}}{1-\eta} \cdot \Big[P_t^{1/(1-\mu)} - \eta Q_{t,t}^{1/(1-\mu)} \Big], \qquad \text{(A12.48)}
\end{aligned}
$$

where we have used (A12.47) in the final step. Rewriting (A12.48) we obtain:

$$
\begin{aligned}
P_t^{1/(1-\mu)} &= \eta Q_{t,t}^{1/(1-\mu)} + (1-\eta)\,[(1+\pi^*)\,P_{t-1}]^{1/(1-\mu)} \qquad \Leftrightarrow \\
P_t &= \Big[\eta Q_{t,t}^{1/(1-\mu)} + (1-\eta)\,[(1+\pi^*)\,P_{t-1}]^{1/(1-\mu)} \Big]^{1-\mu}. \;\text{(A12.49)}
\end{aligned}
$$

The current aggregate price is a CES weighted sum of the currently optimal price, $Q_{t,t}$, and the core-inflation-corrected lagged aggregate price. $(1+\pi^*)\,P_{t-1}$.

(d) Equation (Q12.13) follows from (A12.49) and noting that:

$$
\begin{aligned}
P_t &= \left[P_t^{1/(1-\mu)} \left(\eta \left(\frac{Q_{t,t}}{P_t} \right)^{1/(1-\mu)} + (1-\eta) \left[(1+\pi^*) \frac{P_{t-1}}{P_t} \right]^{1/(1-\mu)} \right) \right]^{1-\mu} \\
&= P_t \cdot \left[\eta q_{t,t}^{1/(1-\mu)} + (1-\eta) \left(\frac{1+\pi^*}{1+\pi_t} \right)^{1/(1-\mu)} \right]^{1-\mu}. \qquad \text{(A12.50)}
\end{aligned}
$$

The expression in (Q12.13), is obtained from (A12.45) by dividing by P_t and writing the numerator in terms of real marginal cost:

$$
\begin{aligned}
q_{t,t} &\equiv \frac{Q_{t,t}}{P_t} = \mu \cdot \frac{\Phi_{N,t}}{\Phi_{D,t}}, \\
\Phi_{N,t} &\equiv \sum_{k=0}^{\infty} (1-\eta)^k\,(1+\pi^*)^{-\varepsilon k}\,D_{t,t+k}\,mc_{t+k} \left(\frac{P_{t+k}}{P_t} \right)^{1+\varepsilon} C_{t+k}, \;\text{(A12.51)} \\
\Phi_{D,t} &\equiv \sum_{k=0}^{\infty} (1-\eta)^k\,(1+\pi^*)^{(1-\varepsilon)k}\,D_{t,t+k} \left(\frac{P_{t+k}}{P_t} \right)^{\varepsilon} C_{t+k}. \qquad \text{(A12.52)}
\end{aligned}
$$

Using (A12.51) we can write $\Phi_{N,t}$ as:

$$
\begin{aligned}
\Phi_{N,t} \quad &\equiv \quad mc_t \cdot C_t + \frac{(1-\eta)\,(1+\pi^*)}{1+R_{t+1}} mc_{t+1} \left(\frac{1+\pi_{t+1}}{1+\pi^*}\right)^{1+\varepsilon} C_{t+1} \\
&\quad + \frac{(1-\eta)^2\,(1+\pi^*)^2}{(1+R_{t+1})\,(1+R_{t+2})} mc_{t+2} \left(\frac{(1+\pi_{t+1})\,(1+\pi_{t+2})}{(1+\pi^*)^2}\right)^{1+\varepsilon} C_{t+2} \\
&\quad + \cdots .
\end{aligned}
\tag{A12.53}
$$

Similarly, we can write $\Phi_{N,t+1}$ as:

$$
\begin{aligned}
\Phi_{N,t+1} \quad &\equiv \quad mc_{t+1} \cdot C_{t+1} + \frac{(1-\eta)\,(1+\pi^*)}{1+R_{t+2}} mc_{t+2} \left(\frac{1+\pi_{t+2}}{1+\pi^*}\right)^{1+\varepsilon} C_{t+2} \\
&\quad + \frac{(1-\eta)^2\,(1+\pi^*)^2}{(1+R_{t+2})\,(1+R_{t+3})} mc_{t+3} \left(\frac{(1+\pi_{t+2})\,(1+\pi_{t+3})}{(1+\pi^*)^2}\right)^{1+\varepsilon} C_{t+3} \\
&\quad + \cdots .
\end{aligned}
\tag{A12.54}
$$

Using (A12.54) we immediately see that (A12.53) can be written recursively as:

$$
\Phi_{N,t} \equiv mc_t \cdot C_t + \frac{(1-\eta)\,(1+\pi^*)}{1+R_{t+1}} \left(\frac{1+\pi_{t+1}}{1+\pi^*}\right)^{1+\varepsilon} \cdot \Phi_{N,t+1},
$$

which is the result to be proved.

Similarly, for $\Phi_{D,t}$ and $\Phi_{D,t+1}$ we find:

$$
\begin{aligned}
\Phi_{D,t} \quad &\equiv \quad C_t + \frac{(1-\eta)\,(1+\pi^*)}{1+R_{t+1}} \left(\frac{1+\pi_{t+1}}{1+\pi^*}\right)^{\varepsilon} C_{t+1} \\
&\quad + \frac{(1-\eta)^2\,(1+\pi^*)^2}{(1+R_{t+1})\,(1+R_{t+2})} \left(\frac{(1+\pi_{t+1})\,(1+\pi_{t+2})}{(1+\pi^*)^2}\right)^{\varepsilon} C_{t+2} + \cdots ,
\end{aligned}
$$

and:

$$
\begin{aligned}
\Phi_{D,t+1} \quad &\equiv \quad C_{t+1} + \frac{(1-\eta)\,(1+\pi^*)}{1+R_{t+2}} \left(\frac{1+\pi_{t+2}}{1+\pi^*}\right)^{\varepsilon} C_{t+2} \\
&\quad + \frac{(1-\eta)^2\,(1+\pi^*)^2}{(1+R_{t+2})\,(1+R_{t+3})} \left(\frac{(1+\pi_{t+2})\,(1+\pi_{t+3})}{(1+\pi^*)^2}\right)^{\varepsilon} C_{t+3} + \cdots .
\end{aligned}
$$

It follows that:

$$
\Phi_{D,t} \equiv C_t + \frac{(1-\eta)\,(1+\pi^*)}{1+R_{t+1}} \left(\frac{1+\pi_{t+1}}{1+\pi^*}\right)^{\varepsilon} \cdot \Phi_{D,t+1},
$$

which is (Q12.16).

Question 6: Monetary policy in the New Keynesian model

(a) Equation (Q12.17) is a first-order expectational difference equation that we can solve forward in time. We show some steps. We know that in period $t + 1$:

$$x_{t+1} = -\phi \cdot [R_{t+1} - E_{t+1}(\pi_{t+2})] + E_{t+1}(x_{t+2}) + d_{t+1}.$$

Substituting this result into (Q12.17) we thus get:

$$
\begin{aligned}
x_t &= -\phi[R_t - E_t(\pi_{t+1})] + + d_t \\
&\quad E_t(-\phi[R_{t+1} - E_{t+1}(\pi_{t+2})] + E_{t+1}(x_{t+2}) + d_{t+1}) \\
&= -\phi[R_t - E_t(\pi_{t+1})] - \phi E_t[R_{t+1} - E_{t+1}(\pi_{t+2})] \\
&\quad + E_t(E_{t+1}(x_{t+2})) + E_t(d_{t+1}) + d_t \\
&= -\phi[[R_t - E_t(\pi_{t+1})] + E_t[R_{t+1} - E_{t+1}(\pi_{t+2})]] \\
&\quad + d_t + E_t(d_{t+1}) + E_t(x_{t+2}),
\end{aligned}
$$

where we have used the fact that

$$E_t(E_{t+1}(\pi_{t+2})) = E_t(\pi_{t+2}), \quad \text{and} \quad E_t(E_{t+1}(x_{t+2})) = E_t(x_{t+1})$$

in the final step (see also Chapter 3). But we can keep substituting, i.e. the next one to substitute would be x_{t+2}. But the pattern should be clear by now. We obtain:

$$x_t = E_t\left[\sum_{i=0}^{\infty} (-\phi \cdot [R_{t+i} - \pi_{t+1+i}] + d_{t+i})\right], \tag{A12.55}$$

i.e. the current gap depends on the expectation of all current and real interest rates and demand shocks.

(b) The standard expectations augmented Phillips curve is the inverse of the Lucas supply curve. We would write the Lucas supply curve, for example, as:

$$x_t = \gamma \cdot [\pi_t - E_{t-1}(\pi_t)] + s_t^*, \tag{A12.56}$$

with $\gamma > 0$. The output gap depends on the expectational error, for example because workers are fooled and supply too much (if $\pi_t > E_{t-1}(\pi_t)$) or too little (if $\pi_t < E_{t-1}(\pi_t)$) labour. Solving (A12.56) for inflation we would get the following standard Phillips curve:

$$\pi_t = E_{t-1}(\pi_t) + \frac{1}{\gamma} \cdot [x_t - s_t^*]. \tag{A12.57}$$

Current inflation depends on what is was expected to be in the previous period, on the current output gap, and on the current supply shock.

By solving (Q12.18) forward in time we obtain for the New Keynesian Phillips curve:

$$\pi_t = E_t\left[\sum_{i=0}^{\infty} \beta^i \cdot [\lambda x_{t+i} + s_{t+i}]\right]. \tag{A12.58}$$

In this specification, current inflation depends on the expectation regarding current and future output gaps and supply shocks.

(c) To solve this problem, we follows the two-step procedure suggested by Clarida et al. (1999, p. 1671). In the first step we let the central banker minimize Ω_t subject to the Phillips curve (Q12.18). In the second step we find the implied optimal interest rate.

The Lagrangian for the first step problem is:

$$
\begin{aligned}
\mathcal{L} \equiv\ & \frac{1}{2}\left[\alpha x_t^2 + \pi_t^2\right] + \mu_t \cdot \left[\pi_t - \lambda x_t - (\beta E_t\left(\pi_{t+1}\right) + s_t)\right] \\
& + \frac{1}{2} E_t\left[\sum_{i=1}^{\infty} \beta^i \cdot \left[\alpha x_{t+i}^2 + \pi_{t+i}^2\right]\right] \\
& + E_t \sum_{i=1}^{\infty} \mu_{t+i} \cdot \left[\pi_{t+i} - \lambda x_{t+i} - (\beta \pi_{t+i+1} + s_{t+i})\right],
\end{aligned}
$$

where μ_{t+i} are the Lagrange multipliers. In principle, the central banker chooses x_{t+i} and π_{t+i} for all $i = 0, 1, 2, \cdots$, but is re-optimizes every period so the only first-order condition of interest in period t is the one pertaining to π_t and x_t (appearing only on the first line of the Lagrangian expression. We easily find:

$$
\begin{aligned}
\frac{\partial \mathcal{L}}{\partial \pi_t} &= \pi_t + \mu_t = 0, \\
\frac{\partial \mathcal{L}}{\partial x_t} &= \alpha x_t - \lambda \mu_t = 0.
\end{aligned}
$$

Combining these expressions we obtain:

$$
x_t = -\frac{\lambda}{\alpha} \pi_t. \tag{A12.59}
$$

This is a policy of leaning against the wind: if inflation is higher than the target (of zero) then the central bank reduces the output gap (by raising the nominal interest rate) and vice versa if inflation is lower than the target level.

To find the expressions for x_t and π_t, we first substitute (A12.59) into the Phillips curve (Q12.18) and then impose the rational expectations assumption. The first step yields:

$$
\begin{aligned}
\pi_t &= -\frac{\lambda^2}{\alpha} \pi_t + \beta E_t\left(\pi_{t+1}\right) + s_t \\
\pi_t &= \left[1 + \frac{\lambda^2}{\alpha}\right]^{-1} \cdot \left[\beta E_t\left(\pi_{t+1}\right) + s_t\right] \\
&= \frac{\alpha \beta}{\alpha + \lambda^2} \cdot E_t\left(\pi_{t+1}\right) + \frac{\alpha}{\alpha + \lambda^2} \cdot s_t. \tag{A12.60}
\end{aligned}
$$

This is an expectational difference equation, the solution of which is child's play. We postulate the trial solution:

$$
\pi_t = \zeta_0 + \zeta_1 s_t, \tag{A12.61}
$$

where ζ_0 and ζ_1 are the unknown coefficients. It follows from (A12.61) and (Q12.20) that $E_t(\pi_{t+1}) = E_t(\zeta_0 + \zeta_1 s_{t+1}) = \zeta_0 + \zeta_1 \rho_S s_t$. Substituting this result into (A12.60) we find:

$$\zeta_0 + \zeta_1 s_t = \frac{\alpha\beta}{\alpha + \lambda^2} \cdot [\zeta_0 + \zeta_1 \rho_S s_t] + \frac{\alpha}{\alpha + \lambda^2} \cdot s_t \qquad \Leftrightarrow$$

$$\zeta_0 \cdot \left[1 - \frac{\alpha\beta}{\alpha + \lambda^2}\right] = \left[\frac{[1 + \zeta_1 \beta \rho_S]\alpha}{\alpha + \lambda^2} - \zeta_1\right] \cdot s_t,$$

which must hold for all s_t. We find that $\zeta_0 = 0$ and ζ_1 is:

$$\zeta_1 = \frac{\alpha}{\alpha[1 - \beta\rho_S] + \lambda^2}.$$

In summary, the discretionary solutions for x_t and π_t are given by:

$$\pi_t = \frac{\alpha}{\alpha[1 - \beta\rho_S] + \lambda^2} \cdot s_t, \qquad (A12.62)$$

$$x_t = -\frac{\lambda}{\alpha[1 - \beta\rho_S] + \lambda^2} \cdot s_t. \qquad (A12.63)$$

The implied optimal solution for R_t is obtained by substituting (A12.62)-(A12.63) into (Q12.17):

$$\phi R_t = \phi E_t(\pi_{t+1}) + E_t(x_{t+1}) + d_t - x_t$$

$$= \frac{\alpha\phi}{\alpha[1 - \beta\rho_S] + \lambda^2} E_t(s_{t+1}) - \frac{\lambda}{\alpha[1 - \beta\rho_S] + \lambda^2} E_t(s_{t+1})$$

$$+ d_t + \frac{\lambda}{\alpha[1 - \beta\rho_S] + \lambda^2} \cdot s_t,$$

$$= \frac{\alpha\phi\rho_S + \lambda(1 - \rho_S)}{\alpha[1 - \beta\rho_S] + \lambda^2} s_t + d_t,$$

or:

$$R_t = \frac{1}{\phi} \frac{\alpha\phi\rho_S + \lambda(1 - \rho_S)}{\alpha[1 - \beta\rho_S] + \lambda^2} s_t + \frac{1}{\phi} d_t. \qquad (A12.64)$$

(d) If the private sector believes the rule, then the Phillips curve can be written as:

$$\pi_t^c = \lambda x_t^c + \beta E_t(\pi_{t+1}^c) + s_t$$

$$= -\lambda\omega s_t + \beta E_t(\pi_{t+1}^c) + s_t,$$

where π_t^c is the inflation rate under the rule. Solving the expectational difference equation (using the trial solution, $x_t^c = \zeta_1 s_t$), we obtain:

$$\pi_t^c = \frac{1 - \lambda\omega}{1 - \beta\rho_S} \cdot s_t. \qquad (A12.65)$$

By substituting (Q12.22) and (A12.65) into the objective function (Q12.21), we can express Ω_t in terms of the choice variable, ω, and the parameters of the model:

$$\Omega_t^c \equiv \frac{1}{2} E_t \left[\sum_{i=0}^{\infty} \beta^i \cdot \left[\alpha \left(x_{t+i}^c \right)^2 + \left(\pi_{t+i}^c \right)^2 \right] \right]$$

$$= \frac{1}{2} E_t \left[\sum_{i=0}^{\infty} \beta^i \cdot \left[\alpha \left(-\omega s_{t+i} \right)^2 + \left(\frac{1 - \lambda \omega}{1 - \beta \rho_S} s_{t+i} \right)^2 \right] \right]$$

$$= \frac{1}{2} \cdot \left[\alpha \omega^2 + \left(\frac{1 - \lambda \omega}{1 - \beta \rho_S} \right)^2 \right] \cdot E_t \left[\sum_{i=0}^{\infty} \beta^i \cdot s_{t+i}^2 \right].$$

The second term in square brackets on the right-hand side is the unavoidable turbulence in the economy due to supply shocks. The first term in square brackets, however, contains the choice variable ω, and the optimal choice of ω minimizes that term:

$$\omega^* = \arg\min \left[\alpha \omega^2 + \left(\frac{1 - \lambda \omega}{1 - \beta \rho_S} \right)^2 \right]. \tag{A12.66}$$

The first-order condition is:

$$0 = \alpha \omega^* - \frac{\lambda \left(1 - \lambda \omega^* \right)}{\left(1 - \beta \rho_S \right)^2} \qquad \Leftrightarrow$$

$$\omega^* = \frac{\lambda}{\alpha \left(1 - \beta \rho_S \right)^2 + \lambda^2}. \tag{A12.67}$$

The resulting optimal rule-based solutions for x_t^c and π_t^c are thus:

$$x_t^c = -\omega^* \cdot s_t = -\frac{\lambda}{\alpha \left(1 - \beta \rho_S \right)^2 + \lambda^2} \cdot s_t, \tag{A12.68}$$

$$\pi_t^c = \frac{1 - \lambda \omega^*}{1 - \beta \rho_S} \cdot s_t$$

$$= \frac{\alpha \left(1 - \beta \rho_S \right) \omega^*}{\lambda} \cdot s_t = \frac{\alpha \left(1 - \beta \rho_S \right)}{\alpha \left(1 - \beta \rho_S \right)^2 + \lambda^2} \cdot s_t \tag{A12.69}$$

(e) Recall from (A12.62) that the discrete inflation rate is given by:

$$\pi_t^d = \frac{\alpha}{\alpha \left[1 - \beta \rho_S \right] + \lambda^2} \cdot s_t. \tag{A12.70}$$

Using (A12.70) in (A12.69) we find:

$$\frac{\pi_t^c}{\pi_t^d} = \frac{\frac{\alpha}{\alpha [1 - \beta \rho_S] + \lambda^2 / (1 - \beta \rho_S)} \cdot s_t}{\frac{\alpha}{\alpha [1 - \beta \rho_S] + \lambda^2} \cdot s_t}$$

$$= \frac{\alpha \left[1 - \beta \rho_S \right] + \lambda^2}{\alpha \left[1 - \beta \rho_S \right] + \lambda^2 / \left(1 - \beta \rho_S \right)} < 1,$$

because $1 / \left(1 - \beta \rho_S \right) > 1$. For a given supply shock, inflation is less severe under the rule than under discretionary policy.

Chapter 13

Exogenous economic growth

Question 1: Short questions

(a) Show that the Solow-Swan model with labour-augmenting technological change can account for stylized facts (SF1)–(SF6) mentioned in the textbook.

(b) "An economy is dynamically inefficient if its citizens are short-sighted and save too little. Savings should be stimulated by the policy maker in a dynamically inefficient economy." Explain and evaluate these propositions.

(c) Explain intuitively why, in the context of the extended Ramsey model, a lump-sum tax-financed increase in government consumption leads to crowding in of private capital and an increase in output. Explain also the transition mechanism.

(d) Does the Cobb-Douglas production function $Y = K^{\alpha} L^{1-\alpha}$ satisfy all the Inada conditions? Are the inputs necessary?

(e) What would happen to the speed of adjustment of output in a Mankiw, Romer, and Weil (1992) (MRW) model of a small open economy which has access to unlimited flows of human capital (at a constant rental rate). The perceived setting is one in which imports (or exports) of smart foreigners (highly skilled workers) is unrestricted.

(f) In the book the concepts of *human wealth* and *human capital* are both used. Explain how these concepts differ.

(g) Explain how the speed of adjustment predicted by the standard Solow-Swan model can be made more realistic.

(h) Explain why dynamic inefficiency is impossible in the *standard* Ramsey growth model as given in Table 13.1 in the book. How could taxes/subsidies affect your answer?

(i) "In the absence of adjustment costs of investment, the convergence speed in a small open economy is infinite." Evaluate and explain this statement.

Question 2: The Harrod-Domar model

[Based on Harrod (1939) and Domar (1949)] One of the key notions underlying the Solow-Swan model is the substitutability between capital and labour incorporated in the aggregate production function [viz. equation (13.1) or (13.6)]. Even before Solow-Swan made their contributions, Roy Harrod and Evsey Domar proposed a growth model which negates the possibility of substitution between capital and labour. They postulated the following aggregate production function:

$$Y(t) = \min \left(\frac{K(t)}{v}, \frac{L(t)}{\alpha} \right), \quad v > 0, \alpha > 0, \tag{Q13.1}$$

where $Y(t)$, $K(t)$, and $L(t)$ are, respectively, aggregate output, the capital stock, and employment, and the coefficients v and α are fixed. The rest of the model is the same as in the text:

$$S(t) = sY(t), \qquad\qquad 0 < s < 1, \tag{Q13.2}$$

$$I(t) = \delta K(t) + \dot{K}(t), \tag{Q13.3}$$

$$I(t) = S(t), \tag{Q13.4}$$

$$\frac{\dot{L}(t)}{L(t)} = n_L, \tag{Q13.5}$$

where $S(t)$, $I(t)$, s, and n_L are, respectively, aggregate saving, aggregate investment, the (constant) propensity to save, and the (constant) growth rate of the population.

(a) Draw the isoquants of the production function given in (Q13.1). Derive expressions for Y/K, Y/L, and K/L under the assumption that both production factors are fully employed. What happens if the actual K/L is less than v/α? What if it is larger than v/α?

(b) Show that, in order to maintain full employment of capital in the model, output and investment must grow at the so-called "warranted rate of growth" which is equal to $[s - \delta v]/v$.

(c) Show that, in order to maintain full employment of labour in the model, output and investment must grow at the so-called "natural rate of growth" which is equal to n_L.

(d) Derive the condition under which the economy grows with full employment of both factors of production. This is called the Harrod-Domar condition. What happens if $[s - \delta v]/v$ falls short of (exceeds) n_L?

(e) Show that a Harrod-Domar like condition also appears in the Solow-Swan model but that the latter model does not suffer from the instability (or knife-edge stability) of the Harrod-Domar model. Make sure that you explain the critical role of capital-labour substitution.

Question 3: The production function

Assume that the production function, $Y = F(K, L)$, satisfies assumptions (P1)–(P3) stated in section 13.2 in the book. Define the per-worker production function, $f(k)$, as in equation (13.8).

(a) Show that the marginal products of capital and labour (F_K and F_L, respectively) can be written in terms of the per-worker production function.

(b) Prove that the per-worker production function has the following properties:

$$f'(k) \geq 0, \quad \lim_{k \to 0} f'(k) = +\infty, \quad \text{and} \quad \lim_{k \to \infty} f'(k) = 0.$$

(c) Assume that the production factors receive their respective marginal products. Derive the expressions for the wage rate, W, and the rental rate on capital, $r + \delta$, when technology is Cobb-Douglas. What happens to (W, r) as $k \to 0$ and as $k \to \infty$? Derive the expression for the *factor price frontier* (FPF), i.e. the expression linking W and r, and illustrate it graphically. Show what happens to the FPF if general productivity increases.

Question 4: The wage-rental ratio

[Based on Burmeister and Dobell (1970)] Assume that the factors of production are paid according to their respective marginal products, i.e. $W = F_L(K, L)$ and $r + \delta = F_K(K, L)$ as in equation (13.79) in the text. Abstract from technological progress.

(a) The wage-rental ratio, ω, is defined as follows: $\omega \equiv W/[r + \delta]$. Show that ω can be written as a function of k only, i.e. $\omega = \omega(k)$. Show that this function can be inverted to yield k as a function of ω. Denote this function by $k = \xi(\omega)$.

(b) Identify the wage-rental ratio in a diagram with k on the horizontal axis and y and $W(k)$ on the vertical axis.

(c) The elasticity of substitution in production is defined as:

$$\sigma_{KL} \equiv \frac{F_L F_K}{F(K, L) F_{LK}}. \tag{Q13.6}$$

Show that the *elasticity* of the $\xi(\omega)$ function, defined as $\dfrac{dk}{d\omega} \dfrac{\omega}{k}$, is equal to σ_{KL}.

Question 5: The Solow-Swan model

Consider the Solow-Swan model discussed in the book in section 13.2. Assume that the economy features perfectly competitive firms.

(a) Derive the phase diagram for the model without technological progress with output per worker, y, on the vertical axis and capital per worker, k, on the horizontal axis. Show that in the balanced growth path the relative output shares of capital and labour are constant. Show those shares in the diagram.

(b) Next assume that there is Harrod-neutral technological progress. Derive the expressions for the rental rate on capital and the wage rate. Show that in the balanced growth path the wage rate grows at the rate of technological progress (n_A). Demonstrate the constancy of income shares and illustrate with a diagram.

(c) Abstract from technological progress but assume that the population growth rate is not constant (as in the standard Solow-Swan model) but instead depends on economic conditions. In particular, assume that n_L is low for low levels of output per worker (y), rises quite rapidly as y exceeds some "subsistence level," and starts to slow down again as y becomes very large. Show that is possible for the model to exhibit multiple steady-state equilibria. Investigate the stability of these equilibria and explain how the model can provide a description of the theory of the "big push" (known from development economics).

Question 6: The Pasinetti model

[Based on Kaldor (1955), Pasinetti (1962), and Samuelson and Modigliani (1966)] Consider the Solow-Swan model discussed in the text in section 13.2. Assume that the economy features perfectly competitive firms and abstract from technological progress. Assume that the savings function takes the form suggested by Nicholas Kaldor:

$$S(t) = s_w W(t)L(t) + s_p \left[Y(t) - W(t)L(t) \right], \tag{Q13.7}$$

where $S(t)$, $W(t)$, $L(t)$, and $Y(t)$ are, respectively, aggregate saving, the wage rate, employment, and output. The propensity to save out of labour income is s_w, and the propensity to save out of profit income is s_p. Both these savings propensities are constant and it is assumed that $0 < s_w < s_p < 1$. The rest of the model is standard and is given by equations (13.3)–(13.6) in the book.

(a) Show that the savings function can be written as $S(t) = s(t)Y(t)$, where $s(t)$ is defined as:

$$s(t) \equiv s_w + (s_p - s_w)\omega_K(k(t)), \tag{Q13.8}$$

and where $\omega_K(\cdot) \equiv (r(t) + \delta)K(t)/Y(t)$ is the income share of capital.

(b) Derive the fundamental differential equation for output per worker. Assume that the production function is CES with substitution elasticity $0 < \sigma_{KL} \leq 1$. Demonstrate stability and uniqueness of the steady-state equilibrium. Illustrate your answer using a diagram with output per worker, y, on the vertical axis, and capital per worker, k, on the horizontal axis.

(c) Show that income shares are constant along the balanced growth path and illustrate this result in the diagram.

Question 7: The Solow-Swan model with population growth

Consider the standard Solow-Swan model in which the population, $L(t)$, grows at a constant exponential rate ($\dot{L}(t)/L(t) = n_L$). Abstract from technological progress and assume that the labour force *participation* rate is a function of the real wage rate, $W(t)$, according to:

$$p(W(t)) = \frac{N(t)}{L(t)}, \tag{Q13.9}$$

where $N(t)$ is employment. Assume that the production function is Cobb-Douglas:

$$Y(t) = K(t)^\alpha N(t)^{1-\alpha}, \tag{Q13.10}$$

with $0 < \alpha < 1$.

(a) Derive the fundamental differential equation for the per capita capital stock ($k \equiv K/L$) and show that it depends on the elasticity of the participation rate with respect to the wage (η_{pW}) and on the elasticity of wages with respect to per capita capital (η_{Wk}).

(b) What are the likely signs of η_{pW} and η_{Wk}? Explain intuitively.

(c) Explain both formally and intuitively what the effect of an endogenous participation rate is on the adjustment speed of the economy.

Question 8: Some mathematics

[Based on Koopmans (1967) and Cass (1965)] In Intermezzo 13.3 we derive the consumption Euler equation (13.68) by means of the *Hamiltonian method*. Study the intermezzo carefully, and answer the following questions.

(a) Derive the consumption Euler equation (13.68) by means of the *Hamiltonian method* explained in Intermezzo 13.3. Explain the steps you make in your derivation. Denote the co-state variable by $\mu(t)$. Which variable is the control variable? Which one is the state variable?

(b) Develop the phase diagram for the Ramsey model with $\mu(t)$ on the vertical and $k(t)$ on the horizontal axis (rather than in the (c, k) space, as in Figure 13.8).

In the text we assume that the representative household has a lifetime utility function as in (13.57). Assume now that the household has a slightly different lifetime utility function:

$$\Lambda(0) \equiv \int_0^\infty L(t)U(c(t))e^{-\rho t}dt, \ \rho > 0, \tag{Q13.11}$$

where $L(t)$ is the size of the population (i.e. the size of the dynastic family). Assume a constant population growth rate, i.e. $\dot{L}(t)/L(t) = n$.

(c) Compare and contrast (13.57) and (Q13.11). Derive the consumption Euler equation for the modified model.

Question 9: Optimal investment

[Based on Intriligator (1971)] Consider the standard neoclassical growth model without technological change. Assume that consumption per worker is fixed (at $c(t) = \bar{c}$), that capital does not depreciate ($\delta = 0$), and that the population grows at a constant exponential rate n_L.

(a) Show that the growth rate of the capital stock, $\gamma_K(t) \equiv \dot{K}(t)/K(t)$, is maximized when this growth rate equals the marginal product of capital, i.e. when $\gamma_K(t)$ equals the interest rate.

(b) Illustrate your result in part (a) graphically. Assume for convenience that technology is Cobb-Douglas. *Hint*: express $\gamma_K(t)$ as a function of the capital-labour ratio $k(t)$.

(c) Generalize your result to the case with a positive depreciation rate ($\delta > 0$).

Question 10: Welfare of future generations

[Based on Ramsey (1928) and Intriligator (1971)] In the original treatment of the problem of optimal economic growth, Frank Ramsey argued on the basis of ethical beliefs that there should be no discounting of future felicity ($\rho = 0$). Since the welfare integral will then not generally converge, Ramsey suggested a different approach. He assumed that there is a finite upper limit for either the production function or the felicity function, in either case leading to a finite upper limit to utility called *bliss*, B:

$$B \equiv \max_{\{c\}} U(c) = U(c_B), \tag{Q13.12}$$

where c_B is the bliss consumption per worker which is assumed to be finite. He then postulated the following (undiscounted) objective function that is to be *minimized*:

$$R \equiv \int_0^\infty [B - U(c(t))]\,dt, \tag{Q13.13}$$

where R is a measure of "regret" (i.e. the social cost associated with deviating from the bliss point). Solve the Ramsey problem of minimizing regret subject to the neoclassical growth model. Assume that there is no technological change and that the population is constant. Illustrate your answer with the aid of a diagram and show that the model is saddle-point stable.

Question 11: The savings function

[Based on Kurz (1968)] One of the objections that has been raised against the Solow-Swan model concerns the *ad hoc* nature of the savings function. In the so-called "inverse optimum" problem we try to determine the class of household objective functions which will in fact yield the Solow-Swan savings function as an optimal policy rule. In this question we study this inverse optimum problem in detail. We consider the following model:

$$\dot{k}(t) = f(k(t)) - c(t) - (\delta + n_L)\,k(t), \tag{Q13.14}$$
$$c(t) = (1-s)\,y(t), \qquad 0 < s < \alpha, \tag{Q13.15}$$
$$y(t) = Ak(t)^\alpha, \qquad 0 < \alpha < 1, \tag{Q13.16}$$

where $k(t)$, $y(t)$, and $c(t)$ are, respectively, capital, output, and consumption per worker. Capital depreciates at a constant rate, δ, and the population grows at an exponential rate, n_L. The savings rate, s, is constant. The economy is perfectly competitive so the usual marginal productivity conditions for the production factors are valid. Household behaviour is described by the Ramsey model of section 13.5.

(a) Show that equation (Q13.14) is a rewritten version of equation (13.59) in the book.

(b) Show that in the steady state, the various parameters are related according to:

$$\frac{\delta + n_L}{s} = \frac{\rho + \delta + n_L}{\alpha}, \tag{Q13.17}$$

where ρ is the rate of time preference.

(c) Show that the only solution for the inverse optimum problem is the family of utility functions featuring a constant elasticity of substitution. Show also that $\sigma = s$ and explain why we need the condition $s < \alpha$ for this result to make sense.

★ Question 12: The savings ratio in the Ramsey model

In the book we develop and solve the Ramsey model in terms of its implications for consumption and capital per worker. In this question we study the Ramsey model in terms of its implications for capital per worker and the savings ratio. Recall that the savings ratio, $s(t)$, is the proportion of income that is saved and invested:

$$s(t) \equiv \frac{S(t)}{Y(t)} = \frac{I(t)}{Y(t)} = \frac{\dot{K}(t) + \delta K(t)}{Y(t)}. \tag{Q13.18}$$

It follows from (Q13.18) that consumption per worker is:

$$c(t) = (1 - s(t)) \, y(t), \tag{Q13.19}$$

where $y(t) = f(k(t))$ is the intensive-form production function. The fundamental differential equation for the capital stock is:

$$\dot{k}(t) = s(t) f(k(t)) - (\delta + n_L) k(t). \tag{Q13.20}$$

Assume that the technology is Cobb-Douglas, i.e. $y(t) = Ak(t)^\alpha$ with $0 < \alpha < 1$, and that the felicity function is iso-elastic with intertemporal substitution elasticity σ. Abstract from technological change.

(a) Solve the optimization problem in terms of the savings rate and the capital stock per worker.

(b) Derive the fundamental differential equations for k and s.

(c) Denote the steady-state value for the savings rate by s^*. Illustrate the phase diagram for the three possible cases, namely case (Q13.18) $s^* = \sigma$, case (Q13.19) $s^* > \sigma$, and case (Q13.20) $s^* < \sigma$. Explain the economic intuition behind the dynamic adjustment for all three cases.

(d) Now solve for the optimal time path of the savings rate if the production function is $f(k(t)) = Ak(t)$.

Question 13: Technological change

Consider the neoclassical growth model with technological progress and assume that the aggregate production function is given by:

$$Y(t) = A_P(t) F(A_K(t) K(t), A_L(t) L(t)), \tag{Q13.21}$$

where $A_P(t) \equiv e^{n_H t}$ summarizes "product augmenting" technical changes, $A_K(t) \equiv e^{n_S t}$ summarizes "capital augmenting" technical change, and $A_L(t) \equiv e^{n_A t}$ summarizes "labour augmenting" technical change. Assume that the representative household has the lifetime utility function (13.57) and faces the budget identity (13.59) and an appropriately defined NPG condition.

(a) Show that the only technical progress consistent with a balanced growth equilibrium is purely labour augmenting ("Harrod neutral") technical change.

(b) Develop the solution to the household optimization problem in the case of Harrod neutral technological change, where $n_A > 0$ and $n_S = n_H = 0$. Assume that the utility function features a constant intertemporal substitution elasticity, σ. *Hint*: recall that the wage rate grows exponentially on the balanced growth path.

Question 14: Constant marginal utility

In the text we focus attention on the case in which household utility features a finite intertemporal substitution elasticity. As an extension we now study the case for which marginal utility is constant. The lifetime utility function (13.57) is replaced by:

$$\Lambda(0) \equiv \int_0^\infty c(t)e^{-\rho t}dt, \tag{Q13.22}$$

where $c(t)$ is consumption per worker. We study the social planning solution to the household optimization problem. The fundamental differential equation for the capital stock per worker, $k(t)$, is:

$$\dot{k}(t) = f(k(t)) - c(t) - (\delta + n_L)k(t), \tag{Q13.23}$$

where $y(t) = f(k(t))$ is output per worker. The production function satisfies the Inada conditions and there is no technological progress. The solution for consumption must satisfy the following constraints:

$$\bar{c} \le c(t) \le f(k(t)), \tag{Q13.24}$$

where $\bar{c}$ is some minimum consumption level (it is assumed that $0 < \bar{c} < c^{GR}$, where c^{GR} is the maximum attainable "golden rule" consumption level).

(a) Set up the appropriate current-value Hamiltonian and derive the first-order conditions. Show that the solution for consumption is a so-called "bang-bang" solution:

$$c(t) = \begin{cases} \bar{c} & \text{for } \mu(t) > 1 \\ \text{free} & \text{for } \mu(t) = 1 , \\ f(k(t)) & \text{for } \mu(t) < 1 \end{cases} \tag{Q13.25}$$

where $\mu(t)$ is the co-state variable.

(b) Derive the phase diagram for the model and show that there exists a unique saddle-point stable equilibrium. Show that this equilibrium is in fact reached provided the initial capital stock per worker lies in the interval (k_L, k_U).

Question 15: Intertemporal substitution

Assume that the lifetime utility function is given by:

$$\Lambda \equiv \int_0^\infty U\left(C\left(\tau\right)\right) e^{\rho\tau} d\tau, \tag{Q13.26}$$

where $U\left(\cdot\right)$ is the felicity function and $C\left(\tau\right)$ is consumption. The intertemporal substitution elasticity between $C(t)$ and $C(s)$ is formally defined as:

$$\sigma\left(C(t), C(s)\right) \equiv -\frac{U'\left(C(s)\right)/U'\left(C\left(t\right)\right)}{C(s)/C(t)} \frac{d\left(C\left(s\right)/C(t)\right)}{d\left[U'\left(C\left(s\right)\right)/U'\left(C(t)\right)\right]}. \tag{Q13.27}$$

(a) Provide an interpretation for (Q13.27) involving the marginal rate of substitution between $C(s)$ and $C(t)$.

(b) Derive expressions for $d\left(C(s)/C(t)\right)$ and $d\left[U'\left(C(s)\right)/U'\left(C(t)\right)\right]$ under the assumption that lifetime utility is held constant (so that the derivatives are evaluated along a given indifference curve).

(c) Prove that in the limit, as $C(s) \to C(t)$, the expression for $\sigma\left(\cdot\right)$ converges to:

$$\sigma\left(C(t)\right) \equiv -\frac{U'\left(C(t)\right)}{C(t)U''\left(C(t)\right)}. \tag{Q13.28}$$

Answers

Question 1: Short questions

(a)
- SF1. Y/L grows at rate n_A in steady-state model with labour-augmenting technological change.
- SF2. K/L grows at rate n_A.
- SF3. K/N is constant in balanced growth path. Rate of interest is then also constant.
- SF4. K/Y is constant.
- SF5. Income shares are constant (since these depend on K/N)

(b) The first statement is false. Dynamic inefficiency deals with *over* saving (not undersaving). The second statement is also false. Saving should be discouraged since the capital stock is already too high.

(c) Normality of leisure is the key. If T ↑ then households feel poorer (drop in human wealth) and cut back both consumption and leisure (C ↓ and $(1 - N)$ ↓). Saving goes up and labour supply rises (as does wage income). Output rises and in the long run the capital-labour ratio is restored. Hence, K ↑ and Y ↑.

(d) The Inada conditions deal with the behaviour of marginal factor products in extreme case (See the textbook, section 13.2.1). We compute:

$$F_L = (1 - \alpha)K^\alpha L^{-\alpha},$$
$$F_K = \alpha K^{\alpha-1}L^{1-\alpha}.$$

Holding constant $K = K_0$, we derive:

$$\lim_{L \to 0} F_L = \lim_{L \to 0}(1 - \alpha)K_0^\alpha L^{-\alpha} = (1 - \alpha)K_0^\alpha \lim_{L \to 0} L^{-\alpha} = +\infty,$$
$$\lim_{L \to \infty} F_L = \lim_{L \to \infty}(1 - \alpha)K_0^\alpha L^{-\alpha} = (1 - \alpha)K_0^\alpha \lim_{L \to \infty} L^{-\alpha} = 0,$$

because $\alpha > 0$. Similarly, holding constant $L = L_0$, we find:

$$\lim_{K \to 0} F_K = \lim_{K \to 0} \alpha K^{\alpha-1}L_0^{1-\alpha} = \alpha L_0^{1-\alpha} \lim_{K \to 0} K^{\alpha-1} = +\infty,$$
$$\lim_{K \to \infty} F_K = \lim_{K \to \infty} \alpha K^{\alpha-1}L_0^{1-\alpha} = \alpha L_0^{1-\alpha} \lim_{K \to \infty} K^{\alpha-1} = 0,$$

because $\alpha < 1$ (so that $\alpha - 1 < 0$).

(e) If there are no adjustment costs on physical capital, both human and physical capital would be jump variables. As a result, there would be no transitional dynamics at all (static model). The speed of adjustment would be infinitely high. In the presence of capital adjustment costs there would be a well-defined investment demand. But the adjustment in human wealth is still instantaneous, so that output would still be able to adjust immediately. Note that the MRW model uses an ad hoc savings rate regarding physical capital accumulation, so that the issue of r equalling the rate of time preference does not play a role.

(f) Human wealth is the market value of the agent's time endowment. Human capital is the agent's stock of (technical and other) knowledge that features into the production function of firms. By accumulating human capital, the agent can affect the path of wages it faces. It can thus also affect the size of its human wealth in that way.

In short, human wealth is a component of the agent's wealth (along with financial wealth). Human capital is a productive input (along with physical capital).

(g) By assuming a higher output share of capital. One way to do this is by assuming that capital is defined in broad terms, as the composite of physical and human capital. This is the trick that Mankiw et al. (1992) use.

(h) As is clear from Figure 13.9 in the book, the Keynes-Ramsey capital stock is smaller than the golden-rule capital stock. Technically, this is because the KR interest rate equals $\rho + n$ whilst the GR interest rate equals n. Since ρ is positive (impatience), there is less capital in the KR case. But this all hinges on the absence of tax distortions. If the government somehow distorts the savings decision, for example with savings subsidies, it may induce people to save too much. In that case, the subsidy-distorted KR equilibrium would lie to the right of the GR point.

(i) In a small open economy, the real interest rate is determined in the world capital market and is exogenous to the domestic households and firms. In the absence of adjustment costs, profit maximizing forms want to set the marginal product of capital equal to the rental charge on capital, i.e. $F_K(K, 1) = \bar{r} + \delta$, where we assume exogenous labour supply for convenience. But this means that any exogenous change in $\bar{r}$ will result in an immediate change in the capital stock. Physical capital is a flow variable in this case, and the adjustment speed is infinite. This is not realistic.

Question 2: The Harrod-Domar model

(a) With full employment of both factors of production we have $Y = K/v$ and $Y = L/\alpha$. It follows that in that case:

$$\frac{Y}{K} = \frac{1}{v}, \qquad \frac{Y}{L} = \frac{1}{\alpha}, \qquad \frac{K}{L} = \frac{v}{\alpha}. \tag{A13.1}$$

In terms of Figure A13.1, the points for which both factors are fully employed lie on the dashed line from the origin. If K/L (the actual capital-labour ratio) falls short of v/α then there will be unemployed labour (see point C). If $K/L > v/\alpha$ (in point B) there will be unemployed capital.

(b) By using equations (Q13.2)–(Q13.4) we get $I = \delta K + \dot{K} = sY$, which implies that:

$$\dot{I} = s\dot{Y}, \tag{A13.2}$$

where we have used the fact that s is constant. With full employment of capital

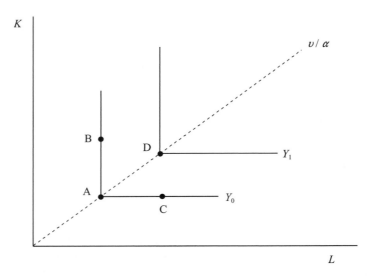

Figure A13.1: Leontief technology

we have $vY = K$ and thus:

$$\dot{Y} = \frac{1}{v}\dot{K} = \frac{1}{v}\left[I - \delta K\right]$$

$$= \frac{1}{v}\left[I - \delta vY\right] \qquad \text{(using } K = vY\text{)}$$

$$= \frac{1}{v}\left[I - \frac{\delta v}{s}I\right] \qquad \text{(using } Y = I/s\text{)}$$

$$= \left(\frac{s - \delta v}{sv}\right)I. \tag{A13.3}$$

Combining (A13.2) and (A13.3) yields:

$$\dot{Y} = \frac{1}{s}\dot{I} = \left(\frac{s - \delta v}{sv}\right)I \quad \Rightarrow$$

$$\frac{\dot{Y}}{I} = \frac{1}{s}\frac{\dot{I}}{I} = \frac{s - \delta v}{sv} \qquad \Rightarrow$$

$$\frac{\dot{Y}}{sY} = \frac{1}{s}\frac{\dot{I}}{I} = \frac{s - \delta v}{sv} \qquad \Rightarrow$$

$$\frac{\dot{Y}}{Y} = \frac{\dot{I}}{I} = \frac{s - \delta v}{v}. \tag{A13.4}$$

The expression in (A13.4) is the so-called *warranted rate of growth*.

(c) With full employment of labour we have $L = \alpha Y$ and thus $\dot{L} = \alpha\dot{Y}$. Since the growth rate of labour is $\dot{L}/L = n_L$ we derive the so-called *natural growth rate*:

$$\frac{\dot{Y}}{Y} = \frac{\frac{1}{\alpha}\dot{L}}{\frac{1}{\alpha}L} = \frac{\dot{L}}{L} = n_L. \tag{A13.5}$$

(d) The Harrod-Domar condition: equality between the natural and warranted growth rates. Using (A13.4) and (A13.5) we can write the HD condition as:

$$n_L = \frac{s - \delta v}{v}. \tag{A13.6}$$

The HD condition is a knife-edge condition as n_L, s, δ, and v are all constants. It follows that for $n_L > \frac{s - \delta v}{v}$ there will be increasing unemployment of labour whilst for $n_L < \frac{s - \delta v}{v}$ there will be increasing unemployment of capital.

(e) In the Solow-Swan model we have a variable capital-labour ratio ($k \equiv K/L$) rather than a fixed one as in the Harrod-Domar model. According to equation (13.7) in the book we have:

$$\dot{k} = s \underbrace{f(k)}_{y} - (\delta + n_L)k. \tag{A13.7}$$

In the steady state we have $\dot{k} = 0$ so that $sy = (\delta + n_L)k$. Rewriting this expression yields:

$$s\frac{y}{k} - \delta = n_L$$
$$\frac{s}{v} - \delta = n_L, \tag{A13.8}$$

where $v \equiv k/y = K/Y$. Equation (A13.8) is the HD condition for the Solow-Swan model. Variations in k (and thus in v) ensure that this HD condition always holds in the steady state. The substitutability of capital and labour thus ensures that the knife-edge problem disappears.

Question 3: The production function

(a) Dropping the time index, we restate (13.8) here for convenience:

$$f(k) \equiv F(k, 1), \tag{A13.9}$$

where $k \equiv K/L$. Obviously, since, $y = f(k)$, we also have:

$$Y = Lf(k), \tag{A13.10}$$

so that:

$$F_K \equiv \frac{\partial Y}{\partial K} = Lf'(k)\frac{dk}{dK} = f'(k), \tag{A13.11}$$

$$F_L \equiv \frac{\partial Y}{\partial L} = f(k) + Lf'(k)\frac{dk}{dL} = f(k) - L\frac{K}{L^2}f'(k) = f(k) - kf'(k), \tag{A13.12}$$

where we use the fact that $dk/dK = 1/L$ and $dk/dL = -K/L^2$.

(b) We have shown in (A13.11) that $f'(k) = F_K$. Property (P2) thus establishes that $f'(k) > 0$, whilst property (P3) ensures that $\lim_{k \to 0} f'(k) = +\infty$ and $\lim_{k \to \infty} f'(k) = 0$.

(c) The marginal productivity conditions for labour and capital are:

$$W = F_L, \qquad r + \delta = F_K. \tag{A13.13}$$

For the Cobb-Douglas production function, $Y = AK^\alpha L^{1-\alpha}$, we find that these expression amount to:

$$W = (1 - \alpha)Ak^\alpha, \tag{A13.14}$$

$$r + \delta = \alpha Ak^{\alpha-1}. \tag{A13.15}$$

The following limiting results can be derived with the aid of (A13.14)–(A13.15):

$$\begin{aligned} \lim_{k \to 0} W = 0, & \qquad \lim_{k \to 0}(r + \delta) = \infty \\ \lim_{k \to \infty} W = \infty, & \qquad \lim_{k \to \infty}(r + \delta) = 0 \end{aligned} \tag{A13.16}$$

For $k \in [0, \infty)$ we can solve from (A13.14)–(A13.15):

$$\left[\frac{W}{(1 - \alpha)A}\right]^{1/\alpha} = k = \left[\frac{r + \delta}{\alpha A}\right]^{1/(\alpha-1)}. \tag{A13.17}$$

Solving the outermost expressions yields the factor price frontier:

$$1 = \left[\frac{W}{(1 - \alpha)A}\right]^{1/\alpha} \left[\frac{r + \delta}{\alpha A}\right]^{1/(1-\alpha)} \quad \Leftrightarrow$$

$$W = A^{1/(1-\alpha)} \left[\frac{\alpha}{r + \delta}\right]^{\alpha/(1-\alpha)}. \tag{A13.18}$$

The factor price frontier has been illustrated in Figure A13.2. An increase in general productivity causes an outward shifts in the factor price frontier, say from FPF_0 to FPF_1.

Question 4: The wage-rental ratio

(a) The wage-rental ratio is:

$$\omega(k) \equiv \frac{W}{r + \delta} = \frac{F_L}{F_K} = \frac{f(k) - kf'(k)}{f'(k)}. \tag{A13.19}$$

Intuitively, ω only depends on k because technology features constant returns to scale so that both F_L and F_K only depend on k. We can invert $\omega(k)$ because its slope, $\omega'(k)$, is single signed. After some manipulations we find:

$$\begin{aligned} \omega'(k) &= \frac{f'(k)\left[f'(k) - f'(k) - kf''(k)\right] - \left[f(k) - kf'(k)\right]f''(k)}{[f'(k)]^2} \\ &= -\frac{f(k)f''(k)}{[f'(k)]^2} > 0, \qquad \text{for } k \in (0, \infty), \end{aligned} \tag{A13.20}$$

where the sign follows from the fact that $f(k) > 0$, $f'(k) > 0$, and $f''(k) < 0$ for $k \in (0, \infty)$.

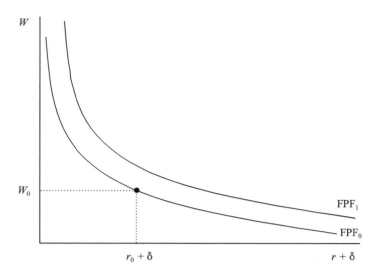

Figure A13.2: The factor price frontier

(b) We illustrate the factor share in Figure A13.3. The capital stock is k^* and the line that is tangent to the production function at point E_0 represents the rental rate on capital, $r^* + \delta$. It follows that E_0D represent the payment to capital, $(r^* + \delta)k^*$, whilst DF is the wage payment, W^*. Since DF is the same as AB, we find that $(r^* + \delta)$ =AB/BC, i.e. the segment BC is the wage-rental ration, $\omega(k)$. Formally, we observe that:

$$r^* + \delta = \frac{f(k^*)}{k - \underline{k}} \quad \Leftrightarrow \quad k - \underline{k} = \frac{f(k^*)}{r^* + \delta} = \frac{f(k^*)}{f'(k^*)} \quad \Leftrightarrow$$

$$-\underline{k} = \frac{f(k^*) - k^* f'(k^*)}{f'(k^*)} = \frac{W^*}{r^* + \delta} \equiv \omega. \tag{A13.21}$$

(c) We must relate the substitution elasticity, defined in (Q13.6), to the properties of the per capital production function, $f(k)$. By straightforward differentiation we find:

$$F_L = f(k) - kf'(k), \tag{A13.22}$$

$$F_K = f'(k), \tag{A13.23}$$

$$F_{LK} = F_{KL} = -\frac{K}{L^2} f''(k), \tag{A13.24}$$

and we recall that $Y = Lf(k)$. By using these results in (Q13.6) we find after some manipulations:

$$\sigma_{KL} \equiv \frac{[f(k) - kf'(k)] f'(k)}{-Lf(k) (K/L^2) f''(k)} = -\frac{[f(k) - kf'(k)] f'(k)}{kf(k)f''(k)}. \tag{A13.25}$$

By using (A13.20) and (A13.25), the elasticity of the $\xi(\omega)$ function can be determined:

$$\frac{d\omega}{dk} \frac{k}{\omega} = -\frac{f(k)f''(k)}{[f'(k)]^2} \frac{kf'(k)}{f(k) - kf'(k)} = \frac{-kf(k)f''(k)}{[f(k) - kf'(k)] f'(k)} = \frac{1}{\sigma_{KL}}. \tag{A13.26}$$

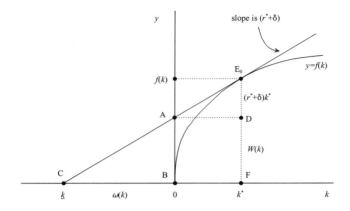

Figure A13.3: Factor shares and the wage-rental ratio

It follows from (A13.26) that:

$$\frac{dk}{d\omega}\frac{\omega}{k} = \sigma_{KL}. \tag{A13.27}$$

Question 5: The Solow-Swan model

(a) The fundamental differential equation is given by equation (13.7) in the book:

$$\dot{k} = sf(k) - (\delta + n_L)k \quad \Leftrightarrow$$

$$\frac{\dot{k}}{s} = \underbrace{f(k)}_{y} - \frac{\delta + n_L}{s}k. \tag{A13.28}$$

We draw the two terms on the right-hand side of (A13.28) in Figure A13.4. The steady-state is indicated by stars (k^* and y^*). Recall that under perfect competition the factor prices satisfy:

$$r = f'(k) - \delta, \tag{A13.29}$$

$$W = f(k) - kf'(k). \tag{A13.30}$$

In point E_0 we have that the slope of $f(k^*)$ equals $r^* + \delta$, i.e. $f'(k^*) = r^* + \delta$. Since the slope is represented by the ratio E_0A/BA we get:

$$r^* + \delta = \frac{E_0A}{BA} = \frac{E_0A}{k^*} \quad \Rightarrow \quad E_0A = (r^* + \delta)k^*. \tag{A13.31}$$

Hence, the line segment E_0A represents the gross income of capital. We derive:

$$\begin{aligned} W^* &= f(k^*) - k^*f'(k^*) \\ &= y^* - (r^* + \delta)k^* \\ &= \text{segment BC}. \end{aligned} \tag{A13.32}$$

The line segment BC thus represents wage income.

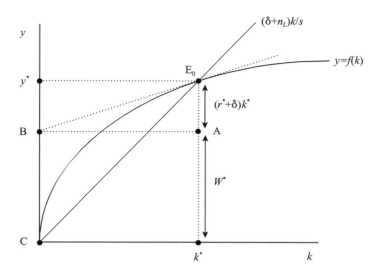

Figure A13.4: Factor shares

(b) With Harrod-neutral technological progress the fundamental differential equation becomes:

$$\dot{k} = sf(k) - (\delta + n_L + n_A)k \quad \Leftrightarrow$$

$$\frac{\dot{k}}{s} = \underbrace{f(k)}_{y} - \frac{\delta + n_L + n_A}{s}k, \tag{A13.33}$$

where $k \equiv K/N$, $N = AL$, and $\dot{N}/N = n_A + n_L$. In the steady state we have:

$$f(k^*) = \left(\frac{\delta + n_L + n_A}{s}\right)k^*. \tag{A13.34}$$

Competitive firms solve the following maximization problem:

$$\max_{\{K,L\}} \Pi \equiv F(K, \underbrace{AL}_{N}) - (r + \delta)K - WL. \tag{A13.35}$$

The first-order conditions are:

$$\frac{\partial \Pi}{\partial K} = 0: \quad F_K = r + \delta, \tag{A13.36}$$

$$\frac{\partial \Pi}{\partial L} = 0: \quad F_N A = W. \tag{A13.37}$$

Since $W^* = AF_N(k^*, 1)$ and k^* is constant along the balanced growth path, we have:

$$\frac{\dot{W}^*}{W^*} = \frac{\dot{A}}{A} = n_A, \tag{A13.38}$$

i.e. the wage grows exponentially at rate n_A along the BGP. Since the production function features constant returns to scale (CRTS) we derive:

$$Y = F_K K + F_N N$$
$$= (r + \delta)K + \frac{W}{A}N$$
$$= (r + \delta)K + WL \quad \Rightarrow$$
$$1 = (r + \delta)\frac{K}{Y} + \frac{WL}{Y}. \tag{A13.39}$$

Along the balanced growth path (BGP) we have $y^* = f(k^*)$ and:

$$\left(\frac{\dot{K}}{K}\right)^* = \left(\frac{\dot{Y}}{Y}\right)^* = \left(\frac{\dot{N}}{N}\right)^* = n_L + n_A. \tag{A13.40}$$

Hence, K/Y is constant as is WL/Y $((\dot{W}/W)^* = n_A, (\dot{L}/L) = n_L$, and $(\dot{Y}/Y)^* = n_A + n_L)$. Next we define $f(k) \equiv F(K/N, 1) = Y/N$. Hence,

$$Y = NF\left(\frac{K}{N}, 1\right). \tag{A13.41}$$

Differentiating (A13.41) with respect to N yields:

$$[F_N \equiv] \frac{\partial Y}{\partial N} = F\left(\frac{K}{N}, 1\right) + NF_K(\cdot)\frac{-K}{N^2}$$
$$= f(k) - F_K(\cdot)k. \tag{A13.42}$$

Differentiating (A13.41) with respect to K yields:

$$[F_K \equiv] \frac{\partial Y}{\partial K} = NF_K(\cdot)\frac{1}{N} = F_K\left(\frac{K}{N}, 1\right). \tag{A13.43}$$

Similarly, since $Y = Nf(k)$, we have that:

$$\frac{\partial Y}{\partial K} = Nf'(k)\frac{1}{N} = f'(k). \tag{A13.44}$$

Combining the results we obtain:

$$W = AF_N = A\left[f(k) - kf'(k)\right], \tag{A13.45}$$
$$r + \delta = F_K = f'(k). \tag{A13.46}$$

We illustrate the factor shares in Figure A13.5.

(c) This question is loosely based on Branson (1972, p. 396). We assume that δ and s are constant but that n_L is an S-shaped function of per capita income. As Figure A13.6 shows, there are three steady-state equilibria: two stable ones (at E_0 and E_2) and one unstable one (at E_1). A less developed country may get stuck in the low-level steady-state equilibrium at E_0. In particular, if it starts out with k less than k_U^* then the population growth rate is too high (relative to saving) to allow net capital accumulation. The economy will move to E_0 as a result. A boost in the savings rate (or a windfall donation of k by rich countries) may get the economy away from the low-level trap.

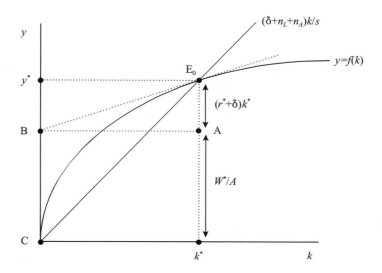

Figure A13.5: Factor shares with Harrod-neutral technical progress

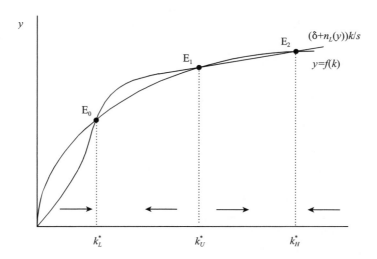

Figure A13.6: Poverty trap and the big push

Question 6: The Pasinetti model

(a) We know that with a constant returns to scale technology and perfectly competitive firms output is fully exhausted by factor payments, i.e.:

$$Y(t) = W(t)L(t) + (r(t) + \delta)K(t), \tag{A13.47}$$

where $r(t)$ is the interest rate and δ is the depreciation rate of capital ($r(t) + \delta$ is the rental price of capital). By using (A13.47) in (Q13.7) we obtain:

$$S(t) = s_w W(t)L(t) + s_p [Y(t) - W(t)L(t)] \quad \Rightarrow$$

$$\frac{S(t)}{Y(t)} = s_w \frac{Y(t) - (r(t) + \delta)K(t)}{Y(t)} + s_p \frac{(r(t) + \delta)K(t)}{Y(t)}$$

$$= s_w + (s_p - s_w)(r(t) + \delta)v(t) \equiv s(t), \tag{A13.48}$$

where $v(t) \equiv K(t)/Y(t)$ is the capital-output ratio.

(b) The fundamental differential equation becomes:

$$\dot{k}(t) = s(t)f(k(t)) - (\delta + n_L)k(t) \quad \Rightarrow$$

$$\dot{k}(t) = [s_w + (s_p - s_w)\omega_K(\cdot)] y(t) - (\delta + n_L)k(t), \tag{A13.49}$$

where $\omega_K(\cdot) \equiv (r(t) + \delta)k(t)/y(t)$ is the share of capital income. For the Cobb-Douglas production function, $y(t) = k(t)^\alpha$, we have that $\omega_K(\cdot) = \alpha$ so that equation (A13.49) simplifies to:

$$\dot{k}(t) = [(1-\alpha)s_w + \alpha s_p] y(t) - (\delta + n_L)k(t) \tag{A13.50}$$

The fundamental differential equation for the Cobb-Douglas case takes the same form as Figure 13.1. For the general CES case, the propensity to save depends on the capital stock. We find that in that case $\omega_K(\cdot)$ can be written as:

$$\omega_K(k(t)) = \alpha \left(\frac{f(k(t))}{k(t)} \right)^{(1-\sigma_{KL})/\sigma_{KL}}. \tag{A13.51}$$

By differentiating (A13.51) we obtain:

$$\frac{d\omega_K(t)}{\omega_K(t)} = \frac{\sigma_{KL} - 1}{\sigma_{KL}} [1 - \omega_K(t)] \frac{dk(t)}{k(t)}. \tag{A13.52}$$

From (A13.52) we find that $\omega'_K(\cdot) > 0$ (< 0) if $\sigma_{KL} > 1$ (< 1). The capital share is increasing (decreasing) in k if the substitution elasticity between labour and capital is larger (smaller) than unity. In the question we consider the case for which $0 < \sigma_{KL} \leq 1$. This means, by equations (14.6)–(14.7) in the book, that $\omega_K(0) = 1$ and $\omega_K(\infty) = 0$.

By using the definition for $s(t)$ (given in (Q13.8)) we can rewrite (A13.49) as:

$$\frac{1}{s(t)}\dot{k}(t) = f(k(t)) - \phi(k(t))k(t), \tag{A13.53}$$

$$\phi(k(t)) \equiv \frac{\delta + n_L}{[s_w + (s_p - s_w)\omega_K(k(t))]}. \tag{A13.54}$$

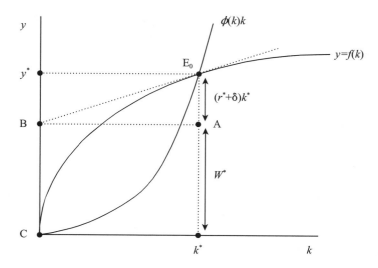

Figure A13.7: Factor shares in the Pasinetti model

It is clear from the results obtained thus far that $\phi(0) = (\delta + n_L)/s_p$, $\phi(\infty) = (\delta + n_L)/s_w$, $\phi(0) < \phi(\infty)$ (since $s_w < s_p$), and:

$$\phi'(k(t)) = -\frac{(\delta + n_L)(s_p - s_w)\omega'_K(\cdot)}{\left[s_w + (s_p - s_w)\omega_K(k(t))\right]^2} > 0. \tag{A13.55}$$

It follows that the phase diagram for the CES case is a drawn in Figure A13.7.

(c) Using the same approach as before, we can identify the steady-state factor shares in Figure A13.7.

Question 7: The Solow-Swan model with population growth

(a) We continue to work with capital per member of the population, i.e. $k(t) \equiv K(t)/L(t)$. Of course, at any moment in time $L(t)$ is predetermined but $N(t)$ can jump. The production function features CRTS and can thus be written as:

$$Y(t) = F(K(t), N(t)) = L(t)F\left(\frac{K(t)}{L(t)}, \frac{N(t)}{L(t)}\right) \quad \Rightarrow$$

$$y(t) = F(k(t), n(t)), \tag{A13.56}$$

where $y(t) \equiv Y(t)/L(t)$ and $n(t) \equiv N(t)/L(t)$. Since $F(\cdot)$ features CRTS we also have:

$$y(t) = F_k(\cdot)k(t) + F_n(\cdot)n(t), \tag{A13.57}$$

where $F_k = F_K$ and $F_n = F_N$.

Competitive firms still hire labour and capital according to the usual productivity conditions:

$$r(t) + \delta = F_K(K(t), N(t)) = F_k(k(t), n(t)), \tag{A13.58}$$

$$W(t) = F_N(K(t), N(t)) = F_n(k(t), n(t)). \tag{A13.59}$$

Of course, since $F(\cdot)$ features constant returns to scale, $F_N(\cdot)$ is homogeneous of degree zero so that (A13.59) implies that the wage depends only on k/n. For the Cobb-Douglas production function we find that (A13.56), (A13.58), and (A13.59) simplify to:

$$y(t) = k(t)^\alpha n(t)^{1-\alpha}, \tag{A13.60}$$

$$r(t) + \delta = \alpha \left(\frac{n(t)}{k(t)} \right)^{1-\alpha}, \tag{A13.61}$$

$$W(t) = (1-\alpha) \left(\frac{k(t)}{n(t)} \right)^\alpha. \tag{A13.62}$$

The labour market is described by (A13.62) and the rewritten version of (Q13.9):

$$p\left(W(t)\right) = n(t). \tag{A13.63}$$

By loglinearizing (A13.62)–(A13.63) around the steady state we find:

$$\tilde{W}(t) = \alpha \left[\tilde{k}(t) - \tilde{n}(t) \right], \tag{A13.64}$$

$$\eta_{pW} \tilde{W}(t) = \tilde{n}(t), \tag{A13.65}$$

where $\tilde{W}(t) \equiv dW(t)/W$, $\tilde{k}(t) \equiv dk(t)/k$, $\tilde{n}(t) \equiv dn(t)/n$, and $\eta_{pW} \equiv Wp'(\cdot)/p(\cdot)$ is the elasticity of the participation rate function. We observe (from (A13.64)) that for the Cobb-Douglas production function $\eta_{Wk} = \alpha$. By solving (A13.64)–(A13.65) we find (provided $1 + \alpha\eta_{pW} \neq 0$):

$$\tilde{n}(t) = \frac{\alpha\eta_{pW}}{1 + \alpha\eta_{pW}} \tilde{k}(t), \qquad \tilde{W}(t) = \frac{\alpha}{1 + \alpha\eta_{pW}} \tilde{k}(t). \tag{A13.66}$$

The first expression in (A13.66) shows that $n(t)$ is some function of $k(t)$ in the generalized model. For future reference, we denote this functional relationship by:

$$n(t) = g\left(k(t)\right), \tag{A13.67}$$

where the elasticity of $g(\cdot)$ is given in (A13.66). The fundamental differential equation for the per capita capital stock is now:

$$\dot{k}(t) = sk(t)^\alpha g\left(k(t)\right)^{1-\alpha} - (\delta + n_L)k(t), \tag{A13.68}$$

where s is the constant savings rate. By loglinearizing (A13.68) around the steady state we find after a number of steps:

$$\frac{d\dot{k}(t)}{k} = s\left[\alpha k^{\alpha-1} g^{1-\alpha} \frac{dk(t)}{k} + (1-\alpha)k^\alpha g^{-\alpha} \frac{dg}{k} \right] - (\delta + n_L)\frac{dk(t)}{k}$$

$$\dot{\tilde{k}}(t) = sk^{\alpha-1}g^{1-\alpha} \left[\alpha\tilde{k}(t) + (1-\alpha)\tilde{g}(t) \right] - (\delta + n_L)\tilde{k}(t)$$

$$= -(\delta + n_L)(1-\alpha) \left[\tilde{k}(t) - \tilde{g}(t) \right], \tag{A13.69}$$

where $\dot{\tilde{k}}(t) \equiv d\dot{k}(t)/k$, $\tilde{g}(t) \equiv dg(t)/g$, and we have used the fact that $sk^{\alpha-1}g^{1-\alpha} = \delta + n_L$ in the steady state. We know from (A13.66)–(A13.67) that:

$$\tilde{g}(t) = \frac{\alpha\eta_{pW}}{1 + \alpha\eta_{pW}} \tilde{k}(t). \tag{A13.70}$$

By using (A13.70) in (A13.69) we find that:

$$\dot{\tilde{k}}(t) = -(\delta + n_L)(1-\alpha) \left[1 - \frac{\alpha\eta_{pW}}{1+\alpha\eta_{pW}} \right] \tilde{k}(t)$$
$$= -\frac{(\delta + n_L)(1-\alpha)}{1+\alpha\eta_{pW}} \tilde{k}(t), \tag{A13.71}$$

where the term in round brackets represents the speed of convergence in the economy. In the standard model, participation is exogenous, $\eta_{pW} = 0$, and the convergence speed is equal to $(\delta + n_L)(1-\alpha)$ (see section 13.3.3 in the book). With endogenous participation, both $\eta_{Wk} = \alpha$ and η_{pW} affect the speed of convergence.

(b) The likely sign of η_{pW} is positive. This is the case if the substitution effect dominates the income effect in labour supply. This is the usual assumption we make, despite the fact that empirical evidence in support of this assumption is rather scarce. For the Cobb-Douglas case we have already seen that $\eta_{Wk} = \alpha$ so that it follows automatically that $0 < \eta_{Wk} < 1$.

For the CES case it is more than likely that $0 < \eta_{Wk} < 1$ continues to hold. This can be shown as follows. We write (A13.59) in implicit form as $W = F_n(k,n)$ and note that:

$$\eta_{Wk} \equiv \frac{kW_k}{W} = \frac{kF_{NK}L}{F_N} = \frac{KF_{NK}}{F_N} = \frac{KF_K}{Y}\frac{YF_{NK}}{F_NF_K} = \frac{\omega_K}{\sigma_{KN}}, \tag{A13.72}$$

where $\omega_K \equiv KF_K/Y$ is the income share of capital and $\sigma_{KN} \equiv F_NF_K/(YF_{NK})$ is the substitution elasticity between capital and labour. Since $0 < \omega_K \ll 1$ and $\sigma_{KN} \approx 1$ it follows that $0 < \eta_{Wk} < 1$ is quite likely.

(c) In part (b) we motivate the assumption that $\eta_{pW} > 0$. It then follows from (A13.71) that the convergence speed is slower in the extended model than in the standard Solow-Swan model. Intuitively, as k rises during transition so does the wage rate and the participation rate. But the additional labour that is thus released needs to be equipped with capital also. The participation response slows down the convergence speed.

Question 8: Some mathematics

(a) The household's lifetime utility function is given in (13.68) which is restated here for convenience:

$$\Lambda(0) \equiv \int_0^\infty U(c(t))e^{-\rho t}dt, \tag{A13.73}$$

with $\rho > 0$. The household budget identity and solvency condition are:

$$\dot{a}(t) \equiv [r(t) - n]a(t) + W(t) - c(t), \tag{A13.74}$$
$$\lim_{t\to\infty} a(t)\exp\left[-\int_0^t [r(\tau) - n]\,d\tau \right] = 0. \tag{A13.75}$$

The current-value Hamiltonian is defined as:

$$\mathcal{H} \equiv U(c(t)) + \mu(t)\Big[[r(t) - n]a(t) + W(t) - c(t) \Big], \tag{A13.76}$$

where $c(t)$ is the control variable, $a(t)$ is the state variable, and $\mu(t)$ is the co-state variable. The (interesting) first-order conditions are $\partial \mathcal{H} / \partial c(t) = 0$ and $-\partial \mathcal{H} / \partial a(t) = \dot{\mu}(t) - \rho \mu(t)$:

$$U'(c(t)) = \mu(t), \tag{A13.77}$$

$$\dot{\mu}(t) - \rho \mu(t) = -[r(t) - n]\,\mu(t). \tag{A13.78}$$

We can rewrite (A13.78) as follows:

$$\frac{\dot{\mu}(t)}{\mu(t)} = \rho + n - r(t). \tag{A13.79}$$

By differentiating (A13.77) with respect to time, we find:

$$U''(c(t))\dot{c}(t) = \dot{\mu}(t). \tag{A13.80}$$

By combining (A13.80) and (A13.77) we find:

$$\frac{c(t)U''(c(t))}{U'(c(t))}\frac{\dot{c}(t)}{c(t)} = \frac{\dot{\mu}(t)}{\mu(t)}. \tag{A13.81}$$

Finally, equations (A13.79) and (A13.80) can be combined to yield the consumption Euler equation:

$$\frac{\dot{c}(t)}{c(t)} = \sigma(c(t))\,[r(t) - n - \rho]\,, \tag{A13.82}$$

where $\sigma(\cdot)$ is the intertemporal substitution elasticity:

$$\sigma(c(t)) \equiv -\frac{U'(c(t))}{c(t)U''(c(t))}. \tag{A13.83}$$

(b) The model consists of (A13.82) and:

$$\dot{k}(t) = f(k(t)) - c(t) - (\delta + n)\,k(t), \tag{A13.84}$$

$$r(t) = f'(k(t)) - \delta. \tag{A13.85}$$

Equation (A13.84) is the capital accumulation equation (see (T1.2) in Table 13.1) and equation (A13.85) is the rental rate expression (T1.3). We assume that marginal felicity is positive throughout, i.e. $U'(c(t)) > 0$ for all $c(t)$. But this means that we can invert $U'(c(t))$ and write (A13.77) as:

$$c(t) = V(\mu(t)), \tag{A13.86}$$

where $V(\cdot) \equiv U'^{-1}(\cdot)$. (For example, if $U(c(t)) \equiv \ln c(t)$ then $U'(c(t)) \equiv 1/c(t)$ and $V[\mu(t)] = 1/\mu(t)$.) We find easily that $V'(\cdot) = 1/U''(\cdot) < 0$ (since $U''(\cdot) < 0$). We illustrate the typical $V(\cdot)$ function in the left-hand panel of Figure A13.8. Note that positive consumption is measured along the horizontal axis in the left-hand panel.

By using (A13.86) in (A13.84) we find that the capital accumulation equation can be written in terms of k and μ:

$$\dot{k}(t) = f(k(t)) - V(\mu(t)) - (\delta + n)\,k(t). \tag{A13.87}$$

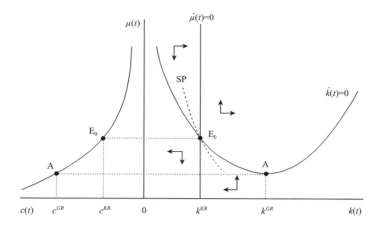

Figure A13.8: Phase diagram in (μ, k) space

The $\dot{k} = 0$ line has been drawn in the right-hand panel of Figure A13.8. Its slope is given by:

$$\left(\frac{d\mu}{dk} \right)_{\dot{k}=0} = \frac{f'(k) - (\delta + n)}{V'(\mu)} \lessgtr 0 \text{ for } k \lesseqgtr k^{GR}, \tag{A13.88}$$

where k^{GR} is the golden-rule capital stock $(f'(k^{GR}) \equiv \delta + n)$. For points above (below) the $\dot{k} = 0$ line, μ is too high (too low), V is too low (too high) and capital increases (decreases). This is indicated with horizontal arrows in Figure A13.8.

By using (A13.85) in (A13.79) we find that the dynamics of μ is given by:

$$\frac{\dot{\mu}(t)}{\mu(t)} = \rho + \delta + n - f'(k(t)). \tag{A13.89}$$

The $\dot{\mu} = 0$ line is vertical and defines a unique capital-labour ratio, k^{KR}, which is smaller than k^{GR} $(f'(k^{KR}) \equiv \rho + \delta + n)$. For points to the right (left) of the $\dot{\mu} = 0$ line, the capital stock is too high (too low) and the marginal product of capital is too low (too high) so that μ rises (falls) over time. This is indicated with vertical arrows in Figure A13.8.

The configuration of arrows confirms that the steady-state equilibrium at E_0 is saddle-point stable. The saddle path is downward sloping and has been drawn as SP in Figure A13.8. For all points on the saddle path we can find the corresponding consumption levels in the left-hand panel of Figure A13.8.

(c) In (13.57) we postulate that household utility depends only on felicity per family member. In equation (Q13.11) we instead postulate that utility depends on total felicity of the family, which is felicity per family member times the number of family members. Equation (Q13.11) is a *Benthamite welfare function* (named after Jeremy Bentham) whereas (13.57) is a *Millian welfare function* (named after John Stuart Mill).

We can restate the optimization problem in a more convenient form by noting that $L(t) = L(0)e^{nt}$ so that (Q13.11) is:

$$
\begin{aligned}
\Lambda(0) &\equiv \int_0^\infty L(0)e^{nt}U(c(t))e^{-\rho t}dt \\
&= \int_0^\infty U(c(t))e^{-(\rho-n)t}dt,
\end{aligned}
\tag{A13.90}
$$

where we have normalized $L(0)$ to unity in the final step. It must be noted that the integral on the right-hand side of (A13.90) only converges if $\rho > n$. Provided this condition holds, and there is not too much population growth relative to the rate of time preference, the problem is again standard. The only thing that is different is that the households adopts a lower discount rate, $\rho^* \equiv \rho - n$, to evaluate future felicity.

The household maximizes (A13.90) subject to (A13.74)–(A13.75), taking initial assets, $a(0)$, as given. The current-value Hamiltonian is still given by (A13.76) but the first-order conditions are now $\partial \mathcal{H}/\partial c(t) = 0$ and $-\partial \mathcal{H}/\partial a(t) = \dot{\mu}(t) - (\rho - n)\mu(t)$:

$$
U'(c(t)) = \mu(t),
\tag{A13.91}
$$
$$
\dot{\mu}(t) - (\rho - n)\mu(t) = -[r(t) - n]\,\mu(t).
\tag{A13.92}
$$

By combining (A13.91)–(A13.92) we find that the consumption Euler equation is now:

$$
\frac{\dot{c}(t)}{c(t)} = \sigma(c(t))\,[r(t) - \rho].
\tag{A13.93}
$$

With the alternative utility function (Q13.11), the rate of population growth vanishes from the Euler equation. As a result, the steady-state interest rate is equal to the rate of time preference, just as in the model with a constant population.

Question 9: Optimal investment

(a) The model in this part of the question is:

$$
Y(t) = C(t) + I(t),
\tag{A13.94}
$$
$$
I(t) = \dot{K}(t),
\tag{A13.95}
$$
$$
Y(t) = F(K(t), L(t)),
\tag{A13.96}
$$

where we have used the fact that there is no government consumption ($G(t) = 0$) and capital does not depreciate ($\delta = 0$). By using (A13.94)–(A13.96) we can derive:

$$
y(t) = c(t) + \dot{k}(t) + n_L k(t),
\tag{A13.97}
$$
$$
y(t) = f(k(t)),
\tag{A13.98}
$$

where $y \equiv Y/L$, $k \equiv K/L$, and $c \equiv C/L$. By substituting $c(t) = \bar{c}$ and (A13.98) into (A13.97) we find that:

$$\dot{k}(t) = f(k(t)) - \bar{c} - n_L k(t) \qquad \Leftrightarrow$$

$$\gamma_k(t) \left[\equiv \frac{\dot{k}(t)}{k(t)} \right] = \frac{f(k(t)) - \bar{c}}{k(t)} - n_L \qquad \Leftrightarrow$$

$$\gamma_K(t) \left[\equiv \frac{\dot{K}(t)}{K(t)} = \gamma_k(t) + n_L \right] = \frac{f(k(t)) - \bar{c}}{k(t)}. \tag{A13.99}$$

By maximizing $\gamma_K(t)$ by choice of $k(t)$ we find from (A13.99):

$$\frac{d\gamma_K(t)}{dk(t)} = \frac{k(t)f'(k(t)) - [f(k(t)) - \bar{c}]}{[k(t)]^2}$$

$$= \frac{1}{k(t)} \left[f'(k(t)) - \frac{f(k(t)) - \bar{c}}{k(t)} \right] = 0. \tag{A13.100}$$

In the neoclassical model (without depreciation) the capital rental rate expression is $r(t) = f'(k(t))$. By using this expression as well as (A13.99) in (A13.100) we find the desired result.

$$\frac{d\gamma_K(t)}{dk(t)} = \frac{r(t) - \gamma_K(t)}{k(t)} = 0 \quad \Leftrightarrow \quad r(t) = \gamma_K(t). \tag{A13.101}$$

According to (A13.101), the growth rate of the capital stock is maximized in a point for which the rate of interest equals this growth rate.

(b) In Figure A13.9 we draw the expression for the growth rate of capital for the Cobb-Douglas case, with $y = k^{\alpha}$. Dropping the time index, we find that for the Cobb-Douglas case, equation (A13.99) simplifies to:

$$\gamma_K = \frac{k^{\alpha} - \bar{c}}{k}. \tag{A13.102}$$

We derive the following properties:

$$\lim_{k \to 0} \gamma_K = -\infty, \qquad \lim_{k \to 0} \gamma_K = 0, \tag{A13.103}$$

$$\frac{d\gamma_K}{dk} = \frac{\bar{c} - (1 - \alpha)k^{\alpha}}{k^2}, \tag{A13.104}$$

$$\frac{d^2\gamma_K}{dk^2} = \frac{(1 - \alpha)(2 - \alpha)k^{\alpha} - 2\bar{c}}{k^3}. \tag{A13.105}$$

It follows from (A13.105) that $d^2\gamma_K/dk^2 < 0$ in the point for which γ_K is optimized, i.e. (A13.101) describes a maximum. We observe, from equation (A13.102), that point k^0 in Figure A13.9 is defined as follows:

$$k^0 \equiv (\bar{c})^{1/\alpha}. \tag{A13.106}$$

The maximum point, k^*, is found by setting $d\gamma_K/dk = 0$ in (A13.104) and solving for k:

$$k^* \equiv \left(\frac{\bar{c}}{1 - \alpha} \right)^{1/\alpha}. \tag{A13.107}$$

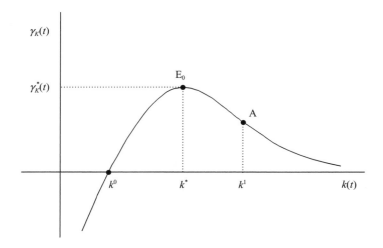

Figure A13.9: The growth rate of the capital stock

Finally, γ_K has an inflexion point for $k = k^1$:

$$k^1 = \left(\frac{2}{2-\alpha}\right)^{1/\alpha}\left(\frac{\bar{c}}{1-\alpha}\right)^{1/\alpha} > k^*. \tag{A13.108}$$

(c) With depreciation of capital, equation (A13.95) changes to:

$$I(t) = \dot{K}(t) + \delta K(t), \tag{A13.109}$$

so that (A13.97) is generalized to:

$$y(t) = c(t) + \dot{k}(t) + (\delta + n_L)\,k(t), \tag{A13.110}$$

and (A13.99) becomes:

$$\gamma_K(t) = \frac{f\left(k(t)\right) - \bar{c}}{k(t)} - \delta. \tag{A13.111}$$

The first-order condition for a maximum of γ_K is now:

$$\begin{aligned}
\frac{d\gamma_K(t)}{dk(t)} &= \frac{k(t)f'\left(k(t)\right) - \left[f\left(k(t)\right) - \bar{c}\right]}{[k(t)]^2} \\
&= \frac{1}{k(t)}\left[f'\left(k(t)\right) - \left(\frac{f\left(k(t)\right) - \bar{c}}{k(t)}\right)\right] \\
&= \frac{r(t) + \delta - (\gamma_K(t) + \delta)}{k(t)} = 0, \tag{A13.112}
\end{aligned}$$

where we have used the fact that $f'\left(k(t)\right) = r(t) + \delta$. It follows from (A13.112) that the depreciation rate drops out of the first-order condition. This is rather obvious as it enters the expression to be maximized linearly–see (A13.111).

Question 10: Welfare of future generations

The fundamental differential equation for capital (per worker) is:

$$\dot{k}(t) = f(k(t)) - c(t) - \delta k(t). \tag{A13.113}$$

The social planner chooses paths for consumption and the capital stock such that R is minimized, subject to (A13.113) and taking as given the initial capital stock, $k(0)$. Of course minimizing R is the same as maximizing $-R$, so the Hamiltonian takes the following format:

$$\mathcal{H} \equiv [U(c(t)) - B] + \mu(\tau)\Big[f(k(t)) - c(t) - \delta k(t) \Big]. \tag{A13.114}$$

The first-order conditions are $\partial \mathcal{H}/\partial c(t) = 0$ and $-\partial \mathcal{H}/\partial k(t) = \dot{\mu}(t)$ (no discounting) so:

$$U'(c(t)) = \mu(t), \tag{A13.115}$$

$$f'(k(t)) - \delta = -\frac{\dot{\mu}(t)}{\mu(t)}. \tag{A13.116}$$

By combining (A13.115)–(A13.116) we find the consumption Euler equation:

$$\frac{\dot{c}(t)}{c(t)} = \sigma(c(t))r(t), \tag{A13.117}$$

where $r(t) \equiv f'(k(t)) - \delta$ is the interest rate and $\sigma(\cdot)$ is the intertemporal substitution elasticity:

$$\sigma(c(t)) \equiv -\frac{U'(c(t))}{c(t)U''(c(t))}. \tag{A13.118}$$

The phase diagram is presented in Figure A13.10. The $\dot{k} = 0$ line is derived from (A13.113) and takes the following form:

$$c(t) = f(k(t)) - \delta k(t). \tag{A13.119}$$

It follows from (A13.119) (and the Inada conditions) that consumption is zero for $k = 0$ and for $k = k^{MAX}$. Consumption is maximized for the golden-rule capital stock, k^{GR}, where $f'(k^{GR}) = \delta$ and $c^{GR} = f(k^{GR}) - \delta k^{GR}$. For points below (above) the $\dot{k} = 0$ line, consumption is too low (too high) and the capital stock rises (falls) over time. This has been indicated with horizontal arrows in Figure A13.10.

According to (A13.118), the $\dot{c} = 0$ line is the line for which the interest rate is zero. This defines a unique (golden-rule) capital stock, k^{GR}. For points to the left (right) of the $\dot{c} = 0$ line, capital is scarce (abundant), the interest rate is positive (negative), and consumption rises (falls) over time. This has been indicated with vertical arrows in Figure A13.10.

Given the configuration of arrows, the steady-state equilibrium E_0 is saddle-point stable and the saddle path, SP, is upward sloping. If the economy starts out with an initial capital stock, k_0, it will gradually accumulate capital until the optimal point E_0 is reached.

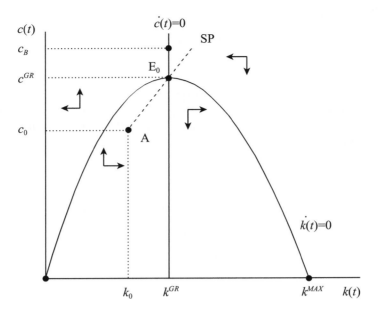

Figure A13.10: The original Ramsey model

Question 11: The savings function

(a) Equation (13.59) in the book is:

$$\dot{a}(t) \equiv [r(t) - n_L] a(t) + W(t) - c(t). \qquad \text{(A13.120)}$$

There is no government debt, so capital is the only asset and $a(t) = k(t)$. There are constant returns to scale and firms are perfectly competitive so the rental expressions are $r(t) + \delta = f'(k(t))$ and $W(t) = f(k(t)) - k(t)f'(k(t))$. Output is fully exhausted by factor payments, so $f(k(t)) = W(t) + [r(t) + \delta] k(t)$. Equation (A13.120) can then be rewritten as follows:

$$\begin{aligned}
\dot{k}(t) &\equiv [(r(t) + \delta) - (\delta + n_L)] k(t) + W(t) - c(t) \\
&= y(t) - c(t) - (\delta + n_L) k(t) \\
&= f(k(t)) - c(t) - (\delta + n_L) k(t). \qquad \text{(A13.121)}
\end{aligned}$$

Equation (A13.121) coincides with (Q13.14) in the question.

(b) In the steady state we have both $\dot{k} = 0$ and $\dot{c} = 0$. For the Cobb-Douglas production function we derive from the fact that $\dot{k} = 0$:

$$sAk^{\alpha} = (\delta + n_L) k \quad \Leftrightarrow \quad \alpha Ak^{\alpha-1} = \frac{\alpha (\delta + n_L)}{s}. \qquad \text{(A13.122)}$$

From the condition $\dot{c} = 0$ we find for the Cobb-Douglas function:

$$r = \rho + n_L \quad \Leftrightarrow \quad \alpha Ak^{\alpha-1} = \rho + \delta + n_L, \qquad \text{(A13.123)}$$

where we used the Euler equation (13.68) (see also (A13.123) below). By combining (A13.122)–(A13.123) we find the result stated in equation (Q13.17) in the question.

(c) The first-order condition for the Ramsey model is summarized by the consumption Euler equation (13.68), which is restated here:

$$\frac{\dot{c}(t)}{c(t)} = \sigma(c(t)) \left[r(t) - (\rho + n_L) \right]$$
$$= \sigma(c(t)) \left[f'(k(t)) - (\rho + \delta + n_L) \right]$$
$$= \sigma(c(t)) \left[\alpha A k(t)^{\alpha-1} - (\rho + \delta + n_L) \right] \qquad \text{(A13.124)}$$

where $\sigma(\cdot)$ is the intertemporal substitution elasticity. We derive from equation (Q13.15)–(Q13.16) that:

$$\frac{\dot{c}(t)}{c(t)} = \frac{\dot{y}(t)}{y(t)} = \alpha \frac{\dot{k}(t)}{k(t)}, \qquad \text{(A13.125)}$$

where we have used the fact that both s and A are constant. By using (Q13.14)–(Q13.16) in (A13.125) we find:

$$\frac{\dot{c}(t)}{c(t)} = \alpha \left[s A k(t)^{\alpha-1} - (\delta + n_L) \right] \qquad \text{(A13.126)}$$

We now have two expressions for consumption growth, namely equations (A13.125) and (A13.126), which must both hold. By equating the two expressions we find:

$$\sigma(c(t)) = \frac{s\alpha A k(t)^{\alpha-1} - \alpha(\delta + n_L)}{\alpha A k(t)^{\alpha-1} - (\rho + \delta + n_L)}$$
$$= \frac{s\alpha A k(t)^{\alpha-1} - s(\rho + \delta + n_L)}{\alpha A k(t)^{\alpha-1} - (\rho + \delta + n_L)} = s,$$

where we have used the expression in (Q13.17) to get to the second line. We reach the conclusion that for a Cobb-Douglas production function, the solution for the inverse optimal problem for a constant savings ratio (satisfying $s < \alpha$) is the constant elasticity of substitution (or iso-elastic) utility function with $\sigma = s$. See Kurz (1968, pp. 166-170) for a more advanced discussion of this issue.

We need the condition $s < \alpha$ because the Ramsey model rules out the emergence of dynamic inefficiency. If s were higher that α then we know from the discussion surrounding equation (13.22) in the book that there would be oversaving. Since this is impossible in a Ramsey model, the inverse optimum problem does not have a solution for $s > \alpha$.

Question 12: The savings ratio in the Ramsey model

(a) We solve the problem directly as a social planning problem. The solution is identical to the solution chosen by the representative household. The social planner chooses sequences for $s(\tau)$ and $k(\tau)$ such that the lifetime utility function of the representative household,

$$\Lambda(t) \equiv \int_t^\infty \left[\frac{[(1 - s(\tau)) f(k(\tau))]^{1-1/\sigma} - 1}{1 - 1/\sigma} \right] e^{\rho(t-\tau)} d\tau, \qquad \text{(A13.127)}$$

is maximized given the constraint (Q13.20) and taking as given the initial capital stock per worker, $k(t)$. The current-value Hamiltonian for this problem is:

$$\mathcal{H} \equiv \frac{[(1-s(\tau))\,Ak(\tau)^\alpha]^{1-1/\sigma}-1}{1-1/\sigma} + \mu(\tau)\,[s(\tau)Ak(\tau)^\alpha - (\delta + n_L)\,k(\tau)],$$

(A13.128)

where $\mu(\tau)$ is the co-state variable, $s(\tau)$ is the control variable, and $k(\tau)$ is the state variable. The first-order conditions are $\partial \mathcal{H}/\partial s(\tau) = 0$ and $-\partial \mathcal{H}/\partial k(\tau) = \dot{\mu}(\tau) - \rho\mu(\tau)$:

$$0 = \left[\mu(\tau) - [(1-s(\tau))\,Ak(\tau)^\alpha]^{-1/\sigma}\right]Ak(\tau)^\alpha, \qquad (A13.129)$$

$$\dot{\mu}(\tau) - \rho\mu(\tau) = -\alpha[(1-s(\tau))\,Ak(\tau)^\alpha]^{-1/\sigma}(1-s(\tau))\,Ak(\tau)^{\alpha-1}$$
$$- \alpha\mu(\tau)s(\tau)Ak(\tau)^{\alpha-1} + (\delta + n_L)\,\mu(\tau). \quad (A13.130)$$

Since the capital stock is strictly positive, (A13.129) can be simplified to:

$$\mu(\tau) = [(1-s(\tau))\,Ak(\tau)^\alpha]^{-1/\sigma}. \qquad (A13.131)$$

Equation (A13.131) says that the marginal utility of wealth (left-hand side) must be equated to the marginal utility of consumption (right-hand side). By using making use of (A13.131), equation (A13.130) can be simplified to:

$$\frac{\dot{\mu}(\tau)}{\mu(\tau)} = \rho + \delta + n_L - \alpha Ak(\tau)^{\alpha-1}. \qquad (A13.132)$$

Equation (A13.132) says that the rate of change in the marginal utility of wealth is determined by the difference between $\rho + n_L$ and the interest rate ($\alpha Ak(\tau)^{\alpha-1} - \delta$).

(b) The fundamental differential equation for the capital stock per worker is given in (Q13.20). The fundamental differential equation for the savings rate is derived as follows. First we differentiate (A13.131) with respect to time:

$$\frac{\dot{\mu}(\tau)}{\mu(\tau)} = -\frac{1}{\sigma}\left[-\frac{\dot{s}(\tau)}{1-s(\tau)} + \alpha\frac{\dot{k}(\tau)}{k(\tau)}\right]. \qquad (A13.133)$$

By combining (A13.132) and (A13.133) we obtain:

$$\alpha Ak(\tau)^{\alpha-1} - (\rho + \delta + n_L) = \frac{1}{\sigma}\left[-\frac{\dot{s}(\tau)}{1-s(\tau)} + \alpha\frac{\dot{k}(\tau)}{k(\tau)}\right] \quad \Leftrightarrow$$

$$\frac{\dot{s}(\tau)}{1-s(\tau)} = -\sigma\left[\alpha Ak(\tau)^{\alpha-1} - (\rho + \delta + n_L)\right] + \alpha\frac{\dot{k}(\tau)}{k(\tau)}. \qquad (A13.134)$$

We derive from equation (Q13.20) that:

$$\frac{\dot{k}(\tau)}{k(\tau)} = s(\tau)Ak(\tau)^{\alpha-1} - (\delta + n_L). \qquad (A13.135)$$

Finally, by substituting (A13.135) into (A13.134) we find the fundamental (nonlinear) differential equation for the savings rate:

$$\frac{\dot{s}(\tau)}{1-s(\tau)} = (s(\tau) - \sigma)\,\alpha Ak(\tau)^{\alpha-1} + \sigma\,[\rho + \delta + n_L] - \alpha(\delta + n_L). \quad (A13.136)$$

(c) We use (A13.134) and (A13.135) to determine the steady-state values for k and s. We find after some manipulations:

$$k^* = \left(\frac{s^* A}{\delta + n_L} \right)^{1/(1-\alpha)}, \tag{A13.137}$$

$$s^* = \frac{\alpha (\delta + n_L)}{\rho + \delta + n_L}. \tag{A13.138}$$

Using these steady-state values, we can rewrite (A13.136) as follows:

$$\frac{\dot{s}(\tau)}{1 - s(\tau)} = (s(\tau) - \sigma) \alpha A k(\tau)^{\alpha-1} - (s^* - \sigma) [\rho + \delta + n_L]. \tag{A13.139}$$

Case (Q13.18). If the steady-state savings rate, defined in (A13.138) above, equals σ then the constant term drops out of (A13.139) so that $\dot{s}(\tau) > 0$ ($\dot{s}(\tau) < 0$) for $s(\tau) > \sigma$ ($s(\tau) < \sigma$). The dynamic behaviour of the savings rate has been illustrated with vertical arrows in Figure A13.11. Note that $0 < s(\tau) < 1$ is ensured because $0 < c(\tau) < y(\tau)$. The $\dot{k} = 0$ line is obtained from (A13.135):

$$s(\tau) = \frac{\delta + n_L}{A} k(\tau)^{1-\alpha}. \tag{A13.140}$$

It follows that the $\dot{k} = 0$ line has the convex shape as drawn in Figure A13.11. It also follows from (A13.135) that $\partial \dot{k}(\tau) / \partial s(\tau) > 0$, i.e. the capital stock increases (decreases) for points above (below) the $\dot{k} = 0$ line. This has been illustrated with horizontal arrows in Figure A13.11. The configuration of arrows confirms that the model is saddle-point stable. The saddle path coincides with the $\dot{s} = 0$ line. If the economy starts out with a capital stock per worker equal to k_0 then it will gradually move from A to E_0 over time. This solution is, of course, the same one we discussed in Question 11 above.

Case (Q13.19). If the steady-state saving rate exceeds the intertemporal substitution elasticity ($s^* > \sigma$) then the constant term does not drop out of (A13.139) and the $\dot{s} = 0$ line can be written as:

$$\begin{aligned} s(\tau) &= \sigma + (s^* - \sigma) \frac{\rho + \delta + n_L}{\alpha A} k(\tau)^{1-\alpha} \\ &= \sigma + \frac{s^* - \sigma}{s^*} \cdot \frac{\delta + n_L}{A} k(\tau)^{1-\alpha}, \end{aligned} \tag{A13.141}$$

where we have used (A13.138) in getting from the first to the second line. The phase diagram for this case is presented in Figure A13.12. The $\dot{k} = 0$ line is still given by (A13.140) whilst the $\dot{s} = 0$ line is given by (A13.141). The latter curve lies everywhere above σ (i.e. $s(\tau) > \sigma$ for all τ) and is upward sloping but flatter than the $\dot{k} = 0$ line. The steady-state is at E_0 and the saddle path is upward sloping. We have already discussed the dynamics of the capital stock (the horizontal arrows in Figure A13.12). The dynamics of the saving rate follows from (A13.139):

$$\frac{1}{1 - s(\tau)} \frac{\partial \dot{s}(\tau)}{\partial k(\tau)} = - (1 - \alpha) (s(\tau) - \sigma) \alpha A k(\tau)^{\alpha-2}. \tag{A13.142}$$

Equation (A13.142) shows that $\partial \dot{s}(\tau) / \partial k(\tau) < 0$ because $0 < \alpha < 1$ and $s(\tau) > \sigma$ for all τ. Hence, the savings rate decreases (increases) over time for points to

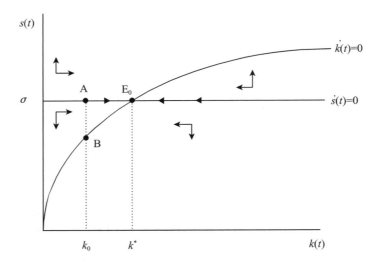

Figure A13.11: Dynamics of $s(t)$ when $s^* = \sigma$

the right (left) of the $\dot{s} = 0$ line. This is illustrated with vertical arrows. If the initial capital stock is k_0, then the economy moves gradually from point A to E_0. When $s^* > \sigma$, the representative household has a relatively weak willingness to substitute consumption through time. Ceteris paribus the interest rate, the household chooses a relatively flat consumption profile. As capital and output increase over time, so does the savings rate.

Case (Q13.20). If the steady-state savings rate falls short of the intertemporal substitution elasticity ($s^* < \sigma$) then the $\dot{s} = 0$ line, given in (A13.141), is downward sloping and lies below σ for all values of the capital stock. The situation has been illustrated in Figure A13.13. It follows from (A13.142) that $\partial \dot{s}(\tau)/\partial k(\tau) > 0$ (because $0 < \alpha < 1$ and $s(\tau) < \sigma$ for all τ), i.e. the savings ratio rises (falls) for points to the right (left) of the $\dot{s} = 0$ line. Combined with the dynamics of the capital stock this confirms that the equilibrium at E_0 is saddle-point stable. With a relatively high intertemporal substitution elasticity, the saddle point is thus downward sloping. Hence, if the capital stock is initially k_0 the economy will move gradually to point E_0 and the savings rate will rise during transition.

(d) By setting $\alpha = 1$ in (A13.136) we find the fundamental differential equation for the savings rate:

$$\frac{\dot{s}(\tau)}{1 - s(\tau)} = [s(\tau) - \sigma] A + \sigma (\rho + \delta + n_L) - (\delta + n_L). \qquad (A13.143)$$

The key thing to note is that (A13.143) does not depend on the capital stock–it is an unstable differential equation in s only. By defining the steady-state savings rate, s^*, as the rate for which $\dot{s} = 0$ in (A13.143), we can rewrite (A13.143) as:

$$\dot{s}(\tau) = (1 - s(\tau)) (s(\tau) - s^*) A, \qquad (A13.144)$$

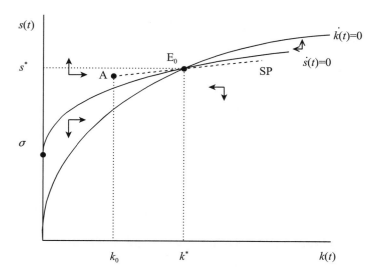

Figure A13.12: Dynamics of $s(t)$ when $s^* > \sigma$

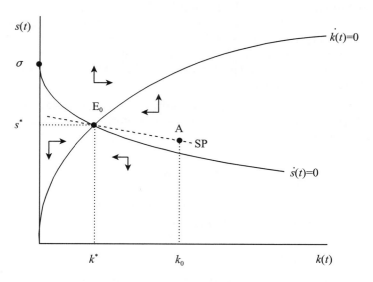

Figure A13.13: Dynamics of $s(t)$ when $s^* < \sigma$

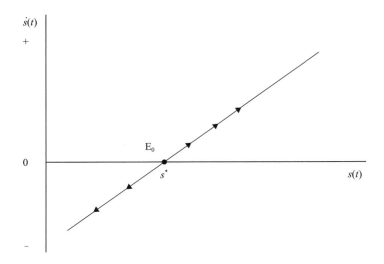

Figure A13.14: Saving rate dynamics with $\alpha = 1$

where s^* is:

$$s^* \equiv \frac{\sigma (A - \rho) + (1 - \sigma) (\delta + n_L)}{A}. \tag{A13.145}$$

The first-order conditions for the optimum will ensure that s^* is feasible, i.e. that $0 < s^* < 1$.

We illustrate the differential equation for the savings rate in Figure A13.14. In view of (A13.144), the savings rate rises (falls) over time if $s(\tau)$ exceeds (falls short of) s^*. Hence, the only stable solution is that $s(\tau) = s^*$ for all τ. There is no transitional dynamics in the savings rate in this 'AK' model. (See also Chapter 14 on this issue.) The constancy of the savings rate does not hinge on the value of σ any longer.

Given that the savings rate is always equal to its steady-state level s^* we can find the growth rate in the capital stock (per worker) from equation (A13.135) with $\alpha = 1$ imposed:

$$\gamma_k(\tau) \equiv \frac{\dot{k}(\tau)}{k(\tau)} = \sigma [A - (\rho + \delta + n_L)]. \tag{A13.146}$$

Equation (A13.146) generalizes (14.10) in the book for the case of an optimally chosen (rather than ad hoc) savings rate.

Question 13: Technological change

(a) We follow the approach of Barro and Sala-i-Martin (1995, pp. 54–55) to answer this question. We write the production function as follows:

$$\begin{aligned} Y(t) &= A_P(t)F\left(A_K(t)K(t), A_L(t)L(t)\right) \\ &= e^{n_H t}F\left(e^{n_S t}K(t), e^{n_A t}L(t)\right). \end{aligned} \tag{A13.147}$$

By dividing both sides of (A13.147) by $K(t)$ we find:

$$
\begin{aligned}
\frac{Y(t)}{K(t)} &= \frac{e^{n_H t}}{K(t)} F\left(e^{n_S t} K(t), e^{n_A t} L(t)\right)] \\
&= \frac{e^{(n_H + n_S)t} K(t)}{K(t)} F\left(1, e^{(n_A - n_S)t} \frac{L(t)}{K(t)}\right) \\
&= e^{(n_H + n_S)t} F\left(1, e^{(n_A - n_S)t} \frac{L(t)}{K(t)}\right).
\end{aligned}
\tag{A13.148}
$$

The population grows at a constant exponential rate, $\dot{L}(t)/L(t) = n_L$, and in the steady state $K(t)$ grows at exponential rate $\gamma_K^* \equiv \dot{K}(t)/K(t)$. It follows that in the steady state the labour-capital ratio is:

$$
\frac{L(t)}{K(t)} = \left(\frac{L}{K}\right)_0 e^{(n_L - \gamma_K^*)t},
\tag{A13.149}
$$

where L_0 and K_0 are the initial labour force and capital stock, respectively. By substituting (A13.149) into (A13.148) we find:

$$
\frac{Y(t)}{K(t)} = e^{(n_H + n_S)t} F\left[1, \left(\frac{L}{K}\right)_0 e^{(n_A + n_L - n_S - \gamma_K^*)t}\right].
\tag{A13.150}
$$

In the balanced growth path we must have that the right-hand side of (A13.150) is constant. There are only two ways in which this is possible.

The *first* case is if technological progress is purely labour augmenting. In this case, $n_H = n_S = 0$ (so that $e^{(n_H + n_S)t} = 1$.) and $\gamma_K^* = n_A + n_L$ (so that the exponential term in (A13.150), $e^{(n_A + n_L - n_S - \gamma_K^*)t} = 1$).

The *second* case is if the term $e^{(n_H + n_S)t}$ is exactly offset by the term $F(1, \cdot)$ in (A13.150) for all t. This is only possible if the production function is Cobb-Douglas. Assume that technology can be written as follows:

$$
Y(t) = e^{n_H t} \left[e^{n_S t} K(t)\right]^\alpha \left[e^{n_A t} L(t)\right]^{1-\alpha},
\tag{A13.151}
$$

so that (A13.150) becomes:

$$
\begin{aligned}
\frac{Y(t)}{K(t)} &= e^{(n_H + n_S)t} \left(\frac{L}{K}\right)_0 e^{(1-\alpha)(n_A + n_L - n_S - \gamma_K^*)t} \\
&= \left(\frac{L}{K}\right)_0 \exp\left[(n_H + n_S + (1 - \alpha)(n_A + n_L - n_S - \gamma_K^*))t\right].
\end{aligned}
\tag{A13.152}
$$

The right hand side of (A13.152) is constant if and only if:

$$
\begin{aligned}
0 &= n_H + n_S + (1 - \alpha)(n_A + n_L - n_S - \gamma_K^*) \qquad \Leftrightarrow \\
\gamma_K^* &= n_L + n_A + \frac{n_H + \alpha n_S}{1 - \alpha}.
\end{aligned}
\tag{A13.153}
$$

But we can always write the Cobb-Douglas production function as involving only labour-augmenting technological progress by appropriately defining the rate of Harrod-neutral technological progress. Indeed, the following production function is identical to (A13.151) and only involves Harrod-neutral technological change:

$$Y(t) = K(t)^\alpha \left[e^{n_A^* t} L(t) \right]^{1-\alpha}, \tag{A13.154}$$

where n_A^* is:

$$n_A^* \equiv n_A + \frac{n_H + \alpha n_S}{1 - \alpha}. \tag{A13.155}$$

(b) The household optimization problem with only Harrod-neutral technological change is solved as follows. The production function can be written in terms of efficiency units of labour ($N(t)$) as:

$$y(t) = f(k(t)), \tag{A13.156}$$

where $y(t) \equiv Y(t)/N(t)$, $k(t) \equiv K(t)/N(t)$, and $N(t) \equiv e^{n_A t} L(t)$. The representative firm hires capital and (raw) labour in order to maximize profit:

$$\Pi(t) \equiv F\left(K(t), e^{n_A t} L(t)\right) - (r(t) + \delta) K(t) - W(t)L(t). \tag{A13.157}$$

The first-order conditions are:

$$r(t) + \delta = F_K(K(t), N(t)), \tag{A13.158}$$
$$W(t) = e^{n_A t} F_N(K(t), N(t)). \tag{A13.159}$$

By using the expressions in (13.79) in the book we find that (A13.158)–(A13.159) can be written in terms of the intensive-form production function:

$$r(t) + \delta = f'(k(t)), \tag{A13.160}$$
$$W(t) = e^{n_A t} \bar{W}(t), \qquad \bar{W}(t) \equiv f(k(t)) - k(t)f'(k(t)), \tag{A13.161}$$

where $\bar{W}(t)$ can be interpreted as the "raw" wage rate. According to (A13.160) the steady-state interest rate is constant. According to (A13.161) the steady-state wage rate grows at the exponential rate n_A, but the raw wage rate is constant.

It is useful to transform the household optimization problem somewhat by measuring consumption and assets in terms of efficiency units of labour. By dividing (13.58) by $N(t)$ we find:

$$\frac{\dot{A}(t)}{N(t)} \equiv r(t)\frac{A(t)}{N(t)} + W(t)\frac{L(t)}{N(t)} - \frac{C(t)}{N(t)} \qquad \Leftrightarrow$$
$$\dot{a}(t) = [r(t) - (n_A + n_L)]a(t) + \bar{W}(t) - c(t), \tag{A13.162}$$

where $a(t) \equiv A(t)/N(t)$ and $c(t) \equiv C(t)/N(t)$. In going from the first to the second line we have used that fact that $\dot{A}(t)/N(t) = \dot{a}(t) + (n_A + n_L)a(t)$, $\dot{N}(t)/N(t) = n_A + n_L$, and $W(t)L(t)/N(t) = \bar{W}(t)$. The key thing to note is that assets accumulate at rate $r(t) - (n_A + n_L)$ in (A13.162). Since consumption per capita features in (13.57) we must rewrite the objective function in terms of consumption per efficiency unit of labour. We find in a straightforward manner that (13.57) becomes:

$$\Lambda(0) \equiv \int_0^\infty U\left(c(t)e^{n_A t}\right) e^{-\rho t} dt, \tag{A13.163}$$

The household chooses sequences for consumption and financial assets such that lifetime utility (A13.163) is maximized, subject to the budget identity, given in (A13.162), and a solvency condition, and taking as given the initial level of assets ($a(0)$). The current value Hamiltonian is:

$$\mathcal{H} \equiv U\left(c(t)e^{n_A t}\right) + \mu(t)\Big[\left[r(t) - (n_A + n_L)\right] a(t) + \bar{W}(t) - c(t)\Big], \tag{A13.164}$$

where $c(t)$ is the control variable, $a(t)$ is the state variable, and $\mu(t)$ is the co-state variable. The first-order conditions are $\partial\mathcal{H}/\partial c(t) = 0$ and $-\partial\mathcal{H}/\partial a(t) = \dot{\mu}(t) - \rho\mu(t)$:

$$e^{n_A t}U'\left(c(t)e^{n_A t}\right) = \mu(t), \tag{A13.165}$$

$$\dot{\mu}(t) - \rho\mu(t) = -\mu(t)\left[r(t) - (n_A + n_L)\right]. \tag{A13.166}$$

We can rewrite (A13.166) as follows:

$$\frac{\dot{\mu}(t)}{\mu(t)} = \rho + n_A + n_L - r(t). \tag{A13.167}$$

By differentiating (A13.165) with respect to time we find:

$$\frac{\dot{\mu}(t)}{\mu(t)} = n_A + \frac{U''(\cdot)}{U'(\cdot)}\left[\dot{c}(t)e^{n_A t} + n_A c(t)e^{n_A t}\right]$$

$$= n_A - \frac{1}{\sigma}\left[\frac{\dot{c}(t)}{c(t)} + n_A\right], \tag{A13.168}$$

where σ is the intertemporal substitution elasticity (which is constant by assumption):

$$\sigma \equiv -\frac{U'\left(c(t)e^{n_A t}\right)}{U''\left(c(t)e^{n_A t}\right)c(t)e^{n_A t}}. \tag{A13.169}$$

By combining (A13.165)–(A13.166) we find the consumption Euler equation:

$$\frac{\dot{c}(t)}{c(t)} = \sigma\left[f'(k(t)) - (\rho + \delta + n_L)\right] - n_A, \tag{A13.170}$$

where we have used (A13.160) in the final step.

Next we derive the fundamental differential equation for the capital stock (per efficiency unit of labour). In the absence of government debt, the capital stock is the only financial asset so $K(t) = A(t)$ and thus also $k(t) = a(t)$. By using this result in (A13.162) we find:

$$\dot{k}(t) = \left[r(t) + \delta - (\delta + n_A + n_L)\right]k(t) + \bar{W}(t) - c(t)$$

$$= f(k(t)) - c(t) - (\delta + n_A + n_L)k(t), \tag{A13.171}$$

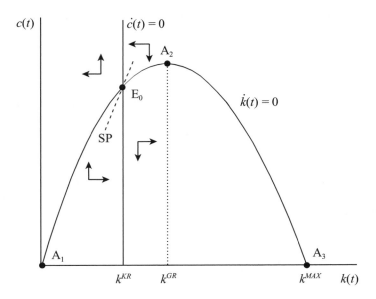

Figure A13.15: Phase diagram

where we have used the fact that $y(t) = (r(t) + \delta) k(t) + \bar{W}(t)$ in going from the first to the second line.

The model is fully characterized by equations (A13.170) and (A13.171). The phase diagram is presented in Figure A13.15. The $\dot{k} = 0$ line has the usual shape and reaches its maximum for $k = k^{GR}$ which is defined implicitly by:

$$r^{GR} \equiv f'\left(k^{GR}\right) - \delta = n_A + n_L. \tag{A13.172}$$

For points above (below) the $\dot{k} = 0$ line, consumption is too high (too low) and the capital falls (increases) over time. This is indicated with horizontal arrows in Figure A13.15. The $\dot{c} = 0$ line is seen from (A13.170) to imply a unique capital stock, k^{KR}, which is defined implicitly by:

$$r^{KR} \equiv f'\left(k^{KR}\right) - \delta = \rho + n_L + \frac{n_A}{\sigma}. \tag{A13.173}$$

It is not difficult to show that k^{KR} falls short of k^{GR}, i.e. that the steady-state equilibrium at E_0 must be dynamically efficient (see the discussion by Barro and Sala-i-Martin (1995)). The consumption dynamics is derived from (A13.170). For points to the right (left) of the $\dot{c} = 0$ line, the capital stock is too high (too low), the interest rate is too low (too high) and consumption falls (increases) over time. This is indicated with vertical arrows in Figure A13.15.

It follows from the configuration of arrows that the steady-state equilibrium at E_0 is saddle-point stable. In the steady state, both k and c are constant so that

K and C both grow at the rate of growth in N (which equals $n_A + n_L$):

$$\gamma_K^* \equiv \left(\frac{\dot{K}(t)}{K(t)}\right)^* = n_A + n_L, \tag{A13.174}$$

$$\gamma_C^* \equiv \left(\frac{\dot{C}(t)}{C(t)}\right)^* = n_A + n_L, \tag{A13.175}$$

We thus reach exactly the same conclusion as we did in the Solow-Swan model with technological progress (see section 13.2.2 in the book).

Question 14: Constant marginal utility

(a) The social planner chooses paths for per capita consumption and the capital stock per worker such that (Q13.22) is maximized subject to (Q13.23)–(Q13.24) and a transversality condition, taking as given the initial capital stock, $k(0)$. The current-value Hamiltonian is:

$$\mathcal{H} \equiv c(t) + \mu(t)\left[f\left(k(t)\right) - c(t) - (\delta + n_L)\,k(t)\right], \tag{A13.176}$$

where $c(t)$ is the control variable, $k(t)$ is the state variable, and $\mu(t)$ is the co-state variable. The current-value Hamiltonian is linear in the control variable so we expect a bang-bang solution. The derivative of the current-value Hamiltonian with respect to consumption is:

$$\frac{\partial \mathcal{H}}{\partial c(t)} = 1 - \mu(t). \tag{A13.177}$$

If $\mu(t) > 1$ then it follows from (A13.177) that $\mathcal{H}$ is decreasing in consumption. The planner sets consumption as low as is feasible, i.e. $c(t) = \bar{c}$ if $\mu(t) > 1$. On the other hand, if $\mu(t) < 1$ then $\mathcal{H}$ is increasing in consumption so it is optimal to set consumption as high as possible, i.e. $c(t) = f\left(k(t)\right)$ if $\mu(t) < 1$. Finally, if $\mu(t) = 1$ then $\mathcal{H}$ does not depend on $c(t)$ so consumption can be freely chosen.

The second first-order condition, $\dot{\mu}(t) - \rho\mu(t) = -\partial \mathcal{H}/\partial k(t)$, determines the optimal path for the co-state variable:

$$-\frac{\dot{\mu}(t)}{\mu(t)} = f'\left(k(t)\right) - (\rho + \delta + n_L)\,. \tag{A13.178}$$

(b) To derive the phase diagram we first establish the boundaries for the capital stock per worker that are implied by the minimum consumption requirement. We derive from (Q13.23) that the $\dot{k} = 0$ line can be written as follows:

$$c(t) = f\left(k(t)\right) - (\delta + n_L)\,k(t). \tag{A13.179}$$

We have drawn the $\dot{k} = 0$ line in (c, k) space in Figure A13.16. By assumption, $\bar{c}$ is less than the golden-rule consumption level so there are two points for which consumption is exactly equal to $\bar{c}$, points A_1 and A_3.

The phase diagram in (μ, k) space is drawn in Figure A13.17. The $\dot{\mu} = 0$ line is derived from (A13.178) and defines a unique capital stock per worker, $k = k^{KR}$. For points to the right (left) of the $\dot{\mu} = 0$ line, the capital stock is too high (too

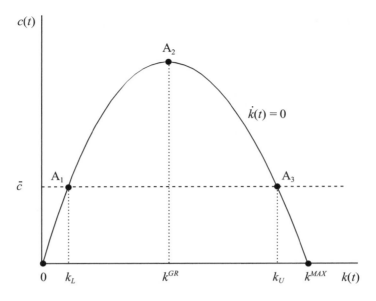

Figure A13.16: The feasible range for the capital stock

low), the interest rate is too low (too high), and μ rises (falls) over time. This has been indicated with vertical arrows in Figure A13.17.

The dynamics of the capital stock depends on the value of μ. If $\mu(t) < 1$ then $c(t) = f(k(t))$ so that it follows from (Q13.23) that $\dot{k}(t) = -(\delta + n_L)k(t)$, i.e. the capital stock falls over time. This is indicated with horizontal arrows in Figure A13.17. If $\mu(t) > 1$, then $c(t) = \bar{c}$ and it follows from (Q13.23) that the capital stock increases over time for $k(t) \in (k_L, k_U)$ but decreases over time for $0 < k(t) < k_L$ and for $k(t) > k_U$. These dynamic effects have been illustrated with horizontal arrows in Figure A13.17.

The configuration of arrows shows that the steady-state equilibrium at E_0 is saddle-point stable. Provided the initial capital stock per worker is within the feasible region, the economy will converge along a unique saddle path to E_0.

Question 15: Intertemporal substitution

(a) We can write equation (Q13.27) as:

$$\frac{1}{\sigma(C(t), C(s))} \equiv -\frac{\widetilde{MRS_{s,t}}}{[\widetilde{C(s)/C(t)}]}, \tag{A13.180}$$

where the marginal rate of subsitution between $C(s)$ and $C(t)$ is denoted by $MRS_{s,t}$ which is defined as follows:

$$MRS_{s,t} \equiv \frac{U'(C(s))}{U'(C(t))}. \tag{A13.181}$$

As usual, the tilde above a variables denotes that variable's proportional rate of change (e.g. $\tilde{x} \equiv dx/x$). Hence, $1/\sigma(\cdot)$ measures what happens (in per-unit

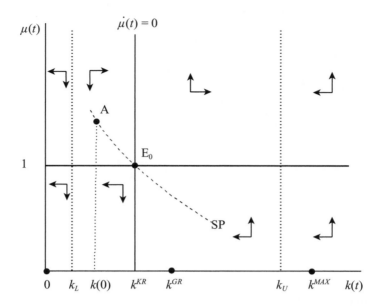

Figure A13.17: Phase diagram when marginal utility is constant

terms) to the marginal rate of subsitution between $C(s)$ and $C(t)$ if the average ratio is changed by one per-unit. Of course, the changes must be evaluated *along* a given difference curve.

(b) The first expression is obtained as follows:

$$d\left(\frac{C(s)}{C(t)}\right) = \frac{C(t)dC(s) - C(s)dC(t)}{[C(t)]^2} = \frac{C(s)}{C(t)}\left[\frac{dC(s)}{C(s)} - \frac{dC(t)}{C(t)}\right]. \quad (A13.182)$$

The second expression is:

$$d\left(\frac{U'(C(s))}{U'(C(t))}\right) = \frac{U'(C(t))U''(C(s))dC(s) - U'(C(s))U''(C(t))dC(t)}{[U'(C(t))]^2}$$

$$= \frac{C(s)U'(C(t))U''(C(s))\frac{dC(s)}{C(s)} - C(t)U'(C(s))U''(C(t))\frac{dC(t)}{C(t)}}{[U'(C(t))]^2}.$$

$$(A13.183)$$

By taking the total differential of (Q13.26), considering only non-zero values for $dC(t)$ and $dC(s)$ we find that the indifference curve implies:

$$d\Lambda = \int_0^\infty U'(C(\tau))dC(\tau)e^{\rho\tau}d\tau = 0 \quad \Rightarrow$$

$$0 = U'(C(t))dC(t)e^{\rho t} - U'(C(s))dC(s)e^{\rho s} \quad \Leftrightarrow$$

$$\frac{dC(s)}{C(s)} = -\frac{C(t)}{C(s)}\frac{U'(C(t))}{U'(C(s))}e^{\rho(s-t)}\frac{dC(t)}{C(t)}. \quad (A13.184)$$

Using (A13.184) in (A13.182) we obtain:

$$d\left(\frac{C(s)}{C(t)}\right) = -\frac{C(s)}{C(t)}\left[\frac{C(t)}{C(s)}\frac{U'(C(t))}{U'(C(s))}e^{\rho(s-t)} + 1\right]\frac{dC(t)}{C(t)},$$

$$\lim_{s\to t} d\left(\frac{C(s)}{C(t)}\right) = -2\frac{dC(t)}{C(t)}. \tag{A13.185}$$

Similarly, using (A13.184) in (A13.183) we get:

$$d\left(\frac{U'(C(s))}{U'(C(t))}\right) = -\frac{C(s)U'(C(t))U''(C(s))\frac{C(t)}{C(s)}\frac{U'(C(t))}{U'(C(s))}e^{\rho(s-t)}\frac{dC(t)}{C(t)}}{[U'(C(t))]^2}$$

$$-\frac{C(t)U'(C(s))U''(C(t))\frac{dC(t)}{C(t)}}{[U'(C(t))]^2}$$

$$= -C(t)\frac{dC(t)}{C(t)}\frac{[U'(C(t))]^2\frac{U''(C(s))}{U'(C(s))}e^{\rho(s-t)} + U'(C(s))U''(C(t))}{[U'(C(t))]^2}. \tag{A13.186}$$

By taking the limit of (A13.186) we get:

$$\lim_{s\to t} d\left(\frac{U'(C(s))}{U'(C(t))}\right) = -2C(t)\frac{dC(t)}{C(t)}\frac{U''(C(t))}{U'(C(t))}. \tag{A13.187}$$

(c) Combining (A13.185) and (A13.187) we find that:

$$\lim_{s\to t}\frac{1}{\sigma(C(t),C(s))} = -\frac{\lim_{s\to t}\widetilde{MRS}_{s,t}}{\lim_{s\to t}[\widetilde{C(s)/C(t)}]} = -\frac{-2C(t)\frac{U''(C(t))}{U'(C(t))}}{-2}$$

$$= -\frac{C(t)U''(C(t))}{U'(C(t))}, \tag{A13.188}$$

from which we derive that:

$$\lim_{s\to t}\sigma(C(t),C(s)) = -\frac{U'(C(t))}{C(t)U''(C(t))}. \tag{A13.189}$$

Chapter 14

Endogenous economic growth

Question 1: Short questions

(a) "Growth models of the capital-fundamentalist type are outrageous because they all predict that the share of labour will go to zero in the long run." Explain and evaluate this proposition.

(b) Why are the models in Chapter 13 called *exogenous* growth models and why are the ones in Chapter 14 called *endogenous* growth models?

(c) "According to Nicholas Kaldor, the real interest rate is constant over very long time periods, even if the capital stock increases by quite a bit. This implies that growth must be of the endogenous growth variety studied in this chapter." True, false, or uncertain? Explain.

Question 2: Endogenous growth

Consider the following growth model of a closed economy. The technology is given by:

$$Y(t) = Z_1 K(t) + Z_2 K(t)^\alpha L(t)^{1-\alpha},$$

where $Y(t)$ is output, $K(t)$ is the capital stock, and $L(t)$ is the employment. The parameters feature the following properties: $Z_1 > 0, Z_2 > 0, 0 < \alpha < 1$. The dynastic family (the population) grows at a constant exponential rate, $\dot{L}(t)/L(t) = n_L$. The lifetime utility function of the dynastic family (the representative agent) is given by:

$$\Lambda(0) \equiv \int_0^\infty \frac{c(\tau)^{1-1/\sigma} - 1}{1 - 1/\sigma} e^{-\rho\tau} d\tau,$$

where $c(\tau)$ is per capita consumption, σ is the intertemporal substitution elasticity, and ρ is the pure rate of time preference. We assume that $0 < \sigma < 1$ and $0 < \rho \ll \infty$. The per capita budget identity is given by:

$$\dot{a}(t) = [r(t) - n_L]a(t) + W(t) - c(t),$$

where $a(t)$ is financial assets, $r(t)$ is the real interest rate, and $W(t)$ is the wage rate. We abstract from a government. All markets are perfectly competitive.

(a) Does technology satisfy constant returns to scale? Derive the intensive-form expression for the production function.

(b) Prove that the dynamic expression for the capital stock per worker can be written as:

$$\dot{k}(t) = y(t) - c(t) - (\delta + n_L)k(t),$$

where $y(t) \equiv Y(t)/L(t)$ and $k(t) \equiv K(t)/L(t)$.

(c) Derive the expression for the consumption Euler equation.

(d) Compute the *long-run* growth rate. Assume that $Z_1 > \rho + \delta + n_L$. Explain what happens to the national income share of wages in the long run. Would you call this model an *exogenous* growth model or an *endogenous* growth model?

(e) ★ Use the following transformed variables: $v(t) \equiv y(t)/k(t)$ and $z(t) \equiv c(t)/k(t)$. Derive the system of differential equation for $v(t)$ and $z(t)$ and draw the phase diagram (Hint: place $z(t)$ on the vertical axis and $v(t)$ on the horizontal axis).

Question 3: Minimum consumption and endogenous growth

[Based on Rebelo (1992)] Consider a simple model of endogenous growth. The representative household has the following life-time utility function:

$$\Lambda(t) \equiv \int_t^\infty \left[\frac{[C(\tau) - \bar{C}]^{1-1/\sigma} - 1}{1 - 1/\sigma} \right] e^{\rho(t-\tau)} d\tau, \tag{Q14.1}$$

where $\bar{C}$ denotes the subsistence (or minimum) level of private consumption. The production function displays constant returns to scale with respect to a very broad measure of capital, i.e. $Y(t) = AK(t)$. Ignore technological change and assume a constant population. Assume furthermore that $r > \rho$ and $(1-\sigma)r + \sigma\rho > 0$ where $r \equiv A - \delta$.

(a) Derive an expression for the intertemporal substitution elasticity and show that it depends on $\bar{C}$. Explain the intuition.

(b) Derive an expression for the growth rate of the economy, both in the short run and in the long run. Show that poor countries grow at a slower rate than rich countries do.

(c) Consider a Ramsey model of classical growth with the same preferences as before, but with a Cobb-Douglas production function and thus decreasing returns to capital, i.e. $Y(t) = F(K(t)) \equiv AK(t)^\alpha$. Derive an expression for the growth rate of the economy, both in the short run and in the long run. Is it now possible for poor countries to grow faster than rich countries and catch up?

Question 4: Asymptotic endogenous growth

Consider the following simple "Solow-Swan style" model of economic growth.

$$
\begin{align}
S(t) &= s\left[Y(t) - T(t)\right], \qquad 0 < s < 1, & \text{(Q14.2)}\\
Y(t) &= C(t) + I(t) + G(t), & \text{(Q14.3)}\\
\dot{K}(t) &= I(t) - \delta K(t), \qquad \delta > 0, & \text{(Q14.4)}\\
\frac{\dot{L}(t)}{L(t)} &= n_L, \qquad n_L > 0, & \text{(Q14.5)}\\
Y(t) &= AK(t) + BK(t)^\alpha L(t)^{1-\alpha}, \qquad A, B > 0, \quad 0 < \alpha < 1, & \text{(Q14.6)}\\
G(t) &= T(t), & \text{(Q14.7)}
\end{align}
$$

where the variables take their usual meaning (see Chapter 13 in the book). The parameters A and B are exogenous constants (features of the technology).

(a) Does the production function satisfy the Inada conditions? Explain.

(b) Derive the fundamental differential equation for the capital stock per worker, $k(t) \equiv K(t)/L(t)$. Assume that $G(t) = gL(t)$ where g is a time-invariant constant.

(c) Derive a condition under which the model behaves like a standard Solow-Swan exogenous growth model. Show that the model is stable and compute the adjustment speed.

(d) Derive a condition under which the model behaves like an endogenous growth model. Compute the asymptotic growth rate. What happens to the national income share of labour in the long run?

(e) Study the effects of a tax-financed increase in government consumption for the endogenous growth version of the model.

Question 5: External effect and endogenous growth

In this question we consider a version of the AK model. Individual, perfectly competitive firms face the following technology:

$$
Y_i(t) = F(K_i(t), L_i(t)) \equiv Z(t)L_i(t)^{\varepsilon_L}K_i(t)^{1-\varepsilon_L}, \qquad 0 < \varepsilon_L < 1, \qquad \text{(Q14.8)}
$$

where $Z(t)$ is the level of general technology (taken as given by individual firms), and Y_i, K_i, and L_i are, respectively, output, capital, and employment of firm i. There are many firms, $i = 1, 2, \cdots, N_0$, where N_0 is the fixed number of firms. The aggregate variables are defined as $Y \equiv \sum_i^{N_0} Y_i$, $K \equiv \sum_i^{N_0} K_i$, and $L \equiv \sum_i^{N_0} L_i$. There is an external effect which ensures that general technology is positively affected by the aggregate capital stock:

$$
Z(t) = AK(t)^{\varepsilon_L}, \qquad \text{(Q14.9)}
$$

where A is a constant. Firms hire factors of production from the households and maximize the stock market value of the firm. Capital depreciates at a constant rate, δ. The household savings function is of the Keynes-Solow type:

$$
S(t) = sY(t), \qquad 0 < s < 1, \qquad \text{(Q14.10)}
$$

where s is the (exogenous) savings rate. We are considering a closed economy. The aggregate labour force (equalling the population) grows at a constant exponential rate, i.e. $\dot{L}(t) = L(t) = n_L > 0$. Assume for simplicity that government consumption is zero ($G(t) = 0$).

(a) Derive the marginal productivity conditions for labour and capital for each firm. Show that firms all choose the same capital intensity, $k_i \equiv K_i/L_i$.

(b) Derive an expression for aggregate output. Prove that there are increasing returns to scale at the macroeconomic level. Prove that the real interest rate would increase exponentially in this economy (contra stylized fact (SF3) in Chapter 13).

(c) Reformulate the formulation of the external effect (Q14.9) in such a way that a standard AK model is obtained. Work with this revised model in the remainder of this question.

(d) Show that the share of labour in total output is equal to ε_L.

(e) Compute the growth rate in per capita output, $\gamma_y(t) \equiv \dot{y}(t)/y(t)$. Prove that there is no transitional dynamics in this model.

(f) Prove that the growth rate in per capita output increases if there is an abrupt and permanent decrease in the growth rate of the population. Explain the economic intuition behind your result.

Question 6: Asymptotic capital fundamentalist model

You are given the following aggregate production function:

$$F(K(t), L(t)) \equiv AL(t) + \left[(1-\alpha) L(t)^{(\sigma_{KL}-1)/\sigma_{KL}} + \alpha K(t)^{(\sigma_{KL}-1)/\sigma_{KL}} \right]^{\sigma_{KL}/(\sigma_{KL}-1)},$$
(Q14.11)

with $A > 0$, $\sigma_{KL} > 1$, and $0 < \alpha < 1$. Production is perfectly competitive. There is no population growth, and the aggregate population is equal to L_0. The representative household's Euler equation is given by:

$$\frac{\dot{c}(t)}{c(t)} = \frac{\dot{C}(t)}{C(t)} = \sigma[r(t) - \rho],$$
(Q14.12)

where $c(t)$ is consumption per households member, $C(t) \equiv L_0 c(t)$ is aggregate household consumption, $\rho > 0$ and $\sigma > 0$. We consider a closed economy and the government consumes a constant proportion of output, i.e. $G(t) = g_0 Y(t)$, where g_0 is exogenous and time-invariant. All markets clear.

(a) Prove that the production function (Q14.11) features constant returns to scale. Compute F_K and F_L and show that they only depend on the capital intensity, $k(t) \equiv K(t) L(t)$.

(b) Derive an expression for the intensive-form production function, $f(k(t)) \equiv F(K(t)/L(t), 1)$.

(c) Derive a condition under which the model displays endogenous growth in the long run. Assume that $\alpha^{\sigma_{KL}/(\sigma_{KL}-1)} > \rho + \delta$. Hint: compute the following limit:

$$\lim_{k(t)\to\infty} f'\left(k\left(t\right)\right). \tag{Q14.13}$$

(d) Prove that an increase in the government's consumption share, say from g_0 to g_1, does not affect the asymptotic growth rate of the economy. Is g completely neutral or does something in the economy react to an increase in g? Explain.

Answers

Question 1: Short questions

(a) False. The statement is correct for the sub-class of models for which easy substitutability between labour and capital gives rise to endogenous growth. In such models labour becomes less and less important as a production factor as time goes on. The AK models based on external effects, on the other hand, are perfectly consistent with a stable (non-zero) share of labour over time.

(b) They key distinction lies in whether or not the *long-run* growth rate is endogenous in the sense that it can be affected by economic policy. In the standard Solow-Swan model, long-run growth equals the sum of the population growth rate and the rate of growth in labour-augmenting technological change. Both these growth rate are exogenously given. This is why we call such models exogenous growth models, even though the transitional dynamics can be influenced by policy.

In the models of Chapter 14, the long-run growth rate typically can be affected by policy instruments.

(c) False. In the standard Ramsey exogenous growth model, the steady-state real interest rate is pinned down by the sum of the rate of time preference and the population growth rate, i.e. $r = \rho + n$. This pins down a unique optimal capital-labour ratio, $k^* \equiv (K/L)^*$. If the population grows, the capital stock will grow at the same rate in the steady state.

Question 2: Endogenous growth

(a) The production function features constant returns to capital and labour:

$$F(\lambda L, \lambda K) = Z_1 \lambda K(t) + Z_2 [\lambda K(t)]^\alpha [\lambda L(t)]^{1-\alpha}$$
$$= \lambda \left(Z_1 K(t) + Z_2 K(t)^\alpha L(t)^{1-\alpha} \right)$$
$$= \lambda F(L, K).$$

The intensive-form production function is obtained by expressing everything in per capita terms. We obtain:

$$\frac{Y(t)}{L(t)} = Z_1 \frac{K(t)}{L(t)} + Z_2 \frac{K(t)^\alpha L(t)^{1-\alpha}}{L(t)}$$
$$y(t) = Z_1 k(t) + Z_2 k(t)^\alpha \equiv f(k(t)).$$

We observe immediately that:

$$f'(k(t)) \equiv Z_1 + \alpha Z_2 k(t)^{\alpha-1}$$
$$\lim_{k(t) \to \infty} f'(k(t)) = Z_1.$$

Hence, one of the Inada conditions does not hold! This smells like a capital fundamentalist model in the long run.

(b) We know that with a constant returns to scale technology and perfectly competitive firms output is fully exhausted by factor payments, i.e.:

$$Y(t) = W(t)L(t) + (r(t) + \delta)K(t),$$

or, in per capita terms:

$$y(t) = W(t) + (r(t) + \delta)k(t).$$

There is no government ($b(t) = 0$) and we are dealing with a single durable asset ($a(t) = k(t)$). Using these results in the budget identity above we find:

$$\dot{a}(t) = [r(t) - n_L]a(t) + W(t) - c(t) \quad \Rightarrow$$
$$\dot{k}(t) = [(r(t) + \delta) - (\delta + n_L)]k(t) + W(t) - c(t) \quad \Rightarrow$$
$$\dot{k}(t) = (r(t) + \delta)k(t) + W(t) - c(t) - (\delta + n_L)k(t) \quad \Rightarrow$$
$$\dot{k}(t) = y(t) - c(t) - (\delta + n_L)k(t).$$

(c) The household chooses paths for $c(\tau)$ and $k(\tau)$ in order to maximize $\Lambda(0)$ given the capital accumulation function, the technology, and a transversality condition. The current-value Hamiltonian is:

$$\mathcal{H} \equiv \frac{c(t)^{1-1/\sigma} - 1}{1 - 1/\sigma} + \mu(t) \left[f\left(k(t)\right) - c(t) - (\delta + n_L)k(t) \right].$$

The state variable is $k(t)$, $\mu(t)$ is the co-state variable, and $c(t)$ the control variable. The first-order conditions are:

$$\frac{\partial \mathcal{H}}{\partial c(t)} = c(t)^{-1/\sigma} - \mu(t) = 0,$$

$$\dot{\mu}(t) - \rho\mu(t) = -\frac{\partial \mathcal{H}}{\partial k(t)} = \mu(t) \left[f'\left(k(t)\right) - (\delta + n_L) \right].$$

Simplifying we get:

$$\mu(t) = c(t)^{-1/\sigma},$$
$$\frac{\dot{\mu}(t)}{\mu(t)} = \left[\rho + \delta + n_L - f'\left(k(t)\right) \right].$$

By eliminating $\mu(t)$ from these expressions we obtain the consumption Euler equation:

$$\frac{\dot{c}(t)}{c(t)} = -\sigma \frac{\dot{\mu}(t)}{\mu(t)} = \sigma \left[f'\left(k(t)\right) - \delta - \rho - n_L \right],$$
$$= \sigma[r(t) - (\rho + n_L)],$$

where $r(t) \equiv f'\left(k(t)\right) - \delta$.

(d) In the long run, the marginal product of capital approaches a constant (as $\lim_{k(t) \to \infty} f'\left(k(t)\right) = Z_1$) so that the interest rate approaches $Z_1 - \delta > 0$. The asymptotic growth rate in per capita consumption is obtained from the consumption Euler equation:

$$\gamma_c^* \equiv \lim_{t \to \infty} \frac{\dot{c}(t)}{c(t)} = \sigma[\lim_{t \to \infty} r(t) - (\rho + n_L)]$$
$$= \sigma[Z_1 - (\delta + \rho + n_L)] > 0.$$

Since $W(t) = F_L$ we find that:

$$W(t) = (1 - \alpha)Z_2 K(t)^\alpha L(t)^{-\alpha}$$
$$= (1 - \alpha)Z_2 k(t)^\alpha.$$

Hence, $W(t)/y(t)$ is equal to:

$$\frac{W(t)}{y(t)} = \frac{(1 - \alpha)Z_2 k(t)^\alpha}{Z_1 k(t) + Z_2 k(t)^\alpha} = \frac{(1 - \alpha)Z_2}{Z_2 + Z_1 k(t)^{1-\alpha}},$$

so that $\lim_{k(t) \to \infty} W(t)/y(t) = 0$. In the long run human wealth (the present value of wages) goes to zero and the household only consumes out of financial wealth, i.e. the ratio between $c(t)$ and $k(t)$ will be constant in the long run, say $z^* \equiv \lim_{t \to \infty} \frac{c(t)}{k(t)}$.

The asymptotic growth rate in the per capita capital stock is:

$$\gamma_k^* \equiv \lim_{t \to \infty} \frac{\dot{k}(t)}{k(t)} = \lim_{t \to \infty} \left(\frac{y(t)}{k(t)} - \frac{c(t)}{k(t)} \right) - (\delta + n_L)$$
$$= Z_1 - z^* - (\delta + n_L) = \gamma_c^*,$$

where the last equality follows from the fact that z^* is constant (so that $\gamma_k^* = \gamma_c^*$). We find that z^* (the propensity to consume out of total wealth) equals:

$$z^* = (1 - \sigma)[Z_1 - (\delta + n_L)] + \sigma\rho > 0$$

This is an endogenous growth model of the capital fundamentalist type.

(e) The system of differential equations is:

$$\frac{\dot{k}(t)}{k(t)} = \frac{y(t)}{k(t)} - \frac{c(t)}{k(t)} - (\delta + n_L),$$
$$\frac{\dot{c}(t)}{c(t)} = \sigma\left[f'(k(t)) - (\delta + \rho + n_L) \right].$$

A phase diagram with $c(t)$ and $k(t)$ on the axes is no good because these variables grow perpetually. By using the transformed variables, however, we can rewrite the equations in stationary format. First we note that $f'(k(t))$ can be rewritten as follows:

$$f'(k(t)) = (1 - \alpha)Z_1 + \alpha\frac{y(t)}{k(t)}.$$

Next we note from the production function that:

$$v(t) = Z_1 + Z_2 k(t)^{\alpha-1}$$

$$\dot{v}(t) = (\alpha - 1) Z_2 k(t)^{\alpha-1} \frac{\dot{k}(t)}{k(t)}$$

$$= (\alpha - 1)(v(t) - Z_1) \frac{\dot{k}(t)}{k(t)},$$

where the one million dollar trick is again to note that $Z_2 k(t)^{\alpha-1} = v(t) - Z_1$. We thus obtain from the capital growth equation that:

$$\dot{v}(t) = (1 - \alpha)[Z_1 - v(t)][v(t) - z(t) - (\delta + n_L)].$$

This is equation (4.57) in Barro and Sala-i-Martin (1995, p. 162). Next we write:

$$\frac{\dot{z}(t)}{z(t)} \equiv \frac{\dot{c}(t)}{c(t)} - \frac{\dot{k}(t)}{k(t)}$$

$$= \sigma[(1 - \alpha)Z_1 + \alpha v(t) - (\delta + \rho + n_L)] - [v(t) - z(t) - (\delta + n_L)]$$

$$= \sigma[(1 - \alpha)Z_1 - (\delta + \rho + n_L)] + (\delta + n_L) + (\sigma\alpha - 1)v(t) + z(t)$$

$$= \sigma[(1 - \alpha)Z_1 - \rho] + (1 - \sigma)(\delta + n_L) - (1 - \sigma\alpha)v(t) + z(t).$$

This is equation (4.58) in Barro and Sala-i-Martin (1995, p. 162). In the final step we can rewrite the system in deviation from the steady-state values z^* and $v^* \equiv Z_1$.

$$\dot{v}(t) = (1 - \alpha)(v^* - v(t))[v(t) - z(t) - (\delta + n_L)],$$

$$\frac{\dot{z}(t)}{z(t)} = [z(t) - z^*] - (1 - \sigma\alpha)[v(t) - v^*].$$

Question 3: Minimum consumption and endogenous growth

(a) The intertemporal substitution elasticity is defined in the book below equation (14.62):

$$\sigma(C(t)) \equiv -\frac{U'(C(t))}{U''(C(t))C(t)}. \tag{A14.1}$$

By using the felicity function stated in (Q14.1) we find:

$$\sigma(C(t)) \equiv -\frac{(C(t) - \bar{C})^{-1/\sigma}}{-(1/\sigma)(C(t) - \bar{C})^{-1/\sigma-1}C(t)}$$

$$= \sigma \frac{C(t) - \bar{C}}{C(t)}. \tag{A14.2}$$

According to (A14.2), the intertemporal substitution elasticity is no longer constant when subsistence consumption enters the felicity function. Indeed, we find from (A14.2) that $\sigma(\bar{C}) = 0$, $\sigma'(C(t)) = \bar{C}/C(t)^2 > 0$, and $\lim_{C(t) \to \infty} \sigma(C(t)) = \sigma$. So poor countries (with a low consumption level) have a lower intertemporal substitution elasticity than rich countries (with a high consumption level) do.

(b) We solve the social planning solution to the optimal growth problem. The social planner chooses paths for consumption and the capital stock such that lifetime utility (Q14.1) is maximized subject to the capital accumulation equation:

$$\dot{K}(\tau) = AK(\tau) - C(\tau) - \delta K(\tau), \tag{A14.3}$$

where δ is the depreciation rate of the capital stock. The initial capital stock, $K(t)$, is taken as given by the social planner. The current-value Hamiltonian for this optimization problem is:

$$\mathcal{H} \equiv \frac{[C(\tau) - \bar{C}]^{1-1/\sigma} - 1}{1 - 1/\sigma} + \mu(\tau) \Big[(A - \delta) K(\tau) - C(\tau) \Big], \tag{A14.4}$$

where $C(\tau)$ is the control variable, $K(\tau)$ is the state variable, and $\mu(\tau)$ is the co-state variable. The first-order conditions are $\partial \mathcal{H} / \partial C(\tau) = 0$ and $-\partial \mathcal{H} / \partial K(\tau) = \dot{\mu}(\tau) - \rho \mu(\tau)$ or:

$$[C(\tau) - \bar{C}]^{-1/\sigma} = \mu(\tau), \tag{A14.5}$$

$$-\frac{\dot{\mu}(\tau)}{\mu(\tau)} = r - \rho, \tag{A14.6}$$

where $r \equiv A - \delta$ is the competitive real interest rate. By combining (A14.5)–(A14.6) we find the consumption Euler equation:

$$\frac{\dot{C}(\tau)}{C(\tau) - \bar{C}} = \sigma [r - \rho]. \tag{A14.7}$$

Since $r > \rho$ (by assumption) the growth rate in consumption is positive for countries with a consumption level above subsistence.

In order to solve for the closed-form solution for consumption we rewrite the Euler equation as follows:

$$\dot{C}(\tau) = \alpha [C(\tau) - \bar{C}], \tag{A14.8}$$

where $\alpha \equiv \sigma [r - \rho]$ is a positive constant. Equation (A14.8) is a linear differential equation with constant coefficients which can be solved in a straightforward manner. We find in a number of steps that:

$$e^{-\alpha\tau} [\dot{C}(\tau) - \alpha C(\tau)] = -\alpha \bar{C} e^{-\alpha\tau} \qquad \Leftrightarrow$$

$$\frac{d}{d\tau} [C(\tau)e^{-\alpha\tau}] = -\alpha \bar{C} e^{-\alpha\tau} \qquad \Rightarrow$$

$$\int_0^t dC(\tau)e^{-\alpha\tau} = -\alpha \bar{C} \int_0^t e^{-\alpha\tau} \qquad \Leftrightarrow$$

$$C(t)e^{-\alpha t} - C(0) = -\alpha \bar{C} \left[\frac{e^{-\alpha t} - 1}{-\alpha} \right]. \tag{A14.9}$$

Simplifying (A14.9) yields the solution for consumption at time t:

$$C(t) = C(0)e^{\alpha t} + \bar{C} \left(1 - e^{\alpha t}\right). \tag{A14.10}$$

To determine $C(0)$ we substitute (A14.10) into the intertemporal budget constraint:

$$
\begin{aligned}
K(0) &= \int_0^\infty C(t)e^{-rt}dt \\
&= \int_0^\infty \left[(C(0) - \bar{C})\, e^{\alpha t} + \bar{C} \right] e^{-rt}dt \\
&= \frac{C(0) - \bar{C}}{(1-\sigma)r + \sigma\rho} + \frac{\bar{C}}{r},
\end{aligned}
\tag{A14.11}
$$

where we have used the fact that $\alpha - r = \sigma(r - \rho) - r = -[(1-\sigma)r + \sigma\rho]$ in going from the second to the third line. (Note that the integral in (A14.11) only exists if r exceeds α.) Using the same methods we find that:

$$
\begin{aligned}
K(t) &= \int_t^\infty C(\tau)e^{r(t-\tau)}d\tau \\
&= \left[\frac{C(0) - \bar{C}}{(1-\sigma)r + \sigma\rho} \right] e^{\sigma(r-\rho)t} + \frac{\bar{C}}{r} \\
&= \frac{C(t) - \bar{C}}{(1-\sigma)r + \sigma\rho} + \frac{\bar{C}}{r}.
\end{aligned}
\tag{A14.12}
$$

By solving (A14.12) for $C(t)$ we find:

$$
C(t) = \bar{C} + [(1-\sigma)r + \sigma\rho] \left[K(t) - \frac{\bar{C}}{r} \right].
\tag{A14.13}
$$

By using (A14.13) in (A14.3) we find that the growth rate in the capital stock is:

$$
\begin{aligned}
\gamma_K(t) &\equiv \frac{\dot{K}(t)}{K(t)} = r - \frac{C(t)}{K(t)} \\
&= r - \frac{\bar{C}}{K(t)} - [(1-\sigma)r + \sigma\rho] \left[1 - \frac{\bar{C}}{rK(t)} \right] \\
&= \sigma(r - \rho) \left[1 - \frac{\bar{C}}{rK(t)} \right].
\end{aligned}
\tag{A14.14}
$$

It follows from (A14.14) that the growth rate of poor countries is lower than that of rich countries. The poor countries save less because they get high utility from the consumption of basic needs. As the countries develop, growth rates catch up. In the long run, both rich and poor countries end up with the (asymptotic) growth rate $\sigma(r - \rho)$. However, poor countries never catch up with the level of wealth of rich countries. This pattern of growth has been illustrated in Figure A14.1.

(c) Intuitively we expect that the long-run growth rate is zero for both rich and poor countries as there is no population growth and no technical change. Formally we can derive this result as follows. The differential equation for consumption, given in (A14.7), becomes:

$$
\dot{C}(t) = \sigma \left[F'(K(t)) - \delta - \rho \right] [C(t) - \bar{C}],
\tag{A14.15}
$$

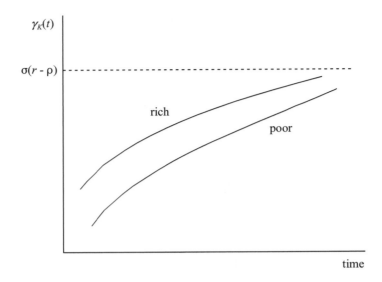

Figure A14.1: Growth rates of poor and rich countries

where $r(t) = F'(K(t)) - \delta$ is the interest rate determined according to the usual rental rate expression. The key thing to note is that $r(t)$ is no longer constant when there are diminishing returns to capital.

The differential equation for the capital stock is:

$$\dot{K}(t) = AK(t)^\alpha - C(t) - \delta K(t). \tag{A14.16}$$

By linearizing (A14.15)–(A14.16) around the steady state (K^*, C^*) (using the approach explained in section 13.6.2 in the book) we find:

$$\begin{bmatrix} \dot{C}(t) \\ \dot{K}(t) \end{bmatrix} = \begin{bmatrix} 0 & \sigma F''(K^*)\,(C^* - \bar{C}) \\ -1 & \rho \end{bmatrix} \begin{bmatrix} C(t) - C^* \\ K(t) - K^* \end{bmatrix}, \tag{A14.17}$$

where we used the fact that the steady-state interest rate equals the rate of time preference, i.e. $r^* \equiv F'(K^*) - \delta = \rho$. The speed of adjustment in the economy (denoted by β in the book) is represented by the stable characteristic root $(-\beta < 0)$ of the Jacobian matrix:

$$\beta \equiv \frac{\rho}{2} \left[\sqrt{1 - \frac{4\sigma F''(K^*)\,(C^* - \bar{C})}{\rho^2}} - 1 \right]$$

$$= \frac{\rho}{2} \left[\sqrt{1 + \frac{4\alpha\sigma(1 - \alpha)(K^*)^{\alpha-2}\,(C^* - \bar{C})}{\rho^2}} - 1 \right]. \tag{A14.18}$$

We derive in a straightforward manner that $\partial\beta / \partial\,(C^* - \bar{C}) > 0$ so the further away the economy is from the subsistence level, the higher is the rate of growth in the economy.

The rate of growth in consumption is:

$$\gamma_C(t) \equiv \frac{\dot{C}(t)}{C(t)} = \sigma \left[\underbrace{F'(K(t)) - \delta}_{(a)} - \rho \right] \left[\underbrace{1 - \frac{\bar{C}}{C(t)}}_{(b)} \right]. \qquad \text{(A14.19)}$$

Term (a) is lower for rich than for poor countries because rich countries have a higher capital stock. Term (b) is lower for poor countries than for rich countries because poor have a lower consumption level. It follows that during transition poor countries may initially grow at a slower rate than rich countries. Eventually, however, poor countries must catch up with rich countries because both types of countries have the same (zero) growth rate.

Question 4: Asymptotic endogenous growth

(a) The Inada conditions deal with the properties of F_K and F_L in extreme points. We find:

$$F_L \equiv (1 - \alpha) BK^{\alpha} L^{-\alpha}, \qquad \text{(A14.20)}$$
$$F_K \equiv A + \alpha BK^{\alpha-1}L^{1-\alpha}. \qquad \text{(A14.21)}$$

It follows that:

$$\lim_{L \to 0} F_L = +\infty, \qquad \lim_{L \to \infty} F_L = 0,$$

so for the marginal product of labour the Inada conditions hold. Also:

$$\lim_{K \to 0} F_K = +\infty, \qquad \lim_{K \to \infty} F_K = A.$$

The last result violates an Inada condition.

(b) By substituting (Q14.3) into (Q14.4) we find:

$$\dot{K}(t) = [Y(t) - C(t)] - G(t) - \delta K(t). \qquad \text{(A14.22)}$$

We know that $Y = C + S + T$ so that $Y - C = S + T$. Substituting this result and (Q14.2) into (A14.22) we find:

$$\dot{K}(t) = s[Y(t) - G(t)] - \delta K(t), \qquad \text{(A14.23)}$$

where we have used (A14.25). Substituting (Q14.6) into (A14.23) we get:

$$\dot{K}(t) = s\left[AK(t) + BK(t)^{\alpha}L(t)^{1-\alpha}\right] - sG(t) - \delta K(t). \qquad \text{(A14.24)}$$

Dividing by $L(t)$ we thus get:

$$\dot{k}(t) = s\left[Ak(t) + Bk(t)^{\alpha}\right] - sg - (\delta + n_L)k(t), \qquad \text{(A14.25)}$$

where $k(t) \equiv K(t)/L(t)$ and $g(t) \equiv G(t)/L(t)$.

(c) The growth rate of $k(t)$ is obtained by dividing (A14.25) by $k(t)$:

$$\gamma_k(t) \equiv \frac{\dot{k}(t)}{k(t)} = sA - (\delta + n_L) + sBk(t)^{\alpha-1} - s\frac{g}{k(t)}. \qquad (A14.26)$$

Diagrammatically we can distinguish two cases–see Figures A14.2 and A14.3.

If $sA < \delta + n_L$ then $\lim_{t\to\infty} \gamma_k(t) < 0$. Of course, this does not mean that growth becomes negative. It means that there is a unique (stable) steady-state level of $k(t) = k^*$ for which $\gamma_k(t) = \gamma^* = 0$. See Figure A14.2. This the case of exogenous economic growth.

The adjustment speed is computed as follows. We know that, around k^*, we have:

$$Ak(t) + Bk(t)^{\alpha} \approx Ak^* + B(k^*)^{\alpha} + \left[A + \alpha B(k^*)^{\alpha-1}\right] \cdot [k(t) - k^*]. \quad (A14.27)$$

By substituting (A14.27) into (A14.25) we find:

$$\begin{aligned}
\dot{k}(t) &= s\left[Ak^* + B(k^*)^{\alpha}\right] + s\left[A + \alpha B(k^*)^{\alpha-1}\right] \cdot [k(t) - k^*] \\
&\quad - sg - (\delta + n_L)k(t).
\end{aligned} \qquad (A14.28)$$

But in the steady state we have that:

$$\dot{k}^* = 0 = s\left[Ak^* + B(k^*)^{\alpha}\right] - sg - (\delta + n_L)k^*, \qquad (A14.29)$$

so that (A14.28) simplifies to:

$$\dot{k}(t) = -\beta[k(t) - k^*], \qquad (A14.30)$$

where β is the speed of adjustment (around the steady state):

$$\beta \equiv (\delta + n_L) - s\left[A + \alpha B(k^*)^{\alpha-1}\right] > 0. \qquad (A14.31)$$

(d) If $sA > \delta + n_L$ then $\lim_{t\to\infty} \gamma_k(t) = sA - (\delta + n_L) \equiv \gamma^* > 0$, where γ^* is the asymptotic endogenous growth rate. See Figure A14.3. The national income share of labour is defined as:

$$\begin{aligned}
\omega_L &\equiv \frac{L \cdot F_L}{Y} = \frac{L(1-\alpha)BK^{\alpha}L^{-\alpha}}{AK + BK^{\alpha}L^{1-\alpha}} \\
&= \frac{(1-\alpha)Bk^{\alpha}}{Ak + Bk^{\alpha}} \\
&= \frac{(1-\alpha)B}{Ak^{1-\alpha} + B}.
\end{aligned}$$

It follows that $\lim_{k\to\infty} \omega_L = 0$ (because $\lim_{k\to\infty} k^{1-\alpha} = +\infty$).

(e) We have already imposed the government budget constraint. An increase in g has no effect on the asymptotic endogenous growth rate, $\gamma^* \equiv sA - (\delta + n_L)$. However, it does affect growth during transition. We find from (A14.26) that:

$$\frac{\partial \gamma_k(t)}{\partial g} \equiv \frac{\dot{k}(t)}{k(t)} = sA - (\delta + n_L) + sBk(t)^{\alpha-1} - \frac{s}{k(t)} > 0,$$

i.e., for a given $k(t)$ the growth rate falls. This effect has been illustrated in Figure A14.3.

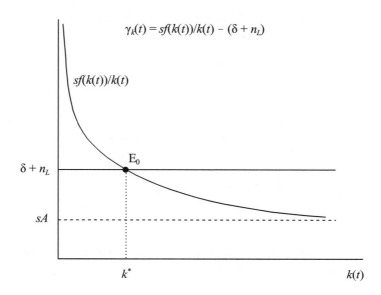

Figure A14.2: Exogenous growth

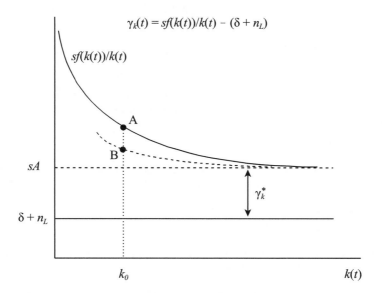

Figure A14.3: Asymptotic endogenous growth

Question 5: External effect and endogenous growth

(a) Each firm i hires capital and labour to equate the rental rates to the respective marginal products:

$$W \quad = \quad \frac{\partial Y_i}{\partial L_i} = \varepsilon_L Z L_i^{\varepsilon_L - 1} K_i^{1 - \varepsilon_L} = \varepsilon_L Z k_i^{1 - \varepsilon_L}, \tag{A14.32}$$

$$R^K \quad = \quad r + \delta = (1 - \varepsilon_L) Z L_i^{\varepsilon_L} K_i^{-\varepsilon_L} = (1 - \varepsilon_L) Z k_i^{-\varepsilon_L}, \tag{A14.33}$$

where $k_i \equiv K_i / L_i$ is the firm's capital intensity. Since W and R^K are the same for all firms (perfect mobility of production factors), we immediately find that:

$$k_i = k, \qquad \text{(for all } i\text{)}. \tag{A14.34}$$

(b) Aggregate output is defined as:

$$Y \equiv \sum_{i=1}^{N_0} Y_i, \tag{A14.35}$$

because the goods are homogeneous. In view of (Q14.8) and (A14.34) we know that $Y_i = Z L_i k^{1 - \varepsilon_L}$. Hence, we find:

$$Y = \sum_{i=1}^{N_0} Z L_i k^{1 - \varepsilon_L} = Z k^{1 - \varepsilon_L} \sum_{i=1}^{N_0} L_i = L Z k^{1 - \varepsilon_L}, \tag{A14.36}$$

where we have used the fact that $\sum_{i=1}^{N_0} L_i = L$ (labour market clearing). From (Q14.9) we find:

$$Z = A K^{\varepsilon_L} = A (kL)^{\varepsilon_L}. \tag{A14.37}$$

Substituting (A14.37) into (A14.36) we find the "macroeconomic production function":

$$\begin{aligned} Y(t) \quad &= \quad L(t) A k(t)^{\varepsilon_L} L(t)^{\varepsilon_L} k(t)^{1 - \varepsilon_L} \\ &= \quad A L(t)^{\varepsilon_L} K(t), \end{aligned} \tag{A14.38}$$

where we have used $K(t) = k(t) L(t)$. There are increasing returns to scale at the macroeconomic level. The interest rate is obtained by substituting (A14.34) and (A14.37) into (A14.33):

$$r(t) + \delta = (1 - \varepsilon_L) A L(t)^{\varepsilon_L}, \tag{A14.39}$$

which grows exponentially because $L(t)$ does. The external effect is too strong and the model runs foul of stylized fact (SF3) in Chapter 13.

(c) A correctly specified external effect sets:

$$Z(t) = A k(t)^{\varepsilon_L}. \tag{A14.40}$$

Productivity depends the stock of capital *per worker*. Using (A14.40) in (A14.32)-(A14.33) and (A14.36) we obtain:

$$\begin{aligned} W(t) \quad &= \quad \varepsilon_L Z(t) k(t)^{1 - \varepsilon_L} = \varepsilon_L A k(t)^{\varepsilon_L} k(t)^{1 - \varepsilon_L} \quad &\Leftrightarrow \\ W(t) \quad &= \quad \varepsilon_L A k(t), \quad & \tag{A14.41} \\ r(t) + \delta \quad &= \quad (1 - \varepsilon_L) A, \quad & \tag{A14.42} \\ Y(t) \quad &= \quad A K(t). \quad & \tag{A14.43} \end{aligned}$$

(d) We can rewrite (A14.41) as $W(t) L(t) = \varepsilon_L AK(t) = \varepsilon_L Y(t)$, i.e. the national income share of labour is equal to ε_L.

(e) We know that $Y = C + S = C + I$ or $I = S$. Also, $\dot{K} = I - \delta K$ so that:

$$\dot{K}(t) = sY(t) - \delta K(t) = sAK(t) - \delta K(t).$$

The growth rate is:

$$\gamma_K(t) \equiv \frac{\dot{K}(t)}{K(t)} = sA - \delta = \gamma^*. \tag{A14.44}$$

Since $Y(t) = AK(t)$ we find that $\gamma_Y(t) = \gamma^*$ also. Output per worker grows according to $\gamma_y(t) = \gamma_y^* = \gamma^* - n_L$. There is no transitional dynamics.

(f) If n_L falls then γ_y^* increases. A given amount of capital accumulation is diluted more slowly by the growth in the labour force. This speeds up per capita growth.

Question 6: Asymptotic capital fundamentalist model

(a) To obtain compact expressions we first define $\zeta \equiv (\sigma_{KL} - 1)/\sigma_{KL}$. Let $\lambda > 0$ and compute $F(\lambda K, \lambda L)$:

$$
\begin{aligned}
F(\lambda K, \lambda L) &= \lambda AL + \left[(1-\alpha)(\lambda L)^\zeta + \alpha(\lambda K)^\zeta \right]^{1/\zeta} \\
&= \lambda AL + \left[\lambda^\zeta \cdot \left[(1-\alpha) L^\zeta + \alpha K^\zeta \right] \right]^{1/\zeta} \\
&= \lambda AL + \lambda \left[(1-\alpha) L^\zeta + \alpha K^\zeta \right]^{1/\zeta} = \lambda F(K, L),
\end{aligned}
$$

i.e. there are constant returns to scale. The marginal product of labour is:

$$
\begin{aligned}
F_L &= A + \frac{1}{\zeta} \cdot \left[(1-\alpha) L^\zeta + \alpha K^\zeta \right]^{1/\zeta - 1} \times \zeta \cdot (1-\alpha) L^{\zeta-1} \\
&= A + (1-\alpha) L^{\zeta-1} \cdot \left[(1-\alpha) L^\zeta + \alpha K^\zeta \right]^{(1-\zeta)/\zeta} \\
&= A + (1-\alpha) \cdot \left[L^{-\zeta} \cdot \left[(1-\alpha) L^\zeta + \alpha K^\zeta \right] \right]^{(1-\zeta)/\zeta} \\
&= A + (1-\alpha) \cdot \left[1 - \alpha + \alpha k^\zeta \right]^{(1-\zeta)/\zeta}. \tag{A14.45}
\end{aligned}
$$

For the marginal product of capital we get:

$$F_K = \alpha \cdot \left[(1-\alpha) k^{-\zeta} + \alpha \right]^{(1-\zeta)/\zeta}. \tag{A14.46}$$

Both F_L and F_K depend on k only (as we know from Euler's Theorem).

(b) The intensive form production function is:

$$
\begin{aligned}
f(k) &\equiv F\left(\frac{K}{L}, 1\right) \\
&= A + \frac{1}{L} \cdot \left[L^{(\sigma_{KL}-1)/\sigma_{KL}} \cdot \left[(1-\alpha) + \alpha k^{(\sigma_{KL}-1)/\sigma_{KL}} \right] \right]^{\sigma_{KL}/(\sigma_{KL}-1)} \\
&= A + \left[1 - \alpha + \alpha k^{(\sigma_{KL}-1)/\sigma_{KL}} \right]^{\sigma_{KL}/(\sigma_{KL}-1)} . \quad\quad\text{(A14.47)}
\end{aligned}
$$

(c) We know (from (A14.46)) that:

$$
\begin{aligned}
f'(k) &= \alpha \cdot \left[(1-\alpha) k^{(1-\sigma_{KL})/\sigma_{KL}} + \alpha \right]^{1/(\sigma_{KL}-1)} \quad\quad\text{(A14.48)} \\
&= \frac{\alpha}{\left[(1-\alpha) k^{(1-\sigma_{KL})/\sigma_{KL}} + \alpha \right]^{1/(1-\sigma_{KL})}} . \quad\quad\text{(A14.49)}
\end{aligned}
$$

If $0 < \sigma_{KL} < 1$ ($\zeta < 0$, difficult substitution between capital and labour), then $k^{(1-\sigma_{KL})/\sigma_{KL}} \to +\infty$ as $k \to +\infty$. It follows from (A14.49) that $\lim_{k\to\infty} f'(k) = 0$. There cannot be endogenous growth because labour gets ever scarcer.

On the other hand, if $\sigma_{KL} > 1$ ($\zeta > 0$, easy substitution between capital and labour), then $k^{(1-\sigma_{KL})/\sigma_{KL}} \to 0$ as $k \to +\infty$. It follows from (A14.49) that:

$$
\lim_{k\to\infty} f'(k) = \frac{\alpha}{\alpha^{1/(1-\sigma_{KL})}} = \alpha^{\sigma_{KL}/(\sigma_{KL}-1)} > 0. \quad\quad\text{(A14.50)}
$$

There is a lower limit to the marginal product of labour and endogenous growth is possible.

(d) We must first compute the asymptotic growth rate, γ^*. The full model is given by:

$$
\begin{aligned}
\dot{K}(t) &= Y(t) - C(t) - G(t) - \delta K(t), \\
Y(t) &= AL(t) + \left[(1-\alpha) L(t)^{(\sigma_{KL}-1)/\sigma_{KL}} + \alpha K(t)^{(\sigma_{KL}-1)/\sigma_{KL}} \right]^{\sigma_{KL}/(\sigma_{KL}-1)}, \\
G(t) &= g_0 Y(t), \\
\frac{\dot{C}(t)}{C(t)} &= \sigma [r(t) - \rho], \\
r(t) + \delta &= f'(k(t)), \\
L(t) &= L_0.
\end{aligned}
$$

In per capita terms we thus get:

$$
\gamma_k(t) \equiv \frac{\dot{k}(t)}{k(t)} = (1 - g_0) \frac{f(k(t))}{k(t)} - \frac{c(t)}{k(t)} - \delta, \quad\quad\text{(A14.51)}
$$

$$
\gamma_c(t) \equiv \frac{\dot{c}(t)}{c(t)} = \sigma [f'(k(t)) - (\rho + \delta)] . \quad\quad\text{(A14.52)}
$$

The asymptotic growth rate is obtained from (A14.52) by letting $k(t) \rightarrow +\infty$:

$$
\begin{aligned}
\gamma^* &= \lim_{k(t)\rightarrow+\infty} \gamma_c(t) = \sigma \left[\lim_{k(t)\rightarrow+\infty} f'(k(t)) - (\rho + \delta) \right] \\
&= \sigma \left[\alpha^{\sigma_{KL}/(\sigma_{KL}-1)} - (\rho + \delta) \right] > 0.
\end{aligned}
\tag{A14.53}
$$

Asymptotically, the c/k ratio is constant, i.e. The $\gamma_k(t) = \gamma^*$ also. We find from (A14.51) that:

$$
\begin{aligned}
\left(\frac{c}{k}\right)^* &= (1 - g_0) \lim_{k(t)\rightarrow+\infty} \frac{f(k(t))}{k(t)} - \gamma^* - \delta \\
&= (1 - g_0) \alpha^{\sigma_{KL}/(\sigma_{KL}-1)} - \gamma^* - \delta,
\end{aligned}
\tag{A14.54}
$$

where we have used the fact that:

$$
\begin{aligned}
\lim_{k(t)\rightarrow+\infty} \frac{f(k(t))}{k(t)} &= \lim_{k\rightarrow\infty} \frac{A}{k} + \lim_{k\rightarrow\infty} \left[(1-\alpha) k^{(1-\sigma_{KL})/\sigma_{KL}} + \alpha \right]^{\sigma_{KL}/(\sigma_{KL}-1)} \\
&= \lim_{k\rightarrow\infty} f'(k) = \alpha^{\sigma_{KL}/(\sigma_{KL}-1)}.
\end{aligned}
$$

An increase in g (from g_0 to g_1) does not affect γ^* but decreases the long-run consumption-capital ratio. The increase in public spending causes a reduction in consumption. Note that there is transitional dynamics in this model (because the marginal and average products of capital are only constant in the very long run).

Chapter 15

Real business cycles

Question 1: Short questions

(a) Real business cycle models are often criticized for their lack of internal propagation. What do we mean by that? How could we improve the internal propagation mechanism?

(b) "Depending on the persistence of a fiscal policy shock, investment may increase or decrease during the early phases of adjustment in the RBC model." True or false? Explain.

(c) "In the unit-elastic RBC model, the long-run fiscal policy multiplier, $dY(\infty)/dG$, is zero if there is no income effect in labour supply." True or false? Explain.

(d) In the unit-elastic RBC model there is a sharp difference in the response of labour supply to (i) a purely temporary productivity increase and (ii) a permanent productivity increase. How do income- and substitution effects explain this difference?

Question 2: Small open economy model

[Based on Kim and Kose (2003), Correia, Neves, and Rebelo (1995) and Schmitt-Grohe and Uribe (2003)] Consider the following model of an infinitely-lived representative household-producer living in a small open economy. The representative household features the following lifetime utility function:

$$E_t \Lambda_t \equiv E_t \sum_{\tau=t}^{\infty} \left(\frac{1}{1+\rho} \right)^{\tau-t} \cdot \ln \left(C_\tau - \frac{\gamma_L}{1+\sigma} L_\tau^{1+\sigma} \right), \tag{Q15.1}$$

where C_τ is consumption, L_τ is labour hours, ρ is the pure rate of time preference, and γ_L and σ are positive parameters. We model the household as a household-producer, i.e. we assume that it makes both the consumption and production decisions. The constraints it faces are:

$$Y_\tau + r_\tau B_\tau = C_\tau + I_\tau + (B_{\tau+1} - B_\tau), \tag{Q15.2}$$

$$Y_\tau = Z_\tau K_\tau^{1-\varepsilon_L} L_\tau^{\varepsilon_L}, \qquad 0 < \varepsilon_L < 1, \tag{Q15.3}$$

$$K_{\tau+1} = (1-\delta) K_\tau + \Phi \left(\frac{I_\tau}{K_\tau} \right) \cdot K_\tau, \qquad 0 < \delta < 1, \tag{Q15.4}$$

where I_τ is gross investment, Y_τ is output, K_τ is the stock of capital at the beginning of period τ, and Z_τ is a stochastic productivity shock. Equation (Q15.2) is the resource constraint. It says that total income (left-hand side) is spent on consumption, investment, or asset accumulation. Here, B_τ is the stock of net foreign assets at the beginning of period τ, and r_τ is the real (world) rate of return on these assets. This rate of return is stochastic and taken as given by the representative household. It is assumed that the mean international rate of return, $\bar{r}$, satisfies:

$$\bar{r} = \rho. \tag{Q15.5}$$

Equation (Q15.4) is the capital accumulation constraint featuring adjustment costs. It is assumed that $\Phi(\cdot)$ is non-negative, concave, $\Phi''(\cdot) < 0 < \Phi'(\cdot)$, and features $\Phi(\delta) = \delta$ and $\Phi'(\delta) = 1$. The household chooses optimal sequences for C_τ, L_τ, I_τ, Y_τ, $K_{\tau+1}$, and $B_{\tau+1}$ in order to maximize (Q15.1) subject to (Q15.2)-(Q15.5).

(a) Solve the household's optimization problem, using the Lagrangian method explained in the text (see equations (15.62)-(15.65)).

(b) Loglinearize the model.

(c) To get to understand the model, first assume that Z_t and r_t are non-stochastic, i.e. $Z_t = 1$ and $r_t = \bar{r} = \rho$. Show that the model displays hysteresis.

(d) Assume that Z_τ and r_τ both follow first-order autoregressive processes of the form:

$$\begin{aligned} \tilde{Z}_t &= \xi_Z \tilde{Z}_{t-1} + \eta_t^Z, & 0 < \xi_Z < 1, & \tag{Q15.6} \\ \tilde{r}_t &= \xi_R \tilde{r}_{t-1} + \eta_t^R, & 0 < \xi_R < 1, & \tag{Q15.7} \end{aligned}$$

with $\eta_t^i \sim N\left(0, \sigma_i^2\right)$ for $i = Z, R$ and $E\left(\eta_t^Z \eta_s^R\right) = 0$ for all s and t (uncorrelated innovations). Derive the system of stochastic difference equations for $\tilde{K}_t$ and $\tilde{X}_t$ (the counterpart to (15.78) in the text).

(e) ★ Solve the system of stochastic difference equations using the method of undetermined coefficients (see Appendix B.2 in Chapter 15 in the textbook.).

Question 3: The non-market sector

It is a well-known fact of life that the non-market sector is quite sizeable in advanced economies. For example, in the United States, an average married couple spends 33 percent of its discretionary time working for a wage in the market sector and 28 percent of its time working in the home. Home production activities can include things like cooking, cleaning, child care, gardening, shopping, etcetera. Similarly, the figures indicate that investment in household capital (such as consumer durables and residential structures) exceeds investment in market capital (producer durables, non-residential structures). In this question we study the effects of introducing home production into the RBC model.

The representative household has the following lifetime utility function:

$$E_t \Lambda_t \equiv E_t \sum_{\tau=t}^{\infty} \left(\frac{1}{1+\rho}\right)^{\tau-t} \ln\left(C_\tau^\varepsilon [1 - L_\tau]^{1-\varepsilon}\right), \tag{Q15.8}$$

where ρ captures the notion of time preference ($\rho > 0$), C_τ is *composite* consumption, $1 - L_\tau$ is leisure, and $0 < \varepsilon < 1$. Composite consumption itself depends on the consumption of a market-produced good (C_τ^M) and a home-produced good (C_τ^H):

$$C_\tau \equiv \left[\eta \left(C_\tau^H \right)^{(\sigma-1)/\sigma} + (1 - \eta) \left(C_\tau^M \right)^{(\sigma-1)/\sigma} \right]^{\sigma/(\sigma-1)}, \qquad \text{(Q15.9)}$$

where $\sigma \geq 0$ is the substitution elasticity between C_τ^H and C_τ^M in composite consumption, and $0 < \eta < 1$. Labour time is spent either in the market sector (L_τ^M) or on home production activities (L_τ^H):

$$L_\tau \equiv L_\tau^M + L_\tau^H. \qquad \text{(Q15.10)}$$

Home-produced goods are only used for home consumption and the technology is given by:

$$C_\tau^H = Z_\tau^H \left(L_\tau^H \right)^\theta \left(K_\tau^H \right)^{1-\theta}, \qquad \text{(Q15.11)}$$

where K_τ^H is the stock of household capital, Z_τ^H is a stochastic productivity term affecting home production, and $0 < \theta < 1$. In addition to household capital, the household also accumulates business (or market) capital, K_τ^M, that it rents out to firms in the market sector. The household budget constraint can be written as:

$$C_\tau^M + K_{\tau+1}^M + K_{\tau+1}^H = W_\tau L_\tau^M + R_\tau^K K_\tau^M + (1 - \delta_M)K_\tau^M + (1 - \delta_H)K_\tau^H, \quad \text{(Q15.12)}$$

where δ_M and δ_H denote the depreciation rates of, respectively, business capital and household capital ($0 < \delta_M < 1$ and $0 < \delta_H < 1$). Furthermore W_τ is the real wage rate and R_τ^K is the rental rate on business capital.

(a) What do we assume about the intertemporal substitution elasticity of the household's felicity function?

(b) Interpret the household budget constraint (Q15.12). What do we assume about the substitutability of the two types of capital?

(c) Solve the household optimization problem using the methods explained in the book (viz. section 15.5.1.1). Interpret the various expressions you obtain.

The representative firm is perfectly competitive and produces homogeneous output, Y_τ, by renting business capital, K_τ^M, and labour, L_τ^M, from the household sector. The production function is:

$$Y_\tau \equiv Z_\tau^M \left(L_\tau^M \right)^\alpha \left(K_\tau^M \right)^{1-\alpha}, \qquad \text{(Q15.13)}$$

where Z_τ^M is a stochastic productivity term affecting market productivity, and $0 < \alpha < 1$. The firm maximizes profit, $\Pi_\tau \equiv Y_\tau - W_\tau L_\tau - R_\tau^K K_\tau$.

(d) Derive the first-order conditions for the firm's optimal plans.

(e) What do we assume about the substitutability of working in the market sector and in home production? Show how you can modify the household utility function to capture the notion that working in the market is actually preferred to working around the home.

Question 4: A general RBC model

In this question we extend the continuous-time RBC model by assuming more general preferences and technology. In particular, the felicity function ($\Phi(\tau)$, appearing in (15.1)) now takes the following form:

$$\Phi(\tau) \equiv \frac{U(\tau)^{1-1/\sigma_X} - 1}{1 - 1/\sigma_X}, \tag{Q15.14}$$

where σ_X is the intertemporal substitution elasticity and $U(\tau)$ is the sub-felicity function which depends on consumption ($C(\tau)$) and leisure ($1 - L(\tau)$):

$$U(\tau) \equiv \left[\varepsilon_C C(\tau)^{(\sigma_{CL}-1)/\sigma_{CL}} + (1 - \varepsilon_C)[1 - L(\tau)]^{(\sigma_{CL}-1)/\sigma_{CL}} \right]^{\sigma_{CL}/(\sigma_{CL}-1)}. \tag{Q15.15}$$

We assume that the production function (15.11) is replaced by a more general CES function featuring a constant elasticity of substitution, σ_{KL}:

$$F[K(\tau), L(\tau)] \equiv \left[\varepsilon_L L(\tau)^{(\sigma_{KL}-1)/\sigma_{KL}} + (1 - \varepsilon_L)K(\tau)^{(\sigma_{KL}-1)/\sigma_{KL}} \right]^{\sigma_{KL}/(\sigma_{KL}-1)}. \tag{Q15.16}$$

The rest of the model is unchanged.

(a) Prove that the extended model incorporates the unit-elastic model studied in the text as a special case.

(b) Use the method of two-stage budgeting (which is discussed *inter alia* in section 16.5.1.1 of the book) to solve the optimal plans of the representative households. Show that the Euler equation for *full* consumption is given by:

$$\frac{\dot{X}(\tau)}{X(\tau)} = \sigma_X[r(\tau) - \rho] + (1 - \sigma_X)\frac{\dot{P}_U(\tau)}{P_U(\tau)}, \tag{Q15.17}$$

where $P_U(\tau)$ is the true cost-of-living index:

$$P_U(\tau) \equiv \begin{cases} \left[\varepsilon_C^{\varepsilon_C} (1 - \varepsilon_C)^{1-\varepsilon_C} \right]^{-1} W(\tau)^{1-\varepsilon_C} & \text{if } \sigma_{CL} = 1 \\ \left[\varepsilon_C^{\sigma_{CL}} + (1 - \varepsilon_C)^{\sigma_{CL}} W(\tau)^{1-\sigma_{CL}} \right]^{1/(1-\sigma_{CL})} & \text{if } \sigma_{CL} \neq 1 \end{cases} \tag{Q15.18}$$

Hint: start by postulating that full consumption and subfelicity are related according to:

$$X(\tau) \equiv C(\tau) + W(\tau)[1 - L(\tau)] = P_U(\tau)U(\tau). \tag{Q15.19}$$

(c) Derive the marginal productivity conditions for labour and capital. Relate the wage rate and the interest rate to, respectively, output per worker and output per unit of capital. Explain the role of σ_{KL} in the factor demand equations.

(d) Show that the "great ratios" result still holds for the extended model studied here.

(e) Derive the long-run output multiplier with respect to government consumption ($dY(\infty)/dG$) and show that it does not depend on the intertemporal substitution elasticity, σ_X. Give an economic interpretation for this result.

Question 5: Government spending shocks in the unit-elastic model

Consider the unit-elastic RBC model discussed in section 15.5.1 of the text. Change the lifetime utility function (15.59) to:

$$E_t \Lambda_t \equiv E_t \sum_{\tau=t}^{\infty} \left(\frac{1}{1+\rho}\right)^{\tau-t} \left[\varepsilon_C \ln\left(C_\tau - \frac{\gamma_L}{1+\theta_L} L(\tau)^{1+\theta_L}\right) - (1-\varepsilon_C)L_\tau\right], \quad (Q15.20)$$

where G_τ is government consumption and α is a constant parameter ($0 \leq \alpha \leq 1$). The felicity function is linear in labour supply so we make use of the lottery model developed by Hansen. The household views G_τ as an uncontrollable stochastic process that is not dependent on any endogenous variables. The stochastic process for G_τ is given by:

$$\ln G_t = \alpha_G + \rho_G \ln G_{t-1} + \varepsilon_t^G, \quad 0 < \rho_G < 1, \quad (Q15.21)$$

where ε_t^G is the innovation term which is identically and independently distributed with mean zero and variance σ_G^2. Technology is deterministic. The rest of the model is unchanged.

(a) Solve the household's optimization problem, using the Lagrangian method explained in the text (see equations (15.62)-(15.65)).

(b) Loglinearize the model. Comment on the differences you find between this model, and the standard unit elastic model of Table 15.4 in the book.

(c) Show that the quasi-reduced form for the interest rate is independent of the capital stock. Solve for the rational expectations solution for consumption. Explain how private consumption depends on government consumption in this model.

Question 6: No wealth effect in labour supply

Consider the extended Ramsey model discussed in sections 15.2–15.4 of the book. Assume that the felicity function (15.2) is changed to:

$$\Phi(\tau) \equiv \ln\left(C(\tau) - \frac{\gamma_L}{1+\theta_L} L(\tau)^{1+\theta_L}\right), \quad (Q15.22)$$

with $\theta_L > 0$.

(a) Solve the household optimization problem.

(b) Incorporate the results derived in part (a) into the model given in Table 15.1. Derive the phase diagram for the model. Show that the model is saddle-point stable.

(c) Loglinearize the model around the initial steady state (i.e., redo the relevant expressions from Table 15.2).

(d) Compute the expressions for the various long-run spending multipliers, like $dY(\infty)/dG$, $dC(\infty)/dG$, $dI(\infty)/dG$ etcetera. Explain the intuition behind your results with the aid of the phase diagram.

Answers

Question 1: Short questions

(a) See pages 15.5.2.1 and 15.5.2.2 of the book. Lack of propagation: output response is virtually identical to shock input (technology shock). The model itself does not add much in that sense. Better propagation:

- Add another slow moving stock variable (e.g. human capital).
- Sticky prices.
- Search unemployment.

(b) True, see Figure 15.6 in the book. If labour supply is highly elastic and the shock is rather persistent, then net investment rises at impact. Output increases a lot and the increase in G does not cause crowding out. The opposite happens if the shock is rather transitory and labour supply is not very elastic.

(c) True, see Footnote 2 on page 502. If labour supply only depends on the wage rate, an increase in lump-sum taxes will not cause labour supply to change. Hence, the adjustment is fully borne by consumption, which is crowded out one-for-one.

(d) For a purely temporary shock, the wage is only abnormally high in the shock period itself. It is thus important to benefit from that high wage in the shock period by working very hard then. This is the case where the substitution effect is dominant. There is of course an income effect, but it is small because the wage is only high in that one period.

The opposite holds for a permanent shock. In this case the income effect is large, and the substitution effect is small (because the wage is higher than before in all periods, so no one period stands out).

Question 2: Small open economy model

(a) The Lagrangian expression is:

$$
\begin{aligned}
\mathcal{L}_t \equiv\ & E_t \sum_{\tau=t}^{\infty} \left(\frac{1}{1+\rho}\right)^{\tau-t} \cdot \left[\ln\left(C_\tau - \frac{\gamma_L}{1+\sigma}L_\tau^{1+\sigma}\right)\right. \\
& -\lambda_\tau \cdot \left[B_{\tau+1} - (1+r_\tau)\,B_\tau - Z_\tau K_\tau^{1-\varepsilon_L} L_\tau^{\varepsilon_L} + C_\tau + I_\tau\right] \\
& \left.-\mu_\tau \cdot \left[K_{\tau+1} - (1-\delta)\,K_\tau - \Phi\left(\frac{I_\tau}{K_\tau}\right)\cdot K_\tau\right]\right],
\end{aligned}
$$

where λ_τ and μ_τ are the Lagrange multipliers for the constraints in period τ. For convenience, we define X_τ as:

$$
X_\tau \equiv C_\tau - \frac{\gamma_L}{1+\sigma}L_\tau^{1+\sigma}, \tag{A15.1}
$$

The first-order conditions for this problem (for $\tau = t, t+1, t+2, ...$) are:

$$\frac{\partial \mathcal{L}_t}{\partial C_\tau} = \left(\frac{1}{1+\rho}\right)^{\tau-t} E_t \left[\frac{1}{X_\tau} - \lambda_\tau\right] = 0,$$

$$\frac{\partial \mathcal{L}_t}{\partial L_\tau} = \left(\frac{1}{1+\rho}\right)^{\tau-t} E_t \left[-\frac{\gamma_L L_\tau^\sigma}{X_\tau} + \varepsilon_L \lambda_\tau Z_\tau K_\tau^{1-\varepsilon_L} L_\tau^{\varepsilon_L-1}\right] = 0,$$

$$\frac{\partial \mathcal{L}_t}{\partial I_\tau} = \left(\frac{1}{1+\rho}\right)^{\tau-t} E_t \left[-\lambda_\tau + \mu_\tau \Phi'\left(\frac{I_\tau}{K_\tau}\right)\right] = 0,$$

$$\frac{\partial \mathcal{L}_t}{\partial K_{\tau+1}} = \left(\frac{1}{1+\rho}\right)^{\tau-t} E_t \left[-\mu_\tau + (1-\varepsilon_L)\frac{\lambda_{\tau+1}}{1+\rho} Z_{\tau+1} K_{\tau+1}^{-\varepsilon_L} L_{\tau+1}^{\varepsilon_L}\right.$$
$$\left. + \frac{\mu_{\tau+1}}{1+\rho}\left(1-\delta+\Phi\left(\frac{I_{\tau+1}}{K_{\tau+1}}\right) - \Phi'\left(\frac{I_{\tau+1}}{K_{\tau+1}}\right) \cdot \frac{I_{\tau+1}}{K_{\tau+1}}\right)\right] = 0,$$

$$\frac{\partial \mathcal{L}_t}{\partial B_{\tau+1}} = \left(\frac{1}{1+\rho}\right)^{\tau-t} E_t \left[-\lambda_\tau + (1+r_{\tau+1})\frac{\lambda_{\tau+1}}{1+\rho}\right] = 0.$$

For the planning period ($\tau = t$) these first-order conditions can be written in a more compact format as:

$$\lambda_t = \frac{1}{X_t}, \tag{A15.2}$$

$$\gamma_L L_t^\sigma = \varepsilon_L \frac{Y_t}{L_t}, \tag{A15.3}$$

$$\lambda_t = \mu_t \Phi'\left(\frac{I_t}{K_t}\right), \tag{A15.4}$$

$$\mu_t = E_t \left[(1-\varepsilon_L)\frac{\lambda_{t+1}}{1+\rho}\frac{Y_{t+1}}{K_{t+1}}\right.$$
$$\left. + \frac{\mu_{t+1}}{1+\rho}\left(1-\delta+\Phi\left(\frac{I_{t+1}}{K_{t+1}}\right) - \Phi'\left(\frac{I_{t+1}}{K_{t+1}}\right) \cdot \frac{I_{t+1}}{K_{t+1}}\right)\right], \tag{A15.5}$$

$$\lambda_t = E_t \left[\frac{1+r_{t+1}}{1+\rho} \cdot \lambda_{t+1}\right], \tag{A15.6}$$

$$Y_t = Z_t K_t^{1-\varepsilon_L} L_t^{\varepsilon_L}. \tag{A15.7}$$

(b) The deterministic steady state has the following features:

$$\frac{1}{\lambda^*} = C^* - \frac{\gamma_L}{1+\sigma}(L^*)^{1+\sigma},$$

$$\gamma_L (L^*)^{1+\sigma} = \varepsilon_L Y^*,$$

$$\frac{\rho+\delta}{1-\varepsilon_L} = \frac{Y^*}{K^*},$$

$$\lambda^* = \mu^*,$$

$$Y^* + \bar{r}B^* = C^* + I^*,$$

$$I^* = \delta K^*,$$

$$\frac{Y^*}{K^*} = \left(\frac{L^*}{K^*}\right)^{\varepsilon_L}.$$

The model features many great ratios, namely $(Y/K)^*$, $(I/K)^*$, $(K/L)^*$, and thus also L^*. The hysteretic property of the model (see below) confines itself to consumption and assets.

The loglinearized model is given by:

$$\tilde{\lambda}_t = -\tilde{X}_t, \tag{A15.8}$$

$$\sigma \tilde{L}_t = \tilde{Y}_t - \tilde{L}_t, \tag{A15.9}$$

$$\tilde{\lambda}_t = \tilde{\mu}_t - \sigma_A \left[\tilde{I}_t - \tilde{K}_t \right], \tag{A15.10}$$

$$\tilde{\mu}_t = \frac{1}{1+\rho} E_t \left[(\rho + \delta) \left(\tilde{Y}_{t+1} - \tilde{K}_{t+1} \right) + \tilde{\mu}_{t+1} + \rho \tilde{\lambda}_{t+1} \right], \tag{A15.11}$$

$$\tilde{\lambda}_t = E_t \left[\frac{\rho}{1+\rho} \tilde{r}_{t+1} + \tilde{\lambda}_{t+1} \right], \tag{A15.12}$$

$$\tilde{Y}_t = \tilde{Z}_t + (1 - \varepsilon_L) \tilde{K}_t + \varepsilon_L \tilde{L}_t, \tag{A15.13}$$

$$\tilde{K}_{t+1} = \tilde{K}_t + \delta \left[\tilde{I}_t - \tilde{K}_t \right], \tag{A15.14}$$

where $\sigma_A \equiv -\delta \Phi''(\delta) > 0$. Of these, the only one that warrants further comment is (A15.11). Differentiating (A15.5) around the deterministic steady state we find:

$$(1+\rho) d\mu_t = E_t \left[(1 - \varepsilon_L) d \left(\lambda_{t+1} \frac{Y_{t+1}}{K_{t+1}} \right) + (1 - \delta) d\mu_{t+1} \right.$$
$$\left. + \mu^* \left(\Phi'(\delta) - \Phi'(\delta) - \Phi''(\delta) \cdot \delta \right) d \left(\frac{I_{t+1}}{K_{t+1}} \right) \right].$$

Dividing by $\mu^* = \lambda^*$ on both sides and simplifying we obtain:

$$(1+\rho) \tilde{\mu}_t = E_t \left[(1 - \varepsilon_L) \frac{\lambda^*}{\mu^*} \frac{Y^*}{K^*} \left(\tilde{\lambda}_{t+1} + \tilde{Y}_{t+1} - \tilde{K}_{t+1} \right) + (1 - \delta) \tilde{\mu}_{t+1} \right.$$
$$\left. - \Phi''(\delta) \cdot \delta^2 \left(\tilde{I}_{t+1} - \tilde{K}_{t+1} \right) \right].$$

By using the definition of σ_A and substituting (A15.10) we arrive at:

$$(1+\rho) \tilde{\mu}_t = E_t \left[(\rho + \delta) \left(\tilde{\lambda}_{t+1} + \tilde{Y}_{t+1} - \tilde{K}_{t+1} \right) + (1 - \delta) \tilde{\mu}_{t+1} \right.$$
$$\left. + \delta \left(\tilde{\mu}_{t+1} - \tilde{\lambda}_{t+1} \right) \right].$$

After some cancellation of terms we obtain equation (A15.11).

(c) To derive the system of (stochastic) difference equations, we first condense the model as much as possible. Using (A15.9) and (A15.13) we find:

$$\tilde{Y}_t = \frac{1+\sigma}{1+\sigma-\varepsilon_L} \left[\tilde{Z}_t + (1 - \varepsilon_L) \tilde{K}_t \right],$$

$$\tilde{Y}_t - \tilde{K}_t = \frac{(1+\sigma) \tilde{Z}_t - \sigma \varepsilon_L \tilde{K}_t}{1+\sigma-\varepsilon_L}. \tag{A15.15}$$

Note that $\tilde{\zeta}_t \equiv \tilde{\mu}_t - \tilde{\lambda}_t$ corresponds to Tobin's q in a decentralized setting. Deducting (A15.12) from (A15.11) we derive:

$$\tilde{\zeta}_t = \frac{1}{1+\rho} E_t \left[(\rho + \delta) \left(\tilde{Y}_{t+1} - \tilde{K}_{t+1} \right) + \tilde{\zeta}_{t+1} - \rho \tilde{r}_{t+1} \right]. \tag{A15.16}$$

The system of difference equations is thus:

$$\tilde{K}_{t+1} = \tilde{K}_t + \frac{1}{\sigma_A} \cdot \tilde{\zeta}_t, \tag{A15.17}$$

$$\tilde{\zeta}_t = \frac{1}{1+\rho} E_t \left[(\rho + \delta) \frac{(1+\sigma) \tilde{Z}_{t+1} - \sigma \varepsilon_L \tilde{K}_{t+1}}{1 + \sigma - \varepsilon_L} \right.$$
$$\left. + \tilde{\zeta}_{t+1} - \rho \tilde{r}_{t+1} \right]. \tag{A15.18}$$

Equation (A15.17) is obtained by substituting (A15.10) into (A15.14), whereas (A15.18) follows from (A15.15) and (A15.16).

For the deterministic case we can drop the expectations operator, $E_t (\cdot)$, and set $\tilde{Z}_t = \tilde{r}_t = 0$. After some manipulations we find:

$$\begin{bmatrix} \tilde{K}_{t+1} \\ \tilde{\zeta}_{t+1} \end{bmatrix} = \Delta \cdot \begin{bmatrix} \tilde{K}_t \\ \tilde{\zeta}_t \end{bmatrix},$$

where Δ is defined as:

$$\Delta \equiv \begin{bmatrix} 1 & 0 \\ \frac{-(\rho+\delta)\sigma\varepsilon_L}{1+\sigma-\varepsilon_L} & 1 \end{bmatrix}^{-1} \cdot \begin{bmatrix} 1 & 1/\sigma_A \\ 0 & 1+\rho \end{bmatrix}$$

$$= \begin{bmatrix} 1 & 0 \\ \frac{(\rho+\delta)\sigma\varepsilon_L}{1+\sigma-\varepsilon_L} & 1 \end{bmatrix} \cdot \begin{bmatrix} 1 & 1/\sigma_A \\ 0 & 1+\rho \end{bmatrix}$$

$$= \begin{bmatrix} 1 & 1/\sigma_A \\ \frac{(\rho+\delta)\sigma\varepsilon_L}{1+\sigma-\varepsilon_L} & 1+\rho+\frac{(\rho+\delta)\sigma\varepsilon_L}{\sigma_A(1+\sigma-\varepsilon_L)} \end{bmatrix}.$$

We find that:

$$\text{tr}\Delta = \eta_1 + \eta_2 = 2 + \rho + \frac{(\rho+\delta)\sigma\varepsilon_L}{\sigma_A (1+\sigma-\varepsilon_L)} > 2,$$

$$|\Delta| = \eta_1 \eta_2 = 1 + \rho > 1,$$

where η_1 and η_2 are the characteristic roots. The characteristic equation is thus:

$$F(s) \equiv |sI - \Delta| = s^2 - \text{tr}\Delta \cdot s + |\Delta| = 0.$$

We find that $F(0) = |\Delta| > 0$, $F(1) = -\left(2 + \frac{(\rho+\delta)\sigma\varepsilon_L}{\sigma_A(1+\sigma-\varepsilon_L)} \right) < 0$, $F'(\bar{s}) = 0$ and $F''(\bar{s}) > 0$ for $\bar{s} = \text{tr}\Delta/2 > 1$ (a minimum). It follows that both roots are positive an lie on either side of unity. The investment part of the model is saddle-point stable. It follows from (A15.8) and the deterministic version of (A15.12) that:

$$\tilde{X}_{t+1} = \tilde{X}_t,$$

i.e. X_t features a unit root. The dynamics of $\tilde{L}_t$ is non-degenerate (proportional to that of $\tilde{K}_t$) so neither is the dynamics in $\tilde{C}_t$.

(d) By rewriting (A15.18) we find:

$$E_t \tilde{\zeta}_{t+1} = (1+\rho) \tilde{\zeta}_t - (\rho+\delta) \frac{(1+\sigma) E_t \tilde{Z}_{t+1} - \sigma \varepsilon_L E_t \tilde{K}_{t+1}}{1+\sigma-\varepsilon_L} + \rho E_t \tilde{r}_{t+1}$$

$$= (1+\rho) \tilde{\zeta}_t - (\rho+\delta) \frac{(1+\sigma) \xi_Z \tilde{Z}_t - \sigma \varepsilon_L \left[\tilde{K}_t + \frac{1}{\sigma_A} \cdot \tilde{\zeta}_t \right]}{1+\sigma-\varepsilon_L} + \rho \xi_R \tilde{r}_t, \qquad (A15.19)$$

where we have used (Q15.6)-(Q15.7). The stochastic system of difference equations is thus:

$$\begin{bmatrix} \tilde{K}_{t+1} \\ E_t \tilde{\zeta}_{t+1} \end{bmatrix} = \Delta \cdot \begin{bmatrix} \tilde{K}_t \\ \tilde{\zeta}_t \end{bmatrix} + \begin{bmatrix} 0 \\ \rho \xi_R \tilde{r}_t - \frac{(\rho+\delta)(1+\sigma)}{1+\sigma-\varepsilon_L} \xi_Z \tilde{Z}_t \end{bmatrix}. \qquad (A15.20)$$

(e) We follow the approach in Appendix B.2 and postulate the trial solution:

$$\tilde{\zeta}_t = \pi_K \tilde{K}_t + \pi_Z \tilde{Z}_t + \pi_R \tilde{r}_t, \qquad (A15.21)$$

where we want to determine the unknown constants, π_K, π_Z, and π_R. It follows that:

$$\begin{aligned} E_t \tilde{\zeta}_{t+1} &= \pi_K E_t \tilde{K}_{t+1} + \pi_Z E_t \tilde{Z}_{t+1} + \pi_R E_t \tilde{r}_{t+1} \\ &= \pi_K \tilde{K}_{t+1} + \pi_Z \xi_Z \tilde{Z}_t + \pi_R \xi_R \tilde{r}_t. \end{aligned}$$

Substituting these results into (A15.21) we find:

$$\begin{bmatrix} \tilde{K}_{t+1} \\ \pi_K \tilde{K}_{t+1} + \pi_Z \xi_Z \tilde{Z}_t + \pi_R \xi_R \tilde{r}_t \end{bmatrix} = \Delta \cdot \begin{bmatrix} \tilde{K}_t \\ \pi_K \tilde{K}_t + \pi_Z \tilde{Z}_t + \pi_R \tilde{r}_t \end{bmatrix}$$

$$+ \begin{bmatrix} 0 \\ \rho \xi_R \tilde{r}_t - \frac{(\rho+\delta)(1+\sigma)}{1+\sigma-\varepsilon_L} \xi_Z \tilde{Z}_t \end{bmatrix}.$$

This gives two expressions for $\tilde{K}_{t+1}$ in terms of $\tilde{K}_t$, $\tilde{Z}_t$, and $\tilde{r}_t$ that must hold for all combinations of these variables. By solving these equations we can express the unknown coefficients in terms of structural parameters. (See Appendix B.2 of Chapter 15 for details.)

Question 3: The non-market sector

(a) The intertemporal substitution elasticity is equal to one. The felicity function is logarithmic.

(b) The representative household makes the consumption and accumulation decisions. Note that (Q15.12) can be rewritten in a more conventional form as:

$$C_\tau + I_\tau^M + I_\tau^H = W_\tau L_\tau + R_\tau^K K_\tau^M - T_\tau, \qquad (A15.22)$$

where $I_\tau^M \equiv K_{\tau+1}^M - (1-\delta_M)K_\tau^M$ and $I_\tau^H \equiv K_{\tau+1}^H - (1-\delta_H)K_\tau^H$ represent *gross* investment in, respectively, business and home capital. This equation is thus a generalized version of equation (15.60) in the book. Since we are adding up the different types of capital, we implicitly assume that the two types of capital are perfect substitutes as far as the household's investment decision is concerned.

(c) The household chooses sequences $\{C_\tau\}_t^\infty$, $\{C_\tau^M\}_t^\infty$, $\{C_\tau^H\}_t^\infty$, $\{L_\tau\}_t^\infty$, $\{L_\tau^M\}_t^\infty$, $\{L_\tau^H\}_t^\infty$, $\{K_{\tau+1}^H\}_t^\infty$, and $\{K_{\tau+1}^M\}_t^\infty$ in order to maximize (Q15.8) subject to the constraints and definitions (Q15.9)–(Q15.12), taking as given the initial stock of total capital, $K_t^M + K_t^H$. It is thus assumed that household capital can costlessly and instantaneously be turned into business capital and vice versa. The Lagrangian expression for this problem is:

$$\mathcal{L}_t^H \equiv E_t \sum_{\tau=t}^\infty \left(\frac{1}{1+\rho}\right)^{\tau-t} \left[\varepsilon_C \ln C_\tau + (1 - \varepsilon_C) \ln[1 - L_\tau^M - L_\tau^H]\right.$$

$$- \lambda_\tau \left(K_{\tau+1}^M + K_{\tau+1}^H + C_\tau^M - W_\tau L_\tau^M - (R_\tau^K + 1 - \delta_M)K_\tau^M - (1 - \delta_H)K_\tau^H\right)$$

$$- \mu_\tau \left(C_\tau - \left[\varepsilon_H \left(C_\tau^H\right)^{(\sigma-1)/\sigma} + (1 - \varepsilon_H)\left(C_\tau^M\right)^{(\sigma-1)/\sigma}\right]^{\sigma/(\sigma-1)}\right)$$

$$\left. - \nu_t \left(C_\tau^H - Z_\tau^H \left(L_\tau^H\right)^{\eta_L}\left(K_\tau^H\right)^{1-\eta_L}\right)\right], \tag{A15.23}$$

where we have substituted the time constraint (Q15.10) into the felicity function. The Lagrange multipliers are denoted by μ_τ, ν_τ, and λ_τ and the (interesting) first-order conditions are:

$$\frac{\partial \mathcal{L}_t^H}{\partial C_\tau} = \left(\frac{1}{1+\rho}\right)^{\tau-t} E_t \left[\frac{\varepsilon_C}{C_\tau} - \mu_\tau\right] = 0, \tag{A15.24}$$

$$\frac{\partial \mathcal{L}_t^H}{\partial L_\tau^M} = -\left(\frac{1}{1+\rho}\right)^{\tau-t} E_t \left[\frac{1-\varepsilon_C}{1-L_\tau} - \lambda_\tau W_\tau\right] = 0, \tag{A15.25}$$

$$\frac{\partial \mathcal{L}_t^H}{\partial L_\tau^H} = -\left(\frac{1}{1+\rho}\right)^{\tau-t} E_t \left[\frac{1-\varepsilon_C}{1-L_\tau} - \nu_\tau \hat{W}_\tau\right] = 0, \tag{A15.26}$$

$$\frac{\partial \mathcal{L}_t^H}{\partial C_\tau^M} = \left(\frac{1}{1+\rho}\right)^{\tau-t} E_t \left[\mu_\tau(1-\varepsilon_H)\left(\frac{C_\tau}{C_\tau^M}\right)^{1/\sigma} - \lambda_\tau\right] = 0, \tag{A15.27}$$

$$\frac{\partial \mathcal{L}_t^H}{\partial C_\tau^H} = \left(\frac{1}{1+\rho}\right)^{\tau-t} E_t \left[\mu_\tau \varepsilon_H \left(\frac{C_\tau}{C_\tau^H}\right)^{1/\sigma} - \nu_\tau\right] = 0, \tag{A15.28}$$

$$\frac{\partial \mathcal{L}_t^H}{\partial K_{\tau+1}^M} = \left(\frac{1}{1+\rho}\right)^{\tau-t} E_t \left[-\lambda_\tau + \lambda_{\tau+1}\frac{R_{\tau+1}^K + 1 - \delta_M}{1+\rho}\right] = 0, \tag{A15.29}$$

$$\frac{\partial \mathcal{L}_t^H}{\partial K_{\tau+1}^H} = \left(\frac{1}{1+\rho}\right)^{\tau-t} E_t \left[-\lambda_\tau + \lambda_{\tau+1}\frac{(\nu_{\tau+1}/\lambda_{\tau+1})\hat{R}_{\tau+1}^K + 1 - \delta_H}{1+\rho}\right] = 0, \tag{A15.30}$$

where $\hat{W}_\tau$ is the *imputed* home wage, i.e. the marginal product of working at home (producing home goods):

$$\hat{W}_\tau \equiv \eta_L Z_\tau^H \left(L_\tau^H\right)^{\eta_L-1}\left(K_\tau^H\right)^{1-\eta_L} = \eta_L \left(\frac{C_\tau^H}{L_\tau^H}\right), \tag{A15.31}$$

and $\hat{R}_\tau^K$ is the imputed rental charge on home capital, which is defined as:

$$\hat{R}_\tau^K \equiv (1-\eta_L)Z_\tau^H \left(L_\tau^H\right)^{\eta_L}\left(K_\tau^H\right)^{-\eta_L} = (1-\eta_L)\left(\frac{C_\tau^H}{K_\tau^H}\right). \tag{A15.32}$$

For the planning period, $\tau = t$, we can simplify these first-order conditions into a number of static conditions and a dynamic condition. By using (A15.25)–(A15.26) we find:

$$\pi_t \equiv \frac{\nu_t}{\lambda_t} = \frac{W_t}{\hat{W}_t}, \tag{A15.33}$$

where π_t is the relative price of home goods. According to (A15.33), labour must be allocated across the two activities such that it yields the same real (imputed) wage. By substituting (A15.24)–(A15.25) into (A15.27) we find:

$$\lambda_t = \frac{\varepsilon_C(1-\varepsilon_H)}{C_t}\left(\frac{C_t}{C_t^M}\right)^{1/\sigma} = \frac{1-\varepsilon_C}{1-L_t}\frac{1}{W_t} \quad \Rightarrow$$

$$W_t = \frac{(1-\varepsilon_C)/(1-L_t)}{[\varepsilon_C/C_t](1-\varepsilon_H)(C_t/C_t^M)^{1/\sigma}}, \tag{A15.34}$$

i.e. the marginal rate of substitution between leisure and consumption of the home good must be equated to the wage rate. Similarly, by using (A15.24) and (A15.26) in (A15.28) we find:

$$\nu_t \equiv \lambda_t\pi_t = \frac{\varepsilon_C\varepsilon_H}{C_t}\left(\frac{C_t}{C_t^H}\right)^{1/\sigma} = \frac{1-\varepsilon_C}{1-L_t}\frac{1}{\hat{W}_t} \quad \Rightarrow$$

$$\hat{W}_t \equiv \frac{W_t}{\pi_t} = \frac{(1-\varepsilon_C)/(1-L_t)}{[\varepsilon_C/C_t]\varepsilon_H(C_t/C_t^H)^{1/\sigma}}. \tag{A15.35}$$

Again, the optimality condition calls for an equalization of the marginal rate of substitution between leisure and home consumption with the relevant wage rate, $\hat{W}_t$. Equations (A15.34)–(A15.35) determine the optimal division between home consumption and consumption of market goods as a function of the relative price, π_t.

Next we use (A15.27)–(A15.28) to deduce a relationship between μ_t and λ_t. Equations (A15.27)–(A15.28) imply:

$$C_t^M = \left(\frac{\mu_t(1-\varepsilon_H)}{\lambda_t}\right)^\sigma C_t, \qquad C_t^H = \left(\frac{\mu_t\varepsilon_H}{\lambda_t\pi_t}\right)^\sigma C_t, \tag{A15.36}$$

where π_t is defined in (A15.33) above. By substituting these expressions into equation (Q15.9) we find:

$$C_t^{\frac{\sigma-1}{\sigma}} = \varepsilon_H\left[\left(\frac{\mu_t\varepsilon_H}{\lambda_t\pi_t}\right)^\sigma C_t\right]^{\frac{\sigma-1}{\sigma}} + (1-\varepsilon_H)\left[\left(\frac{\mu_t(1-\varepsilon_H)}{\lambda_t}\right)^\sigma C_t\right]^{\frac{\sigma-1}{\sigma}}$$

$$1 = \varepsilon_H\left(\frac{\mu_t\varepsilon_H}{\lambda_t\pi_t}\right)^{\sigma-1} + (1-\varepsilon_H)\left(\frac{\mu_t(1-\varepsilon_H)}{\lambda_t}\right)^{(\sigma-1)}$$

$$\frac{\mu_t}{\lambda_t} = \left[\varepsilon_H^\sigma\pi_t^{1-\sigma} + (1-\varepsilon_H)^\sigma\right]^{1/(1-\sigma)} \equiv P(\pi_t), \tag{A15.37}$$

where $P(\pi_t)$ is the true price index of composite consumption. Since (A15.27)–(A15.28) are essentially static decisions, (A15.37) holds not only for period t but also for all other periods, i.e. $\mu_\tau / \lambda_\tau = P(\pi_\tau)$. Note that (A15.24)–(A15.25) in combination with (A15.37) imply:

$$\frac{(1 - \varepsilon_C)/(1 - L_\tau)}{\varepsilon_C / C_\tau} = \frac{W_\tau}{P(\pi_\tau)}. \tag{A15.38}$$

The marginal rate of substitution between leisure and composite consumption is equated to the real wage rate, using the true price index for composite consumption as the deflator. Equation (A15.38) in the counterpart to (15.66) in the book.

Equations (A15.29)–(A15.30) state that the two capital stocks should yield the same *ex ante* rate of return. For period t we find from (A15.29)–(A15.30):

$$\lambda_t = E_t \left[\lambda_{t+1} \frac{1 + r_{t+1}}{1 + \rho} \right] = E_t \left[\lambda_{t+1} \frac{1 + \hat{r}_{t+1}}{1 + \rho} \right], \tag{A15.39}$$

where $r_{t+1} \equiv R_{t+1}^K - \delta_M$ and $\hat{r}_{t+1} \equiv \pi_{t+1} \hat{R}_{t+1}^K - \delta_M$. By using (A15.24) and (A15.37) we find that (A15.39) can be rewritten as:

$$\frac{\varepsilon_C}{C_t} = E_t \left[\frac{1 + r_{t+1}}{1 + \rho} \frac{\varepsilon_C}{C_{t+1}} \frac{P(\pi_t)}{P(\pi_{t+1})} \right] \tag{A15.40}$$

$$= E_t \left[\frac{1 + \hat{r}_{t+1}}{1 + \rho} \frac{\varepsilon_C}{C_{t+1}} \frac{P(\pi_t)}{P(\pi_{t+1})} \right]. \tag{A15.41}$$

Equation (A15.40) is the counterpart to (15.67) in the book. Of course, since capital is perfectly mobile across activities, *ex post* rates of return will also equalize, i.e. $r_\tau = \hat{r}_\tau$ for all τ.

(d) The representative firm makes a static decision regarding output and input demands. In period τ, the realization of the technology shock, Z_τ is known and the firm maximizes Π_τ subject to the technology (Q15.13). The first-order conditions are:

$$\frac{\partial \Pi_\tau}{\partial L_\tau^M} = 0 : \quad \varepsilon_L \frac{Y_\tau}{L_\tau^M} = W_\tau, \tag{A15.42}$$

$$\frac{\partial \Pi_\tau}{\partial K_\tau^M} = 0 : \quad (1 - \varepsilon_L) \frac{Y_\tau}{K_\tau^M} = R_\tau^K. \tag{A15.43}$$

Because the technology features CRTS excess profit is zero ($\Pi_\tau = 0$ for all τ).

(e) Implicit in the formulation of the felicity function is the notion that the household derives disutility from its *total* work effort, $L_\tau^M + L_\tau^H$, regardless of where the work takes place. It follows that L_τ^M and L_τ^H are perfect substitutes to the household. Following Benhabib, Rogerson, and Wright (1991, p. 1171) we can change this aspect of the model by adopting the following felicity function:

$$U_\tau \equiv \varepsilon_C \ln C_\tau + (1 - \varepsilon_C) \ln \left(1 - L_\tau^M - L_\tau^H \right) + \gamma_L L_\tau^M, \tag{A15.44}$$

with $0 < \varepsilon_C < 1$ and $0 \leq \gamma_L < 1 - \varepsilon_L$. With this formulation, the marginal disutility of working at home or in the market are:

$$-\frac{\partial U_\tau}{\partial L_\tau^M} = \frac{1 - \varepsilon_C}{1 - L_\tau} - \gamma_L = -\frac{\partial U_\tau}{\partial L_\tau^H} - \gamma_L.$$

Provided γ_L is strictly positive, working in the market sector is preferred to working around the house. (Note that the sign restriction on γ_L ensures that $-\partial U_\tau / \partial L_\tau^M$ remains positive.)

Question 4: A general RBC model

(a) In the unit-elastic model we have:

$$\sigma_X = 1 \qquad \text{so that} \qquad \Phi = \ln U \tag{a}$$

$$\sigma_{CL} = 1 \qquad \text{so that} \qquad U = C^{\varepsilon_C}(1-L)^{1-\varepsilon_C} \tag{b}$$

$$\sigma_{KL} = 1 \qquad \text{so that} \qquad y = L^{\varepsilon_L} K^{1-\varepsilon_L} \tag{c}$$

There are thus only two types of results to prove, namely results of type (a) and of type (b).

To demonstrate result (a), we can use footnote 18 in Chapter 13. Given the definition of Φ in equation (Q15.14), it follows that both the numerator and the denominator go to zero as $1/\sigma_X \to 1$. We must therefore use L'Hôpital's rule for evaluating limits of the $0/0$ type. We find:

$$\lim_{1/\sigma_X \to 1} \Phi = \lim_{1/\sigma_X \to 1} \frac{-1 \cdot U^{1-1/\sigma_X} \ln U}{-1} = \ln U.$$

To demonstrate result (b) we first take the logarithm of equation (Q15.15):

$$\ln U = \frac{\ln\left(\varepsilon_C C^x + (1-\varepsilon_C)[1-L]^x\right)}{x},$$

where $x \equiv (\sigma_{CL}-1)/\sigma_{CL}$. Both the numerator and the denominator go to zero as $x \to 0$ so we must again use L'Hôpital's rule:

$$\lim_{x \to 0} \ln U = \lim_{x \to 0} \frac{\varepsilon_C C^x \ln C + (1-\varepsilon_C)[1-L]^x \ln(1-L)}{\varepsilon_C C^x + (1-\varepsilon_C)[1-L]^x}$$
$$= \varepsilon_C \ln C + (1-\varepsilon_C) \ln(1-L), \tag{A15.45}$$

where we have used the fact that $\lim_{x \to 0} C^x = \lim_{x \to 0}(1-L)^x = 1$ to get from the first to the second line of (A15.45). It follows from (A15.45) that $U = C^{\varepsilon_C}(1-L)^{1-\varepsilon_C}$.

(b) According to the hint, given in equation (Q15.19), we can write $U(\tau) = X(\tau)/P_U(\tau)$. By using this result, the optimization problem for the household in *stage 1* is to choose paths for $X(\tau)$ and $A(\tau)$ such that:

$$\Lambda(t) = \int_t^\infty \left[\frac{(X(\tau)/P_U(\tau))^{1-1/\sigma_X} - 1}{1 - 1/\sigma_X}\right] e^{\rho(t-\tau)} d\tau,$$

is maximized subject to the household budget identity:

$$\dot{A}(\tau) = r(\tau)A(\tau) + W(\tau) - T(\tau) - X(\tau), \tag{A15.46}$$

and the NPG condition. The household takes as given its initial level of financial assets, $A(t)$. Note that (A15.46) is obtained from (15.3) in the book by using the definition of full consumption given in equation (Q15.19).

The current-value Hamiltonian for this optimization problem is:

$$\mathcal{H} \equiv \frac{(X(\tau)/P_U(\tau))^{1-1/\sigma_X} - 1}{1 - 1/\sigma_X} + \mu(\tau)\left[r(\tau)A(\tau) + W(\tau) - T(\tau) - X(\tau)\right],$$

where $\mu(\tau)$ is the co-state variable, $A(\tau)$ is the state variable, and $X(\tau)$ is the control variable. The first-order conditions are $\partial H/\partial X = 0$ and $-\partial H/\partial A = \dot{\mu} - \rho\mu$, or:

$$\left(\frac{X(\tau)}{P_U(\tau)}\right)^{-1/\sigma_X} \frac{1}{P_U(\tau)} = \mu(\tau),$$

$$-r(\tau)\mu(\tau) = \dot{\mu}(\tau) - \rho\mu(\tau).$$

Combining these first-order conditions yields:

$$\frac{\dot{\mu}(\tau)}{\mu(\tau)} = -\frac{1}{\sigma_X}\left[\frac{\dot{X}(\tau)}{X(\tau)} - \frac{\dot{P}_U(\tau)}{P_U(\tau)}\right] - \frac{\dot{P}_U(\tau)}{P_U(\tau)} = \rho - r(\tau) \quad \Rightarrow$$

$$\frac{\dot{X}(\tau)}{X(\tau)} - \frac{\dot{P}_U(\tau)}{P_U(\tau)} + \sigma_X\frac{\dot{P}_U(\tau)}{P_U(\tau)} = \sigma_X\left[r(\tau) - \rho\right] \quad \Rightarrow$$

$$\frac{\dot{X}(\tau)}{X(\tau)} = \sigma_X[r(\tau) - \rho] + (1 - \sigma_X)\frac{\dot{P}_U(\tau)}{P_U(\tau)}. \tag{A15.47}$$

Equation (A15.47) coincides with the expression in (Q15.17). We must now verify that (Q15.18) is the correct expression for the true cost-of-living index. We do so by solving *stage 2* of the optimization procedure.

In stage 2, the household maximizes subfelicity, U, subject to the constraint $X = C + W(1 - L)$, with X given. The Lagrangian expression is:

$$\mathcal{L} \equiv \left[\varepsilon_C C(\tau)^{(\sigma_{CL}-1)/\sigma_{CL}} + (1 - \varepsilon_C)[1 - L(\tau)]^{(\sigma_{CL}-1)/\sigma_{CL}}\right]^{\sigma_{CL}/(\sigma_{CL}-1)}$$

$$+ \lambda\left[X - C - W(1 - L)\right], \tag{A15.48}$$

where λ is the Lagrange multiplier. The first-order conditions are the constraint as well as $\partial\mathcal{L}/\partial C = \partial\mathcal{L}/\partial(1 - L) = 0$. It follows from the latter two conditions that:

$$[\cdot]^{\sigma_{CL}/(\sigma_{CL}-1)-1}\varepsilon_C C^{(\sigma_{CL}-1)/\sigma_{CL}-1} = \lambda, \tag{A15.49}$$

$$[\cdot]^{\sigma_{CL}/(\sigma_{CL}-1)-1}(1 - \varepsilon_C)(1 - L)^{(\sigma_{CL}-1)/\sigma_{CL}-1} = \lambda W, \tag{A15.50}$$

where $[\cdot]$ is the term in square brackets in equation (Q15.15). By dividing (A15.50) by (A15.49) we obtain the expression for the marginal rate of substitution between leisure and consumption:

$$\frac{(1 - \varepsilon_C)(1 - L)^{-1/\sigma_{CL}}}{\varepsilon_C C^{-1/\sigma_{CL}}} = W. \tag{A15.51}$$

We can use (A15.51) and the constraint to express C and $1 - L$ in terms of X,

W, and the parameters. We show a few steps here:

$$\left(\frac{\varepsilon_C W}{1-\varepsilon_C}\right)^{\sigma_{CL}}(1-L)+W(1-L)=X \quad\Rightarrow$$

$$W(1-L)\left[1+\varepsilon_C^{\sigma_{CL}}(1-\varepsilon_C)^{-\sigma_{CL}}W^{\sigma_{CL}-1}\right]=X \quad\Rightarrow$$

$$(1-\varepsilon_C)^{-\sigma_{CL}}W^{\sigma_{CL}-1}W(1-L)\left[\varepsilon_C^{\sigma_{CL}}+(1-\varepsilon_C)^{\sigma_{CL}}W^{1-\sigma_{CL}}\right]=X \quad\Rightarrow$$

$$W(1-L)=(1-c_X)X,$$

where $1-c_X$ is the full consumption share of spending on leisure. It is defined as:

$$1-c_X=\frac{(1-\varepsilon_C)^{\sigma_{CL}}W^{1-\sigma_{CL}}}{\left[\varepsilon_C^{\sigma_{CL}}+(1-\varepsilon_C)^{\sigma_{CL}}W^{1-\sigma_{CL}}\right]}.$$

Similarly, we can write $C=c_X X$, where c_X is defined as:

$$c_X=\frac{\varepsilon_C^{\sigma_{CL}}}{\left[\varepsilon_C^{\sigma_{CL}}+(1-\varepsilon_C)^{\sigma_{CL}}W^{1-\sigma_{CL}}\right]}.$$

We can now relate U and X and derive the expression for P_U. We find:

$$U=\left[\varepsilon_C C^{(\sigma_{CL}-1)/\sigma_{CL}}+(1-\varepsilon_C)(1-L)^{(\sigma_{CL}-1)/\sigma_{CL}}\right]^{\sigma_{CL}/(\sigma_{CL}-1)}$$

$$=\left[\varepsilon_C (c_X X)^{(\sigma_{CL}-1)/\sigma_{CL}}+(1-\varepsilon_C)\left(\frac{(1-c_X)X}{W}\right)^{(\sigma_{CL}-1)/\sigma_{CL}}\right]^{\sigma_{CL}/(\sigma_{CL}-1)}$$

$$=X\left[\varepsilon_C c_X^{(\sigma_{CL}-1)/\sigma_{CL}}+(1-\varepsilon_C)\left(\frac{1-c_X}{W}\right)^{(\sigma_{CL}-1)/\sigma_{CL}}\right]^{\sigma_{CL}/(\sigma_{CL}-1)}.$$

$$(A15.52)$$

By using the expressions for c_X and $1-c_X$, the complicated term in square brackets on the right-hand side of (A15.52) can be simplified:

$$[\cdot]=\varepsilon_C\left[\frac{\varepsilon_C^{\sigma_{CL}}}{\varepsilon_C^{\sigma_{CL}}+(1-\varepsilon_C)^{\sigma_{CL}}W^{1-\sigma_{CL}}}\right]^{(\sigma_{CL}-1)/\sigma_{CL}}$$

$$+(1-\varepsilon_C)\left[\frac{(1-\varepsilon_C)^{\sigma_{CL}}W^{1-\sigma_{CL}}}{\left[\varepsilon_C^{\sigma_{CL}}+(1-\varepsilon_C)^{\sigma_{CL}}W^{1-\sigma_{CL}}\right]}\frac{1}{W}\right]^{(\sigma_{CL}-1)/\sigma_{CL}}$$

$$=\frac{\varepsilon_C^{\sigma_{CL}}+(1-\varepsilon_C)^{\sigma_{CL}}W^{1-\sigma_{CL}}}{\left[\varepsilon_C^{\sigma_{CL}}+(1-\varepsilon_C)^{\sigma_{CL}}W^{1-\sigma_{CL}}\right]^{(\sigma_{CL}-1)/\sigma_{CL}}}$$

$$=\left[\varepsilon_C^{\sigma_{CL}}+(1-\varepsilon_C)^{\sigma_{CL}}W^{1-\sigma_{CL}}\right]^{1/\sigma_{CL}}. \quad (A15.53)$$

By using (A15.53) in (A15.52) we obtain:

$$U=\frac{X}{\left[\varepsilon_C^{\sigma_{CL}}+(1-\varepsilon_C)^{\sigma_{CL}}W^{1-\sigma_{CL}}\right]^{1-\sigma_{CL}}}=\frac{X}{P_U},$$

where P_U is thus:

$$P_U \equiv \left[\varepsilon_C^{\sigma_{CL}} + (1 - \varepsilon_C)^{\sigma_{CL}} W^{1-\sigma_{CL}}\right]^{1-\sigma_{CL}}. \tag{A15.54}$$

This expression coincides with the second line in (Q15.18). To obtain the first line in (Q15.18) we can let $\sigma_{CL} \to 1$ in (A15.54). This limit can again be determined by using L'Hôpital's rule.

(c) Firm behaviour is still characterized by the usual rental expressions stated in (15.14). By using equation (Q15.16), we find that the marginal product of labour can be written as follows:

$$
\begin{aligned}
\frac{\partial F}{\partial L} &= \left[\varepsilon_L L^{(\sigma_{KL}-1)/\sigma_{KL}} + (1-\varepsilon_L)K^{(\sigma_{KL}-1)/\sigma_{KL}}\right]^{\sigma_{KL}/(\sigma_{KL}-1)-1} \varepsilon_L L^{-1/\sigma_{KL}} \\
&= \left[Y^{(\sigma_{KL}-1)/\sigma_{KL}}\right]^{1/(\sigma_{KL}-1)} \varepsilon_L L^{-1/\sigma_{KL}} \\
&= \varepsilon_L \left(\frac{Y}{L}\right)^{1/\sigma_{KL}}. \tag{A15.55}
\end{aligned}
$$

Similarly, we can write the marginal product of capital as:

$$
\begin{aligned}
\frac{\partial F}{\partial K} &= \left[\varepsilon_L L^{(\sigma_{KL}-1)/\sigma_{KL}} + (1-\varepsilon_L)K^{(\sigma_{KL}-1)/\sigma_{KL}}\right]^{\sigma_{KL}/(\sigma_{KL}-1)-1} (1-\varepsilon_L)K^{-1/\sigma_{KL}} \\
&= \left[Y^{(\sigma_{KL}-1)/\sigma_{KL}}\right]^{1/(\sigma_{KL}-1)} (1-\varepsilon_L)K^{-1/\sigma_{KL}} \\
&= (1-\varepsilon_L) \left(\frac{Y}{K}\right)^{1/\sigma_{KL}}. \tag{A15.56}
\end{aligned}
$$

Intuitively, σ_{KL} measures how easy it is to substitute the production factors for each other. By using (A15.55)–(A15.56) in (15.14) we find the demand functions for capital and labour:

$$\frac{K}{Y} = \left(\frac{r+\delta}{1-\varepsilon_L}\right)^{-\sigma_{KL}}, \qquad \frac{L}{Y} = \left(\frac{W}{1-\varepsilon_L}\right)^{-\sigma_{KL}}.$$

If σ_{KL} is very high then the demand functions are very sensitive to changes in factor prices, i.e. they are very flat. This is because substitution is very easy in that case. Conversely, if σ_{KL} is close to zero, then the demand functions are rather insensitive to changes in factors prices, i.e. they are very steep. Intuitively, this is because substitution is very difficult in that case and the production function features nearly constant input coefficients, i.e. it is close to a Leontief production function (and the isoquants are close to L-shaped).

(d) The great ratios are determined as follows. In the steady state we have $\dot{X} = 0$, $\dot{K} = 0$ (and $\dot{P}_U = 0$) so that it follows from (Q15.17) that $r = \rho$ and from (15.13) that $I = \delta K$. Since $r + \delta = (1-\varepsilon_L)(Y/K)^{1/\sigma_{KL}}$ it follows that Y/K is constant. Hence, I/Y and (by the CRTS production function) K/L are also constant. Since F_L depends on the K/L ratio, it and the real wage are both constants. By (A15.51) we find that $C/(1-L)$ is also constant.

(e) The long-run multiplier can be computed by noting that the supply side of the model fixes the great ratios. Equations (15.17)–(15.18) are all still valid so the multiplier remains as given in (15.19). The intertemporal substitution elasticity does not affect the great ratios at all because these are fixed by the supply side of the model. It does, however, affect the transition path towards the steady state.

Question 5: Government spending shocks in the unit-elastic model

(a) The Lagrangian expression is:

$$\mathcal{L}_t^H \equiv E_t \sum_{\tau=t}^{\infty} \left(\frac{1}{1+\rho}\right)^{\tau-t} \Big[\varepsilon_C \ln\left(C_\tau + \alpha G_\tau\right) - (1 - \varepsilon_C)L_\tau \tag{A15.57}$$

$$-\lambda_\tau \Big[K_{\tau+1} - w_\tau + T_\tau - (R_\tau^K + 1 - \delta)K_\tau + C_\tau + w_\tau(1 - L_\tau)\Big]\Big],$$

where λ_τ is the Lagrange multiplier for the budget identity in period τ. The first-order conditions for this problem (for $\tau = t, t+1, t+2, ...$) are:

$$\frac{\partial \mathcal{L}_t^H}{\partial C_\tau} = \left(\frac{1}{1+\rho}\right)^{\tau-t} E_t \left[\frac{\varepsilon_C}{C_\tau + \alpha G_\tau} - \lambda_\tau\right] = 0,$$

$$\frac{\partial \mathcal{L}_t^H}{\partial [1 - L_\tau]} = \left(\frac{1}{1+\rho}\right)^{\tau-t} E_t \left[-(1 - \varepsilon_C) - \lambda_\tau w_\tau\right] = 0,$$

$$\frac{\partial \mathcal{L}_t^H}{\partial K_{\tau+1}} = \left(\frac{1}{1+\rho}\right)^{\tau-t} E_t \left[-\lambda_\tau + \frac{R_{\tau+1}^K + 1 - \delta}{1+\rho}\lambda_{\tau+1}\right] = 0.$$

For the planning period ($\tau = t$) these first-order conditions can be combined to obtain one static and one dynamic equation (plus a definition):

$$\frac{w_t}{C_t + \alpha G_\tau} = \frac{1 - \varepsilon_C}{\varepsilon_C}, \tag{A15.58}$$

$$\frac{\varepsilon_C}{C_t + \alpha G_\tau} = E_t \left[\frac{1 + r_{t+1}}{1+\rho} \cdot \frac{\varepsilon_C}{C_{t+1} + \alpha G_\tau}\right], \tag{A15.59}$$

$$r_{t+1} \equiv R_{t+1}^K - \delta. \tag{A15.60}$$

The rest of the model is as follows. Technology is deterministic so:

$$Y_\tau = F(K_\tau, L_\tau) \equiv L_\tau^{\varepsilon_L} K_\tau^{1-\varepsilon_L}, \quad 0 < \varepsilon_L < 1, \tag{A15.61}$$

$$w_\tau = F_L(K_\tau, L_\tau) \equiv \varepsilon_L \frac{Y_\tau}{L_\tau}, \tag{A15.62}$$

$$R_\tau^K = r_\tau + \delta = F_K(K_\tau, L_\tau) \equiv (1 - \varepsilon_L) \frac{Y_\tau}{K_\tau}, \tag{A15.63}$$

and we know that:

$$Y_\tau = C_\tau + I_\tau + G_\tau, \tag{A15.64}$$

$$K_{\tau+1} = I_\tau + (1 - \delta)K_\tau, = T_\tau. \tag{A15.65}$$

(b) Loglinearization of (A15.61)-(A15.65) is explained in detail in the text. To log-linearize (A15.58)-(A15.59) we first define the auxiliary variable,

$$B_\tau \equiv C_t + \alpha G_\tau, \tag{A15.66}$$

so that (A15.58) can be written as:

$$w_t = \frac{1 - \varepsilon_C}{\varepsilon_C} B_\tau.$$

This implies that:

$$\tilde{w}_t = \tilde{B}_t. \tag{A15.67}$$

Similarly, (A15.59) can be written as:

$$\frac{\varepsilon_C}{B_t} = E_t \left[\frac{1 + r_{t+1}}{1 + \rho} \cdot \frac{\varepsilon_C}{B_{t+1}} \right].$$

Following the steps leading to (15.71) in the book we thus find:

$$0 = E_t \left[\frac{\rho}{1 + \rho} \tilde{r}_{t+1} + \tilde{B}_t - \tilde{B}_{t+1} \right]. \tag{A15.68}$$

We also note that:

$$\tilde{B}_\tau = \theta_C \tilde{C}_\tau + (1 - \theta_C) \tilde{G}_\tau, \tag{A15.69}$$

where $\theta_C \equiv C^* / B^*$. Finally, we deduce from (Q15.21) that:

$$\tilde{G}_t = \rho_G \tilde{G}_{t-1} + \varepsilon_t^G, \tag{A15.70}$$

so that (A15.68) can be written as:

$$\theta_C \left[E_t \tilde{C}_{t+1} - \tilde{C}_t \right] = (1 - \rho_G)(1 - \theta_C) \tilde{G}_t + \frac{\rho}{1 + \rho} E_t \tilde{r}_{t+1}$$

In summary, Table 15.4 in the book changes to:

$$\tilde{K}_{t+1} - \tilde{K}_t = \delta \left[\tilde{I}_t - \tilde{K}_t \right] \tag{AT4.1}$$

$$\theta_C \left[E_t \tilde{C}_{t+1} - \tilde{C}_t \right] = (1 - \rho_G)(1 - \theta_C) \tilde{G}_t + \frac{\rho}{1 + \rho} E_t \tilde{r}_{t+1} \tag{AT4.2}$$

$$\tilde{G}_t = \tilde{T}_t \tag{AT4.3}$$

$$\tilde{w}_t = \tilde{Y}_t - \tilde{L}_t \tag{AT4.4}$$

$$\rho \tilde{r}_t = (\rho + \delta) \left[\tilde{Y}_t - \tilde{K}_t \right] \tag{AT4.5}$$

$$\tilde{Y}_t = \omega_C \tilde{C}_t + \omega_I \tilde{I}_t + \omega_G \tilde{G}_t \tag{AT4.6}$$

$$\tilde{w}_t = \theta_C \tilde{C}_t + (1 - \theta_C) \tilde{G}_t \tag{AT4.7}$$

$$\tilde{Y}_t = \varepsilon_L \tilde{L}_t + (1 - \varepsilon_L) \tilde{K}_t \tag{AT4.8}$$

(c) To solve for the impulse-response function of the model, we can follow the procedure explained in the text (see from equation (15.72) onward). We show some of the key steps. From (AT4.4), (AT4.7), and (AT4.8) we find:

$$\tilde{L}_t = \tilde{K}_t - \frac{\theta_C \tilde{C}_t + (1 - \theta_C) \tilde{G}_t}{1 - \varepsilon_L}, \tag{A15.71}$$

$$\tilde{Y}_t = \tilde{K}_t - \frac{\varepsilon_L \left[\theta_C \tilde{C}_t + (1 - \theta_C) \tilde{G}_t\right]}{1 - \varepsilon_L}. \tag{A15.72}$$

Using (A15.72) in (AT4.5) we find:

$$\frac{\rho}{\rho + \delta} \tilde{r}_t = - \frac{\varepsilon_L \left[\theta_C \tilde{C}_t + (1 - \theta_C) \tilde{G}_t\right]}{1 - \varepsilon_L}, \tag{A15.73}$$

i.e. the interest rate does not depend on the capital stock! In combination with (AT4.2) this means that we can solve for the path of $\tilde{C}_\tau$ without knowing the path for $\tilde{K}_\tau$. Indeed, by using (A15.73) in (AT4.2) we obtain the following expectational difference equation:

$$\theta_C \left[1 + \frac{\rho + \delta}{1 + \rho} \frac{\varepsilon_L}{1 - \varepsilon_L}\right] \cdot E_t \tilde{C}_{t+1} = \theta_C \tilde{C}_t + \left[(1 - \rho_G) - \rho_G \frac{\rho + \delta}{1 + \rho} \frac{\varepsilon_L}{1 - \varepsilon_L}\right] (1 - \theta_C) \cdot \tilde{G}_t,$$

or:

$$E_t \tilde{C}_{t+1} = \xi_C \tilde{C}_t + \xi_G \tilde{G}_t, \tag{A15.74}$$

with:

$$\xi_C \equiv \left[1 + \frac{\rho + \delta}{1 + \rho} \frac{\varepsilon_L}{1 - \varepsilon_L}\right]^{-1}, \qquad 0 < \pi_C < 1, \tag{A15.75}$$

$$\xi_G \equiv \frac{1 - \theta_C}{\theta_C} \frac{(1 - \rho_G) - \frac{\rho + \delta}{1 + \rho} \frac{\varepsilon_L \rho_G}{1 - \varepsilon_L}}{1 + \frac{\rho + \delta}{1 + \rho} \frac{\varepsilon_L}{1 - \varepsilon_L}}. \tag{A15.76}$$

Several things are worth noting:

- Since $0 < \xi_C < 1$, equation (A15.74) is a stable expectational difference equation that can be solved easily. It converges provided $\rho_G / \xi_C < 1$, i.e. $\xi_C > \rho_G$ (this can be seen by iterating (A15.74) forward in time). Using the trial solution $\tilde{C}_t = \pi_0 + \pi_1 \tilde{G}_t$ we find $E_t \tilde{C}_{t+1} = \pi_0 + \pi_1 \rho_G \tilde{G}_t$. Substituting into (A15.74) we find the implied solution $\tilde{C}_t = (\pi_0 / \xi_C) + [(\pi_1 \rho_G - \xi_G) / \xi_C] \tilde{G}$. It follows that $\pi_0 = 0$ and $\pi_1 = -\xi_G / (\xi_C - \rho_G)$. Hence:

$$\tilde{C}_t = - \frac{\xi_G}{\xi_C - \rho_G} \cdot \tilde{G}_t, \qquad \text{(with } \xi_C > \rho_G\text{)}, \tag{A15.77}$$

is the rational expectation solution for consumption.

- From the stability condition ($\rho_G < \xi_C$) we find:

$$\rho_G \;<\; \frac{1}{1 + \frac{\rho+\delta}{1+\rho}\frac{\varepsilon_L}{1-\varepsilon_L}} \qquad \Leftrightarrow$$

$$\left[1 + \frac{\rho+\delta}{1+\rho}\frac{\varepsilon_L}{1-\varepsilon_L}\right]\rho_G \;<\; 1 \qquad \Leftrightarrow$$

$$0 \;<\; (1-\rho_G) - \rho_G\frac{\rho+\delta}{1+\rho}\frac{\varepsilon_L}{1-\varepsilon_L} \equiv \xi_G.$$

Since ξ_G positive, it follows from (A15.77) that private consumption moves in the opposite direction to public consumption.

Question 6: No wealth effect in labour supply

(a) The current-value Hamiltonian is:

$$\mathcal{H}_C \equiv \ln\left(C\left(\tau\right) - \frac{\gamma_L}{1+\theta_L}L\left(\tau\right)^{1+\theta_L}\right) + \lambda\left(\tau\right)\left[r\left(\tau\right)A\left(\tau\right) + W\left(\tau\right)L\left(\tau\right) - T\left(\tau\right) - C\left(\tau\right)\right].$$

The control variables are C and L, the state variable is A, and the co-state variable is λ. The main first-order conditions are:

$$\frac{\partial\mathcal{H}_C}{\partial C} \;=\; \frac{1}{C\left(\tau\right) - \frac{\gamma_L}{1+\theta_L}L\left(\tau\right)^{1+\theta_L}} - \lambda\left(\tau\right) = 0,$$

$$\frac{\partial\mathcal{H}_C}{\partial L} \;=\; \frac{\gamma_L L\left(\tau\right)^{\theta_L}}{C\left(\tau\right) - \frac{\gamma_L}{1+\theta_L}L\left(\tau\right)^{1+\theta_L}} + \lambda\left(\tau\right)W\left(\tau\right) = 0,$$

$$-\frac{\partial\mathcal{H}_C}{\partial A} \;=\; -r\left(\tau\right)\lambda\left(\tau\right) = \dot{\lambda}\left(\tau\right) - \rho\lambda\left(\tau\right).$$

We define subfelicity as:

$$X\left(\tau\right) \equiv C\left(\tau\right) - \frac{\gamma_L}{1+\theta_L}L\left(\tau\right)^{1+\theta_L}, \tag{A15.78}$$

and write the first-order conditions as:

$$\gamma_L L\left(\tau\right)^{\theta_L} \;=\; W\left(\tau\right), \tag{A15.79}$$

$$\frac{\dot{X}\left(\tau\right)}{X\left(\tau\right)} \;=\; r\left(\tau\right) - \rho. \tag{A15.80}$$

We can now write the budget identity as:

$$\dot{A}\left(\tau\right) = r\left(\tau\right)A\left(\tau\right) + Y_F\left(\tau\right) - T\left(\tau\right) - X\left(\tau\right), \tag{A15.81}$$

where Y_F is full income:

$$\begin{aligned}
Y_F\left(\tau\right) &\equiv W\left(\tau\right)L\left(\tau\right) - \frac{\gamma_L}{1+\theta_L}L\left(\tau\right)^{1+\theta_L} \\
&= \gamma_L L\left(\tau\right)^{1+\theta_L} - \frac{\gamma_L}{1+\theta_L}L\left(\tau\right)^{1+\theta_L} \\
&= \frac{\theta_L}{1+\theta_L}\gamma_L\left(\frac{W\left(\tau\right)}{\gamma_L}\right)^{(1+\theta_L)/\theta_L}.
\end{aligned} \tag{A15.82}$$

Once we know the solution for $X(\tau)$ and $W(\tau)$ we can recover the solution for $C(\tau)$ by noting that in the optimum:

$$
\begin{aligned}
C(\tau) &= X(\tau) + \frac{\gamma_L}{1+\theta_L} L(\tau)^{1+\theta_L} \\
&= X(\tau) + \frac{\gamma_L}{1+\theta_L} \left(\frac{W(\tau)}{\gamma_L} \right)^{(1+\theta_L)/\theta_L} \\
&= X(\tau) + \frac{1}{\theta_L} Y_F(\tau).
\end{aligned}
\tag{A15.83}
$$

(b) The model of Table 15.1 is thus:

$$
\dot{K}(t) = I(t) - \delta K(t) \tag{AT1.1}
$$

$$
\frac{\dot{X}(t)}{X(t)} = r(t) - \rho \tag{AT1.2}
$$

$$
G(t) = T(t) \tag{AT1.3}
$$

$$
W(t) = \varepsilon_L \frac{Y(t)}{L(t)} \tag{AT1.4}
$$

$$
r(t) + \delta = (1 - \varepsilon_L) \frac{Y(t)}{K(t)} \tag{AT1.5}
$$

$$
Y(t) = X(t) + \frac{1}{\theta_L} Y_F(t) + I(t) + G(t) \tag{AT1.6}
$$

$$
W(t) = \gamma_L L(t)^{\theta_L} \tag{AT1.7}
$$

$$
Y(t) = Z_0 L(t)^{\varepsilon_L} K(t)^{1-\varepsilon_L} \tag{AT1.8}
$$

where we need the definition for $Y_F(t)$ to close the model.

To deduce the phase diagram we first compute quasi-reduced form expressions for factor prices $r(t)$ and $W(t)$. We know that $W(t) = \varepsilon_L \frac{Y(t)}{L(t)}$ (labour demand) so that labour market clearing implies:

$$
\begin{aligned}
W(t) &= \varepsilon_L Z_0 L(t)^{\varepsilon_L - 1} K(t)^{1-\varepsilon_L} = \gamma_L L(t)^{\theta_L} \quad \Rightarrow \\
L(t)^{1-\varepsilon_L + \theta_L} &= (\varepsilon_L Z_0 / \gamma_L) K(t)^{1-\varepsilon_L} \quad \Rightarrow \\
L(t) &= (\varepsilon_L Z_0 / \gamma_L)^{1/(1-\varepsilon_L+\theta_L)} K(t)^{(1-\varepsilon_L)/(1-\varepsilon_L+\theta_L)}. \tag{A15.84}
\end{aligned}
$$

Hence, $W(t)$ is:

$$
\begin{aligned}
W(t) &= \gamma_L (\varepsilon_L Z_0 / \gamma_L)^{\theta_L/(1-\varepsilon_L+\theta_L)} K(t)^{\theta_L(1-\varepsilon_L)/(1-\varepsilon_L+\theta_L)} \\
&\equiv \eta_w K(t)^{\theta_L(1-\varepsilon_L)/(1-\varepsilon_L+\theta_L)}. \tag{A15.85}
\end{aligned}
$$

Full income is thus equal to:

$$
\begin{aligned}
Y_F(t) &= \frac{\theta_L}{1+\theta_L}\gamma_L\left(\frac{W(\tau)}{\gamma_L}\right)^{(1+\theta_L)/\theta_L} \\
&= \frac{\theta_L}{1+\theta_L}\gamma_L\left((\varepsilon_L Z_0/\gamma_L)^{\theta_L/(1-\varepsilon_L+\theta_L)}K(t)^{\theta_L(1-\varepsilon_L)/(1-\varepsilon_L+\theta_L)}\right)^{(1+\theta_L)/\theta_L} \\
&= \frac{\theta_L}{1+\theta_L}\gamma_L(\varepsilon_L Z_0/\gamma_L)^{(1+\theta_L)/(1-\varepsilon_L+\theta_L)}K(t)^{(1+\theta_L)(1-\varepsilon_L)/(1-\varepsilon_L+\theta_L)} \\
&= \eta_f K(t)^{(1+\theta_L)(1-\varepsilon_L)/(1-\varepsilon_L+\theta_L)} \tag{A15.86}
\end{aligned}
$$

Similarly, $Y(t)$ can be written as:

$$
\begin{aligned}
Y(t) &= Z_0 L(t)^{\varepsilon_L}K(t)^{1-\varepsilon_L} \\
&= Z_0\left[(\varepsilon_L Z_0/\gamma_L)^{1/(1-\varepsilon_L+\theta_L)}K(t)^{(1-\varepsilon_L)/(1-\varepsilon_L+\theta_L)}\right]^{\varepsilon_L}K(t)^{1-\varepsilon_L} \\
&= Z_0(\varepsilon_L Z_0/\gamma_L)^{\varepsilon_L/(1-\varepsilon_L+\theta_L)}K(t)^{(1-\varepsilon_L)(1+\theta_L)/(1-\varepsilon_L+\theta_L)} \\
&\equiv \eta_y K(t)^{(1-\varepsilon_L)(1+\theta_L)/(1-\varepsilon_L+\theta_L)} \tag{A15.87}
\end{aligned}
$$

and $r(t)$ is given by:

$$
\begin{aligned}
r(t)+\delta &= (1-\varepsilon_L)\frac{Y(t)}{K(t)} \\
&= (1-\varepsilon_L)Z_0(\varepsilon_L Z_0/\gamma_L)^{\varepsilon_L/(1-\varepsilon_L+\theta_L)}K(t)^{-\varepsilon_L\theta_L/(1-\varepsilon_L+\theta_L)} \\
&\equiv \eta_r K(t)^{-\varepsilon_L\theta_L/(1-\varepsilon_L+\theta_L)} \tag{A15.88}
\end{aligned}
$$

The dynamic model is thus given by:

$$
\begin{aligned}
\dot{K}(t) &= Y(t)-X(t)-\frac{1}{\theta_L}Y_F(t)-G(t)-\delta K(t) \\
&= \left(\eta_y-\frac{\eta_f}{\theta_L}\right)K(t)^{(1-\varepsilon_L)(1+\theta_L)/(1-\varepsilon_L+\theta_L)}-X(t)-G(t)-\delta K(t) \tag{A15.89} \\
\frac{\dot{X}(t)}{X(t)} &= r(t)-\rho \\
&= \eta_r K(t)^{-\varepsilon_L\theta_L/(1-\varepsilon_L+\theta_L)}-(\rho+\delta) \tag{A15.90}
\end{aligned}
$$

Despite the fact that labour supply is endogenous, the model looks a lot like the standard Ramsey model with exogenous labour supply. The phase diagram is qualitatively the same as Figure 13.9 in the book (but with X rather than C on the vertical axis). See Figure A15.1.

(c) The changes occur in equations (T2.2), (T2.6) and (T2.7) from Table 15.2 in the book. For book equation (T2.2) we find:

$$
\begin{aligned}
d\dot{X}(t) &= (r-\rho)\,dX(t)+X\,dr(t) \\
\frac{d\dot{X}(t)}{X} &= r\frac{dr(t)}{r} \\
\dot{\tilde{X}}(t) &= \rho\tilde{r}(t) \tag{A15.91}
\end{aligned}
$$

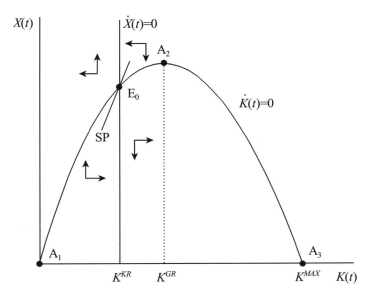

Figure A15.1: Phase diagram: No wealth effect in labour supply

For book equation (T2.6) we obtain:

$$
\begin{aligned}
dY(t) &= dX(t) + \frac{1}{\theta_L} dY_F(t) + dI(t) + dG(t) \\
\frac{dY(t)}{Y} &= \frac{X}{Y}\frac{dX(t)}{X} + \frac{1}{\theta_L}\frac{Y_F}{Y}\frac{dY_F(t)}{Y_F} + \frac{I}{Y}\frac{dI(t)}{I} + \frac{G}{Y}\frac{dG(t)}{G} \\
\tilde{Y}(t) &= \omega_X \tilde{X}(t) + \frac{\omega_F}{\theta_L}\tilde{Y}_F(t) + \omega_I \tilde{I}(t) + \omega_G \tilde{G}(t),
\end{aligned}
\tag{A15.92}
$$

where $\omega_X \equiv X/Y$ and $\omega_F \equiv Y_F/Y$. Of course, Y_F is proportional to Y so we can write:

$$
\begin{aligned}
Y_F(t) &= \eta_f K(t)^{(1+\theta_L)(1-\varepsilon_L)/(1-\varepsilon_L+\theta_L)} \\
&= \frac{\eta_f}{\eta_y} Y(t),
\end{aligned}
\tag{A15.93}
$$

so that $\tilde{Y}_F(t) = \tilde{Y}(t)$ and we can write (T2.6) as:

$$
\left[1 - \frac{\omega_F}{\theta_L}\right]\tilde{Y}(t) = \omega_X \tilde{X}(t) + \omega_I \tilde{I}(t) + \omega_G \tilde{G}(t).
\tag{A15.94}
$$

Finally, for book equation (T2.7) we get:

$$
\begin{aligned}
dW(t) &= \theta_L \gamma_L L^{\theta_L-1} dL(t) \\
\frac{dW(t)}{W} &= \frac{\theta_L \gamma_L L^{\theta_L-1} dL(t)}{\gamma_L L^{\theta_L}} \\
\tilde{W}(t) &= \theta_L \tilde{L}(t).
\end{aligned}
\tag{A15.95}
$$

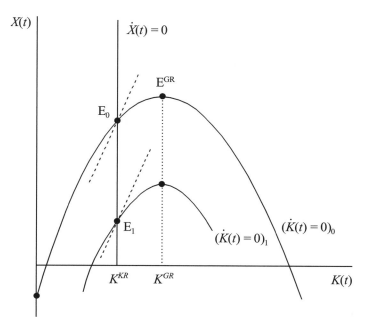

Figure A15.2: Fiscal policy in the absence of a wealth effect in labour supply

(d) We know that in the long run we have $r = \rho$ (i.e. $\tilde{r}(\infty) = 0$) so that:

$$\tilde{Y}(\infty) = \tilde{K}(\infty) = 0.$$

We also have $\dot{K}(\infty) = 0$ so that:

$$\tilde{I}(\infty) = \tilde{K}(\infty).$$

Using these results in (T2.6) we get:

$$
\begin{aligned}
\omega_X \tilde{X}(\infty) &= -\omega_G \tilde{G} \\
\frac{X}{Y}\frac{dX(\infty)}{X} &= -\frac{G}{Y}\frac{dG}{G} \\
\frac{dX(\infty)}{dG} &= -1
\end{aligned}
\tag{A15.96}
$$

The remaining multipliers are easy:

$$
\begin{aligned}
\frac{dY(\infty)}{dG} &= \frac{dI(\infty)}{dG} = \frac{dK(\infty)}{dG} = \frac{dL(\infty)}{dG} = \frac{dW(\infty)}{dG} = 0 \\
\frac{dC(\infty)}{dG} &= -1
\end{aligned}
$$

See Figure A15.2 for an illustration.

Chapter 16

Overlapping generations in continuous time

Question 1: Short questions

(a) Explain how the virtual absence of annuity markets could explain why most countries have significant public pension systems.

(b) Explain the role of the annuities market in the Blanchard - Yaari model. Demonstrate that the insurance firms in the Blanchard - Yaari model make zero pure profits due to the assumption of actuarial fairness.

(c) Assume (realistically) that household mortality is increasing in the age of the household. What would happen to the annuity rate of interest in that case? Explain.

(d) Explain why, according to standard theory, people facing an uncertain lifetime place a positive value on annuities. In reality, however, annuity markets are quite thin. Can you think of some some reasons why this may be so?

(e) Use the standard Blanchard - Yaari model to investigate the effect of a drop in the birth-death parameter β. For simplicity, assume away the existence of a government ($B(t) = G(t) = T(t) = 0$). Explain the intuition behind the effects.

(f) "In a small open economy, the world interest rate must equal the pure rate of time preference. Otherwise, the model is not internally consistent." True, false, or uncertain? Evaluate this statement.

Question 2: The Buiter model

[Based on Buiter (1988)] In the standard Blanchard - Yaari model (reported in Table 16.1 in the book), the crude birth rate and the mortality rate are equal to each other so that the population is constant in size. Buiter has generalized the Blanchard - Yaari model by distinguishing separate parameters for the birth rate, β, and the mortality rate, μ. In the absence of a government, the Buiter model takes the following form:

$$\frac{\dot{c}(t)}{c(t)} = r(t) - \rho - \beta(\rho + \mu) \cdot \frac{k(t)}{c(t)}, \tag{Q16.1}$$

$$\dot{k}(t) = y(t) - c(t) - (\delta + \beta - \mu)k(t), \tag{Q16.2}$$

$$r(t) + \delta = \varepsilon \frac{y(t)}{k(t)}, \tag{Q16.3}$$

$$w(t) = (1 - \varepsilon)y(t), \tag{Q16.4}$$

$$y(t) = Z_0 k(t)^{\varepsilon}, \qquad 0 < \varepsilon < 1. \tag{Q16.5}$$

Consumption, capital, and output are measured in per capita terms, i.e. $c(t)$ is per capita consumption, $k(t)$ is capital per worker (the capital intensity), and $y(t)$ is per capita output. The population growth rate, defined as $n_L \equiv \beta - \mu$, is assumed to be positive, and δ is the positive depreciation rate of capital.

(a) Explain intuitively why the birth rate features in the generational turnover (GT) term in the aggregate "Euler equation"? And why does the mortality rate feature in the GT term?

(b) Derive the phase diagram for the Buiter model. Show that the model is saddle-point stable. Which is the predetermined variable? And which is the jumping variable?

(c) Show the effects of an unanticipated and permanent productivity improvement.

(d) Show that, depending on the parameters, dynamic inefficiency cannot be ruled out in the Buiter model. Derive a condition under which oversaving occurs and show that the model is nevertheless well-defined (saddle-point stable, steady-state $c(t)$ and $k(t)$ both positive, etcetera).

(e) Under Ricardian Equivalence, the basic unit of analysis is the altruistically-linked dynastic family. We usually call this dynastic family the representative agent (RA). Provided no new dynastic families emerge, Ricardian equivalence holds. That is what Robert Barro taught the profession. Show under which parameter setting the Buiter model formally reduces to the RA model with a growing population. Explain. (You may want to use the concepts of population growth on the intensive and the extensive margin.)

Question 3: Endogenous growth

[Based on Saint-Paul (1992)] In this question we extend the Blanchard - Yaari model to allow for endogenous growth. Assume that the private production function, $F(K, L)$, is given by:

$$Y(t) = F(K(t), L(t)) \equiv Z(t)L(t)^{\varepsilon_L}K(t)^{1-\varepsilon_L}, \tag{Q16.6}$$

where $Z(t)$ is the level of general technology (taken as given by individual firms). There is an external effect which ensures that general technology is positively affected by the aggregate capital stock:

$$Z(t) = AK(t)^{\varepsilon_L}. \tag{Q16.7}$$

The rest of the model is unchanged, i.e. the expressions in Table 16.1 are all still appropriate. Assume for simplicity that government consumption is zero ($G(t) = 0$).

(a) Derive the marginal productivity conditions for labour and capital. Show that the real interest rate is constant.

(b) Assume that the government maintains a constant tax rate on labour income, so that $T(t) = t_L W(t)$, where $W(t)$ is the real wage rate. Assume furthermore that the government also maintains a constant ratio between debt ($B(t)$) and aggregate output ($Y(t)$) which we denote by ζ (i.e. $B(t) = \zeta Y(t)$). Derive the growth rate of the economy.

(c) Is the rate of economic growth affected by the birth-death rate, β? If so, explain the economic intuition behind this dependence.

(d) Show that a decrease in ζ increases the rate of growth in the economy. Explain the economic intuition behind the result.

Question 4: The Blanchard - Yaari model without insurance

[Based on Buiter (1990, ch. 7)] In this question we modify the standard Blanchard model by assuming that there are no markets for insuring against the risks associated with an unexpected death. In this case the household will generally make "accidental bequests" which may be positive or negative. It is assumed that the estate of a household who has died accrues to the government. The government reimburses the revenue of this scheme to surviving agents in an age-independent lump-sum fashion. Surviving agents take these lump-sum transfers as given.

(a) Solve the optimization problem for individual households. Explain carefully what the household's budget identity looks like and state the NPG condition that you use.

(b) Derive the aggregate consumption rule and the aggregate consumption Euler equation for this model.

(c) Show that the validity of the Ricardian equivalence theorem hinges on the birth rate and not on the existence of life insurance possibilities *per se*. Explain the intuition behind this result.

Question 5: Technological change

[Based on Buiter (1988)] In this question we modify the standard Blanchard model by assuming that: (i) the probability of death, μ, is not necessarily equal to the birth rate, which we denote by $\beta \geq 0$; (ii) there is Harrod-neutral technological change at an exogenously given rate $n_A \geq 0$. The expected lifetime utility function of a representative household of vintage v in period t is:

$$E\Lambda(v,t) = \int_t^\infty \ln \bar{c}(v,\tau) e^{(\rho+\mu)(t-\tau)} d\tau, \tag{Q16.8}$$

where $\bar{c}(v,\tau)$ is consumption and ρ is the pure rate of time preference. We assume that $\rho > n_L$, where n_L is the growth rate of the population. The budget identity of the household is:

$$\dot{\bar{a}}(v,\tau) = [r(\tau) + \mu]\,\bar{a}(v,\tau) + \bar{w}(\tau) - \bar{z}(\tau) - \bar{c}(v,\tau), \qquad (Q16.9)$$

where $r(\tau)$ is the interest rate, $\bar{w}(\tau)$ is the wage rate, $\bar{z}(\tau)$ is the lump-sum tax, $\bar{a}(v,\tau)$ are real financial assets, and $\dot{\bar{a}}(v,\tau) \equiv d\bar{a}(v,\tau)/d\tau$. The solvency condition is:

$$\lim_{\tau\to\infty} e^{-R^A(t,\tau)}\bar{a}(v,\tau) = 0, \quad R^A(t,\tau) \equiv \int_t^\tau [r(s) + \mu]\,ds. \qquad (Q16.10)$$

The population at time t is denoted by $L(t)$ and the population at time $t = 0$ is normalized to unity ($L(0) = 1$). With a positive birth rate ($\beta > 0$), the cohort born at time v is related to the total population in existence at that time according to $L(v,v) = \beta L(v)$.

(a) Solve the optimization problem for individual households.

(b) The growth rate of the total population is given by n_L. Prove that the size of cohort v at time $t \geq v$ is equal to:

$$L(v,t) = \begin{cases} \beta e^{\beta v} e^{-\mu t} & \text{if } \beta > 0 \\ e^{-\mu t} & \text{if } \beta = 0,\ v = 0 \\ 0 & \text{if } \beta = 0,\ v > 0 \end{cases}$$

Prove furthermore that $n_L = \beta - \mu$. Explain the intuition behind the expressions.

(c) Derive the aggregate consumption rule, the aggregate consumption Euler equation, and the differential equation for aggregate human wealth for this model. Denote the aggregate variables by $C(t)$, $A(t)$, $W(t)$, $Z(t)$, and $H(t)$, etcetera.

(d) The aggregate production function is given by $Y(t) = K(t)^\alpha N(t)^{1-\alpha}$, where $Y(t)$ is aggregate output, $K(t)$ is the capital stock, and $N(t) \equiv A_L(t)L(t)$ is the labour input measured in efficiency units. The index of Harrod-neutral technical change grows exponentially at rate n_A, i.e. $\dot{A}_L(t)/A_L(t) = n_A > 0$. The capital stock depreciates at a constant rate δ and firms are perfectly competitive. Derive the marginal productivity conditions for labour and capital and express them in terms of the intensive-form production function, $y(t) = k(t)^\alpha$, where $y(t) \equiv Y(t)/N(t)$ and $k(t) \equiv K(t)/N(t)$.

(e) Assume that the government budget identity is given by $\dot{B}(\tau) = r(\tau)B(\tau) + G(\tau) - Z(\tau)$, where $B(\tau)$ is government debt and $G(\tau)$ is government consumption. Write the model derived thus far in terms of efficiency unit of labour and state the system of differential equations characterizing the economy. Use the notation $c(t) \equiv C(t)/N(t)$, $a(t) \equiv A(t)/N(t)$, $b(t) \equiv B(t)/N(t)$ etcetera.

(f) Show that the Ricardian equivalence theorem is valid when the birth rate is zero ($\beta = 0$) even if the probability of death is positive ($\mu > 0$ so that lifetimes are uncertain) or there is positive technological change ($n_A > 0$). Explain the intuition behind this result.

(g) Assume that government consumption, $G(t)$, is financed by means of lump-sum taxes, $Z(t)$, and that there is no government debt. Compute the effects on growth in consumption, output, wages, and the capital stock, of a balanced-budget increase in government consumption expressed in terms of efficiency units of labour. Illustrate your answer with the aid of a phase diagram and draw the impulse-response functions.

Question 6: Mandatory retirement

[Based on Nielsen (1994)] In this question we study the effects of social security in a Blanchard - Yaari model of a small open economy with mandatory retirement. The economy under consideration is small in world financial markets and faces a constant interest rate r^*. There is no capital and the production function is:

$$Y(\tau) = ZL(\tau), \tag{Q16.11}$$

where Y is output, Z is an index of productivity (exogenous), and L is employment. Households are as in section 16.4.5 of the book but there is a system of mandatory retirement which prohibits agents older than π to work. Instead such retired agents receive an untaxed pension, P, from the government. The pension system is financed by means of age-independent lump-sum taxes, T, levied on working generations. The income at time τ of a generation born at time $v \leq \tau$ is thus:

$$I(v, \tau) = \begin{cases} W(\tau) - T(\tau) & \text{for } \tau - v < \pi \\ P & \text{for } \tau - v \geq \pi \end{cases} \tag{Q16.12}$$

We abstract from government consumption and government debt. The country is populated by patient agents so that $\rho < r^*$.

(a) Solve the household optimization problem. Explain why human wealth is age-dependent in this case.

(b) Derive the government budget constraint. Show what happens to the lump-sum tax if the retirement age is increased but the pension payment is held constant.

(c) Derive the aggregate consumption rule, the aggregate consumption Euler equation, and the differential equation for aggregate financial wealth for the model. Explain the intuition behind the terms involving the pension system.

(d) Derive the impact, transitional, and long-run effects on consumption and net foreign assets of an increase in the pension payment. Illustrate with the aid of a phase diagram and explain the intuition.

(e) Derive the impact, transitional, and long-run effects on consumption and net foreign assets of an increase in the mandatory retirement age. Illustrate with the aid of a phase diagram and explain the intuition.

Question 7: Public infrastructure

[Partially based on Mourmouras and Lee (1999)] Consider the following Blanchard - Yaari model with productive public infrastructure. Individual households have the utility function (16.29) and face the lifetime budget constraint (16.30). The production function (16.45) is replaced by:

$$Y(t) = Z_0 K(t)^{1-\varepsilon_L} [K_G(t)L(t)]^{\varepsilon_L}, \tag{Q16.13}$$

where Z_0 is a time-invariant index of general technology and $K_G(t)$ is the quantity of productive government services (measured as a flow). There is a general output tax, t_Y, so the objective function of the firm is given by:

$$V(t) = \int_t^\infty \left[(1 - t_Y) Y(\tau) - W(\tau)L(\tau) - I(\tau)\right] e^{-R(t,\tau)} d\tau. \tag{Q16.14}$$

The tax receipts are used to finance government services, i.e. $t_Y Y(t) = K_G(t)$. There is no government debt and lump-sum taxes are zero. Labour supply is exogenous and normalized to unity ($L(\tau) = 1$).

(a) Derive the first-order conditions for the (representative and competitive) firm's optimization problem. Show that factor payments exhaust after-tax revenues.

(b) Show that the marginal product of capital is uniquely related to Z_0 and t_Y only. Derive an expression for the marginal product of labour.

(c) Prove that there is no transitional dynamics in the model.

(d) Show that the model exhibits endogenous growth. Compute the growth rate and show that it depends negatively on the birth-death rate β. Give the intuition for this result.

(e) Characterize the maximum growth rate in this economy. Show that the growth maximizing tax rate does not depend on the birth-death rate. Provide the intuition behind this result. Is the maximum growth rate independent of the birth/death rate?

Heijdra and Meijdam (2002) consider the more realistic scenario in which $K_G(t)$ is the *stock* of public infrastructure (rather than the flow of services) which must be built up gradually with the aid of public investment, $I_G(t)$. The accumulation identity for public capital is:

$$\dot{K}_G(t) = I_G(t) - \delta_G K_G(t), \tag{Q16.15}$$

where δ_G is the constant rate of depreciation of public capital. The government budget constraint is now $t_Y Y(t) = I_G(t)$.

(f) ★ Write down the dynamic system characterizing the macroeconomy. Rewrite the model in stationary format and characterize the steady-state growth rate. Explain intuitively why you expect the modified model to displays nontrivial transitional dynamics. Compute the asymptotic growth rate as a function of t_Y.

Answers

Question 1: Short questions

(a) A public pension system can be seen as a kind of annuity system. Agents pay into the scheme during their youth and middle age, and receive a pension when they are retired. In the absence of a public pension system and an annuity system, it is possible for agents experiencing lifetime uncertainty to run out of saved assets (if they live much longer than they expected). This problem does not exist when there is a public pension system: one gets the pension as long as one is alive. Of course, the pension scheme should be viable, i.e. it should not run out of money.

(b) The annuity market allows the household to insure against the unpleasant aspects of lifetime uncertainty. They don not need buffer stocks of assets anymore (to adhere to the constraint $\Pr\{A(T) \geq 0\} = 1$). This constraint is automatically satisfied with annuities.

(c) Provided age is observable, the annuity rate would increase also. If the probability of death increases the insurance company will demand a higher premium (or pay a higher benefit). Assumption: actuarially fair insurance.

(d) This property was pointed out by Yaari (1965) in his famous paper. In the absence of annuities the agent must hold buffer stock assets to make sure that he/she meets the non-negativity constraint on wealth with probability 1 at each and every moment in time ($\Pr\{A(T) \geq 0\} = 1$). These assets detract from consumption and thus are costly from a utility perspective. With annuities such buffer stocks are not needed. Consumption can be higher, the yield on the assets is higher (because the annuity rate exceeds the rate of interest), and utility is higher. The agent will fully insure. The annuities need not be actuarially fair. Provided r^A exceeds r, it is advantageous to hold wealth in the form of annuities.

Various (not totally convincing) reasons exist to explain the *annuity puzzle*:

- Annuities may not be actuarially fair, due to resource costs of life insurance companies.

- Annuities may not be actuarially fair, due to adverse selection (only people who know they are very healthy will buy annuities; health status is not observable by insurance companies).

- Public pensions may implicitly force agents to annuitize more of their wealth than they would like to.

(e) The model is given in the book:

$$\dot{C}(t) = [r(t) - \rho]C(t) - \beta(\rho + \beta)K(t),$$
$$\dot{K}(t) = F(K(t), 1) - C(t) - \delta K(t),$$
$$r(t) = F_K(K(t), 1) - \delta.$$

The phase diagram is given in Figure 16.7. The $\dot{C} = 0$ line is:

$$C(t) = \beta(\rho + \beta)\frac{K(t)}{F_K(K(t), 1) - (\rho + \delta)}.$$

A decrease in β thus rotates the $\dot{C} = 0$ line in a clockwise direction:

$$\frac{\partial C(t)}{\partial \beta} = (\rho + 2\beta)\frac{K(t)}{F_K(K(t),1) - (\rho + \delta)} > 0.$$

The new equilibrium is associated with a higher capital stock and a higher consumption level. Because people live longer lives they save more (individually and in aggregate). The generational turnover term becomes less important for each level of the capital stock. (Recall that for $\beta = 0$ we recover the RA model, in which the GT term is zero.)

(f) This statement is correct for the representative-agent model but not for the overlapping-generations model. Section 16.4.5 in the book explains in detail why this is the case. Briefly put, with overlapping generations the generational turnover effect ensures that there is no zero-root in the dynamic model, even if the rate of time preference happens to coincide with the world interest rate.

Question 2: The Buiter model

(a) The key difference between the Blanchard model (of Table 16.1 in the book) and the Buiter model is the demographic part. Blanchard assumes that the birth rate is equal to the death rate so that the population is constant and we can work directly in levels of output, consumption, and capital etcetera. In the Buiter model the birth rate is allowed to differ from the death rate, so the population can grow.

Buiter's framework makes a distinction between the probability of death μ (≥ 0) and the birth rate β (≥ 0). Denote the population size at time t by $L(t)$. In the absence of international migration, the growth rate of the population, n_L, is equal to the difference between the birth and death rates:

$$\frac{\dot{L}(t)}{L(t)} = \beta - \mu \equiv n_L.$$

By solving this expression subject to the initial condition $L(0) = L_0$, we find the path for the aggregate population:

$$L(t) = L_0 e^{n_L t}. \tag{A16.1}$$

Like Blanchard, Buiter assumes that the size of a newborn generation is proportional to the current population:

$$L(v,v) = \beta L(v), \tag{A16.2}$$

where $L(v,v)$ is the size of the cohort born at time v. Since the death rate is constant and cohorts are assumed to be large, the size of each generation falls exponentially according to:

$$L(v,t) = e^{-\mu(t-v)}L(v,v), \qquad t \geq v. \tag{A16.3}$$

By substituting (A16.1) and (A16.2) into (A16.3) we finally obtain:

$$\begin{aligned} L(v,t) &= \beta e^{\mu(v-t)}L(v) = \beta e^{\mu(v-t)}L(t)e^{n_L(v-t)} \\ &= \beta e^{-\beta(t-v)}L(t). \end{aligned} \tag{A16.4}$$

The relative size of cohorts is thus given by $l(v,t) \equiv L(v,t)/L(t) = \beta e^{-\beta(t-v)}$. It falls at an exponential rate equal to the birth rate. The mortality rate does not feature because both the numerator and the denominator fall at the same exponential rate (due to age-independent mortality).

An attractive feature of the Buiter formulation is that it nests two influential OLG models as special cases. Indeed, by setting $\beta = \mu$ the Blanchard (1985) model is obtained and by setting $\mu = 0$ the Weil (1989) model is obtained.

In the Blanchard model studied in section 16.3, individual consumption is given by:

$$C(v,t) = (\rho + \mu)\left[A(v,t) + H(t)\right], \tag{A16.5}$$

whilst the Euler equation is given by:

$$\frac{\dot{C}(v,t)}{C(v,t)} = r(t) - \rho. \tag{A16.6}$$

Economy-wide average per capita consumption is now defined as:

$$c(t) = \int_{-\infty}^{t} l(v,t)\, C(v,t)\, dv. \tag{A16.7}$$

To derive the "aggregate Euler equation", we differentiate the expression for $c(t)$ in (A16.7) with respect to time to calculate $\dot{c}(t)$:

$$
\begin{aligned}
\dot{c}(t) &\equiv l(t,t)\, C(t,t) + \int_{-\infty}^{t} l(v,t)\, \dot{C}(v,t)\, dv + \int_{-\infty}^{t} \dot{l}(v,t)\, C(v,t)\, dv \\
&= \eta C(t,t) + \int_{-\infty}^{t} l(v,t)\, \dot{C}(v,t)\, dv - \beta \int_{-\infty}^{t} l(v,t)\, C(v,t)\, dv \\
&= \int_{-\infty}^{t} l(v,t)\,[r(t) - \rho]\, C(v,t)\, dv - \beta \cdot [c(t) - C(t,t)] \\
&= [r(t) - \rho]\, c(v,t) - \beta \cdot [c(t) - C(t,t)], \tag{A16.8}
\end{aligned}
$$

where we have used the fact that $\dot{l}(v,t)/l(v,t) = -\beta$. Since $C(t,t) = (\rho+\mu)$ $H(t)$ (as $A(t,t) = 0$) and $c(t) = (\rho+\mu)\,[a(t) + H(t)]$ we can rewrite (A16.8) to obtain (Q16.1). In this economy there is no debt, so $a(t) = k(t)$.

We are now in a position to answer the questions:

- The birth rate β features in the GT term because the turnover of generations hinges on the fact that new generations are born (not because members of these generations face a finite life).

- The mortality rate μ features in the GT term because the propensity to consume out of total wealth depends on it. Mortality leads to higher discounting of future felicity and raises the effective rate of time preference and the propensity to consume, $\rho + \mu$.

(b) By substituting (Q16.3) and (Q16.5) into (Q16.1) and (Q16.2) we find the system of differential equations for c and k.

$$\dot{c}(t) = \left[\varepsilon Z_0 k(t)^{\varepsilon - 1} - \delta - \rho\right] c(t) - \beta(\rho+\mu)k(t), \tag{A16.9}$$

$$\dot{k}(t) = Z_0 k(t)^{\varepsilon} - c(t) - (\delta + \beta - \mu)\, k(t). \tag{A16.10}$$

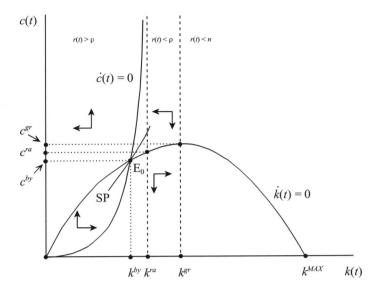

Figure A16.1: Phase diagram for the Buiter model

This model is saddle-point stable, with $c(t)$ acting as the jumping variable and $k(t)$ as the predetermined variable.

The derivation of the phase diagram proceeds along the lines shown in the book, although it is easier here because we are employing a simple, Cobb-Douglas production function. The $\dot{k}(t) = 0$ lines is given by:

$$c(t) = Z_0 k(t)^{\varepsilon} - (\delta + n_L) k(t), \tag{A16.11}$$

which is inverse-U shaped and features zero consumption at $k = 0$ and $k = k^{MAX}$, with:

$$k^{MAX} \equiv \left(\frac{Z_0}{\delta + n_L} \right)^{1/(1-\varepsilon)}. \tag{A16.12}$$

Net investment is positive (negative) for points below (above) the $\dot{k}(t) = 0$ line. See the horizontal arrows in Figure A16.1. The $\dot{k}(t) = 0$ reaches a maximum for at the golden rule capital stock, k^{GR}, where the the interest rate equals the rate of population growth, i.e. $r^{GR} \equiv \varepsilon Z_0 \left(k^{GR} \right)^{\varepsilon-1} - \delta = n_L$.

The $\dot{c}(t) = 0$ line can be written as:

$$c(t) = \frac{\beta(\rho + \mu)k(t)}{\varepsilon Z_0 k(t)^{\varepsilon-1} - (\delta + \rho)}, \tag{A16.13}$$

which is upward sloping, features zero consumption at $k = 0$, and has a vertical asymptote at $\bar{k} = k^{ra}$:

$$\bar{k} \equiv \left(\frac{\varepsilon Z_0}{\delta + \rho} \right)^{1/(1-\varepsilon)}. \tag{A16.14}$$

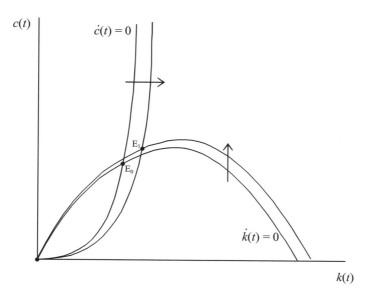

Figure A16.2: A technology improvement in the Buiter model

For points to the right (left) of the $\dot{c}(t) = 0$ line, the GT is relatively strong (weak) and consumption falls (rises) over time. See the vertical arrows in Figure A16.1.

The arrow configuration confirms that the model is saddle-point stable and that the saddle path is upward sloping. On this count, the Buiter model thus looks very similar to the Blanchard model studied in the book.

(c) An unanticipated and permanent productivity shock is captured by a once-off increase in Z_0. The $\dot{k}(t) = 0$ line (A16.11) shifts up, whilst the $\dot{c}(t) = 0$ line (A16.13) rotates in a clockwise direction. See Figure A16.2. Long-run per capita consumption and the capital stock both increase as the economy moves from E_0 to E_1. At impact per capita consumption rises as the wage path is permanently higher than before the shock. (We have not drawn the saddle path to avoid cluttering the diagram.)

(d) With dynamic inefficiency we mean a situation where the steady-state interest rate is less than the population growth rate, i.e. $r^{BY} < n_L$. In Figure A16.1 the steady-state equilibrium is at point E_0, which lies to the left of the golden-rule point, i.e. $k^{BY} < k^{GR}$. But it turns out that the k^{BY} point can also be located to the right of the golden rule point. We present a simple example in Figure A16.3.

As was pointed out above, the $\dot{c}(t) = 0$ locus (A16.13) features a vertical asymptote at $\bar{k}$. As we show in the figure, the $\dot{c}(t) = 0$ has two branches, only one of which is in the economically feasible region (with $c(t) \geq 0$). The example assumes that the parameters are such that $\bar{k}$ is equal to k^{MAX}. Using (A16.12) and (A16.14) we find that this is the case if:

$$\rho = \varepsilon n_L - \delta(1 - \varepsilon).$$

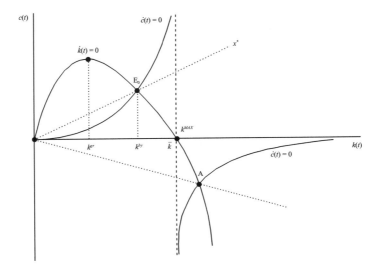

Figure A16.3: Dynamic inefficiency in the Buiter model

The equilibrium is at point E_0 which lies to the right of the golden-rule point. At that point, $0 < \rho < r^{BY} < n_L$. The equilibrium is saddle-point stable.

Of course, this example is quite extreme. But for any case where $\bar{k}$ lies sufficiently to the right of the golden-rule point, the overlapping generations equilibrium exist and will feature dynamic inconsistency.

This property of the Buiter model is due to the arrival of new disconnected generations (non-zero β), not to the fact that lives are finite (non-zero μ). See Weil (1989) and section 13.7.3 of the book on this.

(e) We can capture the growing dynastic family by setting:

- $\beta = 0$: no new, disconnected, generations arrive into the economy. Population growth on the extensive margin is zero. The GT term is absent.

- $\mu = -n_L < 0$: the death rate of dynasty member is negative. This, of course, means that the size of the dynasty grows over time. Population growth is entirely on the intensive margin.

If we plug these parameter settings into the model, we obtain the RA model with population growth:

$$\frac{\dot{c}(t)}{c(t)} = r(t) - \rho,$$
$$\dot{k}(t) = y(t) - c(t) - (\delta + n_L)k(t).$$

Question 3: Endogenous growth

(a) The representative firm faces the technology (Q16.6) and hires capital and labour according to the usual marginal productivity conditions:

$$[F_K \equiv] \quad (1 - \varepsilon_L) Z(t) L(t)^{\varepsilon_L} K(t)^{-\varepsilon_L} = r + \delta, \tag{A16.15}$$

$$[F_L \equiv] \quad \varepsilon_L Z(t) L(t)^{\varepsilon_L - 1} K(t)^{1 - \varepsilon_L} = W. \tag{A16.16}$$

But all firms hire according to (A16.15)–(A16.16). By substituting (Q16.7), normalizing the number of firms by unity, and setting $L = 1$ we find from (A16.15)–(A16.16):

$$r + \delta = (1 - \varepsilon_L) A K(t)^{\varepsilon_L} L(t)^{\varepsilon_L} K(t)^{-\varepsilon_L} = (1 - \varepsilon_L) A, \tag{A16.17}$$

$$W = \varepsilon_L A K(t)^{\varepsilon_L} L(t)^{\varepsilon_L - 1} K(t)^{1 - \varepsilon_L} = \varepsilon_L A K. \tag{A16.18}$$

The aggregate production function is linear in capital:

$$Y = AK. \tag{A16.19}$$

Since δ, ε_L, and A are all constants, it follows from (A16.17) that the interest rate is constant also.

(b) We denote the (common) growth rate by γ^*. We must have that:

$$\gamma^* = \frac{\dot{K}}{K} = \frac{\dot{C}}{C} = \frac{\dot{Y}}{Y} = \frac{\dot{B}}{B} = \frac{\dot{W}}{W}. \tag{A16.20}$$

We can now rewrite the equations in Table 16.1 of the book as follows:

$$\frac{\dot{C}}{C} = [r - \rho] - \beta(\rho + \beta) \left[\frac{K}{C} + \frac{B}{C} \right], \tag{A16.21}$$

$$\frac{\dot{K}}{K} = \frac{AK}{K} - \frac{C}{K} - \frac{\delta K}{K}, \tag{A16.22}$$

$$\frac{\dot{B}}{B} = \frac{rB}{B} - \frac{T}{Y} \frac{Y}{B}, \tag{A16.23}$$

$$r = (1 - \varepsilon_L) A - \delta, \tag{A16.24}$$

$$W = \varepsilon_L A K, \tag{A16.25}$$

where we have incorporated the assumption $G = 0$. But $\zeta \equiv B/Y$ so that $B/C = \zeta A K / C$. Furthermore, $T/Y = t_L W / Y = \varepsilon_L t_L$. We can thus summarize the model by the following expressions:

$$\gamma^* = (1 - \varepsilon_L) A - (\rho + \delta) - \beta(\rho + \beta)(1 + \zeta A)\kappa, \tag{A16.26}$$

$$\gamma^* = A - \delta - \frac{1}{\kappa}, \tag{A16.27}$$

$$\gamma^* = (1 - \varepsilon_L) A - \delta - \frac{\varepsilon_L t_L}{\zeta}. \tag{A16.28}$$

where $\kappa \equiv K/C$. The model is recursive in (γ^*, κ) and t_L. Equations (A16.26)–(A16.27) determine the growth rate γ^* and the capital-consumption ratio, κ, as a function of the parameters; equation (A16.28) then residually determines the tax rate required to balance the budget.

By using (A16.27) in (A16.26) we find the following expression in κ:

$$A - \delta - \frac{1}{\kappa} = (1 - \varepsilon_L)A - (\rho + \delta) - \beta(\rho + \beta)(1 + \zeta A)\kappa \quad \Leftrightarrow$$

$$\frac{1}{\kappa} = (\rho + \varepsilon_L A) + \beta(\rho + \beta)(1 + \zeta A)\kappa \quad \Leftrightarrow$$

$$0 = \beta(\rho + \beta)(1 + \zeta A)\kappa^2 + (\rho + \varepsilon_L A)\kappa - 1. \tag{A16.29}$$

The quadratic function has a unique economically sensible (i.e. positive) solution for κ which equals:

$$\kappa^* = \frac{\rho + \varepsilon_L A}{2\beta(\rho + \beta)(1 + \zeta A)} \left[\sqrt{1 + \frac{4\beta(\rho + \beta)(1 + \zeta A)}{(\rho + \varepsilon_L A)^2}} - 1 \right]. \tag{A16.30}$$

(c) To find the effect of the birth rate on the growth rate it is easiest to first determine the effect on κ^*. By differentiating (A16.29) with respect to κ and β we find:

$$0 = (1 + \zeta A) \left[2\beta(\rho + \beta)\kappa d\kappa + (\rho + 2\beta)\kappa^2 d\beta \right] + (\rho + \varepsilon_L A)d\kappa \quad \Leftrightarrow$$

$$\frac{d\kappa^*}{d\beta} = -\frac{(1 + \zeta A)(\rho + 2\beta)(\kappa^*)^2}{2\kappa^*(1 + \zeta A)\beta(\rho + \beta) + (\rho + \varepsilon_L A)} < 0. \tag{A16.31}$$

The quadratic function determining κ^* shifts upward and the economically sensible solution falls as a result. In view of (A16.27) we find that the growth rate changes according to:

$$\frac{d\gamma^*}{d\beta} = \frac{1}{(\kappa^*)^2} \frac{d\kappa^*}{d\beta} < 0. \tag{A16.32}$$

A lower birth rate leads to an increase in consumption relative to the capital stock which in turn causes a reduction in the rate of economic growth.

(d) Again we approach this problem via the effect on κ^*. By differentiating (A16.29) with respect to κ and ζ we find:

$$\frac{d\kappa^*}{d\zeta} = -\frac{\beta A(\rho + \beta)(\kappa^*)^2}{2\kappa^*(1 + \zeta A)\beta(\rho + \beta) + (\rho + \varepsilon_L A)} < 0. \tag{A16.33}$$

A *reduction* in ζ thus leads to an *increase* in κ^*. In view of (A16.27) we find that the effect on the growth rate is:

$$\frac{d\gamma^*}{d\zeta} = \frac{1}{(\kappa^*)^2} \frac{d\kappa^*}{d\zeta} < 0. \tag{A16.34}$$

A reduction in the debt-output ratio increases the rate of economic growth. The increase in κ^* implies that the C/K ratio falls, i.e. households increase the propensity to save out of capital.

Question 4: The Blanchard - Yaari model without insurance

(a) The lifetime utility function is still as given in (16.29) because the household still faces a non-zero probability of death. There is no life-insurance scheme, however, so the budget identity of the household changes from (16.30) to:

$$\dot{A}(v,\tau) = r(\tau)A(v,\tau) + W(\tau) + Z(\tau) - T(\tau) - C(v,\tau), \qquad \text{(A16.35)}$$

where all variables have the same meaning as in the text and where $Z(\tau)$ are the (age-independent) transfers received from the government. Because there is no annuity market, financial assets attract only the market rate of interest, i.e. $r(\tau)$ and not the annuity rate, $r(\tau) + \beta$, features on the right-hand side of (A16.35). The NPG condition for the household is in this case:

$$\lim_{\tau \to \infty} e^{-R(t,\tau)} A(v,\tau) = 0, \qquad R(t,\tau) \equiv \int_t^{\tau} r(s)ds. \qquad \text{(A16.36)}$$

Following the same steps as in the book, we find that:

$$A(v,t) + H(t) = \int_t^{\infty} C(v,\tau)e^{-R(t,\tau)}d\tau, \qquad \text{(A16.37)}$$

$$H(t) \equiv \int_t^{\infty} \left[W(\tau) + Z(\tau) - T(\tau) \right] e^{-R(t,\tau)}d\tau. \qquad \text{(A16.38)}$$

The key thing to note is that the market interest rate is used for discounting in (A16.36)–(A16.38).

The household maximizes (16.29) subject to (A16.37), taking as given its initial total wealth, $A(v,t) + H(t)$. The (interesting) first-order conditions are $\partial E\Lambda(v,t)/\partial C(v,\tau) = 0$ (for $\tau \in [t,\infty)$) or:

$$\frac{1}{C(v,\tau)} \cdot e^{(\rho+\beta)(t-\tau)} = \lambda(t)e^{-R(t,\tau)}, \qquad \text{(A16.39)}$$

where $\lambda(t)$ is the Lagrange multiplier of the lifetime budget constraint (A16.37). Note that for $t = \tau$, (A16.39) says that $C(v,t) = 1/\lambda(t)$. Retracing the steps in the book (below (16.35)) we find that consumption in the planning period is:

$$C(v,t) = (\rho + \beta) \left[A(v,t) + H(t) \right]. \qquad \text{(A16.40)}$$

For future use, we differentiate (A16.39) with respect to τ to derive the consumption Euler equation:

$$\dot{C}(v,\tau) = C(v,\tau) \left[\frac{\partial R(t,\tau)}{\partial \tau} - (\rho + \beta) \right] \quad \Leftrightarrow$$

$$\frac{\dot{C}(v,\tau)}{C(v,\tau)} = r(\tau) - (\rho + \beta). \qquad \text{(A16.41)}$$

Because there are no annuity markets, the Euler equation for individual generations differs from the one that obtains when such markets do exist (compare (A16.41) and (16.36)).

(b) Using the aggregation scheme exemplified in (16.38) we find that (A16.35) and (A16.40) are aggregated to:

$$\dot{A}(\tau) = (r(\tau) - \beta)\, A(\tau) + W(\tau) + Z(\tau) - T(\tau) - C(\tau), \qquad \text{(A16.42)}$$

$$C(t) = (\rho + \beta)\, [A(t) + H(t)]. \qquad \text{(A16.43)}$$

At each moment in time a cross section of the population dies. Since their assets accrue to the government, the revenue from the estates equals $\beta A(\tau)$ so that the transfers equal $Z(\tau) = \beta A(\tau)$. Using this result in (A16.42) we find that the aggregate asset accumulation is simplified to:

$$\dot{A}(\tau) = r(\tau)A(\tau) + W(\tau) - T(\tau) - C(\tau). \qquad \text{(A16.44)}$$

The key thing to note is that this expression is *identical* to the one that obtains when annuity markets exist (compare (A16.44) and (16.41)). For the aggregate asset accumulation equation it does not matter whether the assets of the dead are redistributed via the insurance companies or via government transfers.

The aggregate consumption Euler equation is derived by differentiating (16.38) with respect to time t:

$$\dot{C}(t) = \beta C(t,t) - \beta C(t) + \beta \int_{-\infty}^{t} \dot{C}(v,t) e^{\beta(v-t)} dv$$

$$= \beta(\rho + \beta)H(t) - \beta(\rho + \beta)\, [A(t) + H(t)] + [r(t) - (\rho + \beta)]\, C(t)$$

$$\frac{\dot{C}(t)}{C(t)} = [r(t) - (\rho + \beta)] - \beta(\rho + \beta)\frac{K(t) + B(t)}{C(t)}, \qquad \text{(A16.45)}$$

where we have used the individual Euler equation (A16.41) to get from the first to the second line and noted that $A(t) = K(t) + B(t)$.

(c) Next we establish that Ricardian equivalence holds if and only if $\beta = 0$. The absence of annuities markets *per se* does not affect the validity of the theorem. The government budget constraint is still given by (16.49). The transfers do not feature in that expression because they are covered by the revenue from the estates of the dead and not by lump-sum taxes. By integrating (A16.44) and imposing the terminal condition $\lim_{\tau \to \infty} A(\tau)e^{-R(t,\tau)} = 0$ we find:

$$A(t) = \int_{t}^{\infty} [C(\tau) + T(\tau) - W(\tau)]\, e^{-R(t,\tau)} d\tau. \qquad \text{(A16.46)}$$

By substituting the GBC (16.49) into (A16.46) and noting that $A(t) = K(t) + B(t)$ we find:

$$K(t) = \int_{t}^{\infty} [C(\tau) + G(\tau) - W(\tau)]\, e^{-R(t,\tau)} d\tau. \qquad \text{(A16.47)}$$

It follows from (A16.45) and (A16.47) that there is only debt neutrality if and only if $\beta = 0$. Only in that case is the aggregate Euler equation independent of $B(t)$. Buiter (1990, ch. 7) presents a more general (discrete-time) model in which birth and death rates differ and proves that it is the non-zero birth rate that destroys Ricardian equivalence.

Question 5: Technological change

(a) Repeating the steps leading to (16.38) in the book we find easily that consumption is proportional to total wealth:

$$\bar{c}(v,t) = (\rho + \mu)\left[\bar{a}(v,t) + \bar{h}(t)\right],\tag{A16.48}$$

where human wealth is defined as:

$$\bar{h}(t) = \int_t^\infty \left[\bar{w}(\tau) - \bar{z}(\tau)\right]e^{-R^A(t,\tau)}d\tau.\tag{A16.49}$$

Human wealth does not feature the generations index because wages, taxes, and the annuity interest rate are all age-independent. It is also straightforward to show that the consumption Euler equation has the usual form:

$$\frac{\dot{\bar{c}}(v,t)}{\bar{c}(v,t)} = r(t) - \rho,\tag{A16.50}$$

where $\dot{\bar{c}}(v,t) \equiv d\bar{c}(v,t)/dt$. For future reference we note that human wealth satisfies the following differential equation:

$$\dot{\bar{h}}(t) = \left[r(t) + \mu\right]\bar{h}(t) - \left[\bar{w}(t) - \bar{z}(t)\right],\tag{A16.51}$$

where $\dot{\bar{h}}(t) \equiv d\bar{h}(t)/dt$.

(b) The second result is easy to prove by looking at the inflow into the population (births) and the outflow out of the population (deaths). If the birth rate is zero ($\beta = 0$) then the population falls exponentially at the rate of deaths, i.e. $n_L = -\mu$. If there is a positive birth rate ($\beta > 0$) then $\dot{L}(t) = \beta L(t) - \mu L(t)$ so that $n_L \equiv \dot{L}(t)/L(t) = \beta - \mu$.

The first result is obtained as follows. If the birth rate is zero then there is only one cohort (the one in place at time $t = 0$) so $L(v,t) = 0$ for $v \neq 0$ and $L(v,t) = L(t) = e^{-\mu t}$ for $v = 0$. With a positive birth rate we know that $L(v,v) = \beta L(v)$ and $L(v,t) = L(v,v)e^{\mu(v-t)}$. Furthermore, by definition $L(v) = L(t)e^{n_L(v-t)}$. By combining these results we find:

$$L(v,t) = \beta L(t)e^{n_L(v-t)}e^{\mu(v-t)}.\tag{A16.52}$$

But $L(t) = L(0)e^{n_L t} = e^{n_L t}$ (since $L(0) = 1$) and $n_L = \beta - \mu$ so (A16.52) can be simplified to:

$$\begin{aligned}
L(v,t) &= \beta e^{n_L t}e^{n_L(v-t)}e^{\mu(v-t)}\\
&= \beta e^{(\beta-\mu)v}e^{\mu(v-t)}\\
&= \beta e^{\beta v}e^{-\mu t}.
\end{aligned}\tag{A16.53}$$

(c) We define the aggregate variables as follows:

$$\begin{aligned}
X(t) &\equiv \int_{-\infty}^t L(v,t)\bar{x}(v,t)dv\\
&= \begin{cases} \beta e^{-\mu t}\int_{-\infty}^t \bar{x}(v,t)e^{\beta v}dv & \text{for } \beta > 0\\ \bar{x}(v,t)e^{-\mu t} & \text{for } \beta = 0 \text{ and } v = 0 \end{cases}
\end{aligned}\tag{A16.54}$$

Using this definition in (A16.48) we find the aggregate consumption rule:

$$C(t) = (\rho + \mu)\left[A(t) + H(t)\right],\tag{A16.55}$$

where $C(t)$, $A(t)$, and $H(t)$ are, respectively, aggregate consumption, aggregate financial wealth, and aggregate human wealth. Aggregate human wealth is related to individual wealth (A16.49) according to:

$$
\begin{aligned}
H(t) &\equiv \beta e^{-\mu t} \int_{-\infty}^{t} \bar{h}(t) e^{\beta v} dv \\
&= \beta \bar{h}(t) e^{-\mu t} \left[\frac{e^{\beta v}}{\beta}\right]_{-\infty}^{t} \\
&= \bar{h}(t) e^{n_L t},
\end{aligned}\tag{A16.56}
$$

where we recall that $n_L = \beta - \mu$.

The aggregate consumption Euler equation is derived as follows. We note that (for $\beta > 0$) $C(t)$ is defined as:

$$C(t) \equiv \beta e^{-\mu t} \int_{-\infty}^{t} \bar{c}(v,t) e^{\beta v} dv.\tag{A16.57}$$

By differentiating (A16.57) with respect to time we obtain:

$$
\begin{aligned}
\dot{C}(t) &= -\mu \beta e^{-\mu t} \int_{-\infty}^{t} \bar{c}(v,t) e^{\beta v} dv + \beta e^{-\mu t} \left[\bar{c}(t,t) e^{\beta t} + \int_{-\infty}^{t} \dot{\bar{c}}(v,t) e^{\beta v} dv\right] \\
&= -\mu C(t) + \beta \bar{c}(t,t) e^{n_L t} + \beta e^{-\mu t} \int_{-\infty}^{t} \left[r(t) - \rho\right] \bar{c}(v,t) e^{\beta v} dv \\
&= \left[r(t) - \rho\right] C(t) + \left(\beta \bar{c}(t,t) e^{n_L t} - \mu C(t)\right).
\end{aligned}\tag{A16.58}
$$

The term in round brackets on the right-hand side of (A16.58) is a generational turnover term. We know that $\bar{c}(t,t) = (\rho + \mu)\bar{h}(t)$ (since $\bar{a}(t,t) = 0$). By using this result and (A16.55)–(A16.56) we can rewrite the generational turnover term as follows:

$$
\begin{aligned}
\beta \bar{c}(t,t) e^{n_L t} - \mu C(t) &= \beta(\rho + \mu)H(t) - \mu(\rho + \mu)\left[A(t) + H(t)\right] \\
&= (\rho + \mu)\left[(\beta - \mu)H(t) - \mu A(t)\right] \\
&= (\rho + \mu)\left[(\beta - \mu)(A(t) + H(t)) - \beta A(t)\right] \\
&= (\beta - \mu)C(t) - \beta(\rho + \mu)A(t).
\end{aligned}\tag{A16.59}
$$

By using (A16.59) in (A16.58) and noting that $n_L = \beta - \mu$ we find:

$$\dot{C}(t) = \left[r(t) + n_L - \rho\right] C(t) - \beta(\rho + \mu)A(t).\tag{A16.60}$$

Equation (A16.60) is compatible with equation (16.43) in the book, but is generalized for population growth and separate birth and death rates.

The differential equation for human wealth is obtain as follows. By differentiating (A16.56) with respect to time we find:

$$
\begin{aligned}
\dot{H}(t) &= n_L \bar{h}(t) e^{n_L t} + \dot{\bar{h}}(t) e^{n_L t} \\
&= n_L H(t) + \left[r(t) + \mu\right] \bar{h}(t) e^{n_L t} - \left[\bar{w}(t) - \bar{z}(t)\right] e^{n_L t} \\
&= \left[r(t) + n_L + \mu\right] H(t) - \left[W(t) - Z(t)\right],
\end{aligned}\tag{A16.61}
$$

where we have used (A16.51) in going from the first to the second line.

Finally, the differential equation for aggregate financial wealth is obtained as follows. We note that:

$$A(t) \equiv \beta e^{-\mu t} \int_{-\infty}^{t} \bar{a}(v,t) e^{\beta v} dv. \tag{A16.62}$$

By differentiating (A16.62) with respect to time, we find:

$$
\begin{aligned}
\dot{A}(t) &= -\mu \beta e^{-\mu t} \int_{-\infty}^{t} \bar{a}(v,t) e^{\beta v} dv + \beta e^{-\mu t} \left[\bar{a}(t,t) e^{\beta t} + \int_{-\infty}^{t} \dot{\bar{a}}(v,t) e^{\beta v} dv \right] \\
&= -\mu A(t) + \beta e^{-\mu t} \int_{-\infty}^{t} \Big[[r(t) + \mu] \, \bar{a}(v,t) + \bar{w}(t) - \bar{z}(t) - \bar{c}(v,t) \Big] e^{\beta v} dv \\
&= r(t) A(t) + W(t) - Z(t) - C(t),
\end{aligned}
\tag{A16.63}
$$

where we have used equation (Q16.9) (and noted the fact that $\bar{a}(t,t) = 0$) in going from the first to the second line.

(d) The derivation is similar to the one leading to (16.64)–(16.65) in the book. The objective function of the representative firm is:

$$V(t) = \int_{t}^{\infty} \left[F\left(K(\tau), A_L(\tau) L(\tau)\right) - \bar{w}(\tau) L(\tau) - I(\tau) \right] e^{-R(t,\tau)} d\tau, \tag{A16.64}$$

where the discount factor, $R(t,\tau)$, and gross investment, $I(\tau)$, are defined as:

$$R(t,\tau) = \int_{t}^{\tau} r(s) ds, \tag{A16.65}$$

$$I(\tau) = \dot{K}(\tau) + \delta K(\tau). \tag{A16.66}$$

The firm chooses paths for capital, labour, and investment such that $V(t)$ is maximized. The current-value Hamiltonian for this optimization problem is:

$$\mathcal{H} \equiv F\left(K(\tau), A_L(\tau) L(\tau)\right) - \bar{w}(\tau) L(\tau) - I(\tau) + \mu(\tau) \left[I(\tau) - \delta K(\tau) \right], \tag{A16.67}$$

where $\lambda(\tau)$ is the co-state variable, $K(\tau)$ is the state variable, and $L(\tau)$ and $I(\tau)$ are the control variables. The first-order conditions are:

$$\frac{\partial \mathcal{H}}{\partial L(\tau)} = A_L(\tau) F_N\left(K(\tau), N(\tau)\right) - \bar{w}(\tau) = 0, \tag{A16.68}$$

$$\frac{\partial \mathcal{H}}{\partial I(\tau)} = -1 + \lambda(\tau) = 0, \tag{A16.69}$$

$$\dot{\lambda}(\tau) - r(\tau) \lambda(\tau) = -\frac{\partial \mathcal{H}}{\partial K(\tau)} = -F_K\left(K(\tau), N(\tau)\right) + \delta \lambda(\tau). \tag{A16.70}$$

It follows from (A16.69) that $\lambda(\tau) = 1$ so that $\dot{\lambda}(\tau) = 0$. Using these results in (A16.70) we find the usual rental rate expression for capital:

$$r(\tau) + \delta = F_K\left(K(\tau), N(\tau)\right). \tag{A16.71}$$

Similarly, (A16.68) can be used to derive the marginal productivity condition for labour:

$$\frac{\bar{w}(\tau)}{A_L(\tau)} = F_N\left(K(\tau), N(\tau)\right). \tag{A16.72}$$

For the Cobb-Douglas production function, (A16.71)–(A16.72) simplify to:

$$r(\tau) + \delta = \alpha k(\tau)^{\alpha-1}, \qquad \frac{\bar{w}(\tau)}{A_L(\tau)} = (1-\alpha)k(\tau)^{\alpha}, \tag{A16.73}$$

where $k(\tau) \equiv K(\tau)/N(\tau)$ is capital expressed in efficiency units of labour. For a constant k, (A16.73) shows that the interest rate is constant but the wage rate grows at the rate of Harrod-neutral technological change (i.e. $\dot{\bar{w}}/\bar{w} = \dot{A}_L/A_L = n_A$ in the steady state).

(e) We use the definitions $a(t) \equiv A(t)/N(t)$, $b(t) \equiv B(t)/N(t)$, $c(t) \equiv C(t)/N(t)$, $g(t) \equiv G(t)/N(t)$, $h(t) \equiv H(t)/N(t)$, $w(t) \equiv W(t)/N(t)$, and $z(t) \equiv Z(t)/N(t)$. Using these expressions, (A16.60), (A16.61), and (A16.63) can be rewritten as:

$$\dot{c}(t) = [r(t) - n_A - \rho]\, c(t) - \beta(\rho + \mu)a(t), \tag{A16.74}$$

$$\dot{h}(t) = [r(t) + \mu - n_A]\, h(t) - [w(t) - z(t)], \tag{A16.75}$$

$$\dot{a}(t) = [r(t) - n_A - n_L]\, a(t) + w(t) - z(t) - c(t), \tag{A16.76}$$

where we use the relationship $\dot{X}/N = \dot{x} + (n_A + n_L)x$ for each of these variables. The government budget identity can be rewritten as:

$$\dot{b}(t) = [r(t) - n_A - n_L]\, b(t) + g(t) - z(t). \tag{A16.77}$$

Since $W(t) \equiv \bar{w}(t)e^{n_L t} = \bar{w}(t)L(t)$ and $\bar{w}(t) = (1-\alpha)A_L(t)k(t)^{\alpha}$ we find that:

$$w(t) = (1-\alpha)k(t)^{\alpha}. \tag{A16.78}$$

Equilibrium on the goods market and on the capital market implies:

$$y(t) = c(t) + i(t) + g(t), \tag{A16.79}$$

$$\dot{k}(t) = i(t) - (\delta + n_L + n_A)k(t), \tag{A16.80}$$

$$a(t) = k(t) + b(t). \tag{A16.81}$$

The full model consists of the first expression in (A16.73) and (A16.74)–(A16.81). The NPG condition for the government is:

$$\lim_{\tau \to \infty} b(\tau) \exp\left[-\int_t^\tau [r(s) - n_A - n_L]\, ds\right] = 0. \tag{A16.82}$$

By integrating (A16.77) forward in time and imposing (A16.82) we find the budget constraint of the solvent government:

$$b(t) = \int_t^\infty [z(\tau) - g(\tau)] \exp\left[-\int_t^\tau [r(s) - n_A - n_L]\, ds\right] d\tau. \tag{A16.83}$$

To the extent that there exists a positive government debt at time t ($b(t) > 0$), the solvent government must cover it in present-value terms by the future primary surpluses (positive right-hand side of (A16.83)).

(f) We can investigate the validity of Ricardian equivalence by noting that (A16.75) can be integrated forward in time:

$$h(t) = \int_t^\infty [w(\tau) - z(\tau)] \exp\left[-\int_t^\tau [r(s) + \mu - n_A]\, ds\right], \tag{A16.84}$$

where we have used the boundary condition (Buiter, 1988, p. 284):

$$\lim_{\tau \to \infty} h(\tau) \exp\left[-\int_t^\tau [r(s) + \mu - n_A]\, ds\right] = 0. \tag{A16.85}$$

According to (A16.84), human wealth is the present value of after-tax wages, using the annuity rate of interest, corrected for productivity growth, for discounting. Ceteris paribus the paths for $r(\tau)$, $w(\tau)$, and $z(\tau)$, the probability of death has a negative effect on human wealth and productivity growth has a positive effect on human wealth. The key thing to note is that the birth rate does not affect human wealth directly because there is no operative bequest motive in this model (See Buiter, 1988, p. 284).

To investigate Ricardian equivalence we recall that consumption is proportional to total wealth, i.e. $c(t) = (\rho + \mu)[a(t) + h(t)]$. By using (A16.81) and (A16.83) we find:

$$a(t) + h(t) = k(t) + \int_t^\infty [w(\tau) - g(\tau)] \exp\left[-\int_t^\tau [r(s) + \mu - n_A]\, ds\right]$$
$$+ \left(b(t) - \int_t^\infty [z(\tau) - g(\tau)] \exp\left[-\int_t^\tau [r(s) + \mu - n_A]\, ds\right]\right). \tag{A16.86}$$

We compare the term in round brackets on the right-hand side of (A16.86) with the government budget constraint (A16.83). Ricardian equivalence holds if and only if the term in round brackets is zero, i.e. if and only if $r(s) + \mu - n_A$ coincides with $r(s) - n_A - n_L$ for all s. This amounts to the requirement that $\mu + n_L = 0$ or, equivalently, that $\beta = 0$. The birth rate must be zero for Ricardian equivalence to hold.

(g) Under the balanced-budget assumption, the model can be condensed to two differential equations in k and c:

$$\dot{c}(t) = [r(t) - n_A - \rho]\, c(t) - \beta(\rho + \mu)k(t), \tag{A16.87}$$
$$\dot{k}(t) = k(t)^\alpha - c(t) - g - (\delta + n_L + n_A)k(t). \tag{A16.88}$$

Equation (A16.87) is obtained by using (A16.71) and (A16.74) and noting that $b(t) = 0$. Equation (A16.88) is obtained by using (A16.79)–(A16.80) and noting that $y(t) = k(t)^\alpha$. The phase diagram of the model, presented in Figure A16.4, looks rather like the one for the standard Blanchard model (see Figure 16.7 in the book). For points to the left (right) of the $\dot{c} = 0$ line, capital is scarce (abundant) and the interest rate is higher (lower) than $\rho + n_A$. Since the golden-rule capital stock is such that $r^{GR} = n_L + n_A$ and consumption equilibrium implies an interest rate of $r^{BY} = \rho + n_A$ it follows from the assumption $\rho > n_L$ that $r^{BY} > r^{GR}$, i.e. $k^{BY} < k^{GR}$. The equilibrium at E_0 is dynamically efficient.

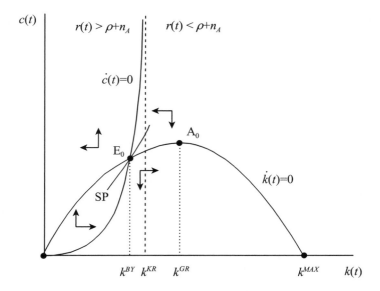

Figure A16.4: Growth and overlapping generations

An unanticipated and permanent increase in government consumption leads to a downward shift in the $\dot{k} = 0$ line. At impact the capital stock is predetermined and consumption jumps down because of the higher taxes. During transition, both consumption and the capital stock fall gradually towards their lower equilibrium values (see Figure 16.8 in the book for an illustration of the adjustment path described verbally here.) The impulse response functions are given in Figure A16.5. The paths for consumption and capital follow directly from the phase diagram. The path for the interest rate follows readily from the fact that $r = f'(k) - \delta = \alpha k^{\alpha-1} - \delta$. It is the mirror image of the path of the capital stock. The path for the wage rate follows from the *factor price frontier* which implies an inverse relationship between the interest rate and the wage rate. Indeed, for the Cobb-Douglas technology the factor price frontier is:

$$\left(\frac{r(t) + \delta}{\alpha}\right)^{\alpha} \left(\frac{w(t)}{1 - \alpha}\right)^{1-\alpha} = 1. \tag{A16.89}$$

Question 6: Mandatory retirement

(a) The budget identity of the household is:

$$\dot{A}(v, \tau) = (r^* + \beta) A(v, \tau) + I(v, \tau) - C(v, \tau), \tag{A16.90}$$

and the NPG condition is:

$$\lim_{\tau \to \infty} A(v, \tau) e^{-R^A(t,\tau)} d\tau, \qquad R^A(t, \tau) = \int_t^{\tau} [r^*(s) + \beta] \, ds. \tag{A16.91}$$

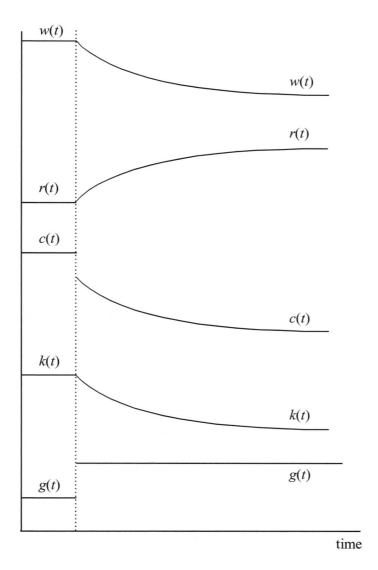

Figure A16.5: Fiscal policy

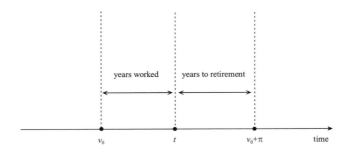

Figure A16.6: Mandatory retirement scheme

In this question the interest rate stays constant so $R^A = (r^* + \beta)(\tau - t)$. Using (A16.90)–(A16.91) we find the household budget identity:

$$A(v,t) + H(v,t) = \int_t^\infty C(v,\tau)e^{-R^A(t,\tau)}d\tau, \tag{A16.92}$$

where human wealth is age-dependent because income is age-dependent:

$$H(v,t) \equiv \int_t^\infty I(v,\tau)e^{-R^A(t,\tau)}d\tau. \tag{A16.93}$$

Following the same steps as in the book (see the discussion leading to (16.37)) we find the consumption rule and the Euler equation:

$$C(v,t) = (\rho + \beta)\left[A(v,t) + H(v,t)\right], \tag{A16.94}$$

$$\frac{\dot{C}(v,t)}{C(v,t)} = r^*(t) - \rho. \tag{A16.95}$$

At time t, the *age* of a generation is defined as the difference between t and that generation's birth date, v. It follows that for working-age generations we have $t - v < \pi$ whereas for retired generations we have $t - v \geq \pi$. See Figure A16.6 for an illustration. At time t, a generation born at time v_0 has already worked $t - v_0$ periods and faces $v_0 + \pi - t$ periods to retirement. Human wealth for the retired generations is thus:

$$H(v,t)|_{t-v\geq\pi} \equiv \int_t^\infty P(\tau)e^{-R^A(t,\tau)}d\tau \tag{A16.96}$$

$$= \frac{P}{r^* + \beta}, \tag{A16.97}$$

where we have used the fact that both P and r^* are time-invariant in the final step. For retired generations, human wealth is the perpetuity value of the pension payment, using the annuity interest rate for discounting.

For working-age generations, human wealth is:

$$H(v,t)|_{0\le t-v<\pi} \equiv \int_t^{v+\pi} [W(\tau) - T(\tau)]\, e^{-R^A(t,\tau)}d\tau$$

$$+ \int_{v+\pi}^{\infty} P(\tau)e^{-R^A(t,\tau)}d\tau$$

$$= \frac{W-T}{r^*+\beta}\left[1 - e^{-(r^*+\beta)(\pi+v-t)}\right] + \frac{P}{r^*+\beta}e^{-(r^*+\beta)(\pi+v-t)}, \quad \text{(A16.98)}$$

where (A16.98) is valid if W, T, P and r^* are time-invariant. In (A16.98), $\pi + v - t$ is the remaining period until retirement. If $\pi + v - t = 0$ then, of course, (A16.98) and (A16.97) coincide.

(b) Each generation supplies one unit of labour during its working age so $L(v,t)$ is:

$$L(v,t) = \begin{cases} 1 & \text{for } t - v < \pi \\ 0 & \text{for } t - v \ge \pi \end{cases} \qquad \text{(A16.99)}$$

Aggregate labour supply is thus:

$$L(t) = \int_{t-\pi}^{t} \beta e^{\beta(v-t)}dv = 1 - e^{-\beta\pi}. \qquad \text{(A16.100)}$$

Note that if $\pi \to \infty$ then $L(t) \to 1$ and we are back in the standard Blanchard - Yaari model. Since the total population equals unity, it follows from (A16.100) that the retired population equals $1 - L(t) = e^{-\beta\pi}$. The government budget constraint (in the absence of debt) is thus:

$$\left[1 - e^{-\beta\pi}\right]T = e^{-\beta\pi}P. \qquad \text{(A16.101)}$$

If the retirement age is increased and the pension payment is held constant then we find from (A16.101) that:

$$\left[1 - e^{-\beta\pi}\right]dT + \beta T e^{-\beta\pi}d\pi = -\beta e^{-\beta\pi}P d\pi \quad \Leftrightarrow$$

$$\frac{dT}{d\pi} = -\frac{\beta e^{-\beta\pi}(P+T)}{1 - e^{-\beta\pi}} < 0. \qquad \text{(A16.102)}$$

The tax falls for two reasons. First, the working-age population increases so a given revenue is obtained by smaller lump-sum taxes per working household. Second, the retired population decreases so less revenue is needed.

(c) Aggregate consumption is defined in the usual fashion:

$$C(t) \equiv \beta \int_{-\infty}^{t} e^{\beta(v-t)}C(v,t)dv. \qquad \text{(A16.103)}$$

By differentiating (A16.103) with respect to t we obtain:

$$\dot{C}(t) = \beta\left[C(t,t) - C(t)\right] + \beta \int_{-\infty}^{t} \dot{C}(v,t)e^{\beta(v-t)}dv$$

$$= \beta(\rho + \beta)\left[H(t,t) - H(t) - A(t)\right] + \left[r^* - \rho\right]C(t), \qquad \text{(A16.104)}$$

where we have used the fact that $C(t,t) = (\rho + \beta)H(t,t)$ (since $A(t,t) = 0$) and $C(t) = (\rho + \beta)[A(t) + H(t)]$. Rewriting (A16.104) somewhat we find the aggregate consumption "Euler equation":

$$\frac{\dot{C}(t)}{C(t)} = r^* - \rho - \beta(\rho + \beta)\left[\frac{A(t) + H(t) - H(t,t)}{C(t)}\right], \qquad (A16.105)$$

where the term in square brackets is the generational turnover term. It differs from the one appearing in the standard Blanchard - Yaari model because human wealth is age-dependent.

Next we work on the term $H(t) - H(t,t)$. We know from (A16.98) that human wealth of a newborn at time t is:

$$
\begin{aligned}
H(t,t) &= \frac{W - T}{r^* + \beta}\left[1 - e^{-(r^*+\beta)\pi}\right] + \frac{P}{r^* + \beta}e^{-(r^*+\beta)\pi} \\
&= \frac{W - T - P}{r^* + \beta}\left[1 - e^{-(r^*+\beta)\pi}\right] + \frac{P}{r^* + \beta}, \qquad (A16.106)
\end{aligned}
$$

where Nielsen (1994, p. 53) calls $W - T - P$ the social security system's "wedge" parameter. Total human wealth can be computed as follows:

$$
\begin{aligned}
H(t) &\equiv \beta \int_{-\infty}^{t} H(v,t)e^{\beta(v-t)}dv \\
&= \beta \int_{t-\pi}^{t}[H(v,t)]_{0 \le t-v < \pi}\, e^{\beta(v-t)}dv + \beta \int_{-\infty}^{t-\pi}[H(v,t)]_{t-v \ge \pi}\, e^{\beta(v-t)}dv. \\
&\qquad\qquad\qquad\qquad\qquad\qquad\qquad\qquad\qquad\qquad\qquad\qquad (A16.107)
\end{aligned}
$$

By using (A16.97) and (A16.98) in (A16.107) we find:

$$
\begin{aligned}
H(t) &= \beta \int_{t-\pi}^{t} \frac{W - T - P}{r^* + \beta}\left[1 - e^{-(r^*+\beta)(\pi+v-t)}\right]e^{\beta(v-t)}dv \\
&\quad + \beta \int_{-\infty}^{t} \frac{P}{r^* + \beta}e^{\beta(v-t)}dv \\
&= \beta \frac{W - T - P}{r^* + \beta}\int_{t-\pi}^{t}\left[1 - e^{-(r^*+\beta)(\pi+v-t)}\right]e^{\beta(v-t)}dv + \frac{P}{r^* + \beta}. \\
&\qquad\qquad\qquad\qquad\qquad\qquad\qquad\qquad\qquad\qquad\qquad\qquad (A16.108)
\end{aligned}
$$

The integral on the right-hand side of (A16.108) is equal to:

$$
\begin{aligned}
\cdots &= \int_{t-\pi}^{t} e^{\beta(v-t)}dv - e^{-\beta\pi}\int_{t-\pi}^{t}e^{-r^*(\pi+v-t)}dv \\
&= \left[\frac{e^{\beta(v-t)}}{\beta}\right]_{t-\pi}^{t} - e^{-\beta\pi}\left[\frac{e^{-r^*(\pi+v-t)}}{-r^*}\right]_{t-\pi}^{t} \\
&= \frac{1 - e^{-\beta\pi}}{\beta} - \frac{e^{-\beta\pi}}{r^*}\left[1 - e^{-r^*\pi}\right]. \qquad (A16.109)
\end{aligned}
$$

By using (A16.109) in (A16.108) we find:

$$H(t) = \frac{W - T - P}{r^* + \beta}\left[1 - e^{-\beta\pi} - \frac{\beta e^{-\beta\pi}}{r^*}\left[1 - e^{-r^*\pi}\right]\right] + \frac{P}{r^* + \beta}. \quad (A16.110)$$

By deducting (A16.110) from (A16.106) we find:

$$H(t,t) - H(t) = \frac{W - T - P}{r^* + \beta}\left[-e^{-(r^*+\beta)\pi} + e^{-\beta\pi} + \frac{\beta e^{-\beta\pi}}{r^*}\left[1 - e^{-r^*\pi}\right]\right]$$

$$= \frac{W - T - P}{r^*}e^{-\beta\pi}\left[1 - e^{-r^*\pi}\right]. \tag{A16.111}$$

Finally, by substituting (A16.111) in (A16.105) we find the ultimate expression for the aggregate consumption Euler equation:

$$\dot{C}(t) = (r^* - \rho)\,C(t) - \beta(\rho + \beta)\left[A(t) - \frac{W - T - P}{r^*}e^{-\beta\pi}\left[1 - e^{-r^*\pi}\right]\right]. \tag{A16.112}$$

Next we derive the differential equation for aggregate financial wealth which, in the absence of capital and bonds, coincides with the nation's current account (i.e. $A(\tau) = A_F(\tau)$ for all τ, where A_F is net foreign assets). Aggregate financial wealth is defined as:

$$A(t) \equiv \beta \int_{-\infty}^{t} e^{\beta(v-t)} A(v,t)\,dv. \tag{A16.113}$$

By differentiating (A16.113) with respect to t we obtain:

$$\dot{A}(t) = \beta\left[A(t,t) - A(t)\right] + \beta \int_{-\infty}^{t} \dot{A}(v,t)e^{\beta(v-t)}\,dv$$

$$= -\beta A(t) + \beta \int_{-\infty}^{t} \left[(r^* + \beta)\,A(v,t) + I(v,t) - C(v,t)\right]e^{\beta(v-t)}\,dv$$

$$= rA(t) + \beta \int_{-\infty}^{t} I(v,t)e^{\beta(v-t)}\,dv - C(t). \tag{A16.114}$$

In view of (Q16.12) we can compute the integral on the right-hand side of (A16.114):

$$\beta \int_{-\infty}^{t} I(v,t)e^{\beta(v-t)}\,dv = \beta \int_{t-\pi}^{t} [W - T]\,e^{\beta(v-t)}\,dv + \beta \int_{-\infty}^{t-\pi} Pe^{\beta(v-t)}\,dv$$

$$= (W - T)\left[e^{\beta(v-t)}\right]_{t-\pi}^{t} + P\left[e^{\beta(v-t)}\right]_{-\infty}^{t-\pi}$$

$$= (W - T)\left[1 - e^{-\beta\pi}\right] + Pe^{-\beta\pi}$$

$$= W\left[1 - e^{-\beta\pi}\right] - \left[T\left(1 - e^{-\beta\pi}\right) - Pe^{-\beta\pi}\right]$$

$$= W\left[1 - e^{-\beta\pi}\right], \tag{A16.115}$$

where we have used the government budget constraint (A16.101) in getting to the final line. By using (A16.115) in (A16.114) we find the differential equation for financial wealth:

$$\dot{A}(t) = rA(t) + W\left[1 - e^{-\beta\pi}\right] - C(t). \tag{A16.116}$$

By using the government budget constraint (A16.101) we find that $T + P = P/\left(1 - e^{-\beta\pi}\right)$ so that (A16.112) can be rewritten in terms of the pension payment only:

$$\dot{C}(t) = (r^* - \rho) C(t) \tag{A16.117}$$

$$- \beta(\rho + \beta) \left[A(t) - \left(W \left[1 - e^{-\beta\pi} \right] - P \right) \frac{e^{-\beta\pi} \left[1 - e^{-r^*\pi} \right]}{r^* \left[1 - e^{-\beta\pi} \right]} \right].$$

(d) The economy is fully characterized by the dynamics of C and A as stated in (A16.116)–(A16.117). In view of the technology (Q16.11), the wage rate is equal to the (exogenous) productivity parameter, i.e. $W = Z$. In Figure A16.7 we present the phase diagram for the case of a patient country (with $r^* > \rho$). The $\dot{C} = 0$ equation is obtained from (A16.117):

$$C(t) = \frac{\beta(\rho + \beta)}{r^* - \rho} \left[A(t) - \left(W \left[1 - e^{-\beta\pi} \right] - P \right) \frac{e^{-\beta\pi} \left[1 - e^{-r^*\pi} \right]}{r^* \left[1 - e^{-\beta\pi} \right]} \right]. \tag{A16.118}$$

The line slopes upward and, under the assumption that $W \left[1 - e^{-\beta\pi} \right] > P$, cuts the horizontal axis for a positive level of financial assets. For points above (below) the $\dot{C} = 0$ line, consumption increases (decreases) over time–see the vertical arrows. The $\dot{A} = 0$ line is obtained from (A16.116):

$$C(t) = rA(t) + W \left[1 - e^{-\beta\pi} \right]. \tag{A16.119}$$

This line also slopes up but cuts the horizontal axis for a negative level of financial assets. For points to the right (left) of the $\dot{A} = 0$ line, financial assets are increased (decreased) over time–see the horizontal arrows. Provided the $\dot{A} = 0$ line is flatter than the $\dot{C} = 0$ line, the two lines intersect once (at E_0) and the equilibrium is saddle-point stable. The stability condition is thus $r^* < \frac{\beta(\rho+\beta)}{r^*-\rho}$ or:

$$r^*(r^* - \rho) - \beta(\rho + \beta) < 0 \quad \Leftrightarrow$$
$$r^* [r^* + \beta - (\rho + \beta)] - \beta(\rho + \beta) < 0 \quad \Leftrightarrow$$
$$r^*(r^* + \beta) - (r^* + \beta)(\rho + \beta) < 0 \quad \Leftrightarrow$$
$$(r^* + \beta) [r^* - (\rho + \beta)] < 0 \quad \Leftrightarrow$$
$$r^* < \rho + \beta. \tag{A16.120}$$

Hence, the model is saddle-point stable provided r^* is less than $\rho + \beta$.

An increase in the pension payment shifts the $\dot{C} = 0$ line up and leaves the $\dot{A} = 0$ line unaffected. In terms of Figure A16.8, the steady-state equilibrium shifts from E_0 to E_1, consumption and financial wealth decrease in the long run. The intuition behind this result is as follows. The increase in P is advantageous to existing generations at the time of the shock, more so the older they are (the retired generations receive a pure windfall gain as they do not have to pay taxes any more). Consumption increases at impact and over time households start to run down financial assets. In the long run, both consumption and assets are lower than before the shock. Newborn generations are worse off as a result of

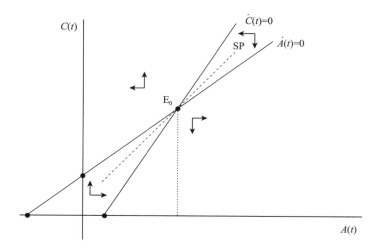

Figure A16.7: Phase diagram of a patient country

the shock. Indeed, by using the result $T + P = P/\left(1 - e^{-\beta \pi}\right)$ in (A16.106) we find:

$$H(t,t) = \frac{W}{r^* + \beta}\left[1 - e^{-(r^*+\beta)\pi}\right] - \frac{T+P}{r^*+\beta}\left[1 - e^{-(r^*+\beta)\pi}\right] + \frac{P}{r^*+\beta}$$

$$= \frac{W}{r^* + \beta}\left[1 - e^{-(r^*+\beta)\pi}\right] - \frac{P}{r^*+\beta}\cdot\frac{1 - e^{-(r^*+\beta)\pi}}{1 - e^{-\beta\pi}} + \frac{P}{r^*+\beta}$$

$$= \frac{W}{r^* + \beta}\left[1 - e^{-(r^*+\beta)\pi}\right] - \frac{P}{r^*+\beta}\cdot\frac{e^{-\beta\pi} - e^{-(r^*+\beta)\pi}}{1 - e^{-\beta\pi}}, \quad \text{(A16.121)}$$

where second term on the right-hand side of (A16.121) is positive, i.e. $dH(t,t)/dP < 0$, because $r^* > 0$ (the equilibrium is dynamically efficient) and the working period is finite ($\pi \ll \infty$). Hence, the policy shock redistributes resources away from the future newborns and towards the currently existing generations.

(e) An increase in the mandatory retirement age affects both the $\dot{C} = 0$ and $\dot{A} = 0$ loci. Starting with the $\dot{A} = 0$ line, it is easy to show that it shifts up. We define $\bar{W} \equiv W[1 - e^{-\beta\pi}]$ and find:

$$\frac{d\bar{W}}{d\pi} = \beta W e^{-\beta\pi} > 0. \quad \text{(A16.122)}$$

The upward shift has been illustrated in Figure A16.9. The effect on the $\dot{C} = 0$ line is much more complicated. First we rewrite the $\dot{C} = 0$ line in short-hand notation as follows:

$$C(t) = \frac{\beta(\rho + \beta)}{r^* - \rho}A(t) - \frac{\beta(\rho + \beta)}{r^*(r^* - \rho)}\left(\bar{W} - P\right)\phi(\pi), \quad \text{(A16.123)}$$

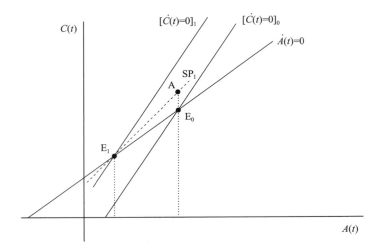

Figure A16.8: An increase in the pension payment

where $\phi(\pi)$ is defined as follows:

$$\phi(\pi) \equiv \frac{e^{-\beta\pi}\left[1 - e^{-r^*\pi}\right]}{1 - e^{-\beta\pi}}. \tag{A16.124}$$

The derivative of $\phi(\pi)$ is:

$$\phi'(\pi) \equiv \frac{\left[1 - e^{-\beta\pi}\right]\frac{de^{-\beta\pi}\left[1-e^{-r^*\pi}\right]}{d\pi} - e^{-\beta\pi}\left[1 - e^{-r^*\pi}\right]\frac{d\left[1-e^{-\beta\pi}\right]}{d\pi}}{\left[1 - e^{-\beta\pi}\right]^2}$$

$$= \frac{e^{-\beta\pi}\left[r^*e^{-r^*\pi}\left(1 - e^{-\beta\pi}\right) - \beta\left(1 - e^{-r^*\pi}\right)\right]}{\left[1 - e^{-\beta\pi}\right]^2} \gtreqless 0. \tag{A16.125}$$

It is thus ambiguous which way the $\dot{C} = 0$ line shifts. The increase in $\bar{W}$ causes a downward shift but this shift may be offset if $(\bar{W} - P)\phi'(\pi) > 0$. Following Nielsen (1994, p.56) we simply assume that $\dot{C} = 0$ line shifts up. In Figure A16.9, the equilibrium shifts from E_0 to E_1. The transition path consists of an impact jump from E_0 to A followed by a gradual move from A to E_1.

Question 7: Public infrastructure

(a) The Hamiltonian is given by:

$$\mathcal{H} \equiv (1 - t_Y)Y - WL - I + \lambda\left[I - \delta K\right], \tag{A16.126}$$

where we suppress the time index for convenience. The control variables are L and I, the state variable is K, and the co-state variable is λ. The first-order

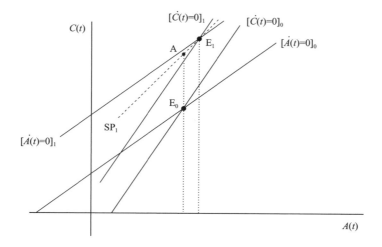

Figure A16.9: Increase in the mandatory retirement age

conditions are: $\partial \mathcal{H} / \partial L = \partial \mathcal{H} / \partial I = 0$ and $\dot{\lambda} - r\lambda = -\partial \mathcal{H} / \partial K$. We obtain:

$$(1 - t_Y) \frac{\partial Y}{\partial L} = W, \tag{A16.127}$$

$$\lambda = 1, \tag{A16.128}$$

$$\dot{\lambda} - r\lambda = -(1 - t_Y) \frac{\partial Y}{\partial K} + \delta \lambda. \tag{A16.129}$$

Combining these results we get the following marginal productivity conditions for capital and labour:

$$(1 - t_Y) \frac{\partial Y}{\partial L} = W, \tag{A16.130}$$

$$(1 - t_Y) \frac{\partial Y}{\partial K} = r + \delta. \tag{A16.131}$$

The production function is linearly homogenous in K and L so we have:

$$\begin{aligned}
(1 - t_Y) Y &= (1 - t_Y) \left[\frac{\partial Y}{\partial L} L + \frac{\partial Y}{\partial K} K \right] \\
&= (1 - t_Y) \left[\frac{WL}{1 - t_Y} + \frac{(r + \delta) K}{1 - t_Y} \right] \\
&= WL + (r + \delta) K. \tag{A16.132}
\end{aligned}$$

It follows from (A16.132) that factor payments fully exhaust after-tax revenue.

(b) By using equation (Q16.13) and noting the government budget constraint, $t_Y Y = K_G$, and the full employment condition for labour, $L = 1$, we obtain for the marginal product of capital:

$$\frac{\partial Y}{\partial K} = (1 - \varepsilon_L) Z_0 \left(\frac{K_G}{K}\right)^{\varepsilon_L}$$

$$= (1 - \varepsilon_L) Z_0 \left(t_Y \frac{Y}{K}\right)^{\varepsilon_L}. \tag{A16.133}$$

We can also write $\partial Y / \partial K$ as:

$$\frac{\partial Y}{\partial K} = (1 - \varepsilon_L) \frac{Y}{K}. \tag{A16.134}$$

By equating the two expressions (A16.133) and (A16.134) we can solve for Y/K:

$$\frac{Y}{K} = Z_0^{1/(1-\varepsilon_L)} t_Y^{\varepsilon_L/(1-\varepsilon_L)} \quad \Leftrightarrow \quad Y = AK, \tag{A16.135}$$

$$A \equiv Z_0^{1/(1-\varepsilon_L)} t_Y^{\varepsilon_L/(1-\varepsilon_L)}. \tag{A16.136}$$

Output is proportional to the capital stock and the factor of proportionality, A, depends only on Z_0 and t_Y.

The marginal product of labour is:

$$\frac{\partial Y}{\partial L} = \varepsilon_L Z_0 K \left(\frac{K_G}{K}\right)^{\varepsilon_L}$$

$$= \varepsilon_L Z_0 K \left(t_Y \frac{Y}{K}\right)^{\varepsilon_L}$$

$$= \varepsilon_L AK, \tag{A16.137}$$

where we have used (A16.135)–(A16.136) in the final step.

(c) The full model is given by:

$$\dot{C}(t) = [r - \rho] C(t) - \beta (\rho + \beta) K(t), \tag{A16.138}$$

$$\dot{K}(t) = (1 - t_Y) Y(t) - C(t) - \delta K(t), \tag{A16.139}$$

$$r = (1 - t_Y)(1 - \varepsilon_L) A - \delta, \tag{A16.140}$$

$$Y(t) = AK(t). \tag{A16.141}$$

Equation (A16.138) in the aggregate Euler equation, (A16.139) is the goods market clearing condition, (A16.140) is (A16.131) combined with (A16.135), and (A16.141) is (A16.135). We define $\theta(t) \equiv C(t) / K(t)$ and note that $\dot{\theta}(t) / \theta(t) \equiv \dot{C}(t) / C(t) - \dot{K}(t) / K(t)$. We can now rewrite the transformed model as:

$$\frac{\dot{\theta}(t)}{\theta(t)} = (1 - t_Y)(1 - \varepsilon_L) A - (\rho + \delta) - \frac{\beta(\rho + \beta)}{\theta(t)} - \frac{\dot{K}(t)}{K(t)}, \tag{A16.142}$$

$$\frac{\dot{K}(t)}{K(t)} = (1 - t_Y) A - \delta - \theta(t). \tag{A16.143}$$

By substituting (A16.143) into (A16.142) we obtain a differential equation in $\theta(t)$:

$$\frac{\dot{\theta}(t)}{\theta(t)} = -\varepsilon_L (1 - t_Y) A - \rho + \theta(t) - \frac{\beta(\rho + \beta)}{\theta(t)}. \tag{A16.144}$$

Equation (A16.142) is an unstable differential equation, the only economically sensible solution of which is the steady state. It follows that $\theta(t)$ jumps to its constant equilibrium level, θ^*. The growth rate in capital, consumption, and output also features no transitional dynamics–see equation (A16.143).

(d) By combining (A16.143)–(A16.144) and setting $\gamma_Y \equiv \dot{K}(t)/K(t)$ we find the expression characterizing the growth rate:

$$[(1 - t_Y) A - (\delta + \gamma_Y)] (r - \gamma_Y - \rho) = \beta (\rho + \beta). \qquad \text{(A16.145)}$$

In the representative-agent model, $\beta = 0$ and (since $(1 - t_Y) A - (\delta + \gamma_Y) r > 0$) the growth rate is given by $\gamma_Y = r - \rho$. Since $r = (1 - t_Y)(1 - \varepsilon_L) A - \delta$ we find that:

$$(\gamma_Y)_{\beta=0} = (1 - t_Y)(1 - \varepsilon_L) Z_0^{1/(1-\varepsilon_L)} t_Y^{\varepsilon_L/(1-\varepsilon_L)} - (\rho + \delta). \qquad \text{(A16.146)}$$

This is just the expression found for the Barro model discussed in Chapter 14.

For the overlapping-generations model, γ_Y is the solution to (A16.145). To derive $d\gamma_Y/d\beta$ we totally differentiate (A16.145) and find:

$$-\left[[(1 - t_Y) A - (\delta + \gamma_Y)] + (r - \gamma_Y - \rho) \right] \frac{d\gamma_Y}{d\beta} = \rho + 2\beta. \qquad \text{(A16.147)}$$

Since the term in square brackets on the left-hand side is positive we conclude that $d\gamma_Y/d\beta < 0$. The higher the birth/death rate, the lower is the rate of growth. It follows from (A16.144) that $dc/d\beta = -(1/A) d\gamma_Y/d\beta > 0$. Hence, the higher the birth/death rate, the higher is the proportion of output that is consumed. Growth is lower because there is less room for capital accumulation.

(e) By defining $x \equiv (1 - t_Y) A$ and noting that $r = (1 - \varepsilon_L) x - \delta$, we can rewrite (A16.145) as follows:

$$\left[x - (\delta + \gamma_Y) \right] \left[(1 - \varepsilon_L) x - (\delta + \rho + \gamma_Y) \right] = \beta (\rho + \beta). \qquad \text{(A16.148)}$$

Equation (A16.148) in an implicit function relating γ_Y to x (and the constant parameters). It is not difficult to show that:

$$\frac{d\gamma_Y}{dx} = \frac{[x - (\delta + \gamma_Y)](1 - \varepsilon_L) + (1 - \varepsilon_L) x - (\delta + \rho + \gamma_Y)}{[x - (\delta + \gamma_Y)] + (1 - \varepsilon_L) x - (\delta + \rho + \gamma_Y)} > 0, \text{ (A16.149)}$$

where we have used the fact that $x - (\delta + \gamma_Y) > 0$ and $(1 - \varepsilon_L) x - (\delta + \rho + \gamma_Y) > 0$. It follows from (A16.149) that the growth rate is maximized if x is maximized. This conclusion is independent of the value of β. Since $x \equiv (1 - t_Y) A$ and $A \equiv Z_0^{1/(1-\varepsilon_L)} t_Y^{\varepsilon_L/(1-\varepsilon_L)}$ we find that γ_Y is maximized if $(1 - t_Y) t_Y^{\varepsilon_L/(1-\varepsilon_L)}$ is maximized, i.e. if $t_Y = \varepsilon_L$ (just as in the Barro model). The corresponding maximum growth rate is of course lower, the higher is the birth/death rate (see part (d) of this question).

(f) The model is now:

$$\dot{C}(t) = [r(t) - \rho] C(t) - \beta (\rho + \beta) K(t), \tag{A16.150}$$

$$Y(t) = C(t) + I(t) + I_G(t), \tag{A16.151}$$

$$\dot{K}(t) = I(t) - \delta K(t), \tag{A16.152}$$

$$\dot{K}_G(t) = I_G(t) - \delta_G K_G(t), \tag{A16.153}$$

$$I_G(t) = t_Y Y(t) \tag{A16.154}$$

$$r(t) = (1 - t_Y)(1 - \varepsilon_L) Z_0 \left(\frac{K_G(t)}{K(t)} \right)^{\varepsilon_L}, \tag{A16.155}$$

$$Y(t) = Z_0 K(t) \cdot \left(\frac{K_G(t)}{K(t)} \right)^{\varepsilon_L} - \delta. \tag{A16.156}$$

As in section 14.2.2.2.1, we rewrite the model in stationary format by defining:

$$\kappa(t) \equiv \frac{K(t)}{K_G(t)}, \qquad \theta(t) \equiv \frac{C(t)}{K(t)}. \tag{A16.157}$$

In the steady state, $\kappa(t) = \kappa^*$ and $\theta(t) = \theta^*$, and we rewrite the model as:

$$\gamma^* = (r^* - \rho) - \frac{\beta (\rho + \beta)}{\theta^*}, \tag{A16.158}$$

$$\gamma^* = (1 - t_Y) Z_0 (\kappa^*)^{-\varepsilon_L} - \theta^* - \delta, \tag{A16.159}$$

$$\gamma^* = t_Y Z_0 (\kappa^*)^{1-\varepsilon_L} - \delta_G, \tag{A16.160}$$

$$r^* = (1 - t_Y)(1 - \varepsilon_L) Z_0 (\kappa^*)^{-\varepsilon_L} - \delta, \tag{A16.161}$$

where γ^* is the common growth rate of $C(t)$, $K(t)$, $K_G(t)$, $I(t)$, $Y(t)$, and $I_G(t)$ along the balanced growth path.

Apart from the generational turnover term in (A16.158), this model is the same as the one studied in section 14.2.2.2.1. We can derive the government capital accumulation (GCA) line by solving (A16.161) for κ^* and substituting the resulting expression into (A16.160):

$$\gamma^* = t_Y Z_0 \cdot \left(\frac{(1 - t_Y)(1 - \varepsilon_L) Z_0}{r^* + \delta} \right)^{(1-\varepsilon_L)/\varepsilon_L} - \delta_G. \tag{A16.162}$$

In the top panel of Figure A16.10, the GCA line represents a downward sloping relationship between the growth rate, γ^*, and the interest rate, r^*.

By using (A16.161) in (A16.159) we find that:

$$\theta^* = \Phi(r^*, \gamma^*) \equiv \frac{r^* + \delta}{1 - \varepsilon_L} - \gamma^* - \delta. \tag{A16.163}$$

Using this expression in (A16.158) we find the modified Euler equation (MEE):

$$\gamma^* = (r^* - \rho) - \frac{\beta (\rho + \beta)}{\Phi(r^*, \gamma^*)}. \tag{A16.164}$$

This is an implicit relationship between γ^* and r^*. Together with (A16.162) it determines the steady-state equilibrium. Differentiating (A16.158) with respect

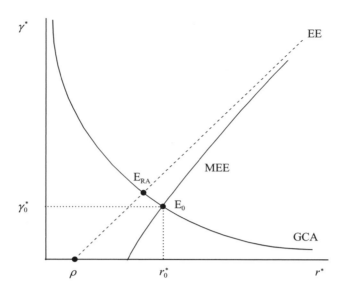

Figure A16.10: Steady-state growth and interest rates

to γ^* and r^* and re-arranging we find the slope of the MEE locus:

$$\frac{d\gamma^*}{dr^*} = \frac{1 + \frac{\beta(\rho+\beta)}{(\theta^*)^2(1-\varepsilon_L)}}{1 + \frac{\beta(\rho+\beta)}{(\theta^*)^2}} > 1. \tag{A16.165}$$

In Figure A16.10, the dashed EE line is the Euler equation for the representative agent model, i.e. $\beta = 0$ and $\gamma^* = r^* - \rho$. The MEE line lies to the right of EE and approaches it asymptotically.

The growth rate for the overlapping generations model is γ_0^* and the interest rate is r_0^*. Growth is lower with overlapping generations than in the representative agent model.

In principle we can use the approach explained in section 14.2.2.2.2 in the book to formally study the transitional dynamics of the revised model. Intuitively, however, it is clear why there is non-trivial transitional dynamics. Both K and K_G are stocks, so their ratio, κ, will also be a sluggish variable. That is the case in the representative-agent version of the model and thus also in the overlapping-generations model.

Chapter 17

Overlapping generations in discrete time

Question 1: Short questions

(a) "In a dynamically inefficient economy it is Pareto-improving to move from a PAYG to a fully-funded pension system." True or false? Explain with the aid of a figure.

(b) Consider an economy with a defined-contribution PAYG pension system and assume that there is a new baby boom. Show what happens to the economy at impact, over time, and in the long run as a result of this baby boom. Explain the intuition.

(c) "PAYG pensions are Pareto efficient." True or false? Explain.

Question 2: Capital fundamentalism in an OLG model

[Based on Jones and Manuelli (1992)] In this question we consider a capital - fundamentalist growth model in which agents have finite lives. We show that intergenerational redistribution of resources from the old to the young is needed to jump-start the growth process. We use a simplified version of the Diamond - Samuelson model considered in section 17.1 of the book. The representative young household has the following lifetime utility function:

$$\Lambda_t^Y \equiv \ln C_t^Y + \frac{1}{1+\rho} \ln C_{t+1}^O, \tag{Q17.1}$$

where Λ_t^Y is lifetime utility, C_t^Y is consumption during youth, C_{t+1}^O is consumption during old age, and ρ is the pure rate of time preference. The household faces the usual budget identities:

$$C_t^Y + S_t = W_t, \tag{Q17.2}$$

$$C_{t+1}^O = (1 + r_{t+1})S_t, \tag{Q17.3}$$

where S_t is saving, W_t is the wage rate, and r_{t+1} is the interest rate. There is no population growth and the size of each generation is normalized to unity ($L_t = L_{t-1} = 1$). Households only work during youth.

The representative firm hires labour L_t (from the young) and capital K_t (from the old) in order to maximize profit:

$$\Pi_t \equiv F(K_t, L_t) - W_t L_t - R_t^K K_t, \tag{Q17.4}$$

where $F(\cdot)$ is a linear homogeneous production function, and R_t^K is the rental rate on capital. It is assumed that the production function features a constant elasticity of substitution:

$$F(K_t, L_t) \equiv A \left[\alpha K_t^{(\sigma-1)/\sigma} + (1-\alpha) L_t^{(\sigma-1)/\sigma} \right]^{\sigma/(\sigma-1)}, \quad 0 < \alpha < 1, \tag{Q17.5}$$

where A is some index of general productivity. It is assumed that capital and labour can be substituted quite easily, i.e. $\sigma > 1$.

(a) Use a simple arbitrage argument to explain why the rental rate on capital is equal to $R_t^K = r_t + \delta$.

(b) Solve the optimization problems for the representative (old and young) households and the representative firm. Show that profits are zero and that saving is proportional to the wage rate. Derive the expression linking S_t and K_{t+1}.

(c) Derive an expression for W_t / K_t. Use your expression to show that:

$$\lim_{K_t \to 0} \frac{W_t}{K_t} = \infty \quad \text{and} \quad \lim_{K_t \to \infty} \frac{W_t}{K_t} = 0.$$

Define the growth rate of capital (per worker) by $\gamma_t^K \equiv (K_{t+1} - K_t)/K_t$ and show that it goes to zero in the long run. Illustrate your answer with the aid of a diagram with K_t on the vertical axis and K_{t+1}/K_t on the horizontal axis.

(d) Why is there no endogenous growth in this model despite the fact that capital and labour can be easily substituted?

Assume that the government introduces an output tax, τ, so that the profit function is now $\Pi_t \equiv (1-\tau)F(K_t, L_t) - W_t L_t - R_t^K K_t$. Assume that the tax revenue, $\tau F(K_t, L_t)$, is rebated to young households in the form of lump-sum transfers. Hence, these transfers are given by $T_t^Y = \tau F(K_t, L_t)$.

(e) ★ Solve the extended model and prove that the long-run growth rate in the capital stock is given by:

$$\gamma_t^K = \max_{0, \gamma^*} , \gamma^* \equiv \frac{\tau A}{2 + \rho} \alpha^{\sigma/(\sigma-1)} - 1. \tag{Q17.6}$$

Explain intuitively why endogenous growth becomes feasible if a sufficient amount of income is distributed to the young.

Question 3: Welfare effects of debt

Consider the basic Diamond - Samuelson model studied in section 17.1 of the book and assume that the felicity function is logarithmic:

$$\Lambda_t^Y \equiv \ln C_t^Y + \frac{1}{1+\rho} \ln C_{t+1}^O, \tag{Q17.7}$$

where Λ_t^Y is lifetime utility, C_t^Y is consumption during youth, C_{t+1}^O is consumption during old age, and ρ is the pure rate of time preference. The technology is Cobb-Douglas and $y_t = k_t^{1-\varepsilon_L}$ where $y_t \equiv Y_t / L_t$ and $k_t \equiv K_t / L_t$.

(a) Introduce government consumption, government debt and lump-sum taxes levied on young and old generations into the model. Denote these variables by G_t, B_t, T_t^Y, and T_t^O respectively. Define per capita debt and government consumption as, respectively, $b_t \equiv B_t / L_t$ and $g_t \equiv G_t / L_t$. Derive and interpret the government budget identity.

(b) Solve the household optimization problem. Establish the link between household saving and the future capital stock. Show that one of b_t, T_t^Y, and T_t^O is redundant to finance a given path for government consumption.

(c) Determine the macroeconomic effects of a once-off increase in government consumption, g, which is financed by means of lump-sum taxes on the young. Abstract from government debt (i.e. $b_t = b_{t+1} = 0$). Derive the stability condition and explain the intuition behind your results.

(d) Redo part (c) but now assume that financing is by means of lump-sum taxes on the old. Comment on the key differences with the earlier case.

(e) Assume that the government is somehow unable to levy taxes on the old (so that $T_t^O = 0$ for all t) and that it maintains a constant amount of debt per member of the young generation (i.e. $b_t = b$ for all t). Show that a once-off increase in b leads to crowding out of capital in the long run in a dynamically efficient economy.

Question 4: Lifetime uncertainty in a two-period model

Consider a two-period setting. An agent faces lifetime uncertainty in the sense that he/she may die after the first period. The probability of death is given by π, with $0 < \pi < 1$. The expected utility of the agent is thus:

$$E(\Lambda) = U(C_1) + \frac{\pi}{1+\rho} U(C_2), \tag{Q17.8}$$

where C_t is consumption in period t, $U(C_t)$ is the felicity function (satisfying $U''(C_t) < 0 < U'(C_t)$), and $\rho > 0$ captures impatience. The household faces the following budget identities:

$$\begin{align} C_1 + A &= W_1, \tag{Q17.9}\\ C_2 &= W_2 + (1+r)A, \tag{Q17.10} \end{align}$$

where W_t is exogenous wage income in period t, A is assets, and r is the interest rate. If $A < 0$ the agent is borrowing.

(a) Compute the optimum consumption-saving plans of an agent whose preferences are such that he/she plans to save during the first period of life. Illustrate your solution with the usual diagram (see Chapter 5) with C_2 on the vertical axis and C_1 on the horizontal axis.

(b) Redo part (a) for an agent who would like to borrow in the first period of life. Is that possible? What is the optimum this agent reaches?

(c) Introduce actuarial notes (as in Yaari (1965)) that yield r^A if the agent survives into the second period, and zero if the agent dies. Derive an expression for the actuarially fair value of r^A.

(d) Show that both initial savers (part (a)) and frustrated borrowers (part (b)) will make use of these actuarial notes. Illustrate your answer in the diagrams and explain. Show that this result also holds if the notes are not actuarially fair, provided $r^A > r$.

Question 5: Pensions in the Diamond-Samuelson model

Consider the Diamond - Samuelson model discussed in section 17.1 of the book. Change the lifetime utility function (17.1) to:

$$\Lambda_t^Y \equiv U(C_t^Y, C_{t+1}^O), \tag{Q17.11}$$

and assume that indifference curves bulge toward the origin (in a graph with C_t^Y on the horizontal axis and C_{t+1}^O on the vertical axis). There exists a pension system so that the agent's budget equations are given by:

$$
\begin{align}
C_t^Y + S_t &= W_t - T, \tag{Q17.12}\\
C_{t+1}^O &= (1 + r_{t+1})S_t + Z_{t+1}, \tag{Q17.13}\\
L_t &= (1 + n_t)\, L_{t-1}, \tag{Q17.14}\\
L_{t-1}Z_t &= L_t T, \tag{Q17.15}
\end{align}
$$

where T is the (exogenous) pension contribution paid during youth, and n_t is the population growth rate in period t ($n_t > 0$).

(a) What kind of pension system have we assumed in this model? Funded or PAYG? Defined-benefit or defined-contribution?

(b) Derive the comparative static effects on the optimal choices of C_t^Y, C_{t+1}^O, and S_t of an increase in the pension contribution ($dT > 0$). Assume that $r_t > n_t$ for all t. Explain the intuition behind your results with the aid of a diagram with C_t^Y on the horizontal axis and C_{t+1}^O on the vertical axis.

(c) Prove that $S_t = (1 + n_{t+1})\, k_{t+1}$, where $k_t \equiv K_t/L_t$.

(d) Close the model with the usual expressions (17.15)-(17.16). Assume that (i) $U(C_t^Y, C_{t+1}^O)$ is homothetic, (ii) the production function is Cobb-Douglas, $y_t = k_t^\alpha$ with $0 < \alpha < 1$, and (iii) the economy under consideration features a single stable steady state. Compute the (local) stability condition that we implicitly assume to hold in this economy.

Question 6: Consumption taxation and redistribution

This question deals with consumption taxation. Consider the basic Diamond - Samuelson model of section 17.1 in the book. There is a (potentially time-varying) consumption tax which is denoted by t_{Ct}. The revenue of this tax is recycled in a lump-sum fashion to existing household, i.e. the government budget constraint in period t is:

$$t_{Ct}C_t = L_t Z_t^Y + L_{t-1} Z_t^O, \tag{Q17.16}$$

where C_t is total consumption, Z_t^Y is the lump-sum transfer to each young household, and Z_t^O is the lump-sum transfer to each old household. The budget identities (17.2)-(17.3) are changed to:

$$
\begin{aligned}
C_t^Y + S_t &= w_t + Z_t^Y, &\tag{Q17.17}\\
C_{t+1}^O &= (1 + r_{t+1})S_t + Z_{t+1}^O. &\tag{Q17.18}
\end{aligned}
$$

(a) Derive the optimizing behaviour of young and old households. Show how the savings equation is affected by the consumption taxes and the lump-sum transfers.

(b) Assume that the substitution elasticities in the utility and production functions are both equal to unity (unit-elastic model). Derive the savings function.

(c) Assume that the entire revenue is given to the young, i.e. $Z_t^O = 0$ in (Q17.16). Derive the fundamental difference equation for the capital-labour ratio.

(d) Now redo part (b) under the assumption that the old receive the entire tax revenue, i.e. $Z_t^Y = 0$ in (Q17.16). Comment on any differences that may exist between the two scenarios.

Answers

Question 1: Short questions

(a) False. It is optimal to *expand* the PAYG system. It constitutes a chain letter. There is too much capital already and an expansion of the system constitutes a move in the direction of the golden rule point. Figure 17.4 shows the adjustment path. The economy is initially at $k = k_0$. Without the PAYG scheme the economy would have converged to point B. When the PAYG scheme is introduced, the economy follows the path from C toward the new equilibrium at E_0. The difference between points A and C is due to the fact that the current young save less than they would have done in the absence of the PAYG scheme.

(b) This is the opposite of the case drawn in Figure 17.6. A baby boom can be modeled as an increase in the birth rate, n. In the long run the capital stock falls. There are more asset-less young people and fewer asset-rich old people. The dependency ratio, $1/(1 + n)$, falls as a result of the baby boom.

(c) This statement is correct in a dynamically efficient economy (with $r > n$) if there are no other distortions that can be reduced by sizing down the PAYG system. In the text we state that an allocation of resources in the economy is called Pareto-optimal (or Pareto-efficient) if there is no other feasible allocation which (i) makes no individual in the economy worse off and (ii) makes at least one individual strictly better off than he or she was. Similarly, a policy is called *Pareto-improving* vis-à-vis the initial situation if it improves welfare for at least one agent and leaves all other agents equally well off as in the status quo. The steady-state generation are better off with a smaller PAYG system but the correct old cannot be compensated (there is no loose change lying around).

Question 2: Capital fundamentalism in an OLG model

(a) The easiest way to derive the expression for the rental rate on capital is to model explicitly the investment process. If an investor purchases K_t units of capital in period t then he will obtain future rental payments, R_{t+1}^K, plus the undepreciated part of the capital stock, $(1 - \delta)K_t$. Hence, the profit from investing is:

$$\Pi_t^I \equiv -K_t + \frac{R_{t+1}^K K_t + (1 - \delta)K_t}{1 + r_{t+1}}, \tag{A17.1}$$

where future revenues are discounted at the real interest rate, r_{t+1}. The investment profit is maximized by choice of K_t and the first-order condition (for an interior solution, with $K_t > 0$) is:

$$\frac{d\Pi_t^I}{dK_t} = -1 + \frac{R_{t+1}^K + (1 - \delta)}{1 + r_{t+1}} = 0, \tag{A17.2}$$

from which we derive that $r_{t+1} = R_{t+1}^K - \delta$.

(b) The household's consolidated budget restriction is obtained by combining equations (Q17.2)–(Q17.3):

$$W_t = C_t^Y + \frac{C_{t+1}^O}{1 + r_{t+1}}. \tag{A17.3}$$

The young household chooses C_t^Y and C_{t+1}^O (and, implicitly, S_t) in order to maximize Λ_t^Y (given in (Q17.1)). The Lagrangian expression for this optimization problem is:

$$\mathcal{L} \equiv \ln C_t^Y + \frac{1}{1+\rho} \ln C_{t+1}^O + \lambda \left[W_t - C_t^Y - \frac{C_{t+1}^O}{1+r_{t+1}} \right],$$

where λ is the Lagrange multiplier. The first-order conditions are the constraint and $\partial L / \partial C_t^Y = \partial L / \partial C_{t+1}^O = 0$:

$$\frac{1}{C_t^Y} = \lambda, \tag{A17.4}$$

$$\frac{1}{1+\rho} \frac{1}{C_{t+1}^O} = \frac{\lambda}{1+r_{t+1}}. \tag{A17.5}$$

By combining (A17.4)–(A17.5) we find the consumption Euler equation:

$$\frac{C_{t+1}^O}{C_t^Y} = \frac{1+r_{t+1}}{1+\rho}. \tag{A17.6}$$

According to (A17.6), if r_{t+1} exceeds (falls short of) ρ, then future consumption will be higher (lower) than current consumption. By substituting (A17.6) into the lifetime budget constraint (A17.3) we can find the solutions for C_t^Y and C_{t+1}^O. For C_t^Y we find:

$$C_t^Y + \frac{C_{t+1}^O}{1+r_{t+1}} = W_t \quad \Leftrightarrow$$

$$C_t^Y + \frac{C_t^Y}{1+\rho} = W_t \quad \Leftrightarrow$$

$$C_t^Y = \frac{1+\rho}{2+\rho} W_t. \tag{A17.7}$$

By using (A17.7) in, respectively, (A17.6) and (Q17.2) we find the expressions for C_{t+1}^O and S_t:

$$C_{t+1}^O = \frac{1+r_{t+1}}{1+\rho} C_t^Y = \frac{1+r_{t+1}}{2+\rho} W_t, \tag{A17.8}$$

$$S_t = W_t - C_t^Y = \frac{W_t}{2+\rho}. \tag{A17.9}$$

We observe that saving is proportional to wage the income of the young.

The representative firm hires capital and labour from the households. After-tax profit is defined as:

$$\Pi_t \equiv (1-\tau) F(K_t, L_t) - W_t L_t - R_t^K K_t, \tag{A17.10}$$

where τ is an output tax used in part (e) of this question. Profit maximization yields the usual first-order conditions:

$$\frac{\partial \Pi_t}{\partial L_t} = 0: \quad (1-\tau) F_L(K_t, L_t) = W_t, \tag{A17.11}$$

$$\frac{\partial \Pi_t}{\partial K_t} = 0: \quad (1-\tau) F_K(K_t, L_t) = R_t^K. \tag{A17.12}$$

Since technology features CRTS, excess profits are zero ($\Pi_t = 0$).

To derive the link between saving by the young and the future capital stock, we need to do some bookkeeping. The economy-wide resource constraint is:

$$Y_t + (1 - \delta)K_t = K_{t+1} + C_t, \tag{A17.13}$$

where C_t is total consumption (by young and old). The young consume $C_t^Y = W_t - S(W_t)$ (where $S(\cdot)$ is given in (A17.9) above) and the old consume $C_t^O = (r_t + \delta) K_t + (1 - \delta)K_t$. Since we abstract from population growth, total consumption is:

$$
\begin{aligned}
C_t &\equiv C_t^Y + C_t^O \\
&= W_t - S(W_t) + (r_t + \delta) K_t + (1 - \delta)K_t. \tag{A17.14}
\end{aligned}
$$

With a zero output tax ($\tau = 0$) we have that $F(K_t, L_t) = W_t + (r_t + \delta) K_t$ so that (A17.14) simplifies to:

$$Y_t + (1 - \delta)K_t = C_t + S(W_t). \tag{A17.15}$$

Finally, by equating (A17.13) and (A17.15) we find the desired expression linking $S(W_t)$ and K_{t+1}:

$$K_{t+1} = S(W_t). \tag{A17.16}$$

(c) According to (A17.11), the wage rate equals the marginal product of capital (recall that $\tau = 0$ here). By using (Q17.5) we find:

$$
\begin{aligned}
F_L(K_t, L_t) &= A \left[\alpha K_t^{(\sigma-1)/\sigma} + (1 - \alpha)L_t^{(\sigma-1)/\sigma} \right]^{\sigma/(\sigma-1)-1} (1 - \alpha)L_t^{-1/\sigma} \\
&= (1 - \alpha)A \left[\alpha K_t^{(\sigma-1)/\sigma} + 1 - \alpha \right]^{1/(\sigma-1)}, \tag{A17.17}
\end{aligned}
$$

where we have substituted $L_t = 1$ in the second line. By using (A17.17) and noting that $W_t = F_L(K_t, 1)$ we find:

$$\frac{W_t}{K_t} = (1 - \alpha)A \frac{\left[\alpha K_t^{(\sigma-1)/\sigma} + 1 - \alpha \right]^{1/(\sigma-1)}}{K_t}. \tag{A17.18}$$

We use (A17.18) to derive the various limits. For the lower limit we find:

$$\lim_{K_t \to 0} \frac{W_t}{K_t} = (1 - \alpha)A \frac{\lim_{K_t \to 0} \left[\alpha K_t^{(\sigma-1)/\sigma} + 1 - \alpha \right]^{1/(\sigma-1)}}{\lim_{K_t \to 0} K_t} = \infty. \tag{A17.19}$$

The upper limit is most easily computed by first rewriting (A17.18) somewhat:

$$\frac{W_t}{K_t} = (1 - \alpha)A \frac{\left[\alpha + (1 - \alpha) K_t^{(1-\sigma)/\sigma} \right]^{1/(\sigma-1)} K_t^{1/\sigma}}{K_t}. \tag{A17.20}$$

By letting $K_t \to \infty$ in (A17.20) we find that:

$$\lim_{K_t \to \infty} \frac{W_t}{K_t} = (1 - \alpha)A\alpha^{1/(\sigma-1)} \lim_{K_t \to \infty} K_t^{(1-\sigma)/\sigma} = 0, \tag{A17.21}$$

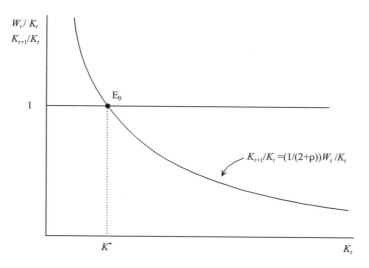

Figure A17.1: Hampered endogenous growth in the OLG model

where we have used the fact that $\lim_{K_t \to \infty} K_t^{(1-\sigma)/\sigma} = 0$ as $\sigma > 1$. It follows that, for $\sigma > 1$, the ratio between wages and the capital stock goes to zero as the capital stock gets large.

In Figure A17.1 we illustrate the dynamic properties of the model. On the vertical axis we measure W_t/K_t and K_{t+1}/K_t and on the horizontal axis K_t. The horizontal line depicts steady states, for which $K_{t+1}/K_t = 1$. The downward sloping line is the graphical representation of (A17.16) (with equation (A17.9) inserted):

$$\frac{K_{t+1}}{K_t} = \frac{1}{2+\rho} \frac{W_t}{K_t}. \tag{A17.22}$$

In view of (A17.19) and (A17.21), this line is vertical near the origin and approaches the horizontal axis as the capital stock gets large. It follows that the model possesses a unique steady state at E_0 and that growth vanishes in the long run, i.e. $\gamma_\infty^K = 0$.

(d) Despite the fact that this is a "capital-fundamentalist" model, with easy substitution between capital and labour, there is no long-run growth. Intuitively this is because the savings rate is too low. Saving depends on wages of the young (see (A17.9)) but as K_t gets large the W_t/K_t ratio (and thus also the S_t/K_t ratio) gets smaller and smaller. This excludes the possibility of endogenous growth as there exists an upper limit on the amount of capital than can be sustained by the savings plans of the young.

(e) The budget identity (Q17.2) is changed to:

$$C_t^Y + S_t = W_t + T_t^Y, \tag{A17.23}$$

so that (A17.3) becomes:

$$W_t + T_t^Y = C_t^Y + \frac{C_{t+1}^O}{1 + r_{t+1}}. \tag{A17.24}$$

By using (A17.6) and (A17.24) we find that consumption during youth increases as a result of the transfers:

$$C_t^Y = \frac{1+\rho}{2+\rho}\left[W_t + T_t^Y\right]. \tag{A17.25}$$

By using (A17.25) in (A17.23) we find that the savings equation is given by:

$$S_t = \frac{1}{2+\rho}\left[W_t + T_t^Y\right]. \tag{A17.26}$$

Hence, saving also increases as a result of the transfers. This is obvious, as the household wants to use some of the transfers to support a higher consumption level during old age.

The government budget identity is given by:

$$\tau Y_t = T_t^Y. \tag{A17.27}$$

For the representative firms the expressions in (A17.11)–(A17.12) are all still valid. The resource constraint is also still as presented in (A17.13). Total consumption, C_t, is now:

$$\begin{aligned}
C_t &\equiv C_t^Y + C_t^O \\
&= W_t + T_t^Y - S\left(W_t + T_t^Y\right) + (r_t + \delta)\,K_t + (1-\delta)K_t. \tag{A17.28}
\end{aligned}$$

We find from (A17.10)–(A17.12) that:

$$(1-\tau)Y_t = W_t + (r_t + \delta)\,K_t. \tag{A17.29}$$

By using (A17.27) and (A17.29) in (A17.28) we find equation (A17.15) again. It follows that $K_{t+1} = S(W_t + \tau Y_t)$ or, by using (A17.26), that:

$$\frac{K_{t+1}}{K_t} = \frac{1}{2+\rho}\left[\frac{W_t}{K_t} + \frac{\tau Y_t}{K_t}\right]. \tag{A17.30}$$

Equation (A17.30) is the fundamental difference equation for the capital stock.

In order to illustrate the possibility of endogenous growth we must first figure out what happens to Y_t/K_t as K_t gets large. We derive from (Q17.5):

$$\begin{aligned}
\frac{Y_t}{K_t} &= \frac{A}{K_t}\left[\alpha K_t^{(\sigma-1)/\sigma} + (1-\alpha)L_t^{(\sigma-1)/\sigma}\right]^{\sigma/(\sigma-1)} \\
&= A\left[K_t^{(1-\sigma)/\sigma}\left(\alpha K_t^{(\sigma-1)/\sigma} + (1-\alpha)L_t^{(\sigma-1)/\sigma}\right)\right]^{\sigma/(\sigma-1)} \\
&= A\left[\alpha + (1-\alpha)K_t^{(1-\sigma)/\sigma}\right]^{\sigma/(\sigma-1)}, \tag{A17.31}
\end{aligned}$$

where we have substituted $L_t = 1$ in getting to the final expression. It follows from (A17.31) that:

$$\lim_{K_t \to \infty} \frac{Y_t}{K_t} = A\alpha^{\sigma/(\sigma-1)} > 0. \tag{A17.32}$$

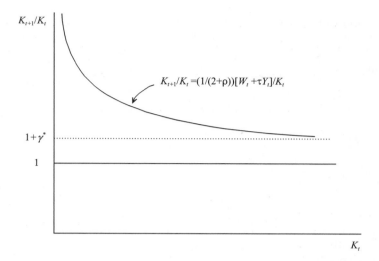

Figure A17.2: Endogenous growth with transfers to the young

By taking limit on both sides of (A17.30) and noting (A17.21) and (A17.32) we find that:

$$\lim_{K_t \to \infty} \frac{K_{t+1}}{K_t} = \frac{1}{2+\rho} \left[\lim_{K_t \to \infty} \frac{W_t}{K_t} + \tau \lim_{K_t \to \infty} \frac{Y_t}{K_t} \right]$$

$$= \frac{\tau}{2+\rho} A\alpha^{\sigma/(\sigma-1)}. \tag{A17.33}$$

There are now two possibilities:

- If the right-hand side of (A17.33) is less than unity, then there is still no endogenous growth. The economy reaches a unique steady state, just as in Figure A17.1.

- If the right-hand side of (A17.33) is larger than unity, then there is endogenous growth as K_{t+1}/K_t is bounded away from the steady-state line.

These two possibilities have been summarized mathematically in (Q17.6). Figure A17.2 illustrates the endogenous growth case. The endogenous growth rate is increasing in the output tax, τ. Intuitively, the output tax redistributes resources from the old (who dissave) to the young (who save). This enables the young to sustain the level of saving required for perpetual growth.

Question 3: Welfare effects of debt

(a) The government budget identity is:

$$G_t + (1+r_t)B_t = L_t T_t^Y + L_{t-1} T_t^O + B_{t+1}, \tag{A17.34}$$

where B_t is the total stock of government debt at the beginning of period t (which is in the hands of the old). The left-hand side of (A17.34) represents total spending on government consumption plus interest payment and debt redemption. The right-hand side represents total government revenue, consisting of tax revenues plus bond sales (to the young). By noting that $L_t = (1+n)L_{t-1}$, $g_t \equiv G_t/L_t$ and $b_t \equiv B_t/L_t$ we can rewrite (A17.34) in per capita terms as follows:

$$\frac{G_t}{L_t} + (1+r_t)\frac{B_t}{L_t} = T_t^Y + \frac{L_{t-1}}{L_t}T_t^O + \frac{L_{t+1}}{L_t}\frac{B_{t+1}}{L_{t+1}} \qquad \Leftrightarrow$$

$$g_t + (1+r_t)b_t = T_t^Y + \frac{T_t^O}{1+n} + (1+n)b_{t+1}. \tag{A17.35}$$

(b) Instead of (17.2)–(17.3), the household faces the following budget identities:

$$C_t^Y + S_t = W_t - T_t^Y, \tag{A17.36}$$

$$C_{t+1}^O = (1+r_{t+1})S_t - T_{t+1}^O. \tag{A17.37}$$

By eliminating S_t from (A17.36)–(A17.37) we find the consolidated lifetime budget constraint:

$$\hat{W}_t \equiv W_t - T_t^Y - \frac{T_{t+1}^O}{1+r_{t+1}} = C_t^Y + \frac{C_{t+1}^O}{1+r_{t+1}}, \tag{A17.38}$$

where $\hat{W}_t$ thus represents after-tax human wealth of the young household.

In view of (17.5) in the textbook and (Q17.7) we find that the consumption Euler equation is:

$$\frac{C_{t+1}^O}{C_t^Y} = \frac{1+r_{t+1}}{1+\rho}. \tag{A17.39}$$

By combining (A17.38) and (A17.39) we find the solutions for C_t^Y and C_{t+1}^O:

$$C_t^Y = \frac{1+\rho}{2+\rho}\hat{W}_t, \tag{A17.40}$$

$$C_{t+1}^O = \frac{1+r_{t+1}}{2+\rho}\hat{W}_t. \tag{A17.41}$$

Finally, by substituting (A17.40) into (A17.36) we find the saving function:

$$S_t = \frac{1}{2+\rho}[W_t - T_t^Y] + \frac{1+\rho}{2+\rho}\frac{T_{t+1}^O}{1+r_{t+1}}. \tag{A17.42}$$

Ceteris paribus, saving depends negatively on taxes during youth and positively on taxes during old age.

To establish the link between saving and capital formation we must do some bookkeeping. The resource constraint is:

$$Y_t + (1-\delta)K_t = \dot{K}_{t+1} + C_t + G_t, \tag{A17.43}$$

where C_t is total consumption. Consumption by the two demographic groups is given by:

$$L_{t-1}C_t^O = (r_t + \delta)K_t + (1-\delta)K_t + (1+r_t)B_t - L_{t-1}T_t^O, \tag{A17.44}$$

$$L_tC_t^Y = L_t\left[W_t - T_t^Y - S(\cdot)\right], \tag{A17.45}$$

where $S(\cdot)$ is the saving function defined in (A17.42) above. According to (A17.44), the old consume their assets (inclusive of interest payments) minus the taxes they face. By using (A17.44)–(A17.45) and noting that $Y_t = (r_t + \delta) K_t + W_t$ we find that total consumption can be written as:

$$
\begin{aligned}
C_t &\equiv L_{t-1} C_t^O + L_t C_t^Y \\
&= Y_t + (1 - \delta) K_t + \left[(1 + r_t) B_t - L_{t-1} T_t^O - L_t T_t^Y \right] - L_t S(\cdot) \\
&= Y_t + (1 - \delta) K_t + B_{t+1} - G_t - L_t S(\cdot),
\end{aligned}
\tag{A17.46}
$$

where we have used the government budget identity (A17.34) in getting to the final expression. By comparing (A17.43) and (A17.46) we find the link between household saving and capital formation:

$$
\begin{aligned}
K_{t+1} + C_t + G_t &= C_t + G_t - B_{t+1} + L_t S(\cdot) \quad \Leftrightarrow \\
L_t S(\cdot) &= B_{t+1} + K_{t+1}.
\end{aligned}
\tag{A17.47}
$$

Equation (A17.47) coincides with (17.62) in the text. Total saving by the young (left-hand side) equals next period's stock of assets, consisting of physical capital and government debt (right-hand side). In per capita terms, equation (A17.47) can be rewritten as:

$$
S(\cdot) = (1 + n) [b_{t+1} + k_{t+1}],
\tag{A17.48}
$$

where $k_t \equiv K_t / L_t$ is the capital labour ratio. To demonstrate the redundancy of one of b_t, T_t^Y, and T_t^O we define following so-called *effective taxes* (Ihori, 1996, p. 201):

$$
\hat{T}_t^Y \equiv T_t^Y + (1 + n) b_{t+1}, \qquad \hat{T}_t^O \equiv T_t^O - (1 + r_t)(1 + n) b_t.
\tag{A17.49}
$$

By using these definitions in (A17.35) we find that the government budget identity can be rewritten as:

$$
\begin{aligned}
g_t &= \left[T_t^Y + (1 + n) b_{t+1} \right] + \frac{1}{1 + n} \left[T_t^O - (1 + n)(1 + r_t) b_t \right] \\
&= \hat{T}_t^Y + \frac{\hat{T}_t^O}{1 + n}.
\end{aligned}
\tag{A17.50}
$$

Similarly, by using (A17.36), (A17.48)–(A17.49) we find:

$$
\begin{aligned}
W_t - T_t^Y - C_t^Y &= (1 + n) [b_{t+1} + k_{t+1}] \quad \Leftrightarrow \\
C_t^Y &= W_t - \hat{T}_t^Y - (1 + n) k_{t+1}.
\end{aligned}
\tag{A17.51}
$$

Equation (A17.44) can be rewritten by using (A17.49) as:

$$
\begin{aligned}
C_t^O &= (1 + r_t)(1 + n) [b_t + k_t] - T_t^O \\
&= (1 + r_t)(1 + n) k_t - \hat{T}_t^O.
\end{aligned}
\tag{A17.52}
$$

Since W_t and r_t only depend on k_t (see (17.15)–(17.16) in the book), the economy is fully characterized by equations (A17.39) and (A17.50)–(A17.52). The key thing to note is that *only the effective taxes appear in these equations*, not the separate components b_t, T_t^Y, and T_t^O. It follows that one of these three components making up the effective taxes is redundant.

(c) The fundamental difference equation for this case is obtained by using (A17.42) and (A17.48) and noting that $T_t^O = T^O$ and $b_{t+1} = b_t = 0$ for all t:

$$k_{t+1} = \frac{1}{(1+n)(2+\rho)}\left[W(k_t) - T_t^Y + \frac{1+\rho}{1+r(k_{t+1})}T^O\right], \qquad (A17.53)$$

where for the Cobb-Douglas technology $W_t = W(k_t) \equiv \varepsilon_L k_t^{1-\varepsilon_L}$ and $r_t = r(k_t) \equiv (1-\varepsilon_L)k_t^{-\varepsilon_L}$. By differentiating (A17.53) with respect to k_{t+1}, k_t and T_t^Y we find:

$$\Delta dk_{t+1} = W'(k_t)dk_t - dT_t^Y, \qquad (A17.54)$$

where Δ is defined as follows:

$$\Delta \equiv (1+n)(1+\rho) + \frac{(1+\rho)\,T^O}{(1+r)^2}r'(k_{t+1}). \qquad (A17.55)$$

If $T^O \le 0$ it follows automatically that $\Delta > 0$ (since $r'(\cdot) < 0$) but if $T^O > 0$ the sign of Δ is ambiguous. We assume that $\Delta > 0$. Since $W'(k_t) > 0$, the stability condition for the model is then:

$$0 < \frac{W'(k_t)}{\Delta} < 1 \quad \Leftrightarrow \quad 0 < \frac{dk_{t+1}}{dk_t} < 1. \qquad (A17.56)$$

In the sequel we assume that (A17.56) is satisfied. By using (A17.35) and noting that $b_{t+1} = b_t = 0$ and $T_t^O = T^O$ we find that the tax on the young changes according to $dT_t^Y = dg$. By using this result in (A17.54) we find the impact and long-run multipliers:

$$\frac{\partial k_{t+1}}{\partial g} = -\frac{1}{\Delta} < 0, \qquad \frac{dk_\infty}{dg} = -\frac{1}{\Delta - W'(k_\infty)} < 0. \qquad (A17.57)$$

At impact, the capital stock is predetermined ($dk_t = 0$) and the increase in government consumption crowds out investment ($\partial k_{t+1}/\partial g < 0$). In the long run the capital stock is crowded out even further because the future wage rate declines and the future interest rate increases (both these effects depress future saving).

(d) The fundamental difference equation for this case is obtained by using (A17.42) and (A17.48) and noting that $T_t^Y = T^Y$ and $b_{t+1} = b_t = 0$ for all t:

$$k_{t+1} = \frac{1}{(1+n)(2+\rho)}\left[W(k_t) - T^Y + \frac{1+\rho}{1+r(k_{t+1})}T_{t+1}^O\right]. \qquad (A17.58)$$

The government budget constraint simplifies for this case to:

$$T_t^O = (1+n)\left(g_t - T^Y\right). \qquad (A17.59)$$

By substituting (A17.59) into (A17.58) we find:

$$k_{t+1} = \frac{1}{(1+n)(2+\rho)}\left[W(k_t) - T^Y + \frac{(1+\rho)(1+n)}{1+r(k_{t+1})}\left(g_{t+1} - T^Y\right)\right]. \qquad (A17.60)$$

The stability condition is still given by (A17.56) and the impact and long-run multipliers are:

$$\frac{\partial k_{t+1}}{\partial g} = \frac{1}{(1+r)\,\Delta} > 0, \qquad \frac{dk_\infty}{dg} = \frac{(1+\rho)(1+n)}{(1+r)\,[\Delta - W'(k_\infty)]} > 0. \quad \text{(A17.61)}$$

At impact there is a positive effect on capital formation because the young anticipate higher future taxes and save more as a result (see also (A17.42) above). In the long run two things happen. First, the wage rises because there is more capital per worker. Second, the interest rate falls (due to capital formation) and the present value of taxes during old age ($T^O_{t+1}/(1+r_{t+1})$) rises. Both effects explain that the long-run effect is larger than the short-run effect on capital.

The lesson we learn from parts (c)–(d) is that the effect on the capital stock of an increase in public consumption depends very much on the financing method employed by the policy maker. If the young must finance this fiscal policy then capital formation is harmed. The opposite holds if the old must pay for the additional public consumption.

(e) Since the government does not possess a full set of age-specific taxes, there is no redundant tax parameter any more. Indeed, in view of (A17.49) and the assumption that $T^O_t = 0$ for all t it follows that changing b must change both $\hat{T}^Y_t$ and $\hat{T}^O_t$. In this setting government debt has real effects. By using (A17.35) we find that the government budget identity simplifies to:

$$g + (1+r_t)b = T^Y_t + (1+n)b, \tag{A17.62}$$

so that the change in taxes on the young satisfies:

$$dT^Y_t = (r_t - n)\, db > 0, \tag{A17.63}$$

where the sign follows from the assumption that the economy is dynamically efficient (so that $r_t > n$). The fundamental difference equation for the capital stock is obtained by using (A17.42) and (A17.48):

$$k_{t+1} = \frac{1}{(1+n)(2+\rho)}\left[W(k_t) - T^Y_t\right] - b. \tag{A17.64}$$

The stability condition for the model is still as in (A17.56) (with $T^O = 0$ imposed). The impact effect on capital of an increase in b is:

$$\begin{aligned}
\frac{\partial k_{t+1}}{\partial b} &= -\frac{1}{(1+n)(2+\rho)}\frac{dT^Y_t}{db} - 1 \\
&= -\left[1 + \frac{r_t - n}{(1+n)(2+\rho)}\right] < -1,
\end{aligned} \tag{A17.65}$$

where we have used (A17.63) to get from the first to the second line. The increase in debt crowds out capital formation because the tax on the young has risen. The long-run effect on the capital stock is:

$$\frac{dk_\infty}{db} = -\frac{r - n + (1+n)(1+\rho)}{(1+n)(1+\rho) - W'(k_\infty)} < 0. \tag{A17.66}$$

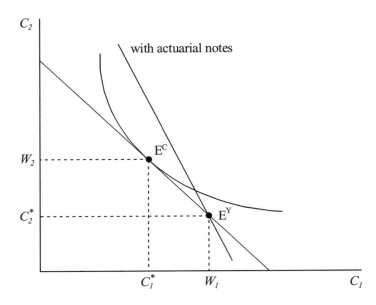

Figure A17.3: A happy mortal saver

Question 4: Lifetime uncertainty in a two-period model

(a) Since $A > 0$ the time-of-death borrowing constraint is not operative. We can combine (Q17.8)-(Q17.9) to obtain the ex ante lifetime budget constraint:

$$C_1 + \frac{C_2}{1+r} = W_1 + \frac{W_2}{1+r}. \tag{A17.67}$$

The agent maximizes (Q17.8) subject to (A17.67). The Lagrangian is:

$$\mathcal{L} \equiv U(C_1) + \frac{\pi}{1+\rho} U(C_2) + \lambda \cdot \left[W_1 + \frac{W_2}{1+r} - C_1 - \frac{C_2}{1+r} \right],$$

and the first-order necessary conditions are:

$$U'(C_1) = \lambda,$$
$$\frac{\pi}{1+\rho} U'(C_2) = \frac{\lambda}{1+r}.$$

Combining we obtain the Euler equation:

$$\frac{U'(C_2)}{U'(C_1)} = \frac{1+\rho}{\pi(1+r)}. \tag{A17.68}$$

The optimum is illustrated in Figure A17.3. The income endowment point is at E^Y whilst the optimal consumption point is at E^C. The horizontal difference between W_1 and C_1^* is optimal saving, A^*, in the first period. (The vertical difference between C_2^* and W_2 equals $(1+r)A^*$.)

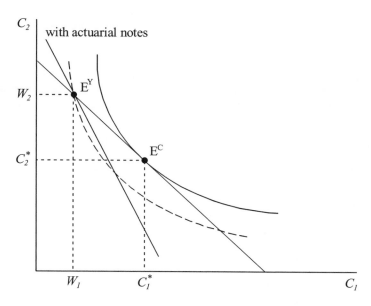

Figure A17.4: A frustrated mortal borrower

(b) Borrowing in the first period is not possible because the agent may die (and not pay back the loan). Hence, the constraint $A \geq 0$ is binding. The best the agent can do is to consume at the endowment point. The constrained optimum is illustrated in Figure A17.4. The agent would like to consume at point E^C but that is unattainable. Consumption takes place at point E^Y.

(c) The life-insurance company breaks even if:

$$1 + r = \pi \cdot \left(1 + r^A\right) + (1 - \pi) \cdot 0,$$

which implies that the annuity rate is:

$$1 + r^A = \frac{1 + r}{\pi} > 1 + r.$$

(d) Initial savers like annuities because $r^A > r$, i.e. they get a higher return on their savings. Initially frustrated borrowers also like them because they can now borrow at a finite rate r^A, whereas they could not borrow at all before (i.e. they faced an infinite borrowing rate). Both types are better off as a result because the choice set is increased for both types. All agents face the following lifetime budget constraint:

$$C_1 + \frac{C_2}{1 + r} = W_1 + \frac{W_2}{1 + r^A}.$$

The Euler equation for both types is thus:

$$\frac{U'(C_2)}{U'(C_1)} = \frac{1 + \rho}{\pi (1 + r^A)} = \frac{1 + \rho}{1 + r}.$$

(The probability of death drops out just as for the Blanchard - Yaari model studied in Chapter 16.)

The effects of the actuarial notes on the optimal choices can be illustrated easily. Because $r^A > r$ the budget constraint rotates in a clockwise fashion around the income endowment points in the two figures. Choice sets are enlarged for both types. This hold as long as $r^A > r$, so also for less-than-actuarially-fair notes.

Question 5: Pensions in the Diamond-Samuelson model

(a)   • This is a PAYG system. The young pay for the pensions of the old.

       • Since T is exogenous (and held constant), this is a DC system. If n_t were to change, then Z_{t+1} would adjust.

(b) From (Q17.14) and (Q17.15) we can deduce that:

$$Z_{t+1} = \frac{L_{t+1}}{L_t} T = (1 + n_{t+1}) T.$$

By substituting this result into (Q17.13) we find:

$$C_{t+1}^O = (1 + r_{t+1})S_t + (1 + n_{t+1}) T. \qquad (A17.69)$$

We can combine (A17.69) with (Q17.12) to eliminate S_t:

$$C_t^Y + \frac{C_{t+1}^O}{1 + r_{t+1}} - \frac{1 + n_{t+1}}{1 + r_{t+1}}T = W_t - T,$$

$$C_t^Y + \frac{C_{t+1}^O}{1 + r_{t+1}} = W_t + \frac{1 + n_{t+1}}{1 + r_{t+1}}T - T,$$

$$C_t^Y + \frac{C_{t+1}^O}{1 + r_{t+1}} = W_t - \frac{r_{t+1} - n_{t+1}}{1 + r_{t+1}}T \equiv \Omega.$$

Since $r_{t+1} > n_{t+1}$, the pension plan makes agents poorer than they would be without such a plan.

The optimization problem features the following Lagrangian:

$$L \equiv U(C_t^Y, C_{t+1}^O) + \lambda \cdot \left[C_t^Y + \frac{C_{t+1}^O}{1 + r_{t+1}} - \Omega \right].$$

The FONCs are:

$$\frac{\partial U(C_t^Y, C_{t+1}^O)}{\partial C_t^Y} = \lambda,$$

$$\frac{\partial U(C_t^Y, C_{t+1}^O)}{\partial C_{t+1}^O} = \frac{\lambda}{1 + r_{t+1}}.$$

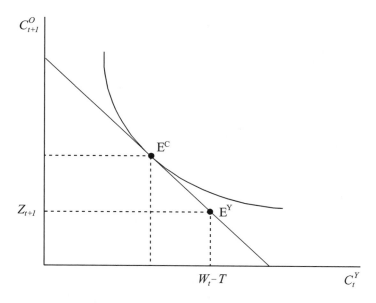

Figure A17.5: Optimal consumption with age-dependent taxes and transfers

plus the lifetime budget constraint. After eliminating λ we obtain the Euler equation:

$$\frac{\partial U(C_t^Y, C_{t+1}^O)}{\partial C_{t+1}^O} = \frac{\frac{\partial U(C_t^Y, C_{t+1}^O)}{\partial C_t^Y}}{1 + r_{t+1}},$$

$$1 + r_{t+1} = \frac{\frac{\partial U(C_t^Y, C_{t+1}^O)}{\partial C_t^Y}}{\frac{\partial U(C_t^Y, C_{t+1}^O)}{\partial C_{t+1}^O}}.$$

In terms of Figure A17.5, the optimum consumption point is at point E^C (the income endowment point is at E^Y).

The comparative static effects are obtained from the following system:

$$C_t^Y + \frac{C_{t+1}^O}{1 + r_{t+1}} = W_t - \frac{r_{t+1} - n_{t+1}}{1 + r_{t+1}} T,$$

$$\frac{\partial U(C_t^Y, C_{t+1}^O)}{\partial C_t^Y} - (1 + r_{t+1}) \frac{\partial U(C_t^Y, C_{t+1}^O)}{\partial C_{t+1}^O} = 0.$$

By totally differentiating with respect to C_t^Y, C_{t+1}^O, and T (holding constant W_t and r_{t+1}) we thus find:

$$dC_t^Y + \frac{dC_{t+1}^O}{1 + r_{t+1}} = -\frac{r_{t+1} - n_{t+1}}{1 + r_{t+1}} dT,$$

$$U_{11} dC_t^Y + U_{12} dC_{t+1}^O - (1 + r_{t+1}) \left[U_{21} dC_t^Y + U_{22} dC_{t+1}^O \right] = 0.$$

This can be written in matrix format as:

$$\Delta \cdot \begin{bmatrix} dC_t^Y \\ dC_{t+1}^O \end{bmatrix} = \begin{bmatrix} -1 \\ 0 \end{bmatrix} \cdot \frac{r_{t+1} - n_{t+1}}{1 + r_{t+1}} dT,$$

where Δ is given by:

$$\Delta \equiv \begin{bmatrix} 1 & \frac{1}{1+r_{t+1}} \\ U_{11} - (1 + r_{t+1}) U_{21} & U_{12} - (1 + r_{t+1}) U_{22} \end{bmatrix}$$

We obtain by Cramer's Rule:

$$\frac{dC_t^Y}{dT} = \frac{1}{|\Delta|} \cdot \begin{vmatrix} -1 & \frac{1}{1+r_{t+1}} \\ 0 & U_{12} - (1 + r_{t+1}) U_{22} \end{vmatrix} \cdot \frac{r_{t+1} - n_{t+1}}{1 + r_{t+1}},$$

$$= \frac{-U_{12} + (1 + r_{t+1}) U_{22}}{|\Delta|} \cdot \frac{r_{t+1} - n_{t+1}}{1 + r_{t+1}},$$

$$\frac{dC_{t+1}^O}{dT} = \frac{1}{|\Delta|} \cdot \begin{vmatrix} 1 & -1 \\ U_{11} - (1 + r_{t+1}) U_{21} & 0 \end{vmatrix} \cdot \frac{r_{t+1} - n_{t+1}}{1 + r_{t+1}},$$

$$= \frac{U_{11} - (1 + r_{t+1}) U_{21}}{|\Delta|} \cdot \frac{r_{t+1} - n_{t+1}}{1 + r_{t+1}}.$$

The effect on saving effect is obtained from (A17.69):

$$dC_{t+1}^O = (1 + r_{t+1}) dS_t + (1 + n_{t+1}) dT,$$

$$(1 + r_{t+1}) \frac{dS_t}{dT} = \frac{dC_{t+1}^O}{dT} - (1 + n_{t+1}).$$

Since $r_t > n_t$ we find that the increase in T would lead to an inward shift of the lifetime budget constraint in Figure A17.5 (not drawn). The new budget line is parallel to the old one because we are keeping r_{t+1} constant in this experiment. What happens to optimal consumption and saving depends on the shape of preferences.

(c) The resource constraint is given by:

$$Y_t + (1 - \delta) K_t = C_t + K_{t+1}. \tag{A17.70}$$

Total consumption is defined as:

$$C_t \equiv L_{t-1} C_t^O + L_t C_t^Y,$$

whereas consumption by the cohort is given by:

$$L_{t-1} C_t^O = (r_t + \delta) K_t + (1 - \delta) K_t,$$
$$L_t C_t^Y = w_t L_t - S_t L_t.$$

It follows that:

$$C_t = (r_t + \delta) K_t + (1 - \delta) K_t + w_t L_t - S_t L_t,$$
$$= Y_t + (1 - \delta) K_t - S_t L_t. \tag{A17.71}$$

By comparing (A17.70) and (A17.71) we get:

$$S_t L_t = K_{t+1}.$$

Dividing by L_t and noting (Q17.14) we obtain:

$$S_t = \frac{K_{t+1}}{L_{t+1}} \cdot \frac{L_{t+1}}{L_t} = (1 + n_{t+1}) k_{t+1}.$$

(d) The marginal productivity conditions are:

$$
\begin{aligned}
W_t &= (1 - \alpha) k_t^\alpha, \\
r_t + \delta &= \alpha k_t^{\alpha-1}.
\end{aligned}
$$

We assume that $U(C_t^Y, C_{t+1}^O)$ is homothetic. This implies that we can write:

$$U(C_t^Y, C_{t+1}^O) = G\left(H(C_t^Y, C_{t+1}^O)\right),$$

with $G'(\cdot) > 0$ and $H(\cdot)$ homogeneous of degree one. We know:

$$
\begin{aligned}
H &= H_1 C_t^Y + H_2 C_{t+1}^O, \\
0 &= H_{11} C_t^Y + H_{12} C_{t+1}^O, \\
0 &= H_{21} C_t^Y + H_{22} C_{t+1}^O, \\
H_{21} &= H_{12}, \\
\sigma &\equiv \frac{H_1 \cdot H_2}{H \cdot H_{12}}.
\end{aligned}
$$

The system can now be written as:

$$C_t^Y + \frac{C_{t+1}^O}{1 + r_{t+1}} = W_t - \frac{r_{t+1} - n_{t+1}}{1 + r_{t+1}} T, \tag{A17.72}$$

$$H_1(C_t^Y, C_{t+1}^O) - (1 + r_{t+1}) H_2(C_t^Y, C_{t+1}^O) = 0. \tag{A17.73}$$

The first line can be written as:

$$
\begin{aligned}
\frac{C_t^Y}{\Omega} \frac{dC_t^Y}{C_t^Y} + \frac{C_{t+1}^O}{(1 + r_{t+1})\Omega} \frac{dC_{t+1}^O}{C_{t+1}^O} &= -\frac{r_{t+1} - n_{t+1}}{1 + r_{t+1}} \frac{dT}{\Omega}, \\
\omega_1 \frac{dC_t^Y}{C_t^Y} + (1 - \omega_1) \frac{dC_{t+1}^O}{C_{t+1}^O} &= -\frac{r_{t+1} - n_{t+1}}{1 + r_{t+1}} \frac{dT}{\Omega}.
\end{aligned}
$$

Differentiating the second line we find:

$$
\begin{aligned}
H_{11} dC_t^Y + H_{12} dC_{t+1}^O - (1 + r_{t+1}) \left[H_{21} dC_t^Y + H_{22} dC_{t+1}^O \right] &= 0, \\
[H_{11} - (1 + r_{t+1}) H_{21}] dC_t^Y + [H_{12} - (1 + r_{t+1}) H_{22}] dC_{t+1}^O &= 0, \\
-\frac{H_1}{\sigma} \frac{dC_t^Y}{C_t^Y} + \frac{H_1}{\sigma} \frac{dC_{t+1}^O}{C_{t+1}^O} &= 0, \\
\frac{dC_t^Y}{C_t^Y} &= \frac{dC_{t+1}^O}{C_{t+1}^O}.
\end{aligned}
$$

(This last result is obvious because we leave r_{t+1} unchanged so the Euler equation for the homothetic case defines a constant ratio between C_{t+1}^O and C_t^Y.)

For the homothetic case, the system is thus:

$$\begin{bmatrix} \omega_1 & 1 - \omega_1 \\ -1 & 1 \end{bmatrix} \cdot \begin{bmatrix} \dfrac{dC_t^Y}{C_t^Y} \\ \dfrac{dC_{t+1}^O}{C_{t+1}^O} \end{bmatrix} = \begin{bmatrix} -1 \\ 0 \end{bmatrix} \cdot \frac{r_{t+1} - n_{t+1}}{1 + r_{t+1}} \frac{dT}{\Omega},$$

Matrix inversion in child's play and we easily find:

$$\begin{bmatrix} \dfrac{dC_t^Y}{C_t^Y} \\ \dfrac{dC_{t+1}^O}{C_{t+1}^O} \end{bmatrix} = \begin{bmatrix} 1 & -(1 - \omega_1) \\ 1 & \omega_1 \end{bmatrix} \begin{bmatrix} -1 \\ 0 \end{bmatrix} \cdot \frac{r_{t+1} - n_{t+1}}{1 + r_{t+1}} \frac{dT}{\Omega},$$

$$= -\begin{bmatrix} 1 \\ 1 \end{bmatrix} \cdot \frac{r_{t+1} - n_{t+1}}{1 + r_{t+1}} \frac{dT}{\Omega}.$$

The saving effect is:

$$\frac{dS_t}{dT} = -\left(1 + \frac{dC_t^Y}{dT}\right)$$

To investigate local stability we write:

$$S(W_t, r_{t+1}, T) = (1 + n_{t+1}) k_{t+1},$$
$$S\left((1 - \alpha) k_t^\alpha, \alpha k_{t+1}^{\alpha - 1} - \delta, T\right) = (1 + n_{t+1}) k_{t+1}. \qquad \text{(A17.74)}$$

Differentiating (A17.74) gives:

$$S_W \alpha (1 - \alpha) k_t^{\alpha - 1} dk_t + S_r \alpha (1 - \alpha) k_{t+1}^{\alpha - 1} dk_{t+1} = (1 + n_{t+1}) dk_{t+1}.$$

By gathering terms (and evaluating around the steady state, $k_{t+1} = k_t = k^*$):

$$\frac{dk_{t+1}}{dk_t} = \frac{-S_W \alpha (1 - \alpha) (k^*)^{\alpha - 1}}{S_r \alpha (1 - \alpha) (k^*)^{\alpha - 1} - (1 + n_{t+1})}.$$

The stability condition is that $|dk_{t+1}/dk_t| < 1$. (Of course, we can deduce the partial derivatives $S_r \equiv \partial S / \partial r_{t+1}$ and $S_W \equiv \partial S / \partial W_t$ from the system (A17.72)-(A17.73) above. (But that is left an exercise to the very keen student.)

Question 6: Consumption taxation and redistribution

(a) To shorten the notation we define $T_{Ct} \equiv 1 + t_{Ct}$, $T_{Ct+1} \equiv 1 + t_{Ct+1}$, and $R_{t+1} \equiv 1 + r_{t+1}$. The utility function is:

$$\Lambda_t^Y \equiv U(C_t^Y) + \frac{1}{1 + \rho} U(C_{t+1}^O), \qquad \text{(A17.75)}$$

and the budget identities are:

$$T_{Ct} C_t^Y + S_t = W_t + Z_t^Y,$$
$$T_{Ct+1} C_{t+1}^O = R_{t+1} S_t + Z_{t+1}^O.$$

The consolidated budget constraint is obtained as follows:

$$S_t = W_t + Z_t^Y - T_{Ct}C_t^Y = \frac{T_{Ct+1}C_{t+1}^O - Z_{t+1}^O}{R_{t+1}}.$$

Hence:

$$T_{Ct}C_t^Y + \frac{T_{Ct+1}C_{t+1}^O}{R_{t+1}} = W_t + Z_t^Y + \frac{Z_{t+1}^O}{R_{t+1}}. \tag{A17.76}$$

The young agent chooses C_t^Y and C_{t+1}^O in order to maximize (A17.75) subject to (A17.76). The Lagrangian is:

$$\mathcal{L} \equiv U(C_t^Y) + \frac{1}{1+\rho}U(C_{t+1}^O) + \lambda \cdot \left[W_t + Z_t^Y + \frac{Z_{t+1}^O}{R_{t+1}} - T_{Ct}C_t^Y - \frac{T_{Ct+1}C_{t+1}^O}{R_{t+1}} \right],$$

whilst the first-order conditions are:

$$U'(C_t^Y) = \lambda T_{Ct},$$
$$\frac{1}{1+\rho}U'(C_{t+1}^O) = \lambda \frac{T_{Ct+1}}{R_{t+1}}$$

Combining we obtain the Euler equation:

$$\frac{U'(C_{t+1}^O)}{U'(C_t^Y)} = \frac{1+\rho}{R_{t+1}} \frac{T_{Ct+1}}{T_{Ct}}. \tag{A17.77}$$

We observe that the optimal choices for C_t^Y and C_{t+1}^O depend on W_t, r_{t+1}, Z_t^Y, Z_{t+1}^O, t_{Ct}, and t_{Ct+1}. The savings function is defined as follows:

$$\begin{aligned} S_t &= W_t + Z_t^Y - T_{Ct}C_t^Y \\ &\equiv S\left(W_t, r_{t+1}, Z_t^Y, Z_{t+1}^O, t_{Ct}, t_{Ct+1}\right). \end{aligned} \tag{A17.78}$$

To find the comparative static effects for S_t with respect to taces and transfers, the following direct approach can be used. Write the utility function in terms of S_t:

$$\Lambda_t^Y \equiv U\left(\frac{W_t + Z_t^Y - S_t}{T_{Ct}}\right) + \frac{1}{1+\rho}U\left(\frac{R_{t+1}S_t + Z_{t+1}^O}{T_{Ct+1}}\right),$$

and note that the first- and second-order conditions are:

$$\Gamma(S_t, \cdot) \equiv -\frac{U'(C_t^Y)}{T_{Ct}} + \frac{R_{t+1}U'(C_{t+1}^O)}{(1+\rho)T_{Ct+1}} = 0,$$
$$\frac{\partial \Gamma(S_t, \cdot)}{\partial S_t} = \frac{U''(C_t^Y)}{T_{Ct}^2} + \frac{R_{t+1}^2 U''(C_{t+1}^O)}{(1+\rho)T_{Ct+1}^2} < 0.$$

The effect of lump-sum transfers is:

$$\frac{\partial S_t}{\partial Z_t^Y} = \frac{\partial \Gamma (S_t, \cdot) / \partial Z_t^Y}{|\partial \Gamma (S_t, \cdot) / \partial S_t|} = \frac{-U'' (C_t^Y)}{T_{Ct}^2 |\partial \Gamma (S_t, \cdot) / \partial S_t|} > 0,$$

$$\frac{\partial S_t}{\partial Z_{t+1}^O} = \frac{\partial \Gamma (S_t, \cdot) / \partial Z_{t+1}^O}{|\partial \Gamma (S_t, \cdot) / \partial S_t|} = \frac{R_{t+1} U'' (C_{t+1}^O)}{(1 + \rho) T_{Ct+1}^2 |\partial \Gamma (S_t, \cdot) / \partial S_t|} < 0$$

The effect of the consumption taxes is:

$$\frac{\partial S_t}{\partial T_{Ct}} = \frac{\partial \Gamma (S_t, \cdot) / \partial T_{Ct}}{|\partial \Gamma (S_t, \cdot) / \partial S_t|} = \frac{T_{Ct} U' (C_t^Y) + U'' (C_t^Y) [W_t + Z_t^Y - S_t]}{T_{Ct}^3 |\partial \Gamma (S_t, \cdot) / \partial S_t|} \gtreqless 0,$$

$$\frac{\partial S_t}{\partial T_{Ct+1}} = \frac{\partial \Gamma (S_t, \cdot) / \partial T_{Ct+1}}{|\partial \Gamma (S_t, \cdot) / \partial S_t|}$$

$$= \frac{-R_{t+1}}{(1 + \rho) T_{Ct+1}^3} \frac{T_{Ct+1} U' (C_{t+1}^O) + U'' (C_{t+1}^O) [R_{t+1} S_t + Z_{t+1}^O]}{T_{Ct}^2 |\partial \Gamma (S_t, \cdot) / \partial S_t|} \gtreqless 0,$$

There are offsetting income and substitution effects.

(b) For the logarithmic case the Euler equation is:

$$T_{Ct} C_t^Y = (1 + \rho) \frac{T_{Ct+1} C_{t+1}^O}{R_{t+1}} \tag{A17.79}$$

Substituting into the budget constraint (A17.76) we find:

$$T_{Ct} C_t^Y + \frac{T_{Ct+1} C_{t+1}^O}{R_{t+1}} = W_t + Z_t^Y + \frac{Z_{t+1}^O}{R_{t+1}},$$

$$\left(1 + \frac{1}{1 + \rho} \right) T_{Ct} C_t^Y = W_t + Z_t^Y + \frac{Z_{t+1}^O}{R_{t+1}},$$

or:

$$T_{Ct} C_t^Y = \frac{1 + \rho}{2 + \rho} \cdot \left[W_t + Z_t^Y + \frac{Z_{t+1}^O}{R_{t+1}} \right], \tag{A17.80}$$

$$\frac{T_{Ct+1} C_{t+1}^O}{R_{t+1}} = \frac{1}{2 + \rho} \cdot \left[W_t + Z_t^Y + \frac{Z_{t+1}^O}{R_{t+1}} \right]. \tag{A17.81}$$

The savings function is:

$$S_t = W_t + Z_t^Y - T_{Ct} C_t^Y$$

$$= W_t + Z_t^Y - \frac{1 + \rho}{2 + \rho} \cdot \left[W_t + Z_t^Y + \frac{Z_{t+1}^O}{R_{t+1}} \right]$$

$$= \frac{1}{2 + \rho} \cdot \left[W_t + Z_t^Y \right] - \frac{1 + \rho}{2 + \rho} \cdot \frac{Z_{t+1}^O}{R_{t+1}}. \tag{A17.82}$$

Some key points about this savings function:

- Consumption tax has no effect on saving (offsetting income and substitution effects).
- Transfers during youth increase saving.
- Transfers during old-age decrease saving.

(c) We must first do some bookkeeping. We know the resource constraint:

$$Y_t + (1 - \delta) K_t = K_{t+1} + C_t, \tag{A17.83}$$

with

$$C_t \equiv L_t C_t^Y + L_{t-1} C_t^O.$$

We also know that:

$$
\begin{aligned}
L_{t-1} C_t^O T_{Ct} &= (r_t + \delta) K_t + (1 - \delta) K_t + L_{t-1} Z_t^O, \\
L_t C_t^Y T_{Ct} &= W_t L_t + L_t Z_t^Y - L_t S_t, \\
Y_t &= (r_t + \delta) K_t + W_t L_t.
\end{aligned}
$$

Hence:

$$
\begin{aligned}
C_t (1 + t_{Ct}) &= Y_t + (1 - \delta) K_t + L_t Z_t^Y + L_{t-1} Z_t^O - L_t S_t, \\
C_t &= Y_t + (1 - \delta) K_t - L_t S_t.
\end{aligned}
$$

Hence, as in the model without taxes, we still have that:

$$L_t S_t = K_{t+1} \qquad \Leftrightarrow \qquad S_t = (1 + n) k_{t+1}, \tag{A17.84}$$

where n is the population growth rate.

For the scenario here we have $Z_t^O = 0$ (for all t) and Z_t^Y is:

$$Z_t^Y = t_{Ct} c_t, \tag{A17.85}$$

where $c_t \equiv C_t / L_t$. From (A17.83) we deduce that c_t can be written as:

$$c_t = y_t + (1 - \delta) k_t - (1 + n) k_{t+1}. \tag{A17.86}$$

Using (A17.84)-(A17.85) in (A17.82) and noting that $Z_t^O = 0$ (for all t) we find:

$$
\begin{aligned}
S_t &= \frac{1}{2 + \rho} \cdot [W_t + t_{Ct} (y_t + (1 - \delta) k_t - S_t)] \\
&= \frac{1}{2 + \rho + t_{Ct}} \cdot [W_t + t_{Ct} (y_t + (1 - \delta) k_t)]. \tag{A17.87}
\end{aligned}
$$

Since $y_t \equiv k_t^{1-\varepsilon_L}$ and $W_t \equiv \varepsilon_L k_t^{1-\varepsilon_L}$ we find that the fundamental difference equation for the capital-labour ratio is:

$$(1 + n) k_{t+1} = S_t = \frac{1}{2 + \rho + t_{Ct}} \left[\varepsilon_L k_t^{1-\varepsilon_L} + t_{Ct} \left(k_t^{1-\varepsilon_L} + (1 - \delta) k_t \right) \right]. \tag{A17.88}$$

(d) If the old get the revenue matters are different. For this scenario we have $Z_t^Y = 0$ for all t and Z_t^O is equal to:

$$Z_{t+1}^O = t_{Ct+1} \frac{C_{t+1}}{L_t} = (1+n)\, t_{Ct+1} c_{t+1}. \tag{A17.89}$$

The other relevant equations are:

$$c_{t+1} = y_{t+1} + (1-\delta)\, k_{t+1} - (1+n)\, k_{t+2}, \tag{A17.90}$$

$$S_t = \frac{1}{2+\rho} \cdot W_t - \frac{1+\rho}{2+\rho} \cdot \frac{Z_{t+1}^O}{R_{t+1}}. \tag{A17.91}$$

Combining results we find that the fundamental difference equation can be written as:

$$(1+n)\, k_{t+1} = S_t = \frac{1}{2+\rho} \cdot \varepsilon_L k_t^{1-\varepsilon_L}$$
$$- t_{Ct+1} \cdot \frac{1+\rho}{2+\rho} \cdot \frac{1+n}{1+r_{t+1}} \cdot \left[k_{t+1}^{1-\varepsilon_L} + (1-\delta)\, k_{t+1} - (1+n)\, k_{t+2} \right] \tag{A17.92}$$

Comparing (A17.88) and (A17.92) we find that the former is a first-order difference equation whilst the latter is a second-order difference equation (which is much harder to analyze analytically).

Bibliography

Azariadis, C. (1993). *Intertemporal macroeconomics*. Oxford: Basil Blackwell.

Barro, R. J., & Sala-i-Martin, X. (1995). *Economic growth*. New York: McGraw-Hill.

Benhabib, J., Rogerson, R., & Wright, R. (1991). Homework in macroeconomics: Household production and aggregate fluctuations. *Journal of Political Economy, 99*, 1166-1187.

Blanchard, O. J., & Fischer, S. (1989). *Lectures on macroeconomics*. Cambridge, MA: MIT Press.

Blanchard, O. J., & Kahn, C. M. (1980). The solution of linear difference models under rational expectations. *Econometrica, 48*, 1305–1311.

Branson, W. H. (1972). *Macroeconomic theory and policy*. New York: Harper and Row.

Buiter, W. H. (1988). Death, productivity growth and debt neutrality. *Economic Journal, 98*, 279–293.

Buiter, W. H. (1990). *Principles of budgetary and financial policy*. New York: Harvester Wheatsheaf.

Buiter, W. H., & Miller, M. (1982). Real exchange rate overshooting and the output cost of bringing down inflation. *European Economic Review, 33*, 143–175.

Burmeister, E., & Dobell, A. R. (1970). *Mathematical theories of economic growth*. London: Macmillan.

Cagan, P. (1956). The monetary dynamics of hyperinflation. In M. Friedman (Ed.), *Studies in the quantity theory of money*. Chicago: University of Chicago Press.

Calvo, G. A. (1980). Tax-financed government spending in a neoclassical model with sticky wages and rational expectations. *Journal of Economic Dynamics and Control, 2*, 61–78.

Calvo, G. A. (1983). Staggered prices in a utility-maximizing framework. *Journal of Monetary Economics, 12*, 383-398.

Cass, D. (1965). Optimum growth in an aggregative model of capital accumulation. *Review of Economic Studies, 32*, 233–240.

Chiang, A. C. (1984). *Fundamental methods of mathematical economics* (third ed.). New York: McGraw-Hill.

Clarida, R., Galí, J., & Getler, M. (1999). The science of monetary policy: a new keynesian perspective. *Journal of Economic Literature, 37*, 1661–1707.

Correia, I., Neves, J. C., & Rebelo, S. (1995). Business cycles in a small open economy. *European Economic Review, 39*, 1089–1113.

Domar, E. D. (1949). Capital expansion, rate of growth, and employment. *Econometrica, 14*, 137–147.

Gandolfo, G. (1971). *Mathematical methods and models in economic dynamics*. Amsterdam: North-Holland.

Harrod, R. F. (1939). An essay in dynamic theory. *Economic Journal, 49*, 14–33.

Heijdra, B. J., & Meijdam, A. C. (2002). Public investment and intergenerational distribution. *Journal of Economic Dynamics and Control, 26,* 707–735.

Hornstein, A., & Wolman, A. L. (2007). *The calvo model without local approximation.*

Ihori, T. (1996). *Public finance in an overlapping generations economy.* London: Macmillan Press.

Intriligator, M. D. (1971). *Mathematical optimization and economic theory.* Englewood Cliffs, NJ: Prentice Hall.

Jones, L. E., & Manuelli, R. E. (1992). Finite lifetimes and growth. *Journal of Economic Theory, 58,* 171–197.

Kaldor, N. (1955). Alternative theories of distribution. *Review of Economic Studies, 23,* 83–100.

Kam, E. (2004). A note on cash-in-advance contraints in continuous time. *Economics Bulletin, 5,* 1–8.

Kim, S. H., & Kose, M. A. (2003). Dynamics of open-economy business-cycle models: role of the discount factor. *Macroeconomic Dynamics, 7.*

Koopmans, T. C. (1967). Objectives, constraints, and outcomes in optimal growth models. *Econometrica, 35,* 1–15.

Kurz, M. (1968). The general instability of a class of competitive growth processes. *Review of Economic Studies, 35,* 155–174.

Ljungqvist, L., & Sargent, T. J. (2000). *Recursive macroeconomic theory.* Cambridge, MA: MIT Press.

Mankiw, N. G., Romer, D., & Weil, D. N. (1992). A contribution to the empirics of economic growth. *Quarterly Journal of Economics, 107,* 407-437.

Mansoorian, A., & Mohsin, M. (2004). Monetary policy in a cash-in-advance economy: employment, capital accumulation, and the term structure of interest rates. *Canadian Journal of Economics, 37.*

Marini, G., & Ploeg, F. van der. (1988). Monetary and fiscal policy in an optimising model with capital accumulation and finite lives. *Economic Journal, 98,* 772–786.

Mark, N. C. (2001). *International macroeconomics and finance.* Oxford: Blackwell.

McCallum, B. T. (1980). Rational expectations and macroeconomic stabilization policy: An overview. *Journal of Money, Credit, and Banking, 12,* 716–746.

McCallum, B. T. (1983). The liquidity trap and the Pigou effect: A dynamic analysis with rational expectations. *Economica, 50,* 395–405.

Mourmouras, I. A., & Lee, J. E. (1999). Government spending on infrastructure in an endogenous growth model with finite horizons. *Journal of Economics and Business, 51,* 395–407.

Nielsen, S. B. (1994). Social security and foreign indebtedness in a small open economy. *Open Economies Review, 5,* 47–63.

Nordhaus, W. D. (1975). The political business cycle. *Review of Economic Studies, 42,* 169–190.

Pasinetti, L. L. (1962). Rate of profit and income distribution in relation to the rate of economic growth. *Review of Economic Studies, 29,* 267–279.

Pissarides, C. A. (2000). *Equilibrium unemployment theory* (Second ed.). Cambridge, MA: MIT Press.

Poole, W. (1970). Optimal choice of monetary policy instruments in a simple stochastic macro model. *Quarterly Journal of Economics, 84,* 197–216.

Ramsey, F. P. (1928). A mathematical theory of savings. *Economic Journal, 38,* 543–559.

Rebelo, S. (1992). Growth in open economies. *Carnegie-Rochester Conference Series on Public Policy, 36,* 5–46.

Saint-Paul, G. (1992). Fiscal policy in an endogenous growth model. *Quarterly Journal of Economics, 107,* 1243–1259.

Samuelson, P. A. (1939). Interaction between the multipier analysis and the principle of acceleration. *Review of Economics and Statistics, 21,* 75–78.

Samuelson, P. A., & Modigliani, F. (1966). The Pasinetti paradox in neoclassical and more general models. *Review of Economic Studies, 33,* 269–301.

Scarth, W. M. (1988). *Macroeconomics: An introduction to advanced methods.* Toronto: Harcourt Brace Jovanovich.

Schmitt-Grohe, S., & Uribe, M. (2003). Closing small open economy models. *Journal of International Economics, 61,* 163–185.

Shapiro, C., & Stiglitz, J. E. (1984). Equilibrium unemployment as a worker discipline device. *American Economic Review, 74,* 433–444.

Turnovsky, S. J. (1979). Optimal monetary policy under flexible exchange rates. *Journal of Economic Dynamics and Control, 1,* 85–99.

Weil, P. (1989). Overlapping families of infinitely-lived agents. *Journal of Public Economics, 38,* 183-198.

Yaari, M. E. (1965). Uncertain lifetime, life insurance, and the theory of the consumer. *Review of Economic Studies, 32,* 137-150.

Yun, T. (1996). Nominal price rigidity, money supply endogeneity, and business cycles. *Journal of Monetary Economics, 37,* 345–370.